597.96   Broekel, Ray.
BRO   Snakes /

251031

DATE
DUE

597.96   Broekel, Ray.
BRO   Snakes /

251031

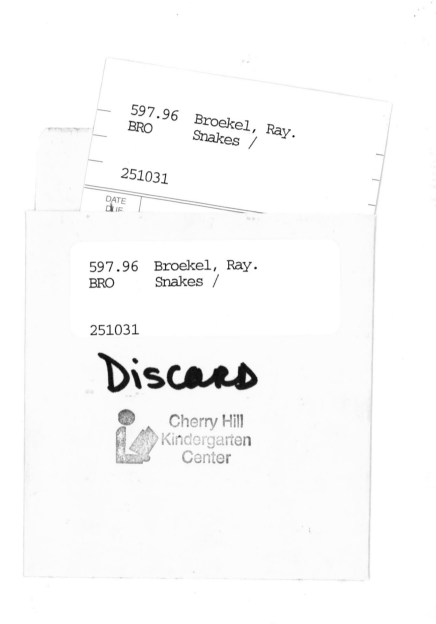

Cherry Hill
Kindergarten
Center

A New True Book

SNAKES

By Ray Broekel

*This "true book" was prepared
under the direction of
Illa Podendorf,
formerly with the Laboratory School,
University of Chicago*

 CHILDRENS PRESS, CHICAGO

Garter snake

PHOTO CREDITS

Lynn M. Stone—Cover, 2, 10, 11, 12, 17, 42

Allan Roberts—9, 14 (bottom), 18, 20, 21, 22, 23, 24, 26 (top), 28 (2 photos), 30, 32, 35, 36 (bottom), 39 (2 photos), 43, 44

James P. Rowan—4, 6, 14 (top), 26 (bottom), 31, 36 (top), 38, 40

Len W. Meents—8

COVER—Corn snake

Library of Congress Cataloging in Publication Data

Broekel, Ray.
    Snakes.   **251031**

    (A New true book)
    Summary: Describes the physiology, habits,
and behavior of snakes.
    1. Snakes—Juvenile literature. [1. Snakes]
I. Title.
QL666.06B864   597.96   81-38487
ISBN 0-516-01649-0   AACR2

TABLE OF CONTENTS

Blair's king snake

WHAT ARE SNAKES?

Snakes have no legs. Yet they can move about. Snakes have no arms or hands. Yet they can catch and eat their food.

Broad-banded copperhead

SCALES

The bodies of snakes have scales on them.

The scales look like little plates. They lie partly over each other.

The scales are dry, not slimy as some people think.

JAWS AND TEETH

Snakes have unusual jaws. Their lower jaws have two bones on each side. Each side of the jaw can move by itself.

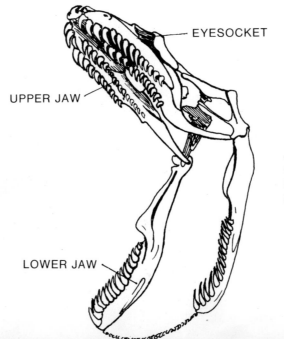

EYESOCKET

UPPER JAW

LOWER JAW

JAWS
OF A
NON-POISONOUS
SNAKE

Common water snake swallowing a fish, head first

The lower jaws are loosely held to the upper jaws. Because of this, a snake can open its mouth wide. A snake can swallow food larger than its mouth.

Hog-nosed snake eating a toad

A snake has small,
hooked teeth, too. Its teeth
and jaws help the snake
pull food into its stomach.

Fox snake

SEEING AND HEARING

Snakes can see things that are nearby.

Some snakes see well at night.

Eastern diamondback rattlesnake

Snakes do not have eyelids that move.

Snakes do not hear as we do. They have no ear openings.

Suppose something near the snakes moves. The snakes feel this movement through their bodies.

Hog-nosed snake

Gray rat snake

TONGUES

The tongues of snakes are forked. They are harmless.

Tongues are used as feelers. They also pick up odors from the air. Then the snakes can tell if the odors came from food or something else.

FANGS

Some snakes are poisonous.

These snakes have large hollow teeth. They are called fangs.

Poisonous snakes bite. Their poison goes into the bite through the hollow fangs.

Fangs and rattle of the Eastern diamondback rattlesnake

Butler's garter snake eating an earthworm

WHAT SNAKES EAT

Snakes eat things that are alive.

Insects are eaten by some snakes.

Worms, frogs, and mice are eaten.

Rats, rabbits, fish, and eggs are eaten, too.

King snake eating a live garter snake

Some snakes even eat other snakes. King cobras and king snakes eat other snakes.

Bullsnakes hatching from eggs

THE YOUNG

Some snakes lay eggs.
Others have their young
alive.

21

Queen snake with her newly-born young

Many snakes have about
12 babies.
Others may have almost
100 at one time.

Cook's tree boa shedding its skin

SHEDDING

What happens when snakes grow?

Their skins become tight.

The snakes shed the tight, old skins.

New skins are under the old skins.

Seventeen-foot python

LENGTH

The longest snakes are anacondas and pythons. They may be almost 30 feet long.

Top: South American anacondas can reach 29 feet in length.   Bottom: Green tree python

The anaconda lives in South America.

The longest python lives in Asia.

The smallest snakes are called thread snakes. They are only about 5 inches long. They are found in the West Indies.

Top: Mangrove snake, found in Asia from Malay Peninsula to the Philippine Islands
Right: Eyelash viper found in jungles from southern Mexico through Central America to Ecuador and Venezuela

WHERE ARE SNAKES FOUND?

Snakes are found all over the world, on land and in the sea.

There are about 3,000 different kinds in the world.

There are about 250 kinds in North America.

Most snakes live on the ground. They find their food there.

Some snakes climb
trees. These snakes often
eat eggs and young birds
in nests.

Yellow
tree boa,
photographed
at night

Northern water snake

    Some snakes live in
fresh water. They live in
ponds, rivers, or lakes.
    These snakes find much
of their food in the water.
They hunt on land, too.

Poisonous sea snake

Some snakes live in salt water. They are called "sea" snakes.

They live in the Pacific Ocean and the Indian Ocean.

Sea snakes are poisonous and have flat tails. They feed mostly on fish.

Some snakes live in deserts.

These snakes move about mostly at night.

They burrow deep into the sand during the day when it is hot.

Western sidewinder rattlesnake

Top: California
mountain
king snake
Right: Goodman's
mountain viper

Some snakes live in the mountains. Mountain air is cool.

In the summer these snakes warm themselves in the sun.

In winter they stay in holes in the ground and caves.

Boa constrictor

Boa constrictors live on the ground and in trees. They squeeze their prey. Then they swallow it.

Left: Cobra in attack position
Above: Closeup showing hood
and tongue of a cobra

Cobras are found in Asia and Africa. They live on the ground.

Cobras are poisonous. Some kinds have hoods. The hoods are spread when the cobras raise their heads.

Puff adder

SNAKES HAVE ENEMIES

Snakes have enemies. They are eaten by birds and other animals. They must protect themselves.

Some snakes are colored like the place they live in. It is hard for their enemies to see them.

Most snakes try to hide or get away from their enemies.

Eastern diamondback giving warning rattle

The poisonous
rattlesnake shakes its tail.
The rattling sound tells the
enemy to stay away or it
will be bitten.

The hog-nosed snake
tries to frighten its enemy,
too. But if this fails, it has
another trick. It rolls over
on its back and plays
dead. Not interested in a
dead snake, the enemy
leaves it alone.

Hog-nosed snake playing dead after its first act
has failed to scare an enemy.

Pilot blacksnake has just swallowed a sparrow or a rodent (see the lump behind its head). Either animal is food for this snake.

SNAKES ARE HELPFUL

Snakes are helpful to humans. They feed on many animals that eat our crops. For this snakes deserve our thanks.

WORDS YOU SHOULD KNOW

burrow(BER • roh) — a hole or tunnel dug in the ground by some animal

constrictor(kahn • STRIK • ter) — a type of snake that kills its food by squeezing

crops(CRAHPZ) — plants grown as food

desert(DEZ • ert) — a dry region of land usually covered with sand

deserve(dih • ZERV) — to be worthy of; to have a right to

eyelid(EYE • lid) — the folds of skin that can cover the eye

fang — a long, pointed tooth

forked(FORKT) — divided into two or more parts

hood — skin on some snakes' necks that flattens out

odor(OH • der) — smell

poisonous(POY • zun • ness) — having poison, something that can harm or kill a living thing

prey(PRAY) — an animal hunted or caught for food by another animal

shed — to lose; drop off

slimy(SLY • mee) — wet and slippery

swallow(SWAHL • oh) — to make food or liquid go from the mouth into the stomach

INDEX

About the author

Ray Broekel is a full-time freelance writer who lives with his wife, Peg, and a dog, Fergus, in Ipswich, Massachusetts. He has had twenty years of experience as a children's book editor and newspaper supervisor, and has taught all subjects in kindergarten through college levels. Dr. Broekel has had over 1,000 stories and articles published, and over 100 books. His first book was published in 1956 (it was published by Childrens Press).

Cherry Hill
Kindergarten
Center

MAXIM GORKY
AND HIS RUSSIA

From the bronze by Valeria Kaun

MAXIM GORKY
And His RUSSIA
BY ALEXANDER KAUN

Benjamin Blom, Inc.
Publishers

First published New York, 1931
Reissued 1968,
by Benjamin Blom, Inc. Bx 10452

Library of Congress Catalog Card No. 67-13330

Printed in U.S.A. by
NOBLE OFFSET PRINTERS, INC.
NEW YORK 3, N. Y.

TO KUDRIK

one immutable friend

PREFACE

NEXT March, Maxim Gorky will be sixty-four. Despite his age and an ancient tuberculosis of the lungs, he is still vigorously creative and keenly responsive to life and its changes. The new, nascent Russia exacts his alert attention and cooperation, and reciprocates by loving him and cherishing his traditional epithet of the Stormy Petrel of the Revolution.

The disadvantage of writing the biography of a man still living and acting is obvious. Not only can the available material not claim finality, but much of it may not be disclosed till after the death of its subject.

Yet I have been prompted to survey Gorky's life, some sixty years of it in any event, as a sharply defined period. The Stormy Petrel of the Revolution lived in, and wrote about, Russia of " on the eve " rather than of " the morning after " the great upheaval. His spectacular public activity passed largely under the old order. As for his literary output, it is confined (except for journalistic writings) to the portrayal of pre-revolutionary Russia. His latest novel, the first two parts of which, *The Bystander* and *The Magnet*, have already appeared in English, sums up Gorky's observations and ends with the death of Lenin. I doubt strongly whether he will venture to depict more recent Russia, for which he lacks both perspective and intimate familiarity.

No author has known pre-Soviet Russia so well, and has described it with such poignant truthfulness, as Maxim Gorky. Surely no author can equal Gorky's dynamic participation in the

movements and currents of his country, or his close acquaintance with its leaders of thought and action. I have chosen to draw a portrait of Gorky the man and writer against the background of Russia in transition from the rule of the tsars to the dictatorship of the Bolsheviks. This scope may explain the comparatively slight proportion of purely literary critique in my work on *Maxim Gorky and His Russia*.

A. K.

Berkeley, California.
Autumn, 1931

CONTENTS

SOURCES AND ACKNOWLEDGMENTS

A minute enumeration of the sources used in the preparation of this work would make the book too cumbrous. I have familiarized myself with every word written by Gorky, and practically with every word written about him — in Russian, at any rate. A summer spent at Capo di Sorrento enabled me to have almost daily conversations with Gorky and his entourage. I am deeply grateful to him for his patience and generosity. I am beholden to a number of people who have helped me accomplish my task, particularly to Mr. Albert Bender and his friends for encouraging my trip to Sorrento. My indebtedness to my correspondents and interlocutors mentioned in the text is too obvious for words. My colleague, Professor G. R. Noyes, has edited, with his customary scrupulosity, the first part of " In the Revolutionary Turmoil." E. Chapman Tracy has read and criticised the whole MS., and G. Graham Bates treated in the same way portions of it. If despite all these friendly endeavours the book suffers from barbarism and gaucheries, the responsibility rests entirely with me.

I have used the twenty-four volumes of Maxim Gorky's *Collected Works,* State Publication (Gosizdat), which contain his fiction and reminiscences. For his essays and journalistic writings I have consulted Russian periodicals, especially the Petrograd daily, *Novaya Zhizn,* 1917–1918, edited by Gorky. Also, his *Stat'yi* (Articles), *1905–1916* (Parus, Petrograd, 1918); *Niesvoyevremennyia mysli* (Thoughts Out of Season), (Kultura i Svoboda, Petrograd, 1918 [?]); *Revolutsia i kultura* (Revolution and Culture), (Ladyschnikow Verlag, Berlin, 1918); *O russkom krestyanstvye* (Concerning the Russian Peasantry), (Ladyschnikow, Berlin, 1922); Gorky's letters to S. P. Dorovatovsky, his first publisher (in the review *Pechat i Revolutsia,* February, 1928, Moscow); Gorky's letters to V. Bryusov (in the same review, May, 1928); Gorky's letters to

M. Kotsyubinsky (in the review *Novy Mir*, January, 1928).

Lenin's letters to Gorky — *Pisma V. I. Lenina k Gorkomu* (Gosizdat, 1924), have been quoted considerably in the text.

Among the writings from which I gleaned factual information about Gorky, I may mention:

I. Gruzdev, *Maxim Gorky: biografichesky ocherk* (a biographic sketch) (Kubuch, Leningrad, 1925).

V. Rudnev, *Gorky Revolutsioner* (Gorky as a Revolutionary) (in the review *Novy Mir*, March–April, 1928, Moscow).

A. Belozerov, *Iz molodykh let M. Gorkovo* (Gorky's Early Years) (April issue of the same review).

Gorky, a miscellany of reminiscences, published by Gosizdat in 1928.

Documents about Gorky and the Department of Police in the review *Byloye*, June, 1918, and Number 16, 1921.

M. Gorky v Nizhnem-Novgorode (M. Gorky in Nizhni Novgorod), (Nizhni Novgorod, 1928).

V. A. Posse, *Moy zhiznenny put* (My Life's Path), (Moscow, 1929).

I. D. Belousov, *Literaturnaya Sreda* (The Literary Wednesdays), (Moscow, 1928).

N. D. Teleshov, *Vse prokhodit* (Everything Passes), (Moscow, 1928).

Other references are mentioned in the text.

There exists no complete biography of Gorky in Russian or any other language. E. J. Dillon's Maxim Gorky (Isbister, London, 1902), treats Gorky's early life and his tramp stories.

Acknowledgment is due to *The Dial*, the *Slavonic Review*, *The University of California Chronicle*, and *Left* for permission to reprint some of my material published in their pages.

A. K.

A LIST OF GORKY'S WRITINGS

in the chronological order of their appearance between 1892 and 1932. Works available in English translation are marked with an asterisk. English titles, when they differ from the original, are put in parentheses.

1892. *Makar Chudra; Of the Siskin that Lied and the Wood-pecker that Loved Truth

1893. Yemelyan Pilyay; Grandfather Arkhip and Lenka

1894. *Chelkash; *Once in Autumn; A Mistake; *The Song of the Falcon

1895. Old Woman Izergil; *The Affair with the Clasps; *On a Raft

1896. *My Fellow Traveller; *The Khan and His Son; *Boles (Her Lover); *Comrades; Heartache; *Konovalov; *Vyvod (An Adulterous Wife; also: The Exorcism); *Varenka Olesova

1897. *The Orlov Couple; *Ex-Men (Creatures that Once Were Men; also: Outcasts; also: Men with Pasts); *Mischiefmaker (An Insolent Man); *In the Steppe; *Malva; The Goltva Fair; *Zazuorina (The Green Kitten); From Boredom

1898. *Chums; *A Shady Character (A Rolling Stone; also: A Strange Companion). A Reader; *Cain and Artem

1899. *Kirilka (Waiting for the Ferry); Concerning the Devil; More Concerning the Devil; Red Vaska; *Twenty Six and One Girl

1900. *Foma Gordeyev

1901. *Song of the Stormy Petrel; *Three of Them

1902. *Smug Citizens (a play); *At the Bottom (also: Lower Depths; also: A Night Lodging; also: Down and Out) (a play)

1903. *Man

1905. January 9 (22); Soldiers; Three Days; Bukoyomov; The Story of Filipp Vasilyevich; The Prison; *Summer Folk (a play); *Children of the Sun (a play)

1906. Comrade!; Enemies (a play); Barbarians (a play); In America: *The City of the Yellow Devil (The City of Mammon); The Kingdom of Tedium; Mob; My Interviews: The Russian Tsar; One of the Republic's Kings; The Masters of Life; A Priest of Morals; Fair France

1907–1908. *Mother

1908. *The Confession; The Last Ones (a play)

1909. *The Life of a Superfluous Man (The Spy); Summer

1910. Okurov Town; Vassa Zheleznova (a play); Queer People (a play)

1911. The Life of Matvey Kozhemyakin

1911–1912. *Italian Tales; *Russian Tales (*both series translated in part as* Tales of Two Countries)

1912. An Incident from the Life of Makar

1913. *Childhood; The Master

1918. *In the World

1919. *Reminiscences of Lev Nikolayevich Tolstoy

1922. *The Old Man (The Judge; a play); Queer People (a play); The Zykovs (a play); Children (a play)

1923–1924. *Notes from My Diary and Recollections (*nearly all translated as* Fragments from My Diary)

1923. *My Universities (*also:* Reminiscences from My Youth); *A Watchman; *The Time of Korolenko; *On the Harm of Philosophy; *First Love; *V. G. Korolenko; N. E. Karonin-Petropavlovsky; A. P. Chekhov; Leo Tolstoy; M. M. Kotsyubinsky; *Leonid Andreyev; *Through Russia: *The Birth of Man; *The Icebreaker; *Gubin; *Nilushka; *The Cemetery; *On a Steamer; *A Woman; *In a Mountain Defile; *Kalinin; They are Coming; *The Dead Man; Hodgepodge; An Evening at Shamov's; An Evening at Panashkin's; An Evening at Sukmomyatkin's; Light-grey and Light-blue; A Book; How They Composed a Song; Birds' Sin; A Silver Ten-Copeck piece; Happiness; A Hero; A Clown; Onlookers; Timka; A Light-minded Man; " Strasti-Mordasti "

(meaningless words of a song) ; By Changul River ; A
Jolly Chap ; A Maiden and Death (a fairy tale in
verse) ; A Ballad of Countess Hélène de Coursi (in
verse)

Stories and Sketches: A Romantic ; A Mordvinian
Woman ; A Little Girl ; A Fire ; A Theft ; Bandits ;
Complaints ; Tales

1925. *The Artamonov Business (Decadence) ; Stories, 1922–
1924: *The Hermit ; A Story of Unrequited Love ; The
Story of a Hero ; *The Story of a Novel ; Karamora ;
*An Incident ; *The Rehearsal ; *The Sky-Blue Life ;
A Story about the Unusual ; Recollections — Stories
— Sketches ; *V. Lenin ; About S. A. Tolstaya ; Leonid
Krasin ; Sergey Yesenin ; N. F. Annensky ; About
Garin-Mikhaylovsky ; The Guide ; Kemskoy ; *Mur-
derers ; *An Emblem ; About Cockroaches ; The False
Coin (a play) ; Notes of a Reader

1927. *The Life of Klim Samgin — Forty Years (The Bystander) — Volume I

1928. *The Life of Klim Samgin — Forty Years (The Magnet) — Volume II

1931. The Life of Klim Samgin — Forty Years — Volume III

IMPORTANT DATES IN GORKY'S LIFE

1868, March 30. Birth of Alexey Maximovich Peshkov, at Nizhni Novgorod.

1869, spring. His parents move to Astrakhan.

1872, fall. Death of father, and return to Nizhni Novgorod with mother.

1874. Grandfather teaches him Old Slavic alphabet.

1876, winter. A few months of school attendance.

1876, through winter of 1877. Life at the Sormovo suburb of Nizhni Novgorod, with mother and stepfather.

1877. Return to grandfather, at the Kanavino suburb.

1878, August. Death of mother.
fall–winter. First job in a shoe store.

1879, fall. Apprentice at the draughtsman's.

1880, spring–summer. Flight from Nizhni Novgorod; dish-washing on a Volga steamer. Influence of Smury.
September. Return to draughtsman's.

1881–1882. Apprentice at icon shop.

1883. Overseer for draughtsman at Nizhni Novgorod Fair.

1884, summer. Leaves for Kazan, " to study."
November. Apprentice at Semenov's bakery. Wages: three roubles per month.

1885, summer. Gardener and janitor at Madame Cornet's.
fall. Hired as tenor for choir.

1886, summer. Assistant baker at Derenkov's establishment.

1887, December 24. Attempt at suicide.

1888, January. Back at bakery.
July 19. Leaves with Romas for Krasnovidovo, for *Narodnik* venture.
August. Kulaks burn Romas out; Gorky leaves Krasnovidovo.
fall. Works at fisheries by the Caspian Sea.

1889. Works on railroads — as night-watchman, entertainer, weigher.

summer. Peddles *kvas* in Nizhni Novgorod.

September–October. Copying documents at Lanin's office.

1889, October 25. Arrested in connection with the Somov case.

November 19. Out of jail, to remain under secret surveillance.

December. Rejected at recruiting office.

1890. Acquaintance with Korolenko. *Song of the Old Oak.*

1891, April. Leaves Nizhni Novgorod. Tramps down Volga and through Ukraine.

July. Witnesses at Kandybovka, Kherson, public beating of an adulteress; is beaten unconscious for interfering. See his *Vyvod.*

August. Starts out from Odessa with Prince Shakro. See *My Fellow-Traveller.*

November. Reaches Tiflis. Works on railroad.

1892, September 24. First printed story, *Makar Chudra,* in Tiflis daily.

October. Back at Nizhni Novgorod, working for Lanin. Published stories in Volga newspapers.

1895, February–May 1896. Journalistic work at Samara.

June. *Chelkash* appears in Korolenko-Mikhaylovsky's *Russkoye Bogatstvo.* Henceforth accepted by all leading reviews.

1896–1904. Mostly at Nizhni Novgorod, working on local *Nizhegorodsky Listok.*

October. Tuberculosis of the lungs.

December. Crimea.

1897, March. Village Manuylovka, Ukraine. Organizes rustic theatre.

1898, April. Discovers Leonid Andreyev.

May 13. Volumes I and II of Gorky's collected stories appear in print.

May 18. Arrested, taken to Tiflis, and incarcerated in Metekh Fortress.

June 10. Freed from jail, to remain under special surveillance.

November. Sends his books to Chekhov; they begin to correspond.

1899, March–April. Crimea. Meets Chekhov.

September. Second edition of Gorky's stories, in three volumes.

October. First visit to St. Petersburg; growing popularity.

1900, January. Calls on Tolstoy, at Moscow.

February. Appearance of his first novel, *Foma Gordeyev*, dedicated to Chekhov.

March–April. Crimea. Urged by Chekhov and Moscow Art Theatre group to write a play.

1900, summer. Manuylovka once more; writes play.

September. Brings to Moscow first version of *Smug Citizens;* dissatisfied, burns it.

1901, January. *Znaniye* brings out a new edition of Gorky's stories, in four volumes.

February–March. St. Petersburg. " Kazan Demonstration." *Song of the Stormy Petrel.*

April 30. Arrested at Nizhni Novgorod; accused of furnishing mimeograph press for revolutionary literature.

May 30. Owing to intercession of Tolstoy, and report of a commission of physicians, is freed from jail; kept under " domestic arrest."

September. Exiled to Arzamas, under open surveillance.

November. Permitted to go to Crimea. Manifestations in his honor.

1902, March 7. Elected Honorary Academician.

March 23. Official annulment of Gorky's election.

April 9. First performance of *Smug Citizens,* in St. Petersburg.

April 30. Ordered to return to Arzamas.

August. Korolenko and Chekhov resign as Honorary Academicians. Success of *Smug Citizens* in Vienna and Berlin.

September. Returns to Nizhni Novgorod.

December 31. First performance of *At the Bottom* (Lower Depths) by the Moscow Art Theatre. Tremendous success. *Smug Citizens* awarded Griboyedov Premium.

1903, summer. In the Caucasus, and tramping along Black Sea.

fall. Gorky's article about the Kishinev massacre appears in *Osvobozhdeniye*.

winter. Confers with Krasin on Party matters. *At the Bottom* in its 14th edition; awarded the Griboyedov Premium.

1904, November 24. Performance of *Summer Folk* at Kommissarzhevskaya's, in St. Petersburg.

1905, January 21–22. Gorky with other writers and prominent citizens calls on ministers to prevent pending bloodshed.

January 24. Arrested, at Riga, and brought to the Peter and Paul Fortress.

January–February. Writes in his cell the play, *Children of the Sun*. Western Europe and America plead for Gorky's release.

March 5. Released under 10,000 rubles bail.

March–May. Crimea.

Summer. In Finland. Writes play, *Barbarians*.

October 21. First performance of *Children of the Sun* in St. Petersburg and Moscow.

1905, October 9–December 15. *Novaya Zhizn*, Gorky's newspaper, edited by Lenin.

December. Takes part in Moscow uprising.

1906, January 3. Gorky's rooms in St. Petersburg searched by police.

February. Flees abroad, from Finland.

April. In the United States. Enthusiastic reception and swift fall.

summer. While in America, writes *Mother*.

October. Settles at Capri.

1907, May. Attends conference of Russian Social-Democratic Party in London.

Beginning of friendship with Lenin.

1908. Negotiations with Lenin. Intra-factional dissentions.

1909, summer. Capri School for Russian workmen.

1913, February. Amnesty. Gorky plans return to Russia.

August. Severe attack of lung trouble. Physicians give him " three weeks."

1914, January 13. Back at home. Settles in Finland.

1915–1917. Edits monthly, *Letopis.* Organizes publishing house, *Parus.*

1917–1918. Head of daily, *Novaya Zhizn.*

1919–1921. At the head of *Vsemirnaya Literature,* World Literature series published by the State.

1921, August. Lenin urges Gorky to go abroad for the sake of his health.

October. Abroad.

1928, spring. Back in Russia. Enthusiastic welcome.

Since then, Gorky divides his time between Russia and Italy.

CHILDHOOD

Nineteen hundred and eight. Maxim Gorky is forty years old. He peers into the past and reconstructs his earliest experiences. To be sure, his memory, however prodigious, must be alloyed by a bit of imaginative licence. How else could he venture to introduce dialogue between quotation marks, to describe with precision atmospheric conditions and other details which inject life and blood into events of the misty past? Yet this alloy affects only the form of the record; substantially the *Dichtung* does not impinge upon the *Warheit*. By a creative touch the scenes and the people are raised from the reality of a coroner's inquest to the *realiora* of Derain's trees.

THE PESHKOVS

THE very first scene impressed on Gorky's memory is replete with significance and portents. The four-year-old boy is convalescing from cholera, the scourge of unsanitary Russia, especially of such fish ports as Astrakhan, famous for its herring and caviar, and as a connecting link between Europe and Asia. The boy has recovered but he has infected his father, whose dead body is stretched out on the floor. Little Alexey does not understand why his father's jolly eyes are now tightly shut and covered with coppers, nor why his mother, always sedate and tidy, is only half dressed and dishevelled, and sheds copious tears while combing the dead man's hair. A new person is present in the room who intrigues him greatly with her spongy nose, black head and funny remarks. This is his grandmother, destined to play an important part in his life. Just as the gravediggers are about to take away the corpse, mother is seized by the pangs of travail. Alexey hides behind the trunk, and from there he watches another mystery, the birth of a man. He next recalls a rainy day at the cemetery, where he and grandmother attend the burial of his father. A deep pit, a yellow coffin on the bottom in the slush, and frogs leaping on the lid. Grandmother weeps. The boy wonders at the sight of grown-up people crying, but he is even more surprised when grandmother asks him why he does not weep. Heretofore he used to be admonished not to cry.

" Why don't you cry a little ? " asked grandmother as we left the cemetery. " You ought to cry a little ! "

" I don't feel like crying," said I.

" Well, if you don't feel like crying, you needn't," she muttered softly.

Such is the opening of *Childhood*. Death and birth. We are plunged without preliminaries into a life of grotesque colourfulness, despite its apparently commonplace drabness. From the outset the people are drawn grippingly with select sure strokes that make even the insignificant, casually mentioned individuals unforgettable. The main characters evolve gradually, as they impress themselves on the mind of the observing boy. And because we see all through the boy's eyes, his own little person occupies a relatively limited place on our retina. It is only in passing, incidentally, that we learn, bit by bit, of his personal traits, his boundless inquisitiveness, keen observation, brooding disposition, and that basic pertness of his which has caused him many blows but which has kept his individuality intact and afloat through his formative years. Only in passing. Our main interest is centred on those persons and scenes, into whose midst the four-year-old lad is thrown after the death of his father, a reality more fantastic than fiction.

A multicoloured, inexpressibly strange life began for me, flowing with terrifying swiftness. I recall it as an austere fairy-tale told by a kind but painfully truthful genius. Now, as I revive the past, it is hard for me at times to believe that all that actually happened, and there is much that I feel like disputing and rejecting — too abundantly cruel is the dark existence of our " stupid tribe." Yet truth is above pity, and besides, it is not about myself that I am writing, but about that narrow stifling environment of dreary impressions, in which the average Russian lived, indeed lives to this day.

Whether heredity and environment are effectual or not, in Gorky's life these elements had such decisive features as to leave, in any event, an inerasable impression, not unlike that of a nightmare or a violent conflagration. His memory of his father is rather dim, but from fragmentary accounts of him scattered through *Childhood* and other autobiographic works of Gorky, one gathers that he possessed at least one trait in common with his son — pert non-conformity. As a boy he ran

away five times from the home of his father, a sadistic soldier of Nicholas I, who pursued his fugitive son with hounds through the forests of Siberia, and upon catching him almost flogged him to death. After many adventures and escapades he finally reached the city of Nizhni Novgorod, at the age of sixteen, apprenticed himself to a carpenter, and in four years became an expert cabinet maker, upholsterer, and decorator. Next door to his shop was the dyeing establishment of the Kashirin family, and this proximity brought about the romance between the young joiner, Maxim Peshkov, and Varvara Kashirina, the eventual parents of Alexey Peshkov, alias Maxim Gorky.

On one of the long evenings, during which grandmother filled little Alexey's avid mind with the beauty and wisdom of her songs, fairy-tales, and reminiscences, she told him of his father's wooing and his married life. Slightly swaying from side to side, sipping vodka from a tea-pot, now and then stuffing snuff into her voluminous nose, an all-understanding and all-forgiving smile playing in the abundant wrinkles of her swarthy face, she held forth in her inimitably colourful way. One day as she was in the orchard, picking raspberries with her daughter, Varvara, Maxim Peshkov came courting. He climbed over the fence, and came up to them, pacing under the apple trees, a stalwart fellow in a white blouse and plush trousers, barefoot and hatless, a leather band holding his long hair in place, Indian fashion. Without preliminaries he asked for the girl's hand. Varvara hid behind an apple tree, her face the colour of the raspberries she had been picking. The proposal was ridiculous, scandalous. Varvara's father had climbed up from the misery of a Volga bargeman to the height of the owner of a dyeing shop, a respectable citizen, president of his guild for three successive terms, and owner of four houses. He had the ambition of marrying his fine looking daughter to a noble. Naturally grandmother was shocked at the impudence of that Siberian vagabond. She was on the point of striking him. Here Varvara confessed that they had been married for some time. Wouldn't she help them now sanction their marriage with the benefit of the clergy? What was grandmother to do?

She gave the two scapegraces a perfunctory beating, and arranged for a clandestine marriage ceremony. But just as she saw Varvara and Maxim drive off on a troika to the church, some rascal of a busybody informed grandfather. The haughty president of the dyers' guild bellowed like a wild beast, when he heard of the affront, summoned his two sons, the informer, and the coachman, armed them, and had his swift horses harnessed for the pursuit of the elopers. According to grandmother, Varvara's Guardian Angel gave her counsel in the nick of time: she got a knife and cut the shaft bands so that they might burst on the way. So they did, well nigh causing the death of the pursuers. By the time they had the thing mended and arrived at the church, Varvara and Maxim had been married. A fight ensued, in which Maxim proved by far the stronger, and made his assailants retreat.

" Your father kept his senses even when in anger. He said to grandfather: ' Drop your hurlbat, don't swing it over me. I am a peaceful man, but what I have taken was given me by God, no one can take it from me, and there is nothing more I want from you.' They left him in peace then, grandfather took his seat in the drozhki, shouting: ' It's good-bye now, Varvara, you are no daughter of mine, and I don't want to see you. I don't care whether you live or croak from hunger.' He came home, and started to beat me and to swear at me, but I just groaned and held my tongue: everything will pass, but what is to be shall be. Later he said to me: ' Well, Akulina, remember now, you have no daughter any longer. Remember that! ' And I thought to myself: ' Chatter away, Redbeard; malice is like ice, it lasts till it gets warm! ' "

The warmth radiating from grandmother's great heart could melt an iceberg. Her irascible husband finally became reconciled to the mésalliance, and permitted the newlyweds to live with them, in the orchard outbuilding. That is where Alexey was born, March 28, 1868. Grandmother recalled with emotion the days when her son-in-law stayed with them, for she loved him dearly, frankly more than her own savage sons, Mikhail and Yakov, whom we shall meet presently. Despite his oppres-

sive childhood and boyhood, Maxim was joyous, vivacious, good-hearted, and respectful of himself and of others — an extremely rare quality amidst those surroundings. Big, handsome, clever, and dexterous, Maxim made life easier, merrier, fuller, what with songs and dances and harmless pranks and jokes. He was devoted to grandmother, carried her in his arms, and teased Varvara by declaring his preference for her mother.

But this lovable Maxim Peshkov was hated by his two brothers-in-law, perhaps because they lacked the very qualities that endeared him to all, and also because they begrudged him the share in their father's inheritance. They lured him to the ice-covered river, ostensibly to skate, and pushed him into an ice-hole. When he tried to climb out they struck at his fingers with the heels of their heavy boots. He managed to hold himself afloat until they had gone, certain of his death, then he clambered up on the ice and dragged himself to the police station, where they rubbed him with brandy and brought him home, bluish-purple, his fingers bruised and bleeding, the hair on his temples turned white. Maxim had the presence of mind not to reveal to the police the cause of his mishap; he pretended to have fallen in by accident. Grandmother and Varvara slapped the faces of Mikhail and Yakov, and grandfather made them beg Maxim's forgiveness, but he bore them no malice. Only to grandmother he would occasionally complain during the long weeks of convalescence: " Why have they done this to me? What have I done to them? Why, mama? " Shortly after this he was given a commission to build a triumphal arch at Astrakhan in honour of the tsar's visit, and with the first boat the Peshkovs left Nizhni Novgorod, to Varvara's unconcealed joy. A few years later Maxim Peshkov fell a victim to cholera, infected by little Alexey, as we have seen. Grandmother arrived to fetch the bereaved family back to Nizhni Novgorod. Alexey enjoyed the trip hugely, watching through the porthole the " silken banks " of Mother Volga and absorbing impressions galore. He was unconscious of the loss of his father, and merely curious about the corpse of his baby brother, who had died on the way, and whom they were to bury at the first stop of the boat, at Saratov.

A buoyant faith in life and mankind, despite disheartening knocks and blows — has not Gorky inherited this trait from the jovial Maxim Peshkov? In any event, he speaks of his father in a tone which, however reserved, suggests love, even pride, and congeniality. As to his mother, although he knew her a longer time and remembers her more distinctly, he has drawn her with aching curiosity, uncertain to the end of his ability to gauge her. It appears that Varvara Peshkova's affection for her firstborn came in rare spasms; most of the time she was either away from him, or regarded him with a coldness which the child felt keenly. Is it possible that Varvara harboured a bitterness against the cause of her great bereavement? On that boat trip from Astrakhan to Nizhni Novgorod, with one corpse behind them and another tiny one with them, Gorky recalls his mother, " her great graceful body, dark iron face, heavy crown of blond braids of hair — all about her powerful and firm — as though through a mist or a transparent cloud, out of which looked distantly and unamiably grey eyes, as large as those of grandmother."

Yet the rare strokes with which Gorky draws his mother are telling enough to make her unforgettable. Amidst the " leaden abominations of Russian life," which Gorky began early to observe at the home of his grandparents, the figure of his mother stands out aloof, different and alien. " At times, for a short while, mother would appear from somewhere. Haughty, severe, she looked at everything with cold grey eyes, like a winter sun, and quickly disappeared, leaving nothing to be remembered by." Reserved and dignified, tastefully dressed (she made her own clothes), Varvara Peshkova seemed out of place among the slovenly and squabbling Kashirins. Her words were few but compelling. On one occasion little Alexey innocently asked grandmother whether uncle Mikhail was going to get a thrashing for having done a misdeed. Uncle Mikhail struck the table with his hand and shouted to his sister that if she did not muzzle her pup he would knock his head off. Varvara's " Try. Touch him." subdued her wild brother and silenced them all. " She had a way of saying short words that seemed to push

people out of her path, to brush them aside and make them shrink."

Varvara dominated even her father, the thundering Zeus of the Kashirin household. Towering above the red-bearded " little goat," as grandmother affectionately called him, his daughter could reduce him to a limp rag, helplessly whimpering in inconsequential rage, and in the end yielding his ground. Thus when once she returned from some town or other, after giving birth to a baby out of wedlock, and her father began to fume and scream in the manner of a Russian patriarch, the wayward widow calmly declared that she would not allow him to shout at her. In the Kashirin world such a declaration was an unheard of affront, a breach of the hoary tradition of woman's inferiority. Her father even collapsed on a chair in astonishment, and mumbled: " Stay — who am I? Eh? How is it, then? " But in the end he gave in, reconciling himself to the fact, pointed out to him by his wonderful wife, that such things (as Varvara's irregularity) happen even among merchants and the gentry.

Yet the old Kashirin was reluctant to give up the idea of his being the *paterfamilias* of the unlimited authority given him by Russian custom, and sanctioned by the *Domostroy*, the domestic code published under Ivan the Terrible. He had been forced to submit to his daughter's elopement with Maxim Peshkov, and later, to the indiscretion of her young widowhood. But he made one more desperate effort to exercise his paternal power: he tried to force her into marriage with a well-to-do watchmaker. Gorky has drawn a portrait of that fellow, one of his numerous grotesques. A quiet, bald, one-eyed man, in a long black frock coat, looking like a monk. " He always took his seat in a corner of the room and assumed a smile, bending his head to one side and oddly supporting it with one finger thrust into his cleft shaven chin. He was a darkish person, and his solitary eye looked at all of us with a peculiar fixity. He said little, and often repeated: ' Do not trouble, it does not matter.' " Little Alexey felt uneasy in the presence of this man, and with curiosity not unmixed with fear he watched him from the opposite corner, where he cuddled up in a spacious easy chair. He observed the mobile face of the watchmaker,

and he tells us that " it was oily, liquescent, melting and float-ing. When he smiled his thick lips shifted over to his right cheek, and his puny nose also wriggled about, like a dumpling on a plate. His big protruding ears moved queerly, now rising together with the eyebrow of the seeing eye, now converging toward the cheekbones. It looked as though he might at will cover his nose with those ears, as with the palms of his hands. Sometimes he sighed, thrust out his dark tongue that was round like a pestle, and with a cunning circular movement licked his thick glossy lips." Gorky adds that all this did not strike him as amusing; it only amazed him and compelled him to watch the man incessantly.

Left a great deal to himself, the boy overheard most of the elders' talk, and while he failed to comprehend everything, he had enough precocity to draw his own conclusions. Once he heard mother's clear voice ring in answer to her father's per-sistent arguments: " I won't! Never! " He also noticed that his mother was growing sullen, circles appeared under her eyes, she walked about disheveled, in an unbuttoned waist. Alexey, who adored his distant mother, and expected her to be always beautiful, severe, different from the rest, was offended by her untidiness. She even shouted at him without cause, while in-structing him in reading. He knew that she was unhappy, and suspected grandfather back of her unhappiness. But when he presumed to tell his mother that she was apparently troubled and not liking it to live with them, she angrily retorted: " Mind your own work." It remained for the lonely boy to watch in silence the course of the drama. The dénouement came one day, when he was with mother in her room, and grandmother thrust a frightened face through the opened door, and vanished after whispering that the watchmaker had arrived.

Mother did not stir or start. The door opened again, grand-father stood on the threshold, and said solemnly:

" Dress yourself, Varvara, and come along! "

Without rising or looking at him, she asked:

" Come where? "

" Come along, in God's name! Don't argue. He is a peaceful

man, a master of his trade, and he'll be a good father to Alexey. . . ."

Grandfather spoke with an air of unusual importance, stroking his sides with the palms of his hands the while, and his elbows, bent backwards, trembled, as though his hands tried to stretch out forward, while he struggled to keep them back.

Mother interrupted him calmly:

" I am telling you, I won't do that. . . ."

Grandfather took a step toward her, stretched his hands out, as if he had gone blind, and arching and bristling he muttered hoarsely:

" Come along! Or I'll drag you to him — by your hair! "

" You'll drag me? " asked mother, standing up. Her face white, her eyes terrifyingly narrow, she swiftly tore off her waist and skirt. Wearing nothing but a chemise, she came up to grandfather and said:

" Drag me! "

He showed his teeth and shook his fist in her face:

" Varvara, get dressed! "

Mother brushed him aside with her hand, and took hold of the door knob:

" Well, come on! "

" I'll curse you," hissed grandfather.

" I am not afraid. Well? "

She opened the door, but grandfather grabbed her by the rim of her chemise, dropped on his knees, and hissed:

" Varvara, devil, you'll be ruined! Don't disgrace us! "

And he whimpered softly, pitifully:

" Mo-ther! Mo-ther! "

Grandmother was already barring mother's way; shooing her back as if she were a hen, she drove her inside the door, growling through her teeth:

" Varvara, you silly, what are you doing? Scat, you shameless hussy! "

She pushed her into the room, and secured the door with the hook. Then she bent over grandfather, helping him up with one hand, and scolding him with the other:

" Ugh-ugh, old devil! You've no sense."

She set him on the couch, and he flopped down like a rag doll, mouth open and head waggling. Grandmother cried to mother:

THE KASHIRINS

GORKY'S recollections of his grandparents are more complete and distinct than those of his parents, for he lived with them longer and shared their daily existence in a much closer intimacy. It is characteristic of Gorky's talent that, as a result of his closer acquaintance with his sitters, the portraits of his grandfather and, even more so, of his grandmother, are his happiest creations. And as in the case of all great portraits, whether by pen or brush or chisel, the individuality of their personal traits and the uniqueness of their presentation do not deprive these portraits of their all-human and universal appeal and value. At the same time, the Kashirin household, individually and collectively, reflects as in a drop of water the Russian people, with all their complexity and contradictoriness, their kindliness and brutality, religiosity and amorality, beastliness and beauty.

From the outset, the five-year-old Alexey was struck by the difference between his two grandparents, with whom he came to live after the death of his father, a difference both external and intrinsic. His very first recorded recollection, at the corpse of his father, is that of holding the hand of grandmother, a " round, large-headed woman, with enormous eyes and a funny spongy nose; she was all black, soft, and wonderfully interesting." He became at once attached to her, and his admiration for her grew as he watched her force combined with geniality at the birth of his little brother, at the funeral of his father, and on the Volga steamer, journeying from Astrakhan to Nizhni Novgorod. He records his first impression of his grandfather as he saw him at the head of the whole Kashirin

family who came to meet them at the wharf : " a small, wizened old man, in a long black coat, with a short beard red like gold, a beak of a nose, and green eyes." The first remark that old Kashirin made about Alexey was that his cheekbones were like his father's. Did he refer to their Asiatic prominence? That feature is too common in Russia to be commented upon. Rather did the remark reflect Kashirin's instinctive misgiving at the boy's resemblance to Maxim Peshkov, a bird of a different feather, hence suspiciously alien. Alexey too felt foreign to that crowd, and was conscious of a particular dislike for his grandfather : he " at once sensed in him an enemy, and began to regard him with a peculiar interest, a wary curiosity."

Grandmother won the heart of Alexey for the rest of his life. Indeed it is difficult not to be captivated by this woman, as described by Gorky. Soft, round, generous, simple, direct, she regarded the world, nature, and all living creatures with wonderment and love, and everything she said and did had a hearty aptness about it. Already on the deck of the boat Alexey began to draw strength and comfort from the proximity of this saintly Pagan. She disarmed all malice and meanness among those around her, conquering the rough sailors by her even kindliness and sparkling humour. The beauty of the Volga shores, of the approaching vista of Nizhni Novgorod with its golden church cupolas, moved her to tears of joy, and she would punctuate her ecstasy by the laconic rhapsody which summed up her whole outlook : " Look, look, how good it all is ! " What fascinated the boy in particular about his grandmother, were her stories. Whether she told fairy-tales about goblins and imps, or legends of saints and warriors, or reminiscences from her own past, Alexey drank in eagerly and asked for more and more. Her language, strong, rhythmic, colourful with folk imagery, is regrettably beyond the ken of the translator. There is no doubt that, when at his best, Gorky is indebted for his style to his grandmother. The effect of her stories on him may be seen from the following passage, relating his experience on the boat :

As she spoke, she sang her words with a peculiar melodiousness, so that they easily took root in my memory, like flowers,

for they were just as caressing, as bright and luscious. When she smiled, the cherry-dark pupils of her eyes dilated and flared up with an inexpressibly charming light. The smile cheerfully revealed her strong white teeth, and despite the multitudinous wrinkles in the swarthy skin of her cheeks, her whole face appeared young and radiant. What spoiled the face was that spongy nose with its distended nostrils and red tip. She snuffed tobacco out of a black snuff-box ornamented with silver. She was all dark, but she radiated from within — through her eyes — with an inextinguishable, joyous, and warm light. Though stooping, almost humpbacked, and very corpulent, she moved lightly and gracefully, for all the world a huge cat — just as soft as that genial beast.

Before she came into my life I seemed to have been asleep, tucked away in darkness. Then she appeared, woke me up, led me into the light of day, linked my surroundings with a continuous thread, wove them into a many-coloured lacework, and made herself my friend for life, the nearest, most understandable, and dearest being. Her disinterested love for the world enriched me and saturated me with stout fortitude for a hard life.

The life upon which Alexey Peshkov was entering at the age of five, was to be hard, indeed, and he certainly needed a goodly store of fortitude to cope with it and not let it submerge him. The light joy and mutual tenderness that had reigned in his parental home and was vaguely remembered by him, gave room to a heavy atmosphere of hatred, mistrust, and coarseness. The orphan was doomed to a childhood whose brutal features adumbrated a similar boyhood and youth, that is to say, to an environment that tended to kill all self-respect and discourage all creative initiative and individuality. Were it not for the buoying influence of his grandmother, who knows whether Alexey Peshkov could have emerged from the " lower depths " and become Maxim Gorky? It would be difficult to find among modern writers one whose formative years were as discouraging of an artist's assertiveness as those of Gorky. Recall Tolstoy's *Childhood, Boyhood,* and *Youth!* Compare the precious ruminations of Marcel Proust, or even the fine torments of the hero of Somerset Maugham's *Of Human Bondage,*

with the overwhelming, staggering, dehumanizing experiences of young Alexey Peshkov.

The precociously observant little boy soon realized that his grandfather's home " was steeped in a hot fog of mutual hostility, of all against all; not only were the grown people infected with it, but even the children played a lively part in this hostility." He later learned that at the time of their arrival from Astrakhan, his Kashirin uncles, Mikhail and Yakov, were in a particularly ugly mood, clamouring for the immediate division of their father's property, including the dowry intended for Varvara and withheld by old Kashirin because of her secret elopement. The following scene is characteristic enough to bear extensive quotation.

Soon after our arrival, during dinner at the kitchen table, a quarrel flared up. Suddenly my uncles leaped to their feet, and leaning across the table, began to howl and snarl at grandfather, plaintively showing their teeth and shaking themselves like dogs. Grandfather, turning quite red, rapped at the table with his wooden spoon and crowed loudly like a rooster:

" I'll turn you out of the house without a penny! "

With her face twisted painfully, grandmother said:

" Give them away everything, father, then you'll have more peace. Give them all! "

" Hist, conniver! " screamed grandfather with flashing eyes, and it was odd that, small as he was, he could scream so deafeningly.

Mother rose from the table, and going unhurriedly to the window, turned her back on us all.

On a sudden uncle Mikhail struck his brother on the face with the back of his hand. The other howled, grappled with Mikhail, and both of them rolled on the floor, growling, moaning, swearing. The children began to cry; aunt Natalia, who was pregnant, shrieked wildly; my mother seized her round her body and dragged her off somewhere; the jovial pock-marked nursemaid, Eugenia, chased the children out of the kitchen; chairs were knocked down; the young broad-shouldered apprentice, Tsiganok, sat astride uncle Mikhail's back, while the foreman, Gregory, a bald bearded man in dark spectacles, calmly tied uncle's hands with a towel.

His neck stretched out, uncle Mikhail scrubbed the floor with his thin black beard and rattled in his throat terrifyingly, while grandfather, running around the table, shrieked plaintively:

" Brothers, eh! Flesh and blood! Ekh, you-u . . ."

As for me, I got frightened at the beginning of the squabble and clambered up the stove. From there I watched with dread and amazement how grandmother washed the blood off uncle Yakov's battered face by the brass washstand, while he wept and stamped his feet. In a heavy voice she boomed:

" Infidels, savages, come to your senses! "

Grandfather, pulling on his shirt torn in the battle, shouted to her:

" Well, witch, fine beasts you've brought into the world! "

When uncle Yakov left the kitchen, grandmother rushed into the corner where the icons hung, wailing heart-breakingly:

" Most Holy Mother of God, bring my children back to reason! "

Grandfather stood with his side toward her, and glancing at the table on which everything was upset and spilled, he said softly:

" Keep an eye on them, mother, or Varvara's life won't be worth much, with her brothers after her."

" What are you saying, God help you! You better take your shirt off, and I'll mend it."

Pressing his head with the palms of her hands, she kissed him on the forehead; and he — so small compared to her — thrust his face into her shoulder. . . .

I turned awkwardly on the stove, and knocked down a flat-iron, which clattered down the steps and flopped into the slop bucket. Grandfather jumped up one step, dragged me down, and began to stare at me as though he saw me for the first time.

" Who got you up on the stove? Mother? "

" Myself."

" You lie."

" No. Myself. I got scared."

He pushed me away, lightly striking me on the forehead with his palm.

" Like father, like son! Get out of here! "
I was only too glad to run out of the kitchen.

This was Alexey's initiation into the Kashirin order of living, that is, the order of the average Russian family of the
lower middle class. The scene described was followed by
many others, even more brutal and sanguinary. The boy could
see and hear things whose eloquent moral was to the effect that
life presented a hard and harsh business, with love and kindness as rare as was beauty in that slough of sordidness. The
stupor of routine and pettiness fettered all minds; imagination
and ingeniousness were shown only when there was an urge
to play a mean trick on someone. Stupidity and sadism coexisted in the same person in equal proportion. Thus uncle
Mikhail, the beastliest of the lot, combined the two traits admirably. It was he who had Yakov's little boy heat Gregory's
thimble red hot, so that the half blind foreman should burn
his finger. It happened that instead of Gregory, it was grandfather who slipped on the thimble, and thereupon danced
around the room in raging pain, to the delight of his sons.
Mikhail then betrayed the culprit, and his little nephew received a cruel thrashing on Saturday night, the traditional
night for patriarchal chastisements at the Kashirins'. We already know how the two brothers tried to drown Maxim
Peshkov in an ice-hole out of envy for his popularity and
greed for his potential share in the inheritance. They were also
responsible for the death of Tsiganok, the jolliest and most
picturesque member of the household, by loading upon him
an enormous oaken cross and letting it crush him when he
slipped under the burden. Incidentally, it was uncle Yakov
who bought that cross and had vowed to carry it on his shoulders to the cemetery, to place it on the grave of his wife, whose
life he had cut short by pommelling her night after night while
lying at her side in bed. Wife-beating among uncultivated
Russians was regarded as a natural outlet for one's bile.
Grandfather indulged in this sport himself, but forbade it to
his sons, and that is why Yakov had to perform his manly
duty secretly, at night and under cover. Mikhail also chafed

under grandfather's injunction, and was compelled to beat his wife only at night. She was charged by grandfather to teach Alexey the Paternoster and other prayers, and the boy was curious about the pale, timid aunt Natalia, with her child-like face and eyes " so transparent that it seemed as though one might see through them what was back of her head." More than once he saw blue swellings under Natalia's eyes and swollen lips on her yellowish face, and grandmother explained to him that these marks were Mikhail's nightly handi-work. Natalia died in childbirth.

How many modern writers could boast of such an instructive environment during their childhood years? There was a wealth of impressions for the painfully curious Alexey to store up in his memory. Men and things. And the landscape! Mikhail and Yakov finally received their shares, established themselves separately, and grandfather bought himself " a large interesting house." There was a saloon on the main floor, and an orchard leading into a rank ravine, from which the neigh-bourhood lads waged stone-throwing battles against the pug-nacious newcomer, Alexey. At his first inspection of the ravine, Alexey was nudged by grandfather, who " merrily winked " at the slopes overgrown with willow shrubs, and referred to the abundance of " switches." Soon, he warned him, he would begin to teach him the ABC, and the willow branches would be in demand.

The garret room was occupied by grandmother and Alexey; bending across the window-sill, the boy supplemented his edu-cation by watching the drunkards wallowing in the street dust, staggering into the saloon, or being thrown out of it " like sacks of flour." The inquisitive boy found it " entertaining to watch all that from above." He took in also the landscape, which was the typical vista of his early life, with variations. He could see the wide street, thickly covered with dust, which led to the city jail, on the one side, and to the fire-tower with the revolving figure of the watchman, like that of " a dog on a chain," on the other side. The main square was criss-crossed with gullies, one of them perpetually filled with greenish water. The discoloured houses on either side of the street, powdered

with dust, were huddled close together, " like beggars on the church porch." The rare pedestrians wended their way slowly and resembled " cockroaches along the hearth of the oven." The odour of onion- and carrot-pies rose to the nostrils of Alexey, intensifying his distress and filling his breast with an oppressive sense of tedium, as if with " molten warm lead."

Before long Alexey's home ceased to be merely a point of neutral observation. " Nearly every Sunday urchins gathered by the gates, and joyously heralded through the street: ' The Kashirins are fighting again! ' " Uncle Mikhail would appear in the evening, sometimes alone, and sometimes with a few other drunken rowdies, and there would begin a siege of the house. The air reverberated with thick oaths and murderous threats, cobble-stones were hurled at the doors and windows, and much damage was done to the shrubs and trees and the outlying bathhouse. It is not clear as to what Mikhail's grievance actually was (presumably he hankered after the rest of his father's property), but he appeared more or less regularly from behind the street corner, bedraggled, filthy, drunk, and lead the attack against his parents' home, calling them bad names, and occasionally bruising them with missiles and clubs. Grandfather, on espying the approach of his magnificent son, would fortify himself with a few assistants and lie in wait for Mikhail, seething with wrath but cool enough to admonish his men to strike the assailant " on his hands and legs, please, but not on his noddle." On one such night grandmother thrust her arms out of a little window, whose pane had been smashed by Mikhail, and implored her son to run for his life, " for Christ's sake," or they would tear his limbs apart. In answer came a torrent of abuse, and Mikhail's stake hit grandmother on the arm and broke the bone. He finally succeeded in smashing through the door, but was at once hurled off the porch " like mud off a spade."

The street enjoyed the spectacle hugely, but took it as a normal occurrence. Alexey had had enough experience to realize the prevailing, practically universal, cruelty and meanness of the people around, their pleasure in hurting one another, bodily or in such delicately indirect ways as poisoning the

neighbour's dog, or cutting the tail off his cat, or killing his chickens, or pouring kerosene into his barrels of pickled cabbage and cucumbers. When he wondered at the cause of their cruelty and asked his grandmother about it, she retorted that they were not malicious but stupid. The stupidity and tedium of their existence, the wretchedness and hopelessness of their drudgery, accounted for the quest of an outlet for their limited fantasy and desire of some change in their humdrum. We shall see Alexey himself on occasion feel the need of avenging himself on life or fate in the same primitive way as we do, when we kick a chair that has offended our toe.

In this environment the uncommonness of decent persons made them fairy-like. The number of such individuals encountered by the child Alexey would not exhaust the fingers of one hand. There was Tsiganok, the swarthy foundling (hence his sobriquet) whom grandmother loved more than her own sons. Gay and dexterous, he good-naturedly let himself be exploited by others, and in the simplicity of his heart put his arm under grandfather's rod, to avert the blows from Alexey. His death under too heavy a load showed the wastefulness and callousness of the Kashirin brothers. When grandfather saw him dying on the floor, he raged at his sons for having ruined a priceless worker. To Alexey the loss of a friend and comrade was irreplaceable. He could not find any joy in the friendliness of Gregory the foreman, a kindly man whom the Kashirins robbed of his health and eyesight. He was well disposed toward Alexey, often spoke to him with admiration of his father, Maxim Peshkov, and made to him many an illuminating remark concerning the Kashirins and their vices. But the colourless sadness of the red-eyed Gregory with his black spectacles, bald head, and straggly beard, depressed the child. When Gregory eventually became totally blind and went about the streets singing and begging for alms, Alexey shuddered at the sound of his voice and avoided meeting him.

Still another "decent" man who flashed for a time on Alexey's horizon of that period was the pale-nosed scientist who boarded with the Kashirins. He was a taciturn man, nick-

named Fine Business, because of his fondness of employing this phrase in answer to all sorts of requests and remarks. Alexey was tremendously intrigued by this odd person, and from the roof of the shed he would watch him through the window of his room littered with books, bottles, lumps of copper and lead. He weighed and measured things and powders, produced abominable smells, boiled and melted metal particles, and altogether justified the suspicions of the regular folk around the house. A Black Magician! At first Fine Business resented Alexey's inquisitiveness, but gradually he learned to like him, and permitted him to spend long hours with him, listened to his chatter attentively and tolerantly, unlike other grown-ups, occasionally making some brief but pertinent remark or retort, and often inviting him to sit quietly and share his silence. It was Fine Business who once, after being moved to tears by grandmother's recital of an old folk-ballad, urged Alexey to learn how to write, and to write down grandmother's stories. It was also he who gave the future writer one of the most useful precepts in literary art — economy. The boy came from the street and gave an account of a bloody scene he had just witnessed. Fine Business was deeply impressed, but when Alexey in his excitement kept up the story, the man embraced him and said: " Enough, there is no need for more! You've already said all that was necessary, brother — all! "

Both grandfather and grandmother disapproved of Alexey's attachment to the queer, shabby individual, and finally they made their boarder move. The parting scene between the boy and his friend was depressing for both. When Alexey asked the man why no one in the house liked him, the scientist hugged the boy to his side, and answered with a wink: " An alien, do you understand? That's why. Of a different kind. . . ." Here we have an early symptom: what to the incurious average appeared objectionable because of its novelty and strangeness, had an especial appeal to the greedy mind of Alexey Peshkov. He raged at his grandparents for having driven away his precious friend, called them " blockheads," and that evening at supper smashed his spoon, for which he was duly whipped.

" Thus ended his friendship with the first of that endless row of aliens in his native land," whom he was to meet in life, — " its best men."

Those were the only people, outside of his grandmother, whom little Alexey regarded with warmth. To be sure his eye was precociously keen and early enough detected the relativity of good and evil. He was to find shadows even in the sun he worshipped most — his grandmother, and he was to learn with amazement that the most obvious villains had attractive features. Thus uncle Yakov proved to be a good-hearted, broadminded, charmingly impractical sort of a man, and Eugene Maximov, the stepfather whom he stabbed with a knife, reappeared later in Alexey's life as a pathetically delicate and complex character. It was grandfather who taught the boy his first practical lesson against thinking in absolute terms and adopting definitive labels. He initiated his five-year-old grandson into the time-honoured system of pedagogy, by beating him till he was unconscious, yet he made him soon realize that " grandfather was neither malevolent nor terrible ! "

Old Kashirin was one of those self-made men who are convinced that their own hardships justify them in tyrannizing over others. Perhaps such people come to look upon hardships as the necessary prerequisite for success. Kashirin was a petty tyrant ; he displayed his wilfulness as long as he met with no resistance, but when he encountered a strong character, as Maxim Peshkov, or his own daughter Varvara, he collapsed like a " rag doll." He was essentially mediocre, too weak for either great malice or intense kindness. The bitter memory of his past privations, coupled with the accepted standard of a Russian patriarch, prompted his desire to lord it over the household and to express his authority in a fashion most eloquent for him — corporal chastisement of those whose resistance was precluded. He beat his wife, whenever he was in need of an outlet for his otherwise impotent rage or chagrin. On Saturday night, before going to vespers, he methodically thrashed his grandchildren for their weekly offences with an unmalicious glee, enjoying his power and at the same time conscious of performing a deed good for the soul of the culprit.

Alexey's first taste of this Saturday night ordeal came as a result of his curiosity at the wonderful colour-transformations of the clothes dipped by the dyers. He was persuaded by his cousin Sasha, uncle Yakov's son, to dip a snow-white table-cloth into a dark-blue dye. Thereupon Sasha informed grandfather of Alexey's attempt. We have a memorable portrait of this Kashirin lad: " lean and dark, with bulging crab-eyes, he talked hastily and softly, choking with his words, and all the time mysteriously glancing from side to side, as though on the point of running away somewhere and hiding himself. His hazel pupils were stationary, but when he became excited they trembled together with the whites." On Saturday night Sasha was the first to be thrashed by grandfather, for the heated thimble that had been intended for Gregory but had inadvertently burned old Kashirin's finger, and also, curiously enough, for informing on Alexey! During the ceremony Alexey was ordered to stand by and look. He was sickened by the humiliation and painfulness of the scene, and when his turn came, he refused to submit, as Sasha did, but fought and struggled, pulled grandfather's red beard, and bit his finger. The patriarch was exasperated by the unexpected opposition. He raged and bellowed, mauled the boy, and finally hurled him against the bench, battering his face and whipping him into unconsciousness.

For several days Alexey lay ill in bed, back upward. He tells us that those were " great days " in his life. In the course of these days he " must have matured greatly and acquired a peculiar sensibility. From that time he began to experience a restless interest in people, and his heart, as though it had been flayed, became unbearably sensitive to any offence and pain, whether his own or that of others." He was to see and know vast varieties of pain in his life, yet his heart apparently never healed, and remained raw to the touch of violence. At the age of sixty, when I visited him, Maxim Gorky, furrowed and battered, rich in heartache and disenchantment, could not control his tears when he spoke of mass cruelties during the revolution, or of the hungry artists and scientists in the time of famine.

As he thus lay in bed, grandfather appeared suddenly, " as though he had jumped down from the ceiling," sat at his side, stroked his head, and began one of those magnificent Russian soliloquies, simple and direct in substance, yet intricate in design and colour-pattern. At first Alexey had a great mind to kick his tormentor, but soon he was fascinated by the little old man, who bristled his red hair, flashed his green eyes, and lowered his high pitch to a deep sonority as he " blared " into the boy's face his " sturdy, ponderous " words, which he " laid one upon the other nimbly and adroitly." He started by admitting that he had overdone, but explained it by losing his temper because of Alexey's scratching and biting. But, then, it does not harm to be beaten by one of your family — " that is not an insult but a lesson." He himself had been flogged and beaten and abused so that " the Lord God himself must have wept looking on. Yet the result! An orphan, the son of a mendicant mother, had risen to his position — head of a guild, commander of men! " One may doubt whether this argument made an impression on the sorely wounded mind of the boy. What caught his imagination was grandfather's account of his early life, when he towed barges up and down the Volga, pulling and tugging from dawn till dark, under the beating sun, with a throbbing head, sweating blood, and sometimes collapsing from exhaustion. " That's how we lived in the sight of God and the gracious Lord Jesus Christ! " Then there followed a description of a summer evening, when the boatmen would build bonfires on a bank of the Volga and strike up a song, so that the river " seemed to flow ever faster, ready to rear on its haunches like a horse, to the very clouds," and all sorrow would vanish " like dust blown by the wind." Grandfather was carried away by his own reminiscences, while Alexey was so thrilled that when they called the old man on business, he begged him to stay. He did.

Alexey discovered that grandfather was " neither malevolent nor terrible. It was difficult, to the point of tears, to recall that it was he who had so cruelly thrashed him, but neither could one forget that." Time and again Gorky speaks of his grandfather with a certain warmth, but on the whole we feel that

he resents old Kashirin's conceit, his domineering tone, superior air, and supercilious refrain: " Ekh, you-u! " We must remember that the boy had before his eyes the two grandparents, could not help comparing them to one another, and in this comparison grandfather was bound to lose on every point. Even as a story-teller, engaging though he was, he yielded in Alexey's eyes to grandmother. She had a variety of story and song, mingled fact with fiction, and imbued everything she told with the poesy of fairyland, while her husband was contemptuous of fairy-tales, and related only what he had seen himself or heard others recount as actuality.

To the observant mind of the boy the old couple presented two different outlooks, two divergent religions. Grandfather worshipped a stern God, a vindictive Jehovah, formal and exacting. He was extremely regular about his prayers, declaimed them endlessly, without the slightest variation, standing always on the same spot before the icons, stiff and severe, like a soldier reading his report to a superior. He spoke of God with awe, using His name as a threat and trying to inspire others with dread of His punitive propensities. His religion was not unmercenary; he expected to be rewarded for his piety, and on occasion would promise some saint or other a candle in return for a favour. Though strictly honest in his direct dealings with people, he did not scruple, toward the end of his life, to lend money on usurious terms. Clever Tsiganok, when sent to market for provisions, used to bring home meats and groceries for an amount many times exceeding the sum given to him for the purchase. He even retained some change from that sum. Tsiganok did that as a trick, enjoying his dexterity and not caring a whit for the money. Mikhail and Yakov greedily danced around the sleigh loaded with partly purloined goods, and managed to wheedle from Tsiganok the change he kept for himself. As to grandfather, he observed the show with ostensible sullenness, mumbled his misgiving, but said no definite word of reproach or enjoinment. His greediness became in the end a regular malady with him. The harsh youth, the uphill climb to prosperity, the disappointment caused by his children, and finally the loss of his property

and money through untoward circumstances and dubious investments, combined to derange his mind and turn him into a morbid miser. He refused to provide for his wife, and made her buy her own food. Ultimately his dementia became indubitable; he begged in the streets, imploring to let him have "a piece of cake," and ending up with the only reminder of his past grandeur, the supercilious refrain: "Ekh, you-u!" His austere God failed him when he broke down materially and mentally.

Grandmother's religion found expression in her frequent exclamation: "How good it is!" Everything in God's world is good, because God is good. Alexey liked her God; He was so intimate, so understanding. He overheard grandmother's long prayers, as she knelt at night on her bedroom floor. She recounted to God the family difficulties, and asked Him in simple words to put sense into the heads of her husband and sons, to "smile a joy" upon poor Varvara, to heal Gregory's failing eyes, to forgive her own sins, knowing that she sins not from wickedness but because of her "silly mind." Her prayers were spontaneous and therefore would not "bore" God, as she feared grandfather's lengthy and stereotyped prayers did. Lying by her side in the large warm bed, Alexey would wind around his neck her "heavy satin braids," and listen, breathless, to her descriptions of God enthroned on a hill, in the middle of a meadow, surrounded by angels who swarm about Him, "like falling snow," and report to Him on the deeds of men. She *knew* all that perfectly, though she admitted not to have seen it. With the Mother of God she was even more intimate, and every morning would address her with fresh endearments, pouring her heart out in such caresses as "Source of joy, immaculate beauty, apple tree in bloom, dear heart pure and heavenly, golden sun," and the like. She requested Her help and protection with more assurance than when she addressed God (she dared not call Him otherwise than Lord, at times Sir), for here she spoke as woman to woman, mother to mother. Her prayer to Jesus for mercy was a plea "for the sake of His Mother."

Grandmother saw all creation permeated with divinity. The

enormous horse, Sharap, the terror of the household, playfully nibbled her shoulders as she spoke to him: " Well, my baby! Well, my kitten! Feeling frolicky? Go ahead, God's plaything! " Another time, while harnessing him, she chatted away: " Why so sad, toiler of God, eh? " And Sharap sighed in reply. The earth and everything on it were God's, in His keeping, and responsible to Him. When she saw the neighbour's cat bring a starling in his mouth, she rescued the benumbed bird, and reproached the cat: " You have no fear of God, you wretched villain! " She told Alexey of the imps and devils that she had encountered at one time or another, and even these appeared amusing rather than evil, these too were God's children. But though genial and accessible, grandmother's God gave no occasion for familiarity or irreverence. Alexey was not afraid of Him, as he was of grandfather's cruel God, but he found it " impossible to lie to Him." He was " ashamed " to hide anything from this good God, and for this reason he " never lied to grandmother." What made Him especially dear to the boy's heart, was the discovery that He was not so forbiddingly omnipotent as grandfather presented Him to be. Once Alexey locked the fat wife of the tavernkeeper in the cellar, in revenge for her having abused grandmother and thrown a carrot at her. Grandmother chided him for interfering in the affairs of grown-up people; besides, it was not for him to know who was guilty or innocent. God alone is entitled to judge and punish. She took a pinch of snuff, half closed her right eye, and musingly added that, in the last account, God Himself is not always able to tell where the guilt lies. But does not God know everything? Softly and sadly she replied that if He knew everything, people would forego doing a great many things which they were doing. She pictured Him, " the Sir Father, as He looks and looks down from heaven on the earth, upon all of us, and once in a while He bursts out weeping and sobbing: ' Oh people, people, my dear people! Okh, how I pity you! ' " Whereupon she too began to weep, and with wet cheeks moved to the corner to pray.

With such a charmingly imperfect, anthropomorphic God, one's religion, or ethical code, could hardly be straitlaced.

Grandmother told Alexey that when his parents were still in disfavour with grandfather, she stole from him as much money and other things as she could, and brought these on the sly to the newlyweds. She added parenthetically that it is permissible to steal, when you're doing it not for yourself. Compare this elastic morality with grandfather's stiff yet mercenary, bookkeeper honesty. Grandfather looked through his fingers at Tsiganok's hazardous purchases, but grandmother refused to talk to her favourite on those days, and growled: " Ehk-khe! We've lots of rules and regulations, but none of truth and right." Like her husband, she had known hardships, had begged for alms with her crippled mother (she is suspiciously silent as to whether she had a father), had known blows and abuse, yet unlike him, she emerged from the crucible mellow and generous, charitable and tolerant.

Her softness, kindliness, and meekness before her husband, did not prevent her from being marvellously aggressive, determined, active and efficient, when those around her showed indifference, or fear and bewilderment. Alexey once accompanied grandmother to the square whence she fetched water, carrying it in two pails on a yoke. They saw five townspeople beat up a peasant; they threw him on the ground and were worrying him as dogs might worry another dog. Grandmother threw the pails down, and brandishing the yoke she rushed at the rowdies, struck them on the heads and shoulders, and finally turned them to flight. Then she set to work to bathe the wounds of the peasant. " His face had been trampled by heavy boots, one nostril was torn off, and he pressed it with a dirty finger, all the while howling and coughing. Blood spurted from under the man's finger over grandmother's face and breast; she trembled, and also cried." An instructive scene for the little boy. Only when the assailants were about to flee, did some other men decide to take grandmother's side. A fight was a free show, and to interfere in one was regarded unconventional and unsafe.

One of Alexey's early experiences at the Kashirin home was a conflagration which broke out at night at the workshop (uncle Yakov surmised that it was Mikhail's handiwork).

Gorky has always been fascinated by such a spectacle, and some of his best pages are those wherein he describes village- or small town-fires. (In 1923, D. I. Chizhevsky, at Marienbad, read Gorky's horoscope, and found that he was " a son of the sun, that his whole life was illuminated by the sun, and that he would meet an unusual death — in fire.") This first fire of his he watched from under the steps of the porch, afraid lest the nursemaid drag him away together with the other children who were bawling in a chorus. To his observant eye grandmother was " as interesting as the fire itself." Surprised while she was kneeling in prayer on her bedroom floor by grandfather's hoarse announcement that " the Lord had visited " them, she leaped to her feet, and became transformed. She gave short stern orders in all directions, used her fist when necessary on those who were in the way or unduly garrulous, flitted about, dark and sure in the glare of the flames, always doing the right thing at the right moment. Grandfather only whined im- potently. Remembering the presence of vitriol in the workshop, his wife rushed into the flames, to the horror of her husband who expected an explosion any minute, but presently she dove out, scorched and singed, hugging an enormous bottle of vitri- olic oil. Paying no attention to her own burns, she shouted to her husband to get the horse out of the barn. Alexey saw the huge Sharap emerge, eyes red with the reflection of the fire, snorting and rearing, and forcing grandfather to drop the reins and call to his wife for help. She rushed in front of the rearing horse, stretched her arms, and the animal whinnied pitifully and followed her meekly to the gate, calmed by her buoying bass: " Don't fear. D'you think I am going to leave you in this horror? Okh, you, little mouse. . . ."

On the same night, after the fire had been put out, grand- mother had to care for Natalia, Mikhail's martyr wife, who was seized with birth pangs, and at the end of several hours of suffering and piercing screams, died. Only toward morning, bruised and burned, exhausted by toil and pain and nervous strain, grandmother " crept into the room, closed the door with her shoulder, leaned back, and stretching her hands out toward the blue flame of the perpetual holy lamp in front of the icon,

muttered softly, with a childlike plaint: ' My little hands! My little hands hurt. . . .' "

Alexey, who admired grandmother's forcefulness and fearless courage, wondered at her meek submissiveness on other occasions. Her unreserved approbation of God's world puzzled the boy whose keen eye could not help seeing that not all was well in life. He once interrupted grandmother's ecstatic panegyric to God's good order reigning in heaven and on earth, by asking her whether all was good at their home. He was thinking of the fights and abuses he witnessed around the house; of Gregory's failing eyesight; of pale aunt Natalia whom he overheard beseeching God to take her away from this world; of all the meanness and cruelty he was seeing daily. But grandmother made the sign of the cross, and said with conviction: " Glory to the most holy Mother of God — all is good! " Alexey, who carried in his breast the embryonic protest and rebellion of Maxim Gorky, fretted at such fanatic loyalty to God and His order.

He was particularly amazed at grandmother's acceptance of wife-beating as normal and natural. After explaining to him the cause of Natalia's battered and swollen face, and sighing over the brutality of Mikhail, she turned with animation to the past:

" Still, men don't beat their wives as they used to! What if they hit you in the mouth, or on the ear, or drag you by the hair for a bit — in old days they used to torture one for hours and hours! Grandfather beat me one Easter Day from early mass till evening. He would beat and beat, get tired and rest, then start again. He beat me with reins and in all sort of ways."

" Why? What had you done? "

" I forget now. Another time he knocked me about till I was half dead, and then kept me without food for five days — I scarcely lived that through. Again, another time . . ."

I was dumbfounded. Grandmother was twice as big as grandfather, and it was incredible that he should be able to get the better of her.

" Is he stronger than you, then? "

" Not stronger, but older! Besides, he is the husband! For me he will answer to God, but my business is to suffer in patience."

The knowledge that she would submit passively to his blows, encouraged the old Kashirin to use his wife as the Azazel of his grievances. The temptation was too great for that weak strutter. In every respect his superior, grandmother humoured his irascibility and conceit, nursed his hurts and disappointments, and, eternal mother that she was, often calmed and soothed him with the balm of her hearty words, in the same way as she managed to tame the savage Sharap. But on occasion the whimpering weakling would become restive under the caressing yoke, and assert his . . . freedom. Alexey once saw her come up to grandfather, who was whining and complaining against fate, and trying to assuage his spleen. The old man swiftly turned around, and struck her face a staggering blow with his fist. She reeled and almost fell over, but with an effort regained her balance, spat blood at his feet and said softly and quietly: " Ekh, you fool." Gorky tells us of his reaction to this scene:

I was sitting on the low stove, more dead than alive, unable to believe my eyes. This was the first time he had struck grandmother in my presence, and the thing was oppressively nasty, it revealed something new in his nature, something with which I could not reconcile myself, and which seemed to have crushed me.

There is a Russian saying: " The first pancake comes out in a lump." Reality trained Alexey to take things stoically by the dint of their repetition, which made them commonplace. Again, grandmother's aquiescence compelled one to regard the beating as a matter of course. When Alexey followed her to her room, and saw her rinsing her bleeding mouth, she gleefully reported that her teeth were all right; only her lip was bruised. She asked him not to worry about it, condoning grandfather's quick temper by the ill turn which affairs had

taken for him. But Alexey was disconsolate; he was "petrified by intolerable grief."

However accustomed he became to beatings, Alexey was not made of the acquiescing stuff. There was another scene of grandfather punishing his wife, in which the Peshkov grandson was unable to maintain the passivity prescribed for such occasions by the Kashirin code. The scene took place, when grandfather discovered that grandmother was keeping Varvara informed of his plot to marry her to the watchmaker.

He burst into the kitchen, rushed up to grandmother [she was sitting by the table and sewing a shirt for her husband], struck her on the head, and hissed as he swung his fist bruised by the blow:

" Don't you chatter of things you shouldn't, you witch! "

" You're an old fool," quietly said grandmother, putting up straight the headgear-pad which he had knocked off her head. " I am not going to keep silent, not by a long shot! I'll tell her always of your plots . . ."

He threw himself at her, and began to pommel rapidly grandmother's large head. Without defending herself or pushing him away, she said:

" Well, beat me, beat me, little fool! Well, go on, beat me! "

From the stove-shelf I threw at him cushions, blankets, boots, but in his frenzy grandfather did not notice that. Grandmother fell to the floor, and he beat her head with his feet till he finally stumbled and fell down, overturning a pail of water. He jumped up, sputtering and snorting, glanced wildly around, and rushed away to his garret room. Grandmother rose with a groan, sat down on a bench, and began to disentangle her matted hair. I jumped down from the stove, and she said to me angrily:

" Pick up the pillows and things, and put them back on the stove! The idea — throwing pillows! Was it your business? And he too, the old demon, he's kicked the traces clear over, the fool."

Suddenly she gasped, wrinkled up her face, and bending her head called to me:

" Come and look: what is it that hurts me here? "

I disentangled her heavy hair, and saw that a hairpin had

been driven deep into the skin of her head. I pulled it out, but finding another one I felt my fingers grow numb.

" I had better call mother. I am scared! "

She waved her hands:

" What now? I'll call you! Thank God that she has not heard and seen a thing, and you now want to call her! Get away now! "

And with her nimble fingers, a lacemaker's fingers, she began to rummage in her thick black mane. I plucked up courage and helped her pull out from under her skin two more thick, bent hairpins.

" Does it hurt? "

" Never mind. Tomorrow I'll heat a bath, wash my head, and all will be well."

And in a caressing tone she began to beg me:

" Now, pigeon-darling, don't you tell mother that he has beaten me, d'you hear? They are cross at one another as it is. So you won't tell? "

" No."

" Well, don't forget! Come now, let us tidy up here. My face is not bruised? Then all is right, and keep mum."

She set to work to wipe the floor, and I cried out from the depths of my heart:

" You're — like a saint. They torture you and torture you, and you don't mind! "

" What nonsense are you jabbering? A saint, indeed! Silly."

Working on all fours, she growled a long time, while I sat by the stove and thought of a way to take vengeance on grandfather.

Apparently grandmother failed to convert Alexey to her sweet religion. . . .

Throughout the account of his childhood the author remains relatively passive and in the shade. For the most part he is an eager observer. He peeps from the barn roof into the window of Fine Business; he watches domestic brawls from under the table or from that Russian paradise — the platform above the huge stove; he takes in with ecstasy the beauty and dread of his first conflagration from under the porch steps; from his garret window he keeps a sharp eye on the rather drab and

sordid Vanity Fair that passes on the street in front of the tavern and in the courtyards among the variegated tenants within the range of his vision and hearing. He looks and listens, annoys the grown-ups by endless questions, and sponges up quantities of information, authentic and valuable as well as spurious and worthless. Gorky compares himself, at that period, to " a hive, into which all manner of simple drab people deposited the honey of their experience and of their ideas upon life, each one generously enriching my soul with what he had to give. The honey was often dirty and bitter, but the knowledge acquired was honey after all."

Though he was as yet unable to discriminate rationally as to the quality of the contributed " honey," he early developed his likes and dislikes, before he could motivate them. These were both decided and intense, despite his outward reserve and taciturnity, which were due to his meditative and reflective nature. He loved grandmother more than any other person, yet he instinctively resented her opportunism and pietistic acquiescence in things patently wrong. Grandfather's accounts of his past fascinated him to the point of making him forgive, if not forget, the pain and humiliation of the first whipping administered by him, and of the many others that followed. But he plainly disliked, and at times passionately hated the ferret-faced little tyrant, together with his unimaginative religion and wrathful God.

For a while Alexey was attached to uncle Peter, a queer little man, with iron grey curls on his head and beard, who had an abundant store of anecdotic recollections from the time of serfdom, which he narrated in a " buzzing " voice, with the mannerisms of old-fashioned Russian speech. Soon, however, the boy began to sense an abyss of cruelty behind the genial garrulity of his uncle. With chuckling glee Peter dwelt on the descriptions of atrocities committed by the gentry upon their serfs, masking his sadism by unctious phrases and caressing intonations. Alexey discovered with what venom and hatred the amiable grey-beard regarded Russian gentlemen and their offspring. To be sure, hostility mixed with fear was the general feeling of Russian commoners toward the nobility, the numeri-

cally small class that enjoyed all cultural and social privileges under a régime based on inequality and favouritism bestowed on certain groups at the expense of the bulk of the people. The boy knew of the existence of another, superior Russia, a well-mannered, well-dressed, sumptuously housed Russia, that was inaccessible to the common folk. The two Russias had grown further and further apart from the time of Peter the Great, when the Europeanization of the upper crust of the nation was inaugurated with an accelerated tempo, whereas the rest of the people were left to vegetate in their semi-Orientalism. Alexey was aware of the wall between the people and the gentry, but he was amazed at the bitter enmity of uncle Peter against that class. When the boy engaged in a surreptitious friendship with the children of a noble family across the fence, and had to suffer pain and shame when found out, uncle Peter upbraided him mockingly for chumming with " the young serpents " of the gentry. He " hissed " long and virulently, urging his nephew to beat up those boys. His wrinkled little face trembled in hatred, and when Alexey retorted that the boys were kind and should not be beaten, his uncle flew into a rage, drove him away, and began to persecute him from that day in a variety of mean and lying ways. This externally pious and meek old man was detected by the police to have belonged for years to a band of thieves, who specialized in robbing churches. Rather than be arrested, he hid in Kashirin's orchard, and there committed suicide. Alexey was all ears and eyes when uncle Peter's body was discovered, as ever drinking in the horrible details with breathless, painful curiosity. His description of that scene shows how vividly he has retained it in his memory:

. . . all ran into the orchard. There, in a hollow softly bedded with snow lay uncle Peter, his back leaning against a charred beam, and his head drooping toward his chest. Under his right ear was a deep gash, resembling a red mouth, from which bluish pieces stuck out, like teeth. From horror I half shut my eyes, and through the lashes I saw on Peter's knees his knife I knew so well, lying close to the twisted dark fingers of his right hand; his left hand was stuck in the snow. The snow had thawed under him, and his tiny body had sunk into deep

sparkling down, looking even more childlike than when he was alive. On the right side of the body a quaint red design was formed on the snow, resemblind a bird, while on the left the snow was untouched, smooth, and dazzlingly bright. The submissively drooping head pressed its chin against the breast, crushing the thick curly beard, and on his bare chest, amid red streams of congealed blood, hung a large brass cross . . .

Alexey's apparent reserve did not mean passivity. On occasion he gave dynamic expression to his sympathies and antipathies, especially to his antipathies. At the risk of limb he cut off the heads of a number of saints in grandfather's calendar, his most cherished possession, in revenge for driving half a dozen hairpins under the skin of grandmother's head. Old Kashirin was almost hysterical on beholding that sacrilege. Mention has been made already of the manner in which Alexey took revenge on the fat wife of the tavernkeeper for insulting grandmother, and of the way he flew with a knife at his stepfather for abusing mother. With all his love for grandmother and her sunny God, he could not help reacting to outrages in the primordial, reflex fashion — by meting out violence for violence. He did not see why grandmother kicked and scolded him for trying to throw at uncle Mikhail the very brick which the latter had just hurled at them through the window, barely missing grandmother.

Alexey's passion for observation and contemplation did not prevent him from taking also an active part in life's spectacle. At the age of six he enjoyed facing a gang of boys in the ravine, who greeted his appearance in the orchard with a hail of stones. " It was a pleasure to stand one's ground single-handed against many, it was a pleasure to see one's well-aimed stone force the enemy to flee and hide behind the bushes." He found plentiful opportunities to display this pugnacious heroism of his. The neighbourhood was rough, he had no chums, and the boys of the street " treated him with hostility." Apparently he did not quite " belong," and they felt an alien in this aggressive big-nosed gawk with the large sad eyes of a dog. He was easily provoked: knowing that he prided himself on being a Peshkov and not a Kashirin, the gang would shout on his emergence

from the house: " Look! There's the grandson of Kashirin the Deathless! " And the fray would start. Alexey was uncommonly strong for his age and a skilled fighter, but since the opponents were many and acted as an organization, he was always beaten, and came home in a sad shape, his clothes torn, his face bruised and bleeding. It was natural therefore that he was forbidden to go outdoors. " The street excited him; he seemed to grow intoxicated by the impressions it produced on him, and he nearly always caused some scandal or row."

It is a characteristic adumbration of the later man that this passion for impressions and self-assertion coexisted in Alexey with a yearning after God, grandmother's God, " that dear friend of all creation." This God filled his heart with a broad sympathy for living things, and with indignation against the prevailing cruelty toward man and beast. Years later, in his obituary note on Lenin, Gorky will note the unfortunate but inevitable interdependence of love and hatred. Alexey did not mind the bruises and scratches he received in uneven battle, but he was " invariably outraged by the brutality of the street sports, the customary brutality which brought him to a state of frenzy. He could not contain himself when the boys set dogs or cocks against one another, tortured cats, chased the goats that belonged to Jews, jeered at drunken beggars." His heart ached for the queer town-characters, half-demented unfortunates, whom the innocently callous boys made the butt of their practical jokes. Those were grateful occasions for his errantry. The Street was thus hateful to him and at the same time a magnet for his insatiable curiosity and an outlet for his pent-up bitterness.

An outlet he needed often enough. He was too young for a calm digestion of the dose of impressions, enthusiasms, and heartaches, which life served him so copiously. He took in and absorbed so much, yet it was seldom that he had an opportunity for giving back, for sharing, for being listened to sympathetically. The grown-ups preferred to instruct and soliloquize, and deigned not to hearken to the youngster. The one notable exception was Fine Business; but even he favoured silent contemplation rather than talk. Alexey was eager for con-

genial chums of his own age, and that is why he was so overjoyed
when he made the accidental acquaintance of the gentry boys
across the fence. But the father of those children, an old
colonel with white moustachios, espied him once in his courtyard, pushed him out of the gate, and with a threatening gesture said: " Don't you dare come to my place! " Humiliated
and chagrined, Alexey pertly retorted: " It isn't to you that
I've been coming, you old devil! " The colonel took him then
to grandfather, with the usual result.

Pertness and pugnacity served to vent his grievances and
repressed aches. This sturdy boy was thirsting after a motherly
caress. Not even grandmother filled this want. The touch of
mother's arms, on her rare visits, thrilled him to suffocation.
But his clumsy attempts at intimacy were met chillily. She
spurned his sympathy, when he tried to voice it at the time of
grandfather's scheming to marry her to the watchmaker.
Exasperated, Alexey avenged himself by being saucy and
unmanageable, thereby further repelling her from him. Especially strained were their relations after her marriage to the
gentleman-student Maximov, when Alexey lived with them in
a dreary, cockroach-ridden house at Sormovo, the factory
suburb of Nizhni Novgorod. The boy chafed under the hateful
régime, and his heart bled for his once majestic and beautiful
mother who now rapidly wilted, paying the price of marriage
to a gentleman. Gorky recalls that period with a bitterness
which time has not allayed:

I was rarely permitted to go out into the street: on each occasion I returned home battered by the boys — fighting was
my favourite, indeed, my only diversion, and I threw myself
into it with passion. Mother whipped me with a strap, but the
punishment only irritated me the more, and the next time I
fought the boys more furiously, and mother gave me a harder
thrashing. One day I warned her that if she did not stop beating me I should bite her hand, run away to the fields, and
freeze there to death. In amazement she pushed me away,
paced the room, and said, panting with exhaustion:
" You little wild beast! "
That living throbbing rainbow of emotions, which is called

love, was fading out in my heart. Poisonous blue flames of resentment flared up ever more often in it, and there smouldered a feeling of oppressive discontent, a consciousness of solitude amidst that drab, lifeless balderdash.

Alexey heartily resented mother's marriage to Maximov, though he never said aloud as much as one word. Everything about the long-legged student, with his pallid face and pointed little black beard, distressed him. He was particularly revolted by Maximov's mother, whose first impression on him was that of a " dry, green old woman." Her portrait is one of the precious grotesques in Gorky's gallery, and one wonders to what extent the author's venom has affected the verisimilitude. We are told that " she was all green — her dress, her hat, her face with a wart under one eye; even the tuft of hair on the wart was like grass. Dropping her lower lip, she raised the upper, and looked at me with her green teeth, shading her eyes with a hand in a black lace mitten." He added a few valuable details later, as her visits became more frequent and gave him an opportunity to complete her portrait. Sitting at the dining table, she made Alexey think of a " rotten picket in an old stockade. Her eyes were sewn on to her face with invisible threads; rolling out readily out of their bony sockets, they moved about with agility, seeing everything, espying everything, rising to the ceiling when she spoke of God, and drooping down to her cheeks when the conversation touched on domestic matters. Her eyebrows seemed to have been made of bran and as though pasted on. Her gleaming wide teeth noiselessly broke in two whatever she shoved into her mouth with a funny curve of her hand, throwing out the little finger, while near her ears little bony balls rolled to and fro under the skin, her ears too moved up and down, and the green hairs on her wart stirred, creeping along her yellow, wrinkled, repulsively clean skin." Alexey hated the conscious cleanliness and gentility of the old woman and her son, his future stepfather. The green lady made efforts at improving Alexey's manners. Once at dinner she said to him, with horribly bulging eyes: " Akh, little Alexey, why do you eat in such haste, and take such great big pieces? You'll

choke, darling!" The pert boy took the piece of food out of
his mouth, mounted it again on the fork, and handed it to her,
saying: "Take it, since you begrudge it." Followed the usual
whipping, which did not stop him from smearing the seats of
Maximov and his mother with cherry gum, and chuckling at
the sight of their getting stuck to the chairs. He was duly
thrashed, but that was his last prank against the hateful Maximovs: his mother came up to his garret room, and with tears
in her eyes asked him why he was causing her so much grief.
He promised to leave the Maximovs alone, and kept his word.

Then he lost all interest in the grown-ups and their oppressive life. A longing for solitude seized him, and he made himself a broad seat in the orchard, covered it with turf, and
stayed there all summer. Grandfather helped him clear up the
ground, and occasionally favoured him with his sententious
wisdom; but the boy was beginning to take his words more
critically. Sometimes grandmother came, spread some hay near
the seat, and lay on her back all night long, keeping Alexey
awake with delicious outcries about falling stars, and other
beauties of the sky, "God's bright vestment." She still told
him fairy-tales from her inexhaustible store, and he listened
enraptured. Embittered and disheartened, thoroughly disgusted
with the deeds and attitudes of the people around him, and
apparently rendered immune to illusion and sentiment, the
boy still succumbed to the charms of fairyland. What other
escape was there for him from the fantastically sordid reality?
He listened to the fairy-tales, and believed in the impossible
and improbable. During that summer, on his solitary couch in
the orchard, he thought and reflected a good deal. He tells us
that it was "the most tranquil and contemplative period of
his whole life; it was during that summer that a sense of confidence in his own strength was formed in him and grew firm."

Looking back on his rather joyless childhood, Gorky recalls
with pleasure those rare evenings, when in the absence of
grandfather, grandmother arranged "orgies." Neighbours and
boarders were invited, vodka and sweet cordials were served,
uncle Peter distributed large pieces of bread lavishly covered
with jam, uncle Yakov came with his guitar, and the atmos-

result the instruction was not always smooth and genial. When his mother arrived, on her last stay before her marriage to Maximov, she undertook to teach her son the secular alphabet, and made him memorize some verses from a school reader. Alexey easily mastered the reading matter, but when it came to the verses, he showed a perverse tendency to change words and lines, and to produce nonsense-verses, assonant and rhythmic, out of the distorted originals. Mother was angry and impatient with his vagaries, and this, coupled with his bitterness at mother's coldness and wretchedness, provoked him to further mutilations of the assigned verses. At night, lying by the side of grandmother in her spacious bed, he would recite the verses correctly, and often compose his own verses, not devoid of metrical form and of a somewhat acrid wit. Grandmother would laugh uproariously.

Alexey's brief school career revealed the same traits of his nature — pertness, non-conformity, and withal brilliance and receptivity. Mother sent him and his cousin Sasha, the son of uncle Mikhail, to a school, but a few weeks later he fell sick with smallpox, and was thus relieved of the irksome duty. All he learned there was that when asked as to his name he must not answer: " Peshkov," but: " My surname is Peshkov." Also, that he must not say to the teacher: " Don't shout at me, brother: I am not afraid of you." About a year later, while he lived with his mother and stepfather in a miserable dark basement, he was sent to another school, and from the first day " it repelled him." Here are some rich details of that experience:

I arrived at school in mother's shoes, in a jacket made over from grandmother's waist, in a yellow shirt and longish pants. My attire was made fun of, and for the yellow shirt I was nicknamed " ace of diamonds " [the badge on a convict's garb]. With the boys I soon made up, but the teacher and the priest took a dislike to me.

The teacher was jaundiced and bald. His nose always bled, and he appeared in the classroom with cotton in his nostrils, conducting the lesson in a snuffling voice. He would suddenly stop in the middle of a word, pull the cotton out of his nostrils, and examine it, shaking his head. His face was flat, a face of oxidized copper, with a greenish tint in the wrinkles. What especially made that face monstrous, was the pewter eyes, looking quite superfluous and out of place; they were glued to my face so disagreeably that I always felt like wiping my cheeks with the palm of my hand.

This teacher pestered Alexey incessantly, snufflingly admonishing him to change his shirt, to keep his feet quiet, to keep his muddy boots off the floor. The pupil repaid him with " savage insolence," playing all sorts of pranks and tricks on him, from fastening over the door a hollowed half of a watermelon which settled on teacher's bald head when he entered the room, to that ancient and international stratagem of sprinkling snuff into his desk drawer. The teacher got such a sneezing spell that he was forced to leave the classroom, and send in his stead a military officer, his brother-in-law, who commanded the boys to sing " God save the Tsar," and rapped with the ruler the heads of those guilty of false notes.

It goes without saying that these diversions had to be paid for by the culprit, both at school and at home, and that the price did not deter him from continuing his ferocious vengeance against the existing order of things, in his family and elsewhere. He did not spare even the handsome young priest, with his luxuriant hair, Christ-like face, and small hands with which he picked up every object caressingly and tenderly, as though it might break. The priest took a dislike to Alexey, because he could not afford to buy the Sacred History of the Old and New Testament, and the boy irritated him further by mocking his manner of speech. A dialogue would take place between the two:

" Peshkov, have you brought that book, or not? Yes. The book."

" No. I haven't. Yes."

" Yes — what ? "

" No."

" Well, then, go home. Yes. Home. For I don't intend to teach you. Yes. I don't intend to."

This did not grieve me much. I went out, and to the end of the class hours kicked my heels in the dirty streets of the suburb, making notes of its noisy life.

The savage street and the restricted classroom competed for Alexey's attention. The former won eventually, but for some two years the boy was compelled to live in a hateful atmosphere, suffer punishment and humiliation, and vent his resentment in petty vindictiveness. He was by no means dull, and easily excelled his classmates in the knowledge of sacred history, prayers, and apocryphal verses, in which the apt listener of grandfather and grandmother showed himself to advantage. In fact, at his completion of the first two grades he was given a laudatory certificate and several books as prizes! The certificate he mutilated by some inscriptions, and handed it to the unsuspecting grandfather who proudly put it away among his treasures. The books he sold for fifty-five copecks, and gave the money to grandmother, who lay ill and penniless, her husband being already in the last phase of his morbid miserliness and refusing her as much as a pinch of tea-leaves. Apparently books had not as yet become of such significance to him as they did a few years later.

His literary taste at that time was still dictated by the fairy-land of grandmother's creation. When the boys at school slighted his fairy-tales, and spoke with admiration of a certain Robinson Crusoe, Alexey decided to find out for himself what it was all about. In a volume of Dumas belonging to his stepfather he discovered two banknotes; he took the one-ruble note, and treated the school to such rare delicacies as white bread and sausage. He had also intended to buy *Robinson Crusoe,* but the very aspect of the lean yellow booklet, with the bearded man in a fur nightcap on the cover, displeased him, and instead he bought two torn old volumes of Andersen's tales. " The Nightingale " gripped him at once with its opening: " In China all the inhabitants are Chinese, and the Emperor himself is a Chinaman." The phrase struck him with its " simple, gaily smiling music, and something else that was marvellously good."

Incidentally, this adventure cost him dearly. When he returned from school and was asked by mother whether he had taken the money, he admitted, and handed her the books. The fact that she gave him a thorough beating with the frying pan, did not hurt him so much as her depriving him for ever of the delicious Andersen volumes. But what caused him the keenest pain was the meanness of his stepfather who spread the rumour of Alexey's misdemeanour among his acquaintances. Through the children of these the story reached the school, and when Alexey came he was greeted with the nickname of " thief." " Brief and clear, but not true, since he did not attempt to deny having taken the money."

The environment did not greatly encourage the observance of the decalogue or of any moral code. When Alexey was thrown back on his grandfather, after stabbing Maximov, he found it necessary to earn some money, in order to provide for himself and grandmother. He chose the profession of a scavenger. Early in the morning on holidays, and after school on week days, he would wander with a sack through the streets and courtyards, and gather bones, rags, paper, nails. The few coppers realized from the sale of these articles he gave to grandmother, who accepted the coins with good grace and words of cheer. But once he espied her holding his coppers in her palm, looking at them, and crying softly; " one muddy tear hung from her pumiceous nose." He soon found it profitable to vary the trade of picking bones and rags with thieving lumber on the banks of the Volga tributary, at the end of the Nizhni Novgorod Fair, when the booths were taken down. This work required cunning, caution, and strength, and Alexey found a gang of accomplices among the boys of the street. Together they performed adventurous raids on the lumber yards, some of the boys teasing the watchmen and drawing away their attention, while the rest dragged off some planks and poles by means of nails fastened to ropes. They easily disposed of the stolen goods, by selling them to respectable householders, and divided the spoils among the six of them, receiving as much as five or even seven copecks apiece!

In the wretched Kanavino suburb where Gorky's early life

passed, the theft of these planks was not regarded as a sin. He tells us that his gang looked with contempt and horror at common thievery, which was the order of the day. The half-starving denizens regarded thieving as " practically their only means for existence." The great yearly Fair provided them with jobs for some six weeks, and the rest of the time they stole from barges and prowled up and down the river on the lookout for anything " loose." On Sundays the grownups boasted of their successes, and the youngsters " listened and learned." The younger generation put their lessons to practice during the busy days before the Fair, when the streets swarmed with artisans, cabmen, and all sorts of working folk. Toward the end of the day, when many of these were drunk and wallowed in the street, the boys rummaged in their pockets, carried off their tools and harnesses, and performed all that before the eyes of their elders " as a legitimate business." Alexey and his gang not only refrained from pocket-picking, but some of them even undertook to drive other boys off the helpless drunkards, and beat them up if they persisted.

The line of demarcation between permissible theft and heinous pillage might appear rather fine for the member of a normally respectable community. In that Nizhni Novgorod suburb the principle of the sanctity of private property was perforce elastic, and the eight- or nine-year-old Alexey Peshkov and his comrades had to fall on their own sense of discrimination between right and wrong. To that period belongs Gorky's early discovery of the eternally human beneath the most unprepossessing exterior. Those five playmates of his certainly did not belong to nice society. Sanka, the son of a Mordvinian woman, a mendicant and perpetual drunkard who gave him a beating if he failed to bring her enough money for a flask of vodka. Kostroma, without any kin, who later, at the age of thirteen, hanged himself at a colony for young criminals, whither he was sent for stealing a pair of pigeons. Khabi, a Tartar lad of great strength, who had been brought to Nizhni Novgorod by his uncle from some city on the Kama River, whose name he did not know. Yaz, an epileptic, the son of the graveyard-digger and watchman. Finally, Grishka, the eldest

of them all, the son of a widow who made her living as a seam-stress. Described by Gorky without the remotest shade of sentimentality, the gang strikes us as likable boys, charming in their straightforwardness, essential honesty of thought and deed, chivalrous friendship for one another, and pathetic yearn-ing after a better life. They are not goody-goody, yet are capable of spontaneous sympathy and tenderness, expressed and acted upon with the directness of primitive animals.

Alexey found this " independent street life " much to his taste and his comrades aroused in him a deep emotion, " a rest-less desire to do something good for them." Indeed, that life was more attractive than what he could see at grandfather's — degrading parsimoniousness and penury, bitterness and re-proaches, and the silently dying mother with her ailing mori-bund baby. At school the final months brought him additional insults: the boys mocked him for being a scavenger and a beggar, and once they told the teacher that it was impossible to sit next to Peshkov, because he smelled of a cesspool. Alexey was deeply offended by this accusation, since he took great care to wash himself every morning before going to school, and even wore different clothes when plying his profession. It was with a sigh of relief that he finished the first two grades, and felt free to join his gang whenever he was not made by grandfather to nurse his sick baby-brother.

After the death of his mother, grandfather said to Alexey that " he was no decoration to hang on his neck," and that it was time for him to go out " into the world."

Childhood came to an end. Alexey had to take care of him-self. The last semblance of a protective home, of shielding kinsfolk to fall back upon, vanished. The boy, not quite ten years old, had graduated into enforced maturity and self-reliance. Indeed, he had been sufficiently forged and hardened for such an undertaking. Discounting as wasted time his two scholastic years, we may regard his other experiences and im-pressions during the five years largely spent at the Kashirins, as a schooling of no mean consequences. He had seen at close hand the average Russian life in its unadulterated coarseness and brutality; on his own back he had learned the harshness

of kin and the wolfishness of man to man; his heart had been scarred unhealably by insults, humiliations, and scenes of savage sadism. Yet he was keen to perceive that nothing is absolutely black, and he had been startled to discover attractive traits in some of the most inveterate villains on his horizon. In starting out on his own, the boy had no illusion as to life being a pretty fairy-tale. He was prepared for a grim struggle, and could boast a decent equipment. He had the tall stature and robust physique of his parents, their fastidiousness, pugnacity, non-conformity; a pledge that he would not easily submerge either beneath material privations or levelling smugness and mediocrity. Grandfather instilled into him a few drops of common sense and the wisdom of the chase, just enough to serve as an alloy for those precious virtues. Above all, his outlook was suffused with the poesy of grandmother's God, a genial divinity, none too rigid, who prompted one to believe, in spite of everything, in beauty and goodness, and even in fairy-tales.

BOYHOOD

FIRST JOB

IN the life of such a precocious individual as Maxim Gorky its division into periods of childhood, boyhood, and youth is even more arbitrary than in the life of an ordinary person. I am using this division for the sake of convenience, taking up successive five-year periods, since it happens that each one of these marks the end of a definite stage in the evolution of Gorky. It is self evident that in our story the child, boy, and youth overlap and tread on one another's heel. It is the child or the boy that attacks the stepfather with a knife for kicking mother in the chest? Is it the child or the boy that helps out grandmother by picking rags and catching birds? Is it the boy or the youth that supervises the construction of huts at the Nizhni Novgorod Fair for two and a half dollars a month plus two cents for lunch? And who is it declaiming and philosophizing before bearded icon-painters, carpenters, hoboes — a boy or a youth or a prematurely grown man?

Childhood, however lacking in the tenderness and privileges we associate with that age, came to an end with the death of Gorky's mother. Grandfather told him to go " into the world." The last shade of a home was denied him, and though he did come back to his grandparents once or twice for a short stay, he was suffered by old Kashirin as an independent outsider who could shift for himself.

His début " in the world " was in the rôle of a " boy " at a bootshop. The master admonished him not to make faces, not to scratch his scabby hands, and to remember that he was employed in a first-class shop on the main street of the town,

where " a boy must stand by the door like a statooy." It was an irksome job after months of free-lancing with the street boys of the Kanavino suburb, but its educative value was not negligible. Not so much in regard to his manners — he was too restlessly dynamic for the poise of a statue. His quick eye grasped the essential traits of business, which in a country so commercially backward as Russia were crudely obvious. The Russian business man flaunts an ancient maxim : " If you don't cheat you won't sell " ; his western confrère would resent such an offensive lack of subtlety. Alexey had seen enough brutality in life, but this was the first time he was to learn of man's vileness under the guise of hypocrisy. Accustomed to crude straightforwardness, the boy was amazed at the unctious obsequiousness with which the master and his clerks treated a customer. His amazement was coupled with revulsion, when after the departure of the customer these men indulged in snickering vilification of their victim, especially if it happened to be a woman. He knew that the clerks stole as much as they could, and he was given to understand that the master knew of that too, since he would not expect them to act differently; he had been a clerk himself. There was no place for loyalty under the circumstances, and when the old church-watchman asked him to steal a pair of goloshes for him, Alexey after some hesitation consented to do that " for the sake of his old age." But there was another lesson in store for him. The old watchman, after coaxing the boy to steal, suddenly asked him whether it had occurred to him that he might inform the master of this. Alexey was frightened and astonished. The old man then drew the boy to him, and chided him for yielding so easily to temptation. " Do you think one can trust a fellow-man ? Akh, you little fool."

This education was coupled with a great amount of tedious labour at the shop and at the master's home, where he slept on the kitchen stove. Before going to the business-place he had to rise at an early hour, brush the clothes and polish the boots of the whole household, prepare the samovar, fetch wood for all the stoves, wash dishes, and do other menial work under the direction of a grotesque wench, the sick and irascible cook. Alexey's bedfellow was cousin Sasha, uncle Yakov's son, a

chip of the old block. Sasha lorded it over his cousin, in the capacity of an assistant-clerk, and prided himself on successfully emulating his superiors in manners, speech, and conduct, including the art of pilfering shoes in his coat sleeves. Had Alexey been a normal boy he would have succumbed to the régime and adapted himself to the situation. But it was his destiny throughout his life to be a non-conformist, to display his pertness before elders, and to remain pugnaciously different. This first contact with business morals filled him with disgust for the respectable and successful tradesmen, and in his small way he indulged in vindictive sabotage. Thus after one particularly nasty treatment of a customer, a beautiful lady, upon whose departure the master and his clerks spurted a stream of filthy insinuations, Alexey managed during the master's afternoon-nap to drop some vinegar into his gold watch. He felt compensated when later in the day the master came into the shop with the watch in his hands, muttering in bewilderment that his timepiece was sweating: might it not be an evil omen?

AN ACCIDENT — AND FREEDOM

DESPITE this occasional joy
of revenge, Alexey decided to run away from the shopkeeper.
But on the very day when he planned to flee, he managed
to upset a pot of boiling cabbage soup on his hands, and had
to be taken to the hospital. The boy had heard lurid tales about
hospitals, where the gentry indulged in cutting up people.
The Russian hospitals of those days, particularly public in-
firmaries, gave sufficient cause for fantastic rumours. Tormented with pain and fear, angry with the whole cruel and
silly world, Alexey faced the dim hospital-hall with its rows
of beds and wriggling grey bodies as a nightmare. His scalded
hands were not to be attended till the next morning, and the
burning and stinging sensation, augmented by the dread and
loneliness of the environment, became unbearable. He tried
to sneak out and run away, but was caught in the corridor by
a grizzly invalid with a bunch of keys at his belt, who spoke
to him kindly, took him back to his cot, and lulled him to
sleep. When he awoke it was daylight, and grandmother sat
by his side. After his hands were bandaged, the two left in
a cab. Spring was approaching, the ice on the Volga was
breaking and roaring, grandmother's colourful words rumbled
on, and Alexey's heart " fluttered like a lark." He was free,
and he was once more with grandmother!

Old Kashirin did not welcome his grandson with any cordiality. He had lost his money by that time, and was obsessed with
a morbid miserliness which eventually turned into a point of
insanity with him. Grandmother was indifferent to material
prosperity, and had always urged her husband to satisfy the

greed of his sons and give them all his property. When he remonstrated with her, and threatened that if they were careless they would become beggars, grandmother simply and earnestly assured him that begging would not be so bad. In fact, she occasionally dreamed aloud of venturing out into God's world again, and go about asking for alms, as she had done in her early girlhood. Now that they had been reduced to penury, aggravated by old Kashirin's obsession, grandmother regarded their straits as God's punishment for her husband's greed and selfishness in times of plenty. In her unostentatious way she tried to atone for his sins by helping the needy.

Gorky describes one of her trips of " silent charity " during his convalescence. She woke him about midnight, and the two set out on a stroll through the poorest street of the neighbourhood. Here and there grandmother would stop by a wretched hut, cross herself three times, and place on the window-sill a five-copeck piece and three cracknels. Then she invoked the Mother of God to help all those who suffer from misery. The boy kept close to grandmother as they walked the dark and deserted streets, and listened to her soft speech, her observations on life, on the rich and the poor, on her own experiences. A stray dog followed them, attracted and reassured by grandmother's kindly tone, and the three of them proceeded in the dark. At last it began to dawn, they sat down to rest on a bench by some gate, and filled with new impressions Alexey " leaned against grandmother's warm body and fell asleep."

The brief intervals between " jobs," which he spent with his grandparents, were not without significance for Alexey, whose congenital curiosity had gradually matured into thoughtful observation of life. He slept with grandmother on a heap of rags in a tiny woodshed, next to a chicken-house. Awakened by the rooster, and unable to endure the stifling fumes rising from the fowl-dung, Alexey would climb up the roof of the woodshed and watch the neighbours waking up, " eyeless, enormous, swollen with sleep." He soon learned to know all the details of the surrounding existence, through direct observation aided by winged gossip. It was a wretched existence, a shallow slough in which drab individuals writhed impotently and joylessly,

seeking relief in drunken forgetfulness, debauch, slander, passionless adultery. Alexey drank in the reality, yet even in this environment he managed to dilute his acrid draught with a few drops of romance. A lame little girl, whose pale sharp-nosed face was illumined by the blue flicker of large deep eyes, shared his thirst for fairyland. They would hide in the bathhouse, and by the dim light of the window she read aloud endless pages of a penny-dreadful. The boy understood almost nothing of the " multitude of incomprehensible and tedious words," but sitting on the floor and looking up at Lyudmila's flickering blue eyes, he wove his own dreams to the accompaniment of the reader's agitated voice. Soon grandmother joined the couple and enriched their comradeship with her warmth, wit, and inexhaustible store of tales.

On the whole, grandmother trained Alexey in the art of discovering romance in reality. Alongside of her fantastic fairy-tales and religious legends, in which nothing improbable was impossible, she helped him plant his feet firmly on the ground and find in his actual environment adventure galore. Simultaneously practical and adventurous, she encouraged Alexey, when in a moment of reckless bravura he accepted the challenge to spend a night in the cemetery, the prize being one whole ruble. Grandmother calmly instructed him to take along an overcoat and a blanket, and to recite an acathistus to Virgin Mary in case he should " see things." The next morning he confessed to grandmother that during the night he had been afraid, and asked her not to tell this to the boys. But she retorted that he need not be ashamed of that, for " if it had not been frightful, there would be nothing to be proud of." She was proud of Alexey's courage and stoicism, which he displayed on numerous occasions when a faint-hearted boy would cry out in pain and terror. Now, after the cemetery exploit, she boomed with satisfaction: " One must experience everything by one's own self, dear pigeon, one must learn to know everything by oneself. If you don't learn by yourself, no one else can teach you to know."

Surefooted and adroit amid the wiles of the city humdrum, grandmother assumed a majestic geniality when beyond the

confines of civilization. Gorky's finest pages are those describing the days spent with his grandparents in the fir- and birchwoods, on the outskirts of Nizhni Novgorod. Even grandfather, whose immediate purpose in going to the woods was prosaic — chopping fallen trees for firewood, even he was transformed as the " the dark army of the forest moved toward them." Dressed in his wife's short coat, an old visorless cap on his head, grandfather blinked, smiled, stepped cautiously, " as if stealthily," and intoxicated by the approaching forest, he would forget his obsession, and rhapsodize about these " gardens of the Lord, planted by no hand, save by God's wind, the holy breath of His mouth." Then he would recall his early days as a bargeman on the Volga, and narrate wonders about the lure of the Volga forests, that harboured from times inmemorial robbers and hermits, the two categories not quite distinguishable in those days. These stories add to the glamour of the forest in Alexey's eyes, and he enters it with reverence and a wish never to leave it again. " In the forest there are no chattering human creatures, no brawls and drunkenness; there you may forget grandfather's disgusting greed, mother's sandy grave, and all the things which hurt and depress your heart with a heavy dreariness."

But it was grandmother who infused intimacy and kinship into one's relations with the forest. Alexey would steal behind her and watch her pick herbs, with a knowing discrimination as to their medicinal properties, or gather mushrooms, all the while conversing with her God in a suggestive undertone, occasionally emitting a sigh of bliss and whispering thanks to the Most Holy Mother, Bright Light of the Earth. " In the woods she behaved as a proprietress, kindred to everything around; she ambled about like a she-bear, seeing all, praising and blessing everything. A warmth seemed to flow from her through the forest, and it was peculiarly pleasing to see how the moss, crushed by her foot, straightened out and stood up again." Always an admirer of grandmother, Alexey regarded her in the forest as a " supreme being, the most kind and wise on earth." Her senses were as keen as those of an animal, and she treated plants and living things with authoritative friendliness. Once

he espied her, sitting on a stump, speaking quietly to a wolf:
" Go away, now, go! Go, and God be with you! " Alexey was
so happy worshipping her that the discovery of ever so slight
a flaw in her annoyed him painfully. Here is a delicious
instance:

Bowing to the black earth sumptuously clad in verdant em-
broidery, she narrates how once upon a time God, in his anger
at mankind, flooded the earth with water and drowned all living things.

" But His Most Sweet Mother had beforehand collected
every seed in a basket and hidden it away. Later she begged the
sun: ' Dry the earth from end to end, and for that people will
sing thy glory.' The sun dried the earth, and She sowed the
seed which She had hidden. And the Lord beheld: once more
the earth was filling with plants, and beasts, and men! ' Who,'
He asked, ' has done this against My will? ' Here She confessed to Him, and as the Lord had been sorry Himself to see
the earth bare, He said to Her: ' Thou hast done well! ' ' "

I like the story, but it perplexes me, and I ask:

" But was that really so? Wasn't the Mother of God born
long after the flood? "

Now it is grandmother's turn to be surprised.

" Who was it that told you that? "

" It is written in the books, at school."

This reassures her, and she admonishes me:

" Now you drop that stuff, forget all those books. They lie,
those books! "

And she laughs softly and gaily:

" The little fools! How's that: there was God, but He had
no mother? By whom was He born then? "

" I don't know."

" That's fine! Your learning brought you to ' I don't
know '! "

" The priest said that the Mother of God was born of
Joachim and Anna."

Now grandmother is angry. She stands in front of me, and
sternly looks straight into my eyes:

" You mean to say, She was plain Maria Joachimovna? If
that is the way you're going to think, I'll slap you good and
hard."

But a moment later she explains to me:

"The Blessed Virgin existed always, before all and everything! Of Her God was born, and then . . ."

"And what about Christ?"

Grandmother is silent, shutting her eyes in confusion.

"And what about Christ? Eh? eh? eh?"

I see that I am the victor, that I have caused her to become tangled up in God's mysteries, and I feel annoyed.

During that summer Alexey had become hardy and "savage"; the forest had estranged him from the boys of his age and their interests. As to Lyudmila, she struck him as "tiresomely clever." Yet even as a hardy savage Alexey failed to free himself from anxiety concerning his fellow-men. Grandfather's stories and the paganized Christianity of grandmother intensified the boy's awe and love for the forest. But how hopelessly Russian were the dreams of this boy! How characteristic of Maxim Gorky the writer, the fighter, the meliorist!

As I stroll through the woods I muse: how nice it would be to be a bandit, to rob the greedy and the rich and give the spoils to the poor — let all be happy, gay, neither envying nor howling at one another like bad-tempered dogs. It would be fine also to go as far as grandmother's God, and her Holy Virgin, and tell them all the truth about the wretched life people live . . . and about all the offensive and hurtful things on earth that are quite unnecessary. If the Holy Virgin believe me, let her give me such a mind as would enable me to arrange everything differently, in some better way. Let her make people obey me confidently — I should most certainly find a way for a better sort of living! It does not matter that I am so small — Christ was only one year older than I am when the wise men listened to Him.

AT THE DRAUGHTSMAN'S

ALTHOUGH grandmother and Alexey sold enough berries, nuts and mushrooms, gathered in the woods, to provide for both of them, and even to leave some for " silent charity," grandfather scolded them as " drones." When rainy autumn came, he found a " real job " for Alexey, at the home of a draughtsman, who was the son of grandmother's sister. The change of the régime was overwhelming. With the pungency of the forest still in his nostrils, the boy was thrown into a hideous city flat, and made to slave for a most dreary lot of people. His master lived with his mother, a querulous old woman, his wife, who resembled a loaf of white bread, and his younger brother, a clownish fop. They lived in uncomfortable, ridiculously furnished rooms, ate to excess, gossiped avidly and salaciously, and quarrelled with one another, especially the women. The old woman roused Alexey at an early hour and kept him busy till late at night. He had to chop and haul wood, prepare the samovar, heat the stoves, scrub the floors and stairs, scour the pans, wash the dishes, peel the vegetables, carry provisions from the market, run all sorts of errands; later he had, in addition, to take care of the babies, and once a week go to the public stream and do some of the family washing. He did not mind the work; in fact it gave him pleasure " to destroy dirt." What vexed him most was the atmosphere of complacent smugness in the house, of indolent satiety and sanctimonious conceit, to which he much preferred the rank depravity of the Kanavino suburb, with its thugs and prostitutes and life of toil and semi-starvation. Listening to his relatives passing judgement on other

people with a sense of superiority and certitude as to the correct rules of conduct, Alexey felt as he did at the shoeshop: a fierce resentment against the " masters' rules," and a pleasurable sensation in breaking these rules.

Such was the job which grandfather Kashirin procured for the eleven-year-old boy, to further his education and fortify his position " in the world." The joy and adventure of the forest receded into the realm of dreams. Actuality was upon him, powerful, inescapable. He was forced to inhale the fumes of the hateful milieu, inside the draughtsman's flat and immediately outside of it. Across the courtyard stood another ugly house, peopled with families of military gentlemen. The affairs of their numerous orderlies and servants with the housemaids, cooks, and laundresses filled the air with sensuality, brawls, tears, obscenity, which reverberated through the neighbourhood and were smackingly reported and commented upon at the tables of the respectable citizenry, such as the draughtsman's family. Where could Alexey find an outlet for his yearning after fairyland? He would flee to the garret, with coloured scraps of paper and scissors, cut out fantastic patterns, and paste them to the rafters.

For a while he was on the verge of discovering another escape. Once he pertly remarked to his master that instead of teaching him his craft they made him empty the slop-bucket. To his surprise he was not fired, but given paper and drawing-instruments, and ordered to copy a façade of a house from another paper. Delighted to do some clean work for a relief, Alexey threw himself into it with zest, but he let his fantasy run away with him: the façade looked to him rather dreary, and he drew all sorts of birds on the roof and cornices, placed on the ground people with crooked legs under umbrellas, and crossed the whole paper with slanting lines, for rain. Despite this inauspicious début, the master continued to give him similar tasks, which he was to do in his spare moments. But here the old woman interfered. This sister of grandmother's was the very antithesis of the latter. Morbidly jealous about the future of her younger son, she feared that it might be endangered by the prospective rivalry of Alexey. She did all in her

power to prevent him from doing the " clean work," by invent-
ing all sorts of household tasks, by spilling oil over his drawing-
papers, and finally by striking and bruising his face and raising
pandemonium in the house. Her son had to yield. Thus ended
Alexey's first attempt at a genteel profession.

On Saturday night and on holidays Alexey was to attend
church. In the golden-bluish haze the boy would stand in a
corner, gaze at the stern icons illumined by wax candles, and
weave his dreams. Away from the hideous actuality of his
daily environment, the boy would recapture the harmonious
God of grandmother, and recite under his breath some of the
verses he had heard from her. He was redolent of her verses " as
a beehive of honey," and they lent form to his musings and
dreams. In place of stereotyped prayers, the boy, his heart
" contracted by some sweet sadness, or bitten and scratched
by petty grievances," would whisper his plaints in the form of
grandmother's folk-verses. Here is one specimen, minus its
rather uncertain meter and rhyme:

> Lord, Lord, I am so miserable!
> If only I could grow up quickly!
> As it is, I can't endure this life,
> I'll hang myself, Lord forgive!

> There's no good trying to study.
> That devil's doll, granny's sister,
> Growls at me like a wolf,
> And my life is so bitter!

Incidentally, Gorky tells us that he remembers a goodly
number of these " prayers," explaining their retention in his
memory by the fact that " the workings of the mind in childhood leave deep scars, which sometimes fail to heal through
one's whole life." He must have felt intensely most of his experiences, to judge by the crisp clearness with which he recalls
them.

Church-going was the only diversion Alexey was permitted
to have. But he went to church mostly on stormy nights, when
the snow whirled madly through the streets. Then the church

seemed cosy; he " rested there as he did in the forest and in the field. His small heart, already familiar with a multitude of grievances and soiled by life's malign coarseness, laved in hazy, ardent dreams." On mild nights he usually played truant, sauntering about the quiet streets, " alone like the moon in the skies," listening and observing. His fantasy fed on the strange and unknown. Unfamiliar odours wafted from some window or other, sounds of unheard of instruments reached his ear, and the boy stood still, sniffed and listened, and tried to imagine that other, different, finer life which those odours and sounds " hinted at." He discovered a house where someone played on a violoncello once in a while, and the place became his Mecca, whither he faithfully wended his way on church nights, in the hope of hearing again the unearthly sounds. He did not mind the beatings which he received at home for coming late.

These night-wanderings not only quenched his thirst for fairyland but also sharpened his sense of reality. With the unscrupulous curiosity of a born artist, Alexey looked into windows and observed the life that was going on there. Since his eye could see only through the uncurtained windows of lower stories or basements, the life displayed before him belonged to the poorer classes. The upper and curtained windows, inaccessible to the naked eye, gave food to his romantic imagination, the weaker side of the future Gorky. Below, his keen eye saw variegated actuality. He " saw people praying, embracing, fighting, gambling, soundlessly uttering anxious words — a penny-in-the-slot panorama of a dumb, fish-like life." Tragedy and comedy intermingled. Life appeared not uniformly coarse, as at the place of his employment. He once espied in a basement a long-haired youth reading aloud to two women; they listened gravely, and one of them of a sudden covered her eyes with her hands, her shoulders trembled, and the youth fell on his knees and began to kiss her fingers. That was real, yet strange and new; the world of books and ideas was still alien to Alexey.

The widened field of observation broadened his understanding of men and things, and taught him critical discrimination. Back at his irksome home, Alexey, enriched with impressions

and discoveries, rose above his surroundings. Unblinded by personal bites and pricks, he managed to regard those about him with detachment and objectivity. He discovered attractive traits in his master. There was a wistfulness about the draughtsman, a vague yearning, that lent him a shade of refinement and, in any event, placed him far above the other members of the family. Alexey could not help sympathizing with him, even when the master acceded to his mother's petulance and stopped teaching the boy how to draw. He felt in the man a fellow-prisoner of smugness and convention. Indeed, later on the man revealed symptoms of rebellion against his environment, and made Alexey the confidant of his dreams and vagaries.

More striking still was the boy's ability to regard coolly his arch-enemy and persecutor, the master's mother. He must have sensed that her cruelty and meanness were not so much signs of natural maliciousness as they were due to a spirit sickened by hardship, drudgery, and loneliness. Exasperated though he was by her mercilessness as a taskmaster and by her unclean gossip, Alexey found in himself enough detachment to be amused by her quarrels with her daughter-in-law, her passion for complaining and cursing, and the multitude of her other extraordinary traits. Her affection for Victor, her youngest son, a silly lummox, was mirthfully intemperate. We have seen how jealousy for his career prompted her to resent Alexey's apprenticeship with violence and hullabaloo. The boy had fun in watching her wheedle some money from her elder son and hand it over surreptitiously to Victor, or hide some dainties for him, which she would bring to his bed at night. Victor treated her roughly, accepted her tokens of affection as a matter of course, and abused her generously. At dawn Alexey would be awakened by the old woman's prayers. In the sickly light he could see her grey shape, in her night-shirt, kneeling on the cold floor, and exhorting God with vehement lamentations. Her God was not grandmother's God; he was more akin to grandfather's vindictive Jehovah. No wonder Alexey often thought it a pity that grandfather did not marry this woman — " how she would gnaw and nag him! " Her prayers were replete with curses heaped upon her enemies, her daughter-in-law included, and

she besought God to visit his ferocities upon them, and to bestow his favours on her darling Victor. Wakened by her howls, Victor growled and bade her shut her mouth. At times she clambered up the stove, where her son slept, and leaning over him she hissed such extravagant endearments as " drop of my blood, pure like a pearl," " light pinion of an angel," " little baby," and prayed to God for his success with girls — " may they run after him in flocks, like ducks after a drake." Victor would wake up and tell his mother to " go to the devil and not to snort into his mug." She meekly retreated, but once in a while she would resent his manner and spurt forth some such philippic as this : " So-o! So you're sending your mother to the devil, you son of a bitch! Akh, you, my midnight shame, accursed heartsore! The devil has planted you in my heart, may you have rotted away before you were born! " Alexey chuckled in his bed by the lavatory door, until the woman turned on him and roused him to start the day's toil. Yet, despite his " pertness " and hostility toward her, he was not immune from a sense of pity for her, as he watched her occasionally get up in the dead of the night, suffering from insomnia, fall on her knees, and whisper a query: " Who loves me, Lord? Who has any use for me? "

If the multitude of impressions and observations broadened Alexey's outlook and discouraged in him the all-human tendency toward sweeping condemnation, they also armed him against unqualified acceptance. His critical discrimination began to manifest itself even with regard to grandmother. He actually " did not like her " on her visits to his employers, when she appeared from the back stairs, meek and retiring, and sat humbly by the slop-bucket in the kitchen. Her younger sister abused and reproached her and her grandson, while the draughtsman's wife treated her with condescension. When left alone with grandmother Alexey reproached her for humiliating herself before those unworthy people. " With a kindly grin on her wonderful face," the old woman embraced him and explained in a rapid whisper that she knew all that, but was forced to act in this manner in order to wheedle out of his master at least one ruble out of the six rubles stipulated as

Alexey's yearly wages. She recounted her difficulties with grandfather and some of her nephews, and begged him " to be patient " and stay a while longer at his place, till he grew strong. He was made to promise patience " for about two more years."

Alexey failed to keep his promise. Despite his love for grandmother and his admiration for her God, he could not subscribe to her opportunism. Her joyous outlook depended on the elasticity of her standards and demands, on her facility of compromise and adjustment without sacrificing anything essential, on her ability to overlook and ignore skin-deep evils and abuses. Her grandson was made of a different stuff, of rigid attitudes, of absolutes. To be sure, for years he bent his head to life's yoke and his will to men's tyranny, but he never bore his subjection with a smile, he never softened his " pertness." Patience, as prescribed by his elders, be it even grandmother, did not appeal to him as a virtue.

FLIGHT: MOTHER VOLGA

So one bright spring morning he absconded with a twenty-copeck piece, with which he was to buy bread for the family breakfast, and fled to the harbour. For several days he hoboed on the bank of Mother Volga, hobnobbing with rough but kindly stevedores, and getting his first taste of the irresponsible tramp-life which he was to learn so well later on. Then he obtained the job of a dishwasher on one of the Volga steamers at two rubles a month, and a new and valuable experience began for the twelve-year-old boy. Life on the steamer, with its constantly shifting scenes and faces, could not but please the immeasurably curious Alexey. As before, he observed and listened, not hesitating to peep through a keyhole when necessary, so as to store in his memory another significant detail, a characteristic trait — the empty-eyed steward for example, praying on his knees before the icon, sighing softly and stroking his bleached beard. But now his hunger for knowledge and understanding received a new stimulus: he began to read books. His immediate boss, the steamer cook, Smury, is credited by Gorky with having turned his mind toward literature. In his first autobiographic sketch for the Press, Gorky wrote:

Mikhail Antonovich Smury, retired corporal of the Guards, a man of fabulous physical strength, rude of manners, well-read, aroused in me an interest for reading books. Heretofore I hated books and all printed matter, but this teacher forced me, by blows and kindness, to realize the great importance of books, and to become fond of reading.

One is tempted to speculate as to what might have been the course of Alexey's development if Chance or Providence had not thrown him into the path of the giant cook. Would his native curiosity and non-conformity have led him inevitably to the life of books? Or would the aversion to books, bred in him by the aridity of grandfather's religious reading-matter and by the hateful school, have caused him to find another than literary outlet for his store of impressions and observations? In fact, the initial steps of Smury in coercing Alexey to read were hardly propitious. He made the boy read aloud to him book after book from his own collection of leather-bound volumes which he kept in his trunk. These consisted of mystic treatises, pseudo-Classic effusions of Free Masons, and similar occult and unreadable stuff. Smury swore and spat as he listened to the teeth-breaking balderdash, yet he insisted on Alexey reading and rereading those works, in his belief that books possess a great secret power, and that the more obscure the book the more valuable it might be. Thus far the ordeal of reading did not augur anything more pleasant than the school experience. But it happened that the captain's wife, who was fond of Smury, gave him Gogol's *Taras Bulba*. The story made Smury roar with laughter and shed copious tears. After that he left his own library in peace, but continued to borrow books from the captain's wife, and made Alexey read to him aloud. This often meant that the boy neglected his work, which Smury imposed on one of his elder assistants. The others resented this favouritism, and tried to avenge themselves on the " bookeater." Alexey felt awkward in the position of a pet, but of course he dared not argue with his gruff and terrifying chief, and besides, he had acquired a taste for reading comprehensible stories, and shared Smury's enthusiasm for such authors as Nekrasov, Walter Scott, or Dumas-*père*.

The tastes of the master and pupil did not always coincide. Thus Alexey found *Ivanhoe* tedious reading, whereas Smury enjoyed the story and proclaimed Richard " a real king." On the other hand, the boy was much attracted to the *Story of Tomas Yones*, an ancient translation of Fielding's *Tom*

Jones, while Smury growled: " Silly stuff! What do I care about Thomas? Of what use is he to me? There must be different books. . . ." And the reading orgy went on *crescendo.* Alexey now opened a book " with delight: the things told in books differed pleasantly from life." For a long time yet books were to feed his nostalgia for otherworldliness, for that which, like grandmother's fairyland, was so dissimilar to his immediate environment.

The environment was a continuation of his educational course in the understanding of the average Russian. He proceeded to come in direct contact with the common people, and to learn to know them as they are, not through literary idealization or caricature. What he saw and heard was, on the whole, depressing. Singly and collectively the mass of humanity that passed before the boy's eyes, the crew as well as the passengers, was as petty and mean as those whom he had observed in Nizhni Novgorod, from the garret window of grandfather's house in the " bad " Kanavino neighbourhood, or from the bootshop on the nice business street, or from the height of smug complacency at the draughtsman's. Unlike the characters of the books he had read, these were so unheroic, so small in their sentiments, in their joys and sorrows, and especially in their vices. That man to man is a wolf, was demonstrated to him abundantly from his early childhood. No mutual trust or respect, but each one trying to outdo or anticipate the other in malice and meanness. The common conception of diversion was a spectacle of cruelty, of suffering and torment on the part of the weak at the hands of the strong, or of the few at the hands of the many. With what sadistic glee the passengers mutilated a couple of suspected pickpockets! And what homeric laughter greeted the hysteria of a clumsy scullion who let the chickens escape from the coop, and who was brought to the verge of suicide by the taunts and jokes played on him by the jeering mob on the deck. Alexey watched the behaviour of the crowd in face of suspected danger, their cowardice, helplessness, beastly selfishness. On quiet evenings he listened to groups of passengers sprawled on the deck and engaged in the Russian pastime of philoso-

phizing. They discussed life, the soul, God, eloquently weaving into their speech folk proverbs whose wisdom vexed Alexey with its submissiveness to fate. At the same time his ears ached from coarse obscenity mechanically used by everyone, and his eyes could not escape the crude relations between men and women and the sexual promiscuity which went on aboard ship. Once the crew tried to force Alexey into " marrying " a young wench whom they had plied with liquor and locked in one of their cabins. Smury rescued him.

Smury was different. Of fierce countenance and thunderous speech, the terror of all who came near enough to hear his oaths and see the havoc wrought by his hairy fists on their victims, inaccessible, dry, and always sober despite quantities of imbibed liquor, Smury was by no means a brute. His little dishwasher was keen enough to discover a warm heart and fine mind beneath the forbidding exterior. He grew bold to ask the cook why, being essentially kind, he tried to scare everybody. Reluctantly the growling giant had to admit that he wore the gruff mask in order to keep people at a distance, for if they knew that he was kind they would crawl all over him. Indeed, his intrinsic kindliness did not prevent him from despising in a pitying way the bulk of his fellow-men. He did not hesitate to use his fists on fools and rascals when they offended his senses, and in dispersing with thrusts of his belly a mob of cowardly sadists. He addressed them all with the collective " blockhead ! " Alexey was drawn to him ; he felt in him an elemental wisdom which reminded him of grandmother, though the outlooks of the two did not always tally. Thus when Alexey failed to pity the clumsy, lacrimose scullion, and remembering grandmother's admonition to pity all men, felt ashamed, Smury pulled him up to himself and said :

" You can't force yourself to have pity, and it isn't right to lie about it — do you get me ? Don't you learn to be a jellyfish, be your own self."

Smury's attitude was more congenial to Alexey than grandmother's sweet, all-forgiving, all-atoning religion. The men around him irritated him, he often felt like hitting them on

the head rather than pitying them and finding solace in the belief that God's creatures and God's ways cannot be wrong. His passion for understanding grew apace, he was surcharged with queries and doubts, and tried to get Smury to answer some of these. " Are men wicked or good? Docile or roguish? And why are they so cruelly, greedily wicked, and so disgustingly docile? " But the all-wise cook failed to quench the boy's thirst. His answer was as evasive as grandmother's relegations to God. Smury, " enveloping his face in the smoke of his cigarette, would say in a tone of annoyance:

' Ekh, what is tickling you? Men, men. . . . Well, men are men. Some are clever, others are stupid. Read your books, and don't mutter silliness. In books, when they're the right sort, everything is said.' "

The anomalous position of Alexey on the boat as reader for Smury came to a long delayed end, and the steward discharged him at Nizhni Novgorod, with the largest sum the boy had ever possessed — eight rubles. Smury picked him up, kissed him, stood him firmly on the landing of his native town, and gave him a parting admonition to be on the alert with people and to read books — " the best thing he could do."

BACK WITH THE GRANDPARENTS

ANOTHER brief interval at his grandparents'. Once more he faces the priestess of a joyous, kindly God of life and love, and the priest of a malignant and vindictively pedantic Jehovah. Alexey no longer suffers arbitrary guardianship. The sturdy boy, enriched in experience and possessor of eight rubles, flaunts his independence by taking out of his pocket a box of cigarettes and smoking in the presence of grandfather (among other things, Smury taught him to smoke, a vice to which Gorky is addicted to this day beyond all reserve). Old-fashioned Russians still regard tobacco as the " devil's weed," one of the Western crazes imported by Peter the Great. When grandfather, outraged by the boy's pertness, threatens him with his tiny fists, Alexey butts him, head into stomach, and makes the old man drop to the floor and sit there with blinking eyes and wide-open mouth. Grandmother gives Alexey a perfunctory beating, pacifies the two, but the pugnacious gesture of the youngster will serve to keep them at a respectable distance from one another.

The boy's pertness and pugnacity were not signs of conceit and self-satisfaction. No, his " irascible militancy " was due to bitterness and bewilderment. Bitterness, because of human injustice. Why was he forced to part with Smury, his guide and protector? They discharged him as a thief, though his only offence was in that he could not bring himself to inform against Smury's assistants who served food and drink to the passengers and pocketed the money. Bewilderment, because of the indigestible mass of impressions he had accumulated in recent months. Impressions of his fellow-men in the every-

though they " had committed something disgraceful and ridiculous."

Alexey mused on the difference between life in books and actuality. How remote, impossible seemed those adventures, those cavaliers and ladies, those magnificent villains, those polite and witty Europeans, in face of the joyless drabness around him. For even vice lacked colour and zest. A drunken debauch, a cheaply bought woman's affection, and then — the sourness of shame and remorse. Take, for example, Zhikharev, the best worker in the shop, who painted in the faces in the images : how depressing his orgies seem! As a rule his restlessness begins when he puts the finishing touches on some icon, and hates the thought of parting with it. The work done, he places the image on the table, and addresses it with ecstatic solemnity :

" Thou art finished, Mother! Like unto a cup art Thou, a deep cup into which the bitter tears of men's hearts shall now flow."

That is the signal for a spree which usually lasts three or four days. They all go to the public baths, returning toward evening steamed and scoured and festive. The workshop too is tidied up for the occasion, and the big table thoroughly cleaned by Alexey and Pavel. Zhikharev arrives, loaded with parcels of food and drink, and with him sails in a gigantic wench with the face and blue eyes of a baby, who utters sweetish banalities in an even, soporific tone. The men regard the woman with curiosity mingled with fear. Her abnormal dimensions, the slowness of her movements, the monotony of her voice, the vapidness of her words, produce a paralysing effect. They eat and drink, they shout and sing, they manage to get drunk and noisy, yet a heaviness hangs over the dimly lit room. Zhikharev makes desperate efforts at merriment, but his face remains melancholy and twisted in a non-comprehending nostalgia. He finally calls for a " Russian dance." The woman deliberately moves to the centre of the room, plants her huge body and lazily sways her hips, her face preserving a sugary stolidity. Zhikharev pirouettes quaintly around the " stony wench," looking earnest and pathetic in his attempt to " express himself." The other

men join in the dance, but their movements and shouts are dis-
jointed, each one speaking of himself and to himself, flaunting
his own grievances and yearnings in drunken morose abandon.
A macabre grotesque.

Alexey felt like weeping over the diversions of these pathetic
men. They were kind to him. Accustomed to play the part of
Azazel to grown-ups, he was grateful to the painters for treating him humanly. And because of this feeling for them, his
heart ached the more sharply for the wretchedness of their
existence and the grossness of their unquenching amusements.
In their misery he was inclined to read the fate prepared for
him too, and at times he was tempted to yield to that fate, to
swim with the current and find comfort in wallowing cosily in
the mire, with and like " everybody else." Pavel, only two years
older than Alexey, behaved like a regular fellow, drank, spat,
and carried on an affair with a servant girl from across the
street. Lying awake at night, amid snoring, groaning, and
grunting men, Alexey was oppressed by his loneliness, and
often made up his mind to merge with the herd and " go on
the next holiday to where all the others went." But he did not
go. His inborn fastidiousness deprived him of the ease which
one attains through being like everybody else. Vodka nauseated
him with its odour and taste, and woman he still associated with
Queen Margot and his book-heroines. When yet on the steamer
with Yakov the stoker, Alexey realized that reading had made
him " different " from the rest, that " books had rendered him
invulnerable to many temptations. Knowing how people love
and suffer, one could not go to a house of prostitution. Sin at
the price of a few coppers could arouse only disgust for it, and
pity for those to whom it was sweet." The only vice in which he
began to indulge was, as we have noted, smoking, and to this
day Gorky is a slave to Lady Nicotine, in defiance of his
squeamish lungs.

One wonders whether Alexey was aware of how much he had
meant to those icon-painters: his reminiscences are modestly
silent on this point. Though only thirteen, he had seen more of
life than any of them, and his reading had widened his horizon
beyond the reach of their imaginations. In their long and varie-

gated discussions, the boy would command attention and compel the bearded masters to listen to him. He imparted to them his passion for reading, and instead of learning their craft he entertained them at work by reading aloud. They were a receptive audience, too impressionable for the good of their labour. Thus when Alexey obtained from a fire-chief (queer land of Russia!) Lermontov's *Demon,* and began to read it in the shop, all work was disrupted. One after another they laid down their brushes and gradually formed a close circle around the boy, whose own voice choked from emotion, and whose eyes were full of tears. Lermontov's quaint demon, not a Mephisto or Lucifer superciliously mocking us mortals, but an immortal stricken with love for a daughter of men, a sower of evil poisoned with a longing for affection, disturbed them all strangely. The precocious muse of the poet — Lermontov began his *Demon* when in his teens — went to their heads like a potent, unknown wine, and for days they moved about as in a daze. The book was carefully locked up in Zhikharev's trunk, and Alexey was made to read the poem again and again, even after most of them had gone to bed. His reading would rouse them, and once more the reader would be surrounded by eager listeners, now half-naked and shivering from cold. In the frosty night, as they came out into the court for their needs, they gazed at the stars in a new way, and Sitanov quoted Lermontov:

> The wandering caravans
> of luminaries
> thrown into space. . . .

There were evenings on which instead of reading, Alexey, with the help of Pavel, entertained the crowd by acting. The lads smeared their faces with soot and with the paints intended for the holy images, and with the aid of hemp transformed themselves into hirsute creatures enacting Russian heroes and villains, Chinese devils, and what not. The unpretentious audience laughed to colicks, and Alexey, encouraged and provoked, would let his imagination go, play fantastic rôles, or vent his disgust with his day-environment by impersonating the stout merchants, or the rustic simpletons fleeced and hoodwinked by

the salesmen, or these latter. Even the grave and pious painters melted into merry laughter — and what higher award could an artist aspire for! They praised the boy vociferously, and urged him to make use of his talent and try to become a circus clown. It is a wonder that this first success did not turn his head and divert him to a theatrical career. With his mobile face, remarkable nose and eyes, his deep bass and histrionic gifts — what an attraction he might have eventually made in Nikita Baliev's troupe.

One scene makes us realize how precious Alexey was to these people. On his name's day the shop presented him with a miniature icon of Alexey the Man of God, and Zhikharev delivered a long and solemn speech. Gorky claims that he remembers the words distinctly.

" Who art thou? " he spoke, with much twisting of fingers and raising of eyebrows. " Nothing more than an urchin, an orphan, thirteen years all in all, yet I, almost four times your age, praise you and approve your way of facing things direct, not sideways! Keep that position all your life, that's fine! "

. . . . At last Kapendyukhin shouted to the orator with annoyance: " O quit your funeral sermon, look — his ears are turning blue."

And slapping me on the shoulder he added his praise:

" What is fine about you is that you are a kinsman to all folks, that's what is fine! One finds it hard to scold you, let alone beat you, even when you give cause for it! "

They all looked at me with friendly eyes, good-naturedly bantering me for my embarrassment. A little more and I should probably have burst out crying from the unexpected joy of feeling that these people had some use for me. . . .

Years later the observation of the cossack Kapendyukhin was re-echoed by the toilers of Russia, when they hailed Maxim Gorky as one of their own, " kinsman to all folks." His love for man, and even men, has always bridged the gulf between him and his neighbours, those at any rate who did not try to ride on his back. Yet, despite the pleasant relations with the icon-painters, Alexey felt more and more dissatisfied with his life. The melancholy of the workshop weighed heavily upon

him, and though he managed occasionally to dissipate it for the others, his personal relief was dubious and at best momentary. The days at the Gostiny Dvor grew ever more oppressive. The salesman, his boss, disliked heartily the unusual lad, pert and untractable, and did his best to oust him, going even the lengths of dropping coins to tempt him into picking them up, so that he might accuse him of dishonesty. The pettiness and unscrupulous enmity of this " businessman " became dangerous, when he persuaded the clerk of an adjoining shop to wheedle out of Alexey an icon, and later an expensive psalter. Apparently the boy's respect for private property was not overdeveloped, for the man's plea to help him and his starving family prevailed against his moral misgivings. But Alexey's geniality prompted the beggar to confess that he was trapping him into a crime at the behest of the salesman. The boy felt alarmed and disgusted at the same time. He had no one in whom he might confide his fears and longings. Grandfather? Alexey met him once on the street, as he strutted solemnly in a heavy fur coat, and hailed him. The old man looked at him from behind his palm: " Ah, that's you. . . . You're a god-dauber now, ah yes. . . . Well, move on, move on! " He brushed him aside, and resumed his stroll. Grandmother was working hard, taking care of her half-demented husband and of her ill-fated grandchildren. Alexey's admiration for her fine spirit had not diminished, but he was now aware that she " had become blinded by fairy-tales and incapable of seeing, understanding life's bitter reality." To all his doubts and complaints she would answer: " One must have patience, little Alexey." This " virtue of donkeys," as Ludwig Börne classifies patience, was grandmother's recipe against all grievances.

That was all she had to say in reply to my accounts of life's hideousness, of people's torments, of my heartaches, of all the things that outraged me.

I was poorly adjusted for patience, and if occasionally I displayed this virtue of cattle, wood, and stone, I did so to test myself, to find out the reserves of my strength, the degree of my stability on this earth. Sometimes youngsters, in silly bravado and from envy for the strength of grown-ups, attempt

to lift, and do lift, weights much too heavy for their muscles and bones. . . .

I too did that, in the direct and figurative senses, physically and spiritually, and it is due only to some chance that I have not ruptured myself to death or mutilated myself for the rest of my life. For nothing mutilates a man so terribly as patience, submission to the force of external conditions.

And if in the end I shall lay myself into the ground mutilated nevertheless, I shall say in my last hour, not without pride, that for forty years good people anxiously endeavoured to distort my spirit, but that their obstinate labour was not altogether successful.

This was written some thirty-odd years after the icon-shop period, when, licking his wounds, Maxim Gorky could speak thus consolingly of his comparatively safe escape from the claws of life. But at the moment of his actual difficulties the youngster was apt to quake before the self-imposed task of endurance as a test of strength. He wanted to flee — from the pathetic God-daubers, from the smug Gostiny Dvor, from Nizhni Novgorod, the city he associated with his wretchedness. The call of spring turned his eyes once more to the Volga, and he planned to work his way on a steamer down to Astrakhan, and thence to go to Persia. Why Persia? Gorky does not recall the exact reason. Possibly, he suggests, because he was very fond of the Persian merchants at the Nizhni Novgorod Fair, as " they sat like stone idols, calmly smoking their nargiles, their dyed beards thrust into the sunlight, and their eyes large, dark, omniscient." In his earliest recollections, when he describes the death of his father at Astrakhan, he refers to the quaint house in which they lived then, with " bearded, dyed Persians living upstairs, and an old yellow Kalmyck selling sheepskins down in the basement." Did this childhood reminiscence vaguely stir in his mind now, when he craved for romance, for an escape from the familiar?

LAST PHASE OF BOYHOOD

BUT he chanced to meet his relative, the draughtsman, who persuaded him to give up his Persian dream, and come back to work for him. He had big contracts to build shops for the annual fair, and offered Alexey the job of an overseer — to watch the carpenters and other workmen that they did not loiter or steal the material. His wages were enormous — five rubles a month plus five copecks a day for dinner! Alexey always liked in the draughtsman a lurking note of recklessness, a secret longing for rebellion against the petty family and social conventions, in which he squirmed like a fish caught in a net. He greeted the boy amiably, they exchanged Easter kisses, with the traditional " Christ has risen " — " In truth, He has risen," and when the man offered him a cigarette as to an equal, Alexey was won over completely. For two more years or so he remained in Nizhni Novgorod, however restive and yearning for change. One need hardly regret this " compromise " of his. In the end it matters little whether he lived in Nizhni Novgorod or in Kazan or tramped on the Black Sea shores or through the Caucasian mountains. Wherever he was he continued perseveringly his education, based on direct observation and analysis. Two more years in his home-town enriched his mind as they would have done in Paris or New York or any place with human material at hand. There is nothing monotonous or banal about his reminiscences of this period ; they fascinate the reader with their throb of life that is beyond space and time.

On his job he came to know closer that Sphinx of Turgenev, the Russian peasant. The carpenters and plasterers came for

the most part from villages, where they had left their families, and whereto they gravitated perpetually. Alexey observed them at work and play, listened to their endless conversations, took part in these, interviewed the men individually, and in the end was baffled by their contradictoriness and ineffability. They seemed at the same time kindly and callous, ingenious and slothful, religious and amoral, mentally quick and stolid, recklessly courageous and passively craven, challenging and fatalistic, brilliantly eloquent and annoyingly obscure and incoherent. Above all, he felt a primitive craftiness about the peasant, a tendency not to reveal himself wholly but to keep to himself a certain something, " and perhaps in that something hidden, unsaid, was the most important thing." In any event, he found the real muzhik infinitely more complex and engaging than the one he had read about in books. That was not the first discrepancy he discovered between books and life!

His reading went on apace. He borrowed books from a cultivated family which tenanted the rooms where Queen Margot once reigned. Russian stories appealed to him: he " always felt in them something familiar and sad, as though amid their pages was hidden the toll of Lenten bells — it would peal forth softly as soon as one opened the book." He read Turgenev with " avidity " and marvelled how " everything about him was intelligible, simple, and as pellucid as autumn." On the other hand, he read with resentment such books as Gogol's *Dead Souls,* Dostoyevsky's *Memoirs from a Dead House,* Tolstoy's *Three Deaths,* and similar books with lugubrious titles whose name in Russian literature is legion. He read and re-read Scott and Dickens. " The books of Walter Scott resembled a festive mass in a rich church — somewhat long and tedious but always solemn. Dickens has remained with me an author before whom I bow respectfully: he has mastered amazingly the most difficult art of love for men." It is quite evident that he was not in a position to digest everything that came his way. His stepfather brought him, about that time, a batch of literary supplements to *Novoye Vremya,* a leading daily, and called his attention to Flaubert's *Temptation of St. Anthony,* that was published there in instalments. Alexey

was not impressed by the story, and frankly preferred to it the *Memoirs of Upilio Faimali, Tamer of Beasts,* printed in the same supplements.

Maximov, his stepfather, had been reduced to poverty, and now worked as a draughtsman for Alexey's master. The boy met the man with an aching heart, recalling his mother's humiliation and suffering. But gradually he came to regard Maximov with respect and sympathy. He was dying of tuberculosis, and stood well the test of good breeding under the circumstances. The draughtsman's family treated the sick man with contempt and hostility; his gentle bearing and independent air irritated them, and they upbraided him viciously for such fastidious manners as brushing his teeth and fingernails.

Alexey enjoyed Maximov's talk, his intelligent remarks on men and books, and especially his tact in keeping the employer's family at a distance. He inherited from his mother that respect for Nobility, that nostalgia for the romance of beauty and gentility, whose absence in the immediate environment enhanced their allurement. To be sure, Maximov typified Russia's decaying nobility, a moribund class, but to Gorky " the crimson agaric is an unwholesome fungus, but at least it is beautiful." He became attached to the dying man, and assisted at his last moments in the hospital, where he found at his bed a comely girl, obviously from the common people. She was pathetic in her grief for her withered, hideously cadaverous lover. Another commoner idealizing a gentleman! There is a good line at the conclusion of that episode:

Stepfather died quickly; he died and at once improved in his looks.

This was one of the many experiences in Alexey's life to teach him the moral of suspended judgement. He saw again and again the blended coexistence of good and evil and the difficulty of discerning one from the other. He constantly heard people judge others, condemn them, and label them definitively, and he himself was prone to form categorical opinions of individuals on the basis of his first impressions. But the longer

he lived and the closer he observed himself and his neighbours, the more often did he feel obliged to revise his verdicts and to strip them of certitude. The paradoxical muzhiks who worked for his kinsman helped greatly to knock the bottom out of that logarithmic table (in Dostoyevsky's phrase) of moral notions which had been thrust upon him from his birth. The dramatic encounter with his dying stepfather gave another jolt to what had seemed a firm conviction with him as to man's goodness or badness.

Shortly after the death of Maximov, Alexey came upon his uncle, Yakov, of whom he had a distinct memory as of a petty, selfish, greedy, cruel and crafty man, who had driven his first wife into the grave and was responsible, together with his brother, Mikhail, for the death of Tsiganok and other unsavoury deeds. He also remembered uncle Yakov with the guitar, singing boisterous and nonsense songs at grandmother's " orgies." Now he was faded and slovenly, an old beggar living on the charity of his son, who treated his father as a servant. Alexey invited his uncle to a tavern, where a decanter of vodka loosened the man's tongue into a Dostoyevskian monologue. The boy had heard from grandmother about the way Yakov had lost his position of assistant to the jail warden, and was glad to hear uncle's own version of the case. Yakov's love for song led him to arrange parties at his home, to which he invited the prisoners. They formed a jolly crowd, many of them fine singers and dancers — Yakov would remove their chains for the occasion. The merry festivities came to an end, when the police arrested one of Yakov's inmates in the art of choking a deacon on the street — he mistook the clergyman for a rich merchant. The jailer, it seems, would let them out for a while on their promise to come back after the transaction of their affairs. Why the authorities, after protracted investigations, set Yakov free, merely dismissing him from his position, cannot be explained by any other reason than, as the saying goes — *nyevozmózhnavo v Rossíyi nyet,* the impossible does not exist in Russia. Western logic flounders helplessly in face of such mental quirks as shown by Russian convicts, jailers, judges.

Alexey absorbed greedily these instructive, broadening impressions. His position as overseer was not interesting in itself, and it rather irked him to spy on the workmen, of whom he was fond. They too liked the unusual hobbledehoy, and good-naturedly jeered at his futile efforts to keep them from stealing and idling. He enjoyed their discourses, provoked them to argue and reveal themselves, in his vain hope to learn the Truth. But sameness bored him, and he restlessly sought after fresh impressions. Many evenings he spent in a low tavern whose owner had a weakness for songs and treated to a glass of vodka any stray singer who managed to delight his " soul." Russians still talk a great deal about the soul, in a rather vague and comprehensive way. Nothing stirs their soul as intensely as a song, " rightly " performed. That tavern had one or two steady visitors, whose songs miraculously transformed the audience — hucksters, street-walkers, the tavern-keeper — into a hushed, sentimental, worshipful crowd. Alexey listened to the untutored singers, and though moved deeply by emotion he managed also to observe the others and record their reactions.

His restlessness and curiosity led him to places and people that were uncommon and irregular. The career of a tramp gave him many a wink before he actually launched into it. He was drawn to Millions' Street, the hunting ground of Nizhni Novgorod's riff-raff, where he could watch the panorama of ex-men. Ardalyon, a forty-year-old peasant, the best mason in his kinsman's employ, suddenly slipped from his path, went on a debauch, from which he never recovered, though he attempted a return to respectability. The lure of irresponsibility, of freedom from things and duties, of comfortable merging with the multitude of fellow-crawlers at life's bottom, drove many an Ardalyon into the ranks of the Golden or Barefoot Brigade, as Gorky was to learn before long. Ardalyon greeted the appearance of Alexey in Millions' Street, and served him as guide and protector during his visits in the not all too safe neighbourhood. Says Gorky:

I diligently observed those people, closely packed into the stony sack of the old and dirty street. All of them were people who had drifted away from ordinary life, but they seemed to

have created a life of their own, independent of any master, and gay. Carefree and bold, they reminded me of the Volga bargemen in grandfather's stories, who easily changed into bandits or hermits. When there was no work they were not too squeamish about petty thieving from barges and steamers, but that did not trouble me. I saw that all life was cross-stitched with theft, like an old coat with grey threads. At the same time I noticed that these people worked on occasion with tremendous enthusiasm, not sparing their strength, as in cases of emergency jobs, or fires, or ice-floes on the river. And altogether they lived more festively than all other people.

Alexey's trips to Millions' Street were reported to his employer. The draughtsman warned Alexey against that street of thieves and harlots, whence " the road led to jail and hospital." The element of risk would not have dampened the boy's curiosity; on the contrary. He soon gave up his pilgrimage to the street of " festive living," but for another reason. It pained him to see that with all their freedom and broadness, the Golden Brigade were weak enough to practise cruelty upon their inferiors, especially against women. After all, these bold fellows were as pettily sadistic as the fat merchants of Gostiny Dvor! The boy's bookish chivalry toward women was outraged at the sight of their treatment, and he often rebelled and challenged the brutal males. The following episode is characteristic of that phase.

Daily Alexey had to pass a " virulent enemy," the janitor of a brothel, whom he once gave a thorough beating for dragging a drunken prostitute by her legs down the cobblestones of the street. The janitor could not understand why anyone should interfere in his legitimate business of taking care of his charges, and he sought to avenge himself on the impudent lad. Every morning he would block his way and start a fight, but as every time he was worsted, the janitor was forced to look for another way in which he might hurt his assailant. On learning to his surprise that Alexey had beaten him because he felt sorry for the prostitute, he asked him whether he would feel sorry for a cat. Alexey admitted that he would. A few mornings later as he was going to work he noticed the janitor strok-

ing a cat. At his approach the janitor jumped up, seized the cat by its legs, and dashed its head at the curbstone, splashing Alexey with " the warm blood." A mad scuffle followed, the two " rolling on the ground like dogs ":

Later, as I sat among the weeds of the square, nearly crazy with unutterable pain, I bit my lips to keep myself from howling. Even now, as I recall that, I am convulsed with sickening disgust, and am wondering how I escaped losing my mind or killing someone.

The hideous environment was becoming unbearable for Alexey, whose fastidiousness grew ever keener with reading and brooding. Seeing all the filth around him, the unnecessary cruelty and meanness, the overpowering boredom responsible for most of the bestialities he observed, Alexey yearned more and more achingly for Civilization, for the clean and decent life he had read about in books. The contrast between what he saw and what he read failed to down his spirit. Despite the overwhelming blows which surrounding reality dealt to his fine sentiments, Alexey stubbornly believed in that other life, the fairyland he had visualized in his contact with grandmother, Queen Margot, and the tantalizing, provocative books. That faith saved him from acquiescence.

I did not drink vodka and had nothing to do with women — books took the place of these two forms of intoxication for me. But the more I read the more difficult it was to live as emptily and futilely as the people I knew seemed to be living.

I had just turned fifteen years of age, but at times I felt like a mature man. I was, as it were, inwardly swollen and heavy with all that I had lived through, read, and pondered restlessly about. Looking into myself, I found my receptacle of impressions resembling a dark storeroom, promiscuously crowded and packed with all sorts of things, which I was neither strong nor clever enough to put into order. At the same time these loads, despite their abundance, did not repose in me solidly, but floated about and swayed me, as water sways a floating crock.

I had a squeamish dislike for unhappiness, ills, grievances. In the presence of cruelty — blood, blows, even verbal abuse

of a person, I experienced an organic repulsion which soon passed into a cold fury, and I myself would fight like a beast, after which I would feel painfully ashamed. There were moments when I was so passionately anxious to beat up a bully, and threw myself so blindly into a fray, that even now I recall those fits of despair born of impotence with shame and grief.

Within me dwelt two persons. One, having learned too much filth and abomination, had somewhat lost courage because of that, and crushed by the knowledge of the ordinary and horrible, had begun to regard life and people with mistrust and suspicion, with a helpless pity for everyone, including himself. This person dreamed of a peaceful, solitary life, without people around, of a monastery, or the hut of a forest guard, a switchman's box, of Persia, or the job of a night-watchman somewhere on the outskirts of a town. Only to see fewer people, to be as far away from them as possible.

The other person, baptized by the holy spirit of honest and wise books, when observing the triumphant power of the ordinary and horrible, felt how easily that power might wring his neck and crush his heart with its filthy boot. Against this he fought strenuously, with teeth set tight and fists clenched, ever ready for dispute and battle. This person loved and pitied dynamically, and as befitted a brave hero of the French novels, he drew his sword from its scabbard at the slightest provocation, and assumed a militant position.

The former self was characteristic of the majority of Russia's intelligentsia — Turgenev's Hamlets, Chekhov's whining knights of futility. The latter self belonged to the category of that handful of Russians who translated words into action and performed seemingly Quixotic feats, those impractical dreamers whom Maxim Gorky glorified in his *Song of the Falcon,* with the slogan that became historic: " We sing a song to the madness of the brave! " It was this pert and pugnacious self in Alexey that impelled him to strike out for larger spaces, to give himself and " the whole earth a mighty kick which would send everything whirling joyously in a festive dance of people in love with one another and with this life incepted for the purpose of another life — beautiful, buoyant, honourable."

In this mood the fifteen-year-old boy made up his mind " to

do something with himself, lest he go to perdition." Swollen with impressions, meditations, and unanswerable questions, with a nose figuratively and literally thrust forward and upward in boundless inquisitiveness, Alexey Peshkov left his native Nizhni Novgorod for another Volga city, Kazan, " secretly hoping that once there he might find a way to do some studying."

YOUTH

KAZAN

KAZAN on the Volga. In the sixteenth century, Ivan the Terrible captured the city from the Khan of the Golden Horde and annexed it, together with the adjacent territory, the "Kazan Tsardom," to Muscovy. Four centuries later, under the Bolsheviks, Kazan once more became a Tatar capital; namely, capital of the Tatar Autonomous Socialist Soviet Republic. In the interval the city had developed as a commercial and cultural centre, the two races living side by side, quite apart yet with no apparent antagonism. As other old Russian cities, Kazan boasts a towered Kremlin, a cathedral and numerous churches; it is an archbishopal see, and has a renowned Theological Academy. At the same time Kazan is regarded as a seat of Mohammedan learning, and abounds in historical places and relics venerated by the Tatars. Altogether it is a city of old and varied traditions, some of which go centuries back antedating the advent of the Tatars; the thirteenth-century ruins of Bolgary, the capital of the original Bulgarians, are still extant in close vicinity. It was in Kazan that Peter the Great launched one of his imperialistic ventures, the building of a fleet for a campaign against Persia along the Caspian Sea. Under Catherine II, Kazan fell into the hands of Pugachev, leader of the rebellious cossacks, and experienced one of the bloodiest *jacqueries* recorded. Kazan was the birthplace of Gavriil Derzhavin, Catherine's bard and flatterer, a fine poet withal, who lived long enough into the nineteenth century to greet and bless Russia's first national poet, Alexander Pushkin. Derzhavin's influence was responsible in a measure for the growth of

Kazan as an intellectual metropolis of eastern Russia, the establishment of its museums and educational institutions, including its university. Among the students of this university walked once a haughty though homely youth, Count Lev Nikolayevich Tolstoy. About half a century later the same university expelled a politically heretical student, Vladimir Ulyanov, after whose death this institution assumed the name of the Lenin University of Kazan.

It was to this city that Alexey Peshkov, not quite sixteen, came from Nizhni Novgorod, in quest of knowledge, university knowledge, in fact. This impertinent ambition was encouraged in him by a kindly high-school student at Nizhni Novgorod, Yevreinov, who had noticed the common lad ever hankering after books. Yevreinov urged him to come to Kazan, where he could stay with his family, cover the matriculation requirements within some six months, then once at the university he was sure to obtain a government scholarship and five years later become a " scientist." Yevreinov was certain that Alexey was " destined by nature to serve science," and he did not fail to draw a comparison with Mikhail Lomonosov, also a son of the people, who back in the eighteenth century rose from the position of an ignorant fisherman to that of a member of the Academy, and whose versatility prompted Pushkin to dub him " a university," hardly by way of praise only. The plan seemed extraordinarily " simple, because Yevreinov was nineteen and kind of heart." Alexey, whose experience might have ensured him against gullibility, found Yevreinov's enthusiasm infectious. In any event, he was tired of Nizhni Novgorod, he needed a change, and Kazan was within closer reach than Persia, and rather oriental at that. It was fitting that this stage of his life should have concluded with the final advice of grandmother, under whose guidance his childhood and boyhood had passed. As she saw him off at the wharf, she said to him:

" Look here, don't you fret at people — you are always cross, and you've gotten stern and pert! You get that from grandfather; well, look at grandfather: he lived and lived and ended as a fool, a bitter old man. Remember one thing: 'tis not God

who judges people, that's the devil's business! Well, good-bye. . . ."

And wiping scanty tears off her brown flabby cheeks, she added:

" We shan't meet again. You, restless fellow, will stray far away, and I — shall die."

Lately I had kept away from the dear old woman and had seen her but seldom, and now I suddenly felt with pain that never again should I meet a person so intimately close to my heart. I stood at the stern and watched her, at the railing of the wharf, as she was making the sign of the cross with one hand, while the other was wiping with the edge of a shabby shawl her face and her dark eyes filled with the radiance of an indestructible love for human beings.

Indeed, that was the last time Alexey saw grandmother. He later heard of her last days, lonely and wretched, yet as ever dedicated to the task of bringing help and cheer to people of a less happy philosophy of life. Alexey had innumerable opportunities to recall grandmother's admonition — not to fret at people, not to judge them, to be less grave and stern. It was not an easy task to follow these Thou shalt not's in face of the experiences that befell him.

At Kazan Alexey soon discovered of what small practical value Yevreinov's kindness and counsel were. In the first place, the authorities were not at all eager to encourage prospective Lomonosovs. Quite to the contrary. The rôle of the educated youth in fomenting revolutionary movements convinced the Government that in Russia enlightenment was inevitably subversive of the established order of things. Based on gross social inequality, propped up by a small minority favoured against a disabled and overwhelming majority, the autocratic monarchy drew its vitality from the backwardness, ignorance and submissiveness of the people. Education menaced this situation, and accordingly its development was deliberately thwarted from above and made as inaccessible as it was expedient with regard to the minimal needs of the state. During the latter third of the nineteenth century, Count Dmitri Tolstoy introduced the so-called Classic system into the secondary schools,

with the object of filling the time and minds of the pupils with difficult and deadly study of dead languages, at the expense of vital and thought-provoking subjects. Furthermore, the lower classes were to be discouraged from seeking instruction. Tolstoy's man-Friday and successor, Count Delyanov, was indiscreet enough to send out confidential circulars to heads of schools, in which he advised them against admitting socially low applicants, branding these as " children of female cooks " ! Today Soviet educational posters present a woman in a red kerchief proclaiming Lenin's slogan: " Every cook must be taught to know how to govern the country." But what chance did Alexey Peshkov have against these indiscriminations and barriers of the eighteen eighties, an untutored child of the despised people?

That was not all. Alexey found within a few days after his arrival at Kazan that Yevreinov's big heart and love for his neighbour combined with the thoughtless callousness of youth toward those nearest to them. The Yevreinovs — a widow with her two sons — lived in a wretched cabin on a niggardly pension. Alexey's eye was keen and experienced enough to sympathize with the widow's frantic efforts to make her mite do for the education of her boys and for the provision of their other needs. Making use of his experience on the Volga steamers, Alexey tried to help his hostess in the kitchen, and there he faced the delicate task of finding a way to fill youthfully avid and blissfully ignorant appetites by means of an extremely limited wherewithal. The hospitality, so generously proffered by young Yevreinov, irked Alexey too much to enjoy it.

So that was the Kazan dream! Romantic and hungry for illusion, Alexey was yet sturdy enough to prick the bubble promptly on discovering it. To avoid invitations to the table, he spent his days outdoors, wandering through town, or, in bad weather, crouching in a dog- and cat-ridden basement of a burnt-down house, next to the Yevreinov cabin. " This basement," Gorky recalls, " was one of my universities." The university of Kazan now an exploded fantasy, he made the best of its substitute, and in the long rainy hours spent in the evil-smelling cellar he pondered and contemplated, as ever mingling

dream and reality. Disillusionment failed to dishearten him. He tells us that the acquired faculty of dreaming about extraordinary adventures and great heroic deeds helped him out during life's difficult hours, and since such hours were multitudinous his aptitude for dreams grew ever keener. He expected no help from the outside and had no hopes for a good stroke of fortune, but " gradually there developed in him an obstinacy of will, and the harder conditions shaped themselves for him the stronger and even wiser he felt to be. He understood very early that man is made by his resistance to the environment."

My Universities, is the title of Gorky's reminiscences dating from the Kazan period. One hardly need look for bitterness in that title. Conceived and written some thirty years after his actual experiences, these memoirs reflect a becalmed look backward, not devoid of philosophical humour. The extramural education proved so much broader and deeper, so much more vital than the formal, diploma-crowned education doled out to the exclusive few by professors supervised and circumscribed by Dmitri Tolstoy and his followers. Finding himself in no position to join the privileged eligibles of illiterate Holy Russia, Alexey resumed his educational training along the lines he had followed as errand boy, scavenger, scullion, and in other capacities accessible even to " children of female cooks." Yet, though still of the high-school age, the fifteen-year-old lanky lad, of homely features and a challenging nose, had by now graduated into full-fledged manhood, as far as toil and endurance were concerned. He now matriculated for a long period of grim study and thorough grilling in a variety of courses of applied values, concepts, and human interrelations. Looking back at his " universities," Maxim Gorky must have felt a deal of satisfaction at the knowledge and experience they had taught him, even if the price of hard knocks he had to pay for his instruction seemed exorbitant at the time.

Of all his universities, Mother Volga had been his truest *alma mater.* On her vast bosom and along her endless shores he learned and absorbed life in diverse shapes and doses. The

port of Kazan called unto him soon after his arrival both because he had to earn for his subsistence and because of the romance Volga and its children had always held for him. Again reality and fantasy commingled in his life. As he tells us, he could always earn fifteen or twenty copecks at the wharf. There, amidst stevedores, hoboes, and men of shady professions, he felt like " an iron bar thrust into red-hot coals " — each day saturated him with a multitude of sharp, burning impressions. Before his eyes circled in a whirlwind men nakedly greedy, men of coarse instincts, and he liked their rancour against life, their mocking attitude toward the world, and their nonchalance toward themselves. " His personal experiences made him long for these men, arousing in him a desire to sink into their acrid midst." As in Nizhni Novgorod, so in Kazan, and in Odessa, and along the Caspian Sea, and all through his " university " period, he was drawn irresistibly toward the men of the fifth estate. Those of a restless introspective nature are familiar with this, temporary or permanent, yearning after a carefree, irresponsible environment, in which to drown their inner voice, still and small but as annoyingly perseverant as a gnat. Vsevolod Garshin, the hypersensitive author of *The Red Flower,* haunted to death by black melancholia over life's cruelty and injustice, felt at ease, physically and mentally, while serving as a private in the war against Turkey. Was it not the blissfulness of ignorance and apathy of the Yasnaia Poliana peasants that seduced Lev Tolstoy into the rustic blouse? The cosiness of the common mire often lured Leonid Andreyev and such of his characters as the terrorist in *Darkness,* as an escape from the chilly peak of self-analysis. No wonder that Alexey Peshkov, precociously observant, bloated with an indigestible mass of impressions, experiences, and bookish notions, sought relief in the I-don't-care milieu of submerged humanity.

The point to be remembered is that although Alexey had probably come closer to the bottom of life than anyone who has lived to tell us of that limbo, he never achieved the comfort of complete sinking, if we may take his word. In moments of the most potent temptations to merge with the irresponsibles,

the critical observer in Alexey held him afloat and kept him from hitting the bottom. Or perhaps it was not so much the critical observer as the romantic dreamer of grandmother's fairyland, the chivalrous knight of Queen Margot that served Alexey as a buoy and held him suspended between the unattainable zenith and the all-too-accessible nadir. An intimate associate of the lowly, sharing their indifference to man-made codes and standards, he yet remained stubbornly squeamish about joining them in their transgressions of the Mosaic commandments, whether it was the sixth or the eighth or even if it was only the seventh. Gorky explains rather vaguely as to why he refused his partnership to some of the Kazan thieves whom individually he admired. "By all the logic of my past experiences," he says, "it would have been quite natural for me to go with them. The explosion of my hope to rise up, to engage in learning, also drove me in their direction. In hours of hunger, bitterness, and heartache I felt quite capable of a crime not only against the sacred institutions of property. However, the romanticism of youth prevented me from turning off the road which I was doomed to follow. Aside from penny-dreadfuls and the humane Bret Harte, I had already read not a few serious books, and these aroused in me a striving for something that was not clear to me, but which seemed more significant than everything I saw in my environment."

Occasional work as a stevedore, and close communion with the harbour riff-raff did not preclude association with the intelligentsia. The former pacified or dulled his mental unrest, the latter stimulated it, but Alexey was not guilty of common sense or logical conduct. Besides, most of the intelligentsia he hobnobbed with were economically and socially not far removed from the wharf worthies. Count Delyanov would have branded them as "children of female cooks." Alexey shared a cot with a student, Pletnev, beneath the staircase of a notorious tenement house, Marusovka. Pletnev was too poor to pay his rent, but he played so well on the accordion and sang such touching songs, that the heart of the landlady, a buxom procuress, melted into warm affection for her penniless tenant. Marusovka was a large tumble-down building, peopled by hun-

gry students, prostitutes, and "ghosts of men who had out-
lived themselves." At Pletnev's suggestion, Alexey began to
study systematically, with the aim of passing an examination
for the certificate of a village teacher. He found this labour
extremely hard and was "particularly vexed by grammar, with
its monstrously narrow, petrified forms, into which he found
it utterly impossible to squeeze the living, difficult, whimsi-
cally flexible Russian language." It may be said here, parenthetically, that in conversation and fiction Gorky's language is
to this day delectably free and flexible, while his publicistic
writings are encumbered with fossilized forms, participles and
gerunds, theological eloquence, and legalistic turns of speech.
Soon, however, Alexey learned that he was under age for a
teacher's position, and it was "with pleasure" that he gave
up this last attempt at regimented education. Instead, he wandered through the corridors of Marusovka and plied his ancient
craft — observation. The place hummed from morning till far
after midnight, and since privacy in that world was neither
feasible nor craved for, the observer easily discerned its sounds
and voices, its comedies and tragedies. As he inhaled the sour,
pungent odours soaring in the dank corridors; as he listened
to the rattle of seamstresses' machines, the exercises of light-
opera chorus girls, the bass gamuts of divinity students — prospective deacons of the Chaliapin diapason, the rasping decla-
mation of some half-mad, alcoholic actor (resurrected in the
Lower Depths), the hysterical screams of drunken prostitutes,
their clients and pimps — Alexey asked himself the old question: "What is the purpose of all this?" No adequate answer
was vouchsafed him, then or later, and as before and as after,
the curiosity of the observer eventually proved more fruitful
and valuable than the querulosity of the truth seeker.

At the Marusovka "university" Alexey had a close view
of a miniature Babel of bewilderingly diversified levels of culture and ethics. A monomaniacal merchant, who lived at
Marusovka for the comfort of his "soul" gave from time to
time Lucullian parties for his fellow-tenants in his dirty room,
and there gathered men and women that might have come
from different planets so far as their outlooks were concerned.

Yet the discerning eye could detect the ultimate oneness of the human race in this grotesque diversity. There was pathos, too, in that grotesquerie, and instructive sermons. It must have been a broadening experience for Alexey to watch the prostitutes leave surreptitiously parcels of food at the door of a tubercular divinity student, an emaciated madman who might have proved the existence of God on a mathematical basis, had he not died too soon.

The intelligentsia whom Alexey came to know through Yevreinov and Pletnev typified the transitional eighteen eighties, later described, not without sarcasm, in the first volume of *Klim Samgin* (*Bystander*). In the preceding two decades Russia's cultivated youth had adopted the view that their privileged position, their knowledge and culture, were acquired at the price of keeping the masses of the people subjected and ignorant. Their sick conscience dictated a policy of atonement, through bringing about the liberation of the people and enlightening them. But liberation depended on enlightenment, and this was impeded by the Autocracy from the motive of self-preservation. To break this vicious circle, the young idealists threw themselves headlong into an unequal fight against the Government, determined to destroy it, or at least force it to yield concessions, by means of revolutionary terrorism. Their love for the mysterious *narod*, " people," they expressed through hatred for the oppressors, and though gentle and tender in private life these privileged children of society proved merciless and iron-willed in shooting and dynamiting the enemy. For several years a handful of young terrorists, undaunted by prison, exile, and execution, carried on its spectacular activity, which culminated in the assassination of Emperor Alexander II, in March, 1881.

The heroic exploits of these revolutionists failed to accomplish either of their purposes. The inertia of the masses was not shaken by the distant rumblings of shots and explosions, and the removal of a score of dignitaries, even of the tsar himself, did not bring the government to terms. On the contrary, the régime of Alexander III was far more reactionary and oppressive than that of his vacillating father. Society, which had

passively applauded the reckless fighters, in the hope of reaping the benefits on the morning after, was now tired from the terrific strain, and craved for peace at any price. Russia's greatest, Tolstoy and Dostoyevsky, had unwittingly struck the keynote for this period of compromise, acquiescence, and common sense, the former by his doctrine of non-resistance to evil, the latter, in his Pushkin speech, by his admonition: " Humble thyself, proud man! " The average citizen used these profound thoughts as a shield for his shallowness and cowardice, marking the eighties as the decade of Small Souls and Petty Deeds. In its mass the intelligentsia presented then those futile whiners whom Chekhov depicted in his stories and plays, notably in *Ivanov*. The sense of futility began to infect even the ranks of the revolutionary youth, the survivors of the smash-up which overwhelmed the Terrorist Organization after the event of March, 1881. Their *narodnik* ideal, that is, the sanctification and idealization of the *narod*, the peasant people, was losing its inviolability. In life and in literature the peasant began to appear in his true colours, belying the poetized muzhik of Turgenev, the perfect Christian prototype of Tolstoy, the lachrymose Job-like sufferer of Zasodimsky, Zlatovratsky, and other *narodnik* gushers. Doubts as to whether the *narod* deserved the sacrifices of the intelligentsia, threatened to poison the revolutionary minds. Moreover, with the growth of industry and the emergence of a city proletariat, Marxian Socialism was gaining ground and dealing blow after blow to the illusions of the *narodniks,* who believed with Alexander Herzen that Russia might skip the stage of industrial capitalism and leap directly into the paradise of village communism.

Alexey came in contact with certain groups of Kazan college students and other intellectuals, who cherished the revolutionary traditions. He was introduced to a *narodnik,* Andrey Derenkov, owner of a general store in one of the quiet back streets. Derenkov gave his whole income to the cause, and used the rooms in the rear of the store for a library of forbidden revolutionary books, and for secret gatherings of friends of the people. Alexey was thankful for the opportunity to attend these clandestine meetings. There was the adventure of mystery and risk

(if apprehended by the police, the participants faced prison or exile, or both), and also there loomed the possibility of finding amidst these learned men answers to his numerous accursed problems. Most of those present were students of the local University, or the Theological Academy, or the Veterinary Institute, with a sprinkling of returned exiles from Siberia and students deported from the capitals. They were young, noisy, excitable, and they carried on heated and vociferous disputes, seeking support for their arguments in the enormous tomes which they brought along. Alexey was ill prepared for their theoretical battles. " Their truths," he tells us, " were lost to me in the abundance of words, as starlets of fat in the thin soup of poor people." But he sensed their devotion to the people, their anxiety for the future of Russia, and their determination to change life for the better. In their words he often heard the sound of his own " silent thoughts, and he regarded these men almost with enthusiasm, as a prisoner to whom they promised freedom." The " almost " is characteristic of Gorky's uneven attitude towards the intelligentsia.

Who and what are the intelligentsia? This bastard term, ungrammatical and un-Russian, acquired its popular usage about the middle of the nineteenth century. To the reactionaries the term embraced all who threatened the existing order of things — revolutionists, radicals, liberals, contemptible democrats, bespectacled bookworms, long-haired men and short-haired women conveniently dubbed nihilists, in a word, those who could read and write and had the temerity to think independently of the grooves prescribed by the Autocrat and the Holy Greek Orthodox Church. When, under Nicholas II, mercenary loyalists known as Black Hundreds were organized into public demonstrations with flags and church banners and the portrait of the tsar and knives and clubs and guns, these patriots rioted and massacred shouting: " Death to the Jews and the intelligentsia! " In November, 1917, the term intelligentsia became synonymous in Soviet Russia with white-collared bourgeois, saboteurs, traitors, cowards, mushy babblers, dry-as-dust highbrows, and altogether useless parasites. On the other hand, the Russian émigrés, even those who by

inclination might have belonged to the Black Hundreds, wrap themselves now in the martyrdom toga of the intelligentsia.

Empirically, then, one may consider non-conformity as an essential trait of the intelligentsia. From the time of Catherine II, the age of Kant, Voltaire, Rousseau, and the Encyclopaedists, the greater part of thinking Russians has stood in opposition to the established order and has championed the cause of the unprivileged classes. Since the ability and opportunity to think had been until lately confined to members of the "better" classes, it follows that the intelligentsia sacrificed their own advantages in pleading the cause of the common people. Their non-conformity was thus inevitably altruistic. Lavrov, and other leaders of revolutionary thought, defined the intelligentsia, or the truly cultured, as critically thinking individuals who dedicate their knowledge and understanding to the enlightenment of the dark people and the betterment of their lot. This formula applies to the best sons and daughters of Russia, who for the last century and a half stimulated thought and action in a land where both of these were prohibited and penalyzed. The Bolshevik revolution has temporarily dethroned and dislodged the intelligentsia, advocating as it does the self-sufficiency of the toiling masses; any activity for the people smacks of superiority, condescension, and bourgeois sentimental idealism. I say "temporarily," because the builders of Soviet Russia, sobered of their early intoxication with self-importance, realize now the need of a new idealistic intelligentsia for the gigantic task confronting them, particularly in the village, the stronghold of stagnation and backwardness.

With all these definitions and formulas, the term intelligentsia as applied in life remains vague and indefinable. When in old Russia you said of a man that he was an *intellighènt,* or of a woman that she was an *intellighèntka,* you probably meant that the person had intellectual and human interests, was morally fastidious and mentally alert, professed an unselfish outlook and practised it in his or her daily commerce with mankind. But you also meant a certain fugitive quality which marked that person with an unmistakable though ineffable ex-

clusiveness, aristocratism. A member of the Black Hundred seldom erred in picking the right head to be smashed by his club: he scented an *intellighènt* as keenly as he did a son of Israel.

Now it is certain that no bloodhound of the Black Hundred would suspect Maxim Gorky, or Alexey Peshkov, of belonging to the intelligentsia. He neither looks nor acts like one of them; above all, he does not feel like an *intellighènt,* and has always been ill at ease in their midst. Not that his " low " origin was responsible for it: Chekhov came from peasant stock, yet he typified the finest Russian intelligentsia. Gorky rose rapidly to fame and popularity, was lionized by the best circles of society, most lavishly supported cultural and revolutionary activities, and after 1917 he used his influence with Lenin and the minor gods to feed and shelter and save from execution scores and scores of Russia's intelligentsia. Yet he has never " belonged " there. Zinaida Hippius (Madame Merezhkovsky) has graphically defined, in private conversation, the attitude of the intelligentsia toward Gorky: he has always appeared to them as a negro in a silk hat. The charm of Gorky is in his rough robustness. He looks like a soldier or a miner, talks and writes in the colourful and sappy Volga Russian, and smells of the forest and the sea. But when he sits amidst intelligentsia, or when he tries to portray them, or when he writes editorials (most of his non-fiction writings are editorials), or when he vehemently battles for Western progress against Asiatic barbarism, he loses his firm ground and flounders.

Gorky has written eloquent passages, as a publicist, on the valuable rôle of the intelligentsia in recent Russian history. But in his fiction, and occasionally in his reminiscences, we meet most virulently suggestive remarks against the intelligentsia as a group and as individuals. One gains the impression that these idealists and altruists may seem a bit presumptuous in the eyes of the common people, on whose misery they batten their virtuousness. The common people are suspicious of too extravagant protestations of love for them (they are rather in doubt as to whether they deserve it), and some of them are impudent enough to resent their self-appointed leaders and

spokesmen. In a number of stories Gorky points out the super-
ficiality of the intelligentsia's affection for the " people," and
its failure to stand a real test. During the Kazan period Alexey
was " almost " enthusiastic about the intelligentsia he met, as
noted. He never felt quite at home with them, at first because
of timidity and awe before the scholarly gentlemen, and later
because he was seeing through them and was resenting some of
their traits.

They treated him as a curiosity, and recommended him to
one another as a " native nugget " and " a son of the people,"
" with the same pride with which street urchins boast of a
copper coin found on the pavement." Alexey did not like that.
Their passionate love for the people touched him deeply; he
felt that in such love one might find and understand the meaning of life. Yet he could not help doubting the reality of the
" people " they were worshipping. " To them the *narod* appeared as the embodiment of wisdom, spiritual beauty, and
kindliness, as something unique and godlike, a depository of
the fundamentals of all that is beautiful, just and grand."
Alexey was unable to associate these conceptions with the *narod*
he had known from his early childhood, the human-all-too-
human sailors, carpenters, plasterers, stevedores, and other
" sons of the people."

It is likely that an altruist may develop a selfish complacency
about his unselfishness. The humility of the *narodniks*, their
prostrations and genuflections before the imaginary people,
savoured at times of conceit and self-slapping on the back for
being so good and kind and humble. They expected the people's
gratitude and reverence, as a matter of course, and if these were
not forthcoming readily, they showed the people their place.
Andrey Derenkov's self-sacrifice — the cause not only took the
income of his store but also exposed him to constant danger
owing to the forbidden library and the secret assemblies he
harboured — was accepted by the young *narodniks* as a natural
duty, and they treated him with condescension, as a menial.
In receiving Alexey Peshkov into their midst they assumed the
right to guide him and show him the light as they knew best.
But when the " nugget " anticipated matters, asked pert ques-

tions, presumed to criticize opinions heard or read, and chose books of his own accord, he was treated as an ingrate, and exhorted to behave properly, to read what was given him by his guides, and to abstain from criticism for the time being. " In order to have the right to criticize one must believe in a certain truth," admonished him a typhoid-ridden student of philology, obsessed with the idea of harmonizing contrasts, freedom and coercion, Marx and Nietzsche. On his death-bed, some ten years later, dying from tuberculosis which he contracted while in prison and exile, this eternal student greeted Alexey with a hoarse exhortation: " Without a synthesis it is impossible to live! "

Alexey could not help being critical and resentful of mentorship, any more than he could mitigate the pugnacity of his nose. Long afterward he displayed with pride a volume of Schopenhauer which he acquired at Kazan by dint of saving coppers, mainly because one of his mentors told him curtly that the book was beyond him and might even prove harmful. As to believing in " a certain truth," he felt rather at sea. He believed blindly yet ardently in the revolution. It was a vast adventure, a mighty undercurrent of whose potency one was aware despite the officially smooth surface of drab reality, and this awareness gave life meaning, zest, and hopefulness. Back in Nizhni Novgorod Alexey had an ear for the dim rumblings of that undercurrent; he took notice of the tolling bells on the assassination of Alexander II, and avidly listened to whispers about dangerous persons and dangerous books that horrified such smug citizens as the draughtsman's family. In Kazan Alexey came within closer hearing of the current. There were searches and arrests made in Marusovka from time to time, some of the victims being obviously innocent of ordinary offences. Once a whole group, including an ex-army officer and an ex-soldier, were seized for attempting to organize a secret printing shop — one of the gravest political crimes in the eyes of the Authorities. On another occasion, when a tall tenant whom Alexey nicknamed " Wandering Belfry " was arrested, Pletnev commissioned his cot-mate with the delicate and dangerous task of warning certain people of this arrest. Alexey

performed his mission with the glee and excitement of one who had but recently pored over Fenimore Cooper, Mayne Reid, and Gustave Aimard. But when he asked Pletnev to initiate him into the mysterious doings in which he was apparently engaged, the student told him that he was still immature and ought to do some studying.

One variety of revolutionary activity consisted in forming small circles of workmen or " sympathizers " for the study of social subjects. The police was hot after these groups, especially after their leaders. The need of secrecy was thus essential, but Alexey's sense of humour revolted against the seeming lack of proportion between the elaborately conspirative methods and the relatively innocent end. He was, for instance, instructed to meet a mysterious man in a cemetery outside of the city limits. After numerous precautions he came face to face with a puny youth of a dry countenance and stern round eyes, who tried to appear grown up and grave. This was a *Kulturtraeger* who guided four or five young men in the intricacies of Adam Smith, supplemented with Chernyshevsky's notes. The long hours in a filthy basement, where this group met, filled Alexey with boredom. The work of Adam Smith did not appeal to him. He tells us that the basic principles of economics soon appeared quite familiar to him: he had acquired them directly, on his own skin, and he saw no purpose in writing a thick book in difficult words on something which is perfectly clear to anyone who wastes his strength for the welfare and comfort of " the other guy." At any rate, Pletnev's admonition to " study " for the revolution proved as little to Alexey's taste as most admonitions did.

From time to time he fled from the intelligentsia to his lowbrow friends at the wharf, both to find relief from the thick air of abstractions, and to earn a few coppers for himself and Pletnev. There is a memorable passage in Gorky's reminiscences, which illustrates the tonic effect of physical labour on one who is intellectually muddled and vexed. He describes an *artel* (a labour union whose members pool their income and expenses) of longshoremen unloading the cargo of a barge that had struck a rock near Kazan. Despite his youth and inexperi-

ence Alexey was allowed to join them. It was a cold and windy autumn night, it rained in torrents, and the longshoremen cursed and growled as they were towed toward the barge. But once on the spot, they threw themselves into work with an ardour and eagerness that surprised Alexey who had just observed their sullen mood. Bales and sacks flew about like feathers, the thick-set men raced one another with merry whoops and roars, cheerful, light, efficient, playing a merry game as it were. " They worked as if they had been famished for labour, as if they had waited long for the pleasure of hurling from hand to hand sacks weighing a hundred and fifty pounds." When the owner of the cargo urged on the men by promising three bucketfuls of vodka, the work assumed the speed and intensity of a hurricane. From midnight until two o'clock in the afternoon, the men laboured, lashed by the wind and drenched by rain, until they had the entire cargo transferred from the ill-fated barge. When towed back to Kazan they fell asleep on the deck like drunkards, anticipating the three buckets of vodka.

I too [recalls Gorky] grabbed sacks, hauled and threw them about, raced up and down, grabbed more sacks — and it seemed to me that I and everything about me were spinning in a stormy dance, that these men might work for months and years as terribly and joyously without tiring, without sparing themselves, that they were capable of pulling away the very city of Kazan to any place they liked, by taking hold of its steeples and minarets.

That night I experienced a joy of living, hitherto unknown to me. My soul was kindled with a desire to spend the rest of my life in this half-mad ecstasy of doing things. Overboard the waves leaped savagely, the rain flogged the decks, across the river howled the wind, and in the grey mist of dawn half-naked wet men raced up and down with unabating speed, shouting, laughing, flaunting their strength, their labour. . . .

One felt like hugging and kissing these two-legged beasts, so clever and deft in their work, so self-forgettingly infatuated with it. It seemed that such a strain of joyously infuriated strength could overcome any obstacle, that it could create miracles on this earth, could cover it in one night with mag-

nificent palaces and cities, as one reads about it in wise fairy-
tales. . . .

" The music of a life of toil," " the heroic poesy of labour "
— this phraseology, if not the very sentiment, belongs to Maxim
Gorky of a much later period. The glorification of work as a
creative collective force came as an idea, years after the actual
experience had receded into a memory. In *Chelkash,* the first
story of Gorky to win universal acclaim, published in 1895, the
author's sympathies are obviously on the side of Chelkash, the
tramp and rowdy who has nothing but contempt for the slaves
of " honest " labour. It was almost ten years later that Gorky
began to formulate his idea of progress and man — " all for
man, all through man," with human endeavour — " ever on-
ward! ever upward! " as the alpha and omega of the scheme.
The remoteness of this idea from the mind of the average workman is illustrated by Gorky himself, in his record of a conversation he held with a leading proletarian, some thirty years
after the " universities " period. The man regarded Gorky's
interest in culture, technical progress, and scientific organization of labour as a sign that Gorky had been poisoned by the
intelligentsia. " You are with us, but no longer one of us," he
chided him, linking him with Christ and other idealists of the
intelligentsia brand who " raise riot for super-earthly aims."
The millions of workmen, according to him, are taking part in
the revolutionary movement not because they desire a socialistic
state, but because they hope to free themselves from the yoke
of labour. " Man wants peace," a simple life, not factories, air-
planes, academies. " All one needs is a quiet nook and — a
woman." The fact that this man was not an anarchistic nihilist
but a " regular " revolutionary workman, set Gorky wondering: " What if, indeed, millions of Russians suffer the bitter
pains of the revolution only because in the depths of their souls
they cherish the hope of liberation from work? A minimum of
labour, a maximum of pleasure — that is quite alluring, as
everything unattainable, as all utopias." The query anticipated
one of the gravest problems with which Lenin had to cope in
his effort to harness the Russian chaos.

But whatever glamour time and change of environment may have lent to Alexey's experiences in the port of Kazan, they were beyond doubt more exhilarating to him than the indoor sports of the prematurely grave intelligentsia. His strong body demanded exertion, especially after his intellect had been administered too generous a dose in the stuffy quarters of the *narodniks*. He vacillated between the two worlds, feeling apparently a need for both in his unsettled existence. With the approach of autumn, however, he was forced to look for a more permanent job than what the promiscuity of supply and demand at the wharf could offer. After serving in turn as gardener, janitor, church-choir singer, he was driven by necessity to learn the baking trade. At the bakery-establishment of Vasily Semenov began one of his most trying yet most instructive, physically and mentally, " universities." This period is powerfully described in *Twenty-Six Men and One Girl*, in *Konovalov*, and in *The Master*. The comparative length of time spent by Alexey at the baker trade, and the intensiveness of the training, have made this period stand out in sharp relief in Gorky's recollections. To this day he dwells fondly on his apprenticeship in bakeries, graphically describing the process of kneading, shoving enormous loaves into the oven, snatching them out at the right second and with precise speed and manner, the result being a " perfect loaf."

Fourteen hours of hellish toil in the basement of Semenov's bakery (at the honorarium of three rubles a month) kept Alexey " quiet," for a time. He had to give up his visits to the Derenkov gatherings, which proved a severe privation in his humdrum existence. Whatever leisure was left him after performing the variegated tasks around Semenov's household and business (one of these duties consisted in feeding the master's pets, gigantic Yorkshire hogs which took especial delight in annoying Alexey while he fed them) he spent in sleep or with his fellow-workers. At first these regarded him with curiosity, as a freak, but his extraordinary, for them, erudition and experience, his infectious youth and ardour, his sincerity and serious-mindedness won gradually their affection and respect. What commanded the amazed admiration of these wretched

slaves was the dignity with which the lad fought a long battle against the all-powerful, awe-inspiring master, and ultimately won the latter's recognition. That Vasily Semenov, an ingenious sadist, devoid of scruples and convictions, a scoffer and gloater, evil-minded when drunk and coldly callous in the rare intervals of sobriety, a rich man risen from the lowest ranks and the more mean and blood-sucking for that; that this man should be brought to bay by the sheer mettle of a youngster receiving three rubles a month, and tacitly bow to his superiority, struck the bakers as an unheard of victory of spirit over matter. They were compelled to listen, while kneading dough or shaping cracknels, as one of their lowest held the floor, pouring out unto them the gems he had garnered in books or overheard amidst the intelligentsia. The master once surprised them at such a seance, and he nicknamed the offensive orator " Grokhalo " (" Rattle "). The name clung to him for years, and was recorded by the secret police as one of his " underground " pseudonyms. " The devil knows," Gorky recalls, " what it was that I talked about to those people, but certainly it had to do with whatever inspired hope in a different, easier, and more meaningful life. At times I succeeded in that, and seeing how the bloated faces were illuminated by human sorrow, and their eyes flashed with resentment and anger, I felt in a festive mood and thought with pride that I was ' working among the *narod* ' and ' enlightening ' them."

But these festive moods were rare. More frequently Alexey felt his helplessness against the inertia and ignorance of these people, who were in need of a brighter torch than the one Alexey could proffer them in order that their darkness might be dissipated. He was unable to jolt them out of the cattle-like patience and submissiveness with which they slaved for their half-demented master. What could he muster to say by way of reproach for the only diversions they knew and could assimilate — wineshops and houses of prostitution? He went along, the curiosity of the observer as ever drowning the squeamishness of the truth-seeker. The harlots did not favour the big-nosed lummox who, for all they knew, might have been the chaperon of his mates, since he remained stubbornly chaste. In the end

even the bakers bade him stay away, and not accompany them
to "houses of consolation," for, as one of them put it, they
"did not feel right with him," "as if they were in the presence
of one's father or a priest."

Alexey regretted this result of the awkward sensations he
had caused, for wherever he went he managed to learn a thing
or two. Sexual relations alarmed and interested him keenly,
his own conception of the matter presenting a strange *mélange*
of the crudest he had seen and heard around him with the
idealized and sublimated he had imaged out of books and
dreams. In the cheap resorts frequented by men of the bakers'
calibre, where one ruble could buy a woman for a whole night,
Alexey faced vice that was coarse and boisterous but rather
joyless. He saw shame and embarrassment on the faces of his
fellow-workmen, though they affected cynical nonchalance. It
surprised him painfully to find that in these places the so-called
intelligentsia had a rather poor record. To be sure, the illusion
of escape promised by the call of the flesh might have its appeal
to college students as it did to bakers and stevedores. The
dreadful thing was to hear the forelady and the harlots dis-
course on the relative merits of their clients, and conclude that
divinity students, government clerks, and the "clean public"
in general, were prone to commit excesses, to abuse and mal-
treat the women in a variety of cruel and perverse fashions.
Alexey was hurt in a sensitive spot. Had he not enlarged on
the fine and noble intelligentsia and their unselfish endeavours
to improve the life of the people? Now his listeners, always
dubious about the gentry and their incomprehensible follies,
guffawed in response to his eulogies. They knew better. Did
they not hear what the girls told of the learned gentry and
their behaviour? Low taverns and houses of prostitution served
as universities for the bakers and others of their ilk. Out of
the darkest holes and filthiest cracks of city civilization oozed
a mass of apocryphal information into the receptive minds of
the ignorant, and poisoned them. Envy and hatred served as
nimble conductors of such poison, and envy and hatred are
most readily directed against those who are different and non-
understandable. That is why Jews fall so easily victims of mis-

information. Also the intelligentsia. In no Western country
was the gulf between the cultivated and unlettered so un-
bridgeable as in old Russia. With eighty-five per cent of the
population illiterate, a person who could read and write was
looked upon with wonder and awe, not unmixed with suspicion.
The organizers of Black Hundreds had no difficulty in recruiting members among the attendants of those " universities."
Alexey heard the bakers talk with glee of how they were going
to help beat up college-students with iron weights. He raged,
he who stretched like a thin thread between the two Russias; he
raged, but felt utterly helpless in face of the wall of ignorance
and lack of understanding which separated them.

The experience he had acquired at the Semenov bakery was
to be utilized for the Cause. Derenkov's general store yielded
too small an income for the ever growing needs of the local
narodniks. As many impractical dreamers, Derenkov was redolent with schemes, mathematically calculated to bring huge
profits — for the Cause, of course. He now proposed to open
a bakery, with Alexey as assistant, in order that he, as " one
of us," might contribute to the productivity of the business,
and incidentally prevent the chief baker from stealing.
The business, indeed, soon proved so profitable that they
moved to larger quarters. But as for watching the morals of his
chief, Alexey had to admit defeat. The baker (his portrait:
" grey temples, a pointed beard, a dry face the colour of cured
ham, dark pensive eyes, and an odd mouth: small like that of
a perch, its thick puffy lips shaped as though in an imaginary
kiss. And something derisive gleaming in the depth of his
eyes ") put aside, during the very first night of their work, a
goodly amount of eggs, flour, and butter. " For a slip of a girl,"
he replied amiably to Alexey's inquiry: " a f-f-fine little girl! "
Alexey's sermonizing attempt was treated with such genuine
amazement, and was ignored so matter-of-factly that he was
thenceforth reduced to passive observance of the chief's
" asides " as well as of his amorous practices with the " slip
of a girl " (" . . . a short-legged girl; composed of vari-

dimensioned hemispheres, she resembled a sackful of water-melons ").

We are not told what were Alexey's wages in the *narodnik* bakery. Indirectly we may gauge them from the baker's promise that he would recommend his fee as senior-assistant in the larger bakery to reach ten rubles a month! One thing is certain: Alexey had no chance to loaf on his job. His regular hours were from six in the evening till noon, and the chief found him so apt that he relegated to him practically all the work. Besides kneading and baking, Alexey had to carry the baked goods to Derenkov's store, and to distribute large basketfuls of them to various institutions. These errands fed the unquenchable curiosity of the observer in Alexey. At the refectory of the Theological Academy he supplied buns to the students, on credit and for cash, and making the rounds of the breakfast tables he took in their talks and disputes, on Tolstoy, for example, or, more discreetly, on political subjects. Incidentally, Alexey concealed beneath the buns forbidden books and conspirative notes which he circulated as directed by the *narodniks*.

Miles apart, literally and figuratively, were such places as the Academy, the Insane Asylum, where the psychiatrist Bekhterev (subsequently an international celebrity) demonstrated maniacal patients for the students, or the Institute for Daughters of the Nobility. The assistant-baker would record such impressions as this one: " Once Bekhterev was showing a megalomaniac. When, in the doors of the auditorium, there appeared a long individual in a white robe, with a stocking-like cap on his head, I could not help grinning, but stopping for a second alongside of me the man gazed into my face, and I jumped away, as though with the black but fiery point of his look he pierced my heart. All the while that Bekhterev, pinching his beard, respectfully conversed with the patient, I kept on quietly rubbing my face with the palm, as though it had been scorched with hot dust."

It was so educative, all of this business. The clear-eyed, angelic daughters of the nobility, while picking out with their pink fingers butter-horns from the boy's basket, managed to

leave on the bottom pretty notes, in which they addressed the ugly duckling of a baker with such obscene remarks that he, who had visited " houses of consolation," blushed awkwardly. Alexey looked at these prototypes of Pushkin's Tatyana, Turgenev's Liza, Tolstoy's Natasha, as they bent over the basket, and tried to divine the scabrous authors amidst the innocents who scarcely understood the meaning of their pornography. His inborn nostalgia for the fine and noble urged him to regard the notes as childish pranks. Yet he was destined to learn (always learn!) that some of these children had been seriously wounded by Eros. He tells us of one occasion, on which an angelic brunette persuaded him, in her misery, to carry her frantic message to a university student, who was responsible for her plight.

His limited leisure Alexey spent in talking and listening to a wide variety of people, and also in reading. On the quiet he was already venturing with the pen: at night, while waiting for the dough to rise, he scribbled verses, mostly in a sardonic vein. Aside from the intelligentsia back of Derenkov's shop, Alexey's circle of acquaintances now included a few interesting workmen and artisans, some grotesque characters from all classes of society, and of course his comrades of the wharf adventures and his former fellow-bakers. All of these contributed in a large or small measure to the understanding of Russia and humanity, which he was pursuing in his " universities," and which he was to display so forcefully as a writer.

How variegated were his " courses " at that time! Among his Kazan acquaintances was a policeman, Nikiforych. One must note that in old Russia a policeman was the most universally and heartily hated and despised creature, one of his numerous nicknames being Pharao. But as a " student," Alexey had no choice of subject. Moreover, it was not he who had chosen Nikiforych, but the other way round. The silver-haired, silver-bearded, stalwart and gallant Pharao had made it his business to keep an eye on the suspicious youth of his precinct. Marusovka was his favourite and fruitful hunting-ground. He it was who caused time and again arrests among its political inhabitants, and it was he who patiently watched the movements of young Pletnev, the pet of the neighbourhood,

and finally pounced on him as he was about to print underground proclamations, and had him arrested and transported
to St. Petersburg. Of course, he had noticed the conspicuously
unusual lad, Alexey Peshkov, chum of stevedores and harbour-
thieves, comrade of bakers and other workmen, and friend of
the accursed intelligentsia. It so happened that the " slip of a
girl," the paramour of the chief baker, was Nikiforych's god-
daughter. This remote " kinship " was enough of a pretext for
the policeman to spread his net for the assistant of the baker
who admired the rotundities of Nikiforych's god-daughter.
After a few would-be casual conversations on the street, in
which the Kazan Sherlock Holmes tried to worm out of Alexey
a confession to having read the works of Count Tolstoy
(Alexey had; but what concerned the questioner were Tolstoy's
forbidden pamphlets, and these " seemed boring " to the
youth), the Pharao invited him to call at his house, for " a cup
of tea." Even a less alert person than Alexey would have
understood the purpose of Nikiforych's flirtation, but he was
curious to go, and besides, the Derenkov group, with whom
he took counsel, decided that his refusal would augment the
suspicions of the policeman against the bakery establishment.

" And so " [Gorky recalls] " I am on a visit at Nikiforych's.
One third of the small hole is occupied by a Russian stove,
another third by a double bed behind chintz curtains, with
a mountain of pillows in red fustian cases, and the rest of the
space is ornamented by a cupboard, a table, two chairs, and
a bench by the window. With his uniform-coat unbuttoned,
Nikiforych sits on the bench, screening with his body the only
little window, and at my side sits his wife, a full-bosomed
woman of about twenty, rosy-faced, with sly and malicious
eyes of a strange lavender colour; her bright-red lips pout
capriciously. . . ." In this environment, further coloured by
Madame's coarse flirtations with the visitor under the table,
and in the open when her old Mars is not looking, Alexey attends a " course " in the political outlook of the average Russian standpatter. Here is a delectable sample:

" An invisible thread — understand? " he asks me and looks
into my face with eyes grown round, as if he had become

frightened by something. " Suppose you take the Lord Emperor for a spider. . . ."

" Oy, bless you! " cried his wife.

" Shut up, you! That's said for clearness, you fool, not in derogation, you mare. Take away the samovar! "

Drawing his eyebrows together and half-closing his eyes, he proceeds solemnly:

" An invisible thread — like that of a cobweb — emanates from the heart of His Imperial Majesty Lord Emperor Alexander III and so forth, it passes through the gentlemen ministers, through His High Excellency the Governor and all the ranks down to myself and even the lowest private in the army. All is bound and knit by that thread; it is by its invisible strength that our Lord's tsardom is upheld for ever and eternity. And as to the mangy Poles, Jews, and certain Russians — they are bribed by the perfidious Queen of England, they try to break the thread where there's a chance, pretending that they're for the *narod.*"

With all deference to his guides and teachers from the intelligentsia, Gorky later stated that none of them gave him so definitive and graphic an exposition of the mechanism of the state as did Nikiforych. He began to feel more and more palpably the fine meshes of the " invisible thread " emanating from the heart of the central spider — Nietzsche's " cold monster." Strangely enough, the outlook of the old policeman touched in more than one point on that of the Philosopher of the Hammer. For example, commenting on the arrest of Pletnev, Nikiforych delivered himself of a Nietzschean diatribe against the Christian virtue of pity and charity. " There is much pity in the Gospel," he said, " and pity is a harmful thing. That's the way I think. Pity demands enormous expenditures on unnecessary and even pernicious people. Poorhouses, jails, madhouses. One should give aid to strong healthy people, so that they should not waste their strength in vain. Whereas we are helping the weak — can one ever make a weak man strong? Because of this hodge-podge the strong grow weak, and the weak sit on their necks. Here is a matter worth taking up. There's a lot to be reconsidered. One must

realize that life has long turned away from the Gospel, it
has a course of its own. Take, for instance, Pletnev — for
what good did he ruin himself? Because of pity! We give
alms to beggars, and let students go to perdition. Is that
reasonable, eh?"

These words made a deep impression on Alexey. They were
a far cry from grandmother's religion of kindliness and compassion. Experience had already helped to raise doubts in his
mind as to the efficacy of grandmother's attitude. In the words
of Nikiforych he " felt a certain truth, but was annoyed that
its source should be a policeman." Orientation on the side of
the strong against the weak became a recurring motive in
Gorky's tramp stories, and some critics saw in them the influence of Nietzsche. Gorky tells us that seldom did he come in
books on ideas which he had not previously heard in life. Both
life and books affected him, doubtless. The effect of books remained bookish, however, while things observed and gone
through in life have retained in his presentation an authentic
vitality. That is why the Nikiforych episode was of much
greater consequence for the development of Gorky and his
talent than volumes of subsequently read Nietzsche could be.

Alexey was in the throes of working out a *Weltanschauung,*
and the suggestive words of Nikiforych had touched upon a
sensitive spot. He was eagerly seeking for a formula. The
phraseology of the *narodniks* was not real to him, nor could
he find in his heart a clear response to the arguments of their
opponents, the nascent Marxians. He went to one of the midnight gatherings in an abandoned house on the outskirts of the
city, where George Plekhanov's *Our Divergences* was read and
discussed with vehement acerbity. The last flash of *narodnik*
heroism had illumined the drab skies of the eighties, with the
execution of young Alexander Ulyanov and his accomplices, all
former students of the Kazan university, for an attempt against
the life of Alexander III. From abroad came the voices of
Plekhanov, Axelrod, Deutsch, Zasulich, former *narodniks* who
had been cured of romantic dreams and were now calling the
revolutionary youth under the banner of Marxian Socialism.
A decade later the new movement was to count among its

leaders the younger brother of Alexander Ulyanov, Vladimir, better known as Nikolay Lenin. The problem under discussion was of great importance. Rural or urban Russia — which was to prevail in the near future? The agricultural peasant or the factory workman — which of the two demanded the immediate attention of the revolutionary movement? If Marx were right, and economic determinism reduced the rôle of the individual to zero, then the individual heroism of the *narodniks* was child's play. But that meant blasphemy against the memory of the martyrs! Alexey listened, but heard only personal quibs, bitter accusations of one another, blatant exaggerations on either side, with the truth of the matter hidden in the mist of words and the thick smoke of cigarettes.

Into these discussions as to the more adequate revolutionary methods for the overthrow of the autocratic régime, trickled in the thin voice of Tolstoyan non-resistance. Alexey attended a secret gathering of the more respectable intelligentsia, at the home of a professor, which was addressed by an apostle of the Yasnaya Polyana hermit. A tall, sinewy, swarthy man, with a goat-like black beard and the thick lips of a negro, spoke with a passionate hatred in his eyes on the fundamental principles of the Gospel, and in conclusion hurled at his listeners: " And so, are you with Christ or with Darwin? " Alexey, who had recently read a book about the struggle of Roman Catholicism against science, reflected that the fiery Tolstoyan was " one of those fierce believers in the salvation of the world through the power of love, who out of loving-kindness for men are ready to slaughter and burn them alive." Yet, in restless quest after a formula, Alexey sought out the prophet of love, and called on him the next day. The description of the Tolstoyan with the invidious name of Klopsky (*klop* means bedbug) is not without venom. After scattering stock phrases about love as the essence of life, he listened to Alexey's story of his circumstances and doubts, and commented on the fact that man is man wherever he be, and that one should strive not for a change of one's place in life but for the education of one's mind in love for men. " The lower man is situated the nearer is he to life's genuine truth, to its holy wisdom." Alexey

was rather doubtful as to Klopsky's acquaintance with this " holy wisdom " of life. He frankly gloated when Klopsky's scandalous conduct forced him to leave town.

To be sure, Tolstoy was as little responsible for Klopsky as Christ was for Alexander Borgia. Tolstoy was probably in dead earnest when he jested that he was not a Tolstoyan, or that he would be bored to extinction if he were condemned to dwell among simon-pure Tolstoyans. Klopsky was not an exception but rather a type. Countess Tolstoy speaks with understandable disgust of the " dark ones," though unfortunately she does not distinguish between Klopsky and Chertkov. In his reminiscences of Tolstoy (the *Dial*, June, 1927), Ivan Bunin speaks of Klopsky and other Tolstoyans of his personal acquaintance, and one gathers the distinct impression that the average disciple of the man known as " Russia's conscience " was skin-deep and apt to prove a hypocrite and parasite. The pseudo-Tolstoyan was characteristic of the shallow decade represented by Chekhov's " idealist " who filled his belly with cucumbers (vegetarianism!) and thereupon considered himself the saviour of mankind.

Both the revolutionary *narodniks* and Tolstoy idealized the common people, the peasants, and accentuated the rôle of unselfish love. Alexey could not help seeing the profound discrepancy between these conceptions and reality. He knew what beasts the common people could be, and he saw precious little love and compassion in actual life. He observed that " life unrolled as an endless chain of enmity and cruelty, as an incessant filthy struggle for the possession of trifles." People who talked of charity and love aroused his suspicions. He knew a tailor, Mednikov, a pious little man, who recited by heart all the acathistus hymns to the Holy Virgin, and was in the habit of whipping his son and daughter with a three-thonged lash, while for his wife he reserved the exotics of beating the calves of her legs with a bamboo stick. Mednikov came to personify for him the externally meek and charitable Christians, and he agreed with one of the tailor's apprentices, another unsuspecting Nietzschean, who thus spoke of his master: " I am afraid of such meek people as are pious! A boisterous man you can

see at once, and there is time to hide from him, while the meek one creeps up to you invisible like a perfidious snake in the grass, and of a sudden stings you in the most open spot of your soul. I am afraid of the meek."

Alexey pondered over the Christian virtue of meekness and hesitated: " At times it seemed to me that the meek, mellowing like lichen the stony heart of life, render it softer and more fruitful. But more often, observing the abundance of meek people, their nimble adjustability to vileness, the imperceptible changeableness and elasticity of their souls, their gnat-like whimper — I felt like a hobbled horse amidst a swarm of gad-flies."

Life was becoming more and more complicated for Alexey. His doubts and questions multiplied, and it was getting more difficult to find answers to them, and even to discuss them. Because of Nikiforych's interest in the bakery, the students found it unsafe to frequent the place. Alexey longed for the students, and in his heart of hearts he envied them poignantly. The students were rioting at that time, for political reasons as well as for purely collegiate motives. Alexey could not understand how anyone enjoying the privilege of studying at a university could have complaints and grievances. He tells us that if at that time he were offered the opportunity to study, for the fee of being beaten with sticks every Sunday in public, on the Nicholas Square, he would have accepted that condition without a murmur.

" What shall I do with myself? " he kept on soliloquizing — there was no one to ask for advice. Tall, of extraordinary physical strength, he was clumsy and self-conscious. As in the case of Tolstoy in his youth, he did not like himself: he saw an adolescent gangling, " funny, crass. A Kalmuck-like face, with prominent cheekbones; an intractable voice." In conversation he employed words " of his own," heavy, sharp, at times " deliberately coarse, in protest against something alien, irritating." One of his " guides," a student, remarked about his vocabulary: " The devil knows how you talk! You use not words but weights! " If he were of a boisterous disposition, or given to debauch, he might have found an outlet in his surcharge of

physical power. But he had become too ratiocinative for that — and too genteel. He embarrassed his workmen friends by addressing them in a polite " you," instead of the common Russian " thou ": result of bookishness and longing for " civilization." There were numerous occasions when, out of *noblesse oblige,* he controlled his fists and deprived himself of a much needed relief. When he surprised his violin teacher (out of ennui he began to study music) stuffing his pockets with money out of the bakery cash-box, he felt like hitting him, but to prevent himself from doing it he sat down on the floor, his fists under his thighs, and ordered the thief to unload.

He did not always practise complete non-resistance, however. His heart heavy over the death of a chum in the hospital, he could not stomach the silly superiority of the nurse and the importunity of the janitor, so he lifted the latter bodily, carried him outdoors, and set him down into a mud-puddle. To his chagrin, the janitor failed to provoke further violence, for he calmly remained sitting in the mud, then got up, saying indifferently: " Eh, you dog! " Alexey's itching fists were given a chance the same night, when he joined a friend, an old workman, in a street fight. The issue mattered little — a crowd of factory hands defended a brothel against a band of sailors. It was one of those Russian mass-fights, described by Gorky in such stories as *Andrey Kozhemyakin,* where surplus energy is given vent in mighty gloveless blows, administered lustily and withal amiably and, after a fashion, fairly.

" What shall I do with myself? " queried the big-nosed lummox, still in his teens yet burdened with problems and impressions and experiences; overflowing with energy, strength, masculinity, yet sexually chaste, clumsy and shy; communicative, eager to share his doubts and musings but pathetically lonely. He had recently come on a drunkard wallowing in the slush and muttering French phrases. Alexey picked him up and carried him to where he lived with his demented wife: he always managed to enlarge his collection of grotesques. Halfsobered the man delivered a dramatic monologue, of which one passage particularly impressed Alexey: " Progress — that has been invented for self-consolation! Life is not reasonable; it

is devoid of meaning. Without slavery there is no progress, without the submission of the majority to the minority mankind will be arrested in its march. Desiring to alleviate our life, our labour, we only make life more complex and increase our labour. Factories and machines exist only in order to produce more and more machines — that is stupid. The number of workmen is ever growing, while only the peasant is needful, the the producer of bread. Bread is the only thing which ought to be obtained from nature through labour. The less man needs the happier he is, the more desires the less freedom." This concoction of Schopenhauer-Tolstoy ended with an outcry: " Men seek forgetfulness, consolation, but not knowledge ! " To the impressionable Alexey these ideas, heard for the first time in their blunt directness, were an icy shower on his cherished dreams. Life was, indeed, losing its meaning.

It was then that he received a note from one of his cousins in Nizhni Novgorod, informing him of the death of grandmother. She had been begging alms, with which she supported a number of lazy young kinsmen. While begging she slipped on the church porch, broke her leg, and, unattended, died shortly from gangrene. Alexey was chilled by that news. He sat at night in the courtyard on a stack of firewood, stifling the desire to talk to someone about his wonderful grandmother. Years later, when he read Chekhov's sketch, *Grief,* in which a cabman finds in his horse the only listener to the story of his son's death, Gorky recalled that he had neither horse nor dog to share his pent-up sorrow. A few days later the lady who took charge of the Derenkov household asked Alexey:

" Why are you so morose ? "

" My grandmother died not long ago."

This struck her as amusing, and she asked with a smile:

" Did you like her very much ? "

" Yes. Anything else you want ? "

" No."

This lady was typical of the intelligentsia, as far as their interest in Alexey's intimate life was concerned. No wonder that these people, who regarded him as " raw material in need of elaboration," roused no sympathy in him, nor did they

prompt confidences. Whenever Alexey would begin to talk on something that did not interest them, they cut him short: " Drop that ! "

Alexey's multifarious activities in connexion with the *narodnik* bakery were, meanwhile, losing their glamour of " serving the cause." The good-hearted Derenkov meekly confessed to Alexey that they were facing bankruptcy: the *narodniks* milked the business without any sense of measure. Money was drawn out of the cash-box for various purposes, so that not enough was left to pay for the flour. Life was losing its meaning.

To top it all, Woman had to be dragged into the case. Gorky recalls:

I thought that I was in love with Derenkov's sister, Maria. I was also in love with Nadezhda Shcherbatov, a saleswoman in our shop, a buxom, red-cheeked girl, with an invariably genial smile on her bright-red lips. I was in love, generally speaking. My age, my character, my entangled existence demanded my communion with woman; it was high time, rather than too early. I was in need of a woman's caress, or at least of a woman's friendly attention. I was in need of talking freely about myself, of finding my bearings in the mix-up of incoherent ideas, in the chaos of my impressions.

On the threshold of disenchantment and scepticism, alone with his physical and mental longings and pertubations, Alexey decided on a step which must have been suggested to him by books: it seems so unreal. In December, 1887, he bought an old revolver, which once belonged to a military drummer, and fired it, aiming at his heart. The bullet pierced one lung and lodged conveniently in the back. His robust constitution asserted itself, and within one month he was well and working again in the bakery. A contemporary recalls that " Grokhalo's " attempt produced quite a commotion among the Kazan intelligentsia. Lenin had just been expelled from the university along with other students, and a chum of his, M. G. Grigoryev, treated the Grokhalo episode as a symptom of the time in an address on " Suicide and Nirvana."

Gorky's story, *An Incident in the Life of Makar,* sheds light

on that episode. Gorky himself does not like the story, though he admits its factual truth, but his self-criticism is always extremely severe. Minus its occasional verbosity — a defect which mars more than one of Gorky's stories — *An Incident in the Life of Makar* is a gripping tale, of many excellencies. It is true that the motivation of Makar's attempt at suicide is neither clear nor convincing, but then Alexey's own gesture was apparently bookish and from the head. In the absence of an English version of the story, and because of its value as marking a crisis in the life of Alexey, it may not be amiss to dwell on it for a space at this juncture.

Makar is introduced to us as a self-taught youth in his nineteenth year. He performs his physical work with abandon and joy, infecting the others with his spirit, and hopefully dreaming of arousing mankind to a collective effort at self-liberation, at the destruction of all that oppresses and distorts their life. Makar reads books, and at night, instead of finding rest from his labour in sleep, he weaves dreams and shapes thoughts. The more he reads and thinks, the less congenial does he seem to his fellow-workmen, and he begins to suspect that he bores them. He, then, goes to the intelligentsia in quest of communion and understanding, but finds them more alien than the unlettered labourers. Their curiosity about his being a self-taught son of the *narod* annoys him, he does not quite grasp their dead, bookish language, and he feels that they fail to understand him. At the same time, he thinks he is in love, but is not sure whether it is in Tanya or in Nastya (the Maria and Nadezhda in real life). He does not hide his feelings from them, and they are amused. " He approached them as a homeless man, frozen to the bone, comes up on a winter night to a bonfire at the crossing of roads; he thought that these clever girls — it did not matter which of them — might tell him some word of their own, a woman's caressing word, which would at once dissipate in his breast the oppressive feeling of abandonment, loneliness, dreary yearning." But they make fun of him, remind him of his eighteen years, and advise him to read serious books. Makar's head is tired, he cannot digest any more book-wisdom, and he lives in ruminating the endless mass of " abuses

and scratches " which life has dealt him at one time or another. He decides that he is not good for anything or for anyone. Recalling the fiery words with which he buoyed his fellow-workmen, and the grateful feeling of hope which those words roused in them, he sees himself as a deceiver, and resolves to shoot himself.

He buys an old rusty revolver at the second-hand market, studies in an anatomical atlas the position of the heart in the breast, and prepares for the solemn occasion by going to a public bath and getting well steamed and scrubbed. He comes to his " home ": it consists of the space between the back of a showcase in the bakery-shop and a windowless wall. The door into the shop is curtained with a piece of felt. Along the back of the showcase stands Makar's cot, in front of it a box takes the place of a table; there are a few books on it, a tiny oil lamp, and an engraving of Robert Owen torn out of a book he once bought for five copecks. On the wall hangs an old lithograph of Julie Récamier, and also " the prickly, bird-like face of Belinsky." The wind blows through the cracks in the showcase, every time they open the door from the street into the shop. In this cheery atmosphere Makar prepares for his long journey. He shows his bookishness in that he follows the tradition of suicides, and tries to leave a proper note behind him. In turn he writes and rejects as inadequate: " I am dying because I no longer respect myself "; " No one loves me, no one needs me "; " Life has become too hard to bear "; " I am dying because no one needs me and I need no one." It then occurs to him that he has no one to whom he might address his note.

The screechy door from the shop opened, the rusty felt swayed, and from behind it appeared the rosy gay face of Nastya, the salesgirl. She asked:

" What are you doing? "
" I am writing."
" Verses? "
" No."
" Then what? "
Makar shook his head and to his own surprise admitted:

"A note about my death. And I don't seem to be able to write it."

"Ah, how clever!" exclaimed Nastya, twisting her little nose, which was also rosy. She stood, one hand resting on the knob of the door, the other holding off the felt curtain; she leaned forward, stretching her fair throat with a velvet band around it and shook her dark, smoothly combed head. Between her stretched arm and graceful body hung her long, thick braid.

Makar looked at her, feeling how a tiny, timid hope flared up in him suddenly, like the flame of a holy lamp, while the girl, after a moment's silence, smiled and said:

"You'd better polish my high shoes — Strelsky is playing Hamlet tomorrow, and I am going to see him. Will you?"

"No," said Makar with a sigh, extinguishing the hope.

She moved her thin eyebrows in astonishment.

"Why not?"

Then he said quietly, persuasively, and as if apologizing:

"Upon my word, I am going to shoot myself tonight. I am leaving this minute!"

She swayed back and vanished, leaving behind her a grumble:

"Fi, what a bore you are!"

Another grim touch of humour is suggested by the dialogue between Makar and Nastya, as he goes through the shop on his way to commit suicide. She is sitting behind the counter, reading a book.

"Whither now?" she asks, without raising her head, only slanting her eyes and imperceptibly smiling her familiar smile, usually followed by a bantering word.

"On business of my own," answers Makar.

"A rendezvous?"

"With death," Makar was on the point of blurting out, but he controlled himself.

No, that Makar did not read out of a book. Alan Seeger, American, young, beautiful as a Greek god, was not to sing his own epitaph for another three decades!

Makar walks through the December night toward the Volga.

He knows of a steep bluff, where he intends to shoot himself, so that his body would roll down and probably be buried in the snow, till the awakening of spring would cause his corpse to float out on the river. A fine detail is that of Makar passing an old Tatar night-watchman worrying over a tiny kitten which someone had left to freeze. In broken Russian the Tatar seeks advice, how to save the animal. Makar suggests that he shove it into his bosom: the kitten will be saved and the old man will feel warmer. Later, when he is picked up, bleeding from the wound and scorched badly by his sackcloth shirt which caught fire as Makar pulled the trigger, the Tatar watchman accompanies the wounded to a clinic, and on the way he laments plaintively: " For cats, for beasts he has pity, for himself he has no pity at all! Ugh, head without sense! "

The scene in the hospital, the extraction of the bullet, Makar's rage against the jocose surgeon, his dreams and hallucinations, his fellow-patients in the common ward — are described vividly though not without gall. He does not record in the story the actual detail that on being examined in the hospital by Professor N. I. Studantsky, Alexey heard him pronounce the seemingly unconscious patient hopeless. Then he heard a young intern suggest to extract the bullet since it was so near the surface. The professor agreed to that, sceptically.

As Makar convalesces, we are subtly given to understand that though he is disgusted with himself for having made a mess of his attempt, and is resolved to kill himself at the first chance, his resolution emanates from the head, while his heart vaguely but insistently yearns for life and a human caress. This comes at last. Nastya arrives, and her healthy, merry face makes him want to shout: " Hello! " But he notices Nastya's frowning little nose, the squeamish twirl of her upper lip, her averted eyes because of his bare arms and shoulders. The conversation that follows is just small talk, and when she leaves, Makar realizes " clearly that life is an insult, that it is not worth living." His next visitor also belongs to the intelligentsia — a medical student. He is dreadfully curious about Makar's case, asks questions and shakes his head affirmatively when he finds the answers conforming with his text-books. Makar is

vexed with people, and even the visit of the kindly old Tatar watchman, who invites him to come and drink tea with him in his hut by the monastery cesspools, fails to cheer him. A feeling of self-contempt grows in him, a sense of his uselessness, and the futility of striving for beauty and goodness amidst prevailing meanness and victorious vulgarity: the thought of death looms up as the only reasonable way out.

. . . But suddenly something simple and unexpected happened, which all at once put him on his feet: into the ward entered three familiar men [from Semenov's bakery] — the jolly, gipsy-black baker and two others: a lop-sided youngster with the face of a weasel, and a healthy, broad-shouldered, angrily frowning young fellow.

Smiling guiltily, genially blinking their eyes, embarrassed by the cleanliness of the hospital interior, they stopped in the door, examining the cots.

" There he is! " cried the baker softly, pointing at Makar and showing his white teeth.

As though afraid of breaking through the floor, they came up on tiptoe, hiding behind their backs their grimy hands that held parcels. Two of the men were smiling amiably, while the third smiled sullenly and as if resentfully.

" The-e-ere he is," repeated the baker, drawing in his lips like an old woman, and plucking at his black little beard with a red scorched and scarred hand. The youngster meanwhile shoved unto Makar a paper parcel, and choking on his words he spoke softly and in haste:

" Lemons, excellent ones . . . you'll have 'em with tea."

" Hello! " said the broad-shouldered fellow, angrily shaking Makar's hand. " Well, how are things? You've grown skinny. . . ."

" Not much! " broke in the baker. " Sure thing, sickness is no caress, but never mind! We'll get well — ho, and how! Well, here's for you: a bagful of cracknels, again — sugar, sure thing. . . ."

" Do they let you smoke? " asked the angry fellow, thrusting his hand into his pocket.

" Brothers, how glad I am," muttered Makar, moved to the point of tears.

" They don't let you — smoke? " looking to one side queried

morosely the angry fellow, his hand stirring in the pocket of his blue-linen pants. " Well, to the dogs with them! I've provided both tobacco and lollipops: when you feel like smoking, suck a lollipop, it'll make it easier for you, though it's not the same thing, by a long shot! What cleanliness you're having here, my — my. . . ."

Makar could see how two of his visitors were desperately pretending to be jolly and at ease, while the third strained himself to perspiration, trying to appear calm, and none of them was good at the game: three pairs of eyes were pitifully blinking, tossing, rolling from side to side, in an effort not to meet one another's eyes and not to see Makar's.

" Well, thanks! " he muttered, choking.

They sat down, two of them on the cot, and one on the stool. The youngster chirped most merrily:

" When will they discharge you? "

Said the baker:

" Why ask? You see for yourself, he is ready this very minute! "

The third counselled in a business-like tone:

" As soon as you raise anchor, brother, shoot straight to our place! "

And the three of them broke in all at once:

" Sure thing."

" We'll provide you with an easy kind of work."

" The holidays are almost here, Christmas."

" Is it tiresome to lie here? "

" Sure thing, why ask? "

" So that's how it is."

With trembling hands Makar caught at their callous hands, laughing, sobbing:

" Ah, brothers . . . devil take you! "

They suddenly grew silent, and through his tears Makar noticed that their assumed animation had disappeared, three pairs of eyes reddened, and a soft whisper gripped at his heart:

" Eh-ehkh, you! How could you, eh? "

" You've stru-uck us a blo-ow. . . ."

A third voice added also softly but with grave emphasis:

" Yet you used to say ' Brothers.' . . . Used to say ' Truth.' . . . Used to say. . . ."

" Is this a right thing to do, eh? "

" ' Brothers,' you used to say, and then you go and. . . ."

Laughing, crying, suffocating from joy, squeezing different pairs of hands, seeing nothing and feeling with his whole being that he had recovered for a long, stubborn life, Makar was speechless.

Meanwhile the angry fellow, covering up Makar's bare breast in a business-like way, growled:

" Yes, brother, you talked and talked, yet yourself now. . . . But look here, we must not let you catch a cold, we're folks from the outside, from the cold. . . ."

Beyond the windows thick snow was falling, burying the past.

Alexey-Makar " recovered for a long, stubborn life." The melodramatic experience hardened him for the struggle which he was to wage intermittently to the end. It was the head, the intellect, that had brought confusion into his existence, that drew him to the highfalutin' intelligentsia, that caused him loneliness and humility, that finally drove him to the bookish act of suicide. He " recovered for a long and stubborn life," because with all his heart, with all his strong and hungry body, with his insatiable curiosity for things and people, he cried " Yes! " to life. The visit of his former comrades from Semenov's bakery must have impressed him deeply. The pathos of kinship, the naturalness of relations which he missed so utterly in the intelligentsia, came upon him now overwhelmingly, as a warning and a demand. He was shown clearly where he " belonged " and where he did not " belong." As already observed, and as we shall note again and again, Gorky, despite his long co-operation with the Russian intelligentsia and his prodigious efforts in its behalf, especially after 1917, has remained suspicious and ill at ease when with them or when writing about them. On the other hand, the clumsy, elemental " brothers," who brought with them a current of invigorating fresh air into the sickly cleanliness of the hospital, exacted by implication Makar's self-dedication to them. He belonged to them, he knew their misery, their groping ignorance, their yearnings and plaints inexpressible except in Russian song. He was theirs yet he differed from them in that he

had risen from the stagnant bottom, had acquired wings, had become articulate. " ' Brothers,' you used to say . . . ' Truth,' you used to say. . . ." The privileged distinction he had won placed upon him a double responsibility: to share his wings, his " truth," with his dark brothers, and to tell of their life and real selves to the world, to the intelligentsia, the lovers of the people, the *narod*.

The Kazan period of Alexey's " universities " drew to a significant end.

IN A VILLAGE

AMONG the intelligentsia who gathered in the rear of Derenkov's shop, Alexey had noticed a stalwart, big-chested man, with an expansive blond beard, and a smoothly shaven head, like that of a Tatar. Encased in a tight-fitting grey cossack smock, hooked all the way to his chin, he sat in a corner, sucked his short pipe, and took all in with his calm, grey eyes. What was most extraordinary about this man is that in the midst of those passionate talkers and arguers he seldom opened his mouth. Alexey wondered: "What is this bearded giant silent about?"

He was known as the "Khokhol," the nickname given to Ukrainians by Great Russians. Khokhol means a lock of hair; in old times Ukrainian cossacks shaved their heads, leaving a tuft of hair at the crown. In their turn, the Ukrainians dub the Great Russians "katsaps," meaning goats, because of their beards which seldom know a razor. The Khokhol had recently returned from the Yakut province, in remote Siberia, where he had served a term of ten years' exile for his *narodnik* proclivities. From time to time Alexey found the calm gaze of the silent giant on himself, and he felt with embarrassment that he was being "taken in."

A few weeks after his return to Derenkov's bakery from the hospital, Alexey was approached in the shop by the Khokhol, who laconically offered to take him to the village Krasnovidovo, on the Volga, where he had a general store. Alexey was to help him with the business, and as that would not require much time, he would be able to make use of the owner's good library. It goes without saying that, in view of his recent experience,

Alexey eagerly grasped the opportunity to leave Kazan. Two days later they floated on a raft down the Volga, some forty miles below Kazan, and Alexey breathed in the spring exuberance of his native river. It seemed an auspicious starting-point for his " recovery."

Krasnovidovo (Fairview) is situated on a steep bluff and is one of the admirable spots within the vision of Volga travellers. The few months of Alexey's sojourn there provided him with another " university course " of indubitable value. He learned to know the Russian village, directly and unsentimentally. Essentially, Krasnovidovo is typical of rural Russia, allowing for economic and psychic variants which differentiate the Volga from the Dnyeper khokhol, the Black Sea cossack from the pioneer-like Siberian, or the antediluvian peasant of Archangel and Olonetz from the muzhik of Tula, the province of samovars and of Tolstoy's Yasnaya Polyana. In Krasnovidovo, as in a drop of water, Alexey could see a reflection of Russia's peasantry, with its lights and its shadows.

He also gained much from his nearness to Mikhail Antonovich Romas, as the Khokhol was really called. A man of wide and thorough knowledge, he guided Alexey's reading in a practically helpful way. Among the authors he read there, aside from such Russians as Pushkin, Goncharov, Nekrasov, Chernyshevsky, Pisarev, Dobrolyubov, were Buckle, Hobbes, Lecky, Lubbock, Taylor, Mill, Spencer, Darwin, Macchiavelli. Romas emphasized the importance of reading on natural science, and Alexey greedily devoured what was new to him — factual knowledge of the universe and of life. His guide warned him against allowing books to " hide men." He quoted with approval an old sectarian to the effect that all teaching emanates from man. " Men," concluded Romas, " teach more painfully, they teach crudely, but their instruction bites deeper and firmer." This Alexey had had ample opportunity to learn on his own skin.

Romas was a *narodnik,* and paid dearly for his views, but he differed greatly from those lovers of the people whom Alexey had met in Kazan. Himself the son of a blacksmith, Romas had no reason to sentimentalize or idealize the common people. He

spoke with scorn of the students who chatter about " love for the people." " I tell them: one cannot love the people. . . . To love, that means: to approve, to be lenient, to overlook things, to forgive. With such a feeling one goes to a woman. But how can one overlook the ignorance of the people, approve the errors of their mind, be lenient toward their ruffianism, forgive their brutality? " He had no patience with those who flattered the peasant and sang Nekrasov's lines about the " suffering muzhik." His suggested line of talk to the peasant was this: " You, brother, are not so bad a man, yourself, but you live badly and you don't know how to manage things so that your life might become easier, better. The beast, most likely, takes more reasonable care of itself than you of yourself; the beast defends itself better. Yet it is out of you, muzhik, that everything has grown and blossomed: the nobility, the clergy, the men of learning, the tsars, all of them were once muzhiks. Do you see the point? Do you understand? Well, then, learn to live so as not to let them chaw you."

Romas opened a store in Krasnovidovo with the intention of creating an enlightening centre. As in all small places the world over, a general store becomes a club for the exchange of opinions. Romas hoped to attract the local population by selling commodities at a very low profit, and in general by dealing with them fairly and treating them as equals and friends. The porch of the store became a gathering place for the village wags and characters, and as Alexey listened to their talk, he wondered why Romas sucked at his pipe in silence and did not utilize the numerous chances for putting in a word of enlightenment. When alone, he asked him to explain his reserve. Romas frankly assured the impatient youth that he was not anxious to get back to the Yakuts in Siberia, which would be his fate if he spoke to the peasants as Alexey expected him to. He knew the peasant as a cautious, mistrustful individual, who is afraid of himself, of his neighbour, especially of a stranger.

The peasants were set free in 1861, and had not yet understood clearly the meaning of their " freedom." To them freedom literally meant the right of everyone to do as he pleased,

yet the numerous authorities that they encountered threw a
close net of prohibitions over life. Consequently, freedom was
not yet. Now the peasant was a tsarist. He believed in the
tsar's mysterious power over all and everything, and in his
benevolent attitude toward the peasants. Yes, the tsar was
the father of the people, a tsar-muzhik; that is why he freed
the peasants from the land-owning nobility and took them
under his personal protection. The tsar could do what he
pleased; he might take away the steamers and the shops from
the merchants as he took the land and the serfs from the gentry.
It is he alone who will give the peasants the *real* freedom, on
the day when he destroys completely the power of the gentry
and of the authorities — his enemies and the enemies of the
people. On that day the people will grasp everything in sight,
and a general distribution of all property will take place on
an equal basis. " Black Partition," the peasants called that
final and just division, a name adopted by the group of George
Plekhanov in 1879 in opposition to the Terrorist group of the
" Will of the People."

Mikhail Romas knew how stolid was the peasant, and how
solid were his beliefs and superstitions. To destroy his trust
in the tsar momentarily, as so many of the fiery revolutionists
tried to do, appeared to him as futile folly. The peasant had to
be humoured, intelligence had to be percolated into his brains
in homeopathic doses, and the propaganda was to adapt itself
to his traditional views, however erroneous. Romas told Alexey
that as an initial step one should gradually instil into the mind
of the peasant the desirability of his right to elect his Authorities, from the constable, through the governor, to the tsar himself. When Alexey exclaimed impatiently that that meant a
slow process, for a hundred years perhaps, Romas retorted
seriously:

" Did you intend to have it all done by Whitsuntide? "

It required great patience, perseverance, common sense,
coolness, and above all a rocklike conviction in the justness and
ultimate triumph of the cause, to follow Romas's tactics. The
majority of the *narodniks* were too young and flamboyant to
accept such a modest and slow policy. When the Marxian

Socialists came to the fore, they did not have the temerity to
cope with the peasant issue, and determined to adopt the slogan of Plekhanov: " The Russian revolution will succeed as a
revolution of the working class, or will not succeed at all." The
narodniks made fun of this notion of overlooking the elephant
for the sake of the gnat — as the proletariat seemed to them
at the time, numerically and psychologically. Lenin proved the
correctness of Plekhanov's prognosis, but in order to make the
victory of the proletariat in 1917 more than ephemeral, he was
forced to embrace the Romas platform, namely, constant compromise with the peasant, and concessions to his age-honoured
views and prejudices.

Romas and his small retinue had to face the suspicions and
hostility of the village. Despite all his caution and reserve,
the peasants sensed in him a " foreign " element. His very
kindliness and readiness to help and co-operate, without obvious gain in prospect, singled him out as a different and therefore questionable character. There were two other storekeepers
in the village, and these naturally resented the intrusion of a
third, specially of one who undersold them. Romas began to
organize the orchard-growers into an *artel,* a pooling association, in order to safeguard them against the exploiting middle-
men. Such enterprises made him obnoxious to the local rich
and mighty, and to their kotower, the priest. The village community, or *mir,* as a rule produced a few peasants who, by hook
or by crook, managed to rise above the misery of their
brothers, to acquire property at the expense of the non-aggres-
sive and fatalistic muzhik, and then to prove much more
vicious exploiters of their class than the gentry or the merchants. In their colourful parlance, the peasants named these
freaks *kulaks* — fists, or *miroyeds* — *mir*-eaters, and more
often than not they treated them with respect and were even
proud of them, as of members of their own estate whose good
fortune and rise in the world afforded them a sense of compensation for their own misery. I have used the past tense
with regard to these lucky dogs, because of their practical dis-
appearance from the Soviet village, as a result of Stalin's efforts
to carry out Lenin's legacy, namely: to support the poorest

peasantry and the middle farmer, and to fight relentlessly the
kulak.

In Krasnovidovo, Romas, Alexey, and three or four sympathizers, had to be constantly on the lookout against foul play.
When they ventured out of the house on a dark night, they
were prepared to be attacked by ambushed rowdies armed
with clubs; Romas had to fire his revolver, into the air of
course, before he succeeded in scattering such a band. As to
Alexey, he was hit in the leg and limped for some time, as a
penalty for his nocturnal vigils by the bank of Mother Volga,
where he weaved dreams in solitude or with a friendly
fisherman. Once an explosion occurred in the stove of Romas's
kitchen, which caused rather small damage because the amount
of powder loaded by an ingenious enemy into a hollowed piece
of firewood proved too small. The landlord of Romas, a shrewd
and intelligent young peasant who was on his side, gauged the
situation succinctly: " war! " which was, indeed, a proper
definition for all the big and petty annoyances inflicted on
Romas's undertaking by the villagers. The definition was
proper, but it did not help Alexey, still reminiscent of the
Kazan *narod*-idolators, to understand, and even less to forgive,
this demonstration of repaying good with evil on the part of
the alleged paragons of virtue.

On the whole, Alexey was ridding himself of the illusion,
borrowed from books and city intelligentsia, to the effect that
people on land live more healthfully and blandly than in the
city. He saw before him sullen, lustreless slaves of the soil,
seldom gay, many of them broken in health from inclement
toil, especially the women, prematurely aged and possessed of
all sorts of ailments, due to overwork, to lack of proper care
during and right after confinement, and to the blows which
they received from their husbands as a matter of course: " For
whom else shall a man beat when his soul is outraged? " as
one of Gorky's tramps was to ask, years later. The life of the
peasant did not impress Alexey as simple: " it demands a
strained alertness toward the soil, and much keen craftiness
in one's relations with human beings." Above all, he observed
that the peasants live neither genially nor reasonably, but

" gropingly, like blind men, always afraid of something, mistrustful of one another; there is something wolfish about them." The more he saw of village life, the more respect he had for that of the city, where work does not lower one so hopelessly to the ground, and where one feels " a thirst for happiness, a bold inquisitiveness of the mind, a multiplicity of aims and tasks." Even the alleged moral corruption of the city could not be much worse than in the village, not more vulgar, at any rate. One of the accepted jokes of the young rustics was to catch some girls in the field, turn up their skirts (their only garment), and twist them tightly above their heads. This was called " to launch a girl as a flower." Naked from their toes up to their waists, the girls screamed and swore, but it was apparent that they enjoyed the game — " they noticeably untied their skirts more slowly than they could have done it." True, church-going was more common in the village than in the city, but : " At night-mass in church, the young fellows pinched the girls' buttocks — that seemed the only reason for their attendance. On Sunday, the priest addressed them from the pulpit : ' You beasts ! Can you not find another place for your abominations ? ' "

As a writer Maxim Gorky decidedly favours the city over the village, and has been often accused of exaggerated generalizations. The Krasnovidovo experience must have left in him an after-taste, from which he never freed his palate. Even in such a late panegyric of his to the awakening village as *Summer,* the emphasis on the changing new accentuates the blackness of the old.

To be sure, even in hostile Krasnovidovo Alexey managed to draw close to a few natives who were not without attractions. The very first evening of his arrival he met one of Romas's staunchest helpers, Izot, a tall, spare fisherman, with rosy cheeks, bright blue eyes, a large straight nose, a curly beard, and a mass of reddish hair on his head. His costume consisted of a shirt and drawers; his feet and head were invariably bare. Of extraordinary strength, handsome and intelligent, he was feared in the village, and his whole-hearted support of Romas made him also hateful to them. On those

evenings, when the few intimates did not listen to Romas's informal discourses on history or other subjects, Alexey instructed Izot in the art of reading. The pupil proved quick and eager, and it gave the teacher keen satisfaction to watch Izot's transports of naïve glee when he discovered his ability to read a few lines of verse from a book. He was disappointed when his teacher failed to explain the mystery of reading. " Explain it to me, brother," he queried, " how does the thing happen, when all is said? You look at little lines, these shape themselves in words, and I know them — living words, our own words! How do I know them? No one whispers them to me. If they were pictures, I would understand how it is. But here, it seems as if the very thoughts are printed — how is that? "

Alexey valued Izot's understanding of the village, its needs and peculiarities, and his sound judgements about groups and individuals. His one weakness was with women. He was popular with them, and quite insatiable. There was nothing boastful or caddish about his conquests, and he seemed innocent of religiously moral scruples on this score. " Of course," he confessed good-humouredly, " I am spoiled in this matter. There is offence in that for the husbands, in their place I myself should feel offended. Yet again, one cannot help taking pity on a wench; a wench, you know, is sort of your second soul. She lives without holidays, without a caress; works like a horse, and that's all she knows. The husbands have no time for love, while I am a free man. Many a wife is fed by her husband's fists, the very first year of their marriage. Well, yes, that's my soft spot, I do fool around with them. Only one thing I ask of them: don't be sore at one another, wenches — I'll last for all of you! Don't be jealous of one another, you're all alike to me, I feel sorry for you all."

More than one thousand years of formal Christianity have failed to uproot the paganism of the Russian common folk, images and crosses and other externals notwithstanding. One is reminded of that delectable pagan, Yeroshka, lovingly portrayed from life by Leo Tolstoy, himself a pagan if there ever was one, his Christianity being exclusively a matter of reason

with him. What innocence of the sense of shame or sin, and what an absence of prurience, in Izot's account of one of his incomplete adventures: " One time I almost had a frolick with a certain lady — she was staying at the summer villa, the lady was. A beauty, white like milk, and her hair — like flax. And her eyes, they were bluish, kindly. I was bringing her fish to sell, and used to stand and look at her. ' What is it you want? ' she asks. ' You know yourself,' says I. ' Well, all right,' she says, ' I'll come to you tonight. Wait up for me! ' And sure enough, she came! Only — she was uneasy about the mosquitoes. They bit her and bit her, well, nothing came of it. ' I can't,' she says, ' they bite so ' — she almost wept tears. Next day her husband arrived, a judge, or something. Yes, that's the kind they are, ladies, I mean," he concluded with sadness and reproach. " Mosquitoes don't let them live."

At night Alexey sometimes found Izot at his side, on the river-bank. Izot would dream aloud, in the softness of the night becoming even kindlier and mellower. One of his ambitions was to learn wisdom from books, then wander along rivers, and teach people. " It's fine, brother, to share your soul with another man! Even wenches — some of them, if you talk to them with an open soul — even they understand! " Typically Russian, this desire to teach others, as well as the preoccupation with one's soul. More often Alexey enjoyed Izot's silent presence, rarely punctured by a sigh, a phrase, an exclamation — an *obbligato* to the waning Volga night.

Powerfully flows the velvet ribbon of dark water, above it curves the silver ribbon of the Milky Way, large stars sparkle like golden larks, and one's heart sings unwise songs about life's mysteries.

Far away above the meadows the rays of the sun burst out of reddish clouds, and behold, the sun has spread across the skies its peacock tail.

" That's wonderful — the sun! " mumbles Izot, smiling blissfully.

.   .   .   .

Apple trees are in bloom, the village is enveloped in pinkish snowdrifts, and is saturated with an acrid aroma, which penetrates everywhere and drowns the odours of tar and manure. Hundreds of blossoming trees, festively arrayed in the pinkish satin of their petals, recede in regular rows from the village into the fields. On moonlit nights a light breeze stirs the moth-like blossoms and rustles them softly; the village seems to be flooded with golden-blue, heavy waves: untiringly and passionately the nightingales sing. During the day starlings tease provocatively, and invisible larks pour down on the earth their continuous tender bells.

On holiday-evenings girls and young married women strolled through the streets, sang songs with their mouths wide open like those of fledglings, and languidly smiled with drunken smiles. Izot, too, smiled, as if drunk; he had become thin, his eyes had sunk into dark caverns, his face had grown more serene, more handsome, and — more saintly. All day long he slept, appearing on the street only toward evening, preoccupied, softly pensive. Kukushkin made fun of him, coarsely but amiably, and Izot, grinning confusedly, said:

" Keep mum. What's to be done? "

And rhapsodized:

" Oh, how sweet it is to live! And oh, how lovingly one can live, what hearty words there are! There're words — you won't forget them to your grave, and when you're resurrected from the dead, first thing you'll remember those words! "

" Look sharp, you'll get a beating from the husbands," Romas warned him, also grinning amiably.

" I sure deserve it," agreed Izot.

Indeed, before long someone hacked off the back of Izot's head, from behind, as he was fishing in his boat. Apparently, Romas and his household had reasons to suspect that the murder was committed not by a cuckold, though the number of these must have been legion. Romas spoke bitterly of the multitude ever destroying those who are different, its prophets and saints, implying that Izot was killed because he stood out in the village with his courage, unbending freedom, and intelligence unfettered by tradition. He told an illuminating

story in connection with this popular tendency: " When I was
marching on foot to Siberia, a fellow-convict narráted this to
me. He had been the leader of a band of robbers, five of them.
All of a sudden one of these began to exhort them: ' Brothers,
let us give up robbing. We don't seem to get anything out of
it anyhow, and our life is rotten! ' For that they strangled
him, when he was asleep. The convict praised the murdered
comrade very highly to me: ' I've killed three men after that,'
he said, ' and I don't care, but my chum I feel sorry for to
this day, he was a fine chum, clever, jolly, a clear soul.' ' Why,
then, did you kill him? ' I asked. ' Were you afraid that he
might inform on you? ' He felt downright insulted. ' No,' he
said, ' he wouldn't have betrayed us for any money in the
world, not for anything! But — well, somehow, it didn't feel
right to chum with him any longer, we all of us sinners, and
he, as it were, a saint. It wasn't right.' "

Alexey was apparently fond of Izot more than of any other
Krasnovidovan. Their landlord, Pankov, an intelligent young
muzhik, who defied his father and local standpatters, and
rented his place to Romas, impressed Alexey as almost too
practical, too sensible. At least, that is the feeling one gets
in reading Gorky's reminiscences, in which his reserve toward
Pankov is not explained. The only other villagers he favoured,
more or less, were, again as in the case of Izot the fisherman,
not tillers of the soil, but landless and homeless fellows, " good
for nothings," from the point of view of any respectable house-
owner. Are we to conclude that precisely those peasants who
had ceased being peasants, that is, those who had freed themselves from the harrowing, narrowing, and enslaving Power
of the Soil (the phrase of Gleb Uspensky, the disenchanted
narodnik writer who died in an insane asylum), were alone
possessed of attractive traits?

To take Kukushkin and Barinov, for example. In any community they would be looked down upon, as propertyless fail-
ures, and men of uncertain occupations. Furthermore, they
were both notorious liars. Yet Kukushkin, despite his dis-
reputable rags and ever blue-and-black face, was uncommonly
skilful with his hands, and performed with equal perfection a

variety of odd jobs, from laying out a stove to taking care
of a beehive. In the conversations which Romas held with his
few trusties, Kukushkin, though illiterate, displayed rare acumen and brilliance, in grasping the meaning of facts and
drawing his conclusions. His main weakness, next to getting
into all sorts of unwarranted scraps, as a result of which his
face was perpetually marked and bruised, was a passion for
news. He elbowed his way into groups of people, or button-
holed some individual, eagerly inquiring for fresh tidings
and as eagerly commenting on them (that was one of the
commonest ways for him to get in trouble). In the absence
of such news, Kukushkin would supply some startling intelligence from his own inexhaustible stock of fantasies. Without any connexion with the topic of conversation he might
blurt out the hypothesis that if people ceased fishing for herring for two or three years, the sea would overflow and cause
a deluge. Or he would ask Romas whether he had heard that
the deputy-constable of the adjacent county had decided to
become a monk, because his conscience gnawed him for abusing the peasants. Kukushkin's fiction, as a rule, belonged to
the happy-ending variety. His villains ultimately tired of doing
evil, disappeared " without trace," but more often they were
relegated by the author to a monastery. Here is a sample story
about a wicked lady-landowner:

" She was such a villainess that the governor himself, notwithstanding his high position, called on her: ' Milady,' he
said, ' watch out. Rumours,' says he, ' about your villainous
wickedness have reached even St. Petersburg ! ' Of course, she
treated him to cordials, and said to him: ' Go back, in God's
name. I am not able to break my nature ! ' Three years and a
month passed, when of a sudden she calls the muzhiks together: ' Here,' she says, ' you may have all my lord, good-bye,
forgive me, as I am going . . .'
" To a nunnery," prompts Romas.
Kukushkin gives him an attentive look, and confirms:
" Quite so, as an abbess ! So you, too, have heard about
her ? "
" I have never heard anything about her,"

" Then how do you know? "
" I know you."
The fantast mumbles, shaking his head:
" How you do mistrust people! "

The villagers treated Kukushkin with utter scorn and did
not believe one word of his, yet they listened to him with open
mouths, and in spite of themselves were carried away by his
imagination and enchanted by it. In the same way they relished
the fancies of Barinov, a restless tramp, a laggard, gossiper,
braggadocio, and altogether an undependable chap. Always
dishevelled and ragged, he looked at the world with childlike
blue eyes from a handsome face framed by a curly " merry "
beard; for the delight of his contemptuous listeners he embel-
lished the things he had actually seen on his wanderings. Moscow, apparently, did not treat him kindly, for he spat whenever he spoke of it, and the things he said of the pious city
were not at all charitable:

" A hellish town! Bedlam! Fourteen thousand and six
churches, yet the people are scoundrel upon scoundrel! And
they are all scabby, like horses, by God! Merchants, military
gentry, burghers — all like one walk about and scratch themselves. Yet, 'tis true, they do have there the Tsar-Cannon, an
enormous affair! Peter the Great cast it himself, to fire at the
rioters: a certain wench, a noblewoman, raised a riot against
him, from her love for him. He had lived with her exactly
seven years, day in day out, then he dropped her, with three
kids. She got sore, and — started a riot! Well, brother, as he
went bang from that cannon at the riot — nine thousand three
hundred and eight men he laid out at once! He got scared
even himself: ' No,' says he to Metropolitan Philaret, ' I must
spike the damned thing, against temptation! ' He spiked the
thing . . ."

When Alexey protested that it was all nonsense, Barinov
grew indignant: " Oh, Lord God! What a nasty character you
have! This story was told me in detail by an educated gentleman,
and you. . . ." He had a manner of sustaining his fabrications
by elaborate figures, by way of substantial proof. Thus the

city of Kiev, whither he made a pilgrimage " to the saints,"
appeared in his description fantastic yet figure-proof:

" That city is like our village — also on a hill, and there is
a river too, I forget the name though. Against Volga it's just a
puddle! A confusing town, to tell the truth. All streets are
crooked, and creep uphill. The people are of the khokhol kind
though not the same blood as Mikhail Antonovich, but half-
Polish, half-Tatar. They don't talk, but bla-bla. An unkempt
people, and filthy. They eat frogs, each frog weighs about ten
pounds. They ride on bulls and even plough with them. Their
bulls are remarkable, the smallest is four times the size of ours.
Weighs three thousand three hundred and twenty pounds. As
to monks, there are fifty-seven thousand two hundred and
seventy-three archbishops, and . . . You funny fellow, how
can you argue? I have seen everything with my own eyes, and
you — have you been there? You haven't? Well, there you are!
I love precision, brother, more than anything."

It is such liars as Kukushkin and Barinov that represent
the unlettered artists of the people, weavers of fairy-tales and
romances and travels and history, which in the West are no
longer created but are a recorded memory, from Homer to
Baron Münchhausen. That is why these men are in vogue even
among those who despise and doubt them: much is forgiven
for a good story.

Meanwhile the enemies of Romas were determined to put
an end to his heretical, because uncommon, activities. One
clear August morning the barn, in which Romas kept kerosene
and other inflammable liquids, was set on fire. Within a few
minutes all the buildings were burning, bursting, and threatening the whole village. Rural Russia is wooden, and all Russia
burns down about once in seven years. Few peasants carry
insurance, and yet in time of a fire they stand apathetic, fatal-
istically resigned to the havoc brought by the Red Cock.
Romas tried in vain to whip the peasants into some semblance
of an organization to corral the fire, to draw bucketfuls of
water from the Volga, down at the foot of the village, to hack
down some of the hedges and barns already on fire, and thus
save the rest of the huts. They obeyed his commands, as they

always do an authoritative voice, but they worked perfunc-
torily, and as soon as sparks from the advancing fire reached
them, they scattered. It fell to Romas and Alexey, with some
assistance from Kukushkin and Barinov, to bear the brunt of
the fire. Alexey, we may recall, even in his childhood found
conflagrations marvellous, and later he devoted many loving
pages to descriptions of fires. He now threw into the fight all
his great strength, all his loyalty to Romas, and all his hatred
for the inertia and stupidity of the people. More than once he
lost consciousness and almost perished in the flames, and each
time after they poured water on him he rushed forth with renewed ferocity at what personified to him the enemy on that
occasion.

The fire was finally checked. Although Romas lost everything, his rivals and adversaries insinuated that it was he who
had set his place on fire, having previously concealed the goods
in the bath-house. An enraged crowd surrounded Romas, led
him to the bath-house, broke the lock, and even when convinced that there was nothing hidden, their ugly mood did
not pass away. Romas and Alexey, armed with clubs, stood
back to back, to forestall a blow from behind, and faced the
senseless, ferocious mob. An ax stuck in Alexey's belt cooled
them a bit; the inherent cowardice of the mob came to the
surface. Then a small, lame peasant, dancing on his wooden
leg, screamed frantically: " Bricks at them! From afar! Hit
them at my risk! " Indeed, he was the first to aim a brick
at Alexey's abdomen, but Kukushkin flew at him from above;
they clinched and rolled down the ravine, still embraced. A
few other sympathizers of Romas appeared on the scene, and
the crowd dispersed.

Thus ended Romas' undertaking. Shrewd Pankov, his landlord, decided to take over the business, and even invited Alexey
to stay with him. We already know that Alexey did not like
Pankov, and to him the Krasnovidovo chapter ended with
Romas. On the eve of the latter's departure, as they lay at
night on the floor, Romas asked:

" Are you angry at the muzhiks? Don't. They are only
stupid. Malice is stupidity! "

His words failed to console me, they could not soften my bitterness and the poignancy of my hurt. I saw before me bestial hairy maws ejaculating a vicious screech:

" Bricks at them! From afar! "

He mused over the peasants, those quaint children, naïve and kindly individually, but sheepishly cringing and hypocritical before the mighty of the land when in a mass, or ferocious like savage wolves. He felt that he could not live with these people, and spoke to Romas of his disenchantment with the *narod*. Romas reproached him for rushing into " premature conclusions," and said in parting:

" Don't be in a hurry to condemn! To condemn is the simplest thing to do — don't let it tempt you. Look at everything calmly, remembering this: everything passes, everything changes for the better. Slowly? But on the other hand firmly! Peer into all nooks, scrutinize and touch everything, be fearless, but — don't be in a hurry to condemn. Till we meet again, old man! "

They met again fifteen years later, in the Polish town of Sedletz, where Romas lived in exile, after having served ten more years in the Yakut province for organizing the secret printing press of a *narodnik* group. The parting words of Romas were not unlike those of grandmother, who also had faith in ultimate amelioration, and also warned Alexey against judging and condemning people, this being not God's but the devil's business. Although Alexey never changed his opinion of the peasants — after 1917 he published a bitter and sweeping philippic against them, under the title *The Russian Peasantry* — he felt beholden to Romas in many ways. His advocacy of slow but firm implantation, little as it might appeal to a nineteen-year-old impatient youth, became later the basis of Gorky's plea for cultural work in Russia. The Krasnovidovo conversations solidified much of Alexey's haphazardly garnered knowledge.

Left alone in Krasnovidovo, Alexey felt " like a puppy that had lost its master." For a while he stayed with Barinov, in his bath-house. They wandered through villages, worked for

kulaks, threshed, dug potatoes, pruned orchards. Barinov at last persuaded him to start off on a long tramp, with the Caspian Sea as their final objective. Alexey had not yet seen the sea, which he was later to extol rhapsodically. Though the Caspian Sea is, in reality, only an enormous lake, in the description of Barinov it eclipsed the Atlantic Ocean. " The sea, brother," he used to say, " is not like anything you know. You're like a gnat before it! You look at the sea, and you dwindle away. And life is so sweet there. All sorts of people gather. Once even the head of a monastery came there. 'Twas all right, he worked as everybody else! Then there was a cook, she had been a magistrate's mistress in some town — what more could she desire? But no, she could not stand it: ' I am awfully fond of you, Magistrate, but yet and still — good-bye! ' Because he who once saw the sea is always drawn to it. The expanse there! As in the skies, there's no crowding by the sea! "

In the company of Barinov, Alexey began to make his way down the Volga. Now working on a barge, now stealing a ride on a passenger steamer, now lingering at some port, they slowly plowed southward to the mouth of Mother Volga. At the Caspian Sea they joined an *artel* of Kalmuck fishermen.

The wandering epopee of Alexey Peshkov had begun.

AS NIGHT–WATCHMAN

From the Caspian fisheries Alexey wandered up to the station Dobrinka, on a branch Volga railroad, and found employment there as night-watchman. From six in the afternoon till six in the morning he walks, a stout stick in his hand, around the warehouses, trying to discern sounds of thievish humans through the howl of winds and snowstorms and the clanking of trains which speed and whirl up and down the steppe. Once in a while he espies crouching figures behind a snowdrift — they are cossacks who come to steal sacks of flour. On being surprised, they wheedle and whine, promise him even half a ruble, but Alexey is adamant: he knows that they steal not from want but for drunken debauches. Sometimes the cossacks negotiate through the good-looking Lyoska. She unbuttons her sheepskin coat and blouse, demonstrates her " horizontal " supple breasts, and bargains with the more susceptible watchmen for a sack of flour. Her advances to Alexey are unsuccessful; he still has his ideals, scruples, and dreams, he still reads and thinks and queries and tries to find a formula in life. But he is curious as ever, and a chat with Lyoska on the steps of the warehouse adds a bit or two to his stock of observations. Here are the cossacks — a pious, conservative lot; Lyoska is afraid to smoke in their presence, as they would not stand for such levity in a woman. Yet they encourage her to sell her fine body for a sack of flour with which they might buy a bottle of vodka. A lesson in morals. The university never closes.

Incidentally, it is to this job that Maxim Gorky owes his deep bass. While in Kazan he had a tenor, and he even made

practical use of his voice, next to trying the work of a gardener and a janitor, in the intervals between free-lancing at the harbour and his final landing in the bakery of Semenov. A sign, " Men Wanted for Choir," attracted his hungry eye one day, he ventured inside, and to his surprise was hired. At the same time another tall blond youth, who came in with him, was rejected; this was Feodor Chaliapin. At Dobrinka, on a windy and rainy autumn night, Alexey climbed a tall stack of sacks to cover them up with a tarpaulin. A gust of wind enveloped him in the tarpaulin, and hurled him down on the railroad bed. He struck the rails, lost consciousness, and for some time afterwards suffered from an enormous swelling in his throat. He tells us that when the doctor lanced the sore, there flowed so much pus that he was afraid of choking on it. His voice was gone completely for a time, and when he finally recovered it the tenor had given place to a husky bass.

It was probably before this accident that his voice stood him in good stead with the station-master of Dobrinka, who released him from duty on certain nights that he might come to his home and entertain the parties with songs. Gorky's description of these parties lends a curious detail to his mosaic of pre-revolutionary Russia. Even now, in grim and ascetic Soviet Russia, there appear from time to time exposés (Soviet publicity is merciless) of secret orgies carried on by more or less responsible officials, usually in some Gopher Prairie, where boredom and remoteness from central supervision must not be overlooked among the motives for their misdemeanour. The Russian " whoopee " is particularly striking for its combination of savage joy and black melancholy, of brutality and coarseness with tenderness and fine sensitiveness; in a word, Russian joy-making is aptly expressed in its song and dance.

The revelers whom Alexey entertained with songs belonged to the masters in old Russia, officials with shoulder-straps, money-bags, ecclesiastics. To be sure, the distinction of this *élite* in tiny Dobrinka was a matter of relativity. The host, Afrikan Petrovsky, station-master, of powerful build, with an enormous black beard, and bulging dark eyes, was a notorious scoundrel. He hit his subordinates in the teeth and the ears,

and was said to have beaten his wife to death. At his command the clerks opened the freight-cars that passed through from the Caspian ports, and stole for him silks and delicacies. These he sold, and used the money for the " Monastic Life," as he named the orgies. Some years later Petrovsky was sued for his numerous offences, but he had a " pull " on the railroad board, and in old Russia that meant immunity. Here is another delicious, Russian touch. When they came to Petrovsky's office with a search-warrant, he reached for a paper in his drawer, and handed it to the investigator, with the words: " Here I have honestly written down everything I have stolen." Dostoyevsky's Russia, land of honest thieves and saintly murderers!

Off duty, Petrovsky doffed his uniform with its glittering buttons, and arrayed himself in a scarlet silk Russian shirt, black velvet breeches of great width, thrust into Tatar high boots of green morocco, and on his crown of black curls he wore a flat eastern cap of dark purple embroidered in gold. His guests were:

the assistant district chief of police, Maslov, bald, round, smooth-shaven like a Catholic priest, with the beak of a bird of prey, and foxy little eyes of a whore; he was a spiteful, crafty, and treacherous man, nicknamed the " Actress." Then there was the owner of the local soap-works, Tikhon Stepakhin, an imposing red-haired muzhik, heavy like an ox, who always looked half-asleep; at his works the men were poisoned by some fumes and rotted away, and though he had been sued several times for injuries to his employes, he was not bothered beyond fines. There came also Voroshilov, a one-eyed deacon, a drunkard, always filthy and greasy, an excellent player on the guitar and accordion; his pock-marked face with high cheekbones was all covered with grey hairs, thick as the needles of a porcupine, he had small, well-cared-for hands of a woman, and one beautiful dark-blue eye — he was, indeed, nicknamed " Stolen Eye."

The ladies consisted of lively girls from the village and the cossack settlement, including Lyoska. They sat around a table groaning under heavy food which they dispatched with the

aid of a goodly quantity of vodka. He of the soap-works began to belch, and at this signal they went to another room, more spacious, where to the accompaniment of the deacon's guitar they all sang. As a rule Russians sing well in chorus; they naturally use their voices in unison and harmony. Gorky has the gift to transmit in words the power of song and dance, as we have had occasion to note previously. He makes us visualize the Petrovsky crowd, overfed and overdrunk, yet solemnly, as at a liturgy, singing grippingly sad songs. The deacon strikes up a dancing tune, and the heavy Stepakhin dances alone, revealing an unsuspected elasticity, a beast-like gracefulness, and the rhythm of his fanciful movements brings the others into an ecstacy of joy. Tears, embraces, shouts, and one after another they dance, singly and collectively, to the music of the indefatigable deacon. At Petrovsky's command, Alexey sings song after song from his large repertoire; he selects the saddest and most disturbing ones, and moves them all to tears and frantic outcries. " Undress the wenches! " howls Petrovsky, and Stepakhin slowly performs his function, folds the skirts, shirts, and the rest of the clothes, and puts them away in a corner, business-like. The men examine the women, criticize and praise their bodies as ecstatically as they do a song or a dance. Then they go to the smaller room, again eat and drink, " and there begins something indescribable, nightmarish."

There was nothing blithesome about those orgies. The Moscow merchant, in the old days, who under the influence of drink and a gipsy chorus smashed mirrors with bottles of champagne and showered hundred-ruble bills right and left, was not a mirthful sight. The Petrovsky group, in the same way, voiced a longing for they knew not what, a desire to escape out of their own skins, to drown their ineffable fears and pains and discontent. Here is Petrovsky dancing stormily, " as though tearing and breaking something invisible which restrains him." He howls ferociously, vindictively: " Ekh-ma! I am perishin-ing! "

One can hear him grit his teeth. In this furious merriment there is no laughter, no light, winged joy that raises man

above the earth. It is an almost religious ecstasy; it resembles the rites of the Khlysts [Russian flagelants], or the dances of Dervishes in Transcaucasia. A crushing power is felt in this whirlwind of bodies, and its frantic, aimless tossing seems to me nearing despair. All these men are gifted, each in his way, drearily gifted. They intoxicate one another with their vehement love for song, for dance, for woman's body, for the triumphant beauty of movement and sound. What they are doing resembles a religious ceremony of savages.

Alexey attended those parties, staying to the end, even to the " indescribable and nightmarish," when frenzied bodies writhed in sadistic and masochistic convulsions. The artist's curiosity justifies peeping through keyholes and eavesdropping and going through all imaginable hells. But Gorky always, and not with even success, defends his curiosity by some moral or didactic reason. He tells us that at the time those tumultuous " feasts of the flesh " aroused in him disgust and pain, mixed with pity for the men and especially for the women. Yet he refused to stay away from the " Monastic Life," because he " suffered from the fanaticism of knowledge." He recalled the parting words of Mikhail Romas, to the effect that you must peer into cracks and pits, for perhaps somewhere in there may be tucked away a truth you will find needful; that you must live fearlessly, not shunning the disagreeable and the terrible — what is not understood is usually regarded disagreeable and terrible. Says Gorky: " I did peer everywhere, without sparing myself, and have thus learned many things which for me personally it would have been better not to know, but of which it is necessary to tell other people, because that is their hard life, the filthy drama of the animal struggling in man against his effort at victory over the elemental in himself and outside of himself." And so forth, in the typical vein of Gorky's gritty philosophastry.

Alexey was forced to part with Dobrinka for another reason. Petrovsky's cook, a gigantic woman with green little eyes, became incensed at Alexey who ventured a slighting remark about her servility to Maslov, the " Actress." She worshipped the police-official, and regarded Alexey's affront as sheer blas-

phemy, for which she determined to take perpetual and un-abating revenge. "How could I have guessed," apologizes Gorky, "that this mass of fat and flesh deposited upon enor-mous bones contained something untouchable and so precious for her? Thus life taught me to understand the equable value of all human beings, to respect what abides in them secretly, to regard them more carefully, more painstakingly." But he had to pay the price for this lesson. Maremyana, as that Fury was called, placed on Alexey so many house- and stable-duties at the end of his twelve-hour service that there was left no time for him either to sleep or to read. The litterateur in Alexey was beginning to show his hoofs; in poetry and in prose he wrote to his superiors at Borisoglebsk a petition, in which he de-scribed the tyranny of Maremyana, asking naïvely whether the daily emptying of the station-master's slops was part of his duties. The composition was his first literary success, if success be judged by results: Alexey was transferred to the freight-station of Borisoglebsk and placed in charge of guard-ing and repairing the sacks and tarpaulins.

An entirely different crowd he faced at his new place of service. There was a group of some sixty men, nearly all of them political offenders, former prisoners and exiles, who were recruited by an enterprising man, Adadurov, for the purpose of stamping out thievery and graft on that branch of the Volga railroad. The administration consented, with certain misgiv-ings, to try the extraordinary experiment of employing official " enemies of the fatherland " for the protection of the father-land. The result was encouraging. The " Adadurovans " betook themselves earnestly to the task, and within a short time they brought to the light of day the system of chicanery and fraud practised by the railroad officials, among whom they were employed in a variety of functions. To be sure, by their education, knowledge of languages, high ideals, and un-usual ability these men were worthy of more dignified work. But, then, in autocratic Russia such a phenomenon had the value of a sign and symbol, like Zedekiah's horns or Jehezkel's yoke: it showed the true colours of a government which de-clared as enemies the most capable and patriotic sons of the

people, and kept them in dungeons and enforced inactivity. Characteristically, as in the case of Romas in Krasnovidovo, these obviously honest men were disliked, and even feared and hated, by the population. Aside from the motive which prompted the robbers to strangle their would-be righteous chum, there was another reason for the general resentment against the activity of the " Adadurovans ": they were engaged in an unpopular cause. So ingrained had been before the revolution the conviction that the government and the people were antipodal in their gains and advantages that the average Russian had no scruples about cheating the state or state-controlled enterprises. It would have been regarded as uncalled-for meanness, for example, to betray a " hare " (a ride-stealing passenger) on the train, or to expose a conductor who suffered a passenger to pay, to the conductor, one half of his fare. Precisely in that light was considered the cleansing work of the " Adadurovans."

With these intelligentsia Alexey hoped to find a relief from the people of the Petrovsky calibre, with whom he had associated for months, and whose like he continued to meet among the average. The discrepancy between books and life grew sharper with the years. While watching sacks and tarpaulins against predatory cossacks, Alexey found time to dip into Shakespeare and Heine, and to " dream of great heroic deeds, of life's brilliant joys." Meanwhile around him —

In the town, thoroughly permeated with odours of grease, soap, and rotten meat, the mayor summoned the clergy to his courtyard, to serve mass for the purpose of driving the devils out of his water-well.

A certain teacher of the municipal school lashed his wife in the bath-house every Saturday. At times she broke away, and, stout and naked, she ran around the orchard, her husband chasing her with rods in his hands. The teacher's neighbours invited their acquaintances to watch the spectacle through the cracks of their fence. I too went to look — at the spectators, got into a fight with some one, and with difficulty escaped the police. One of the citizens exhorted me:

" Now why are you so excited? Wouldn't anybody be in-

terested to see such a thing? Even in Moscow they won't show you such a trick! "

A railroad clerk, from whom I rented a cot at one ruble per month, earnestly assured me that all Jews are not only crooks but bisexual to boot. I argued with him. During the night he stole up to my bed, accompanied by his wife and brother-in-law, with the intention of inspecting me: wasn't I a Jew myself? To get rid of them, I had to wrench the clerk's arm and smash the face of his brother-in-law.

The cook of the district chief of police, trying to arouse a tender feeling in a railroad engineer, treated him to cookies, into which she had mixed her menses. The cook's chum told the engineer of this horrible witchcraft, the poor fellow became frightened, came to the doctor and announced that something was fussing and grunting in his belly. The doctor laughed at him, but he came home, and hanged himself in the cellar.

These *ordinary* events of town life in Russia weighed heavily on the mind and conscience of the railroad-watchman who had the privilege of communing with Shakespeare and Heine. He would come to the intelligentsia and with anxiety and indignation recount to them the horrors of everydayness. To his surprise, they estimated his stories as funny or flat anecdotes, and accordingly greeted them with outbursts of laughter or with disappointed reserve. They failed to see, as Alexey did, that it was life itself that he was observing and describing to them, and of course they were too far removed from life to be able to explain its " anecdotes." When he gave them an account of the Petrovsky orgies, he " felt in these men of ' culture ' a hidden envy for the diversions of those savages."

Indeed, the more he studied these intelligentsia, the more " awkward and alarmed " he felt. Life on a higher plane, discussions of Mikhaylovsky, Spencer, and the rôle of the individual in the process of history, did not make them attractive or enviable to the young seeker. Their existence seemed drab and tedious, even more colourless than the reality from which they were divorced. At their parties they flirted bookishly with anaemic epicene women and sang banal student jingles. In spite of himself, Alexey preferred to these flaccid highbrows the Dobrinka orgiasts, with the exuberant display of their in-

stincts sublimated by the beauty of sound and movement. Decidedly, Alexey Peshkov, as later Maxim Gorky, did not " belong " with the intelligentsia!

In the spring Alexey was transferred to the station Krutaya, on a Volga-Don branch, and promoted to the post of freight-weigher. But the railroad university had, apparently, reached the point of saturation with our student. He was becoming restless. Furthermore, he was over twenty, and approaching the time when every Russian had to appear at his birthplace to be examined as to his fitness for the army of the tsar and autocrat of all the Russias.

In May, 1889, Alexey set out from Tsaritsyn (now Stalin-grad), hoping to reach Nizhni Novgorod by September. Most of the way he tramped on foot, earning his food at villages, cossack settlements, or monasteries. At night he occasionally rode on freight-trains. From Ryazan he turned aside, down the Oka tributary of the Volga, and walked to Moscow, where he called at the home of Lev Tolstoy. He was not destined, how-ever, to meet the great man till years later, as he was away at that time, on a visit to the Trinity Monastery.

At the Moscow freight-station Alexey gained the consent of a cattle driver to let him join a band of eight bulls that were being transported to Nizhni Novgorod for slaughter. Five of these behaved properly, but the rest for some reason did not fancy Alexey, and all the way they tried to cause him " all sorts of disagreeable things; when they succeeded in this, they snorted and bellowed contentedly." At certain stops the driver shoved in armfuls of hay, and shouted: " Entertain them! "

Thirty-four hours I spent with the bulls, naïvely imagining that never again shall I meet more brutal bullies than those.

NIZHNI NOVGOROD REVISITED

IN his native city Alexey was given a not altogether pleasing reception: he was made to perform what Leonid Andreyev called the obligation of every Russian citizen, namely, to spend some time in jail. Upon his arrival at Nizhni Novgorod, Alexey was sheltered by a former Kazan acquaintance, Somov, who had recently returned from exile in Siberia, and now lived with another political suspect, Chekin, once a village-teacher. In October, the chief of the Nizhni Novgorod Gendarmerie, General Poznansky, received an order from St. Petersburg for the arrest of Somov. This order " pleased " the General, as he reported to the local governor, because he had long suspected the three occupants of that flat, who had been visited by politically " unsafe " persons, kept no servant, and did not permit even the servant of their landlord to tidy their rooms. The order from St. Petersburg gave the General a good pretext for searching the place. As it often happened in Russia on such occasions, the gendarmes were " a bit late," Chekin and Somov having departed before their visit. During the search Alexey came in, and was subjected to an examination. The report stated that " Peshkov conducted himself with extreme impertinence and effrontery." They tried to learn from him of Somov's whereabouts, and kept him in jail until news arrived about the arrest of Somov at Kazan.

In this connexion the police archives recently published in Soviet Russia contain the first official characterization of Alexey, as given by General Poznansky:

" In answer to my inquiry, the Chief of the Kazan Gendarmerie has informed me concerning Peshkov's record in Kazan,
supporting my long established opinion that Peshkov presents
a convenient soil for co-operation with the politically unsafe
elements of the population. I learned from that reply that at
Kazan Peshkov worked in a bakery, set up for disloyal purposes; was acquainted there with disloyal persons, in whose
midst he was known under a certain nickname; read books
of a specific nature, not quite desirable, nor quite correspond-
ing to the stage of his cultivation and the education he had
received. . . ."

Such is the official tone of the report. Gorky himself gives
a few human touches in his description of the case and of
General Poznansky, as he can be depended upon to give even
in the least expected instances. The prisoner was kept in one
of the four towers of the Nizhni Novgorod jail. On the iron
door he found scratched an inscription, which in his ignorance
of biology he took for a witticism: " Every living thing comes
from a cell." Summoned to the office of General Poznansky, he
found before him an eccentric old man, corpulent, untidy, with
a purplish face and " moist, muddy eyes that looked sad and
tired." Alexey had heard of some drama in his family and of his
being a morphinist. The General won his heart by praising his
verses which were brought to him together with the other
papers found during the search. " What sort of a revolutionist
are you? " grumbled the old man squeamishly. " You are not
a Jew, nor a Pole. Here, I see that you do some writing, well,
why not? When I let you out, show your manuscripts to
Korolenko — are you acquainted with him? No? He is a most
important writer, not worse than Turgenev." Alexey was bored,
he looked around him, and became interested in some medals
in a glass case that stood by the desk. The General noticed
his glance, got up, and began to take out medal after medal
from the case, talking about them with the enthusiasm of a
collector. Before sending him back to his cell, the General happened to ask whether he liked singing birds. Alexey, who was
once a professional catcher of songsters, proved so entertaining on the subject that he kept the General standing and

listening to him for a long time in the doorway, while the military guard stood at attention, waiting for his prisoner. A few days later Alexey sat once more in front of the General. The latter grumbled crossly: " Of course you knew where Somov had gone; you ought to have told me, and then I should have let you go at once. And too, it was not necessary for you to make sport of the officer who searched your place. And, in general. . . ." Then suddenly he bent over to Alexey and asked good-naturedly: " Don't you catch birds nowadays? "

It is seldom that Russian writers, especially those of revolutionary tendencies, treat officials sympathetically. Certainly Turgenev and Tolstoy snubbed them with aristocratic disdain. A notable exception may be found in Andreyev's *The Governor*. Gorky, who had no reason or inclination to whitewash the henchmen of the old régime, has on several occasions (*Memoirs of a Superfluous Man*, in translation: *The Spy*, for example) approached them with his wonted impartial curiosity. The Poznansky incident has an odd epilogue. About ten years later Alexey found himself again in the Nizhni Novgorod jail. At the Gendarmerie, awaiting his examination, he was addressed by a young adjutant: " Do you remember General Poznansky? He was my father. He was very much interested in your fate, followed up your literary success, and not infrequently observed that he was the first to sense your talent. Shortly before his death, in Tomsk, he asked me to hand over to you the collection of medals which you seemed to like, if, of course, you would care to take them." Gorky tells us that he was " sincerely moved." After his release from prison he gave the medals to the Nizhni Novgorod Museum.

Life was still a tangled-up affair to our youth: he had found no formula as yet. Consequently he was still longing for fantastic escapes. His ancient dream of Persia was now replaced by a desire to join a military expedition to Pamir for the study of the Afghan frontier. The desert! The Himalayas! But the jolly doctor at the recruiting station rejected Alexey Peshkov: a perforated lung and an extended vein on his leg. We know the story of his perforated lung. As to his leg, it

still troubles him on occasion and keeps him in bed. At such moments he is likely to recall the cause of his extended vein.

I got it [recalls Gorky] while working as longshoreman on the Volga. I was about twenty years old and had more strength than I could use. Once we went swimming. I undressed, and as I tried the water with my foot, an old Volga stevedore shouted to me:

" Look here, Alexey : you've ruined your leg. See that tumour ? Now tell me which foot do you put forward when you carry a load ? "

" The right foot."

" That's it ! You must step with your left foot first. Well, your song is finished : no good stevedore will come out of you, by God, no. Ekh, what a pity ! "

Meanwhile Alexey had become acquainted with an army officer, a member of the Pamir expedition, who drew luring pictures of Russia's Central Asia. He suggested that Alexey register as a volunteer for the Topographical Section, promising to arrange the red tape formalities, including a postponement of the required examinations. A few days later the officer told him with embarrassment that Alexey had a record of " political disloyalty," and reproached him for having concealed that matter from him. It was a surprise for Alexey himself : he had not suspected the thoroughness with which the " invisible thread " of the Central Spider enmeshed His Majesty's subjects ! General Poznansky ? Another proof that he was a gentleman and a — gendarme.

Another dream exploded, Alexey adjusted himself, more or less, to Nizhni Novgorod, where he remained now for nearly two years. Job followed job : rolling beer barrels in a damp cellar, in addition to washing bottles and bottling beer ; peddling *kvas,* a Russian variety of fermented cider, made of cereals or fruit ; clerking in a distillery office — they chased him out from there, because with the blow of his mighty fist he killed the mistress's wolfhound that had attacked him. He finally began to work in the office of an attorney, A. I. Lanin. In his first autobiographical sketch Gorky wrote about Lanin : " His influence on my education was immeasurably great. He

was a highly cultivated and most noble man, to whom I owe
more than to anyone else." Gorky's gratefulness often led
him to exaggeration, but that he felt beholden to Lanin may
be seen from the fact that his first collection of stories — his
first fabulous success — he dedicated to A. I. Lanin.

While travelling in the company of eight bulls to Nizhni
Novgorod, Alexey hugged one cherished possession against the
frolics of his fellow-passengers: a copybook with his lyrics
and "an excellent poem in prose and verse, *The Song of an
Old Oak*," of which latter Gorky tells us, as usual, unsparingly: "I had never suffered from self-conceit, especially in
those days, when I felt half-baked, but I sincerely believed myself to have written a remarkable production. I had squeezed
into it all of my thoughts for a decade of a varicoloured, difficult
life. I was convinced that upon reading my poem humanity
would be salutarily amazed by the novelty of the things told by
me; that the truth of my tale would convulse the hearts of all
the inhabitants of the globe, and that immediately after that
an honest, clean, and joyous life would spring forth. I desired nothing else or more than that."

After weeks of hesitation Alexey called with his poem on
Vladimir Korolenko, the writer whom Poznansky had recommended as "not worse than Turgenev." Korolenko had already become famous, both as a political martyr and as an
author. He had recently returned from his exile in remote
northern Siberia, and the fame of the story *Makar's Dream*
clung to him even then, though by that time he had written
better things. A stocky, curly-bearded, hazel-eyed Volynian,
Korolenko had been the most popular man of letters in Russia,
beyond peradventure. His name brought to mind not so much
a good writer — opinions differed as to the merits of his
fiction, as a man of a big heart, unquestionable integrity, and
eager readiness to help others. One of the few Russians to
voice in his stories a note of faith and hope, he was not a
syrupy optimist or passive non-resister, but on the contrary,
because of his faith in man's ultimate goodness, he fought all
his years against what he regarded as life's mere excrescences.
Russian reality, opulent with persecution, prejudice, tyranny,

and the general dominance of might over right, furnished Korolenko with issues and causes to fight for till his very death. This is said literally, for even on his death-bed he championed the oppressed against the privileged, the latter then being the victorious Bolsheviks. He died from exhaustion (1921), characteristically refusing to be treated with discrimination, and rejecting the extra medical help and food proffered him by the Soviet authorities in the year of Russia's blockade and famine.

Vladimir Korolenko was also the most popular man among his fellow-writers, which is to say a good deal, in any country where the jealous muses flourish. As co-editor, with Mikhaylovsky, of the monthly review, *Russkoye Bogatstvo* (*Russia's Riches*), he helped in many ways the beginning authors, especially if they happened to come up from the submerged ranks. In unparliamentary Russia public opinion found its indirect, veiled expression in the few monthly magazines which were reluctantly and grudgingly suffered by the authorities. The public, trained in the art of reading between the lines, perused the reviews from page to page, detecting in apparently innocent stories or book-reviews or an essay on the agrarian problem in Brazil, words of guidance and elucidation on burning national issues. Such literary critics as Belinsky, Pisarev, Chernyshevsky, Dobrolyubov, Mikhaylovsky, Plekhanov, " condemned to bark like dogs when they craved to howl like jackals " (Belinsky's plaint), moulded the political opinion of several generations in Russia. A monthly review, therefore, was an important institution, a " parliament of opinion," as it was often called, not without bitterness and yearning after a " real " parliament. The truth must be told, that with the passing of Autocracy, Russian magazines, and for that matter literature as a whole, began to lose, for better or worse, their rôle of political leadership. Korolenko, in any event, as co-editor of the *Russkoye Bogatstvo*, exercised a tremendous influence on public opinion in Russia, and in introducing new authors on the pages of his review he thereby anointed them as priests of that exclusive and martyred temple, the temple of Russian letters.

In his already mentioned autobiographical sketch Gorky assigned to Korolenko the responsibility for his literary profession and success. He hardly could have predicted such a statement after his first encounter with Korolenko, delightfully described in his reminiscences, as ever without sparing his own clumsiness and immaturity. I am tempted to quote a few passages:

Vladimir Galaktionovich [Korolenko] lived on the outskirts of the city, on the second story of a wooden house. On the pavement in front of the porch the snow was being dexterously shovelled away by a thickset man in a queer fur cap with ear-laps, in a short poorly made sheepskin coat, and heavy felt-boots from Vyatka.

I stormed a snowdrift to get to the porch.

" Whom do you want? "

" Korolenko."

" I am Korolenko."

Out of thick, curly whiskers richly ornamented with frost, fine hazel eyes looked at me. . . . Leaning on his shovel, he listened in silence while I explained the reasons for my visit, then he screwed up his eyes, recalling something.

" Your name sounds familiar. Was it not about you, some two years ago, that Romas, Mikhail Antonovich, wrote to me? So! "

Coming up the staircase, he asked:

" Are you not cold? You are very lightly dressed."

.   .   .   .

In his small room, wiping with a kerchief his wet beard and paging my thick copybook, he said:

" Let us read a bit! Strange handwriting, yours — looks simple but is difficult to read."

The manuscript lay on his knees, he cast side glances at it, at me — I felt embarrassed.

" Here you write ' zizgag,' that's, evidently . . . a slip of the pen, there is no such word, there's ' zigzag.' "

The short pause before the phrase " a slip of the pen " gave me to understand that V. G. Korolenko knew how to spare the feelings of his neighbour.

" Romas wrote to me that the muzhiks tried to explode him with powder, and later they set him on fire. Wasn't it so? "

He spoke while perusing the manuscript.

" Foreign words should be used only in cases of absolute necessity, on the whole it is best to avoid them. The Russian language is sufficiently rich, it possesses all the means for the expression of the finest sensations and shades of meaning."

This he said in passing, while asking questions about Romas and the village.

" What a severe face you have! " he exclaimed unexpectedly, and asked with a smile: " Living conditions pretty hard? "

His soft speech was quite different from the Volga talk with its robust, rounded " o " sound, yet I saw in him a strange resemblance to a Volga pilot. I saw it not only in his solid, broad-chested figure and in the keen gaze of his wise eyes, but also in his benign serenity, common to people who observe life as a movement along the winding bed of a river through hidden shallows and rocks.

" You often employ coarse words — is it because they appear to you strong? That happens."

I told him that I was aware of coarseness being natural with me, but that I had had neither the time for enriching myself with soft words and feelings, nor the place where I might have done so.

He looked up at me, and continued gently:

" You write: ' I have come into this world in order to disagree.' . . ." Further down it appeared that someone in my poem sat " like an eagle " on the ruins of a temple.

" A place scarcely appropriate for such a pose, and the pose is not so majestic as it is indecent," said Korolenko smiling. Then he found another " slip of the pen," and another, and another. I was crushed by their abundance, and must have crimsoned like a red-hot coal. On noticing my condition, Korolenko narrated laughingly about some errors of Gleb Uspensky, which was magnanimous, but I no longer listened or understood anything, desiring only one thing — to flee from my disgrace. It is well known that literati and actors are as touchy as poodle dogs.

I went away and spent several days in gloomy depression.

From these passages it is evident that Korolenko was by no means a " pampering papa " with beginning writers. In fact, not for six more years did Gorky appear in *Russkoye*

Bogatstvo. What was novel to Alexey in Korolenko's re-marks, was the criticism of form rather than content. Among his acquaintances the critical criteria were still of the Pisarev-Dobrolyubov variety, epitomized in the aphorism: " A pair of boots is worth more than Pushkin." The writer was expected to tell a gripping message — the " how " did not matter and was even deliberately neglected, lest the composition savour of aestheticism. Alexey was told at that time by a *narodnik* au-thor: " The story must strike at the reader's soul as with a stick, in order that the reader may be brought to feel what a brute he is! " Korolenko made Alexey realize many lin-guistic gaucheries in his poem, about which none of his in-telligentsia friends at the time would have bothered.

The prevailing literary standards were pretty low in Russia during the eighteen eighties. Turgenev and Dostoyevsky were dead, Tolstoy was endeavouring to emasculate himself as an artist (happily without success), Chekhov was writing his jewelled trifles of which the leading critic of the period, Mikhaylovsky, wrote: " I know of no sadder spectacle than that of Chekhov's talent going to perdition. What is it he wants to tell us? " Mikhaylovsky dictated the literary tastes of his contemporaries, and was primarily a publicist, a *narodnik* revolutionist, the literary value of a story being of secondary consideration to him. It must he said in passing that Mikhay-lovsky was occasionally, in spite of himself, a keen appraiser of literature, and what he wrote about Dostoyevsky, Tolstoy, Gorky, and even Andreyev, holds water to this day. It was the school that mattered, the doctrine as to the Sabbath and the man.

During that decade, and especially toward its end, a group of writers, poets for the most part, were interested in formal beauty, and produced fine prose and verse, reminiscent of the French *Parnassiens*. One may mention the old Fet, friend of Turgenev and Tolstoy, the young Fofanov, Minsky, Merezh-kovsky, Sluchevsky, and other forerunners of the Symbolists. These authors were ignored and ridiculed in the periodical press and in public, since in their preoccupation with form they could hardly answer adequately Mikhaylovsky's moni-

torial query: " What is it he wants to tell us? " When a keen young critic, Volynsky, came out with a series of articles, in which he suggested a revision of Russia's critical standards, or rather absence of such, and dared to praise some authors who had been ignored by the critics because of their political conservatism, he was branded as a traitor and actually ostracized for years. Korolenko, and, needless to say, *Russkoye Bogatstvo,* held no brief for the authors suspected of upholding the banner of " Art for art's sake," but he had an inherent sense of form and knew the Russian language from much wandering and travel, hence he cared for the formal aspect of literature more than it was safe for an orthodox *narodnik.* In fact, the zealots did suspect him of heresy.

Alexey's " gloomy depression " was not dissipated when in about a fortnight he received his manuscript back, with Korolenko's inscription on the folder:

It is hard to judge by " The Song " of your ability, but I think that you have one. Write about something you have lived through, and show it to me. I am no appraiser of verses, yours seem unintelligible to me, though some single lines are strong and brilliant. Vl. Kor.

Alexey could not understand what Korolenko meant by asking him to " write about something he had lived through ": had he not lived through everything of which he wrote in his " Song " ? He felt hurt and humiliated. Especially chagrined was he at Korolenko's reference to his verses: these had gotten into the manuscript by accident, they were Alexey's secret, he would not have wished any of his serious friends to suspect him of such frivolity as versification. He seized the manuscript and threw it into the burning stove. Thus he " offered up his wisdom as a sacrifice to the all-purifying fire," and for the remainder of that sojourn in Nizhni Novgorod he wrote not a single line of either prose or verse, " though at times he had a great desire to do so."

But even if he was so peeved as to refrain from calling on Korolenko, Alexey could not help being aware of the presence of the " Volga pilot " in the city. Nizhni Novgorod of the

period between 1886 and 1896, lived "under the sign of Korolenko," since he made himself felt by all classes of the population and by the Administration. No public evil escaped his eye, and as a pursuer of the wrongdoer and champion of the victim Korolenko knew no rest or fear until he obtained as much publicity and redress as was available under the political régime. Among the common people a legend spread about Korolenko being an "English prince," or the nephew of a foreign king (*Korol* means king), who had been authorized to keep an eye on the Authorities and on powerful citizens. The Volga merchants had a constant grudge against Korolenko, ever ready to expose their greed and dishonesty, but they also respected his courage and disinterestedness. One of these, an ancient greybeard, Zarubin, after listening, while ill in bed, to the reading of Korolenko's *Makar's Dream*, was so deeply moved by the author's faculty of sympathy for the lowly that his whole outlook changed. His new views made him enemies among his fellow-merchants, they got him into difficulties and caused him to serve nearly three years in prison. Upon his release, he tried to see Korolenko, but failing in this went to Yasnaya Polyana, where he received Tolstoy's approval. He spent the rest of his life as a militant Tolstoyan, defying officialdom, conventional society, and the all-powerful money-bags of the Volga. It must be added that, as in the case of the "Adadurovans," Korolenko's energy and gifts had no proper outlet and were forced by the conditions of the auto-cratic régime into a shallow channel. Abroad he would have un-doubtedly become a leader of international dimensions.

Among the intelligentsia Korolenko had an exceedingly small circle of friends, who jointly formed what was jestingly known as the Society of Sober Philosophers. Nearly all of them had *narodnik* leanings, but they were all free from in-discriminating " love " for the people, and regarded the village with open eyes. For this very reason Korolenko and his friends aroused the suspicions of the rank and file *narodnik* intelligentsia. To be sure, Korolenko had his long exile and *Makar's Dream* back of him, yet his " sober " attitude toward the muzhik in fiction and by word of mouth placed him under

a shadow. "He is writing from the head," they grumbled, "while the *narod* you can understand only with your soul."

Alexey was becoming interested in the "iron logic" of Karl Marx, and belonged to a small group where they studied and debated the theories of *Das Kapital*. The number of true Marxians was still insignificant in Russia, where they were outstripped by the traditionally still strong *narodniks* and by the epigoni characteristic of all periods of transition. The heroic individualism of the Terrorists, which consisted in unselfish self-expression, had dwindled into a pseudo-individualistic tendency toward personal safety and self-gratification. On the threshhold of two decades there emerged a pronounced cynicism among the young people, some of whom justified their shallowness by facile sophistry, such as combining the alleged individualism of the *narodniks* with the determinism of the Marxians. If progress is determined by historic necessity, they argued, individual effort is futile and uncalled for; therefore let us "thrust our hands into the pockets and whistle indifferently." In Russia, where thinking and educated men were at a premium, such a passive attitude spelled social stagnation and personal solipsism. Alexey felt uneasy with the facetious youths who with an air of worldly wisdom made fun of the "duties of the intelligentsia," and spoke derisively of the "legatees of the heroic epoch." Says Gorky:

My sympathies were precisely on the side of those "legatees," oddish people, true enough, but amazingly high-minded. They seemed to me almost saint-like in their infatuation with the *narod*, the object of their love, anxieties, and heroic sacrifices. Though there was a touch of the comic about their heroism, I was attracted by their romanticism, or, to be exact, by their social idealism.

Attending various gatherings of the intelligentsia, listening to their heated discussions and unnecessarily truculent arguments, Alexey felt more and more entangled in his inner contradictions. One summer night, as he sat on a steep bluff overlooking the Volga, he was nudged by a sturdy shoulder, and recognized Korolenko in the man who took a seat next

to him. He told the older man of his misgivings and of his grievances against the intelligentsia, a foreign element in their own country, divorced from reality and hated by the average citizenry. Korolenko found Alexey's observations correct, but he suggested less gloomy conclusions. The intelligentsia has always and everywhere been divorced from the people, but that is because it marches ahead, such is its historic mission. The intelligentsia, he said, are "the leaven in every popular fermentation, and the first stone in the foundation of every new constructive undertaking. Socrates, Giordano Bruno, Galileo, Robespierre, our Decembrists [in the uprising of December, 1825] Perovskaya and Zhelyabov [leading Terrorists, implicated in the assassination of Alexander II], all those who are now starving in exile, those who this very night are bent over books, preparing themselves for a struggle in the cause of justice, and necessarily, of course, for prison, all these are life's most vital force, its keenest and most sensitive instrument." He added that "mankind began to create its history on the day when the first *intellighènt* made his appearance; the myth about Prometheus was the story of a man who found means of procuring fire and thereby once and for all separated men from beasts."

Alexey was deeply moved by the sincere tone of Korolenko; again he was admonished, as formerly by grandmother and by Romas, against judging on the basis of obvious shortcomings. He was moved, but not comforted. His state of mind was even more confused and depressed than in the late Kazan period. He now, more than then, felt overburdened with ideas and impressions, unable to pacify his inner contradictions, still lacking a formula which might place him in a position to translate thought into action and give vent to his pent-up energy. "I had none of the discipline," recalls Gorky, "or more correctly, of that technique of thinking which one acquires at school. I had accumulated a great deal of material which demanded serious working over, but for such work leisure was necessary, and I had none. I was tortured by contradictions between the books in which I believed almost immutably, and real life of which I had already a fair knowledge. I

realized that I was growing wiser, but felt that something about this very process was spoiling me: like a carelessly loaded ship I heavily heeled to one side."

Alexey suffered from acute mental indigestion. In a humorous sketch, *On the Evils of Philosophy*, he relates of the curious effect his conversations with an erudite student, Nikolay, had on him (incidentally, Nikolay translated to him fragments from Nietzsche). At his request Nikolay began to expound to him the history of philosophy, but by the time he reached the outlook of Empedocles, Alexey fell subject to hallucinations. The world had lost all unity, and before his eyes floated faceless heads, palms of hands, roots of trees resembling enormous spiders, eyeless faces of great bulls, with their round eyes dancing in terror above them. His mentor accused him of possessing an unbridled imagination, and reluctantly truncated his exposition of Empedocles. He was called away to Moscow, and poor Alexey was left alone with his chaos. In his sleep and while awake he was pursued by horrible fragments of images, disconnected, maddening, which caused him to cry out, waken his landlady from her sleep, or disturb, while on a stroll, the old Tatar watchman, who would bring him home and urge him to go to bed, " because a sick man should be lying in bed, at home." He felt madness approaching, and bravely struggled to regain his equilibrium. It became embarrassing when his employer, A. I. Lanin, complained that in copying legal documents Alexey inserted irrelevant and meaningless verses concerning his torments, his inability to pray, and so on. In moments of clarity he dreaded the possibility of going insane, and would have entertained suicide were it not for his experience of two years previously, when he " became convinced of the humiliating stupidity of suicide."

He was finally prevailed upon to seek a physician's advice. An expert psychiatrist examined him for two hours, and then said to him:

" First of all, my friend, you must send to the devil all books and all this nonsense you feed on. By your constitution you are a healthy man, you ought to be ashamed to go to pieces

like that. You need physical labour. What about women, eh? So! That won't do either! Let others practice continence, but as for yourself get to know a woman, one who is eager for the game of love — it will do you good! "

He gave Alexey a few other advices, " equally disagreeable and unacceptable," and wrote out a prescription. Gorky tells us, rather abruptly, that a few days later he left Nizhni Novgorod for a Tolstoyan colony in the province of Simbirsk; when he came there the colony had already been destroyed. He never was attracted by the " simplification " and " non-resistance " sides of Tolstoy's teaching; on the contrary, culture and civilization were his ideal, for himself and for mankind, and dynamic resistance to existing evils he regarded as a categoric imperative. For a short while he dreamed of an escape from masters and humiliations through joining a colony of Tolstoyan agriculturists, where he might " plough, and plant the earth and with his own hands gather its fruit," but mainly — rest and think matters over.

What Gorky fails to mention is that his departure from Nizhni Novgorod was precipitated by a woman, in the same way as his Kazan crisis with its tragi-comic shooting act had come to a head with the unwitting encouragement of a woman. In *On the Evils of Philosophy* he describes one of the phantoms that worried his febrile imagination:

. . . Then Nobody would appear. . . . He was round like a soap bubble, without arms, a clock dial in place of a face with carrots for hands: from my childhood I felt an intense dislike for carrots. I knew that this was the husband of the woman I loved, who had disguised himself that I might not recognize him. Now he was changing into an actual man, small and fattish, with a blond beard and a soft glance in his kindly eyes; smilingly he was telling me all the evil and unflattering things which I had been thinking of his wife, and which could not be known to anyone but myself.
" Get out! " I shouted at him.

We recognize in this phantom the Pole, Boleslaw, the husband of Alexey's *First Love,* somewhat virulently drawn in

the sketch under this title. Boleslaw belonged to those under-ground revolutionists, who were engaged in theoretic discus-sions rather than in any practical activity. He was passionately argumentative, slovenly in dress and careless in his toilet (he " forgot " food in his silken whiskers and moustachios, thereby providing a trap for flies), and innocently unaware of being a parasite on his wife. She had been brought up in an Institute for Daughters of the Nobility, studied midwifery and paint-ing in Paris, then joined the migratory career of Russia's revolutionary Bohemia, bore a baby-girl somewhere between two romances, and was now living with her daughter and Boleslaw in a tiny cellar of a decrepit old house. Pretty, clever, gifted in many small ways, she was of a happy disposition and did not seem to mind either her surroundings or the fact that she was busy from morning till night, cooking and washing and copying portraits from photographs and taking care of the child and, on occasion, computing some statistics for Boleslaw, while the latter fought somewhere verbal battles over the policies of Gladstone and the tactics of Parnell.

Alexey lost his heart to this woman with all the unreason-ing ardour of a passionate chaste youth. Her noble origin, her life in Paris, Vienna, Berlin, and other fascinating places visualized by him through books, her graceful charm and girl-ishness despite her being ten years his senior, her vivacious wit and exuberance in face of poverty and squalor, captivated our knight of Queen Margot completely. She liked him, his inno-cence, his strength, his devotion, his freshness not yet spoiled by books and discussions. A normal youth would have had no difficulty in arranging a *liaison* with the woman, which in that milieu would have been regarded as a matter of course. But Alexey, who had seen the manifestation of sexual relations in their coarsest form, had created for himself too lofty a mys-tery of woman, too divine a conception of her rôle and poten-tial effect on man, to be content with the prose of an every-day affair. " I have come into this world to disagree," was his slogan of unacceptance and non-conformity. " I do not un-derstand," confesses Gorky, " how this romantic dream could have taken shape and live in my mind, but I was firmly con-

vinced that behind that which was known to me there existed something unknown, in which was hidden the lofty, mysterious meaning of communion with woman; that something great, joyous, and even terrible lurked behind the first embrace, and that the experience of that joy completely regenerated man."

Alexey's ardour won the woman's heart, but when she had a frank talk with Boleslaw on the subject, the blond-bearded, blue-eyed Pole shed tears, poured out a torrent of sentimental phrases, and threatened that if left alone he would perish " like a flower without sun." She tried to persuade Alexey that it would be wrong to hurt Boleslaw who was so weak and helpless, whereas Alexey possessed youth and power. It was then, he tells us, that he felt for the first time an intense hostility against weak people. Later in life he had many occasions to observe " the tragic helplessness of strong men when hemmed in by weaklings, and the waste of valuable energy of heart and brains in support of the fruitless existence of those doomed to ruin." He must have recalled sympathetically the Nietzschean aphorisms of Nikiforych.

Alexey was to meet that woman again, and consummate with her First Love. But at this juncture, tormented by hallucinations that resulted as much from ideological indigestion as from thwarted emotions, he felt impelled to leave Nizhni Novgorod. In his autobiographic sketch he states: " In 1890 I began to feel not in the right place among the intelligentsia, and I started off wandering." Another attempt at becoming a member of the intelligentsia ended in failure!

WANDERJAHRE

IN the next two years Alexey tried to purge his mind and body of the decidedly uncongenial intelligentsia diet. In one of his letters he wrote: " My wandering through Russia was prompted not by a lust for tramping but by a desire to see the land I was living in and the people around me." As usual, Gorky employed ratiocination to explain, and perhaps sublimate, his impulse. There must always be found a higher " purpose " in his natural inclinations and actions. Whatever the motive and aim, Alexey spent the twenty-first and twenty-second years of his life as a member of the international order of hoboes. The enormous distances he covered show how restless he had been at that time, how reluctant to settle at any place or tie himself to any occupation. Early in the spring of 1890 he left Nizhni Novgorod, tramped down the Volga as far as Tsaritsyn, by May he was in the Don District, crossed the Ukraine, visited Bessarabia (now annexed by Rumania). A police report, in 1898, to the Department of Police, insinuated that from Bessarabia Peshkov attempted to steal across the border to Rumania, with the intention of proceeding thence to Paris, and on being thwarted in his attempt, he turned off to the Crimea. Gorky himself has not committed himself regarding the truth of this accusation. He did tramp from Bessarabia to the province of Kherson, spent some time in its port of Odessa, then crossed to the Crimea, as inviting a country for tramps as California, wandered along the shore of the Black Sea, through the North Caucasus, and finally, in the fall of 1891, he reached Tiflis, the capital of Georgia.

These *Wanderjahre* furnished Alexey with a wealth of impressions. Gorky's literary fame was originally based on these stories and sketches, in which he presented bits of that kaleidoscopic Russia of his. His first romantic tales, his tramp stories and that whole world of " ex-men " culminating in the play *At the Bottom* (*Lower Depths*), and the numerous stories collected late in his career in *Through Russia,* were drawn from the inexhaustible store of his memories of those wandering years. The horse thief's tale about the terrific love of the gipsies, Zobar and Radda, overheard by Alexey at a bonfire in the steppe, forms the subject of his first published story, *Makar Chudra.* In the hot Bessarabian vineyards he gathers his realistic-romantic material for *The Old Woman Izergil,* and in the ports of Nikolayev and Odessa he meets the prototypes of his *Chelkash. Once in Autumn,* cold and hungry, looking for shelter from the incessant rain, he crawls under an upturned boat on the shore, and finds himself side by side with a girl, also an outcast, also cold and hungry, but one who, in her eternal womanhood, comforts him in his loneliness, warms him with her body, and dries his tears of chagrin and humiliation. In port and on the wide plain, under the floor of a farm barn and in a night lodging he meets his *Malva* of the green eyes, and the callous " student " of *In the Steppe,* and the cynical intellectual hobo of *A Shady Tramp,* and that picaresque gallery of *Ex-Men,* who are free from conventions and codes, from possessions and prejudices, from ambitions and aspirations. Not from his head but from improbable reality does he draw the *Little Girl,* an eleven-year-old tot, playing with a rag-doll in the back of a tenement house, who in a matter-of-fact tone invites him to " come with her." And *The Birth of a Man* takes place on the Caucasian shore of the Black Sea, when Alexey becomes a midwife and helps an unknown peasant woman deliver herself of a Russian citizen, and immediately resume her hike in search of work. *The Adulterous Wife* is not an imaginary horror; in a village in the province of Kherson he witnesses a local custom: a large crowd merrily follows an entirely naked young woman tied to a horse-driven cart. The woman is whipped methodi-

cally by her offended husband, as she moves slowly on, dragging with difficulty her bruised, bleeding body. What the author does not tell here in the story is that the curiosity of an impartial observer failed him on that occasion, that he tried to interfere in the ordeal, and as a result was beaten unconscious by the indignant muzhiks.

This panorama is so vivid, so exhilarating and dynamic despite its spots of gloom and misery, that Gorky has been accused of idealizing his tramp characters and the tramp life in general. The truth is that nowhere does Gorky slur over the dark and bestial features of hoboing. His is not the " Gipsy Trail " strewn with roses born in the imagination of a man sated with city civilization, who enjoys a temporary vacation in unconventional surroundings. Not only does he portray truly the discomfort of being hungry and roofless — privations that might be compensated by the negative freedom from conventions, acquisitiveness, and proprietorship, but he does not hesitate to suggest that even in the midst of the Barefooted Brigade one may strike upon narrowness, selfishnes, jealousy, meanness, disloyalty, and other traits of smug society. Himself a son of the people, Alexey nevertheless was made to feel at times by the submerged ex-men that they regarded him as an alien and suspected him of being unwilling to sink with them to the cozy bottom of irresponsible existence.

In a story, *At the Salt Mines,* written in 1895 and never reprinted, he recalled an incident illustrative of this attitude. When he joined the workers at the mines and began to haul the salt, he discovered that they had done something to the wheelbarrow, so that his hands were pinched in the handles. A burning pain in the palms forced him to cry out and drop the wheelbarrow, but the pain redoubled, and he was able to get his hands free only by leaving their skin in the handles. " Shouts, laughter, and whistling greeted him from every direction, and everywhere he saw malignant, triumphant faces. . . . He looked around him dully and senselessly, feeling the rise of indignation, of a desire for vengeance, and of hatred for these people." He threw himself on the ground in despair, and through his tears he asked them why they had hurt him. They

came closer, and one of them said to him earnestly: " Go away from us, go your own way! "

No, the years of tramping were not unmixed peace and joy. Material privations and collisions with his fellow-men failed to drown his inner doubts and discrepancies. For a space, so he tells us, " a fierce outburst of religious ecstasy " overwhelmed him; he wandered from monastery to monastery, had long talks with hermits and monks, but " it did not help." One recalls this experience in reading Gorky's *Confession*.

It is needless to dwell on the fact that this period was one of Alexey's most valuable " universities." He learned much and fundamentally. Toward the end of this period he had a memorable experience, described by him in *My Travelling Companion*. While working at the port of Odessa as stevedore, he befriended a Georgian youth who attracted his attention as a conspicuously well-dressed idler among the wharf denizens. The Georgian told him that he was the son of a wealthy prince in Tiflis, that he was stranded, robbed, penniless, and homesick. Alexey volunteered to tramp with him the long and difficult journey back to Tiflis. On the way Alexey did all the work and worry, while the prince remained idle and forbearing, let his companion feed him, even cheated and abused him, and to top it all, openly made fun of Alexey's soft-heartedness and gullibility. From time to time the prince regaled Alexey with stories about his wealth and high connexions, and promised that once in Tiflis his father would generously compensate his son's guide and saviour. After many arduous weeks they reached Tiflis. The prince was ashamed to enter his native town in his tattered clothes, asked Alexey to wait till nightfall, and then he slipped away and vanished in the dark. " I never met him after that," wrote Gorky, " this companion of mine for nearly four months, but I often recall him with a pleasant feeling and with a merry laugh. He has taught me much, something one does not find in the heavy tomes written by wise men, for the wisdom of life is always deeper and vaster than the wisdom of men."

In that story the author appears, indeed, irritatingly soft and an " easy mark," so that one almost sympathizes with

the mocking jeers of Prince Shakro. That the episode was not mere fiction was proved in a curious fashion. After *My Travelling Companion* had appeared in a Georgian translation, a certain Tsulukidze wrote in a Tiflis newspaper a " refutation " of Gorky's story. As a matter of fact, he did not refute anything of importance, but on the contrary confirmed the basic elements of Gorky's version. He described the same itinerary, and admitted that " Peshkov alone provided money and food " out of pity for Tsulukidze, consoling him that he need not worry, since he " was not used to work." In Tiflis they " somehow " separated — so ends the prince's " refutation."

This incident closed the tramping epopee of Alexey, for two years at least. The chance meeting with the dandified Georgian at the port of Odessa resulted in our wanderer's trip into the heart of the Caucasus, where he was destined to begin his literary career, to publish his first story, and sign his name for the first time as Maxim Gorky.

TIFLIS

ALEXEY'S dreams of going to Persia, his dream of joining an expedition to Pamir, failed to realize. But having crossed into Transcaucasia, he found himself as close to his conception of exotic Asia as any of his dreams ever approached actuality. From the Volga valleys, from the almost level Russian Plain, from the melancholy monotony of the endless steppes, he leaped into a region of snow-capped mountains (Elbruz! Kazbek!), primeval forests, turbulent torrents, glaciers, sub-tropical luxuriance, and the most bewildering array of mountaineer tribes. He found himself in the heart of the Caucasus, in Georgia — the Gurjistan of the Persians, the Gruzia of the Russians, an ancient country known historically for over two thousand years, with memories of the conquest of Alexander the Great, invasions by Pompey and Trajan, contact and collisions with Byzantines, Persians, Armenians, Turks, and finally Russians. The Georgians pride themselves on being descendants of Thargamos, great grandson of Japhet; they pride themselves on representing the handsomest men and prettiest women of the Caucasian race; on the antiquity of their conversion to Christianity — at the beginning of the fourth century; they pride themselves on being fine riders, brave fighters, excellent singers, unrivalled drinkers. The Georgians are proud for innumerable reasons. Every Georgian gentleman is a " prince," and in old Russia one was not infrequently served in a restaurant by a Caucasian prince. The Georgians have played a notable part in recent Russian history. Their king voluntarily transferred his crown to the Russian tsar on the threshold of the nineteenth century, pressed

as he was now by Turkey now by Persia. The tsars used the Caucasus, incidentally, as a place of exile for over-boisterous poets, and as a result we have Pushkin's *Prisoner of the Caucasus* and Lermontov's *Demon, Mtsyri,* and other fine " Caucasian " poems. Mistreated by the Russian autocracy for over a century, the Georgians furnished the revolutionary ranks with a disproportionately large number of fighters and leaders — the president of the Petrograd Soviet after the overthrow of the Tsar was Chkheidze, and the present master of the Soviet Union is Dzhugashvili, better known as Stalin. Following the revolution of 1917, there were several attempts at the establishment of an independent Georgian republic, and for a time such a government functioned, heartily (i.e., militarily and financially) supported by the British. In 1921, Georgia became a federated member of the Union of Soviet Republics, upon the withdrawal of the disinterested British (to be sure, Georgia lies between the oil-fields of Baku and the port of Batum).

Alexey, who had made the acquaintance of a representative Georgian prince in Odessa, reached at last the capital of Georgia, Tiflis — the Persian Tphilis. Though connected by railroad with various centres of civilization (Baku and Batum among them), Tiflis still possesses a medieval charm, in its ancient cathedrals and squares, market-places and coffee-houses. The city is located at the foot of high mountains, on both banks of the Kura River, and rises three hundred feet above the Black Sea. Its picturesqueness and mild climate could be appreciated by the youth from flat and inclement Russia. Here and there in his writings Gorky touched upon the scenery of the Caucasus, but only in passing. In one of his early sketches he described a public execution of two mountain-bandits in a town of the Tiflis province. The description is pedestrian, and perhaps that is why it was not reprinted in Gorky's works. The scene presented a bit of exotic local colour that must have been eagerly absorbed by Alexey, and added to his store of impressions.

Alexey's orientation in Tiflis began at a police station, where he chanced to find himself in connexion with a street brawl,

in which he, of course, tried to take the part of the offended side. His impudent face, irreverent bearing, and the rags that had borne the brunt of an arduous tramp from Odessa to Tiflis, did not appeal to the " Pharaos." They demanded to know who he was, and who could vouch for his dependability, political and otherwise. Luckily Alexey recalled the name of Mikhail Nachalov, an official of the Transcaucasian railroad, whom he had known in Nizhni Novgorod. Convoyed by two policemen, he sought the man out, obtained his identification, and was given the freedom of the city of Tiflis, in the extremely limited sense of this phrase.

For the Tiflis period of Alexey's peregrinations we have rather fragmentary information. His own statements refer only to the latter part of the period, and mainly to his literary debut. We also have the recently published secret documents of the Police Department, whose paternal eye was never removed from the " Nizhni Novgorod guildsman," Alexey Peshkov, and a pamphlet, *Gorky in Tiflis*, published in 1928 by the " All Georgian Union of Writers." As against the dry and matter-of-fact tone of the police reports, the pamphlet is composed in the hyperbolic style which marks everything Caucasian — whether it be its mountains, its fauna and flora, or its anecdotes. The author rhapsodizes about the " sun-giving " Tiflis, implying not too subtly that were it not for Tiflis Alexey Peshkov might never have become Maxim Gorky.[1] I shall confine my gleanings from these and other sources to what seems factual.

Mikhail Nachalov helped Alexey find employment with the Tiflis railroad-shops as clerk in the paymaster's office. This was, for him, a comparatively genteel occupation, enabling him to devote his leisure to intensive reading and other " cul-

[1] Gorky himself assumes a hyperbolic tone in his congratulatory message to the Georgian republic, at its tenth anniversary. One cannot take seriously such a passage of his as this:

" I never forget that it was in this very city [Tiflis] that I took my first unsure step on the road which I have been following these four decades. One might think that the majestic nature of the land and the romantic softness of its people gave me the jolt which changed me from a tramp into an author."

tural activities." Thus, when, in 1892, the police searched the rooms of a suspect in Rostov-on-the-Don, they found there several letters of Peshkov, in one of which he wrote: "I am sprinkling decent little ideas from the watering pail of enlightenment, with perceptible results." He complained there of the paucity of "capable workers," giving their number as "six or eight." In another of those letters he said that he and his comrades were expecting a visit from "the shiny buttons."

This Æsopian language of Underground Russia might give an exaggerated notion of Alexey's revolutionary work which beckoned a visit from the gendarmes ("shiny buttons"). He did take an active part in the readings and discussions that were organized in the "commune," as they called a rather large basement flat, where he with two chums lived noisily enough to attract the "shiny buttons." Altogether more than two hundred individuals attended those gatherings in the course of the existence of the "commune." Most of the time they read and discussed *narodnik* literature, chiefly fiction, only rarely taking up social and political topics. Alexey Peshkov enjoyed a certain popularity in the "commune," owing to his vast experiences which he recounted with considerable colour, according to contemporary testimony. He is described by one eye-witness as "a tall youth, broad-shouldered and of athletic build, with a broad, coarse, Russian face, and long hair. . . . It was not a jovial face; its intelligent thoughtful eyes expressed strength and the presence of a determined will."

Incidentally we can judge of his extraordinary physical strength at that time from a case which he described in his story *A Mistake*. One of his Georgian acquaintances, Gigo Chitadze, a young peasant who carried on an energetic propaganda of Marxian Socialism among the Tiflis workmen, lost his mental balance from overwork. Until they could find a place for him in the hospital, his comrades took turns in watching by his bed-side. He became so violent, however, that no one dared stay with him, and Alexey alone remained with him for nine days. Several times Chitadze attempted to kill his guard. During the last night of his vigil, the sick man picked up a couch, broke it, and with a board in his hands

rushed at those who came into the room. Alexey managed to repress him and put him into bed securely bound.

In the summer of 1892, the "commune" broke up, and Alexey accepted the offer of a separate and quiet room in the residence of Alexander Kalyuzhny, a revolutionary of the "Will of the People" group, who was deported to Tiflis after serving six years of hard labour in the Kara mines of Siberia. Kalyuzhny, owner of a large library, has been regarded by Gorky as third in the order of those who influenced his education, the first being Smury, the cook on the Volga steamer, and the second, the attorney Lanin (Korolenko takes the fourth place). According to the pamphlet, *Gorky in Tiflis*, Kalyuzhny discouraged Alexey's intentions to study "arithmetic and cosmography" and other high-school subjects, and urged him to read good fiction instead. Alexey had been writing verse on the quiet, after recovering from Korolenko's drubbing, but his first prose story, *Makar Chudra*, was written under the direct suggestion of Kalyuzhny. The pamphlet protests against the statement of I. A. Gruzdev (author of a biographical sketch of Gorky) to the effect that Kalyuzhny locked up Alexey in his room and made him write the story. "Ridiculous and absurd," exclaims the Tiflis pamphlet. Yet Gorky told me this very version, namely, that Kalyuzhny, after hearing him tell the story of Makar Chudra, locked him up in his room and made him write down his narrative.

The story appeared in the local official daily, *Kavkaz* (*Caucasus*), in the issue for September 24, 1892. It was signed "Maxim Gorky" — Maxim the Bitter. Gorky assures me that the name occurred to him at random, when, in the office of the newspaper, they pressed him to sign his story. Late in the fall of the same year he left on the last steamer for Nizhni Novgorod, upon the receipt of a telegram from Lanin who offered him once more a position at his office.

One need not exaggerate the importance of Gorky's first literary step, but there is no doubt that the appearance of his story in print had a stimulating effect on his efforts. As to the rôle of Kalyuzhny in his career, the following letter, writ-

ten to him from Sorrento, on October 25, 1925, speaks eloquently:

My dear friend and teacher, Alexander Mefodievich.

Thirty-four years have passed since I had the good fortune to meet you. Our second and last meeting took place twenty-two years ago.

During that time I have met hundreds of people, among them big and brilliant men. Yet, believe me, not one of them has dimmed your image in my heart's memory.

That is because you, dear friend, were the first man to treat me with genuine humaneness.

You were the first to have looked at me with the memorable kind glance of your soft eyes, that regarded me not as a chap from some queer biography, an aimless tramp, something amusing but dubious. I remember your eyes when you listened to my stories about the things I had seen, and about myself. I understood then that I must not boast of anything in your presence, and I think that owing to you I have never since boasted of myself, never exaggerated my self-estimate, nor the sorrows with which life had generously saturated me.

You were the first, I must say, who made me regard myself seriously. I owe it to your incentive that for the last thirty years I have been honourably serving Russian art.

I am glad at the opportunity to tell you this in so many words — let people know what a fine thing it is to treat one's neighbour with human cordiality.

My old friend, my dear teacher, I firmly grip your hand.
                                        Alexey Peshkov.

With all due allowance for Gorky's aptness to let the pen run away with him in non-fiction writing, especially when his sense of gratitude is involved, we must agree that Kalyuzhny deserves mention for having delicately fostered the diffident plant of Alexey's literary proclivities. From now on we are dealing with — Maxim Gorky.

FROM TRAMP TO WRITER

BACK IN NIZHNI NOVGOROD

ONE may imagine the elation of Alexey Peshkov at the sight of his first printed story. In a country of prevalent illiteracy, such as Russia was at that time, the printed word inspires awe and reverence. We have noted Alexey's worshipful attitude toward books and authors, and it is therefore easy to surmise that the appearance of his *Makar Chudra* in the *Kavkaz* was eventful to him. The tramp, the stevedore, the luckless " Makar," was now mystically joined to the sacred order of word-magicians. To be an author, one of those wonder-workers who from the time of cook Smury and Queen Margot transported him into different worlds, away from the filth and smugness of the average Russia! What a pity that grandmother was dead; how she would have rejoiced, and how she would have glorified her genial God and her darling Mother of God because They had guided her grandson safely through the crooked pathways of life. Even grandfather, had he been alive, would stroke his red beard with satisfaction: for was he not the one to instruct Alexey in the reading of Church Slavic characters and the reciting of prayers and psalms? Peshkov, by his passport a member of the dyers' guild (owing to his kinship with Kashirin), an author!

What undoubtedly sobered his enthusiasm was the continued struggle for material existence, which he was forced to carry on despite the magic signature of " Maxim Gorky " in print. In fact, upon his return to Nizhni Novgorod he could no longer remain indifferent to his prosaic needs: he was now burdened

with family responsibilities. The woman, the heroine of his sketch *My First Love,* had re-entered his life.

Throughout his wanderings Alexey kept the image of that woman alive in his memory, and — who knows, if it was not her image, as formerly that of Queen Margot, that had held him aloof and afloat in his Dantesque ramblings through life's hells? The intensity of his affection for her can be seen from Gorky's admission that when he learned of her arrival at Tiflis — it was shortly after his literary debut, he — " a strong youth of twenty-three, fainted away for the first time in his life." Her husband had stayed in France, while she returned to Russia with her little daughter, for a fresh experience. She was glad to find Alexey at Tiflis as naïvely and clumsily worshipful of her as more than two years previously, and she graciously accepted his verses, in which he spoke of himself as her " merry slave," and referred to her heart as " the loveliest of all flowers that grew on this earth so poor in flowers." But when he gathered up courage to blurt out his offer that she live with him, she retreated into the corner of her room, and then suggested for him to proceed alone to Nizhni Novgorod, and there await her decision. He did so. In the winter of that year, 1893, she joined him there with her daughter. Within a few months Alexey had attained the glory of authorship and the bliss of " ideal " love consummated!

Alexey spent his honeymoon in rather paltry quarters. His wages at Lanin's office, augmented by his literary earnings, must have been exceedingly limited, to judge by the fact that he could afford only two rubles as monthly rent for his love-nest. The place was a bath-house in the garden of an always inebriated priest, who refused to let them cut down the heavy bushes that surrounded the walls and darkened the tiny windows. The two ladies occupied the bath-house proper, and their knight the anteroom. It was so cold and draughty there that while working at night Alexey had to wrap himself in all the clothes available, with the carpet on top of them, and yet even then he contracted very bad rheumatism. This ailment struck him as " well nigh supernatural," since he had prided himself on his health and power of endurance. A few years

later he must have been even more surprised to discover that the price of his endurance was tuberculosis.

It was warmer in the bathroom, where the ladies dwelt, but each time he lighted the stove the whole place would be filled with a stifling odor of rot, soap, and soaked bath-brooms with which the priest's family had anciently steamed themselves in the Russian style. In the spring the bath-house was invaded by spiders and sow-bugs, causing the mother and her daughter convulsions of dread; Alexey battled them intermittently with a rubber golosh.

Alexey suffered humiliation and chagrin because of his poverty, his inability to provide his beloved with better quarters and more nourishing food, or to buy a toy for the little girl. For himself he did not worry: he had been accustomed to privation, but it pained him to subject to misery the frail, genteel woman and her pretty child. Yet the woman proved quite plucky. She never complained, and helped out by doing a variety of odd jobs, such as copying portraits, drawing maps, or concocting Parisian hats for the women of the neighbourhood. Of a happy disposition, she appeared not to mind their penury, and managed to fill her lover with contentment and joy. Whenever they had a few extra rubles, they arranged Russian feasts (despite her noble origin and life abroad she was fond of purely Russian dishes), to which they invited about a dozen people of her acquaintance, gastronomically inclined; she dubbed them the Order of Greedy Stomachs.

For more than two years Alexey lived with this woman. He does not name her, but the recently published documents of the Department of Police make further anonymity the secret of Polichinelle. She was Olga Kaminsky, the wife of a Polish political emigrant, Boleslaw Korsak, an urbane woman of physical charms and quick intelligence. It would have been difficult for any woman to approach the ideal which the twenty-four-year-old chaste youth had erected for himself as an antithesis of all the coarseness and shallowness he had seen most of his life. His powerful body demanded the caresses of a female, which he had spurned heretofore in his extraor-

dinary squeamishness. This thirst Olga Kaminsky quenched willingly and capably enough. But Alexey wanted more than physical satisfaction. His woman was to combine the virtues of all the fair ladies he had read about before and during the Queen Margot period. Concretely, she was to be a mother and a source of creative inspiration — that was the minimum program. Shortly after their marriage, when between embraces on a moonlit night he expounded to her his ideal of sex relations, she looked at him with wide-open, sceptical eyes, and asked: " Are you in earnest? Do you really think so? "

He was in earnest, hence disenchantment was inevitable. She was light-hearted, easy-going, and rather Gallic than Russian in her tastes and in her not over-developed introspectiveness. To his Balzac and Flaubert she preferred Octave Feuillet and Paul de Kock. He saw nothing interesting in the members of the Order of Greedy Stomachs, while to her all men presented potential " perch " to be angled by her coquetry. Her gaiety, suppleness, and wit made her irresistible to the rather shallow Greedy Stomachs, and on more than one occasion Alexey was obliged to restrain the less reserved victims of her angling. He did that not always mildly enough, and there were complaints and grievances. One gentleman whose ears he had pulled none too gently grumbled: " Well, suppose I am to blame — I plead guilty. But to pull my ears! Am I an urchin? Why, I am almost twice as old as that savage, and he dares to pull my ears! He might have struck me, that would have been more proper at least! "

When she asked him whether he was jealous, he indignantly brushed the accusation aside. No, he tells us, he was " too young and self-confident to be jealous." It annoyed him to think that in a moment of intimacy with another man she might betray to him his, Alexey's, own thoughts and feelings, that which one entrusts only to a woman one loves: " There is such a moment of communion with a woman, when you become a stranger even to yourself, and open your heart to her as a believer opens his heart to his God." Apparently aware of producing the impression of protesting too much his immunity

from jealousy, Gorky soliloquizes: " Perhaps it is this fear
[of betrayal] that lies at the root of jealousy? "

Even if we should accept unquestioningly Gorky's assurances of his freedom from jealousy, there is hardly any doubt
as to the annoyance that Olga's flirtations caused him. The gay
parties in the bath-house, with the occasional " corrections "
administered by Alexey to the ardent wooers of Olga, engaged the attention of Nizhni Novgorod gossips, who, it goes
without saying, spread the rumour with unstinted embellish-
ment. Aside from this unpleasant notoriety, Gorky found that
under those conditions of domestic life he was unable to write,
yet in his heart he was beginning to suspect that literature
was his " only place in life." The suspicion was, it is true,
rather vague as yet, if we are to believe his unconvincing pro-
testation that Olga's indifference to his literary efforts did not
vex him in the least, because he " did not believe himself at
that time that he could be a serious writer, and regarded his
newspaper work merely as a means of livelihood, though " —
mark this " though " ! — he " already experienced not infrequently hot waves of inspiration flooding his soul." He was
decidedly hurt, in any event, when one morning, while reading
to Olga his *Old Woman Izergil* written by him during the
night, he noticed that she was fast asleep, " breathing evenly
and peacefully like a baby." Recalling this incident thirty
years later, " with a smile," he admitted that at the time " the
indisputable right of a person to sleep when feeling sleepy
chagrined him deeply."

He continued to be charmed by Olga's cleverness, good
humour, physical and mental neatness — in a word, by her
urbanity — but their basic divergence of outlooks became more
and more oppressively clear to him. One case cited by him
illustrates amply this difference of views and attitudes:

One day in the market-place a policeman beat up a beautiful old man, a one-eyed Jew, accusing him of having stolen a
bunch of horse-radishes from a tradesman. I came upon the
old man in the street, as, after he had been dragged in the
dust by the policeman, he was walking slowly with a certain

picturesque solemnity. His large black eye was sternly fixed on the hot clear sky, and from his battered mouth thin streamlets of blood were trickling down his long beard, staining the silver of the hair a bright crimson.

This happened thirty years ago, yet even now I see that gaze directed skyward in speechless reproach, I see the silver needles of his eyebrows quivering on the old man's face. Unforgettable are the insults inflicted on a human being, nor shall they be forgotten!

I arrived home completely crushed, my face distorted with misery and anger. . . . It was in moments like this that I realized with special clearness how remote from me was the being I held nearest in the world.

When I told her about the beaten Jew, she was greatly surprised:

" And is that why you are so frantic? Oh, what weak nerves you have! "

Later she asked:

" Did you say he was a beautiful old man? But how could he be beautiful if he had only one eye? "

Gorky tells us that no serious row took place between them, because in the course of his life he had learned to regard people with tolerance, and to realize that " all people were more or less sinful before the unknown God of absolute truth." They both agreed that it was best for them to part, and shortly afterward Gorky went to Samara. Olga Kaminsky also left Nizhni Novgorod, having joined a theatrical troupe. She is no longer among the living.

Once more, while in Nizhni Novgorod, Gorky came under the observation of Vladimir Korolenko. A number of Gorky's sketches and stories which appeared in the Kazan daily, *Volzhsky Vestnik (Volga Messenger)*, signed " M.G." or " G-y," came to the attention of Korolenko, a regular contributor of that paper. The tyro was invited to call on the prominent editor and author, and again Korolenko assumed the rôle of guide and critic toward the morose chap with the pugnacious nose, who did not always accept criticism graciously. At their first meeting Korolenko congratulated him on having broken into print, and mentioned that he had been

just reading his allegory, *About the Siskin that Lied*. Recalling probably the thrashing he gave the young man a few years previously for his *Song of the Old Oak,* he now remarked about his obstinacy in writing allegories, adding that even an allegory may be good if it is witty, and that obstinacy is not a bad quality. At parting he invited Gorky to bring his manuscripts and talk them over with him.

Korolenko's offer to tutor his early steps did not meet with Gorky's whole-hearted enthusiasm. Though he left him "envigorated," feeling like one who had "bathed in the cool water of a woodland stream after a hot and very tiring day," he was dimly aware of being out of sympathy with his host. "The probable reason for that," muses Gorky, "was that masters and tutors were becoming somewhat irksome to me by that time. I longed for a rest from them, for a simple, friendly talk with a good man about what was troubling me mercilessly. When I brought the material woven of my impressions to my instructors, they cut it out and sewed it up in accordance with the fashion and traditions of the political-philosophical concerns, whose cutters and tailors they happened to be. I felt that they were quite sincerely incapable of sewing and cutting out in any other way, yet I saw that they were ruining my material." Are we to conclude from this passage that the "university" days were over for him, that Alexey Peshkov, the "native nugget" whom every *narodnik* saw fit to maul and mould *ad majorem populi gloriam,* had grown up into Maxim Gorky, graduated and self-sufficient?

In any event, Korolenko's goodwill and genuine friendship soon disarmed Gorky's misgivings. Even his severe criticism and ironic remarks were voiced with such directness, such candid concern, such humorous winks of the hazel, Ukrainian eyes, that the pupil was won over wholly and for the rest of his life. When he came to hear Korolenko's judgement of his fairy-tale *About the Fisherman and the Fairy* and of *Old Woman Izergil,* he found the bearded Volynian tinkering with an ax on the staircase, and was told that though the weapon was not for his benefit "some decapitation" was in store for him. Of the fairy-tale he said: "If it had been written by a

young lady who had read too much of Musset's poetry. . . .
I should have said to the young lady : ' Not bad, but still you
had better get married ! ' But for a fierce lummox like you to
write tender little verses is almost abominable, and in any
case criminal." Korolenko had apparently heard a great deal
about Gorky's love-affair and its vicissitudes, for when the
author admitted that he had written the fairy-tale while in
Tiflis, his host chuckled, explaining the effusion by a case of
love pessimism. *Old Woman Izergil* he found as " written better, more seriously," but even then it was an allegory ! It
savoured of romanticism, a Lazarus who hardly merited resur-
rection. " You don't seem to me to be singing in your own
key. You are a realist, and not a romanticist — a realist ! "
Korolenko then asked him point-blank whether the Pole in
the story had not been drawn with personal malice, and on
Gorky's confirmation he shouted that anything narrowly personal was inadmissible in fiction.

Korolenko touched here on two of Gorky's weak spots. That
early romanticism of his, an inevitable and salutary emesis
of his ill-digested dreams and fantasies, lingered on in his
writings too long, and deserved rough treatment. The personal
element in Gorky's works is both his forte and his vice. His
strongest characters are those drawn from his own memory,
from his actual experience. But the abundance of his impressions and reminiscences tempts him sometimes to be anecdotic
and " narrowly personal," as Korolenko observed about the
way Gorky ill-used Boleslaw, Olga's husband, as the Pole in
Old Woman Izergil. It speaks much for Gorky's brave frankness that he does not try to soften his own negative traits in
his recollections of Korolenko. Thus he cites a case from his
later experience as a newspaper writer in Samara, when in connexion with a dubious pun which he elaborated in an attack
against a local versifier, he received a scathing letter from
Korolenko, the burden of his sermon being that even in abusing
people one must " maintain a sense of proportion." That was
good advice, sorely needed by Gorky the journalist even more
than by Gorky the fiction writer.

Meanwhile Gorky's stories appeared in Volga papers with

growing frequency, and his story *Emelyan Pilyay* was published, in 1893, in the Moscow daily, *Russkiya Vyedomosti* (*Russian News*), the most serious liberal organ in Russia till the very revolution of 1917. Korolenko apparently followed Gorky's development closely, for at their meetings he displayed an acquaintance with every story of his, and unsparingly pilloried all his stylistic weaknesses. In a story called *An Exceptional Case* (not reprinted) Gorky described a group of peasants weeping over the grave of a member of the intelligentsia, whose cultural rôle they had come to realize. Korolenko, the veteran *narodnik*, who had paid dearly for his infatuation with the *narod*, detected the false note in Gorky's story, and told him in a tone of good humour that must have sounded murderous: " Now, that you have concocted badly. Such tricks you had better give up." He finally urged him to write something for his review, *Russkoye Bogatstvo*: " When they print your work in a monthly magazine, you will, I hope, begin to regard yourself more seriously." This proposal must have meant a great deal to Gorky, for he came home and at once sat down to write *Chelkash,* the story told him by an Odessa tramp at the port of Nikolayev. He finished it in two days and delivered it to Korolenko. A few days later Korolenko congratulated him on having written " not a bad thing, in fact a fine story, all hewn out of one block." The same evening when they sat in his study he went on praising the story: " Not at all bad! You know how to create characters, and your people talk and act of their own accord, naturally, without your interference in the course of their thoughts and the play of their feelings. Not everyone succeeds in that! The best thing about this is that you value the individual as he is. I have told you that you are a realist! " That was generous praise from such a truculent critic as Korolenko, who did not omit to reproach him for a bit of romanticism protruding from the story, and also mentioned that he had corrected several damaging " collisions with grammar " in the manuscript. In conclusion he told him that *Chelkash* would appear in *Russkoye Bogatstvo,* and have the distinction of being printed in the first place!

This formal introduction of Gorky to the exacting and hyper-

critical Russian audience did not take place for another year, not till June, 1895. With the opening of the pages of *Russkoye Bogatstvo* to him, which implied the sanction of Vladimir Korolenko and the all-powerful literary dictator, Mikhaylovsky, his success was assured. Yet it took a few years before Gorky could devote himself to the writing of fiction exclusively; he was obliged to engage in journalistic work, in order to eke out a tolerable existence. A note from Gorky to Korolenko, written in October, 1894, complains of his ill health (pain in the legs and in the chest), of being driven from his rooms for unpaid rent, and of not hearing from *Russkoye Bogatstvo* in regard to his other story, *By the Sea,* which he had sent to the editors. The note also asked for some advance money on *Chelkash*. It is evident that Mikhaylovsky was more reserved about the new contributor than his co-editor; he writes to him about that time: "If you happen to see Peshkov (Gorky), tell him, please, that his other story, *By the Sea,* will not be printed. . . . He is a queer fellow; beyond doubt he is gifted, but at the same time so affected and purposeless that one despairs of him." Mikhaylovsky was severe with those who lacked a definite "purpose" (as in the case of Chekhov), and he probably objected to Gorky's impressionistic style as "affected." Gorky's next attempt to storm *Russkoye Bogatstvo* failed again. In April, 1905, Korolenko informed Mikhaylovsky that he had "a tearful letter" from Gorky about his story, *A Mistake,* having been returned to him "without a word of explanation." It appears that Korolenko approved of the story, and had sent it on to his colleague; he now pleaded with him to write to Gorky, or at least to Korolenko, "two or three words," giving his reason for rejecting the piece which, in his opinion, "does betray talent, and though written on an uncommon theme it is composed forcefully." Mikhaylovsky wrote back that he recalled the story only dimly, but he was sure that it was "quite devoid of a purpose, a lack that was redeemed neither by beauty nor by truthfulness; the thing presented an invented, arbitrary psychology of two madmen. . . . The author is undoubtedly gifted, but if he is going to stagnate in such drawn-out and

decadent pieces as *By the Sea* and *A Mistake,* he is a lost
man. He has strength, but there is no sense in waving his
arms in empty space, however strong his arms be." In the
case of *A Mistake,* one cannot but wonder how Korolenko
could have recommended such tedious drivel, its autobiographic value (noted in the Tiflis chapter) being beside the
point. Curiously enough, *A Mistake* was published in *Russkaya
Mysl* (*Russian Thought*), an important Moscow monthly, in
September of the same year, that is, three months after
Chelkash had made its bow in Mikhaylovsky's review.

The difficulty of breaking into the big reviews explains the
fact that the bulk of the material in the first two volumes
of Gorky's stories was reprinted from daily papers, chiefly
of the Volga region. The compensation for newspaper fiction
was decidedly insufficient, however, and Gorky was forced to
look for the position of a feuilletonist, as the Russians, after
the French, call the journalist who in this column, or more
often, in the lower half of the page, discourses lightly on every
question of the day. Here again Korolenko took a hand in
directing his protégé.

On several occasions he let Gorky know that rumours of
his " orgies " and scandals in the bath-house had reached him,
and that he did not approve of his mode of living. Though
Gorky was extremely touchy on the subject, and impatient
with meddlers, he was moved by Korolenko's genuine concern about his well-being, and gave him a frank account of
the situation. The older man urged him to drop that life and
go away from Nizhni Novgorod, and promised him a recommendation to the editor of the *Samarskaya Gazeta* (*Samara
Gazette*). His oft-reiterated counsel eventually coincided with
Gorky's own decision to put an end to his romance with Olga
Kaminsky, and in February, 1895, he came to Samara.

SAMARA

NIZHNI NOVGOROD — Astrakhan — Nizhni Novgorod — Kazan — Nizhni Novgorod — Astrakhan, then back to Nizhni Novgorod — Samara — Nizhni Novgorod. . . The line of Alexey Peshkov's and of the early Gorky's peregrinations lay chiefly along the Mother Volga. A little over a year he spent in Samara, on the southern Volga. Samara is a typical Russian provincial town, inhabited by Russians and Mongols, famous for its *kumys* (fermented mare's milk; Tolstoy took at one time the *kumys* cure in the Samara steppes), its fine port, its commerce with Siberia and Central Asia, and its being the capital of a province of an exceedingly fertile soil and of recurrent famines — one of Old Russia's characteristic paradoxes. Like other Volga ports, Samara had a powerful class of old-fashioned opinionated merchants at the top of the social ladder and a nondescript mass of the submerged riff-raff at the bottom, with the classless if not declassed intelligentsia in between. At the recommendation of Korolenko, Gorky was given a position as *feuilletonist* on one of the two local dailies, the *Samarskaya Gazeta*. He received one hundred rubles a month, and in addition three copecks per line of fiction.

Looking back at that period Gorky spoke of "writing daily bad *feuilletons* under the good pen-name of 'Jehudiil Chlamyda'" [the Greek "chlamys, chlamydes"]. Jehudiil, Gorky tells me, is an apocryphal priest, the only one of the twelve priests at Jesus' trial to pronounce him not guilty. In his paper on the talented writer, Garin-Mikhaylovsky, he has

another suggestive judgement about his journalistic activity in Samara:

A man in the uniform of a railway engineer [Garin-Mikhaylovsky] came up to me, looked into my eyes, and spoke rapidly and unceremoniously:

" Are you Gorky? Yes? You write not badly. But as Chlamyda — badly. You are Chlamyda too, aren't you? "

I knew myself that Jehudiil Chlamyda wrote badly, was keenly vexed by that, and for this reason the engineer did not find favour in my eyes. And he kept up leeching me:

" As a *feuilletonist* you are feeble. A *feuilletonist* must be somewhat satirical, and you haven't that in you. There is some humour in you, but of a crudish sort, and you are not using it with skill."

It is quite unpleasant when an utter stranger jumps on you in this fashion and starts out to tell you the truth to your face. If he had only misstated the facts, but — no, he made no mistake, all that was true!

Under the title of *Among Other Things* Jehudiil Chlamyda discussed such local themes as the municipal horse-car, the board of aldermen, public entertainments, occasional accidents, brawls, and other events of similar inportance. He also wrote unsigned *Sketches and Draughts,* almost daily. The tone of those writings was of an unrelieved gloom, and their total impression is that of deadly boredom and shallowness. In the issue of August 25, 1895, we find a typical passage: " It appears that during the last twenty-four hours, as also in the course of the past two years, life has not moved in any direction. To be sure, there is movement in it, but that is only because it is decomposing. You observe this and you muse: ' Very sad but quite natural.' " From time to time Jehudiil becomes aware of the futility of his denunciatory efforts, since he lives among people " who are absolutely indifferent as to whether they are being denounced in the press or not, in view of the fact that they are illiterate and for that reason read no newspapers."

That the Samara period was not fruitless for Gorky is evident from the fact that during that time he wrote about a score of stories, among them *Once in Autumn, The Song of the*

Falcon, On a Raft, The Adulterous Wife, and *The Affair of the Clasps.* His first two novels, *Foma Gordeyev,* and *Three of Them,* were based on his observations of Samara merchants and Samara slums. Life, regardless of place and conditions, continued to feed the unquenchable curiosity of our observer. An episode from that period, which he jotted down some thirty years later, shows him in a characteristic light:

One night I was walking along the Volga shore, when I heard a cry: " Help! Good people, help! " It was dark, cloudy, with huge barges silhouetted on the water. Something was struggling in the water near one of the barges. I jumped in, reached the drowning man, grabbed him by the hair, and pulled him out on the shore. Thereupon he caught me by the scruff of the neck and began to scold me: " Hey, you! What right have you to drag people by the hair? " I was surprised: " Weren't you drowning? Didn't you shout for help? " " You head of a devil! How could I drown when I stood in the water just to my shoulders and held on to the safety rope? Are you blind? " " But you did shout for help, didn't you? " " What if I did? Suppose I shout that you are a blockhead, would you believe me? Come on, give me a ruble, or I'll haul you to the police station. Come now! " I argued with him for a while, then realized that in his own way he was right, and gave him all I had on me, about thirty-five copecks. I went home that much wiser.

From reminiscences of contemporaries we learn that in the eyes of the average Samaran, Gorky, or rather Jehudiil Chlamyda, as he was better known locally, was far from prepossessing. His very appearance disturbed the conventional. Tall and broad-shouldered, with the stoop of a stevedore, he was constantly seen marching through the streets, peeping into taverns and shops and stores and barges and steamers and wherever there was life and movement. He wore an oldish dark dolman, whose wings flopped as he walked, wide cossack trousers of blue calico billowing over soft Tatar knee-boots that were ornamented with bits of green, red, and yellow leather, and over the trousers he had a Russian blouse with a narrow Caucasian belt. He always carried a stout, knotty

cane, and long wisps of fair hair hung from under a black soft hat, whose broad brims drooped from having known much rain. This ferocious individual took upon himself to expose daily Samara's shortcomings and offences against decency and humaneness. It is noteworthy that even at that early stage Gorky used the word " Asiatic " to epitomize the backwardness and passivity of his compatriots. Late in life, in 1915, to be precise, he elaborated this point in his essay, *Two Souls,* an analysis of the European and Asiatic elements in the Russian nation, the author's preference emphatically given to the former.

Conventional Samara naturally did not take to Jehudiil Chlamyda. The rival daily, *Samara Vestnik (Samara Messenger),* made Chlamyda the butt of its attacks, and gave Gorky a pungent foretaste of the verbal battles he was to wage for the greater part of his literary career. The *Vestnik* pretended to stand for Marxian principles, which did not prevent it from luring subscribers by the offer of a " phototyped portrait of the Emperor " as a premium. Jehudiil Chlamyda drew upon himself the sarcasms of his fellow-*feuilletonists* on the *Vestnik,* who endeavoured to keep the public informed as to the past of the " enormous guy in the hat of a Turkish bandit, looking like a plantation-owner from the Southern States, and wearing an exceptionally stout stick which, for all we know, might be blood-stained." The readers were advised of such germane details as the mendicancy of Chlamyda's grandmother and the dementia of his grandfather. His long intimacy with riff-raff and tramps, " with whom he wallowed in cesspools," was brought forth as the reason for his " lack of principles " and for his " presenting a dangerous element of degeneration in the Press." Nor was his fiction spared : it was accused of eroticism and leanings toward the Decadent school. He was lampooned as an Italian, Pascarello, a barrel-organist and dog-trainer, who was hired by a certain Balalaykin to write for his paper all sorts of " literature." " Being the only representative in Samara of the only healthy current in literature — Decadence, he has created an especially appetizing cult of feminine beauty. . . . Touchingly and gracefully he has glorified woman in a damp

skirt clinging to all the charming details of her slender form (*vide* the inspiringly artistic product of his pen, entitled *Love for Another's Wife on a Raft*)." The reference was obviously to Gorky's *On a Raft*. The polemic was by no means one-sided, for Jehudiil Chlamyda responded as sardonically and provincially, though less personally.

The war with the *Vestnik* had no bad effects on the fortunes of the *Gazeta*: its circulation exceeded by five or six times that of its rival. But Chlamyda's exposés of economic exploitation and dishonesty on the part of the local administration and capitalists placed the publisher of the *Gazeta* in a delicate position. Letters of protest were addressed to the publishers against Chlamyda, who was branded as " a noxious bacillus in the healthy organism of the Press." Gorky himself recalls good-humouredly an encounter he had as a result of criticizing a rich Samaran, Lebedev:

Lebedev, owner of a cast-iron foundry, hired two workmen to beat me up. They tore off the lapel of my overcoat, and I, who at that time carried a cane because of rheumatism in my knee-joints, was forced to break that cane in the battle with my assailants. Some time later I became friendly with one of these, and learned from him that they had been hired to do the dirty work for three rubles. Four or five years previously a sweet woman offered me fifty copecks to dispatch her husband [cf. Gorky's sketch *Yeralash* (*Hodgepodge*)]. That's how rapidly wages rose in the 'nineties!

The publisher of the *Gazeta* did not cherish the prospect of losing favour with the powerful of Samara. Gorky was dismissed as " too bitter," and his place was given to a more diplomatic and more experienced journalist, a certain A. A. Drobysh-Drobyshevsky. Korolenko, who felt responsible for Gorky, was apparently chagrined by Gorky's " too bitter " tone, for we find him writing to Drobyshevsky in the summer of 1896: " I am glad for you and for the paper that in this fight you won and not he [Gorky]. Of course, it would have been best not to have had any fight, had he written under an editor's firm brakes. Well, things went differently, what

can be done? He is, after all is said, a man of talent, only he was in great need of an editor's instructions."

Few people in Samara appreciated Gorky. "He lived there truly as a prophet in his own country," remarks a contemporary. There was a handful of young men who ventured to call on Gorky, in the basement of a dilapidated house overlooking the Volga. If the caller wished to know whether the host was at home, he had to squat on the sidewalk and peep down the small windows of the basement, trying to discover at the table a shaggy head bent over book or writing paper, or to discern a husky bass calmly rumbling in a rounded "o" accent. Inside they found warmth and hospitality without stint. Despite his comparatively decent earnings, he was usually penniless, because he gave away what he had right and left. A. Treplev recalls that if a caller praised any of Gorky's books or things, the host would invariably force these on him, paying no heed to refusal. Pressing a broad palm to his chest and shoving the praised object to the victim, he would protest: "But I don't need it any more! Upon my word, honestly! May I be damned if I do! That's a fact!" The recalcitrant visitor would eventually discover the object in the pocket of his overcoat left in the hall. This explains why Gorky seldom possessed a watch. Chekhov chided him: "An author and without a watch! For shame," and presented him with an old-fashioned silver time-piece. On the inside of the lid were engraved the words: "From Doctor Chekhov."

Gorky's few callers discovered to their amazement that the erstwhile baker and tramp was better read than any of the local intelligentsia. He knew well Shakespeare, Hugo, Byron, Goethe, Schiller, Maupassant, Dickens, Thackeray, and of course such Russians as Dostoyevsky. The contemporary who gives this list, adds that Gorky was the first to introduce to the Samarans Stendhal, Mérimée, Gautier, Flaubert, Balzac, Baudelaire, Poe, Verlaine, and the Russian poets who were just then launching the Symbolist movement — Merezhkovsky, Minsky, Fofanov, Balmont, Bryusov. Gorky was probably responsible also for the appearance in the *Samarskaya Gazeta* of excerpts from *Thus Spake Zarathustra,* in the translation

of a fellow-journalist, Zimmermann. It is evident that in his insatiable reading Gorky was still seeking, and seeking vainly, that answer to his questions, that " formula " of life, for which he had desperately craved from his childhood, through his arduous boyhood and the " universities " of his grave youth.

His contact with the higher Samara intelligentsia was confined to the gatherings at the home of Judge Yakov Teitel, where he met such writers as Chirikov and Garin-Mikhaylovsky, and where the best minds of the town exchanged views, often in violently earnest disputes. Gorky recalls warmly the kindly, white-haired host and the lavishly hospitable hostess who helped to mollify sharp differences and to create an atmosphere of congeniality in divergence. It may be true that when three Russian intellectuals meet they voice at least four different opinions, but it is also true that Russian intellectuals occasionally display an astonishing tolerance and respect for their however deadly opponents.

Yakov Teitel occupied an exceptional position: he was one of the few Jews — their number could be counted on the fingers of one hand — to have retained an official judiciary post under the Jew-baiting régime of Alexander III and Nicholas II. In his interesting memoirs, *From My Life,* Teitel recalls Gorky's regular attendance of those gatherings at his home. " Alexey Maximovich," he writes, " spoke simply, thoughtfully, and often with extreme acrimony. He seldom took part in the disputes, but preferred to listen, leaning with both elbows on the table, and when the arguments reached red white heat, he would drop a dexterous word or phrase of pristine folk-usage, and not infrequently it served to silence the dispute."

As an example of Gorky's earnestness, Teitel records that his interest in the Jewish question went further than what was regarded as the duty of a liberal writer. In his effort to gauge the substance of Jewry, he even took up the study of the Hebrew language. In one of our talks Gorky confirmed Teitel's statement and drew an unforgettable portrait of his teacher, Lieberman. He was a watchmaker, with a narrow face, long beard, burning eyes, hectic spots on his cheeks; he spat blood, and seemed to be always flying. To my inquiry as to his suc-

cess as a pupil, Gorky stopped (we had been strolling on the
Capo di Sorrento road), his nose wrinkled up ferociously, and
his eyes blazed. How could he learn anything, when Lieberman spoke in such a way that he, the pupil, " would stop breathing." His imagination — precisely, imagination, not intellect —
knew no bounds or obstacles. No mystery was inaccessible to
him. Garin-Mikhaylovsky tried, unsuccessfully in his own opinion and in that of Gorky, to tell in the local *Gazeta* of Lieberman, *The Genius*. The gist of the sketch was to the effect that a
half-educated, tubercular Jew had been working in figures for
twelve years, and discovered differential calculus. When he
learned that he had been anticipated long ago, he was deeply
grieved, and fell dead at the Samara depot from a haemorrhage
of his lungs.

In Samara Gorky went through his first and (thus far) only
marriage ceremony. At one of the Teitel evenings Gorky became acquainted with Katerina Pavlovna Volzhina, a pretty
girl who had just graduated from high school. Katya Volzhina, as she was called at the Teitels, was proof-reader on
the *Samarskaya Gazeta,* and in that capacity became intimately acquainted with Gorky. Their marriage deeply chagrined Katya's parents, a proud though poor couple from the
gentry. This took place in 1896, and the result of the union
is Gorky's only son, Maxim. Though the Peshkovs separated
nearly thirty years ago, they have retained excellent relations,
and Gorky speaks of his wife with warmth and respect. In
1925, on the occasion of the birth of a child to young Maxim,
Katerina Pavlovna travelled from Moscow to Sorrento, to
greet her grandson.

In May, 1896, Gorky and his wife moved to Nizhni Novgorod, to work on the daily, *Nizhegorodsky Listok* (*The
Nizhni Novgorod Leaf*).

THE LAST PULL

FROM 1896 to 1904 Gorky lived for the most part in and about Nizhni Novgorod, with occasional trips to other parts of Russia, undertaken not always from free choice, as we shall see. During most of these years Gorky, along with expanding and improving his output of fiction, was quite active as a journalist. He wrote chiefly for the *Nizhegorodsky Listok,* the most radical and progressive daily on the Volga, which boasted among its contributions Korolenko and his group, and with the advent of Gorky, also Chirikov, Skitalets, Leonid Andreyev, and others of the " Under-Maxim " clan. Gorky's *Rambling Notes* discussed an endless variety of local and national questions, within the limitations of the censor's pencil. Whether he attacked in veiled terms the evils of administrative arbitrariness and corruption, or the flabbiness of the verbose intelligentsia, or the stagnancy of the smug citizens; or whether he championed the poor children and the tramps of the wharf, urging homes and measures of enlightenment for the submerged elements of society, Gorky performed a function which Korolenko defined as " a morally sanitary task." Russian reality presented an inexhaustible field for such a task, and Gorky, who had gone through the " lower depths " of life, and who had an editorial bee from his early years, did his work with gusto and vehemence.

One of the editors of the *Nizhegorodsky Listok,* S. D. Protopopov, recalls Gorky's frequent (" almost daily ") visits to the office of the paper, where he took an active part in the meetings and consultations of the staff, " all of whom worked from idealistic motives, in harmony and with enthusiasm, con-

tent with the smallest compensation." The paper adopted a radical direction, going just as far as the wall of censorship permitted. Protopopov tells us that the staff at times debated as to whether it was best to guard the paper, lest it be suspended by the Authorities, or " to rattle off uncensored one decent issue and perish with honour." Curiously enough Gorky voted against such heroic harakiri, and even signed his name to a contract, jointly with Protopopov, Korolenko, and others, which obliged the signatories to continue the publication of the daily in the capacity of contributors and shareholders.

From this incident it is evident that at that time Gorky agreed with Korolenko, who disparaged underground revolutionary activity, but advocated a slow, *legal* course of action against the existing order. " Autocracy," said Korolenko, " is a diseased but still firm tooth, and its root is branched and deeply embedded. It is not for our generation to pull this tooth out, we must first loosen it, and for that more than one decade of legal work is required." Before long Gorky will discard this view and will help to loosen the tooth of Autocracy by more violent means, but for the time being he remained a Korolenko-man. Yet even then he did not always conform with the faith in man's goodness that formed the core of Korolenko's outlook. Thus, when at one of the meetings of the editorial board the question of the paper's attitude toward Christianity was raised, and someone suggested to follow Christianity according to the " fifth gospel of Renan," and advocate the useful doctrine of love for one's neighbour, Gorky boomed forth: " Love your neighbour? All too often one should thrash one's neighbour! "

The rôle of a journalist in Russia, in the opposition press, was delicate and difficult. The Russian reader expected a meaty and suggestive diet, a comment on all the burning issues of the day, which had to be conveyed adroitly enough to pass the censor's hyper-suspicious eye and yet to enable the subtle reader to draw his inferences. In the lower half of the newspaper was printed the *feuilleton*, a French feature, not unlike the American " column," but in view of the Russian circumstances more grave in subject-matter and treatment. As a rule, the Russian " colyumnist " managed to insinuate some politically

subversive ideas in his lines, whether he discussed a literary production or something new on the stage or local graft or Lord Kitchener or the discovery of a new comet. In a light vein, in a veiled style that resembled Aesop's fables, the writer was expected to show his omniscience, to comment on everything, and above all to thump his nose at the censor. Russia has produced a number of brilliant *feuilletonists,* such as Doroshevich, Amfiteatrov, Homo Novus, Burenin, and that strange genius, V. V. Rosanov. But there also appeared a legion of imitators, of pedestrian scribblers who attempted acrobatic stunts, tried to be funny at any price and clever with a vengeance. The *feuilleton,* a masterpiece at its best, produced also an epidemic of cant, of hackneyed inversions and allegories, of cheap jeremiads wrapped in jejeune burlesquerie, and altogether a lot of tedium served under the sauce of grave comedy.

More than one Russian writer had to serve his journalistic apprenticeship at one time or another, but the effect on his talent was not always equally pernicious. Leonid Andreyev, failing as a lawyer, became a court reporter, then a *feuilletonist,* and finally a writer of fiction. In the last capacity he never betrayed his earlier profession. In fact, it is difficult to realize that the same Andreyev had written the clever, flippant, glib journalistic bits and the literary productions weighed with pensiveness and devoid of verbal fluency. Not so with Gorky. The journalistic experience has left an indelible mark on his literary talent. Perhaps this is due to his inborn didacticism which found an ample outlet in journalistic sermons, and which is seldom absent from his stories and plays. Whenever in reading Gorky we come upon a turgid passage, garnished with highfalutin' words and phrases, suffused with supercilious intellectualism, and laboriously attempted to be humorous, we can see the ears of the journalistic ass protruding through the skin of the lion of fiction.

During the summer of 1896, the All-Russian Exposition took place at the Nizhni Novgorod Fair. The concluding pages of the first volume of *Klim Samgin* (*Bystander*), written thirty years later, give a suggestive description of that imperial exhibitionism. The young tsar, Nicholas II, attended the event,

and the sight of that puny nonentity as the crowned head of more than one-half of Europe and nearly one-half of Asia, aptly symbolized one of the contradictions in Russian life that augured the inevitable explosion. Gorky wrote at the time on various aspects of the exposition, not overlooking the signs of Russia's industrialization — the triumph of the policy of Sergey Witte (later Count Witte), whose gigantic stature completely overshadowed his small blond sovereign.

Among other things, Gorky's *feuilletons* dealt with the pavilion of Russian art, and since he was expected to know everything, he did not hesitate to deliver himself of a thunderous philippic against the painter Vrubel, and in that connexion against modern tendencies in art, generally. Today Mikhail Vrubel is acknowledged as a genius whose versatility vied with his dexterity and depth. In conversation with me Gorky humbly admitted his error: " I am guilty, guilty! I have overlooked Vrubel and Gallen." In *Klim Samgin* the reporter Inokov speaks of " a certain Vrubel, a painter of great power, apparently. . . . I do not understand anything about painting, but I understand power wherever it be." But three decades previously the reporter Gorky saw in Vrubel only signs of decadence, and he hurled him, together with the Symbolist poets of the time, into the dustbin. " There is enough," he pontificated, " in life of things obscure and vague, morbid and depressing, without the fabrications of the firm of Vrubel, Balmont, Hippius, & Co. Life demands light and clarity and has not the slightest need of misty and ugly paintings and of nervously morbid verses, devoid of all sociological significance and infinitely remote from genuine art." Such was the aesthetic criterion of Gorky the critic at that time, and such it remained, basically, throughout his life. The " sociological significance " of a work of art decided its acceptance or rejection on the part of Russia's leading critics, and the same yardstick was applied by the jacks-of-all-trades in the lower limbo of the daily press.

Four years later Gorky modified his sweeping rejection of the modernists, and in reviewing the poems of Balmont and Bryusov, he praised their beauty and power, and with his wonted coarseness of expression, even defended them against those

" literary policemen who pretend to guard the legacies of true poetry, the traditions of Pushkin, and other fine things befouled by their touch, and expectorate in every direction the malodorous gall of their pedestrianism." But even though his appreciativeness expanded, he continued to look for, and discover, the primarily " sociologic significance " in whatever appealed to him in literature. Thus Rostand's *Cyrano de Bergerac* interested him as a protest against the acceptance of life as it is, and Cyrano's bellicosity served him as a text for advocating the defence of one's dignity, particularly needed in these " days of slavery and spiritual corruption." In the same way he suggested a veiled reference to conditions in Russia, when he reported on the Nizhni Novgorod presentation of Hauptmann's *Before Sunrise*. While commending the slogan of the Socialist character in the play: " My fight is a fight for universal happiness," Gorky was still Nietzschean enough at that time to regard the death of Helen without regret: " One does not feel sorry for her; he who must perish perishes, and no pity can prevent his destruction. The death of one who is incapable of living for the good of life, need not be regretted."

Chekhov's *In the Ravine* brought Gorky's warm appraisal of the story and its author. He saw the " terrific force " of Chekhov in that he never " invents," but presents actuality. Yet, unlike most of the critics who accused Chekhov of indifference, of sheer photography, Gorky credited him with a " lofty point of view," from the height of which he observed life and illuminated its boredom, its absurdities, its chaos. In his stories he felt " a sad but poignant and well-aimed reproach to people for bungling their lives," " compassion for human beings," " something simple, forceful, reconciling all and everything." It is not easy to see wherein Chekhov voices a note of reconciliation; but Gorky managed to read into him even " a note of buoyancy and love for life." It was about that very time that Leonid Andreyev, a budding Moscow *feuilletonist* signing his name " James Lynch," commented on the passing of the Chekhov mood of hopelessness and its being supplanted by a new note, the " buoyant note of Gorky." There is no doubt that as an outsider Andreyev was in a better position to

gauge the relative rôles of Chekhov and Gorky in the formation of public moods.

It is worth mentioning another subject touched by Gorky in his *feuilletons:* allegory. Though Korolenko disapproved of Gorky's addiction to this form of composition, it remained a favourite with him for many years. In his review of Olive Schreiner's tales Gorky sought to justify his own preference for the allegoric form, which enables one to " say what one wants to say with greater ease and simplicity," and to say it " schematically." One may go a bit further and suggest that Gorky's frequent employment of allegory was a matter of expediency. No other form lent itself to such a " schematic " yet popular treatment of political and philosophic questions, as one finds in *The Song of the Falcon, The Fayence Pig, The Song of the Stormy Petrel,* or *Facing Life,* where the author was hampered both by fear of the censor and by the vagueness of his own positive ideas. The leading motive of Gorky's allegories was the glorification of heroism and battle as against the security of stagnant vegetation.

In the fall of 1896, Gorky fell ill as a result of overwork, and the physicians diagnosed his case as tuberculosis of the lungs. Years of privations, of irregular shelter and insufficient food, of worry and heartache, coupled in all probability with the effect of the clumsy attempt at suicide, in 1889, finally began to undermine the extraordinary physique of the former stevedore. One of those physicians, Dr. V. N. Zolotnitsky, asserts in a recent paper that Gorky inherited his predilection for tuberculosis from his mother, and possibly also from his father (" according to his relatives, he [the father] coughed violently when he left Nizhni Novgorod for Astrakhan "). Among the circumstances which favoured the development of this ailment in his organism, he mentions a serious beating with a cudgel administered to Gorky by a bedfellow, when he worked on a Volga wharf, and the even more severe beating he courted at the village Kandybovka in attempting to protest against the lashing of an adulterous wife, of which we have already spoken. Dr. Zolotnitsky found his patient working away (" he had to! ") with a temperature of 103, his tuber-

cular condition complicated by pleurisy; at night his body was
drenched with perspiration. The case was serious, and aroused
apprehension. Yet Gorky's constitution has remained to this
day powerful enough to defy a perforated and withering lung
for nearly four decades, and to belie repeated death sentences
by specialists.

At this point Vladimir Posse appears on the stage. A young
St. Petersburg university graduate, a journalist of Marxian
leanings and with good connexions, Posse noticed two of
Gorky's stories, *Chelkash* and *Heartache,* and in the monthly
Obrazovaniye (*Cultivation*) he wrote what was the first note
on Gorky in the Russian press. He praised the stories and
ventured a guess that the author was " from the low ranks
of the people, a man who must have gone through, and who
may still be going through, the hard road of privation." " It
would be sad," he went on to say, " if the development of his
talent should be arrested because of the lack of leisure, so
necessary for earnest literary efforts." Shortly after that
Obrazovaniye received a letter for Posse from a Nizhni Novgorod physician, who confirmed his surmise about the straits
of Maxim Gorky, and advised him that the young author was
not only poor but ill with tuberculosis besides, and in urgent
need of a trip to the south of Russia, which he could not undertake for lack of funds. Posse succeeded, through his influential
brother, in having the Literary Fund, an organization for the
aid of authors, send Gorky eight hundred rubles as a loan.
He also had the review, *Novoye Slovo* (*New Word*) accept
Gorky's story, *Konovalov,* and send him the fee of one hundred and fifty rubles in advance.

Gorky was thus enabled to come early in 1897 to Crimea,
Russia's main region of health resorts. He fretted a good deal
in the uncongenial though sunny atmosphere, and in May we
find him away in the Ukraine, in the hamlet of Dr. Orlovsky
near a village in the province of Poltava. His health showed
improvement, which he ascribed to the friendly relations of
the local people and the pleasure he took in communing with
them. From among the peasants of the neighbourhood he
organized a theatrical troupe, which lived on for years, and

produced some noteworthy actors on the Ukrainian stage. It was there that Gorky wrote his sketch, *The Goltva Fair,* a hymn to the joy of life and the exuberance of Ukraine's colour. He liked the place enough to come there again in 1900, to write his first play, *Smug Citizens,* in the stillness and wholesome environment of the Poltava country, sung by Pushkin and beloved by Korolenko, who spent his last years there.

After spending the winter of 1897 in the province of Tver, with a friend who worked in the laboratories of a paper factory, Gorky returned to Nizhni Novgorod, with whose *Listok* he kept up uninterrupted relations. His return visit was roughly cut short, however. In May, 1898, his rooms were searched by the police at the request of the Tiflis Chief of Gendarmerie. Gorky was arrested and sent to Tiflis, where he was incarcerated in the Metekh Fortress. The secret archives of the Department of Police, published by Soviet investigators, provide us with curious material concerning Gorky. The " invisible thread " of the Central Spider had not let loose of the " Nizhni Novgorod burgher, member of the dyers' guild, Alexey Peshkov," from the time of his connexion with the Derenkov bakery in Kazan. Every movement of his was watched and recorded by spies, the reports piling up into an imposing heap of documents in the central Department of Police in St. Petersburg.

It seems that, back in 1892, a letter addressed from Tiflis to Pletnev, in Kazan, was intercepted by the police, who endeavoured to find its author. The letter stated: " I am working on the railroad, getting forty-three rubles a month. Yesterday they searched my room — let them! They have reduced my wages to thirty-five rubles. I conduct readings with students of the Institute and of the Seminary. I do not preach anything, but advise them to understand one another. I am also reading and conversing with the railroad workmen. There is a workman, Bogatyrovich, a fine fellow. We are close chums. He says that there is nothing good in life; but I say — there is, but it is hidden, lest every trash grab it. . . ." That was the time when Alexey was " sprinkling ideas from the watering pail of enlightenment," as he wrote

in a letter I have already quoted in the chapter on Tiflis. The police reported that the author of that letter to Pletnev was undoubtedly Alexey Peshkov, proceeding to describe him as "a very tall youth of twenty-four, cultivated, of a fine handwriting, who wears glasses and long hair," and has a wide acquaintance among the young people. Further investigation came to a stop with Peshkov's departure from Tiflis, but in 1897 his name once again engaged the police bloodhounds, in connexion with the case of a "criminal society organized to spread Social-Democratic propaganda among the working people for the purpose of arousing discontent with the existing order and governmental policy, and of overthrowing the imperial autocratic power in the more remote future." The head of this group was a certain F. E. Afanasyev, with whom five or six years previously Alexey Peshkov had lived in the "commune." The search of Afanasyev's rooms revealed among other things a photograph with the inscription: "To dear Fedya Afanasyev from Maximych." Afanasyev claimed that he had forgotten the real name of "Maximych," but the police had no difficulty in establishing his identity as that of Alexey Maximovich Peshkov. From the testimonies of various persons who attended the readings at the "commune" the police learned that Peshkov was a dangerous man, well-read and much-travelled, and that he was responsible for converting Afanasyev and other workmen to "criminal" ideas. Peshkov was arrested and brought to Tiflis, together with the enormous correspondence found in his rooms, some five hundred letters.

From the documents of the voluminous "case" it is clear that Gorky endeavoured to convince the police of his indifference to political questions. His wanderings he explained by his "very depressed state of mind that was due to his solitude and utter unfitness for life among cultivated people with their peculiar ways and notions." In another document his wanderings and depression were motivated by "an unsuccessful love affair." Though nothing criminal was found in his correspondence, and though he could not be accused of anything beyond

questionable talk to workmen, the Tiflis gendarmerie tried to create a *cause célèbre*, with Gorky as its pivot.

Again Vladimir Posse played the good fairy. A letter from Katerina Pavlovna advised him of the " terrible night " they had, when the gendarmes invaded their house at midnight, turned everything upside down in search of incriminating matter, and finally took away her husband along with all his correspondence. At the time of the arrest the Peshkovs possessed about fifty copecks in cash. Posse set out to find his well-connected brother, and discovered him opportunely at an exclusive banquet. On hearing Posse's plea his brother there and then spoke of the matter to Senator Tagantsev, member of the Imperial Council. Tagantsev, who had risen to a high position from among the peasants of Penza, promised to wire to the Tiflis prosecuting attorney his request to hasten the inquiry and free the prisoner, if possible. Posse was counselled by his brother to see also Senator Koni, an influential liberal. Koni, in his turn, promised to do all he could for the imprisoned author. Twenty years later, under the Bolsheviks, it fell to the lot of Gorky to intercede with the new Authorities for members of the erstwhile privileged class. Things move speedily in Russia. In passing we may remark that Senator Tagantsev was executed by the Bolsheviks, along with the poet, Gumilev, and other intelligentsia, as the alleged head of an anti-Soviet plot.

The intercession of the two senators must have had a magic effect on the slow and arbitrary justice of old Russia, for the case against Gorky was suddenly dropped, and he was permitted to go back to Nizhni Novgorod, there to abide under police surveillance, to be sure. The Tiflis gendarmerie was reprimanded by the state Department of Police for having made a mountain out of a molehill. Captain Konissky of the Tiflis gendarmerie was forced to send explanations and apologies. This arrest of Gorky was typical of the régime of arbitrariness before the revolution; that Captain Konissky had acted quite in tune with the Authorities is evident from the fact that, despite the reprimand, he attained the position of

Chief of Gendarmerie in St. Petersburg. Gorky himself adds a delightful touch to this drab affair in his paper on Korolenko:

Early in the spring of 1897 [1898?] I was arrested in Nizhni Novgorod and taken off, not very politely, to Tiflis. At the Metekh Fortress, Captain Konissky, while examining me, said mournfully:

"What fine letters Korolenko writes to you. And he is the best writer in Russia now!"

The captain was an odd man: small of stature, his movements were soft, cautious, as though uncertain, his monstrously large nose drooped sadly, while his brisk eyes did not seem to belong to his face, and their pupils now and then hid amusingly somewhere under the bridge of his nose.

"I am a fellow-countryman of Korolenko, also a Volynian. I am a descendant of that Bishop Konissky who made the celebrated speech to Catherine II — do you remember? 'Let us forsake the sun,' and so forth. I am proud of it!"

I inquired politely who made him feel proudest — his ancestor or his fellow-countryman.

"One as much as the other. Of course, one as much as the other!"

He drove his pupils under the bridge of his nose, but the next moment he sniffled loudly, and the pupils sprang back into their proper place. Feeling ill and therefore angry, I remarked that I failed to understand his being proud of a man whose life had been so greatly interfered with by the extravagantly polite attention of the gendarmes. Konissky retorted piously:

"Each one of us is doing the will of Him who sent us, each and every one! Let us proceed. So you maintain . . . whereas we are informed. . . ."

That was not Gorky's last encounter with the Russian police. He did not disentangle himself from the "invisible thread" till the very revolution of 1917.

Meanwhile, between attacks of lung trouble and of the over-zealous police, and along with journalistic work, Gorky continued to write, and publish, stories of an ever improving quality. After his debut in *Russkoye Bogatstvo* he had slight difficulty in having his manuscripts accepted by other leading

reviews, notably by the liberal *Russkaya Mysl,* the decadentish *Severny Vestnik (Northern Messenger),* the first Marxian monthly *Novoye Slovo,* and its successor, *Zhizn (Life).* Already such of his characteristic stories from the life of the submerged had appeared as *The Orlovs, Konovalov, Ex-Men, The Mischief Maker,* and *Malva.* The censor mutilated without mercy the aggressive text, but even then the fresh note of Gorky's writings, and the comparative novelty of his characters — ex-men! — attracted the attention of the reading public. Though describing misery and penury, he voiced an affirmation of life and a challenge to mould and shape life, new motives in Russian literature of the time, the Chekhov period. The Marxian *Novoye Slovo* was aware of Gorky's importance for the awakening of society, and on the receipt of his *Ex-Men,* the editors wrote to him:

The editors send you their profoundest gratitude for the manuscript just received. At this moment there are in our literature so few talented writers who may influence the reader with the truthfulness and depth of their images that one can easily understand how valuable and desirable for the *Novoye Slovo* is your regular co-operation. Your *Konovalov,* even in its form after the outrageous operation performed over it [by the censor], still produces a powerful and complete impression on thousands of readers.

Curiously enough, Posse had a hard time in persuading Gorky to write for *Novoye Slovo.* Apparently Gorky was still wavering between the *narodniks* and the Marxians, with his heart beating more warmly for the heroics of the former. In an early letter to Posse he wrote that in his opinion Marxism " lowered one's individuality," and urged Posse not to join the " counsel of the wicked." Still Gorky let the Marxians have his *Konovalov,* and shortly after the suspension of *Novoye Slovo,* in December, 1897, he felt enough sympathy for them to enter the editorial board of the next Marxian venture, the monthly *Zhizn.*

As yet Gorky felt dissatisfied with his writings — at least he stated so. In 1897, S. A. Vengerov, the indefatigable chroni-

cler of Russian literature and collector of autobiographies, wrote to Gorky, at the suggestion of Korolenko and his friends, for his autobiography and " his works." Gorky, recommended to Vengerov as a " self-taught writer " of " quite an uneven talent," sent in a brief autobiography, but at the end of it he wrote: " Thus far I have not written a single thing to my own satisfaction, and for that reason I have not preserved my writings: *Ergo* I am unable to send them to you." Note the bookish *ergo* of the erstwhile stevedore.

In January, 1898, one of the ex-editors of *Novoye Slovo* wrote to Gorky:

It is about time for you to publish a collection of your stories. Surely you can find more than enough for a volume the size of a volume of stories by Garshin or Chekhov. The moment is propitious. There is a decided interest in you: readers are hunting for your stories in old magazine issues, and your fellow-writers begin to speak of you with circumspection. . . . The readers need the volume, and you — the money. It is high time.

Gorky knew the truth of the last statement very well. His lungs had laid him low the preceding autumn, he needed money for a trip to Crimea, while the fees he had been eking out for his daily contributions and even for his occasional stories in the " big " reviews barely sufficed to cover the ordinary expenses of his family life. He began to negotiate about a publisher. Posse received from him a package of newspaper clippings containing his stories, with the request to find a publisher and obtain from him an advance for his trip to Crimea. Posse, who, in his own words, " was greatly infatuated with the talent of this scarcely known writer," approached a number of publishers with the suggestion to publish a volume of Gorky's stories. It proved to be a difficult task. The name of Gorky meant little as yet, and had no commercial value. Even in his native Nizhni Novgorod his talent was appraised with considerable reserve, typified in the answer of a local authority to an inquiry of S. A. Vengerov: " He has talent, though there is no doubt that nothing big will ever come out of it." Posse had managed to

obtain the consent of two separate publishers, but both of them changed their minds after due consideration. Thus Mme. O. N. Popov, who had agreed to publish two volumes of Gorky's stories and to send the author five hundred rubles in advance, withdrew her consent, under the pretext that she had undertaken several big publications, among them the works of Charles Darwin. She added privately that her firm found it " inconvenient to publish provincial *feuilletons* " and that even the stories of Ivan Bunin, " who was incomparably more talented than Gorky," had no sales.

The kind-hearted Posse suffered refusal after refusal, and was made the butt of jokes because of his infatuation with Gorky. The publishers rejected his offer as unprofitable from the business point of view. The ailing Gorky wrote Posse a letter of despair, and when Posse had almost given up hope, he happened to come in contact with two idealists who decided to take a risk on Gorky. They were S. P. Dorovatovsky and A. P. Charushnikov, active revolutionists during the eighteen seventies and eighties, who had preserved enough radicalism to sense the rebellious note in Gorky. The impractical idealists proved more perspicacious than the experienced veterans of the publishing game.

In March, 1898, the two volumes of Gorky's *Sketches and Stories* were off the press, each volume in the amount of thirty-five hundred copies. At first it was hard to get retail booksellers to buy the books, even on a commission basis. Such big stores as that of Suvorin demanded a rebate of 50%. Suvorin, by the way, had refused to publish Gorky. He was editor and publisher of the most important Russian daily, *Novoye Vremya* (*New Time*), an unscrupulous reactionary paper, and also owner of a theatre, a large bookstore, and a publishing house. His influence on the conservative elements was enormous, and his paper persistently attacked Gorky as an author and as a rebel. Whether Suvorin's reluctance to gamble on Gorky was due to ideologic or commercial motives, is immaterial.

The venture of the radical publishers proved a success. Within a year the two volumes appeared in a second edition, simultaneously with a third volume of *Sketches and Stories,*

and by the summer of 1900 they were sold out completely. According to S. A. Vengerov, " for the first time in the history of the Russian book trade, Gorky's volumes began to sell in tens of thousands of copies, reaching before long the colossal figure of 100,000." One must remember the small number of literates in Russia at that time, and also the fact that each copy was read by at least five persons.

From Dorovatovsky's recent statement we learn that Gorky received one thousand rubles for the first edition of both volumes, one thousand for the second edition, and eight hundred rubles for the first edition of the third volume. We need not trace the growth of Gorky's income after that, but the initial " enrichment " of the struggling writer was truly spectacular. A Nizhni Novgorod neighbour tells us of the day when Gorky received his first fee from the publishers. He seemed more surprised than pleased, as he came to the neighbour's mother, and stood before her with his legs wide apart, his bass booming: " Look here, they gave me a whole thousand, devil take it! " He looked at his palm, as though it had the money in it, and continued to wonder: " They gave me a thousand. What for? " The neighbour adds what has been known universally; namely, that from that moment Gorky began to squander his money lavishly on a variety of things that did not concern his personal pleasure.

In money matters Gorky has been as innocent as a babe, and to this day he depends on others to take care of his financial affairs. That these " others " have not always been dependable, need hardly be said. Gorky has never been able to refuse a request for money or for help in any form, such as intercession with people of authority, and this softness has cost him much time and energy. His readiness was especially prompt when the request concerned such a cause as homeless children or poor students or the revolutionary movement.

And so, in 1898, at the age of thirty, Alexey Peshkov had no further doubts or vacillations as to his road in life: he was to march on as Maxim Gorky. The two volumes of his stories, eagerly bought by the public and seriously received by the critics, had placed him definitively among Russia's writers, a

position of which Alexey the labourer and the tramp had hardly dared dream in his most fantastic reveries. Even two or three years previously he was not quite certain of his vocation, and at times regarded his writings as primarily a means of livelihood, more genteel though not necessarily more remunerative a means than hauling sacks of flour at the wharf. He could not have conceived of anything more miraculous than actually becoming one of those very creators of books who filled him with wonder and hope during the most depressing moments of his life. Now all barriers and doubts were left behind: he was an author, a Russian author, the nobility of whose calling was equalled only by its obligations and responsibilities. Smury-Lanin-Kalyuzhny-Korolenko, these four men Gorky proclaimed as his guides and teachers, who had implanted in him a love for books. He might have mentioned also his grandmother, who taught him to dream and to live eagerly and uncomplainingly. And what of Queen Margot, whose aristocratic beauty had burned into the heart of the " monstrosity " of a boy, and made him fastidious and ambitious amidst the drabness and filth of the Lower Depths?

SUCCESS AND FAME

THE swiftness with which Gorky's fame and popularity spread has hardly any precedent or parallel. Within one year after the publication of his first two volumes, the name of Gorky became known throughout Russia, bordering on notoriety. Everywhere one could see his picture — on postal cards, cigarette- and candy-boxes, and in endless cartoons. Shady characters stopped citizens in the street and asked for, or rather demanded, " a bottle of vodka in the name of Maxim Gorky." Some of these tramps went further, and requested money " for a revolver against the scoundrels, our ministers," also in the name of Gorky, the alleged patron of hoboes and rebels. In various cities there even appeared pseudo-Gorkys, who posed as the original and tried to make use of his popularity. Gorky's costume — a Russian blouse and high boots, became the vogue, and even society ladies considered it fashionable to lisp French phrases concerning those charming *bosyaks*. The word *bosyak* means barefooted, and is broadly applied to signify one of the social riff-raff.

One can hardly doubt that the initial popularity of Gorky was due not only to the quality of his stories, but in a large measure to their subject-matter and to the author's biography. There was a touch of the sensational, if not scandalous, about the introduction into the exclusive salon of Russian letters of the *bosyaks* — not merely as unfortunates to arouse our pity, but as pugnacious individuals, lustily proclaiming their contempt for smug respectability. The additional information that the author himself had only recently risen from the ranks of

the fifth estate, intensified public curiosity. There had been before Gorky two or three writers who described the scum of society, but they had done it with condescending pity, or in the tone of a denunciatory sermon. The tone of Gorky had the challenge of a spokesman, not a denouncer of the submerged elements. " I have come from below," says one of his characters (in the unfinished *Muzhik*), " from the bottom of life, where filth and murk prevail. . . . I am the truthful voice of life, the husky voice of those who have stayed down there, below, and have sent me to testify about their vicissitudes."

The majority of the literary critics received Gorky favourably. I have already mentioned the fact that the word " literary " did not often apply to Russia's critics, who appraised a writer primarily and chiefly for his social message. In the case of Gorky, his " message " pleased everybody. The *narodnik* critics found in his tramps a demonstration of the degenerating effect of city civilization upon the children of the soil, and drew the triumphant conclusion that Russia must remain rustic and agricultural and shun industrialization. The Marxians gleefully pointed out the superior intelligence of Gorky's tramps, their alertness and freedom from stale traditions and conventions, ascribing these virtues to the influence of the city which rapidly transformed the stolid peasant into a nimble proletarian: hence — Russia must be urbanized. In the conservative press Gorky was thanked for having shown the beastly face of the *Lumpenproletariat*, which they confused with the proletariat, and proceeded to argue for the necessity of treating the masses with " porcupine gloves " for the good of their souls. Most astounding, in Prince Meshchersky's *Grazhdanin* (*Citizen*), organ of the most reactionary court circles, a certain Count burst into a sentimental rhapsody concerning our rebellious commoner: " Mr. Gorky presents the only case, heretofore unknown in Russia in the person of an artist, of an *apostle of love for man,* and this lofty mission will certainly sooner or later be recorded to his credit, as a great factor in Russia's spiritual enlightenment and salutariness. . . . For such a missionary of the literary profession as Maxim Gorky we need an adequate sculptor-critic who would crown his brow with laurels and place him

before the people on a suitable pedestal, thus erecting during his lifetime a worthy monument for the powerful and brilliant Russian toiler in *belles-lettres*." This turgid quotation is typical of the tastes among the highest Russian aristocracy, and is indicative of the extent of Gorky's vogue.

All the leading Russian critics spoke of the new writer with serious consideration. N. K. Mikhaylovsky wrote several articles on Gorky in his review, *Russkoye Bogatstvo*, this in itself being a token of recognition. The veteran *narodnik* sensed in Gorky an enemy of the idealized village, but despite this bias he analysed his stories with keen objectivity. He concluded his essay with the statement that in Gorky we have " a great artistic force," after having criticised adversely the author's aptness to philosophize too much and vaguely, and his occasional lapse into flowery language. Mikhaylovsky hated the Decadents and Symbolists, and he suspected in Gorky a leaning in that direction. He quoted one of the characters in *A Mistake*: " The Decadents are subtle. Subtle and sharp like needles, they thrust themselves deeply into the unknown." This alarmed Mikhaylovsky more than Gorky's other faults. At the same time he pointed out to the excellencies in *The Goltva Fair* and *Out of Boredom,* stories that have no tramps in them and which have for that reason been overlooked by other critics.

It is worth noting that N. Minsky, a leader in the so-called Decadent movement that developed into the significant Symbolist current of literature, reviewed Gorky's stories rather tolerantly. He took exception to the young author's exaggerations and loudness, and questioned the probability of south-Russian tramps echoing Nietzsche and Ibsen, but at the end of his article, " The Philosophy of Yearning and the Thirst after Freedom," he asserted that Gorky appeared to him to be " a serious literary phenomenon, if only because the young author had dared to look at life independently, minus those blinkers with which various invited and uninvited teachers and mentors so zealously endeavour to limit the horizon of Russia's intelligentsia. There is much daring in Gorky's designs, and one wishes to believe that this daring is a sign of unusual strength."

Radical anti-*narodnik* critics like Vladimir Posse, the enthusiast who finally succeeded in finding a publisher for Gorky's stories, or like Angel Bogdanovich, editor of the nearly Marxian review, *Mir Bozhy* (*God's World*), emphasized the novel, urban motives in Gorky's writings. Posse, who knew of Gorky's personal circumstances, pointed out that the young author " wrote with his heart's blood," that he was " a vivifying protest against the tedium and peace of Russia's communal-village life . . . a reaction against Slavic amorphousness, softness, and docility," and he ended with a note of hope in Gorky's creative future — " if he only had enough vigour and health! " Bogdanovich called attention to " the new and unexpected " in Gorky's depiction of the tramps, and concluded his review with the statement that " Most of Gorky's stories breathe the freedom of steppe and sea, one feels in them a buoyant mood, which distinguishes them sharply from the stories of other authors who have touched on the same world of beggars and outcasts. This mood is transmitted also to the reader, which lends Gorky's stories the charm of freshness, novelty, and vital truthfulness."

As against the numerous praises, which were often extravagant and irrelevant (Prince Vladimir Baryatinsky compared Gorky to Lomonosov, in an article in *Severny Courier*), the first volumes of Gorky received also a certain amount of adverse criticism. He was accused of condoning and even championing hooliganism and lawlessness. Even such an earnest liberal review as *Russkaya Mysl* had an article by M. A. Protopopov, who reproached Gorky for " praising drunkenness," gravely reminding him that drunkenness is worse than robbery. The most serious unfavourable critique was written by a pillar of Suvorin's *Novoye Vremya*, M. Menshikov, under the title " Pretty Cynicism." Like Mikhaylovsky, he noticed the Nietzchean outlook of Gorky's characters, and he accused the author of deliberately prettifying vice and ridiculing accepted morality. " In contrast to the *narodnik* writers of the eighteen sixties, who sought for the man in the beast, Mr. Gorky eagerly looks for the beast in man, and on finding it he triumphs strangely and sadly. If the beast is good-looking, strong,

young, unemotional, the author's sympathies are on the side of the beast." Aside from this obvious reference to the ethically vulnerable aspect of the early Gorky, Menshikov must be credited with a few keen observations. To him Gorky's past, his toil and poverty, gave no cause for rejoicing and admiration. On the contrary, had he been born in a well-to-do and cultured family, he would have had better taste, and would not have been forced to write so much and so unevenly. Menshikov was quite right in suggesting that Gorky's volumes contained poor stories, whose inclusion was probably due to " material want, the temptation of popularity, importunity of the publishers, a low self-appraisal — roughly speaking, to a lack of taste — a thing that requires special cultivation." In such stories as *Old Woman Izergil* or *Makar Chudra,* Gorky abused the " economy of emotions," and in such as *About the Devil* or *A Reader,* the " economy of ideas." Menshikov considered among Gorky's weaknesses his bookish education, which blighted the freshness and originality of his talent: " all his merits were inherently his own, all his faults he has acquired in educated circles." These " educated circles," the intelligentsia, Menshikov regarded just as un-national, as different and divorced from the real Russian people, as Gorky's tramps. Hence Gorky, both in his bookishness and in his portrayal of the tramps, must not pass as a son of the people, nor must his voice be accepted as the voice of the people. " Yet," concluded Menshikov, " that voice deserves to be listened to."

I have quoted a few representative critics not so much for the value of their opinions as because they reflected the variety of public attitudes toward Gorky. The effect of the critiques on Gorky's talent was probably *nil ;* he was most likely in sympathy with Chekhov whom he quoted as saying: " Critics are like horse-flies which prevent the horse from plowing. . . . For twenty-five years I have read criticisms of my stories, and I don't remember a single remark of any value or one word of valuable advice. Only once Skabichevsky wrote something which made an impression on me . . . he said I would die in a ditch, drunk." Incidentally, this Skabichevsky, a verbose and shallow tester and appraiser from the " radical " point of view,

treated Gorky kindly from the start, and wrote about him long and tedious articles.

That Gorky was in need of advice and criticism at the beginning of his career, is patent. His sudden transition from manual toil to the writing profession was felt in his early works — in the lack of ripeness and sureness of technique. He had much to say, but he had had no training in composition. Exaggeration and gaudiness, what Menshikov aptly called the lack of economy in emotion and thought, were some of the most conspicuous shortcomings of the beginning writer, exuberant and surcharged with ideas and impressions but as yet too timid to express himself simply and directly. Gorky was fortunate in having two friendly critics at this tender and susceptible stage — Korolenko and Chekhov. We have already seen Korolenko's genially severe treatment of the young man's digressions into versification, allegories, and romanticism. Chekhov, a superior and more fastidious artist than Korolenko, but more retiring and indifferent to his fellow-men and fellow-writers, came to Gorky's help only because of the latter's request. In November, 1898, Gorky sent Chekhov his books and a letter, on December 3, Chekhov wrote back, and thus there began a correspondence and friendship that ended all too soon for the younger writer with Chekhov's death, in 1904. Chekhov's first letter is characteristic of his gentleness and keen judgement, delicately and subtly combined. Most of it follows:

You ask for my opinion of your stories. My opinion? An unquestionable talent, and a real, a great talent at that. In the story *In the Steppe,* for instance, there is so much power that I even became envious that I was not its author. You are an artist, a clear-eyed man; you feel keenly, you are plastic, i.e., when you picture a thing, you see and feel it with your hand. This is real art. . . .

Shall I now speak of your defects? This is not so easy. To speak of the defects of a man of talent is the same as to speak of the defects of a big tree that grows in the garden; the main reality here is not in the tree but in the emotion aroused in him who looks at the tree. Isn't it so?

I shall begin by saying that you, in my opinion, have no

self-restraint. You are like the spectator in a theatre who expresses his delight so unreservedly that it prevents himself and others from listening. This lack of self-restraint is especially evident in the descriptions of nature with which you interrupt the dialogue; as one reads these descriptions one wishes that they were more compact, shorter, say about two or three lines or so. The frequent mention of ' softness,' ' whisper,' ' velvety smoothness,' etc., impart to these descriptions a certain floridness, monotony — they cool one's ardour and almost tire one. The lack of self-restraint is felt also in the portrayal of women (*Malva; On a Raft*), and of love scenes. It is not a free swing, a broadness of the brush, but precisely the lack of self-restraint. Then, too, there is a frequent use of words entirely out of place in stories of your type. " Accompaniment," " disks," " harmony " — such words are disturbing. In your delineation of the intelligentsia there is something forced, as if you felt a sense of uncertainty. This is due not to lack of study of the intelligentsia; you know them, but it seems as if you do not know from what angle to approach them. . . .

The early Gorky, as we have already seen in the case of his relations with Korolenko, was supersensitive to criticism. He must have taken Chekhov's remarks peevishly, for in his next letter Chekhov endeavoured to explain that he did not accuse his correspondent of " coarseness," but of using needlessly foreign words, which in Gorky's stories seemed incongruous and " jarred fearfully." " Of course," he added, " it is a question of taste, and perhaps this is only a sign of excessive fastidiousness in me." Evidently aware of Gorky's uneasiness because of his lack of education, Chekhov assured him that in his stories he appeared as " an ' educated ' man in the truest sense." Then he proceeded to mingle honey with vinegar :

Nothing is less characteristic of you than coarseness; you are clever and subtle and delicate in your feelings. Your best things are *In the Steppe* and *On a Raft* — did I write to you about that? They are splendid things, masterpieces; they show an artist who has passed through a very good school. I don't think that I am mistaken. The only defect is the lack of restraint, the lack of grace. When a man spends the least

possible number of movements over some definite action, that is grace. One is conscious of superfluity in your expenditure.

The descriptions of nature are the work of an artist; you are a real landscape painter. Only the frequent personification (anthropomorphism) when the sea breathes, the sky gazes, the steppe barks, nature whispers, speaks, mourns, and so on, — such metaphors make your descriptions somewhat monotonous, sometimes sweetish, sometimes not clear; beauty and expressiveness in nature are attained only by simplicity, by such simple phrases as " The sun set," " It was dark," " It began to rain," and so on — and that simplicity is characteristic of you in the highest degree, more so perhaps than of any writer. . . .

By constantly assuring Gorky of his merits, Chekhov apparently hoped to bring these merits to the surface, if they were latent in him. That he did believe in Gorky's talent is evident from his letters to Suvorin and others, written about the same time, in which he urges them to read *In the Steppe* and *On a Raft*, labelling the former story " wonderful work," " a model," " an ace." He took the trouble to write to Gorky an especial letter to tell him that he had just read *The Goltva Fair* and " liked it very much." In March, 1899, Gorky came to Crimea for a few weeks, and the two consumptives met in person. Chekhov wrote to a friend: " Gorky is in Yalta. In outward appearance he is a tramp, but inside he is a man of taste — and I am glad. I want to introduce him to women, believing that they will be useful to him, but he bristles up, like a porcupine."

His friendship and solicitude became ever warmer. He urged Gorky to leave the provincial Nizhni Novgorod, and move to Moscow or St. Petersburg, where the literary atmosphere would be beneficial to him. Chekhov did not seem to relish Gorky's outlandishness and deliberately democratic exterior; it must have annoyed him, as everything " ultra-Russian " did. In 1901 Chekhov was in Tiflis, and conversed with Kalyuzhny, Gorky's literary godfather, about the latter's talent. " It is high time for Alexey Maximovich to don a frock-coat," said Chekhov, to the indignation of Kalyuzhny, who

insisted that the Russian blouse suited Gorky best, keeping
him in touch with the native source from which he drew
" handfuls of material and bright colours." When in Moscow,
Chekhov tried to entice Gorky to come there by all sorts of
inducements, such as a ticket for the private performance of
Uncle Vanya and a joint visit to Tolstoy.

In answer to Gorky's request for permission to dedicate to
him his forthcoming first novel, *Foma Gordeyev,* Chekhov
wrote that he was against dedications to living people, but that
this dedication gave him " great pleasure and honour." He then
proceeded to give him practical advice about the publisher,
and about cutting out dispensable words, " a host of concrete
nouns," when reading the proofs:

You have so many qualifications that the reader's mind
finds it a task to concentrate on them, and he soon grows tired.
You understand it at once when I say: " A man sat on the
grass " ; you understand it because it is clear and makes no
demands on the attention. On the other hand, it is not easily
understood and it is difficult for the brain when I write: " A
tall, narrow-chested, middle-sized man, with a red beard sat
down on the green grass, already trampled by pedestrians, sat
down silently, shyly, and looked around him timidly." That
does not settle down in the brain at once, and good fiction
should settle down at once, in a second.

One who has read Gorky's early stories will readily see that
Chekhov hit on the soft spot of the beginning writer — his lack
of simplicity. Gorky was aware of his failing. Already Korolenko had chastised him for his employment of words and
phrases which he would not think of using in conversation;
anything pretentious and elaborate ill fitted his robust and
straightforward personality. Even before Chekhov's gentle " advice," Gorky began to weed out unnecessary words in his
stories, and to replace foreign and bookish words with their
native and common equivalents.

While reading the proofs of the first edition of his books, he
cut unsparingly. In the proofs of *Konovalov,* for example,
which have been preserved by the son of his first publisher,
Dorovatovsky, we find the author's corrections nearly on every

page, all in the direction of simplification. Fewer adjectives
and adverbs, the toning down of loud attributes, and such
substitutions as " my listeners " for " my auditorium,"
" beauty " for " poesy," " openly " for " demonstratively," " in
such words " for " approximately in such a style," " through
towns and villages " for " through Holy Russia." He was paying the penalty for having read too many books to the detriment of his inborn directness and unornamented vitality of
style. The ailment had settled rather deeply, if Chekhov could
diagnose its persistent symptoms for a long time yet. In a
letter dated January 2, 1900, after praising Gorky's *My Travelling Companion* (he compares its strength with that of *In the
Steppe*), Chekhov tells him mildly what, in effect, Menshikov
had put rudely: " If I were you, I should take the best things
out of your three volumes and republish them in one volume
. . . and that would be something really remarkable for vigour
and harmony. As it is, everything seems shaken up together in
the three volumes; there are no weak things, but one gets the
impression as though the three volumes were not the work of
one man but of seven."

No one was more conscious than Gorky of the importance
of an author's rôle, especially in Russia, where the author was
the only citizen permitted to speak publicly, in however veiled
and censored a manner. The imperfections of his composition
worried him not so much as the contents of his stories — their
purpose and social value. He could not help demanding of himself that which he preached to others, in his critical *feuilletons*.
" The rôle of art is a pedagogic one," he wrote in the *Nizhegorodsky Listok* at the time of the Fair, in 1896. During the heated
polemic which his remarks on Vrubel's paintings aroused in
the press, Gorky asked concerning the modern schools of
painting and poetry: " What relation can have the paintings
of Vrubel and Gallen, the poetry of Hippius and Balmont, and
in general all the things that are being done in the field of art
by people who seek the non-existent and who yearn ' beyond
the confines of the finite,' what relation can they have with
social values, with real art whose purpose is the education of
man's mind and emotions, and the ennoblement of life? "

In that very year of 1898, when his profession as a writer became definite and irretrievable, he wrote a lyrical allegory, *A Reader*. It presents Gorky's literary profession of faith, which he has consistently maintained to this day. Were it not for its length I should be tempted to reproduce the sketch whole, so characteristic is it of the young author's outlook and aspirations. The mysterious " reader," who encounters Gorky one night after he has read a story to a circle of admirers, is his conscience — a merciless, sarcastic interlocutor. At first the author feels annoyed by the uninvited companion who has the impudence to quiz him on his aims and tendencies, and is about to turn his back on him, but is warned: " If you leave me now we shall never meet again." The word " never " sounded like " the toll of a funeral bell," and it made him stop and listen to the stranger's long queries or rather soliloquies. He assented to the Reader's definition of the aim of literature as " the ennoblement of man." Literature must " help man understand himself, rouse his faith in himself and make him strive for truth, wage war against vulgarity in men, discover what is good in men, provoke in their minds shame, wrath, courage, and do everything that may make them nobly strong and capable of imbuing their life with the holy spirit of beauty." Granted this lofty aim of literature, the writer must answer the question whether he is in a position to serve it adequately. The impertinent Reader whistled a familiar tune, which the author recognized as that of a song about a blind man who undertook to lead a multitude of blind. " How can you be a guide, when you are not acquainted with the road," were some of the words of that song.

Leadership, guidance — that was the traditional purpose of literature in Russia, where it served as the main outlet of the nation's mind, its aspirations, grievances, doubts. A writer without such a purpose was regarded as anomalous, an unnecessary luxury (Mikhaylovsky upbraiding Chekhov for " wasting " his fine talent). Gorky could not be satisfied with writing for the pleasure of self-expression, as a relief for his creative urge. He must teach and guide. And when the Reader

demanded to know whether he had the right to teach, whether he could name his God, he had to hang his head:

For the first time in my life I gazed so attentively into my depths. Do not imagine that I am elevating or debasing myself in order to attract people's attention: one does not ask beggars for alms. I discovered in myself not a few kind feelings and desires, not a little of what people are wont to label as good, but I failed to find in myself an emotion that would unify all that, a sure and clear thought that would embrace all life's phenomena. . . .

Again we face Gorky's frantic and futile effort at finding a formula, an all-uniting and all-embracing emotion or idea. Lacking this, how can he presume to teach, hence to write? The Reader, who compliments him on having the courage to listen to him, that is, to his conscience, harangues him without mercy for his weakness and lack-lustre. He speaks of the great writers whose books will never be " touched by oblivion," because they contain " eternal truths " and " imperishable beauty." He tells Gorky that though he has drawn from those writers " food for his soul," his soul seems undernourished; his words about truth and beauty sound false and laboured. His light is dull and cold, like that of the moon which reflects a light not of its own.

Beneath the turgidity of this effusion we may discern the misgivings of the young writer as to his fitness for the high mission of an author. He is aware of his indebtedness to books, but he also feels that he has not digested them properly, and above all, that he has not succeeded as yet in reconciling his bookish wisdom with the experience he has drawn from life. His conscience tells him that it is not enough to follow the example of other Russian writers, big and small, and to expose the seamy side of existence only. He feels that by constantly harping on man's weakness, wickedness, stupidity, and his helplessness against circumstances, the writer destroys in man all hope in the possibility of being different. The Reader doubts whether his, Gorky's, portrayal of life can arouse in man " a

vindictive shame and an ardent desire to create different forms of living "; whether he is capable of " accelerating the beating of life's pulse, of instilling energy into it," whether he can arouse in people " sincere emotions, with which as with hammers they should smash and destroy life's strait forms and create in their place other, freer forms," whether, finally, he is in a position to provoke " joyous, soul-cleansing laughter."

The majority of Russian writers followed Gogol in depicting the negative traits of the nation. Gogol felt uneasy about his one-sided power of observation — his grim laughter at the foibles of his countrymen he called " laughter through tears " — and he exerted himself to counteract his evil characters by the creation of a gallery of good and noble Russians. We know how utterly he failed in his effort, how feeble, vapid, and flaccid his " good " men and women appeared in his much-burned and rewritten second part of *Dead Souls*. We also know how the craving to be patriotic and violate his talent broke Gogol's spirit and body and drove him into the grave at the age of forty-three.

When Gorky appeared on the stage, the Chekhov mood of winglessness prevailed in literature, whereas life was showing symptoms of awakening among the Russian people. The famine of 1890–1891 had roused the thinking part of society to the realization of the country's backwardness and the need of overthrowing the obsolete Autocracy. The rapid industrialization of the country, fostered by the policy of Sergey Witte, brought about the increase of factory workmen, an inflammable element, and simultaneously the spread of Marxian Socialism and of its protagonists, who made use of the inflammable element. Life was bursting its " strait forms." Gorky felt the need of responding to the new moods and the fresh demands, but the life he knew and could portray did not seem to possess any comforting features, anything to provoke " joyous laughter." Like Gogol, he deplored his " one-sidedness," and from time to time attempted to atone for his dark canvases and present radiant Russians, made-to-order fine men and women. As we shall see in the case of *Mother,* his success in this attempt was partial, if any. What the young writer failed to realize is that he need not have bothered about his fitness

for the high mission. Like Gogol, he was of the greatest service to his country, to mankind, to literature, when he followed the dictates of his talent and presented life as he saw it. Both of them pilloried man's petty vices and both aroused in the reader "vindictive shame," with the difference that Gogol's aloof laughter suggested neither sympathy nor hope, while in Gorky's gloom one sensed a heartfelt compassion and a challenge to smash and destroy life's "strait forms."

Young Gorky, in *A Reader* at all events, sounded quite melancholy, doubtful, and diffident. He was not even sure whether he "loved men," when the Reader inquired about it, yet love for one's neighbour was a trait taken for granted in a Russian writer, the champion of the "humiliated and offended." Instead of giving a direct answer to this question he mused: "One who watches himself carefully will ponder a long time before he will make bold to say: I love men. Everybody knows how remote from each one of us is our neighbour." He was uncertain as to the road he was to indicate for his readers to follow, as these expected him to do. "One thing I know: it is not happiness we ought to aspire for. . . . The sense of life is not in happiness, and man shall not be satisfied with self-contentment: he is above that, after all. The sense of life consists in the beauty and power of striving after goals, and one must try to make every moment have its own high goal. That might be possible, but not within the old confines of life, so tight and narrow, with no room for man's spirit."

This suggested a road and a doctrine! But the young author did not have the temerity to voice his musings aloud. He remained silent, and the Reader departed. "'Already?' I asked softly. However terrible he was for me, it was even more terrible to face myself, alone. 'Yes, I am going. . . . But I shall yet visit you, more than once. Expect me!'"

Despite Chekhov's repeated urgings to settle in one of the capitals, St. Petersburg or Moscow, Gorky clung to his native city till the end of 1904, with occasional trips to other places. His childhood and youth had been stamped with Nizhni Novgorod impressions, and it must have meant much to him to

have risen from the lower depths to the position of an important figure in the very same city. Aside from his work on the *Nizhegorodsky Listok,* Gorky took an active part, and often the initiative, in whatever local social undertakings the existing régime permitted. He readily co-operated in organizing help for the local youths who studied in various universities and came home for the Christmas and summer vacations. Recalling his own vain ambition to enter a university, he sympathized with those who defied poverty and a low social status and donned the coveted blue and green uniform of Russian universities, or that of technical colleges. A considerable portion of Russia's students was always active in the revolutionary movement, and especially after 1898, students joined workmen in forming the vanguard of the movement. Naturally, this appealed to Gorky and enhanced his eagerness to help the students.

Another of his " hobbies " was children. Mindful of his own childhood, he did his utmost to better the conditions of poor children at home and in school. Once a year he organized a Christmas Tree celebration for children of the poor, particularly for the homeless ones, gathering as many as one thousand of them in the large halls of the Nizhni Novgorod kremlin. Gorky had his wealthy friends from among the merchants donate goodly quantities of food and wearing apparel for the occasion. Katerina Pavlovna sewed shirts and blouses from donated dry-goods, and helped in other ways to make the celebration a success. The ragged tots were cheered by the genial bass of their host, by the unheard-of goodies, by the warm clothes they were given, and especially by the brand-new felt boots that were to protect many a pair of frost-bitten purple feet. The organizers were somewhat uneasy as to the possible conduct of the Kanavino boys, denizens of the evil district, who were proficient in fist-fights and in the more gentle art of picking pockets. But the loyalty of the Kanavinites to the host, their erstwhile fellow-citizen, saved the situation, and all went off peacefully and with tolerable decorum.

Gorky's local patriotism was shown also in the numerous gifts he presented to the Nizhni Novgorod Museum, among

these being paintings by such prominent painters of the time as Vasnetzov, Makovsky, Levitan and others. He was instrumental in the establishment of various public institutions, such as dormitories and a People's Palace. The public library had set aside a special section of the books donated by Gorky while sojourning in the city. A list of these books (681 volumes in all), recently made public, includes Nietzsche's *Zarathustra,* James's *Psychology,* works by Darwin, Reclus, Buyot, and other foreign and Russian tomes over which the omnivorous Gorky pored during those years, before passing them on to the library. His passion for books never abated, and he importuned his early publishers with numerous requests for the purchase of volumes and sets, authorizing them to pay sums that were rather extravagant for his income at the time.

The unprecedented, for a beginning author, success of his first volumes brought him considerable money, but not enough to cover his extraordinary expenditures. What with medical treatment and trips to the Crimea, the Ukraine and other places, what with purchases and gifts of paintings and books, and his all too ready response to all sorts of requests for aid, his budget rose prodigiously, and his publishers were taxed with the constantly demanded advances. His house was furnished expensively, with much concern for aesthetic values. Unlike Tolstoy and Korolenko, whose studies were rigoristically simple, Gorky spared nothing to surround himself with things of beauty, for which he had starved so many years. His hospitality was of the truly Russian broadness. Contemporaries tell us that " from morning till evening the most variegated public filled his residence. At the dinner table there were always present, besides Alexey Maximovich and his family, a dozen or fifteen outsiders, some of whom the host did not know even by name. The house was known for its lavish hospitality and the cordial attitude of the host and the charming hostess, Katerina Pavlovna." Others recall that if not for Katerina Pavlovna's strenuous efforts to keep the visitors away from her husband's study, Gorky would have had no chance to write a line.

Gorky's home at Nizhni Novgorod became a Mecca for

admirers and curiosity seekers. Idlers would stroll by or stand opposite the windows, in the hope of catching a glimpse of the much photographed long-haired, big-nosed, black-bloused Maxim Gorky, or of some of his celebrated visitors. Not infrequently the bass of Chaliapin rolled across the street through the open windows, rousing the wild applause of the uninvited enthusiasts. One of these, now an orthodox Bolshevik, asks caustically: " Well, now, let Chaliapin say whether that applause was not better than the one he is getting now from the American mushroom-millionaires bloated with postwar fat."

Vladimir Posse tells a characteristic anecdote of Gorky at that time. Always on the lookout for Man, he discovered a " second Chaliapin " in a Tatar stevedore, and decided to pull him up to the Imperial Conservatory. It occurred to him that as a singer in the cathedral choir the Tatar would have a better chance than as a stevedore. He persuaded him to accept Christianity, and in order to hasten matters he went to the Archbishop to plead for a prompt conversion of the Mohamedan. Now Gorky to this day often uses in conversation the phrase *chort vozmi,* which means " devil take it." He let the phrase slip his tongue while petitioning the Archbishop. The latter remarked: " I must ask you not to express yourself in this manner in my presence." Gorky: " Forgive me, Your Holiness! It is, *chort vozmi,* a habit with me." " In that case keep your habit and your Tatar. We are in no need of dubious and counterfeit adherents." " You are quite right, *chort vozmi.* You have enough of these as it is."

Posse was one of the first " celebrities " to come down to Nizhni Novgorod and pay homage to the object of his literary " infatuation." In his recently published memoirs he recalls with delight meeting the red-moustachioed, slightly stooping, low-voiced Maxim Gorky, and his wife, " an attractive brunette that looked like a high-school girl, though she was already the mother of a sizeable yearling who greatly resembled his father." He describes Gorky's residence, spacious, disorderly, haphazardly furnished. The host's tastes had apparently not settled yet. One room in the house Posse found occupied by songsters;

they flew from their cages and perched on the shoulders of their master. The bird-catcher in Gorky still asserted himself.

Gorky was not only a hearty host to fellow-writers, but he took upon himself, quite early in his career, the rôle of a talent-discoverer among obscure beginners, a rôle which he has not abandoned to this day. One of these discoveries was Leonid Andreyev. Like all opposition periodicals, the *Nizhegorodsky Listok* was subjected to a variety of penalties on the part of the Authorities, one of them being a temporary suspension for some impertinent utterance or other. During one of these suspensions, the publishers arranged for copies of a Moscow daily, the *Courier,* to be sent to its subscribers. This is how Gorky happened in the Easter issue of the *Courier* (1898) to come upon a story, *Bargamot and Garaska,* signed by Leonid Andreyev. This was Andreyev's first story, written to order. Gorky sensed something out of the ordinary about this seemingly traditional Easter story, and he wrote to inquire about its author. A correspondence began between the two men, which resulted in a mutually significant friendship, not unmixed with flashes of hostility, especially in later years, during war and revolution. In his autobiography Andreyev acknowledged his indebtedness to Gorky, both for his encouragement to write and for his help in placing his stories.

One of Gorky's satellites was Petrov, better known as Skitalets (Wanderer). He has written some poems and stories in Gorky's vein, and has been known as " Gorky's shadow," because of his resemblance to him and because he imitated him in everything, from his bass voice and long hair to the black blouse and high boots. Skitalets was not an exception, however. The writer Ivan Belousov recalls that Gorky's costume was adopted by members of the Moscow " Wednesdays," an intimate group of writers, with whom he spent many hours on his visits to the ancient capital. Such of its members as Leonid Andreyev and Feodor Chaliapin added to the blouse and high boots the *poddyovka,* a long coat, tight-fitting in the waistline, with a wide skirt and a standing-up collar. One of the most popular prints of the time was that of a group of " Wednesday "

friends — Teleshov, Chirikov, Bunin, Gorky, Andreyev, Chaliapin, and Skitalets, most of them dressed *à la* Gorky.

The " Wednesdays " cannot be overlooked in any survey
of modern Russian literature. In this informal, unincorporated
club there met the best of Russia's young writers and other
artists. Older writers (Boborykin, Korolenko, Chekhov) kept
in touch with the group and visited their gatherings whenever
in Moscow. Authors read their manuscripts, and criticized
one another without any reserve. The nicknames given to the
members endured, and the critical verdicts were often final.
Leonid Andreyev, introduced to the " Wednesdays " by Gorky,
read there practically every work of his, and when abroad he
sent in his manuscripts, requesting that they be read and criticized: " Without your judgement," he wrote to Teleshov, the
guiding spirit of the group, " I cannot regard any of my works
as finished." Once he read there a story, *The Shrew*. It was
murdered by the mockery of those present. Years later, when
every word of Andreyev commanded attention and high compensation, he was asked by a member of the " Wednesdays "
to donate *The Shrew* for a miscellany that was to be published
for some charity purpose. Andreyev promised a story, but was
indignant at the idea that he might consider the publication of
a work that had been condemned at the " Wednesdays."

Literature was not the only muse worshipped at their
gatherings. Young Russians seldom get together without sooner
or later breaking into song. The " Wednesdays " usually
mingled music with literature. Skitalets could sing and accompany himself on the *" gusli "* (an ancient string instrument) with a success that was more invariable than that of
his stories or verses. In fact, the success of his public recitals
bordered on *succès de scandal*. His uncouth shaggy exterior,
his black blouse, and roaring bass gave the audience a pleasurable shock (it was Gorky who nicknamed his horrendous
friend " a tiger from a furrier's "). He thus appeared once
at a fashionable soirée organized for some charity, where everyone on the program was asked to wear evening dress. Skitalets
ignored this request, and throwing his mane back, he came out
on the stage and roared forth verses of contempt for the public.

" No, I am not with you! " ran some of the lines: " I hate all of you, hate you profoundly, passionately. You are toads in a slimy bog! " The audience applauded. But when Skitalets went on to hurl invectives at the public and threaten it with the oncoming storm (meaning, of course, the revolution), which would " sweep them off the face of the earth like rats," the police-officer in the hall made him stop, and ordered the lights to be turned off. Andreyev, in whose name the permit for the soirée had been obtained, had to appear in court, and Skitalets was deported from Moscow.

Chaliapin was a frequent and welcome guest at the " Wednesdays." He often disrupted literary programs with his outbursts of a singing mood. Chaliapin was then at the height of his power and charm, his peasant naïveté not yet spoiled by success and facile victories over feminine hearts. One evening, Teleshov recalls, Chaliapin appeared in their midst and shouted: " Brothers, I want to sing! " Usually he accompanied himself, but on that occasion he rang up Rachmaninov: " Sergey, I want to sing, deadly! Take a *likhach* [a special drozhka-driver with a swift horse] and gallop to the ' Wednesdays.' We'll sing all night." Rachmaninov came, and Chaliapin did not give him time even to have a glass of tea, but shoved him toward the piano, made him play, and " something wonderful began," says Teleshov. " Chaliapin was inspired. Never and nowhere was he so enchanting, so fine." The singer himself felt his excellency, and cried: " That's where you must hear me, not at the Grand Theatre." The two artists " teased and egged on one another." The authors forgot about the manuscripts they were to read and discuss, and sat enraptured, their eyes glued to the corner, where they could see by the piano the close-cropped head of Rachmaninov, his swiftly moving elbows and his long fingers fluttering over the keyboard. At his side, facing the audience, stood Chaliapin, tall and slender, in high boots and a splendid black *poddyovka*. His face was severe and spiritualized, with no trace of his wonted levity and grossness, but strained in the expectation of the moment when he was to come in.

Gorky's visits to Moscow, legally or in defiance of official

prohibition, were not infrequent. Moscow has been the heart of Russia, the real capital of Russia, especially of the central and Volga provinces. The capital which Peter the Great had built in a Finnish marsh, literally on the bones of hundreds of thousands of serfs, was a superimposition, and never took deep root in the national consciousness. The Muscovites regarded St. Petersburg as a parvenu, a city of pedants, officials, soulless regularity, and barrack-like prose. In their turn, the Petersburgians loved their " Pieter " (the founder gave his capital a Dutch name; the anti-German sentiment behind its change to Petrograd was misplaced), and looked down upon " granny " Moscow, as slow, old-fashioned, provincially hospitable, and Asiatic. Politically, of course, " Pieter " was more important than Moscow, as the centre of both the Autocracy and the revolutionary movement.

Gorky's first visit to St. Petersburg occurred in 1899. He stopped with Posse, who took upon himself to introduce his friend to the intelligentsia of the capital, from the religious mystics of Merezhkovsky's circle to the semi-revolutionary liberals of Milyukov's clan. As editor of the recently established Marxian review, *Zhizn,* Posse arranged in the editorial rooms a banquet in honour of his guest, to which came the most prominent writers of the time. The affair must have caused Posse considerable embarrassment, for the guest of honour showed a lack of manners and tact. To the warm greetings of Mikhaylovsky, Korolenko, and other coryphaei, who welcomed him into their midst and highly praised his talent, Gorky replied brusquely. He was undoubtedly shy and uncomfortable as the centre of attention, and he hid his shyness behind pugnacity. Using common speech and folk-proverbs, he explained to the assembly that his success was due not to his personal gifts, but to the fact that " where there are no fish, even a crayfish is a fish," and " in the village even Thomas is a squire." This was an affront from an upstart that was neither forgotten nor forgiven by many of the intelligentsia. Years later, after the Bolshevik revolution, that offence was included in the list of Gorky's other crimes for which he was indicted by Chirikov, the man who some four decades previously had

introduced Alexey Peshkov to a group of Kazan students as a chap "thirsting for knowledge" and worthy of enlightenment by the intelligentsia!

As he was leaving, Gorky said to Posse: "I have liked three things about your St. Petersburg. First, its smoked whitefish. Second, Merezhkovsky, for his being in earnest about believing in the immortality of the soul. Third, Milyukov's teeth, with which he will some time eat us all up." This frivolous remark need not belittle the importance of the connexions which Gorky established on that visit. Two of these must be mentioned especially: his assuming the literary editorship of *Zhizn,* and his becoming a shareholder of the *Znaniye* publishing house.

His association with *Zhizn* placed a label on his political platform, and though he never became a strict party member, his patent preference for the Marxians dates from that time. Marxism promised him the long and painfully sought "formula." He hoped that the review would become his exclusive "home," forgetting that the Authorities were bound to cut short the life of such a periodical. On two future occasions, in 1905 and 1917, with the relaxation of censorship, Gorky will found a Marxian daily, under the reminiscent name of *Novaya Zhizn (New Life).*

Among the writings of Gorky to appear in *Zhizn* was the unfinished *Muzhik.* The story, or novel, was long and verbose, and the fact that it was never republished need not be lamented. Its interest is largely autobiographic. The hero, Shebuyev the architect, has come up from the "lower depths," from the muzhiks, and like his author, he overbubbles with ideas and impressions. The endless monologues and dialogues are highfalutin', in an allegedly intelligentsia tone, with scarcely any action as a relief. The story, and particularly Shebuyev, must have served as a safety valve for Gorky at the time. One passage from Shebuyev's harangues reflects clearly Gorky's quest of a synthesis, and foreshadows his *Man,* that profession of his faith which appeared about three years later:

"Kants and Spinozas are only enormous heads, Beethoven is only amazingly developed ears and fingers. But life demands

a harmonious man, in whom intellect and instinct should merge as a perfect whole, whose equally developed faculties, mutually complementary, should always react in unison to every impression. A man is wanted who is not only intelligent but also kind, who not only understands everything but also feels everything. . . . Man must be all-sided, only then will he be both vital and active, that is, only then will he be able not only to adjust himself to life but also to alter its conditions in accordance with the growth of his ego."

One of the editors of *Zhizn,* E. Solovyev-Andreyevich, a critic of the ultra-sociologic school, took exceptional delight in the *Muzhik,* and awaited the continuation of its instalments impatiently. He happened to be in one of his periodical drinking spells, when, in the absence of his co-editors, he took charge of the editorial rooms. He set out to bombard Gorky with telegram after telegram, demanding further copy of the story. Gorky must have surmised from the tone of the messages as to their author's state, for he ignored them. Finally, after weeks of expectation, Solovyev received a package from Nizhni Novgorod. He opened it: *Muzhik!* The editor sobered up at once. He rushed the manuscript to the printer, and ordered him to set it up immediately in place of another story. To Gorky he wired again, this time a volley of thanks for the additional chapters. Gorky shrugged his shoulders: he could not have sent any copy, since he had discontinued the story. Just then a beginning writer, A. Svirsky, came to the office of *Zhizn,* and noticing on the desk the galley proofs of *Muzhik,* he avidly began to read them. It was sheer nonsense! He had a hard time finding someone of authority to stop the printing of the stuff. A letter soon came from Gorky, in which he told of an inmate in a madhouse, who had read the first chapters of *Muzhik,* and then wrote, and forwarded, the " continuation," which the over-eager Solovyev swallowed hook and line.

Svirsky, by the way, tells us an illuminating detail concerning Gorky as an editor. Though Svirsky had appeared in print before Gorky, he regarded the latter as his master, and brought him a story from the life of the tramps. The pedagogue protruded from Gorky most obviously when he was a young and

recent arrival in the literary ranks. He gave Svirsky a lecture on the writer's two chief companions, labour and patience, implying that work is more important than talent, and that perseverant labour may raise even a mediocre gift to the heights of genius. Some time later Svirsky called to learn of the fate of his story. Gorky told him that he had read it, found it forceful, but that he took the liberty to " comb it up a bit." " Please, forgive me," he boomed amiably, " and do not think that I am playing schoolmaster. I am aware that for years you have tramped and know that life not worse than I do. But in presenting these tramps you still cling to the old traditions. Your tramps are so debased, so insignificant, that it is hardly worth writing about such microbes." Svirsky read his " combed-up " story and could not recognize it. He had written of two tramps who, driven by hunger and autumn winds, came to one of the Donetz coal mines in search of work. But when they came face to face with the miners, Russia's " white negroes," and when they peered into the dark pits and heard stories about fires and cave-ins occurring underground, they lost courage, and fled. " My *bosyaks*," says Svirsky, " appeared just as I knew them and still know them to be — that is, as good-for-nothing abortions of life — whereas the workmen, though crushed by capital, yet had a glint of a better future in their eyes. Gorky recast the story into something different. With a few apt phrases and witty sayings he managed to array my *bosyaks* so niftily and wrap them into such knightly cloaks, that I positively did not recognize my hoboing idlers." Svirsky withdrew his story, and published it elsewhere.

That was Gorky's pedagogic application of his view on literature. At all events, that is what his view seemed to be about 1900, when Gorky's " formula " was as yet not clear-cut. He was still favouring his Chelkashes and Malvas against the stupid slaves of labour. Some years later, after his " proletarian " *Mother, Enemies,* and other glorifications of the working class, he will change his treatment, and his tramps, in a receded retrospective, will be portrayed less romantically if as colourfully.

The *Znaniye* venture proved more enduring and profitable

than *Zhizn,* whose publication was suspended after the issue of April, 1901, which contained Gorky's *Stormy Petrel.* While in St. Petersburg, Gorky was courted by the house of O. N. Popova, the lady who once had a quick change of mind about bringing out in book-form his reprints from provincial newspapers. She was now willing to be his exclusive publisher. Gorky humbly stated that all he asked for was to be spared the constant worry about daily bread for himself and his family, and requested a regular monthly fee of two hundred rubles. Popova agreed to send him this amount, as part of the income from his books, out of which the publisher was to retain only ten per cent. This seemed generous to Gorky, and Posse urged him to accept the offer. But a newly acquired friend, K. P. Pyatnitsky, a scholar of practical acumen, persuaded Gorky to join *Znaniye* as a shareholder, the shares to be paid for later from his fees. Gorky's name, and his interest in the concern, soon made *Znaniye* one of the most popular and influential houses in the country. The green paper covers of its books began to be seen everywhere, containing between them the best of fiction and popular science. *Znaniye* paid higher fees and royalties than any other firm, and urged authors to become shareholders and thus co-owners of their publications. An idea arose at the Moscow "Wednesdays" to issue from time to time, through *Znaniye,* miscellanies, a favourite form of book in Russia, with contributions from members and first-rate outsiders. The *Znaniye Miscellanies* appeared for a number of years (there were forty of them in all), giving the public the finest prose and poetry from the pens of Chekhov, Gorky, Andreyev, Veresayev, Bunin, Kuprin, and other non-Symbolists, and of such foreigners as Sholom Ash, Knut Hamsun, Walt Whitman, and Émile Verhaeren. Teleshov recalls how astonished and incredulous the public was about the *Znaniye* slogan: "The whole profit from a book should belong to the author, not to the publisher." He assures us that the group made every effort to live up to the slogan, and that after the demise of *Znaniye,* owing to internal dissensions and jealousies, its policy was continued by its successor, the Moscow Authors' Publishing House. Another novel feature introduced by *Zna-*

niye was the sharing of its profits with various worthy undertakings and institutions. To be sure, its monetary contributions
to the revolutionary movement were kept secret, but there were
also " legal " causes deserving support. The first *Miscellany*
announced that a goodly portion of the profits from its sales
would go to certain institutions; thus, one thousand rubles
apiece to the Literary Fund, the Higher Courses for Women,
the Women's Medical Institute, and so forth.

Gorky, ever moved by kindliness and affection, could not
help enjoying his acclamation, which was all but universal.
In his native city he was hailed by all save officials and prigs.
The Volga merchants were proud of Gorky, a product of the
Volga and Nizhni Novgorod, and many of them were on
friendly terms with him. He who had worked on their steamers
and wharfs, who had spent many a night in cheap lodgings
built with their money for homeless beggars and tramps, was
now cordially received in their inordinately hospitable homes.
Gorky came to know well these eccentric millionaires, whose
savagery and greed, not unmixed with generosity and a yearning after better things, he depicted with a power and skill
unequalled by his descriptions of other Russian classes.

To hear Gorky reminisce aloud about the Volga merchants
is a rare treat. His intonation, his gestures, his mobile nose
and eyebrows, his everchangeable eyes lend his oral descriptions a graphic convexity which is apt to be lost in print. He
makes you see and hear, by means of impersonation, the
innumerable oddities he has known. Here is A. M. Gubin, the
mayor of the city of Nizhni Novgorod, forced to resign for
dragging a respectable deacon by his long hair during the
church service. One of Gubin's diversions was to sit by the
window and fire small-shot at the water-carrier's barrel as it
passed by — there were no waterworks in the city then. The
water-carrier finally noticed who was causing the leak in his
barrel, and asked Gubin to leave him in peace. The bearded
scamp gave him a silver ruble in expiation. When asked at
the Merchants' Club as to why he indulged in such pranks,
Gubin replied simply: " To assert myself."

Another scene: Gorky in the company of fat merchants. They talk, or rather listen to him talk, of Tolstoy, of beauty. The voice of a public baths proprietor breaks in: "What are you talking about! Beauty is rubbish. Look at the skies: what a vast empty space, useless too. Here is where one should put up a great sign: ' Commercial Baths of Ivan Petrov.' " The gentleman did not refer to electric signs, for electricity was unknown in Nizhni Novgorod in those days.

The Annual Fair served as an escape for the Nizhni Novgorod merchants from their boredom and drabness, from their unimaginative stout wives and colourless shops. During the brief period of the Fair they would often burn up the savings of a whole year's drudgery, in some *café chantant,* whose gaudy veneer of Europeanism provoked the Asiatic abandon of the Russians. Women of all nationalities reaped a rich harvest at those orgies. Hundred-ruble notes were shoved by unsteady fingers behind the corsages of painted girls, German, Roumanian, Chinese, French, or — most favourite of all — American. Some peasant maid from Tambov would lisp: "I am Amelican," and the merchants showered on her bills and champagne and kisses. The spirit of recklessness would wax toward the closing hours, when buckets of champagne were poured into the throats of the merchants' horses, these to be driven at a mad speed to some public baths, for their masters " to wash off their sins." Accompanied by the " Amelican " girls, and loaded with parcels of food and drink, they would rent a whole bathing establishment, and continue their orgy. " And straight from the baths — to holy mass, at the cathedral."

It goes without saying that Gorky was the idol of the young generation, the students in particular. The lower classes, workers and those who chose not to work, regarded him as one of their own, and were of course proud of his fame and success. His acquaintance with the Nizhni Novgorod factory workers gave Gorky most of the material for the characters in *Mother* and his other writings dealing with the awakening Russia. As to the revolutionists, they made vast use of Gorky's sympathies for the cause and his hatred for things-as-they-are. He helped

them readily with money, with his pen, with advice, in defiance of the police surveillance which was constant and unrelenting.

It must be noted that his two latter offerings were received not without reserve. The very fact that he supported more than one revolutionary party made him unsafe in the eyes of party members whose loyalty to their cause spelled hostility for their rivals and opponents. Gorky remained incurably romantic in his worship of heroism as such. The Marxian Social-Democrats resented his friendly attitude toward the heretical Socialist-Revolutionists, who questioned economic determinism and went so far in sanctioning individual effort as to employ terror against government officials. To this day some of his Bolshevik admirers relate half-pityingly, half-sneeringly, with what enthusiasm Gorky, at Nizhni Novgorod, greeted a Socialist-Revolutionist who wore an iron corset as a result of the treatment administered to his ribs by the police while he was in Siberia. Aside from his sin of political inconstancy, Gorky's confidence in human nature militated against him in the eyes of all revolutionary groups, whose organization and very existence demanded caution and extreme conspiratoriness. What could they do but reject such advice of Gorky as the utilization for party purposes of a certain Nikitin, a celebrated Nizhni Novgorod robber, whose integrity the author guaranteed most warmly, from his personal knowledge of the professional criminal?

Though popularity could not but warm the heart of the man who had known so much loneliness and callousness, it assumed at times such vile forms as to nauseate its victims. Multitudinous photographs and cartoons of Gorky had made him familiar enough to be recognized on the street or in public places, and to be pointed at and scrutinized unceremoniously as if he were some white raven. In St. Petersburg and Moscow the crowds seemed more inconsiderate in their curiosity than in provincial Nizhni Novgorod. Gorky narrates some amusing stories about being inspected and commented upon by passing

strangers in Russia's capital cities. The inquisitiveness of the common people annoyed him probably less than that of the so-called educated public. Newspaper reporters gave him no rest, spied upon him, and described his minutest movements and actions, making an issue of his manner of eating sardines. At the Moscow Art Theatre, during the performance of Chekhov's *Uncle Vanya,* crowds of spectators besieged the box where Gorky and Chekhov sat, thronged after Gorky during the intermissions, and vexed him so much that finally he lost all patience and upbraided them in no gentle terms. The press pounced upon the incident, exaggerated it in a variety of fantastic distortions, and presented the case as the impudent haughtiness of an erstwhile hobo innocent of good manners and tolerance. Gorky found it necessary at length to write a letter to the editor of *Severny Courier:*

. . . Someone published the other day a note in *Novoye Vremya* about certain words I had with the people that were in the corridor of the Moscow Art Theatre. The author of the note states that he was there in person, but this is probably not true, or he did not hear right, because he gives my words in the completely distorted version of the Moscow paper, *Novosti Dnya* [*News of the Day*].

In addressing the crowd I did not employ such expressions as " you're gaping," " you look into my mouth," nor did I say that they were hindering me from drinking tea with A. P. Chekhov, who was at that moment behind the stage.

What I said was this:

" Your attention flatters me — thanks! But I do not comprehend it. I am not the Venus of Medici, nor a conflagration, nor a ballerina, nor a drowned man: what is there of interest in the exterior of a man who writes stories? Wait till I write a play, then clap [literally: slap] as much as you like. As a professional writer I feel hurt that while attending a highly significant play by Chekhov you spend the intermission in trifles."

After saying that I apologized, though I should not have done so. This letter of mine is a protest against the distortion of my words, but it is not an apology. As to the newspapermen who have inflated this puny incident, I ask them in

all earnestness: are you not ashamed, gentlemen, to spend your time in such trifles?

This letter failed to put an end to the storm. The public, *el gran Galleoto*, raged, and its purveyors, the gentlemen of the press, continued to whet its appetite by spicy morsels about the Hobo Who Forgot Himself. One may question Gorky's taste in this affair; it is unthinkable that Chekhov could have acted in that way, and if under a momentary impulse he should have spoken his mind to the annoying crowd, he certainly would not have condescended to write explanations for the press. But Gorky has not learned, not even to this day, to control his public utterances. He likes a scrap, and the journalist in him has never quite died.

The incident gave Gorky a memorable taste of publicity. It demonstrated to him the value of public acclaim. He wrote then a sketch *About a Writer Who Became Conceited*, in which he addressed the readers in these words: " It seems to me that you like me because I do not wear a frock-coat, and because in my stories I use impolite words. And at times I even think that were I to learn how to write lyrics with my left foot, you would regard me more affectionately and with greater interest."

Gorky's life and work seemed to have been destined to arouse sensation, violent reaction, scandal. He " has come into this world — to disagree." As Alexey Peshkov or as Maxim Gorky, with the smug citizens of Nizhni Novgorod, or with the gaping would-be intellectuals of Moscow and St. Petersburg, with the would-be Puritans of New York, with the police of the Russian autocracy or with the henchmen of Lenin and Zinoviev, his pugnacity was bound to get him into trouble and provide copy for the newspapers.

TOLSTOY AND GORKY

RUSSIAN literature is unthinkable without the figure of Lev Tolstoy looming across its horizon. For six decades his presence was vividly felt by would-be ancestors (how eagerly, and vainly, Turgenev tried to assume the rôle of Tolstoy's literary midwife!) and by contemporary descendants. Even today, twenty years after his death, one of the LEF (Left Front) critics complains that too many of the Soviet novels savour of *War and Peace*. Yet it was Tolstoy's living presence that marked with especial significance the life of Russian letters — indeed, all mental life in Russia. Thinking Russia felt, with Chekhov, that as long as Lev Nikolayevich breathed there was a chance for redemption from the reign of vulgarity, pettiness, and sham. A living conscience dwelled in Yasnaya Polyana; one basked in its rays, and one feared its searchlight, for it filled one not only with comfort but also with responsibility. Writers, in particular, were drawn to that mighty source, seeking courage, unadulterated truth and, above all, the glow of a beautiful personality. Garshin, Korolenko, Chekhov, Gorky, Andreyev, Bunin — not one of these and numerous other writers professed Tolstoyanism, yet their pilgrimages to the great hermit were prompted by the need of communion with a higher man.

Gorky paid his first visit to Tolstoy in 1889. The gawky youth, we may recall, tramped his way from Tsaritsyn to Nizhni Novgorod, and at Ryazan he turned down one of the tributaries of Mother Volga, and made his way to Moscow. He wanted to see Tolstoy. Perhaps he hoped that the sage would help him disentangle the maze of questions and doubts in which he floundered helplessly: his perforated chest still

reminded him on occasion of his clumsy attempt at suicide three years previously, as a way out of that maze. He also had a tangible reason for seeing Tolstoy, which he explained later in a letter to him (the letter remained unanswered). It seems that while working on the Tsaritsyn railroad, he and a few other employes caught the infection of Tolstoyan " simpli-fication," then still in vogue, and, in the words of the letter, " infatuated by the idea of independent, personal labour, and rustic life, [they] decided to become tillers of the soil." They requested of Tolstoy " purely material help," in the form of granting them a piece of land, since they had heard that he possessed much uncultivated land. Above all, they hoped for his " spiritual help, counsel and directions that would facilitate the attainment of [their] aim," and they also asked that he send them his *Confession, My Religion,* and " other works for-bidden for circulation." How passing this infatuation was can be seen from the fact that one talk with the writer Karonin, at Nizhni Novgorod, " decapitated " Gorky's dream of settling on the land.

In the back yard of Tolstoy's Moscow house the young tramp came upon the Countess, who informed him that the Count was away, at the Trinity Monastery, and took him to the kitchen for a treat of rolls and coffee. Gorky states that she received him " genially," though, goodness knows, the Countess had been vexed exceedingly by the multitude and variety of stray callers on her husband. In fact, while Gorky greedily and gratefully dispatched his meal, the hostess ob-served that altogether too many " shady knaves " prowled about the place trying to meet Lev Nikolayevich, and that Russia on the whole was redolent of idlers and knaves. The visitor swallowed his food safely, and politely assented to the observation of the Countess, for the correctness of which he could vouch from abundant personal experience.

Ten years pass. The erstwhile tramp has already published two volumes of stories, and is the most talked of and most photographed man in Russia. Chekhov corresponds with him, urges him to exchange his Nizhni Novgorod backwoods for Moscow, and entices him with tickets to *Uncle Vanya* at the

Art Theatre, and with other allurements. He finally plays a trump card:

The day before yesterday I was at L. N. Tolstoy's; he praised you very highly and said that you were a " remarkable writer." He likes your *Goltva Fair* and *On the Raft,* but he does not like your *Malva.* He said: " You can invent anything you like, but you cannot invent psychology. In Gorky one comes across sheer psychological inventions; he describes what he has never felt." So much for you! I told him that next time you were in Moscow we would come together to see him. . . . Tolstoy has been asking about you for a long time; you arouse his curiosity. He is evidently impressed.

Such attention on the part of Lev Tolstoy would turn the head of any writer, especially that of an upstart who was diffident and timid with all his pugnacity. But what with police difficulties and family burdens (he was by now husband and father), Gorky did not find his way to Tolstoy until the month of January, 1900. Tolstoy was glad to see him; he was extremely curious about native talent emanating from the idealized " people." It was about that time that Feodor Chaliapin — not long before a fellow-tramp of Gorky's, now also a rising star — called, and regaled the Count with many a song. And now he faced another autochthonous artist, by passport a Nizhni Novgorod guildsman, in appearance an authentic peasant with pugnacious nose, Asiatic cheek-bones, and a big body, all bone and muscle. A fine specimen in the eyes of the aristocratic populist. In his diary Tolstoy jotted down: " Gorky called. We had a fine talk. And I liked him. A genuine man of the people."

As to Gorky, he must have felt hot and cold by turn during that visit. Self-conscious and ill at ease, even unto this day, in the presence of the " well-born," he writhed under the piercing bearish eyes that saw through one. The conversation seemed to him more like an examination, and what particularly exasperated him was the suspicion that out of condescension to him the Count adopted " some sort of a 'popular style,'

speaking in the language of the street and market-place." Even in later days, when the first flush of " curiosity " gave place to a genuine and mutual interest between the two, Gorky suspected that Tolstoy's interest in him was purely ethnologic, as for a species of an unfamiliar tribe. But that first meeting! He will always remember it.

Tolstoy leads him to his study, seats him down, and facing him closely plunges into an analysis of Gorky's tale, *Varenka Olesova*. That girl, Varenka, pictured as buxom and healthy yet sexually indifferent and resenting the young professor's advances — she is improbable! A girl past fifteen and in good health longs to be embraced and touched — the old man uses such direct terms that Gorky is embarrassed, though he is no tenderfoot and has heard foul language from his childhood. Is the Count trying to be coarse for his sake? Now he is talking about Gorky's *Twenty-Six Men and One Girl*. Worse and worse. Tolstoy's words and turns of speech are downright improper, obscene; in fact this " popular style " strikes Gorky as cynical. Yet it is he, Gorky, who is being branded in the press for employing vulgar language; it is he whom Korolenko has suggestively warned that rudeness does not necessarily spell force. Gorky feels insulted.

Later Gorky came to know that Tolstoy was guilty neither of condescension nor of cynicism, that he preferred direct, " unmentionable " terms, peasant expressions, for their precision and pointedness. An incurable pagan, Tolstoy to his last day took delight in manifestations of nature, his ascetic sermons notwithstanding. In intimate conversation he minced no words, sending a blush to the tough cheeks of Gorky, let alone the shy and fastidious Chekhov. The three of them were strolling one day in the Almond Grove, in Crimea, when Tolstoy asked Chekhov point-blank about his sex experiences in his youth, and noticing his confusion, he spoke of his own indefatigability, using " salty " words. On that occasion Gorky observed that the most indecent words lost their coarseness and sounded natural and simple when they came from Tolstoy's " shaggy lips." Characteristically germane is a scene described to me by Gorky, as he recalled his Crimean days:

One day Sulerzhitsky and I were walking up the coast. At the turn of the road we observed on the upper terrace — Tolstoy. There he stood, a smallish old man with a soft Crimean hat on his head, winking with one of his piercing grey eyes. He was winking at a cooing pigeon that wooed a dove in the middle of the road. A wise old man, winking knowingly.

But this understanding of Tolstoy came to Gorky later. On his first visit to the revered and feared author he merely suspected condescension and secret contempt for his coarseness, clumsiness, his ungainly figure and too conspicuous nose. It did not occur to him that at his age Tolstoy was just as self-conscious and just as fretful over his homely features, particularly his broad, flat nose.

Tolstoy notices his visitor's uneasiness, and graciously drops the sex question. He asks Gorky about his life, his adventures, the writers he has met. Is it true that Korolenko is a musician? He does not think so? But he likes Korolenko's stories? Yes? Apparently by contrast to his own stories. Has he read Weltmann? He is sometimes better than Gogol, who imitated Marlinsky (a second-rate scribbler). Gorky begins to feel more at home; he shows off a bit. Gogol, he says, was influenced by Hoffmann, Sterne, and perhaps by Dickens. The old man looks up sharply and snaps: " Have you read that somewhere? No? It is wrong. Gogol scarcely knew Dickens. But you must have, indeed, read a good deal; look out, it is noxious! Koltsov ruined himself by it." The reference to Koltsov, a self-taught poet from the commoners, irks Gorky. He is sick and tired of being treated as a " native nugget." And perhaps he is half aware himself of having read too much: his bookishness often dilutes the strong wine of his robust talent. The host, again, tries to mollify his bluntness. He sees the lummox to the door, embraces and kisses him, and gives him his blessing:

" You are a real muzhik! You will find it hard to get along with writers, but don't you fear anything, and always say things as you feel them: never mind if it will come out rude! Sensible people will understand."

A polite exchange of notes between the two writers followed

(these and the other letters reproduced below have been published only recently, and are here for the first time given in English) :

Gorky to Tolstoy:

Thanks, hearty thanks for all the things you have said to me, Lev Nikolayevich! I am glad to have seen you, and am very proud of it. Although I knew that you treated people simply and cordially, still I must confess that I did not expect you to meet me so kindly.

Please send me your picture, if you are in the habit of doing so. I beseech you, let me have one. . . .

I bow low to you,
M. Gorky

Tolstoy to Gorky:

Forgive me, my dear Alexey Maximich (if I have made a mistake in your name, forgive me again), that I have not answered you for a long time, and have not sent you my picture. I was exceedingly glad to learn to know you, and am glad to have grown fond of you. Aksakov used to say that some people are better (he said — cleverer) than their books, and some worse. I have liked your writings, but have found you to be better than your writings. You see what a compliment I am paying you; its main value is in its being sincere. There now, good-bye, I grasp your hand with friendly feelings.

Lev Tolstoy

Gorky to Tolstoy:

Many thanks, Lev Nikolayevich, for your portrait, and for your fine and kind words about me. I do not know whether I am better than my books, but I know that every writer must be higher and better than his writings. For what is a book? Even a great book is only a dead, black shadow of the word and only a hint at the truth, whereas man is a depository of the living God. By God I understand one's untamable yearning for self-perfection, for truth and justice. Therefore even a bad man is better than a good book. It is so, isn't it?

I deeply believe that there is nothing better than man on earth, and I even say, paraphrasing Democritus: Only man exists, the rest is a point of view. I have always been and shall

be a man-worshipper, only I cannot express it with adequate force.

I am terribly anxious to call on you again, and am very grieved by my inability to do it right now. I cough, my head aches, am working full speed, writing a story about over-wise people, the kind I don't like. In my opinion they are the basest sort . . . but lest I tire you, I am going to stop. I bow low to you and firmly grasp your hand. My regards to your family.

> I wish you good health!
>
> A. Peshkov

Despite the unpleasant impression of his first visit, Gorky calls shortly afterward at Yasnaya Polyana. He is drawn to Tolstoy, irresistibly. He joins him on his walks, watches him commune with nature, stroke lovingly the satin trunks of his birches, grow excited, huntsman-like, at the sight of a rabbit, scare off a hawk hovering over the chicks. The magnificent old pagan rouses Gorky's never sated curiosity, and he observes avidly. But he is also aware of being observed; he is still under examination, subject to blunt remarks and admonitions. Tolstoy is opinionated, impatient of contradictions, sweeping in his judgements. Gorky's characters are strange to him, hence he regards them as " invented." " You're an inventor," he snaps, " and all these Kuvaldas of yours are inventions."

As a matter of fact, Kuvalda, the keeper of the night-lodging in *Ex-Men,* has been drawn from life, and to this day Gorky delights in recalling bits of wisdom from the lips of that gentleman in rags, who gave up a military career for the freedom of Hoboland. I have it on his word that all the characters in *Ex-Men* (*Creatures that once were Men,* in some English translations) are real, and that Gorky himself figures there under the name of Meteor. He speaks to Tolstoy of the original Kuvalda, and makes him laugh to the point of tears. The old man is hugely amused, and remarks (as probably many who have come in contact with Gorky have noted) that his visitor is better in conversation than in writing. But just the same — he, Gorky, is an inventor, a romanticist, and as a romanticist he is a dubious socialist: all romantics have been monarchists. What — Hugo? Hugo was no good: a noisy chap.

" Now your story, *My Travelling Companion,* is not invented; it is good because it is not invented. But when you think, you beget knights, Amadises, and Siegfrieds."

Dead right! Tolstoy put his finger on Gorky's chief defects — his bookishness, and his sterile imagination. Whenever Gorky draws on his personal experiences, as in *My Travelling Companion,* he is on firm soil. As soon as he begins to imagine characters, from unfamiliar environments, he flounders helplessly, as in *Varenka Olesova.*

Tolstoy reprimands Gorky for his exaggerations. True, he knows his tramps and riff-raff, but he lends them heroic qualities. That's false. There are no heroes, but just people, nothing else. And here he suddenly smiles, and apropos of the second part of Gogol's *Dead Souls* he says good-naturedly: " We are all of us horrible inventors. I myself, when I write, at times feel a sudden pity for one of my characters, and then I give him some good trait, and from someone else I take away a good trait, so that the former may not appear too black in comparison with the others." And immediately he adds sternly: " That's why I say that art is a lie, an arbitrary deception, and is harmful. . . ."

Tolstoy is doubtful about the reality of Gorky's merchants, thinks that they too are invented. He probably refers to *Foma Gordeyev.* Gorky pours out his abundant observations of the Volga merchants at Nizhni Novgorod, Kazan, Samara, and elsewhere. Tolstoy is impressed. He is particularly touched to the quick by Gorky's account of three generations of a merchant family which went through a merciless process of decadence. His bear eyes flash, and he tugs Gorky's sleeve excitedly: " That ought to be written! A big novel written briefly, do you see? Without fail! " But what of the knights that he may beget? queries Gorky. The old man is annoyed. That is a serious matter. He must write it. Ah, that's fine: the one who becomes a monk, to pray for the sins of the rest of the family. And the other, the one who is bored, and hoards, and builds — wonderful! The mouth of the novelist waters. . . . Twenty-odd years later Gorky followed Tolstoy's behest in his novel *The Artamonov Business* (*Decadence,* in the English version).

In the spring of 1901 (to anticipate matters somewhat), Gorky was arrested and placed in the Nizhni Novgorod prison for his anti-government activities. Told of his predicament by K. P. Pyatnitsky, Gorky's literary manager, Tolstoy at once interceded in his behalf with Prince P. D. Svyatopolk-Mirsky, Associate Minister of the Interior, and with Prince P. A. Oldenburgsky, brother-in-law of the Tsar. As a result Gorky was released from jail within a month. Although Tolstoy did not know Prince Mirsky personally, his letter to him had an immediate effect, and Mirsky promised Pyatnitsky to take the necessary steps. Prince Oldenburgsky had previously called on Tolstoy, and had a long talk with him. Part of the correspondence in this connexion follows:

Tolstoy to Prince Oldenburgsky:

Your Highness, that very writer, Gorky (his real name is Alexey Maximovich Peshkov), of whom you and I talked last year, and whose writings you particularly liked, is now in a terrible state: he has been torn away from his family, from his wife, who is in the last stage of pregnancy, and without trial put in the Nizhni Novgorod jail, horrible in its anti-hygienic conditions, especially for one who is sick with tuberculosis of the lungs.

His wife and friends, knowing how much I love him both as a man and as a writer, have requested me to help in his and their sorrow as much as I can. I am turning to you, with the firm hope that you will do what you can to relieve him and his family from the dreadful position in which they are at present. I am certain that you will not shun an opportunity for performing a good deed.

With perfect esteem and devotion, Your Highness' humble servant,   Lev Tolstoy

Tolstoy to Prince Svyatopolk-Mirsky:

Your Serenity: The wife of A. M. Peshkov (Gorky) and his friends have requested me to intercede with whomever I can for the prevention of his murder before the trial, and probably without trial, through being kept, while sick and consumptive, in the Nizhni Novgorod jail which, I am told, is horrible in

its anti-hygienic conditions. I know Gorky personally and love him not only as a gifted writer esteemed throughout Europe, but also as an intelligent, kind, and attractive man. Although I have not the pleasure of knowing you personally, I somehow believe that you will take an interest in the fate of Gorky and his family, and will come to their aid in as much as it is within your power.

Please do not disappoint my expectations. . . .

Gorky to Tolstoy:

Many thanks, Lev Nikolayevich, for your intercession in my behalf. I have been released from jail and am under " domestic arrest," which is a fine thing, in view of my wife's approaching confinement. In all I spent only one month in prison, without any harm to my health, I think. Nor has the affair affected my wife's health very much, so all is well. The investigation is not finished yet but, as far as I am concerned, it will result in a trifle; they will most probably expel me from Nizhni Novgorod, and place me under police surveillance.

Once more — I thank you! I am sorry that you became involved in this mess. . . . It is terribly funny to be under " domestic arrest "! There is one policeman in the kitchen, another on the porch, and one in the street. I may take a walk only accompanied by a policeman, and then only around the house; I am not allowed on the busy streets. Even the policemen feel funny to watch a man who not only has no intentions to flee from town, but who does not want to leave it of his own free will. Well, best regards, good health, vigour, peace! I firmly grasp your hand.

A. Peshkov

Shortly after this, Tolstoy fell seriously ill, and Russia was alarmed. On his recovery he received numerous congratulations — " messages of love from all directions," as he noted in his diary of July 16 (29), 1901. One of these was from a group of " Nizhni Novgorodians," the first signature being that of M. Gorky:

Lev Nikolayevich!

Overjoyed at the safe turn in the course of your illness, we send you, great man, our fervent wishes that you live long

and in good health for the sake of the triumph of truth on earth, and that you may as tirelessly continue to expose falsehood, hypocrisy, and malice with your mighty word.

In 1901–1902 Tolstoy was convalescing from his severe illness in Gaspra, in Crimea. Part of this time Gorky lived near by, in Oleiza, trying to heal his tubercular lungs in the rays of the southern sun. The two men saw a great deal of one another, and were often joined by Chekhov, also driven to Crimea by tuberculosis. It was then and there that Gorky jotted down his fragmentary notes on Tolstoy. These reminiscences are valuable both because they give us the first human portrait, not icon, of Tolstoy, and because their author is extremely candid about himself, even when this is not to his advantage. Thus we see clearly and unretouched both Tolstoy and Gorky.

Once Gorky espied Tolstoy on the road to Dulber, alone, his fingers thrust inside his belt, quietly watching a lizard as it lay basking on a stone. " Feeling fine, eh? " he softly asked the lizard. Then he cautiously looked around, and confessed to the bland reptile: " As for me, I am not."

From close and intimate observation Gorky came to see Tolstoy's utter loneliness and unhappiness. He felt that, aside from all he spoke and wrote, the old man kept silent on what was to him most essential, and which he did not confide even to his diary. Despite his religion, his vehemently accentuated faith (had he not protested too much?), Tolstoy seemed in the eyes of Gorky to be peering into the abyss of nothingness. This esesntial something of which he kept silent, Gorky regarded as a certain " negation of all affirmations, the deepest and most malignant nihilism that had sprung from the soil of a boundless despair and a loneliness which probably no man before him had experienced with such terrifying clearness."

In conversation with his close friends Tolstoy would occasionally lift the edge of the veil that hid his gloom. Thus when Chekhov remarked that he did not like the book of Lev Shestov, *Good and Evil in the Teachings of Nietzsche and Count Tolstoy,* Tolstoy retorted that the book was amusing and interesting: " I surely like cynics, when they are sincere. He [Shestov] says: ' Truth is needless,' and he is right: of

what good is truth to him? He will die all the same." Then, to make himself clear, he added with a sharp grin: " Once a man has learned to think, no matter what he may think about he is always thinking of his death. That is true of all philosophers. And what truths can there be, if there is death? "

Death, then, the old scarecrow that threatened to paralyse Levin-Tolstoy and drive him to suicide, had not been downed by the arduously won faith! How much of that faith was absolutely genuine? Perhaps there was a bit of overdone self-flagellation in the words he once said to Chekhov and Gorky: " The Caliph Abdurahman had during his life fourteen happy days, but I have most probably not had as many. And this is because I have never lived — I am not capable of living — for myself, for my soul; I live for display, for others." Perhaps.

Gorky watched and observed and spied on Tolstoy not only because of his artist's curiosity, but because he had been, and still is seeking, and " will be seeking until death," for a man with " a living, and genuine faith." That is why he was pained, even outraged, by his discovery that not all was well with Tolstoy the preacher: it spelled the futility of Gorky's quest. How cold and wooden were Tolstoy's words when they touched on God, on love for one's neighbour, and other tenets of his faith. Cold, because his faith was neither " genuine " nor " living." In old Luka, of his *At the Bottom*, Gorky wanted to depict such a sermonizer, a dispenser of consoling nostrums, which amounted to alms bestowed with hidden squeamishness and aversion, as if he meant to say: " Leave me in peace! Love God or your neighbour, but leave me alone! Damn God, love not your neighbour but the stranger, but leave me alone! Leave me in peace, for I am a human being and hence doomed to death! "

Small wonder that Tolstoy was sceptical about Tolstoyans, whom Gorky compared to tiny dogs running in a circle beneath a great booming bell and trying to whine in tune. Once in Yasnaya Polyana such a Tolstoyan rhapsodized over his happiness and spiritual purity, which he acquired after " taking " Tolstoy's doctrine. Tolstoy bent over to Gorky and said softly: " The rogue is lying all the time, but then, he does it

for my pleasure." On this point — Tolstoyans — Gorky agreed with the Countess, whom he disliked otherwise (the antipathy was mutual). Years later, when it became fashionable to abuse and blame her for the death of her husband, he even wrote an article in defence of the Countess. Gorky credited her with having tried to save Tolstoy from the onslaught of Tolstoyans, of parasites, of " asinine hoofs ":

Like all great men [he wrote] Tolstoy dwelled on the highway, and each passer-by deemed it his lawful right to touch the unusual, wonderful man in one way or another. It is beyond doubt that Sofia Tolstaya repulsed from her husband not a few filthy and greedy hands, and brushed away a multitude of indifferently curious fingers intent on rudely probing the depth of the wounds of the spiritual rebel, the man who was dear to her.

With the Countess, and with most of the admirers of Tolstoy the artist, Gorky deplored his digression from the road of creative literature to the by-paths of moralism. But few gauged, as he did, the chaos of contradictions that raged within Tolstoy and made him so complex, so tragic, and so lonely. Surely no one has expressed this complexity so succinctly as Gorky, in his suggestion that Tolstoy had in him the traits of three characteristic Russians:

The bold and inquisitive malapertness of Vaska Buslayev [a legendary rogue of medieval Novgorod], and a particle of the stubborn soul of Arch-priest Avvakum [a fanatical Old Believer, executed under Tsar Alexis in the seventeenth century], while somewhere above or on the side lurked the scepticism of Chaadayev [a brilliant thinker declared insane by the government of Nicholas I for his *Philosophical Letters*]. The Avvakum element did the preaching, and tormented the artist; the Novgorodian malapert threw down Dante and Shakespeare, while the Chaadayev element scoffed at these diversions of his mind and, incidentally, at its agonies.

To be sure, these three personalities do not exhaust the pluralistic self of Tolstoy. They do not include the artist, for one thing. Or the aristocrat, for another. Gorky noted the

latter trait acutely. Tolstoy's sermon of simplification and his democratic, peasant exterior deceived many of his visitors. Shallow persons, on finding the celebrated count so " ordinary," so muzhik-like, would be tempted to assume the kind of familiarity which the common folk of Russia call *amico-chonery*. On such occasions, Gorky tells us, " . . . suddenly from behind his muzhik beard and crumpled democratic blouse there would rise the old Russian lord, the magnificent aristo-crat." Then the noses of the overbold visitors became purple with instant frost. Gorky, who has always, perhaps by contrast, admired blue blood, chuckled with delight at this display of social superiority, performed with grace and measure, with just enough force to squash those fellows and make them " shrink and squeak."

One wonders whether Gorky himself had not felt a vic-tim of this dormant but by no means extinguished aris-tocratism. Vladimir Posse describes a joint visit of theirs to Tolstoy's Moscow home, in the spring of 1900. As they sat around in the drawing-room, Gorky was on the point of striking a match, to light his cigarette, when he was suddenly stopped by a sign on the wall: " You are requested not to smoke." Tolstoy told him to go ahead and smoke, and to dis-regard the sign. He even spoke to him in the familiar " thou." Emboldened by the host's geniality, Gorky ventured to ask him whether he had read *Foma Gordeyev*, his first novel, which had just been published. The answer was: " I had begun to read, but was unable to finish it: the thing is tediously in-vented. Yes, the whole thing is invented. No such things ever happened or could have happened." Gorky, meekly: " It seems to me that Foma's childhood is not invented." Tolstoy: " No, everything about it is invented! Pardon me, I do not like it. Now you have a story, *The Goltva Fair*. That I liked very much. Simple, truthful. That bears re-reading."

Gorky hardly enjoyed his smoke. Asked by Tolstoy how long he was going to stay in Moscow, Gorky replied that he would be glad to depart at once, had he not promised to appear at a literary evening and read some of his works. Is he a good reader? No, not very. Then why appear? For show? Gorky

stammers that he has no wish to appear, but the Moscow youth insist. . . . It makes no difference who insists, it is wrong to make a show out of oneself. And Tolstoy admits that once he made a show of himself, but involuntarily. Professor Timiryazev went with him to a congress of physicians and naturalists, and took him right up the platform. The audience recognized him and began to applaud. Timiryazev nudged him: " It is you they are applauding. Bow to them, Lev Nikolay-evich! " He protested: "What wrong have I done that I should have to bow for? "

Gorky's great nose must have turned blue with chill. Tolstoy was apparently aware of having squashed the plebeian, for speaking to Posse on the morrow he said:

I am afraid last night I hurt your friend. I did not tell him the main thing: a great service will forever remain to his credit. He has shown us a living soul in the tramp. Dostoyevsky has shown it in the criminal, and Gorky in the tramp. Only it is too bad that he invents a good deal. . . . Of course I refer to psychologic invention.

Even if we should allow for Vladimir Posse's occasional in-accuracies, the plausibility of his account of that meeting is patent. His version of Tolstoy's estimate of Gorky is borne out in various testimonies. The pianist A. B. Goldenweiser, for example, has recorded more than once the opinions he heard Tolstoy voice concerning Gorky, and these agree in substance with those cited by Posse. Time and again he noted in his diary Tolstoy's criticism of Gorky's " poorly developed sense of measure," his psychologic errors, his lack of restraint, his anthropomorphic descriptions of nature (" The sea laughed ") — on the latter point he is quoted also by Posse. Again, Golden-weiser recorded the fact that with all these, and other stric-tures, Tolstoy credited Gorky with a great service, chiefly in that he " had begun to describe in its full length the world of desolate tatterdemalions and tramps, of which heretofore hardly anyone had spoken. In this respect he did what Tur-genev and Grigorovich had once done for the peasant world." In his diary for May 11 (24), 1901, Tolstoy wrote: " We all

know that tramps are human beings and our brothers, but we know that theoretically, whereas he (Gorky) has shown them to us full length and lovingly, and he has infected us with this love. Their talk may be untrue, exaggerated, but we forgive him everything for having broadened our love."

To be adversely criticized by Tolstoy was equivalent to being scrapped with Shakespeare and Wagner and most of the world-famous artists; in other words, it meant to be placed in rather fine company. But though one must take Tolstoy's critical views, especially his sweeping generalizations, with a big grain of salt, one cannot gainsay the basical truth of most of the strictures in *What Is Art?* and in the numerous conversations recorded by his secretaries and interlocutors. In the case of Gorky, his multiple and varied experience may shield him against the accusation of " invention," repeatedly hurled at him by Tolstoy, whose contact with people outside of his own class was rather limited. The question of " psychologic invention " is too subjective for any categorical judgement. But where Tolstoy touches on concrete points, such as language and portraiture, his arguments are seldom refutable.

Goldenweiser heard Tolstoy praise Chekhov's language for its " simplicity, conciseness, and pictorial force," and condemn the language of Gorky as " artificial and turgid." Gorky tells, with humble frankness, of reading to Tolstoy his story, *The Bull,* which made the old man laugh heartily and compliment the author on his knowledge of " the tricks of language." Then he went on to reproach him for having all his peasants speak cleverly. He assured him that in life peasants deliberately talk in a silly way and incoherently, because of their inborn secretiveness and suspiciousness. They do not confide even in their own wives. Gorky's peasants appear outspoken, and deliver wise aphorisms. That is not true to life! Furthermore, " you touch everything up, people as well as nature — especially people ! "

The pertinence of these remarks is obvious. The later Gorky, from *Childhood* on, shook himself free from many of his early defects, but these were glaring even in some of his best works of the time when his conversations with Tolstoy took place. As

he read to Tolstoy some scenes from his *At the Bottom,* Tolstoy remarked with displeasure that its dialogue was too tricky and racy, unlike the real talk of common people. He also took exception to Gorky's effort at " filling all grooves and cracks with his own paint " and projecting himself through his characters, with the result that they were not characters at all, but made of the same cloth. As to women, he, Gorky, apparently did not understand them, for they did not come off with him, not one of them: one failed to remember them. The creator of Natasha Rostov and Anna Karenina was fastidiously exacting. Indeed, has any writer of fiction " understood " women as uncannily as Tolstoy?

Tolstoy did not like the play. It irritated him; old Luka, especially, annoyed him: he did not trust " his kindliness." One wonders whether Tolstoy vaguely felt the kinship with Luka, of which Gorky spoke in his notes. He certainly must have seen through the unctious tramp with his ingratiating ways and consoling lies. Did he detect in him a vicious caricature of the " genuine son of the people," Platon Karatayev, who caused the " conversion " of Pierre Bezukhov in *War and Peace?* Essentially Luka is not unlike Andreyev's pasquinade on Tolstoy, the spokesman of *My Memoirs* (in English, *The Man Who Found Truth*), who is a past master in hiding the truth behind a screen of logical sophistry.

As time went on, Tolstoy's criticisms of Gorky's writings became more and more adverse. In a letter to Korngold (November 10 (23), 1902), he accused Gorky of " unwittingly paying tribute to the fashionable teaching of Nietzsche, which is extremely revolting to me." On the margins of Gorky's stories he jotted down such remarks as " false," " disgusting " (*The Orlovs*), " nasty " (*Varenka Olesova*), and the like. Of *The Confession* he said, according to his friend and physician, Dr. D. P. Makovicky: " This is something beyond comprehension. A medley of words *à la* Maeterlinck or Balmont." Goldenweiser records that while reading Gorky's *Confession* Tolstoy " emitted ah's! and other sounds of terror." During the last two years of his life he recorded in the diaries his repeated attempts at reading and re-reading Gorky: his conscience ap-

parently was uneasy about disliking him. Thus: " Read Gorky. Very bad. The worst thing is that such an untrue estimate displeases me: one should see only good in him " (January 12 (25), 1909). Or: " In the evening I read Gorky. He knows the dark people, he uses fine language, that is, the speech of the people. But the psychology is absolutely arbitrary and unjustifiable, in the, for the most part heroic, feelings and thoughts which he lends his characters; besides, the environment is exceptionally immoral " (October 9 (22), 1909). One month later : " Evening at home, finished reading Gorky. Nothing but imaginary, artificial, tremendous, heroic emotions; sound false. But a big talent. Neither he nor Andreyev have anything to say. They ought to write verse or, which Andreyev is doing, plays. In verse one is saved by permissible vagueness, and in drama, by the scenery and actors." He even preferred Artsybashev and Kuprin to either Gorky or Andreyev, presumably because of their realistic clarity.

Tolstoy was fond of Gorky, as a " son of the people," and he appreciated his " service " as a sympathetic portrayer of social outcasts, but at the same time he could not rid himself of a certain uneasiness of his relations with the young author. Of course, he tried to rationalize this feeling. In Goldenweiser's diary we find recorded a typical Tolstoyan homily:

" Generally speaking, fame, popularity, is a dangerous thing. One of its harmful effects is that it prevents one from treating celebrities simply, Christian-like. Gorky, for instance, pleases me greatly as a man, yet I cannot treat him with complete sincerity: his fame does not let me. He seems to be not in his right place. And this fame is harmful for himself too. His novels are worse than his small tales, his plays are worse than his novels, while his appeals to the public [journalistic writings? — A.K.] are simply repellent."

In Tolstoy's diaries we find contradictory reactions to Gorky, seemingly whimsical fickleness. After Gorky's first call he entered, as we have seen, the words " I liked him." A little later he enumerated the visitors of the previous day, classifying them as " agreeable," and adding that Posse and Gorky were

" less agreeable." We are told (by I. Ilyinsky) that on that occasion Gorky's manners were rather conspicuous. He showered abuse on one of the guests, repeatedly " combed " his hair with his five fingers, and at dinner he half reclined in his chair and brandished the knife. The Countess Tolstoy asserts that these external trifles reflected in the eyes of her husband Gorky's inner lack of restraint. Hence the " less agreeable." But before long the diary tells us: " I am glad that both Gorky and Chekhov are pleasing to me, especially the former." In view of Tolstoy's extraordinary fondness of Chekhov, this admission is especially notable. About the same time (the fall of 1901) he wrote from Crimea to V. G. Chertkov: " I see here now and then Chekhov, an utter atheist but a kindly soul, and Gorky who has considerably more *fond*, even though he has been overpraised."

We have also Chekhov's word for Tolstoy's " uneven attitude " toward Gorky. With tears of amusement in his laughing eyes Chekhov tells Gorky of a conversation he has just had with Tolstoy, in which the later confessed that he " could not treat Gorky sincerely," himself not knowing why. And again an effort at rationalization: " Gorky is a malicious fellow. He resembles a theological student who has been made a monk against his will, and is therefore sore at the whole world. He has the mind of a spy; he has come from somewhere into the land of Canaan, which is alien to him, he scrutinizes everything, observes everything, and reports everything to some god or other of his. And his god is a monster, something like a wood-demon or water-devil that village wenches believe in." When Chekhov assures Tolstoy that Gorky is kind-hearted, the old man shakes his head: " No, no, I know better. He has a nose like the beak of a duck; such noses belong only to misfits and malicious chaps. Then, again, women don't take to him, and women, like dogs, have a scent for a good man. . . ." Granted that Tolstoy was half-joking, what about the earnest half?

From Gorky's own notes, fearlessly honest notes, it is quite evident that he did not enjoy Tolstoy's unmixed sympathy, as did Chekhov, for instance, for whom the elder man had a tender and immutable affection, even though he told him that his

plays were worse than Shakespeare's. Toward Gorky, Tolstoy often assumed the air of a mentor, now scolding him, now making fun of him, and in all cases suggesting a whiff of contempt for him. Thus he harped on his addiction to book reading, tracing it to his lack of self-confidence. Sensitive to sound harmony, Tolstoy could not bear the juxtaposition of common and bookish words, and he mercilessly ridiculed such cacophonies in Gorky. In Gorky's robust Russian, Tolstoy refused to stomach such foreign words as " absolutely " or " subject," which have Russian equivalents. He probably suspected, and with good reason, that the plebeian author now and then succumbed to the temptation of displaying his bookish genteelness. This was abhorrent to Tolstoy who, if anything, sinned in the opposite direction, often going out of his way to find a folk word or phrase to replace his natural vocabulary of the *salon*.

Gorky's grave countenance and earnest quest after truth at times amused the veteran seeker who " knew all about it." Tolstoy himself could talk and write in dead seriousness on spiritual topics, but in others this tone was apt to offend his aristocratic skepsis. In such cases he might be even frivolous toward his own views. On one occasion he and Gorky listened to a bird singing in the bushes. Tolstoy tried to whistle in tune, with indifferent results. Gorky, the one time bird-catcher, explained that the bird was a finch, and went on describing its characteristic trait of jealousy. " All life long one tune, and yet jealous. Man has hundreds of songs in his breast, yet he is blamed for being jealous," mused Tolstoy and proceeded to chat on jealousy in a way that seemed contradictory to his point of view in *The Kreutzer Sonata*. Gorky called his attention to this contradiction. Then Tolstoy " spread the radiance of a smile across his beard, and replied: ' I am not a finch.' "

Once Gorky asked Tolstoy whether he agreed with Pozdnyshev's (in *The Kreutzer Sonata*) opinion that physicians have destroyed and are destroying thousands and hundreds of thousands of human lives. Tolstoy looked at him quizzically: " Are you very anxious to know? " " Very! " " Then I shan't tell you! " A grin around the bearded mouth, the thumbs twirling amusedly.

Tolstoy treated Gorky much more cordially when the topic of conversation was not literary or abstract. He enjoyed Gorky's accounts of his past, praised his vivid vocabulary, and often laughed heartily over picturesque or spicy details. He laughed himself almost to a pain in his chest listening to Gorky's description of his battle with the widow of General Cornet at Kazan. Gorky was employed by the widow — a French woman with a past — as janitor and gardener. In her broken Russian the widow, always tipsy, swore volubly at her tenants, three genteel young princesses in poor circumstances, and abused them at every opportunity. Her janitor-gardener was young, chivalrous, and romantic, and, one day, on seeing his mistress insult the three princesses and drive them out of the garden, he interceded for the victims. When his verbal ex- hortation provoked a fresh stream of oaths and an extremely indecent gesture, the young knight grasped the widow by the shoulders, turned her around, and struck her with his shovel just below the back, so that she skipped out of the gate, crying out in surprise " Oh! Oh! Oh! " Tolstoy, choking with laughter and pain, could only scream in a thin voice: " With the shovel! . . . Over her buttocks with the shovel, eh? . . . Over her very buttocks? " Was it a broad shovel? " He visualized sharply every detail, and drew some piquant conclusions as to Madame Cornet's intentions. Gorky's naïveté and chivalry evidently touched him, for in conclusion he said:

You are funny. Don't be offended, you are very funny! And it is quite odd that in spite of everything you are good- natured, when you have the right to be full of malice. Yes, you might well be malicious. . . . Your mind I don't under- stand — it's a very tangled mind, but your heart is wise . . . yes, a wise heart!

What was Gorky's attitude toward Tolstoy?

The " unevenness " of the attitude was mutual. In a detached way, Gorky condemned vehemently Tolstoy the teacher, his nihilism, his anarchism, his " Chinaism," his whole system of passivity. A congenital rebel (" I have come into this world — to disagree! "), an active sympathizer with the revolutionary

movement in Russia, Gorky could not but deplore the will-paralysing effect of Tolstoy's non-resistance doctrine. He was fairly incensed against his followers, that swarm of Lilliputian pseudo-Tolstoyans who hid their craven shallowness behind the great man's tenets.

The difference between their outlook is illustrated in the following episode, narrated by Dr. K. V. Volkov. Tolstoy at the time was writing an introduction to the Russian version of Wilhelm von Polenz's novel, *Der Büttnerbauer,* and he spoke to Gorky with rapture about the " artistic truth of the scene, in which the wife, beaten up by her drunken husband, puts him to bed with tender care, and places a pillow under his head." Gorky said nothing. On the way back from Tolstoy's villa Gorky growled to Dr. Volkov: " A pillow under his head! She had better wallop him with a cudgel on his noddle! " Gorky has seen enough wife-beating in his life to appreciate the degrading masochism of Polenz's sweet scene.

Again, one could hardly expect the over-sensitive young writer not to resent Tolstoy's disapproval of his ways and writings, and particularly the tone of his disapproval, in which Gorky sensed contempt and disgust. Now Gorky has never been a good Christian, in the sense of forgiving, let alone loving, those who hurt him. He can hate in a subtle way, under the guise of solemn objectivity. I well remember his parenthetic remarks on the sexual impotence of Merezhkovsky, the permanent virginity of Zinaida Hippius, the running ears and bad teeth of Artsybashev, and similar irrelevant, as it were, darts, which nevertheless served to prick into nothingness the literary *raison d'être* of writers against whom he had a grudge. But Tolstoy had won Gorky's heart wholly, in defiance of reason and logic and peevish grievances. He did not realize the intensity of his affection for Tolstoy till the news of Tolstoy's death reached him, when he wept and sobbed like a baby — in fact, felt " orphaned."

As we read Gorky's reminiscences of Tolstoy, we visualize the great man with his contradictions and weaknesses. Gorky does not spare him, does not " retouch " him. Yet the reminiscences, and subsequent additions and fragments, and bits of

conversation, are all suffused with a glow of admiration and delight, of the kind that one may feel for a sweetheart or a child. Indeed, the very gaucheries of Tolstoy are lent a disarming charm, as if the beholder were facing the capers of an unusual child. How easily Gorky might have suggested the air of arrogance in the scene where Tolstoy reads aloud from his *Father Sergius*, then stops, lifts his head, and declares with conviction: " The old man wrote it well, quite well! " But to Gorky —

He said it with such amazing simplicity, his delight in beauty was so sincere, that I shall never forget the ecstasy I felt then, an ecstasy which I could not, did not know how to express, but which I was able to restrain only by a supreme effort. My heart even stopped beating, and then everything around me became revivingly fresh and new.

The words may sound a bit hyperbolic, but only the words. Gorky makes you aware of the magic force emanating from Tolstoy, of his power to enchant you, to lift and crush you, to draw out your best and worst, and above all to make you discard sham and veneer. Posse tells us of Tolstoy coming up to Gorky, who was hunched up in his chair, gloomy, like a storm-cloud, and asking him: " You don't like me, Alexey Maximovich? " To which Gorky: " I don't, Lev Nikolayevich! " Posse states that Gorky said it " half in jest, half in earnest," but Gorky himself records such cases, when he found it impossible to answer untruthfully, and there was not a shadow of " jesting " about the performance. " You do not like me? " and Gorky *had* to admit that at the moment he did not. " You do not love me? " " No, today I do not love you."

Gorky could not apply the common yardstick to Tolstoy, and however realistically he has drawn him, he has given him extraordinary, heroic dimensions. Here is, for example, an unforgettable portrait of Tolstoy in Crimea:

I was walking over to him at Gaspra along the coast, and below the Yusupov estate, on the very shore, I discovered among the stones his small, angular figure in grey, mussed clothes and a crumpled hat. He sat, his cheek-bones leaning on his hands, the silvery strands of his beard streaming through

his fingers, and was looking far out to sea; greenish wavelets rolled up docilely to his feet and fondled them, as though telling something about themselves to the old wizard. It was a speckled day, cloud shadows glided over the stones, and together with the stones the old man appeared now bright, now dark. The stones were enormous, riven by cracks and covered with smelly seaweed; there had been a high tide the day before. He, too, seemed to me like an ancient stone come to life, that knows all the beginnings and goals, and muses as to when and what will be the end of the stones, of the grasses of the earth, of the waters of the sea, of man and of the whole universe, from the stone to the sun. And the sea is part of his soul, and everything around him is of and from him. In the pensive immobility of the old man I fancied something of a diviner, a magician, something that plumbed the darkness beneath him and inquiringly soared in the blue void above. It seemed that it was he, his centred will, that was summoning and repelling the waves, that was charging the fleeting clouds and shadows which stirred the stones and woke them to life. Suddenly, in a momentary madness, I felt that in a minute — it was quite possible! — he might stand up, wave his hand, and the sea would congeal, become glassy, while the stones would stir and cry out, and all things about would come to life, make a noise, speak in different voices about themselves, about him, against him. I cannot express in words what I felt then. There were both ecstasy and dread in my soul, and then everything blended in one happy thought:

"I am not an orphan on the earth, so long as this man lives on it!"

Such passages as this might be expected in a panegyrical recital of some disciple and worshipper, but there is no hagiolatry in Gorky's notes on Tolstoy. The more striking therefore are these hyperboles, interlaced as they are with bits of matter-of-fact observation and criticism. Gorky was anxious lest Tolstoy be canonized, made into a legend, and he painstakingly built his great portrait out of everyday, concrete stuff, that the world might see Tolstoy, the flesh and blood individual. He has succeeded admirably in his task, and the achievement is not marred by occasional notes of adoration, which seem to

break forth in spite of himself. In conclusion I wish to cite a note, a surprising note from one who so violently opposed Tolstoy's religion:

. . . Suddenly he asked me, as if dealing me a blow:
" Why don't you believe in God? "
" I have not faith, Lev Nikolayevich."
" That is not true. You are a believer by nature, and you cannot get on without God. You will come to realize this before long. Your disbelief comes from obstinacy: the world is not what you would like it to be. Some people do not believe also from shyness; it happens with youths who admire a woman but do not want to show it from fear that she won't understand, and also from want of courage. Faith, like love, requires courage, daring. One must say to oneself, I believe! and all will be well. . . . You were born a believer, and it is no use pretending that you are not. You say — beauty? and what is Beauty? It is the highest and most perfect — God."

He hardly ever spoke to me on this subject, and its seriousness and suddenness somehow crushed and overwhelmed me. I kept silent. He was sitting on the couch with his legs drawn under him, and with a triumphant smile radiating in his beard he said, shaking his finger at me:
" You won't get away from this by silence, no! "
And I, who do not believe in God, gazed at him very cautiously for some reason, and a little timidly. I looked and thought:
" This man is godlike! "

IN THE REVOLUTIONARY TURMOIL:

I. THE INVISIBLE THREAD

ON THE EVE

MEANWHILE, as we watched the evolution of Alexey Peshkov the tramp into the celebrated Maxim Gorky, other eyes had watched him closely. The Central Spider had not relaxed the hold of its Invisible Thread upon one of its numerous victims, Alexey Maximovich Peshkov, member of the dyers' guild at Nizhni Novgorod by his passport, and an author by occupation — hence a doubly suspicious character. The biographer of Gorky cannot help feeling indebted to the meticulous care with which the Russian police recorded his actions and movements, from his bakery days at Kazan to the outbreak of the revolution of 1917. From various parts of the empire, and later from abroad, flowed the reports of secret and open watchers into the vast files of the central Department of Police in St. Petersburg. Part of this material, now published by Soviet archivists, forms a valuable addition to the extant data on Gorky's life, with allowances for the occasionally fanciful imagination of over-eager agents of the Invisible Thread. We shall now trace Gorky's connexion with the revolutionary movement, the most conspicuous chapter in his story.

As we have seen, Gorky was not born into a proletarian or revolutionary-minded family. His grandfather and uncles, with whom most of his childhood was spent, belonged to the artisans of the God- and Tsar-fearing lower middle class, from whose ranks were recruited the reactionary bands of Russia's Black Hundreds. His employers and fellow-employees on the motley jobs that filled his boyhood and youth were similarly of the " smug citizen " variety. Nor could the tramps and " ex-

men " of his vagabondage period pass for either proletarian or revolutionary; if anything they were *Lumpenproletariat,* and as unpolitical as they were unmoral. Gorky's only claim to membership in the proletariat, the aristocracy of Soviet Russia, might be based on his apprenticeship in the Kazan bakeries, when he was in his teens. Indeed, this membership was recently given formal sanction by the bakers' union, which presented Gorky with the card of an Honorary Red Baker.

Yet, as we have also seen, Gorky was a rebel almost from his swaddling clothes, with " I have come into this world — to disagree " as his life's motto. Instead of subduing him, the environment provoked in him resentment and enmity. He refused to accept as sanctified by tradition such traits as wife-beating, drunken debauches, oaths, gossip, cheap and joyless vice. Not only did he refuse to accept these conventions, but even at a tender age he ventured to combat them, incurring the wrath and rod of his seniors. By the same token he eagerly sympathized with whatever differed from and militated against " things as they are," and was naturally condemned and persecuted by their upholders. From the age of twelve, when he avidly caught whispers about the assassination of Alexander II, he was drawn to the underground revolutionary movement. Five years later, at Kazan, his interest in the great adventure caught the eye of the Spider, which followed him ever after, through his experiences at Krasnovidovo, Borisoglebsk, Tiflis, Nizhni Novgorod, and other points west of the Volga.

At the height of his Success and Fame, in 1899, the police recorded Gorky's sojourn in St. Petersburg and the fact that he was made the centre of attention on the part of the intelligentsia. According to " confidential information," he read a story about prostitutes, that had been forbidden by the censor, at a memorial meeting for N. G. Chernyshevsky. Other prominent radicals were reported to have been at that meeting, such as Tugan-Baranovsky, Struve, and Posse. The literary banquet arranged by *Zhizn* in Gorky's honour, of which we have spoken before, came to the knowledge of the police

through an intercepted letter of a St. Petersburg revolutionist to a comrade in Zurich. The author of the letter stated that for a fortnight the literary circles fussed about Gorky, that Gorky was bored by the intelligentsia, " felt sick of the reigning banality," and finally, at the banquet, he " exploded " in " loudly abusing those things before which we have been accustomed to burn incense," and branding the intelligentsia and men of letters " as bourgeois, stagnant and vulgar like the lowest of the low." Those present at the banquet were " outraged by such blasphemy," but to the writer of the letter Gorky's words were " fiery letters on our dead tables," and they " sounded like a revolutionary summons."

The Department of Police was becoming alarmed by the growing political significance of Gorky as a figure and a symbol, particularly in Nizhni Novgorod, where he served as a centre for revolutionary workmen, students, and deported politicals. Intercepted letters from his native city contained references to Gorky as " the publicist of Young Russia," representative of the democracy of the free Russian people who are beginning to wake up from their sleep of centuries," " characteristic of the present moment, a moment of rebirth." The Department instructed the Nizhni Novgorod Gendarmerie to keep Gorky under strict supervision, especially to watch " his relations with the college youth."

Russian colleges have always provided a restless, revolutionary element from among those who deemed education not only a privilege but also a responsibility. The efforts of the Government to hold the students under a severe régime, compelling them to wear a uniform, and forbidding them any sort of initiative and organization, whetted their discontent and resentment, which grew in scope and violence toward the end of the eighteen nineties. In 1897, Maria Vetrova, a college girl, was imprisoned in the Peter and Paul Fortress, where she committed suicide under mysterious circumstances. For sixteen days the authorities kept her death a secret, and then the Vetrov relatives were notified that Vera had poured kerosene over her body and burned herself to death. Violence and foul play were suspected, and the incident served as a spark

to set the student body aflame with indignation. Throughout Russia disturbances took place in the higher schools of learning, and by 1899, thirty colleges with more than twenty-five thousand students were involved. As a rule the college administration acted hand in glove with the Authorities, and for this reason purely local and academic issues assumed unduly exaggerated proportions. The rectors did not scruple about employing police and military force to keep the lectures going and to disperse student mass assemblies. On occasion the cossacks attacked student gatherings and brutally assaulted the unarmed young people with their notorious *nagaykas* — braided-leather whips with metal tips. The beating of the university students in St. Petersburg on February 8, 1899, has been commemorated in a college song which has been sung by all Russia. It has a rollicking refrain:

Akh, little nagayka, little nagayka, sweet little nagayka!
Thou has strolled over our backs on February the eighth.

Both the college administrators and the imperial government acted with tactless severity. The decree of the Government to mobilize the rioting students as privates roused protests from every corner, including the military, who resented the idea of using the army as a punitive institution. Bogolepov, the Minister of Education, was shot and killed by Karpovich, an expelled student, and shortly afterward the famous " Kazan Demonstration " took place. Thousands of men and women gathered in front of the Kazan Cathedral in St. Petersburg to protest against " the violation of human rights." Mounted cossacks galloped into the midst of the crowd, and without giving warning attacked them. A considerable number of prominent people were injured. The " Union of Writers " sent to the Minister of the Interior a signed protest against the conduct of the Administration, and a demand for a judicial investigation. In response, the Union was ordered to disband, and many of its members were exiled from the capital, together with quantities of students, who were to spread the gospel through the length and breadth of Russia.

Gorky reacted to these events vigorously. The police intercepted a letter which he wrote early in 1901 to Teleshov of the Moscow literary " Wednesdays ": " My dear, good man, we must raise our voices in behalf of the Kiev students. We must circulate a petition for the annulment of the mobilization decree. I implore you: do what you can! Some cities have already begun to act." About the same time, he wrote a typical Gorky note to Valery Bryusov, leader of the Moscow symbolist poets and editor of a precious miscellany, *Severnyie Tsvety* (*Northern Blossoms*):

I am in the mood of a beaten and chained dog. . . . If you love man, Sir, you will understand me, let us hope. You see, I feel that to force the students into the soldiery is an abomination, an infamous crime against personal liberty, an idiotic whim of blackguards oversated with power. My heart is boiling, and I should gladly spit into the impudent mugs of those men-haters who will read your *Severnyie Tsvety* and praise them, as they have been praising me too. The thing is outrageous and atrocious, to the point of making me ragingly mad at everything and everybody . . . even at Bunin: I love him, but I cannot understand why he fails to sharpen like a dagger his talent, which is as fine as mat silver, and thrust it in the needed direction.

The Department of Police had information that in February, 1901, Gorky came to St. Petersburg, specifically " in order to attend a meeting of the ' Union of Writers ' to commemorate the fortieth anniversary of the liberation of the peasants." At that meeting, and after its conclusion, in the Palkin restaurant, Gorky behaved in a " revolutionary manner." He was also reported to have taken part in the " Kazan Demonstration," and to have signed the protest of the " Union of Writers." A certain Gurevich, a radical journalist in the secret service of the police, informed the Department that Gorky had given two thousand rubles to the Students' Agitation Committee, and a similar sum to the Fighting Union for the Liberation of the Working Class, the money coming " from honoraria for his stories." The same informant asserted that Gorky belonged

to a number of revolutionary organizations, which he supported in a variety of ways.

In March, 1901, the Chief of the Nizhni Novgorod Gendarmerie received a telegram from the Director of the Department of Police, to the effect that Gorky and his protégé, Petrov-Skitalets, had acquired in St. Petersburg a mimeograph-press " for the purpose of printing proclamations to the workmen of Sormovo," an industrial suburb of Nizhni Novgorod. The precise dimensions of the case in which the criminal article was expressed, were given, as well as the address of the drug-store where it was to be delivered. The Chief was instructed to watch closely the peregrinations of the mimeograph-press, and to plan the arrest of Gorky and Skitalets simultaneously with that of the printers of the proclamations. Had someone played a hoax on the Director, or had the contents of his confidential message leaked out prematurely — or in time? At all events, the Nizhni Novgorod Gendarmerie was obliged to report its failure to discover the alleged case, despite the meticulous inspection of all incoming goods. Nevertheless, on his return to Nizhni Novgorod in April, Gorky was arrested, together with a group of fellow-conspirators, in connexion with the mythical mimeograph.

Among these was, besides Skitalets, a youth by the name of Zinovy Sverdlov, who was one year later adopted by Gorky, and who is now known as Major Zinovy Pechkoff of the Foreign Legion of the French Army, author of *The Bugle Calls,* a eulogy of the Legion. Zinovy was one of Gorky's " finds," a would-be dramatic talent. Gorky tried, through Chaliapin, to put Zinovy into the Moscow " Philarmonia," but as a Jew Sverdlov had no chance. Hence the " adoption."

Gorky on that occasion was charged with a number of political offences, among them the authorship of a *Refutation of the Official Account of the Kazan Demonstration,* and of a poem, *To the Tune of the Marseillaise.* He was also accused of trying to organize in his native city an anti-government demonstration on the anniversary of the death of Lieven, a Nizhni Novgorod student of the Moscow university who committed suicide while in prison by burning himself alive; of

arranging boating parties on the Volga for the purpose of "discussing a question of tendentious nature"; also of planning the clandestine publication of a miscellany which was to contain articles of a "tendentious nature."

We know now that practically all of the charges against him were true. It is doubtful whether he was the author of the poem *To the Tune of the Marseillaise*: it was too drab a banality. But he had certainly written the *Refutation,* which read in part: "We were eye-witnesses of the brutal actions of the police at the Kazan Cathedral, and we hereby assert that the official account of the deportment of the general public and college students on March 4th, is a deliberate lie, and it flagrantly distorts the actual events." It denied the official version which alleged that the students behaved improperly inside the church, smoking cigarettes with their hats on; among those who were present in the Cathedral and categorically testified against the official version, the *Refutation* cited Professor Petrushevsky, formerly the Emperor's tutor, and Lieutenant-General Wasmund. "We further assert," ran the text, " . . . that the police and cossacks had been secretly stationed since early morning in private courtyards: Prefect Kleigels had planned a trap for the students. . . . Some of the young people had been lured to the Cathedral by leaflets that emanated from the Secret Service. We state, on the basis of words of cossacks who had taken part in the outrage, that on the preceding day officers assured their soldiers that ' the students intended to kill the Emperor, and that they should be beaten without mercy.' We assert that on March 4th, the police and cossacks were given vodka, in order to rouse them. . . . We assert categorically that . . . the cossacks appeared on the square at the silent signal of Kleigels, immediately dismounted, and began to beat the crowd right and left with their *nagaykas,* having in no way warned them of their intentions. . . . Thus Prince Vyazemsky, member of the State Council, witnessed the beating of the writers Peshekhonov and Annensky, and his efforts at exhorting the drunken mob were of no avail: cossacks grabbed women by the hair and whipped them with their *nagaykas.* . . . The purpose of Kleigels' action

is evident: by utilizing the students' vexation at the mobilization decree, he endeavours to lend a revolutionary character to their movement, and by quelling this self-made revolution to reap the laurels. . . ."

Posse adds a few interesting details regarding the Kazan Demonstration. It appears that many authors, even elderly men, resolved to take part in the demonstration, in the hope that their presence might " abate the energy of the police." When the police and cossacks began to beat the crowd, Korolenko's friend and collaborator, " old Annensky, his face flushed, his grey beard entangled, his eyes flashing, rushed up to Kleigels, who proudly towered on his magnificent horse, and shaking his unarmed, senile hand, demanded that he put a stop to the outrage. A policeman knocked the old writer down with the blow of his fist. The enormous blue-black circle around his eye played a decisive rôle, when he removed the bandage at the evening meeting of the Union of Writers [referring to the protest sent by the Union to the Minister]. Peshekhonov was also beaten and bruised, but he received the blows on his back."

Nor was the Department of Police wrong about the mimeograph-press. It has recently been established that Gorky did buy such a press and had it sent with a trusted man to Nizhni Novgorod, where it lodged at the home of B. V. M., now a professor in an American university. There they printed revolutionary proclamations, Gorky's uncensored writings, and such illegal pieces as *The Demolished Dam*, by the celebrated revolutionist, Gershuni. The police intercepted a letter written by B. V. M. to his revolutionary friends in Moscow, in which he advised them: " If you have not enough of proclamations, we can send you some from Nizhni Novgorod." Shortly afterward Gorky helped the Nizhni Novgorod Social-Democrats buy a real printing-press, which was placed in a government vodka-shop; its official keeper was Lebedev, a member of the Party. Both Lebedev and the press disappeared after a robbery had occurred in the vodka-shop, and just before the police came to investigate.

Proofs of Gorky's actively sympathetic attitude toward the

revolution were hardly necessary. There was enough incendiary matter in the legal, signed writings of Gorky to brand him as a dangerous enemy of the régime. Phrases and passages from Gorky were universally cited and circulated as militant slogans, such as " To the madness of the brave we sing a song," or " In the madness of the brave is the wisdom of life," from the allegoric *Song of the Falcon.* At the time of his arrest there was published in the Marxian review *Zhizn* his *Song of the Stormy Petrel,* another allegory which was shortly on everyone's tongue in Russia, and which caused the suspension of *Zhizn.*

The poem, written in metric prose, was composed by Gorky during a meeting of the *Zhizn* contributors, in February, 1901. A. Svirsky tells us that while they were discussing a paper read by E. Chirikov, Gorky excused himself and went into the adjacent room. About forty minutes later he came back, and read aloud the *Song,* which he had just " jotted down." When he finished, he wiped his tear-stained eyes with his fist, and said " with childlike simplicity: ' Well written, *chort vozmi!* ' "

" The storm! Soon the storm will break forth! . . . Let the storm break mightily! " The meaning of such phrases in the *Song* was obvious enough to be appreciated by a grammar-school pupil. Allegories of this sort, with their transparent references to the revolutionary struggle, were manna to the Russian reader. He felt as a fellow-conspirator when poring over Gershuni's *Demolished Dam,* for instance, a poetic allegory of the advent of the Socialist-Revolutionary Party. He chuckled at Repin's literary painting, *What Expanse!* in which a young couple, collegiates, ecstatically gaze upon a stormy sea. Aside from their quality of reserved emotion, these compositions offered the public a piquant taste of forbidden goods, of dangerous ideas smuggled through and delivered under the very nose of the censor. The sensation was not unlike that experienced by schoolboys making faces in the presence of their teacher.

Yet despite the obviousness of Gorky's revolutionary proc-livities, and their anxiety to silence such a pernicious enemy,

the Authorities lacked substantial proofs for their accusations against him. To be sure, the Russian administration had exiled and imprisoned thousands of offenders without the benefit of of court or trial, and it would not have scrupled to treat Gorky in the same manner, had he not become so inconveniently notable a person. The country was getting aware of the preciousness of Gorky's life and freedom, and his arrest had caused a commotion even among influential citizens. From reports to the Department of Police we learn that the manifestation in honour of the student Lieven did not take place, because on the eve of the anniversary a meeting of Nizhni Novgorod citizens, arranged with the permission of the Governor, resolved to call off the manifestation. Their chief motive was the fact that Gorky had been too deeply involved in the organization of the affair, and that its consummation imperilled his safety. The police also knew that although Gorky's home was watched day and night, and spies followed all his visitors, they were unable to trace a single political offender of importance to his door: the revolutionary parties were careful not to compromise Gorky. There were also personal intercessions in his behalf, notably one from Yasnaya Polyana. Tolstoy, who had met Gorky shortly before his imprisonment, interceded in his behalf with Prince Oldenburgsky and with Prince Svyatopolk-Mirsky of the Ministry of the Interior, as we have had occasion to note.

The Administration was forced to treat the imprisoned Gorky humanely. But at first Gorky had a taste of the petty arbitrariness of official Russia. His correspondence, for example, reached him belatedly or not all. Thus a letter from J. Rode, from Berlin, offering to publish abroad his works forbidden by the censor, was not delivered to him. The same fate befell a letter to him from Herman Rosenthal, head of the Slavonic Section of the New York Public Library, who informed him of the favourable impression his *Foma Gordeyev* had made on the American public. Gorky was constrained to scribble a note to the warden: " If the outrageous system of opening letters and telegrams is necessary and is sanctioned

by law, can you not at least deliver me telegrams without delay?" Aside from this complaint, Gorky behaved "properly." Years later, when the Nizhni Novgorod revolutionary youth "raised Cain" in jail, and listened to no reason, the hoary jailer would use the one effective argument: "Shame on you! Mister Gorkov used to stay in this very tower — not the like of you, but a writer! Yet he was polite and decent, and made no noise. Surely he was more important a political offender than you, I'll bet on that. Ekh, you!" The young prisoners, we are told by one of them, would, indeed, quiet down.

At the request of Katerina Pavlovna, the prison physician examined Gorky, and pronounced his condition fair enough. In fact, his report implied that the prison régime affected Gorky's health favourably. Katerina Pavlovna requested the prosecutor for a re-examination of the prisoner. The Department of Police, probably owing to Tolstoy's intercession, supported her request, and consequently a commission of seven physicians examined him in prison, and reported the condition of his lungs to be extremely poor. He was released from jail to remain under "special supervision." His presence in Nizhni Novgorod appeared quite undesirable in the eyes of the Governor, and he was soon exiled to the neighbouring small town of Arzamas, where it was easier to keep an eye on him and his visitors. At the same time, the Governor advised the Special Council of the Ministry of the Interior that it was "absolutely necessary to forbid Peshkov to reside in the Nizhni Novgorod province, where his influence among the workmen might easily express itself in a form quite undesirable for the public safety and order."

Gorky took his exile philosophically. Arzamas was quiet and isolated, and Gorky was enabled to do a good deal of writing. He also enjoyed the occasional visits of such friends as Leonid Andreyev, and of some rare local characters who had the temerity to call on the exile in defiance of the openly glowering police. "They have assigned to me several spies," Gorky wrote to Nemirovich-Danchenko. "Some of them are not a bad lot; they come to talk to me. Others stroll in front of the windows.

I hail one of them, and ask: ' Are you a spy? ' ' No.' ' You lie. You are a spy.' ' No, as God lives, I am not.' ' Have you been long on the job? ' ' Not so long.' "

Meanwhile the condition of his health grew markedly worse, and Gorky petitioned the Minister of the Interior to permit him a sojourn in Crimea. In November, 1901, he was allowed to reside in Crimea until the following April, with no right to stop at Yalta, probably because of its central situation and its proximity to the summer villas of the Imperial family.

Gorky's departure from Nizhni Novgorod was made use of by his local admirers for political purposes. The banquet in his honour was enlivened by revolutionary speeches, and it was concluded with revolutionary songs. Gorky sat at the main table with the " Girondists," as the local liberals were dubbed by the radicals, the " Montagnards," who occupied the back tables. Attorney Yavorovsky, representing the former, delivered a brilliant address, composed out of Gorky's texts, with the leading motive of " To the madness of the brave we sing a song," from the *Song of the Falcon.* In response, the revolutionist Kolosov, for the " Mountain," caustically hurled at the liberals the aphorism of Gorky from the same *Song:* " He who is born to crawl, is not able to fly." He proceeded to protest against the violence of the Government. When Gorky was asked to speak he begged to be excused from making a speech, and instead he read the manuscript of his sketch, *About a Writer Who Became Conceited.* It was a bitter and ungracious bit to be offered at a banquet. A coquettish young lady reproved Gorky: " Look here, Alexey Maximovich, we are fêting you, and you abuse us! " He answered grimly: " Your actions deserve it. Or rather your inaction."

On the day when he took the train, hundreds of people gathered at the station, shouted greetings to him, sang forbidden songs, and circulated secretly printed leaflets in which Gorky was hailed as the champion of the " madness of the brave." The report of the Department of Police gave a detailed account of the behaviour of the crowd, the songs it sang, the slogans it shouted, and the route it followed, after leaving the station, through the main streets, continuing to shout and sing.

According to this report, Gorky " appeared several times on the steps of the car, and begged the crowd to discontinue the singing, saying that he had not expected such a leave-taking, that the conduct of the demonstrators might have bad consequences for them, which would pain him greatly, and that, finally, the songs made him feel sad. To this the crowd answered with shouts of ' Hurrah,' ' Long live Gorky,' and . . . Zinovy Sverdlov shouted: ' Long live liberty! ' "

An authoritative eye-witness corrects the police report, asserting that it was not Zinovy who shouted the criminal phrase, but his brother, Yakov, the well-known Chairman of the All-Russian Executive Committee during the earlier part of the Bolshevik régime. The same Yakov made another daring sally about a fortnight later. He stood up in the gallery of the Municipal Theatre, when the lights were turned off, and harangued the Government for persecuting the writers, citing the case of Gorky, who, he alleged, was deported from Nizhni Novgorod without trial.

The police were, evidently, unprepared for the manifestation at the depot. According to I. Gruzdev, " most of them had foregathered in the Cathedral for vespers, as it was the eve of the day of the Archangel Michael, patron of the police." Later a score of students and other citizens were arrested in connexion with this event. The young generation found in Gorky an incentive for rebellion against existing conditions, and used his name as a symbol. Typical of their enthusiasm and tendency to exaggerate, is the proclamation circulated in Moscow by Nizhni Novgorod students on the day before the demonstration at the train:

Tomorrow morning, November 8th, on the eight o'clock mail train Maxim Gorky will arrive at Moscow on his way to Crimea. He is being deported from Nizhni by order of the Administration, that is to say, arbitrarily and unlawfully. All Nizhni is outraged by this fresh manifestation of violence against our beloved poet, the singer of struggle and freedom and the madness of the brave. . . . Tomorrow we are arranging a farewell demonstration for him, in which all classes of society will unite under the common banner of open protest.

We do not know how this will end; perhaps they will crush us, but we will be there to the last man. We now appeal to the Moscow college youth and to all Moscow society with a request to join our protest, to extend it, and to endeavour to arrange similar demonstrative farewells in the cities through which Gorky will pass. He is on his way to Crimea *via* Kharkov. Let the road of the fighter for the freedom of human individuality be the triumphal march of a conqueror; let society once again respond with a bold and open protest against the challenge of the Government. Let thinking Russia show that it has sufficiently advanced and grown strong enough to battle for its rights, unafraid of crude force. Forward, comrades! A great and dark power is against us, but the dawn of freedom and a new life is already rising.

What if Gorky was not deported but allowed to proceed to Crimea at his own request? The fact of the matter was not important, as long as the affair could be utilized as a symbol of official tyranny, on the one hand, and of awakening public consciousness, on the other hand. The Government, however, was not going to let Gorky's journey become a " triumphal march." Moscow, in particular, could be depended upon to thwart public manifestations. The old capital was in the hands of the Grand Duke Sergey, one of the Tsar's uncles, perhaps the most despotic and perverse of the tribe. To the very end he opposed liberal reforms and urged his nephew and sister-in-law-niece (his wife was the sister of the Empress) to remain staunchly autocratic. In 1905 he was literally blown to pieces by the bomb of Kalyayev, and popular rumour had it that the Grand Duke's right hand was discovered in a coffer of Red Cross funds, of which he had been the honorary president. Sergey was ably assisted by the chief-of-police, Trepov, a member of an illustrious family of the Tsar's policemen. His father had the distinction of having unwittingly inaugurated the terroristic period of the *narodnik* revolutionists. In 1878, his maltreatment of political prisoners, while he was chief-of-police in Petersburg, provoked a nineteen-year-old girl, Vera Zasulich, to fire at him. The popularity of the wounded Trepov may be judged from the fact that Vera Zasulich was acquitted by the jury, though she admitted her attempt at killing him. Now his

son was in charge of the Moscow police, and was to climb higher and higher. During the revolution of 1905 he was governor-general of Petersburg, and made himself notorious by his laconic order to the troops that were to pacify the enthusiastic crowds on the publication of the Constitutional Manifesto: " Spare no cartridges! " Public demands forced the Tsar to remove him, but he rewarded his loyalty by appointing him commandant of the palace, responsible for the safety of the Imperial family.

Turning again to the abundant material of the Department of Police, we find that the director of the Moscow Art Theatre had petitioned His Imperial Highness, the Governor-General, to permit Gorky a sojourn of three or four days in Moscow, when on his way to the Crimea, for the purpose of " changing the fourth act of a comedy which he had composed." The reference was apparently to the play *Smug Citizens,* which Gorky had just finished and forwarded to Nemirovich-Danchenko. The request was, of course, not granted. Furthermore, General Trepov skilfully prevented a demonstration in honour of Gorky, describing his method at length and not without glee in his report to the Director of the Department of Police.

In view of the fact [begins the report] that the Nizhni Novgorod guildsman, Alexey Maximovich Peshkov (Gorky), as one under indictment for a serious political crime, does not possess the right to stop at this capital, and also since, according to advices, agitators had managed to recruit toward the evening of November 7th, about three hundred persons who consented to take part in a manifestation appointed for November 8th, at the time of the arrival of Gorky at the Moscow depot. . . .

The General's period is interminably long-winded, and we have sampled it enough. Briefly, Trepov gave orders to detach from the train the car in which Gorky and his family were travelling, about two miles from Moscow; then transfer them to a passenger car specially attached to a freight train, and have them taken to the station of Podolsk, beyond Moscow, there to change again for a train going south to Kharkov. Gorky's wife was allowed to stop at Moscow for a few hours

and arrange her husband's affairs. According to Trepov, about five hundred persons, mostly students, had gathered at the Moscow depot, looking in vain for Gorky among the arrivals. Princess Shakhovskoy, in charge of the information bureau, advised the crowd that Gorky's car had been detached at the station Moscow Second; they all proceeded thither, to discover that Gorky had already left for Podolsk. Nothing was left for them to do but to disperse, adds the General in a tone of mock sympathy. He also states that Chaliapin and several writers journeyed from Moscow to Podolsk to bid good-bye to Gorky.

N. Teleshov gives some curious details concerning this visit to Gorky at the station of Podolsk. Besides Teleshov, there were Ivan Bunin, Leonid Andreyev, K. P. Pyatnistky, F. Chaliapin, and Gorky's German translator, Scholtz, who " had come from Berlin for the special purpose of meeting Alexey Maximovich in person, and of seeing with his own eyes how prominent writers live in Russia." Gorky was overjoyed to see his friends trooping into the tiny Ladies' Room, his place of confinement at the station, which he had been pacing up and down " like a beast in its cage." They obtained the permission of the railroad gendarme to spend the remaining few hours in the town, and drove to the best restaurant available, where the seven of them proved too big a crowd. While they were waiting for dinner, the local population got wind of the celebrities in their midst, and besieged the station in expectation of catching a glimpse of them. The German Scholtz felt rather nervous on discovering, when he peeped into the entry of the restaurant, that gendarmes were searching their overcoats. The Russians assured him that it was " a common occurrence." A moment later the owner of the place entered their room in great embarrassment and requested all present to sign their names and addresses in the guest book. The purpose of this procedure was obvious to any citizen of a *Polizeistaat*. Chaliapin rose and thundered at the poor fellow that he alone would sign his name, the rest being his personal guests. His basso and the signature of an " Artist of the Imperial Theatres " extinguished the involuntary agent of the police. When they re-

turned to the depot, the gendarmes forced them " very politely " through the waiting throng into the Ladies' Room, where they remained until the arrival of Gorky's train.

Trepov telegraphed Gorky's itinerary to the governors of the provinces of Orel, Tula, Kursk, Kharkov, and Simferopol, in order that they might prevent demonstrations in his honour. The Chief of the Kharkov Gendarmerie reported to the Department of Police that about three hundred students attempted to greet Gorky at the depot; but since they were not allowed to enter the station grounds, they retreated to a neighbouring railroad bridge where they awaited the train. At its approach they sang the *Dubinushka* and shouted Hurrah, but the engine began to whistle so loudly that the " demonstrative ovation was drowned by the noise." The Governor of the Kharkov province, in his report, adds a delectable touch to this victory of Autocracy over its foe, stating that the crowd on the bridge " was bombarded by the engine with such a volume of steam that it was forced to take flight." Both sides seemingly indulged in boyish pranks, which they took seriously.

The same incident is described by Gorky in a letter to Posse:

At Kharkov I was ordered to remain in the car. I went out, though, and found the depot deserted, except for a throng of policemen. Outside of the station was gathered a large crowd of students and others, held back by the police. There were shouts and noise; someone was being arrested. The train starts off. It is one o'clock; a dark night. Suddenly Pyatnitsky and I, standing on the open platform of the car, hear in the darkness above our heads a powerful, juicy, militant roar. It appears that the railroad bridge is thronged with people. That was fine, old chap. The bridge was high above, and the shouts were stormy, buoyant, and in unison. I am telling you this not for the aggrandizement of Gorky in your eyes, but in testimony of the state of mind that is taking hold of the better part of the public. . . .

After a few similar incidents — at the Kursk depot the demonstrators were reported to have stopped the train — Gorky finally reached sunny Crimea, where he spent a few months in communion with Tolstoy, Chekhov, and other writ-

ers who could afford to live there. It was a restful sojourn, save for the never abating surveillance of the Invisible Thread, and — the Academy scandal.

At the end of February, 1902, Gorky received a letter addressed " To the Honorary Academician Alexey Maximovich Peshkov," in which A. Veselovsky, chairman of the branch of Russian language and literature of the Imperial Academy of Sciences, informed him officially of his election as Honorary Academician in *belles lettres*. In a private letter Veselovsky wrote to Gorky: " My sincere sympathy with your work prompts me to nominate you as an active member of the oldest Russian literary society, which once saw among its ranks Gogol and Pushkin, and at present is proud to count Leo Tolstoy as a member. . . ." The election took place at the joint assembly of the Academicians of Russian language and literature and of *belles lettres.*

The unprecedentedly rapid rise of the erstwhile tramp and stevedore to the summit of Russian literature was astonishing in itself, but that within four years after the publication of his first volume of stories, Maxim Gorky, plebeian and rebel by word and action, should be elevated to the rank of Honorary Academician, member of an Imperial institution under the presidency of the Grand Duke Constantine, seemed amazing, and struck some people as a fairy-tale, and others as a nightmare. Prince Meshchersky, in his weekly *Grazhdanin,* voiced the nightmare-reaction of the aristocratic circles to the " terrible " news which " made his eyes grow dim " :

I thought I was delirious, and that the words I was reading were not actually printed but were an optical illusion . . . my delirium frightened me. At that moment a friend rushed in, exclaiming: " Have you read the news? They have had the audacity to elect Maxim Gorky Academician! " Then it was not a delirium, I mused with a pain of dread in my heart, it was a fact, then! The affront hurled at all cultivated Russia, at the Russia of Pushkin and Karamzin, at all *loyal* Russia, by the Academy of Sciences, was an historical fact! The mockery over talent, the defamation of two hundred years of

the Academy had actually happened! " Good Lord! " cried my friend, " what are we coming to? Maxim Gorky — an Academician! "

The fairy-tale — or the nightmare — did not last long. About a fortnight after Gorky's election the *Pravitelstvenny Vestnik* (*Official Gazette*), contained the following news: " In view of the elucidation of certain circumstances that had been unknown to the assembly . . . in the Imperial Academy of Sciences, the election as Honorary Academician of Alexey Maximovich Peshkov, who is indicted under Article 1035 of the Criminal Code, is declared non-valid." At his resort in Crimea, Gorky received a " confidential " letter from the Acting Governor of Crimea (Tauris), in which he was asked to comply with the request of the Imperial Academy of Sciences for the return of the notice of election. In a very serious tone Gorky replied to the Acting Governor that since he had received the notification directly from the Academy, he would also return it upon the Academy's own direct request, with its precise and legal motives for such a request. The notification remained in Gorky's possession, to be made public more than a quarter of a century later. The farce ended there, but the press continued to comment on the clumsiness of the Authorities, certain organs chuckling over the discomfiture of Gorky — the " Academic abortion," the " Academician for a fortnight."

Anton Chekhov addressed the following letter to the Grand Duke Constantine:

Your Imperial Highness: Last December I received a notification of the election of A. M. Peshkov as Honorary Academician, and I hastened to call on A. M. Peshkov, who was then in Crimea, being the first to bring him the news of his election and the first to congratulate him. Shortly thereafter I read in the newspapers that in view of the fact that Peshkov was awaiting trial under Article 1035, his election was invalid. It was definitely stated that this announcement was issued by the Academy of Sciences, and since I am an Honorary Academician, the announcement emanated in part from myself. It was I who congratulated him and it was I, too, who declared his election invalid — such a contradiction was be-

yond my understanding, and I could not reconcile my conscience to it. A perusal of Article 1035 explained nothing to me [the Article deals with state offences — A.K.]. After long consideration I could only arrive at one decision, extremely depressing and sad for me; namely, to petition Your Imperial Highness for the suspension of my status as Honorary Academician.

Vladimir Korolenko also renounced his rank of Honorary Academician, and he explained his reasons in a long letter to A. Veselovsky, from which I quote:

Late last year I was invited to take part in the elections for the branch of Russian language and literature and the branch of *belles lettres*. Complying with the invitation I gave my vote for A. M. Peshkov (Gorky) among others; he was elected and, as far as I know, received the customary notification of election. Later there appeared an announcement from the Academy of Sciences . . . to the effect that when we voted for A. M. Peshkov (Gorky), we did not know that he was to be tried under Article 1035, and that once we had learned of this, we, as it were, considered the election invalid.

It seems to me that, having taken part in the election, I also had a right to be invited to discuss the question of its annulment, if that annulment was to be made in the name of the Academy. Then I might have had an opportunity to exercise my inviolable right to enter a special opinion on that question, since when voting for A. M. Peshkov, I did know that he was under trial for a political matter (this was widely known), yet I did not regard that circumstance as an obstacle to his election.

My opinion may be erroneous, but I still maintain it, namely, that the Academy ought to take into consideration only the literary activity of the candidate, ignoring the secret inquiries of an ungermane department. Otherwise, the very nature of the Academic elections is substantially distorted, and they lose all value. . . .

There was much speculation at the time as to what was the attitude of Leo Tolstoy toward this matter. He made no statement, and we find no record of his opinion either in his diaries

or letters. In the recently published diary of Alexey Suvorin, editor of the daily *Novoye Vremya,* we find an entry for September 4, 1902, in which Chekhov is quoted as saying to him that Tolstoy had been approached on the subject of sending in his resignation, but that he replied that " he did not regard himself as an Academician."

Tolstoy's indifference to rank and decoration had been expressed by him on many occasions, and seemed in keeping with his teaching. Suvorin, however, goes on to quote Chekhov: " Yet I know that he (Tolstoy) has cast his vote for Boborykin, which means that he does regard himself as an Academician." Tolstoy's reluctance to " join " any movement might be advanced as a plausible reason for his neutrality in this case.

The underlying intrigues in this tragicomic affair have become known only recently, since the publication of the secret police archives. Four days after Gorky's election, the Department of Police added to the voluminous Gorky file a newspaper clipping concerning that event, with a note: " He is under indictment, accused of carrying on revolutionary propaganda among the workmen, and is under special police surveillance. While some lower him, others elevate him." In this melancholy aphoristic vein the Department presented the case to the Minister of the Interior, who in his turn informed the Tsar of the Academy's act and of Gorky's record. Nicholas II, innocent of familiarity with contemporary Russian literature, was merely shocked by the discovery that a Nizhni Novgorod guildsman, accused of revolutionary tendencies and activities, had been elected to membership in an august institution honoured by the attribute " Imperial." The laconic Tsar inscribed the words: " More than odd! " on the vellum paper upon which the Minister had the newspaper clipping pasted. This " resolution " had its immediate effect. General Vannovsky, Minister of Education, wrote to Grand Duke Constantine:

Your Imperial Highness! His Majesty has deigned to give me His All-Highest command that in the next issue of the *Pravitelstvenny Vestnik* be printed the following announce-

ment of the Imperial Academy of Sciences: " In view of the elucidation " . . . [see the text of the announcement above]. Informing Your Imperial Highness of this, I bespeak Your orders for the fulfilment of the All-Highest command.

Thereupon the grand-ducal President of the Academy summoned K. Sluchevsky, a writer of fine prose and verse who was then the editor of the *Pravitelstvenny Vestnik,* and ordered him to announce on the morrow the annulment of Peshkov's election. Two days later a similar announcement appeared in the name of the Academy.

Poor Academy! The mockery of its rights and independence was duplicated in 1929, when the Soviet authorities practically coerced the Academy to elect as members certain individuals whose chief merit consisted in their Marxian orthodoxy. In 1902 there were Korolenko and Chekov to express their disgust with the Academic farce; in 1929 only the octogenarian Ivan Pavlov had the courage to protest publicly against the reduction of the Academy to the rôle of a tool of the Government.

Korolenko suffered keenly from this disgraceful affair; he was particularly chagrined by the lukewarm indifference of other Academicians to the stand taken by him and Chekhov. To Gorky he wrote consolingly:

. . . I have read about the " annulment " of your election. . . . . After all is said, one thing is patent: the substance of the election is in the election itself; it involves no rank, no salary, no duties. The fact of the election cannot be annulled in any way. " Annulment," indeed!

In 1917, shortly after the March revolution, the Academy passed a resolution to the effect that since the Academy had never actually excluded Gorky from its midst, he was to be regarded as an Honorary Academician, and to receive regular notices about the meetings of his Section. As to Korolenko, in view of his voluntary resignation, it was necessary to reelect him, which the Academy did unanimously in May. Korolenko, however, was not reconciled to the conduct of the Academicians. Replying to Academician Ovsyaniko-Kuli-

kovsky, a well-known professor of literature, who informed
him of the Academy's resolution to re-elect him, he made clear
that his resignation was prompted not by the Tsar's order but
by the way the Academy reacted, or rather failed to react to
his order. He cited the case of Z. Siebel, whose election as
member of the Berlin Academy was not approved by the Kaiser.
The Academy sent their condolences to Siebel, but he assured
them that he was not bothered by such a trifle: " It would have
been far more grievous if the Kaiser had elected me and the
Academy declined its approval." In a *P.S.* Korolenko added
musingly: " Chekhov and I resigned by joint consent. We
cannot come back jointly. . . ." Chekhov had been dead thirteen years. It may be noted to the honour of the Academy
that they upheld the motion of Academicians Shakhmatov and
Koni (the Senator), made in 1914, to leave two vacancies un-
filled until the eventual return of Korolenko and Gorky.

Obviously the Academy scandal did not hurt Gorky. Just as
the " excommunication " of Leo Tolstoy by the Russian Synod
only added to his popularity at home and abroad, so did the
blundering clumsiness of the Authorities in the Gorky case
contribute to his fame and endearment. One may see the uneasiness of the Administration in regard to Gorky's popularity
in the following note written on March 11, one day after the
Grand Duke's cancellation of Gorky's election, by Prince
Svyatopolk-Mirsky, Associate Minister of the Interior, to the
notorious Zubatov, then Vice-Director of the Department of
Police: " The Minister has instructed me to confer with thee,
with Kleigels (Prefect of the city of St. Petersburg) and with
Prince Shakhovskoy (Associate Minister of Education), concerning the question as to whether we should permit the
presentation of Gorky's play at the Panayev Theatre." This
conference took place on March 12, but the police records say
nothing of its proceedings or recommendations. Nemirovich-
Danchenko fills the gap. The play referred to was *Smug
Citizens,* Gorky's first dramatic attempt, written at the urgent
requests of Chekhov and the directors of the Moscow Art
Theatre.

Vladimir Nemirovich-Danchenko recalls the difficulties

which he had to go through in connexion with the production of that play in St. Petersburg. Afraid that the audiences would use the occasion to protest against the arbitrary action of Grand Duke Constantine, Minister of the Interior Sipyagin forbade the presentation of *Smug Citizens* (presumably as a result of the conference of March 12). Danchenko fought this decision with all the energy and perseverance of which he is capable. One of his arguments against the Minister's *veto* was that the guest performances of his theatre in St. Petersburg had been subscribed for, and that the omission of one of the promised plays was equivalent to a breach of contract. In addition to this legal argument, he had a talk with Prince Svyatopolk-Mirsky, a man exceptionally enlightened and liberal for a Russian bureaucrat. At the end of the conversation the Associate Minister said to Danchenko: " You have convinced me, and I believe that I shall succeed in convincing the Minister. I hope that we shall permit the performance." Shortly afterwards permission was given for a dress-rehearsal of the play, which was attended by a number of Ministers, their wives and friends. Says Danchenko: " Though persecuted by them, Gorky attracted their interest in an extraordinary measure, and for some reason, the especial interest of high society ladies. It is quite probable that the dress-rehearsal decided the fate of the performance, because on the whole the show produced an enormous impression on that exclusive audience." Indeed, the presentation of *Smug Citizens* was officially permitted, but the director's troubles were not ended there: he had further conflicts with the police.

One of these took place in connexion with General Kleigels' order to have uniformed policemen take up the admission tickets, to prevent non-subscribers from attending the performances (Danchenko admits that non-subscribers did filter in, to the number of five hundred for each performance). The audience felt nervous in the presence of the " Pharaos," and Danchenko ordered these out of the theatre. An affront to the all-powerful Kleigels! It was that very Kleigels of whom Alexey Suvorin complained in his diary that as Prefect of the city he had the advertisements in *Novoye Vremya*

severely censored; forbidding, for example, one about a sale of apples, since "something else might be understood by apples" (bombs?). Count Witte, in his *Memoirs*, characterized Kleigels as "a very limited man, of scanty culture, one who was far more familiar with the nature of stallions than with that of human beings." The fierce general summoned the director for an explanation, and after some arguments they compromised on letting the policemen take up the tickets, but in evening dress. Nemirovich-Danchenko records that the audiences appreciated the director's difficulties, and refrained from embarrassing demonstrations.

In April, 1902, Gorky's right to stay in Crimea expired, and he was forced to return to the town of Arzamas. Nemirovich-Danchenko had to travel to those backwoods in order to confer with Gorky about the staging at the Moscow Art Theatre of *At the Bottom* (*Lower Depths*), which he was completing in his enforced seclusion. In December the play was given with enormous success. The following February the Administration forbade its performance in any of the Imperial Theatres and in the provinces. Nizhni Novgorod managed to obtain a special permit to present her native son's masterpiece, in which a good deal was recognized as both local and autobiographic. The production of the play in St. Petersburg by the visiting troupe of the Moscow Art Theatre was met with the open resentment of the Conservative press. In reporting this attitude to the Moscow *Courier,* the writer Serafimovich expressed his opinion that "the St. Petersburg newspapers were guided not by a sincere appraisal, but by special considerations." Neither the Administration nor the reactionary journals could find anything politically or morally objectionable in the play, and their "special considerations" must have been based on their fear of Gorky's revolutionary personality and its effect on the public, regardless of the nature of his writings. The Russian reader and spectator could be depended upon to read into Gorky's lines things probably undreamed of by the author and certainly unsuspected by the lynx-eyed censor. The persecution of the play coincided with its receipt of one of the highest literary awards in the country, the Gri-

boyedov prize, the same prize having been awarded but a few months previously to *Smug Citizens*.

There was no doubt of it. Gorky had become a symbol around which clashed the old, apparently firmly entrenched Russia, and the nascent revolutionary Russia. The moribund order was keenly sensitive to its enemies, and was certainly on the right track in suspecting Gorky. The veteran Bolshevik, P. Lepeshinsky, in his study, *Na Povorote (At the Turning Point)*, cites a comrade's letter sent in 1902 from Russia to Nürnberg, concerning Gorky's practical support of the Leninist group. Characteristically for the conspirative nature of the revolutionary movement, a copy of that very letter has been preserved in the archives of the Department of Police, whose text is more complete than the one cited by Lepeshinsky. The correspondent described a secret meeting with Gorky, at which the latter avowed his faith in the solidity of the *Iskra (Spark)* — the underground organ of the Social-Democratic organization, and his contempt for the Socialist-Revolutionaries and for the group of Peter Struve's Liberal-Constitutionalist *Osvobozhdenie (Liberation)* — published at Stuttgart and later in Paris. Gorky offered to help the *Iskra* in every way possible, such as carrying out secret errands, attracting wealthy backers, and giving personal support with pen and purse. Gorky was further quoted to the effect that he had been spending on himself not more than thirty per cent of his income, the rest going to all sorts of organizations. He promised the *Iskra* a minimum of five thousand rubles annually, and hoped to increase this sum.

The Invisible Thread was taut. Agents of the Spider continued to report on Gorky's movements, occasionally varying fact with fiction. In the fall of 1902 the Moscow secret service informed the Department of Police that one of the proclamations issued by the Moscow Committee of the Social-Democratic Party " belonged to the pen of Alexey Maximovich Peshkov (Maxim Gorky), who in all probability had also composed the enclosed text of a proclamation ' To the Public,' signed by a ' Group of Intelligentsia.' " A perusal of the latter by one acquainted with Gorky's style casts a doubt on the

agent's perspicacity. As a matter of fact, as we have noted once before, the revolutionists were reluctant to utilize Gorky's too conspicuous, too identifiable pen. More plausible sounded the report of the chief of the Tiflis secret service for July, 1903, in which Gorky was alleged to have given, during his visit to that city, three hundred rubles to the local committee of the Social-Democratic Party. It has been recently established also that at the end of the same year he gave twenty-five hundred rubles to the Fighting Organization of the Social-Democratic Party at Nizhni Novgorod.

The revolutionary movement was, clearly, absorbing much of Gorky's time and energy, and offering him the comfort of a " formula." He was gradually mastering the " formula " and applying it with growing sureness in his utterances. At a banquet in honour of Chaliapin, in 1902, he addressed his friend and one time fellow-hobo with words of affection and admiration, tempered with a significant But. " Yes," he said, " you are a talent. Yes, you are a genius. But your songs do not reach the toiling masses. Your songs are lost in the gilded apartments of Moscow's fat merchant-wives. Strike enthusiasm in the hearts of those who are wretched and low of spirit. Then only will you be truly great."

At the same time it is evident from his correspondence with Posse that Gorky's impractical dreaminess was giving place to a rather sober interpretation of the " formula." Posse gives the impression that he was peeved by Gorky's " inconsistency." It appears that Gorky, annoyed by the censorship conditions, had proposed to move *Zhizn* abroad and publish it there as an openly revolutionary organ. After the suspension of the review Posse went abroad, expecting Gorky to join him shortly and arrange for the publication of *Zhizn*. Posse waited in vain for many months, and even his letters remained unanswered. At last a melancholy-mystic letter of his brought a reply, in which we find some curious adumbrations of Gorky's later views on man and religion. Thus: " You say that one cannot live without a religion? To the devil with Struve and Fichte! . . . I want my mood to be my philosophy, that is, that guidance which they choose to call religion. . . . I am fond

of life, I love life, I feel a delight in being alive. . . . What devil of good can any brand of a religion do you, if you do not feel in a position to create your own religion? And how can you accept anything not of your own creation, when you are yourself a god and a Kant and the source of all wisdom and nastiness? Only man exists, all the rest is only a point of view. You say that a rational being is a misunderstanding of nature. Granted, but since such a being does exist it is a reality, and being cognitive it is at liberty to create a life of its own choosing. As to God, man creates him after his own image and likeness! "

In his hatred of the Russian Autocracy Gorky was apt to idealize the West and use it as a model for propaganda purposes. He wrote to this effect to Posse, and upbraided the American correspondent, Hourwich, who committed the " political tactlessness " of informing his Russian readers of certain inefficiencies in the United States. " The point is," Gorky argued, " that . . . . the Russian average citizen, on reading such descriptions of Western imperfections, will justly conclude that life is not any better in America than with us, and upon making such a conclusion he will calmly lie down to snooze. . . . One should write of what is good in the West, of what may arouse in our citizen envy, covetousness, a sense of abuse, and similar progressive emotions and sensations. It is necessary that in every letter from abroad the citizen should see above all the advantages of Western life." Posse does not deny himself the pleasure of reminding us that as soon as Gorky found himself abroad he began to " spit into the eyes of Beautiful France," and the American civilization he branded as a Yellow Devil. Gorky was not the first Russian to seek for the Promised Land in the West and discover there the reign of the goddess of mediocrity, Cabell's Sereda. Like Alexander Herzen and Dostoyevsky, Gorky received a violent jolt when he found his ideal polluted, but he recovered eventually and turned an ardent worshipper of the West and denouncer of the East — the " two souls " of Russia.

To come back to Posse's grievance: his urgent and repeated requests that Gorky live up to their " agreement " and come

abroad for open revolutionary work were of no purpose, except that in the end they exasperated Gorky. Posse received an " unfriendly " letter, written in a woman's handwriting and signed " A." (presumably, Maria Andreyeva, Gorky's second wife). This was a definite refusal to go. " Understand this: from here I am not going to co-operate with you, and to you I shall come only when to work here will become utterly impossible for me. I regret to say that I shall probably not have to wait long for that." Posse's exhortations in the name of the cause failed to move Gorky. He wrote: " I should not advise you to speak heroic words; we have at present an abundance of such words — they are cheap. . . . This is my sincere conviction: if at this moment a certain Gorky should be killed during a street brawl, the fact would be more useful for the so-called Russian society than if the same Gorky took it into his head to play a Herzen, even if he performed this rôle with success. . . . So — for the time being leave me do my work, and you go on doing your own work, bearing in mind firmly that both your road and mine lead to Rome."

The relations between the two friends assumed in the end an ugly aspect, when Pyatnitsky had Gorky buy out Posse's shares of the *Znaniye*, " for the good of the further growth of the publishing business," as Gorky explained. Posse accused him of having changed, but the retort was: " No, I have hardly changed, unless it be that my scepticism toward you, intelligentsia chaps, has grown more intense." The Posse episode, in its final stages, decidedly fails to contribute a feather for Gorky's cap.

During the Easter days of 1903, a massacre of Jews took place at the Bessarabian city of Kishinev, which shocked the world with its unprecedented cruelty. The rôle of the Administration in this pogrom was quite unsavoury. A telegram from Minister of the Interior von Plehve to von Raaben, Governor of Bessarabia (note the abundance of " vons " among the tsar's henchmen: one reason for the initial popularity of the war against Germany among the Russians), *two weeks* before the massacre, spoke of the imminent " riots." The

minister urged the governor to refrain from taking too severe measures for the suppression of the rioters, " in order not to enrage the populace against the Government." The governor interpreted this diplomatic note liberally, and permitted the massacre to go on for three days without interference. Leaflets were freely circulated through the province, containing the sentence: " The tsar has given permission to beat the Jews during the first three days of Holy Easter." At a given signal the massacre began, and the ruffians performed their ghastly work calmly and undisturbed. The city was laid waste, the streets were littered with broken furniture, shattered stoves, torn feather beds and pillows. Official figures gave the number of killed and mutilated Jews as forty-five, and over six hundred wounded. Babies were smashed at curbs, pregnant women were ripped open and stuffed with feathers, nails were driven into old men's nostrils, and other ingenious atrocities committed. In his *City of Slaughter,* Khayim Nakhman Byalik, the Hebrew poet, draws a memorable picture of Kishinev:

From steel and iron — cold and hard and dumb —
Forge thou for thee a heart, O man, and come!
Come, follow me into the dreadful town,
And with thine own eye see,
And with thine own hands feel
On hedge and post, on gate and wall,
On city pavements, and all the boards
The black-hardened blood, the very marrow
That from thy brethren's heads and necks did gush.
And wander then amidst the ruins
Through broken walls and crooked doors,
Past shattered stoves and half-burned bricks,
Where yesternight the fire and ax and iron
Upon this bloody revel a wild dance played;
Through broken roofs and ancient garrets creep
And into all the gloomy corners peep —
For these are wounds, open, black, and dumb,
That wait no more for healing in this world —
And wend thy way through streets with feathers flooded,
And bathe thee in a stream, a white stream,
White from the bloody sweat of tortured bodies.

(From the translation of S. Roth)

The Jews have been accustomed to play the part of Azazel. In the early eighteen eighties a wave of pogroms swept the south and south-west of Russia. The Authorities used this blood-letting device for diverting the grievances of the masses from their true oppressors against the Jews, their alleged exploiters. In those days the Government felt obliged, however reluctantly, to quell the riots and punish the offenders. The governor-general of Warsaw pointed out in his memorial that "the Authorities were vexed by their enforced rôle of defenders of the Jews against the Russian populace." On the margin of the memorial Alexander III noted: "That, indeed, is the sad thing about all these Jewish disturbances." Alexey Suvorin quotes from Lyubimov's intimate diaries: "General Gurko was telling the Tsar, in 1884, that he found it difficult to undertake measures for the prevention of anti-Jewish riots: the troops rejoiced when they saw the Jews beaten up. The Tsar interrupted Gurko: "I confess that I myself rejoice when Jews are beaten."

Twenty years later Autocracy had an additional reason for favouring Jewish pogroms: vengeance for the participation of Jews in the revolutionary movement. Crowded like herring within the restricted Pale of Settlement, ousted from all productive occupations, limited in educational opportunities, abused and insulted in every way, the Jewish population naturally furnished a considerable proportion of the malcontents who saw their salvation in the overthrow of Autocracy. Von Plehve merely reflected the sentiments of his sovereigns when he attempted to "drown the revolution in Jewish blood." Kishinev was the first pogrom in which the Authorities did not have to be "vexed by their enforced rôle of defenders of the Jews." It was followed, and eclipsed in cruelty and in the connivance of the military and the police, by the pogroms of Homel, Zhitomir, Belostok, Odessa, and a host of others. In regard to the Kishinev massacre, Nicholas II remarked to General Kuropatkin: "The Jews deserve a lesson."

Maxim Gorky belongs to those Russians who look upon the Jewish question as on a Gentile rather than a Jewish question, since it primarily involves the conduct of the Gentiles. This note he has sounded again and again in his vigorous

fight against anti-Semitism. For the benefit of the Kishinev victims he wrote a story, *The Pogrom,* in which he described an anti-Jewish riot in the Kanavino suburb, during the early 'eighties. He also composed, in the form of an article, a fiery condemnation of the instigators and perpetrators of the Kishinev affair. The article was widely circulated in hecto-graphed copies, and was reprinted in Struve's *Osvobozhdenie.* In this paper Gorky claimed that the true culprits were not the ignorant mobs tempted by plunder and rape and promised immunity, but those Judeophobe journalists who had been per-sistently poisoning the minds of their readers by blaming the Jews for all evils and calamities. He named about half a dozen of these Jew-baiters, among them Alexey Suvorin and Victor Burenin, the latter one of the most talented and most un-scrupulously virulent contributors to the *Novoye Vremya.* The official and conservative press launched a storm of attacks against Gorky. The cleverest stroke was dealt by Burenin in his *Rejoinder to Mr. Maxim Gorky,* where he named Gorky as the real culprit in the Kishinev pogrom: had it not been carried out by his Chelkashes and Konovalovs, the very char-acters whom Gorky had " crowned with the halo of power and grandeur " ?

True enough, Gorky's tramps, sick with a restless, vague yearning after they knew not what, and their moral and social moorings snapped long ago, formed a ready soil for the re-cruitment of hooligans and thugs. In the original version of Gorky's *The Orlovs,* Grigory Orlov gives vent to his heart-ache in forcible terms. Born with " restlessness in his soul," he craves after extraordinary feats: " To smash the whole world, or to get together a band of mates, and kill every Jew alive, or anyhow to do some such thing that would make me rise above all men and spit down on them." In subsequent editions the phrase about the Jews was deleted, though it sounded quite natural in Orlov's mouth.

The point is, of course, that Gorky does not " crown his characters with the halo of power and grandeur," as Burenin and other critics have accused him of doing. They may ap-pear " powerful and grand " in comparison with the " smug

citizens," slaves of conventions and the acquisitive instinct. In themselves, Gorky's tramps are either potential men or ex-men. Negatively free from codes and standards, they lack positive power and purpose, they are amorphous, and though individualistic on the surface they typify the will-less mob that can be as easily swayed to massacre Jews as gentry, to burn synagogues as readily as palaces, to storm the Bastille as lustily as headquarters of the I.W.W. Gorky perhaps portrayed his tramps rather romantically, but he did not glorify them, and he is as much responsible for the misdeeds of his Chelkashes, Konovalovs, and Orlovs as Willa Cather is for the actions of her Nebraskans, New Mexicans, and French Canadians.

THE efforts of von Plehve to drown the revolution in the blood of national minorities, on the principle of " divide and rule," proved ineffectual. The inner contradictions of the Russian state were too deep to be solved by the temporary deviation of public sentiments. The empire had outgrown its paternalistic government, the national organism chafed within the autocratic strait jacket and made desperate endeavours to stretch. The strait jacket was cracking and splitting. To hold its place in the concert of modern empires the Russian empire was forced to encourage capital and industry. This encouragement was given in artificially large doses, out of proportion to the backward conditions of the country, and at the expense of the rural elements which formed more than four fifths of the population. The young industry, which flourished owing to Government bounties, soon found itself languishing from the lack of markets. The home market, made safe from foreign competition by a wall of prohibitive tariff protection, proved exhausted of purchasing power. Impoverished by taxation, suffering from insufficient allotments and obsolete methods of cultivation, the bulk of the nation, the peasantry, could furnish precious few customers for the highly priced domestic manufactures. The logical step would have been a campaign for the betterment of the economic and cultural status of the people, but an enlightened people spelled the doom of an autocratic régime. The Government chose what seemed an easier way: territorial expansion into Central and Far-Eastern Asia, for the conquest and monopolization of new markets. Indeed, for a long period this course presented smooth

sailing: Russia's frontiers came alarmingly close to British India, and the line of the Russian Pacific extended ever farther south. By the end of 1903 Russia was in practical control of northern and southern Manchuria, and was encroaching on Korea under personal orders of Nicholas II, who combined weakness of will and gullibility with compensatory pugnacity.

Japan's resentment of this encroachment on what she regarded as her spheres of influence was taken lightly by the Russian Government. And when, provoked by procrastinations and offensive superciliousness, Japan opened hostilities, the Russian court chuckled over the foolhardiness of the puny island kingdom. The war promised to be " a military promenade," in the expression of Minister of War Kuropatkin, and its prospective results made the mouths of Russian expansionists water. Witte alone, as Minister of Finance, had misgivings, but as against his pessimism there was the enthusiastic support of the tsar's militancy on the part of von Plehve, who now saw the opportunity to drown the opposition in a wave of war patriotism and in the fresh triumph of Autocracy — the victorious outcome of the conflict was taken for granted.

The war proved an acid test for the empire. It brought to light the inefficiency, corruption, and backwardness of its civil and military authorities, and demonstrated to the world that autocratic Russia was a colossus of clay. Japan was victorious on land and on sea, and in the end Russia lost virtually her whole fleet, tens of thousands of men, her Southern Manchurian railroad, Port Arthur and Port Dalny, the southern half of Sakhalin and her prestige in Asia and Europe. At home the disastrous campaign with its resultant miseries and hardships united the nation in its opposition to the criminally stupid régime. Throughout the years of 1904 and 1905 Russia was in a turmoil of labour strikes, disturbances in the army and navy, peasant riots, conferences and banquets of professionals, parties and groups of all hues and programs, with the common demand that Autocracy must go and be replaced by a constitutional order.

The revolutionary parties gained momentum, especially the Socialist-Revolutionists, whose fighting organization carried

out a number of spectacular acts of terror, killing, among others, the all-powerful Minister von Plehve and the Grand Duke Sergey, Governor-General of Moscow. The movement culminated in October, 1905, when a general strike of unprecedented dimensions and comprehensiveness forced Nicholas II to issue a manifesto granting constitutional liberties.

One of the significant episodes during this brief but eventful period was the Red Sunday, January 22, 1905, in St. Petersburg, in which Maxim Gorky was seriously involved. On that day a procession of workmen was to march to the Winter Palace and hand a petition to the tsar. The workmen did not belong to any revolutionary party; on the contrary, they had been organized by the notorious Zubatov of the Department of Police for the purpose of opposing revolutionary tendencies. Zubatov had experimented in various parts of Russia with his scheme of encouraging workers' economic organizations and using these as strongholds against political groups. In nearly all cases his plan failed, since the line between economic and political demands was too vague and it vanished in face of actuality. The St. Petersburg experiment was a classic example of this dangerous play with fire. The leader of the organization was a loyal priest, Georgy Gapon, who had set out to do Zubatov's work with ardour and devotion. By January, 1905, it had become evident to Gapon and his flock of loyalist workmen that the economic and military disasters of Russia were caused by the same evil — the despotic Autocracy and its incapable and dishonest functionaries.

On January 16 a strike began in one of the munition factories, which spread rapidly. The strikers drew up a petition to the tsar, in which they addressed him in naïve but courteous terms, recounting their material difficulties and imploring him to convoke a constituent assembly from among all the classes of the nation. The petition also asked the tsar to take measures against the poverty, ignorance, and legal disability of the common people, and against the oppression of labour by capital. " These [the petition concluded], Sire, are our main wants, with which we have come to thee. Swear to order them

fulfilled, and thou wilt make Russia happy and glorious, and thy name will be stamped in our hearts and the hearts of our descendants for eternity. But if thou wilt not grant, wilt not respond to our prayer, we shall die here on this square in front of the Palace. We have no other place to go to, and no use in going anywhere else. We have only two roads: either to freedom and happiness, or to our graves."

The Authorities had been advised of the procession that was to take place for the purpose of presenting the petition to the tsar. No order forbidding the procession was issued, and on Sunday, January 22, thousands of workmen, with their wives and children, carrying crosses, holy images, and portraits of the emperor and empress, began to march toward the Winter Palace from various corners of the capital. The crowds of un-armed, worshipful subjects of the tsar were met by volleys of bullets, and very few of the marchers actually reached the Palace Square; when they arrived there, they were given the same reception. The snow of the St. Petersburg pavements was crimsoned with the blood of the tsar's faithful citizens. This blood awakened the masses to the realization of their folly in trusting the ruler; thenceforth the Russian proletariat was to have no further illusions on this score. The Authorities contributed grandly to the revolutionization of the class which proved victorious twelve years later.

Maxim Gorky arrived at Petersburg three days before the fateful Sunday. His rôle in those events is made clear in the Declaration, of which he was the author, and which served as one of the reasons for his arrest and imprisonment two days subsequently. Its hastily written, slipshod text follows:

We, the undersigned, regard it as our moral duty to advise our Russian citizens and public opinion in Western countries of the following:

Knowing that the St. Petersburg workmen had decided to march on January 22nd in a solid mass to the Winter Palace, in order to call on the tsar and hand him a program of State reforms;

Knowing that the workmen had no intention to lend a revolutionary character to their peaceful manifestation;

that, rather, they still had faith in the tsar's power and authority, and had hoped that he would trustingly receive them and listen to their plea;

We, the undersigned, went on the evening of January 21st to the minister of the interior, to request that to avoid bloodshed he issue an order against bringing the troops out on the streets the following day, and that the workmen be permitted to talk freely to their tsar.

When, with this purpose in mind, we came to the minister, we were told that he was not in, and were directed to his associate, M. Rydzevsky, who at first refused to receive us; later he admitted us, listened to our request, said that the matter did not concern him, and with an indifferent shrug of the shoulders he left us.

We then called on the prime minister, S. J. Witte, and made him the same declaration; namely, that it was necessary to inform the emperor and the minister of the interior of the workmen's peaceful state of mind, that the workmen should be permitted to present to the tsar their plan of reforms, that the troops and police should be enjoined from interfering with the workmen's intention to address the emperor, that otherwise, we were sincerely convinced, blood would be shed, and that this would arouse a natural mood for revenge — that is, a widespread tendency for terroristic acts on the part of the workmen.

M. Witte replied that Ministers Svyatopolk-Mirsky [of the interior] and Kokovtsev [of finance] had more precise information than we about the state of affairs, that in his opinion the emperor too must have been advised of the workmen's intentions, and that he, Witte, was powerless to do anything for us.

We then asked him to arrange for us a meeting with Svyatopolk-Mirsky, to which M. Witte consented, and in our presence he telephoned to M. S.-Mirsky, asking him whether he would agree to receive us, representatives of a group of writers and scientists, for the discussion of the pending bloody events of January 22nd, and of the measures for their prevention.

M. Svyatopolk-Mirsky declined to receive us.

On January 22nd there began in various parts of St. Petersburg a movement of workmen, who were peacably marching towards the Winter Palace. The undersigned have

partly seen with their own eyes, partly heard from other eye-witnesses, such facts as these:

When the workmen of the Putilov Factory, with church banners and portraits of the emperor and empress in their hands, led by the priest Georgy Gapon, who wore his sacerdotal vestments and carried a cross, approached the Narva Gates, they were fired upon in three volleys without any warning on the part of the commanding officers or the police. Scores of people fell wounded and dead, while the rest of the crowd turned to run or lay down on the pavement to escape the bullets. As soon as they rose, however, they were again attacked with three volleys. This was repeated twice.

When the workmen of the Petersburg Side came up to the Troitsky Bridge, they were fired upon, again without any preliminary request to disperse; about sixty were wounded and killed.

One of us saw in a heap fourteen wounded (five of them being women) and three killed. He also witnessed a cavalry attack near the Police Bridge on the Nevsky Prospect, and saw a mounted soldier fire at a man who had already fallen to the ground.

Also at the Admiralty, on the Moyka, the troops fired at the workmen and the general public, and slashed them with swords. As yet we have no precise figures of the killed and wounded, but this is not what we deem important in the matter.

We feel impelled to declare to all Russia and Western public opinion:

1) that Minister of the Interior Svyatopolk-Mirsky had been warned by us of the workmen's peaceful intentions and calm state of mind, and of their full confidence in the tsar, whom they were desirous to see;

2) that we had requested the minister to keep the troops off the streets;

3) that we had urged the need of advising the tsar of the state of affairs, and of convincing him that it was necessary to admit the workmen to the Palace and hear their petition;

4) that the workmen had, indeed, behaved quite peaceably, and did not provoke the troops;

5) that the commanders of the troops gave orders to fire at the people and attack them, without warning them to disperse.

Such treatment of the procession of workmen we cannot in all conscience call anything but a prearranged slaughter; and therefore, we, the undersigned, before all Russian citizens and Western public opinion, accuse Minister of the Interior Svyatopolk-Mirsky of the deliberate, uncalled for, and senseless murder of a multitude of Russian citizens.

And since Nicholas II had been advised of the nature of the workmen's movement, and of the peaceful intentions of his former subjects killed in innocent blood by the soldiers, and since though knowing that he permitted their slaughter, we accuse him also of the murder of peaceful men who in no way provoked such measures against them.

At the same time we declare that such an order of things must not be further tolerated, and we call upon all the citizens of Russia to an immediate, persistent, and united struggle against Autocracy.

This hastily prepared draught was in substance a correct account of the events. It could not help being inaccurate in minor details, which have been cleared up only subsequently, upon the publication of secret data and documents. Recent testimony by survivors of the procession on that Red Sunday suggests that in some places the commanding officers did order the workmen to disperse, but their voices were not heard by the multitudes that pressed on ahead. The firing of the soldiers was preceded by a bugle signal, the significance of which was probably unknown to the crowd. As to the personal responsibility of Svyatopolk-Mirsky, one may presume that his liberal tactics having proved distasteful to the Court, he was at the time of those events actually though not yet officially released from his duties as minister of the interior. The master of the situation was not Prince Svyatopolk-Mirsky, still less S. Witte, but the uncle of the tsar, Grand Duke Vladimir, commander of the St. Petersburg troops. Dr. E. J. Dillon, at that time correspondent of the *London Daily Telegraph*, wrote for his paper:

I asked a gentleman of the Court why unarmed workmen and students were being killed today without any formalities. He answered: " Because all civil law has been superseded by military law. You are surprised that no one knows of this, and your astonishment is natural; but here in Russia we cannot regard things as you regard them in England. Last night His Majesty resolved to put aside the civilian authorities, and to entrust the task of upholding public order to Grand Duke Vladimir, who is very well read in the history of the French Revolution, and is not going to allow any reckless laxity. He is not going to commit those errors of which the entourage of Louis XVI were guilty: he will show no weakness. In his opinion the hanging of a hundred malcontents in the presence of their comrades would be a sure method of curing the people from constitutional schemes, but heretofore his advice was not heeded. Today His Highness is invested with supreme authority and is in a position to test out his method as fully as he pleases. Grand Duke Vladimir has an excellent opportunity for displaying his gift as a statesman and his Napoleon-like qualities, and he is not in the least uneasy about the results. No matter what happens, he will persist in quelling the riotous spirit of the crowds, even if for that purpose he should have to direct against the population all the troops at his disposal." [1]

On January 24 Gorky was arrested in the city of Riga, and the next day the commandant of the Peter and Paul Fortress reported to the director of the Department of Police: " I have the honour to inform Your Excellency that by order of the Department of Police the writer Alexey Maximovich Peshkov, arrested for a crime against the state, was this day brought to the Fortress and incarcerated in a separate cell, number 39 of the Trubetskoy Bastion. Simultaneously with this I have reported the matter to His Majesty the emperor." The Trubetskoy Bastion has seen within its grim walls many victims of the tyrannical régime (by way of retribution, after the revolution of 1917 it housed the tsar's ministers, and later, prominent anti-Bolsheviks), and it was no mean honour to find

[1] Retranslated into English from the Russian, in Struve's *Osvobozhdenie*, No. 64, 1905.

oneself a fellow-martyr of the Decembrists, of Michael Bakunin, Chernyshevsky, Pisarev, and the leading Russian revolutionists of the last three decades. Built by Peter the Great in his newly conceived, fantastic capital, the fortress named after his two favourite apostles sprawls on an islet in the Neva, and its spire dominates St. Petersburg. At noon and midnight the tower clock used to chime a religious hymn, reminding the Petersburgians of the ever wakeful guardians of Autocracy and of the fate of those who dared to challenge the régime. At present the chimes play the " Internationale."

Maxim Gorky was accused of several grave political offences. The police tried to present the deputation to the ministers as a " provisional government " which, they alleged, had begun to function on the eve of the Red Sunday and subsequently agitated in favour of an armed uprising through Russia, even going the length of sending delegates abroad to establish connexions with sympathizers, and among other things, to raise with the aid of the German Social-Democratic party an interpellation in the Reichstag concerning the methods of the Russian Government in suppressing the manifestation of January 22. Aside from belonging to this deputation, Gorky was accused also of having delivered incendiary speeches at various meetings in St. Petersburg, during and after Red Sunday, and of having signed, together with four hundred and fifty-six others, a proclamation issued at a gathering in the Free Economic Society on the evening of that Sunday. That proclamation ended with an invitation to the army officers " to remove their uniform and put down their arms."

While at the Fortress Gorky was summoned three times before the prosecutor, and a verbatim record of his testimony on each occasion has been preserved in the police archives. He could hardly be expected to tell the whole truth to his captors, yet much in his answers is illuminating and basically candid. He admitted his sole authorship of the Declaration and his original intention to send a copy to Svyatopolk-Mirsky and to have the thing published in the St. Petersburg press. He also acknowledged having been the initiator of the idea to send a deputation to the minister.

On January 21st [he testified] about seven or eight o'clock in the evening, I happened to call at the editorial rooms of the daily *Nashi Dni* (*Our Days*), and found there a large gathering engaged in a lively discussion of the workmen's procession that was planned for the following day. I took part in the discussion, and suggested to those present that they send a deputation to the minister of the interior, with the purpose of presenting to him all the known facts . . . . and also to request him, as a minister and as a man, to undertake all possible measures for the prevention of the almost certain collision between the workmen and the soldiers and police. My proposal was accepted, and a deputation was at once elected. I remember that with me were elected K. K. Arsenyev; the historians, Kareyev and Semevsky; the writers, Peshekhonov, Myakotin, and Annensky; the lawyer, Kedrin, and one workman of the Gapon organization, whose name I do not know. [The name of this workman, an intimate of Gapon, was Kuzin, who subsequently proved to be a *provocateur*].

His departure for Riga on the morrow of the manifestation, Gorky explained by the " severe and dangerous illness of his close kinswoman, Maria Feodorovna Andreyeva," of which he had just been notified. He referred to the actress of the Moscow Art Theatre, who became his intimate friend and helper, and who, as Gorky's unofficial wife, caused the notorious scandal in New York.

As a reason for the sharp tone of the Declaration Gorky gave the freshness of his recent impressions in the streets of St. Petersburg, where he had seen many wounded people and excited crowds. Near the Police Bridge a dragoon fired at a man who had fallen down at Gorky's feet. The police report does not cite any other impressions of Gorky, though he must have mentioned a number of these, judging from his vivid descriptions of them in *Klim Samgin* (*The Magnet*), and the even more vivid ones he enacts in conversation. The latter group includes such unforgettable snapshots as one of a young girl onlooker caught on the points of an iron fence and crucified on the spot by a shower of bullets; or that of an urchin who had climbed up the equestrian statue of Przewalski, to get a better view of the procession, and was hurled by a volley against

the horseman's breast. Gorky (the testimony ran on) returned to his rooms greatly agitated, and in that mood wrote the Declaration. In the evening he went to the meeting at the Free Economic Society, in the hope of finding some members of the deputation to the ministers, whom he wished to consult on the Declaration. He did find one and gave him the manuscript, but it was not the lawyer Kedrin in whose possession the police found the Declaration. Gorky asserted that he spent only a few minutes at the Free Economic Society, and denied having made any speeches. " You tell me that you have information to the effect that at that Society I read publicly a letter of the priest Gapon — that is sheer fancy, of course."

In the reminiscences of D. Sverchkov, *Na Zare Revolutsii* (*At the Dawn of the Revolution*), published by the Commission for the History of the October Revolution, the author describes the meeting at the Free Economic Society on the night of Red Sunday. " Suddenly [he narrates] in the back of the hall rose the familiar figure of M. Gorky. He announced that one of Georgy Gapon's close friends wished to make a declaration in his name. Alongside of him stood up the man he spoke about. It was Georgy Gapon himself, his hair now clipped short and his priest's robe changed to secular clothes. He began to speak. His pale face showed the traces of intense suffering. His eyes burned. His voice trembled. He said that Georgy Gapon had managed to escape, that he would now continue the struggle with different methods, and that he had written a letter to the workmen, a copy of which could be made public. He then read a letter, which began with the words: ' Dear, blood-welded brothers! ' The letter spoke of the tsar's brutality, hurled curses on his head, and called on the workmen to join a revolutionary open struggle. That letter, as I learned later, had been just composed on the spot by M. Gorky. It was widely circulated in Petersburg, and later throughout Russia, along with the workmen's petition to the tsar and a description of the events on January 22nd." In his *Vospominaniya ob A. Bloke* (*Reminiscences of Alexander Blok*) Andrey Bely describes that meeting, at which he heard Gapon speak, and saw

at his side Maxim Gorky who, so they told him, had brought over the disguised priest.

General A. Spiridovich, in his well-informed *Istoria Bolshevisma v Rossii* (*History of Bolshevism in Russia*), also connects Gorky with Gapon: "When a throng of workmen [he relates] marching toward the Narva Gates with Gapon at their head was met with volleys of the troops, Gapon fled into a courtyard, where they clipped his hair and changed his clothes, whereupon he found shelter in the residence of Maxim Gorky." Finally, Gorky himself, in the second volume of his *Klim Samgin,* indirectly confirms his association with Gapon. His self-portrait in that passage is unmistakable: ". . . a tall, high cheek-boned man, with reddish moustachios, in a queer buttonless coat hooked on the left side, in high boots; despite his long straight hair, he suggested a soldier in disguise." The scene described apparently takes place in the rooms of this man, which served as a sort of headquarters on January 22nd. The Moscow millionaire, Savva Morozov, is there, and Gapon, shorn and bedraggled, comes in, and betrays a pathetic bewilderment and nervousness. Incidentally, General Spiridovich establishes Gorky's responsibility for Morozov's interest in the revolutionary movement. He states:

. . . Gorky performed a great service for the Social-Democrats. Having gained the confidence of . . . . Savva Morozov, Gorky obtained considerable sums from him, and part of these he handed over to the Party.

It was also in a large measure under his influence that shortly before his mysterious suicide Savva Morozov had his life insured for a large sum in favour of the Social-Democratic Party. This gift the Party was enabled to receive through the efforts of Gorky and Krasin.

In his obituary note on L. B. Krasin, Gorky narrates of his intimate acquaintance with Morozov, and how he arranged for an interview between him and Krasin, in 1903. Krasin obtained Morozov's agreement to give two thousand rubles a month to Lenin's faction.

In his last testimony Gorky had to answer the accusation of helping a number of organizations and individuals with books and money. He admitted his readiness to come to the aid of all seemingly worthy petitioners, but protested that he had little knowledge of his money affairs and contributions, relegating them to K. P. Pyatnitsky, manager of the *Znaniye* publishing house. " I repeat [he said in conclusion] that in my views I am a liberal, even a radical — this I have never concealed and am not denying now; my previous testimony, and my literary activity show it amply. But I must categorically assert that I have never taken any direct part in anti-governmental activities, and that I do not regard myself capable, by my spiritual makeup, of such activities. As to the composition of the manuscript, for which I am under arrest, that action was caused by the pressure of the horrors which I experienced on January 22nd, as an eye-witness of the terrible events that took place in the streets of St. Petersburg."

It is quite obvious that Gorky had no intention of displaying heroic veracity before the state prosecutor. By simulated frankness he adroitly endeavoured to minimize his actual participation in the political events. Nevertheless the prosecutor, toward the end of his lengthy indictment, arrived at a rather grave conclusion; namely, that " on the basis of the foregoing, the Nizhni Novgorod guildsman, Alexey Maximovich Peshkov, aged thirty-five, is accused of having composed on January 22, 1905, with the aim of circulating it, a proclamation which instigated the overthrow of the existing social order. The dissemination of said proclamation did not materialize because of circumstances which did not depend on Peshkov's volition." The turgid document went on to say that on the basis of such and such statutes and articles and clauses, the aforesaid Peshkov was to be tried at the St. Petersburg Judicial Chamber, without the participation of public representatives, and behind closed doors. That sounded quite ominous in the ears of those familiar with the made-to-order justice of Autocracy in its fight against its enemies.

O. O. Grusenberg, the celebrated defender in political trials, who took up Gorky's case, pleaded for a public trial on behalf

of his client. " Maxim Gorky [he argued] has distinguished himself by sincerity and candidness in all his activities. Even at the moment when the people's blood shed in the streets of the capital had splashed at his sensitive soul and inundated it with pain, horror, and indignation; even then he wrote his Declaration with the explicit intention of having it signed by himself and the other members of the deputation. A writer who has acted so openly has the right to expect that his trial will not take place behind closed doors."

The Government would have probably ignored Grusenberg's plea, as it was bent on ignoring all expressions of public indignation against the arrest of Gorky; but the timid protests of the Russian public were unexpectedly joined by those of the western civilized world. Unexpectedly, because one remembered with what indifference the world literary congress in Vienna, in 1881, had met the proposal of the Russian delegates to plead with their Government for the alleviation of the fate of Nicholas Chernyshevsky, who had been languishing in Siberia on trumped-up charges. The proposal was tabled at the insistence of the valiant Polish delegates, who feared punishment at the hands of the Russian Government. Yet Chernyshevsky was one of the foremost economists of the time, and a prominent editor and author. Twenty-five years later the arrest of Gorky and his imperilled fate (rumours circulated abroad that he was threatened with execution) brought a warm response from the western world, showing plainly what an important place Russian letters had conquered since the death of Dostoyevsky.

Meetings and manifestations in honour of Gorky took place in various foreign cities. Anatole France voiced the prevailing sentiment, when he stated in a public speech that Gorky " belonged not to Russia alone but to the whole world." An address of sympathy was sent to Gorky from Paris, which was signed by such names as Curie, Huysmans, Henri Poincaré, Anatole France, Brunetière, Claretie, the Marguerite brothers, Countess de Noailles, Paul Adam, Octave Mirbeau, Rodin, Monet, Charpentier, Marcel Prévost, and by the protean Aristide Briand. A society of *Les Amis du peuple russe et des*

peuples annexés was founded, counting among its members Georges Clemenceau, Professors Langlois, Seignobos, Painlevé, and other prominent Frenchmen. This society circulated through France a letter of protest against the imprisonment of Gorky, which was covered by thousands of signatures. The Dutch liberal paper, *Pays et Peuple,* launched a similar movement in Holland. In Berlin a play, supposedly based on Gorky's life, was produced, with Korolenko and Chaliapin among the *dramatis personae.* The Goethe Association and the *Berliner Tageblatt* circulated petitions to the Russian Government for the release of Gorky. The copy sent to the minister of the interior was signed by one hundred and sixty-nine prominent writers, scientists, capitalists, journalists, actors, statesmen, including Ernst Haeckel, Gerhart Hauptmann, Hermann Sudermann, Hugo von Hofmanstahl, and other celebrities. A number of deputies of the Italian parliament signed a memorial, in which they requested the Government to " use its good offices with the Russian Government to save the life of Maxim Gorky." *Listok Osvobozhdeniya,* Struve's organ (Number 25), carried the following message: " Progressive Czechs, assembled in Prague on January 30th [1905] proclaim their hearty sympathies with the workmen and intelligentsia who are fighting and suffering for the liberty of Russia. They denounce the inhuman treatment and the slaughter of peaceful citizens. Long live Maxim Gorky! Down with Tsarism! (signed) Professor T. G. Masaryk."

There were a few dissenting voices in this chorus of protests against the Russian autocracy. A number of French periodicals endeavoured to take the side of official Russia, the ally of the Republic; in any event they advocated non-interference in the internal affairs of a foreign country. Maurice Barrès refused to sign a petition for the release of Gorky. One of the German dissenters, who deserved and commanded the most serious attention, was Maximilian Harden. His *Zukunft* was probably the best informed foreign periodical on things Russian during the early part of the twentieth century. In his leading article, *Rusz,* on March 11, 1905, Harden reviewed the Gorky affair at length, and in his wonted truculent manner

he made some observations whose correctness cannot be gain-said. His main point was that Gorky was persecuted not for his artistic productions, but for his political activities. Harden, who had been penalized for *lèse-majesté* by German courts, appreciated the comparative lenience of the Russian Government toward certain writers: " *Die launische Autokratie, die dem alten Tolstoi eine Redefreiheit gewährt, wie sie in keinem Lande Europens auch nur vier Wochen lang denkbar wäre, liesz auch den jungen Gorkij ruhig seine Sturmvogellieder singen. Oft mussten wir, im Genusz unserer für Rede and Schrift konstitutionell verbürgten Preussenfreiheit, ihn benei-den, oft wünschen, nur vierzehn, nur acht Tage lang unange-fochten reden zu dürfen wie er.*" He went on to say that it was preposterous to expect a government to treat one who con-spired against it not as a political offender, but as one to be accorded the *Narrenprivilegium*. With devastating sarcasm he upbraided Ludwig Fulda, Sudermann, and other champions of Gorky for being cowards at home and valiant assailants of despotism from a safe distance: " *Die richtige, aufrichtige Schluss dieser hochtragenden Knabenstümperei wäre gewesen: Wir Alle, die wir nicht das Maul aufzuthun wagen, wenn bei uns ein Schriftsteller wegen einer nicht ganz sänftiglichen Kritik kaiserlicher oder ministerieller Handlungen und Reden eingesperrt wird, wir Alle, die für die edelsten Güter der Menschheit noch nie einen Finger gerührt, sondern stets in warmer Sonne Gunst und Profit gesucht haben, freuen uns heute der Gelegenheit, die uns erlaubt, ohne die allergeringste Gefahr die muthigen Schützer der Freiheit zu mimen.*" Why were there no protests, Harden queried, when the German Gov-ernment incarcerated the septuagenarian Liebknecht, or Thomas T. Heine, or Frank Wedekind? He cited the case of the imprisonment of Déroulède in France and of Oscar Wilde in England, and recalled his own note of two years previously, apropos of the fate of Gorky and Wilde: " *Der erste Pro-letarier der Weltliteratur mag sich auf der schwarzen Erde des Lebens freuen: der britische Majestät Cant ist der Kün-stlervolk ein noch viel härterer Herr als der weisse Zar.*" Fur-thermore, Harden claimed that all the foreign agitation and

protests, far from helping Gorky, were apt to harm him, since they exaggerated his importance and dangerousness in the eyes of the Russian Government. In his opinion, which may be questioned on this point, Gorky might have been released four weeks earlier than he was, had it not been for the foreign interference.

One must recall the isolation of Russia and its unpopularity during the war with Japan, coupled with internal disorders and acute economic difficulties, to understand why the Autocracy discarded on this occasion its wonted arrogance and indifference to public opinion, domestic or foreign. The Gorky case proved too messy a business at a time when official Russia was in dire need of financial and moral support from the outside world. However much they resented foreign interference, the Authorities were forced to accept it with a *bonne mine,* especially when it came from the political and financial ally, France. The redoubtable General Trepov, appointed Governor-General of St. Petersburg after Red Sunday, *smilingly* reassured the representative of the *Petit Parisien* that " Maxim Gorky would not be shot or hanged, as the Russian Law did not admit of such punishment." The smiling general forgot to add that the Administration had had a long experience in suspending the " Russian Law " in political cases. But it was clear that the pressure of foreign opinion would compel the Government to relent and let go its victim and enemy.

The condition of Gorky's health, indeed, demanded attention. He took his imprisonment lightly, made use of his unaccustomed leisure to write a play (*Children of the Sun*), and indulged in hilarious jokes and laughter which shocked as unseemly levity both the Fortress officials and his fellow-prisoners. His physique, however, was at a low ebb. The rack of the recent experiences, and the serious illness of Maria Andreyeva, from whom he was forcibly separated when arrested at Riga, had their effect. He did not even know for certain of Andreyeva's whereabouts. Among the police documents there is a scrap of paper, on which Gorky wrote in his cell the text of a telegram to Dr. Kanegisser, in care of the Gynecologic Institute, City: " I have no news about Maria's health. Where

is she; in Riga, or in your infirmary?" We do not know whether the telegram had been sent off. Nor did the régime in the ever damp Fortress help his tubercular lungs. Occasional visits were permitted to his wife, Katerina Pavlovna, with their seven-year-old son, and to K. P. Pyatnitsky. Katerina Pavlovna finally petitioned for her husband's release in view of the fact that he " suffered from tuberculosis, that lately his temperature had been rising in the evening, and that he had lost weight considerably." The Fortress physician examined the prisoner and diagnosed " a catarrh in the upper portion of the left lung."

By order of the Department of Police, Gorky was transferred from the Fortress to the Preliminary Detention Prison. The commandant of the Fortress forwarded to the Department two copybooks in which Gorky had written his " tragicomedy," as the commandant classified *Children of the Sun,* with the following note: " The fine and quite illegible writing has made it impossible for me to read carefully Peshkov's composition, but a rapid perusal of it impels me to suggest that it ought to be subjected to censorship." In March Gorky was released on ten thousand rubles bail, the sum having been furnished by the eccentric Savva Morozov. At first Gorky was made to sign a pledge not to leave St. Petersburg; then the governor-general ordered him deported to Riga.

Ill and restless, Gorky soon left Riga, and proceeded to Crimea, without waiting for an official permit. On March 22nd, the Moscow Prefect wired to the Department of Police: " To-day 3 P.M. Alexey Peshkov arrives Moscow from Riga. Intends stop here five days. I find such stay absolutely undesirable. Please notify immediately who permitted him come to Moscow. . . . Kindly request minister's instructions." Associate Minister of the Interior, Rydzevsky, replied at once: " If you find Peshkov's stay at Moscow dangerous for public peace, you may apply point four article sixteen Defence Law. Have no information who permitted his arrival Moscow." For a whole month a lively correspondence went on among various departments as to who was responsible for Gorky's departure from Riga; it did not occur to them that Gorky might have ignored all rules and taken French leave. At last

the matter was cleared up in K. P. Pyatnitsky's petition to the Department of Police, in which he wrote:

Alexey Maximovich Peshkov suffers from tuberculosis of the lungs. This is confirmed by an enclosed certificate from Dr. Golzinger. His confinement at the Fortress of Peter and Paul has caused a revival of the tubercular process. This process continued to advance after his release from the Fortress and he began to spit blood. Physicians who examined him insisted on his immediate departure for Crimea, where the progress of his illness could be arrested. Such was also the opinion of Professor Shchurovsky, whom Maxim Gorky consulted while in Moscow; Professor Shchurovsky's certificate is available. In view of the foregoing, and of the patient's continuous haemorrhage, it has been necessary to send him to Crimea with all possible speed. Now, at the request of Alexey Maximovich Peshkov, I petition the Department of Police to permit his stay in Crimea for treatment, as that is the only place in Russia where they may be able to stop the progress of his ailment, which endangers his life.

On May 17th, the Department of Police informed the chief of the Crimean gendarmerie that 'the minister of the interior had permitted the author Alexey Peshkov (Maxim Gorky) a temporary sojourn in Crimea for a climatic cure of the chronic tuberculosis of his left lung, under the condition, however, of a strict secret surveillance by the local police of his private life and activity."

Despite the " strict surveillance," the police overlooked the visitation of Gorky's Crimean resort by Vladimir Bonch-Bruyevich. In the spring of 1905 Bonch-Bruyevich called on Gorky at the request of Lenin, for a final arrangement of Gorky's proposal to have his works and those of Andreyev, Kuprin, Bunin, Skitalets, Chirikov, and other members of the Znaniye group, published abroad, the income to revert to the Bolshevik faction.

The treatment of Gorky by the Authorities was, indeed, strikingly mild and considerate. Meanwhile the prosecutor had composed a voluminous act of accusation against him, and presented it to the Judicial Chamber of St. Petersburg. Owing

to the defendant's stay in Crimea, the trial was postponed till May 16, but on May 19 it was ordered deferred indefinitely, "for further investigation." Actually the case was quashed. Public opinion had one of its rare victories over Autocracy.

The summer of 1905 was replete with revolutionary portents. The Red Sunday reverberated throughout the empire in the form of strikes and riots, burning estates, sporadic murders of landowners and officials, organized terror on the part of the Socialist-Revolutionists, with such incidental repercussions as the revolt of the cruiser *Potemkin* in the Black Sea waters. Discontent was general. The disgraceful Portsmouth peace with Japan pained the patriots and added fuel to the rage of the liberals and radicals over the costly adventure in Manchuria. Sergey Witte, who negotiated the treaty, was sourly rewarded by the tsar with the title of count. The public referred to him as Count Portsmuthsky, or Semi-Sakhalinsky (Russia having lost by the terms of the treaty the southern half of Sakhalin to Japan). The demobilized Manchurian army was moving homeward across the vast plains, further aggravating the popular state of mind by its wretched aspect and tales of woe and misery, on the one side, and of treachery, cowardice, theft, and corruption, on the part of the Authorities. Came October, and the Russian method of passive resistance in the form of an unprecedented general strike, which paralysed the whole empire and brought it to the verge of bankruptcy, proved successful where years of revolutionary activity had failed. The autocrat renounced his autocratic privileges, and granted the country a constitutional form of government and those elementary liberties for which generations of Russian men and women had fought and died. The strike ceased, and the rejoicing was universal and unreserved. It could have been foreseen that as long as the autocrat was strong enough to grant favours to his subjects, the limitation of his power was far from complete. In fact, the Manifesto of June, 1907, which mutilated the constitution and drastically modified the electoral law, contained a justification to the effect that what the tsar bestowed he could likewise take away. The day after the

declaration of the October liberties, there began throughout Russia a series of officially organized massacres of Jews, students, and all those suspected of liberal and radical tendencies. These amateur performances were followed in the ensuing months by punitive military expeditions to various parts of the empire, by the installation of field courts martial for the speedy execution of apprehended suspects, in a word, by the régime of wholesale shootings and hangings, which provoked Lev Tolstoy's helpless outcry, " I Cannot Be Silent! " and which was branded by the Duma deputy Rodichev as the era of " Stolypin's necktie."

During that summer Gorky lived in Kuokkala, Finland. Though annexed to Russia and gradually reduced to the status of a Russian province, Finland enjoyed for the moment a greater degree of political liberty than any part of the empire. While there Gorky frequently met such friends as the painter Repin, the critic Stasov, the writers Andreyev, Kuprin, Skitalets, and he also gained the friendship of many Finns, notably of the painter Axel Gallen. The Department of Police received reports of Gorky's participation in various literary and musical programs arranged in Finland, together with other Russian radical artists, Maria Andreyeva among them. At Kuokkala Gorky completed, by August, his play *Barbarians,* which the Authorities forbade for presentation. Gorky's plays were causing too much annoyance for the police. Even such an innocent play, politically speaking, as *Children of the Sun,* shown in the fall of that year in St. Petersburg and Moscow, produced hysterical scenes. *Children of the Sun* provoked similar disturbances in the provinces, as for example, in Nizhni Novgorod, where it was given on November 21.

The police must have been too preoccupied and bewildered during the last three months of the year 1905, to report on Gorky's movements. Shortly after the October Manifesto Gorky organized a daily paper in St. Petersburg, *Novaya Zhizn* (*New Life*), with the collaboration of prominent authors, and such Social-Democrats as Lenin, Lunacharsky, Avilov, Bazarov, Rozhkov, and their foreign comrades, Kautsky, Liebknecht, Rosa Luxembourg, Marcel Cachin, Guesde, Lafargue,

and others. The nominal editor of the paper was N. M. Minsky, the poet, and the publisher, Maria Andreyeva; beginning with the sixth number, its actual editor was Lenin. In the third number Gorky began the series of his *Notes on Smugness*. Freedom of the press, proclaimed in the Imperial Manifesto, was exemplified in the case of *Novaya Zhizn* most eloquently. The very first issue was confiscated, and hardly an issue thereafter escaped persecution. N. M. Minsky was subjected to trial for " circulating writings that incite to the overthrow of the existing order of state and society," and was eventually imprisoned for one year. On December 15, the paper was suspended.

In the second volume of *Klim Samgin* the events of October-December are laid in Moscow, and their description is too vivid not to have been made by an eye-witness. Gorky must have been fleeting from capital to capital during those eventful weeks, for he appeared ubiquitous, editing *Novaya Zhizn* in St. Petersburg, and watching the October manifestations and the December barricades in Moscow. In conversation Gorky recalls curious details from his observations in those days. From the window of his centrally located Moscow rooms he saw the procession at the funeral of Bauman, the revolutionist killed by the Black Hundreds at the celebration of the October Manifesto. " All Moscow marched after the coffin. . . . Here glimmers the white head of Stanislavsky; there towers Chaliapin with his broad nostrils; there is the painter Serov, there is Bryusov." The procession resulted in fresh attacks by the Black Hundreds against the intelligentsia, and Gorky again had a vantage point by his window. Chaliapin rushed in, ecstatic, dishevelled, his hat way on the back of his head. He gushed: " Ah, Alexey, do you see how fine it is, never has there been anything so fine, do you understand? But no, you could not understand that. Think: we have freedom, equality! Ah, my God, how remarkable it is! " " Suddenly," adds Gorky, " a volley crashed at the window panes, and bits of glass showered all around us." The finale was symbolic of the ephemeral " freedom and equality " at which Chaliapin and thousands of other Russian prematurely rejoiced.

It is definitely established that Gorky took an active part in organizing and supporting the Moscow barricade struggle in December. His part in this movement could not remain a secret for long, and indeed, on January 2, 1906, his rooms in St. Petersburg were searched by the police. Early in February Gorky was in the capital of Finland, Helsingfors. Colonel Gerasimov, of the Secret Service, reported to the minister of the interior that Finnish students and Red Guards greeted Gorky with music and songs, to which he responded with shouts: " Long live the free people of Finland." He was also reported to have made a speech for the Russian students at Helsingfors. Warned of imminent arrest, Gorky left Finland for western Europe.

Gorky's implication in the Moscow uprising became serious during the examinations of Nicholas Schmidt, a Moscow manufacturer arrested for his part in the organization and support of that uprising. Schmidt testified, according to the Chief of the Moscow Secret Service, that Gorky had been instrumental in collecting funds for arms, giving readings at many places where a part of the admission fees went for " avowedly revolutionary purposes." It appeared also that Schmidt was introduced to Gorky in September, 1905, in connexion with the proposed publication of *Novaya Zhizn*. Schmidt admitted to have loaned Gorky fifteen thousand rubles for the paper. (In his note on Krasin Gorky states that *Novaya Zhizn* in St. Petersburg, and *Borba* (*Struggle*), in Moscow, were organized in 1905, " with the help of Savva (Morozov)." He does not mention Schmidt.) Furthermore, Schmidt testified that he had given Gorky twenty thousand rubles as a fund for the purchase of arms for the uprising. In his subsequent testimony Schmidt tried to clear Gorky, but without success. Incidentally, Schmidt acknowledged having attended at a private residence a reading by Gorky (he read his *Children of the Sun*), at which twenty-five rubles were levied from everyone present " for arms." Altogether, it would seem that Gorky's departure for Helsingfors and thence for western Europe was undertaken none too soon.

GORKY AND THE STAGE

IN the preface to the American version of his play, *The Judge,* Maxim Gorky deprecates his dramatic talent quite sweepingly. He admits that not one of his plays satisfies his own standard of a good play, and pleads guilty to didacticism and verbosity. " The characters of a drama [he writes] should all act independently of the volition of the dramatist, in accordance with the law of their individual natures and social environment; they must follow the inspiration of their own destiny, and not that of any other destiny arbitrarily imposed upon them by the writer. They must, driven by their own inner impulses, create the incidents and episodes — tragic or comic — and direct the course of the play, being permitted to act in harmony with their own contradictory natures, interests, and passions. The author throughout should act like a host at a party to which he has invited imaginary guests, without in any way interceding, no matter how one guest may worry or torment any other — be it physically or morally: and finally, it is his business cold-bloodedly to describe the manner in which they all behave." Gorky tells us that he does not know of a single European (how flattering for the rest of the globe!) play written according to that standard, and asserts that he himself " could never write one."

Allowing for the Russian trait of self-castigation, which amounts at times to haughty humility, we still cannot gainsay the relative truth of Gorky's verdict. His plays are imbued with his robust sense of reality, but they all suffer from his avowed weakness for long-winded sermons. The initial success of his dramas was not a little a *succès de scandal,* and above all it

was due in a large measure to the sponsorship of the Moscow Art Theatre.

It was Anton Chekhov who persistently urged Gorky to write for the stage. From their first meeting, in 1899, Chekhov launched into the task of urbanizing the erstwhile hobo. He admired Gorky personally and as a writer, but he deplored the provincialism that protruded now and then in his manners and utterances, taking the form of what Chekhov regarded as a heinous vice for an artist — lack of restraint and measure. He had to go about his task with extreme delicacy, considering Gorky's hypersensitiveness as a newcomer among the intelligentsia. The shy yet pugnacious longshoreman would have been keenly hurt, and hardly helped, if Chekhov told him directly, as he did to Olga Knipper, to Stanislavsky, and others, that he could not get accustomed to Gorky's ostentatious folk-blouse, that he did not like his solemn sermonizing, that, like Tolstoy, he could hardly finish *Three of Them*, and similar truths. In his letters to Gorky, Chekhov voiced a number of strictures, but he did so in a subtly genial manner, though even then he was constrained time and again to mollify and " explain " a word or a phrase that peeved the touchy Maxim. Chekhov was convinced that Gorky needed polish, and that he could obtain this by rubbing elbows with wide-awake and cultivated people. With this in view, he repeatedly charged him to leave the backwoods of Nizhni Novgorod for Moscow or St. Petersburg, where he would live in a proper environment. Largely for the same purpose he introduced Gorky to the Moscow Art Theatre crowd, when they paid a visit to the ailing author of *The Seagull* in the Crimea.

" Write a play! Write! Write! Write! " This became a refrain in Chekhov's letters to Gorky, with disregard for the latter's protestations of not knowing how. Indeed, Gorky had had a rather limited acquaintance with the stage, save for a summer in the Ukrainian village of Manuylovka, where he organized a company of local amateurs. Chekhov coaxed and exhorted, volunteered to read the script, and assured him that even if his first production should fail, the harm would not be great (remembering his own heartache at the fiasco of *The*

Seagull in the Alexandrine Theatre of St. Petersburg, Chekhov, physician that he was, used this prophylaxis). He gave Gorky no rest until *Smug Citizens* and *At the Bottom* were actually written and performed. With what anxiety he followed, from his Crimean retreat, the performances of Gorky's plays! He bombarded Stanislavsky, Nemirovich-Danchenko, his own wife — Olga Knipper — and other actors, with letters, suggestions, complaints, and appeared more concerned than when his own works were being produced. And with what triumphant joy he greeted the success of his protégé!

On the other hand, Chekhov was eager to help the Moscow Art Theatre by recruiting new playwrights for its repertoire. In a letter to Olga Knipper, written after the production of *Smug Citizens,* he said in his wonted tone of earnestness mixed with mischief: " I have been egging on all our best authors to write plays for the Art Theatre. Gorky has already done so, Balmont, Leonid Andreyev, Teleshov, and others have begun to write. It would not be amiss to appoint a fee for me, if only one ruble per nose."

The Moscow Art Theatre was entering the new century armed with enthusiasm and daring. Its quests and innovations appealed to the progressive elements of society, and in its turn the Theatre endeavoured to meet the expectations of the public. Russia lived in the mood of a protracted " on the eve." The chaotic present, what with economic cataclysms, political restiveness, and coexisting extremes in currents of thought, presaged an eventful future. Stanislavsky and Nemirovich-Danchenko felt bound to reflect that mood on the stage. And who but Gorky represented the *Zeitgeist,* as singer of the oncoming storm and of the Madness of the Brave? Who but Gorky could satisfy Stanislavsky's idea of a play which would express the public " discontent, protest, and dreams of a hero boldly speaking the truth " ?

This is why the directors of the Theatre and the whole troupe pounced on Gorky during their visit to the Crimea, and for two weeks beguiled him, and finally won his promise to write a play for them. He attracted them all by his youthfulness, force, non-conformity, and wealth of experience that de-

manded expression. Let me try to transmit his impression on Nemirovich-Danchenko, in the peculiar language of this " Grand Duke " of the Theatre:

A quizzical impetuosity, directed inward. Along with a calm exterior, an enormous store of unspent power ready to hurl itself down the first road prompted by intuition. A keen and precise eye from under a frowning brow, a swift appraisal and sorting out of observations. Concentration, cogitation, and a quick discard of what is obvious and outworn. Side by side with the good taste of modesty, an elemental faith in his self, or at least in his *Weltanschauung*. An agreeable singsong bass, a Volga ' o ' accent, and an enchanting smile that caressingly embraces you all at once. A peculiar, angular gracefulness of movements. . . . Thus I picture Maxim Gorky as I recall our first meetings.

Other members of the troupe were equally struck and captivated by the extraordinary Volgar. Olga Knipper has written some warm pages of reminiscences about meeting Gorky, both in company with her celebrated husband, and behind the stage of the Moscow Art Theatre. She recalls with what care he taught her (she was to play Nastya, the street-walker) how to make a " dog's paw " out of paper, how to drop coarse tobacco, " makhorka," into it, how to roll it into a cigarette, and how to smoke it properly. He offered, " naïvely," to bring a girl from the night-lodging for a short stay with the Chekhovs, to enable Olga Knipper to " get a deeper insight into the psychology of a hollowed soul." She sums up the impression he produced on them in these words: " Like a rocket he flew from somewhere into our quiet intelligentsia life, and stirred us with his tales of an unknown life." Naturally, it was this " unknown life " that interested them all more than anything, but Nemirovich-Danchenko made them realize that at the moment the censor would oppose the portrayal of that life, especially by such a dangerous author as Gorky. It was agreed therefore that in his first play Gorky refrain from bringing in the *bosyaks*.

Gorky's permit for a sojourn in Crimea expired, and the Authorities once again made him stay at Nizhni Novgorod, and shortly after, in the near-by town of Arzamas. Chekhov kept up his refrain. Nemirovich-Danchenko made special trips to the home of the political suspect. Gorky was engaged in writing *Smug Citizens,* but his heart and mind strayed to the subject of his next play, *At the Bottom.* In the former he presented the drabness of mediocrity, of the average existence. In the latter he was to depict the comparative colourfulness of human flotsam free from the moorings of property and convention — a subject of reminiscent warmth to him.

His first drama was praised by Chekhov, again and again, and was received by the Moscow Art Theatre " with joy," as Stanislavsky recalls: anything by Gorky would have carried the day. His name stood for romance and rebellion, and in admiring him the public found compensation for what it lacked, and anticipated, in reality. The somewhat belated performance of *Smug Citizens* in St. Petersburg, in the winter of 1902, threatened to prove a political rather than theatrical event. We may recall that it came shortly after the scandalous annulment of Gorky's election to the Imperial Academy, when the Authorities feared demonstrations against Grand Duke Constantine during the presentation of Gorky's play, and forbade it. It required all the tact and vigour of Nemirovich-Danchenko to have this order rescinded, and to run the play — considerably doctored by the censor, to be sure, and strapping policemen taking up the tickets at the entrances.

Despite the political sensation, and the splendid acting of the company, the success of the play was " moderate," according to Stanislavsky. It hardly deserved anything more than that. There is not enough action in the play, and whatever action there is savours of melodrama. Lack of action in Chekhov's drama is repaid by the mood of inner experience, which insinuates itself into the audience and grips their hearts. In Gorky's first play tedium and lifeless words prevail, only faintly relieved by two or three good parts and a few brilliant situations. Yet there was so much in the name of Gorky that *Smug Citizens* had considerable runs in Russia, wherever the police permitted

its production, and it gained a certain acclaim in Vienna and Berlin, shortly after its showing in St. Petersburg and Moscow.

Meanwhile Gorky had completed his other play, which had a much greater interest both for himself and for the Moscow Art Theatre. In September, 1902, Gorky managed to come to Moscow for a short stay, and he read the manuscript for the company. There were also present Chaliapin, Andreyev, Chirikov, and other artists. Kachalov tells us that he read " beautifully." " When he began to read the scene in which Luka consoles Anna on her death-bed, we held our breaths, and a wonderful stillness reigned. Gorky's voice trembled and broke. He stopped, remained silent for a moment, wiped a tear with his finger, and tried to resume his reading, but after the first few words he stopped again and wept almost aloud, wiping his tears with a handkerchief. ' Ugh, devil,' he mumbled smiling in embarrassment through his tears, ' well written, by God, well done.' "

The reading produced a memorable effect. The actors felt not only enthusiasm for the freshness and originality of the play, but also a new responsibility: they were to portray an utterly unfamiliar *milieu*. No one appreciated the difficulties more than Stanislavsky, who both as actor and director strove above all after truth on the stage. To show Gorky's tramps and outcasts as flesh and blood individuals despite the super-clever and occasionally highfalutin' speeches which the author makes them deliver, was not an easy task. Then, again, the play lacks unity and concentration, and presents a series of loose episodes; to knit these together and instil into them a dramatic cohesion incurred the danger of falling into artificiality and melodrama. Stanislavsky employed his unfailing method of getting saturated with the subject-matter. Not only did he have interminable talks with Gorky, during which the author told of his own experiences with the submerged, and supplied biographical details and characteristics of the members of the cast, but he went into the very midst of that life. With the aid of Gorky and Gilyarovsky, another writer with a " past," expeditions were arranged into the worst dens of Moscow. Nemirovich-Danchenko, Stanislavsky, half a dozen actors, and the painter

Simov, were guided into the dank and gloomy cellars, where their extreme tact, enforced by a generous treat of vodka and sausage, helped them to set the denizens at ease and make them act and talk naturally. The visitors observed, studied, and made notes.

As expected, the play met with the opposition of the censor, and Nemirovich-Danchenko had to muster all the political pull and high connexions available. He is still of the impression that the ultimate grant of the permission to produce the play was due to the conviction of the Authorities in its inevitable failure. Luzhsky recalls the numerous changes in the text demanded by the censor, such as the replacement of " police station " by " precinct," or the deletion of such phrases as " jail won't teach you anything good." In the original version Satin addresses Kleshch, right after the sound of a factory siren: " My advise to you is this: don't do anything." On reaching this place, one of the influential friends of the theatre who tried to help them get the permission, looked quite worried: " What's that? A hint at labour strikes? "

At the Bottom of Life, or in Nemirovich-Danchenko's version, *At the Bottom,* was finally performed at the Art Theatre, in December, 1902. Never before or after did the Theatre reap such a thunderous triumph. Both Gorky and the actors were given endless ovations. To this day *At the Bottom* is the biggest trump in the repertoire of Stanislavsky's company, at home as well as abroad. Its success is due not only to the mastery with which Gorky drew the quintessential epitome of his experience as a vagabond, but in a very large measure also to the sympathetic understanding and tireless efforts at attaining the Truth on the part of the performers.

When at the rehearsal Gorky watched Kachalov in the rôle of the Baron, he boomed: " I wrote nothing of the sort! " But he added: " Only — that is far greater than what I wrote. Of that I have not even dreamed." Kachalov created an unforgettable part not merely by means of his keen intuition: he studied the details of the life of Baron Bucholz, the prototype of Gorky's Baron, and profited from his trips to the Moscow dens, where he met an ex-guardsman who had been sucked in

by the Bottom. In the end Kachalov was able to transcend
Gorky in making us visualize the metamorphosis of the titled
noble into a ragged hobo and pimp. The same is true about
the other parts in the play, major or minor. Whether Stanislavsky as Satin, or Moskvin as old Luka, Luzhsky as Bubnov,
or Olga Knipper as Nastya, each one became reincarnated
into the person portrayed. Even such a seemingly unimportant
part as that of the Tatar was made into a gem by Vishnevsky,
who lived the part for weeks and weeks before the performance.

The success of the performance would not have been what
it was had the actors employed the same naturalistic, " Meinin-
gen," method as they had recently done in Tolstoy's *Power of
Darkness*. Stanislavsky realized that *At the Bottom* called for
something more than ethnic verismilitude. In probing the
depths of the play, in listening to Gorky's tales, in observing
the dwellers of the Moscow night-lodgings, Stanislavsky
reached the conclusion that the " spiritual substance " of the
play could be expressed in the slogan, " Freedom — at any
price! " Alongside of its crass reality, *At the Bottom* is pregnant with symbolic undertones, and these undertones could
not be transmitted by merely adhering to the external Truth.
The flexibility of the Moscow Art Theatre was admirably
shown on this occasion, when they not only presented a night-
lodging " as it is," but also shot across the footlights and into
the hearts of the audience what Stanislavsky called " the public mood of the moment and the political tendency of the
author." No naturalism could convince an audience that a
hymn to man and his potential power might sound forth from
the bottom of life, from a den of ex-men, pick-pockets, prostitutes, and pimps. When in the final scene, as usual in his cups,
Satin-Stanislavsky speaks his monologue on Man (" M-a-n!
That sounds proud! "), he infects the listeners with his sincerity, whereas on a different stage, even at Reinhardt's Kleines
Theater in Berlin, that monologue sounds like turgid decla-
mation.

At the Bottom produced the impression of an epochal event.
There were some enthusiasts who compared the evening of its
production, December 31, 1902, with the evening of February

25, 1830, when Victor Hugo's *Hernani* inaugurated the Romantic revolution on the stage of the Paris Comédie. One read in some accounts that a new aesthetics had been born. *Mercure de France* cited what was the prevailing reaction to Gorky's play in Russia: " What happened would have been unbelievable one day before: genuine life invaded the stage as a vast torrent, sweeping away all its conventions, hurling aside all its forms, and filling the cleared space with cruel artistic truth. It seemed as though the old theatre had ceased to exist. The curtain rose — and there appeared a new theatre. A revolution had been accomplished in the name of the rights of life and the rights of man. . . ."

With the public, the success of the play was overwhelming. Beyond doubt the feeling that it was revolutionary, not only in the aesthetic sense, helped not a little the general enthusiasm. As to the critics, if we discount the exaggerations, both pro and contra, there was a definite cleavage between those in Moscow and St. Petersburg. The former voiced, on the whole, their delight in the novel experiment of proclaiming a hymn to man from the lowest depths. Even the reserved monthly, *Russkaya Mysl*, by no means a champion of Gorky, had to admit that " a sincere hymn to love sounded triumphantly " in the play, and that " the picture of human misery was illuminated by faith in the human soul, and it was this combination that acted irresistibly on the audience." On the other hand, the prevailing opinion of the St. Petersburg critics was adverse. Gorky was reproached for " playing on the base and nasty strings of the human soul," for attempting to put into a form of art certain " horrors of reality, which no matter how much they be stirred up, cannot be crystallized into an artistic idea." " There are hidden recesses of despair, vice, penury," complained one critic, " which cannot be laid publicly bare to the bottom without artificially provoking the most negative results." A. A. Stolypin, brother of the future prime minister, declared that never before had he " felt a more humiliating sensation than at the contemplation of Gorky's *Bottom*, a sensation of being forcibly ducked in a cesspool." Need one add that such reports failed to affect the box receipts adversely?

In its printed form, *At the Bottom,* brought forth the commendation of the best critics, and had fourteen editions in 1903 alone.

None of Gorky's other plays enjoyed anything but a moderate success. The production of *Summer-Folk* at the theatre of Kommissarzhevskaya in St. Petersburg, in November, 1904, gained a certain notoriety, because a portion of the audience hissed the author's treatment of the intelligentsia. Gorky came out to acknowledge the applause and the hisses. In Russia whistling takes the place of hissing. As whistlers the anaemic intelligentsia were no match for the Volga stevedore. There he stood before the footlights, over six feet tall, bowing and whistling. " And I certainly outwhistled that learned bunch," he recalls with a sly wink.

About one year later his *Children of the Sun* was played simultaneously at Kommissarzhevskaya's and at the Moscow Art Theatre. Gorky had written it, we may recall, while incarcerated in the Peter and Paul Fortress, after the Red Sunday events. The name of the author, the place where the play was written, and the troublous weeks of October, 1905, combined to bring into the theatre an electrified audience. The realistic acting of the Moscow Art Theatre made the spectators lose all discrimination between stage and actuality, and during the scene of a riot, in which Gorky has the mob attack a group of intellectuals, the audience went wild and hysterical. The curtain was lowered, but shouts from the public demanded to know whether Kachalov (who played the chemist) had been hurt, and how Maria Andreyeva and the rest fared after the onslaught from the Black Hundreds. The actors had to come out and show themselves to their vociferous admirers.

Early in the next year Gorky left Russia, and the censors were little inclined to pass plays by a political refugee. The one subsequent play by him which won certain praise, and which of course was forbidden for the stage in Russia, was *Enemies.* It is, indeed, a keen appraisal of the clash between the employers and employés. In portraying the factory owners and their workmen, the author does not conceal his sympathies for the latter. His workmen are presented as calm fighters, certain

of their right and of inevitable victory. The leader of the Marxian Socialists, George Plekhanov, wrote a laudatory essay on *Enemies,* though formerly he disparaged Gorky's " Socialism."

Recently Gorky's novel, *Mother,* has been dramatized, both for the stage and the screen. Small wonder that in Soviet Russia Gorky has a hearing, especially through those of his works where he portrays the lower classes and their revolt against smugness and exploitation. Of course, their artistic value does not improve by reason of their popularity.

ABROAD (1906-1914)

THE Russian Authorities might have exclaimed: " Good riddance! " at the news of Gorky's flight across the border. His presence in Russia was the cause of much disturbance and annoyance. The hands of the Administration itched to lay hold on the meddler and muzzle him, yet the international situation made it imperative to heed Gorky's numerous admirers abroad, and to treat him with undeserved considerateness. Now that he was out of the country, though free to speak and act, he was considerably less dangerous than when surrounded with the halo of a martyr at home. Perhaps official Russia foresaw that in direct contact with Gorky the western world would soon discover that as a politician he ranked pathetically below Gorky the fiction writer.

Yet the Invisible Thread did not quite relinquish its hold on Gorky even when he was beyond the frontiers of Russia. The representatives of the Russian government abroad had to watch the mischief which Gorky endeavoured to work against Autocracy, and to counteract or at least neutralize it by all the means at their disposal. Russia was then seeking a loan, and the moment was far from propitious: what with the ignominious peace treaty with Japan, and the recent internal disorders, Gorky's voice of unreserved hatred for the existing order, his passionate appeal for the support of the revolutionary movement, and against propping up the tottering Autocracy by way of loans and investments, was not to be ignored. The more so since his voice was not a cry in the wilderness, but was echoed by numerous liberal and radical

men of prominence, both Russian and western, such as Paul Milukov and Jean Jaurès.

Gorky's stay in Berlin presented an unbroken triumph for the revolutionary cause. Though his presence coincided with the performances of the Moscow Art Theatre, with *At the Bottom* in their repertoire, he was fêted and glorified more as a symbol of struggling Russia than as an author. Kachalov recalls a Gorky evening organized at Charlottenburg, at which Gorky read his *Stormy Petrel* and *Falcon,* Schildkraut some of Gorky's tales in a German translation, and Kachalov himself read *The Goltva Fair.* " During the intermission a crowd of excited Social-Democrats appeared behind the scenes to express their admiration for Gorky; they were lead by the young, merry, black-moustachioed Karl Liebknecht and the grey-bearded, solemn and bespectacled Karl Kautsky. When Gorky was reading his *Stormy Petrel,* the Crown Prince could be seen looking with keen attention from the box nearest the stage; in the depth of the box shimmered the monocles, epaulets, tinselled collars of his resplendent suite." The Berlin reception was symptomatic of the way the western world was going to treat Gorky, and official Russia looked with uneasiness to this progress through Europe and across the Atlantic.

Gorky's trip to the United States for the purpose of securing goodwill and financial support for the revolutionary movement, augured success. American public opinion had been overwhelmingly opposed to the Russian autocracy, both in its war with Japan and in its struggle against the people. Gorky's name had figured prominently and sympathetically in press dispatches ever since the Red Sunday. During his imprisonment at the Peter and Paul Fortress, leading American editors (Richard Watson Gilder of the *Century,* Charles Scribner of *Scribner's,* W. C. Allen of *Harper's*) declared their readiness to join the movement in behalf of Gorky, launched by Dr. Theodore Barth of the Berlin *Nation.*

Gorky's sojourn in the United States promised to be a series of banquets and public meetings, with the participation of many notables. Mark Twain and William Dean Howells were to represent American letters at a reception and dinner in the

guest's honour, and an invitation to the White House was rumoured to be pending from President Roosevelt.

The Invisible Thread got busy. The Russian embassy at Washington endeavoured to counteract Gorky's influence by discrediting him personally. Their effort at inducing the immigration officers to bar the entrance of Gorky to the country as an anarchist, failed. To the customary question of the Authorities as to whether he was an anarchist and an enemy of law and order, Gorky replied that he was a socialist, that he stood for law and order, and therefore was " fighting the tsarist government which was nothing but organized anarchy." Nor did the embassy succeed in its attempt to " inspire " the American press with the notion that it was " inadmissible " to collect dollars for arms against a " friendly " government. Mark Twain, a vigorous champion of the Russian revolution, parried that argument by reminding his compatriots of the help they received from France during their revolutionary struggle. There came then a " special despatch " from St. Petersburg advising Gorky's admirers that he was not merely a liberal or a reformer, but a dangerous and desperate " social revolutionist." This scare proved also ineffective, for in 1906 the word " revolution " was still acceptable in the average American household, even among the D.A.R. The embassy decided to play its trump card and strike at the most vulnerable spot of the native — his scrupulosity in regard to sex morality.

It was only necessary to intimate that the lady registered as Gorky's wife was in reality Madame Andreyeva, whose close and to all intents and purposes matrimonial, relations with the author had not been sanctioned by the clergy. Gorky's reputation dropped to zero point by virtue of that bit of intelligence. Society turned its back upon the erstwhile " distinguished visitor," receptions, invitations, banquets, meetings were cancelled, and the yellow press had its innings. The Gorky party was ejected from one hotel after another, and was finally given shelter at a private home.

Aside from the false step of bringing along Maria Andreyeva and introducing her as his wife, Gorky committed another *gaucherie* while a guest in the " land of the free." He openly

championed the cause of American labour, and took sides with the striking miners. This offence, coupled with the moral issue, may account for the sudden and utter reversal of the public attitude in America toward Gorky. His mission had been dealt a mortal blow; the Invisible Thread was triumphant.[1]

During the summer of 1906, while in America, Gorky published a number of articles, in which he urged the civilized nations to refuse the Russian Government in the ardently sought loan. When the loan was eventually contracted, with the French bankers as its chief subscribers, Gorky burst out with a shower of protests. Anatole France replied to his personal letter in a tone of sympathy and condolence, expressing his profound chagrin over the success of the Russian Government. Gorky published a virulent sketch, *Fair France*, in the somewhat grandiloquent style of his early allegories. He spoke of the great revolutionary past of France, of her cultural leadership, and of her present misconduct, her greed for gold, and her disgraceful support of the Russian despoty. He concluded:

The blood of Russian people will once more be shed, with the aid of thy gold. May, then, this blood suffuse with the red of eternal shame the flabby cheeks of thy lying face.

My beloved! Accept also my spit of blood and gall into thy eyes!

The French press replied to Gorky's outburst with indignation and reproach. René Viviani chided Gorky for writing " an article that might only serve the counter-revolution in Europe, through humiliating a country, which, in spite of all, remains at the vanguard of all nations." Most of the writers reminded Gorky of his popularity in France, and of the wide-spread movement in his behalf, when he lay in prison. Gorky published an open letter " To the Journalists of France," in which he bluntly told them not to boast of having once behaved humanely, and not to expect his gratitude. As to their alleged love for him: " Gentlemen, I tell you frankly: the love of a bourgeois is deeply offensive to an honest writer and so-

---

[1] A fuller account of Gorky's sojourn in U.S.A. is given in the Appendix, I.

cialist." One can imagine official Russia gleefully rubbing their hands; when at large Gorky the politician was as tactful as a drunken muzhik.

The historian Aulard, writing in the *Dépêches* of Toulouse, expressed his sympathy with Gorky's indignation against the granting of the loan. "What," he asked, "would have happened if, in June, 1789, England or Austria had loaned money to Louis XVI?" Yet he resented Gorky's implication that all of France was guilty of mercenariness; in his opinion the French Government approved of the loan " against the convictions of the flower of the republic." Gorky's spit at France he regarded as " the spit of a sick man, inebriated with ink." In his reply to Aulard, Gorky asserted that he was not so naïve as to hurl his accusation at the French people; he had meant, of course, the France that had spat at Émile Zola, and he now gave warning to the financiers who were helping with blood money " the band of robbers and murderers, in other words, the government of Russia ":

The Russian revolution will grow slowly and a long time, but will end in the victory of the people. . . . When power and authority are in the hands of the people, they will be reminded of the French bankers who helped the Romanov family to fight against the freedom of justice and truth, and to retain their rule, whose barbarian and anti-cultural rôle is clearly seen and felt by all the honest eyes and hearts of Europe. I am certain that the Russian people will not return to France the loans already repaid with their blood. They will not!

In this connexion it is pertinent to quote Trotsky's *My Life*. After recounting the story of the St. Petersburg Soviet (under his presidency) in 1905, and of its manifesto which declared the inevitable bankruptcy of Tsarism and warned foreign financiers that the victorious Russian people would not repay the loans incurred by their enemy, the Autocracy, Trotsky proceeds:

The French *Bourse* answered our manifesto a few months later with a new loan of three quarters of a million francs.

The liberal and reactionary press poured sarcasm over the important threat of the Soviet against the tsar's finances and the European bankers. In later years the manifesto was successfully forgotten, but it recalled itself to mind. The financial bankruptcy of Tsarism, prepared for by its whole past history, coincided with the military *débâcle*. And later, after the victories of the revolution, the decree of the Soviet of People's Commissaries, issued in February 10, 1918, declared all the Tsarist debts annulled. This decree remains in force even to this day. It is wrong to say, as some do, that the October revolution does not recognize any obligations: its own obligations the revolution recognizes to the full. The obligation that it took upon itself on December 2, 1905 [the date of the Soviet manifesto. A.K.], it carried out on February 10, 1918. The revolution is fully entitled to remind the creditors of Tsarism: " Gentlemen, you were warned in ample time."

In August, 1906, the chief of the Podolia gendarmerie reported to the Department of Police, on the basis of a clipping from the *Kurjer Lwowski,* that Maxim Gorky had addressed the French workmen with the following appeal:

The hour of a general uprising in Russia is close at hand. If you do not wish your Russian comrades to go into battle with bare hands, give them money for arms and munition; this is the best way in which you can help them in their struggle for freedom.

The political activity of Gorky seemed to have terminated in October, 1906, when he settled on the island of Capri, with the intention of devoting himself to literary work under peaceful and healthful surroundings. But already on January 22, 1907, State Secretary Muravyev, Russian Ambassador at Rome, wrote a confidential report to Prime Minister Stolypin, in which he spoke of Gorky as the leader of the revolutionary emigrants, who " willingly played the rôle of ' teacher ' " to the numerous admirers that visited him at Capri. The Ambassador went on to say that a letter of Gorky's had been published in the Italian press, which " in the form of a solemn proclamation or manifesto, with boundless, at times absurd, conceit and impudence,

thanked the Italians for their attention and hospitality, glorified the Russian revolutionists, and incidentally committed in a few lines a genuine *lèse-majesté*. I make bold to suggest that the latter circumstance deserves the attention of our Authorities at the expected return of Gorky to Russia." Muravyev complained of the great ado the Italian socialists and radicals made about Gorky, even inviting him to preside at a public meeting in Rome for the commemoration of the Red Sunday. Minister of the Interior, Giolitti, whom Muravyev described as a bitter enemy of the socialists, informed him that Gorky had " wisely " declined the invitation.

About one month later the chief of the gendarmerie of Finland communicated some documents to the Department of Police, with a note: " Inclosed a photographic reproduction of Maxim Gorky's original letter to the famous Finnish painter, Axel Gallen, and a copy of Gorky's newspaper article sent with it. I wish to report that we have succeeded in purchasing the original letter for a very brief time, in order to have it photographed at our bureau." The article (which Gorky endeavoured to publish in the press of Italy, France, and England) dealt with the rumoured intention of the Russian Government to " launch a barbarous attack against little Finland." It recounted the cultural achievements of Finland, such as equal suffrage, universal education, notable contributions to the arts, and presented their assailants as " a government of half-literate officials and illiterate generals, a government composed of extremely cruel men and not quite dexterous thieves." The best men of Europe were called upon to protest against the attempt of official Russia at reducing Finland to the position of a Russian province, bereft of all liberties; to shout an " awe inspiring ' Hands off! ' to the profligates and hangmen of the Romanov House, and those with them."

Much warmer and more outspoken was Gorky's personal letter to Axel Gallen, whom he had come to admire as artist and man. The letter was in the handwriting of Maria Andreyeva, and signed by Maxim Gorky. The expressions he used about the Romanovs aggravated his old offense and constituted a serious *lèse-majesté*. Gorky felt pained by the expected in-

vasion of his " dear, precious Finland " by the " Petersburg Ravens." The rulers of Russia were " stupid gluttons and syphilitics of the Romanov dynasty, who had ruined and disgraced the country; their flunkeys — generals from among the Baltic Germans, ready to do anything, even to the murder of thousands of people and the plunder of entire provinces; they are all ignoramuses, barbarian half-beasts rather than human beings. Their one ideal is to guttle, their pleasure — to dominate over people, and they are obsessed with a morbid passion for torture, blood, cruelty. If they be men, which you and I may well doubt, they are sick men, sadists, madmen, who should be treated medically, or should be destroyed, as one destroys mad wolves, dogs, swine." Toward the end of his letter Gorky deplored the fact that the wealthy Finns are ready to compromise with their oppressors, in their fear of revolutionary socialism. He assures the Finns that the Russian revolutionists are their only friends, and calls on them to unite and join their fighting allies.

In the spring of the same year, Gorky attended as a non-voting delegate the London conference of the Russian Social-Democratic Party, at which the divergence between the Plekhanov-led Mensheviks and the Lenin group of Bolsheviks assumed a sharp and definitive form. Gorky's co-operation turned out to be more than platonic. The Conference was originally called at Brussels, but owing to the presentations of the Russian Government its sessions were forbidden by the Belgian police. The Conference was moved to London. The unforeseen additional expense drained the pockets of the delegates, and they faced starvation and an indefinite postponement of their return to Russia. The organizers tried to negotiate with an English bourgeois for a loan, but there were only two delegates present, whose signatures would carry weight: Plekhanov and Gorky. Plekhanov refused to lend his name, and the needed sum was borrowed under Gorky's indorsement. The benevolent bourgeois exacted an odd price for his kindness: he demanded the signatures of all delegates — perhaps as a souvenir. At any rate, when the Central Committee of the Party eventually paid the debt, it retrieved the list of signa-

tures, an extraordinary document, what with the autographs of such men as Lenin, Martov, Trotsky, Plekhanov, and the variety of alphabets represented, from Armenian and Georgian to Lettish and Yiddish.

Gorky attended the sessions of the Conference regularly, and could always be seen in the dark corner of the church, where the meetings took place, eagerly listening to the debates, and expressing his sentiments by applause or disapproving remarks. In the intermission he invariably conversed with groups of Bolshevik workmen in the court of the church, pumping them for information about themselves and their shops, and telling them amusing stories. It was there too that he became acquainted with Trotsky. Here is Trotsky's account of their meeting:

On one of the first days of the Conference I was stopped in the church vestibule by a tall, angular man with a round face and high cheek-bones, who wore a round hat. " I am your admirer," he said, with an amiable chuckle.

" Admirer? " I echoed in astonishment. It appeared that the compliment referred to my political pamphlets that had been written in prison. My interlocutor was Maxim Gorky, and this was the first time I ever saw him. " I hope it is not necessary for me to say that I am your admirer," I said, answering the compliment with another. In that period Gorky was close to the Bolsheviks. With him was the well-known actress, Andreyeva. We went about London together.

" Would you believe it? " said Gorky, as he glanced at Andreyeva in amazement, " she speaks all languages." He himself spoke only Russian, but well. When some beggar would shut the door of the cab behind us, Gorky would plead: " We ought to give him some of those pence." To which Andreyeva would answer: " They have been given, Alyosha dear, they have been given."

In the eyes of the Department of Police, Gorky's participation in the London conference assumed an exaggerated importance. Its over-zealous agents supplied at times fantastic reports. Thus the chief of the Finnish gendarmerie solemnly

stated that "the information alleging that the London conference had passed a resolution against an armed uprising for the present, is not correct; only the Mensheviks are of that opinion. . . . At a separate gathering of Bolsheviks, the following resolution prepared by Kropotkin, Gorky, Aladyin, Alexinsky, and others, was passed: 'An armed uprising must begin simultaneously and in various places, among others in the fleet. Most likely to join the revolution are the south-eastern provinces, also the Caucasus and the Baltic provinces. Expropriations shall be directed mainly against state treasuries and arsenals. Those arsenals which for some reasons could not be utilized by the revolutionists, shall be destroyed. Telegraph and telephone works shall be put out of commission; railroad bridges, dynamited. At the same time, a general strike must begin everywhere. The Finns have promised to join the revolution as soon as the general strike commences, and they have offered their national militia. . . . A republic will be declared in Russia, and members of the reigning house shall be exiled or murdered.' "

The visit of the Tsar to Italy, in 1909, caused considerable fuss among the Russian police, especially in view of the open opposition to that visit on the part of the Italian socialists. The presence of Gorky in Capri appeared irksome to them. Russian and foreign papers printed a variety of rumours concerning the alleged deportation of Gorky from Italy at the request of St. Petersburg. Gorky was finally constrained to deny these rumours in the *Wiener Zeit, Nasha Gazeta,* and elsewhere.

Gorky was concerned about the goodwill of the Italian authorities in view of his efforts at that time to establish at Capri a school for Russian workmen. The Department of Police kept a special file on the Capri school. In June, 1909, its vice-director, Vissarionov, reported to the minister of the interior on Gorky's negotiations with the Central Committee of the Social-Democratic Party regarding his offer to bring to Capri at his cost ten workmen, " to be trained as Bolshevik propagandists, the main lecturers to be Lenin (Ulyanov) and Lunacharsky." Later reports had it that Nikitich (the party name of Krasin) was

in charge of transporting the workmen abroad and bringing them back to Russia. The Department issued secret orders to have the candidate-students, as well as the organizers of the plan, arrested.

In 1912, shortly after the shooting of more than two hundred workmen at the Lena goldfields, Gorky composed for the Bolsheviks the First of May proclamation. The following year he undertook to edit the literary department in the Bolshevik journal, *Prosveshcheniye* (*Enlightenment*). Yet this loyalty to the Bolsheviks did not prevent him from contributing to other parties and party organs, even such moderate reviews as *Vestnik Evropy* (*European Messenger*). Victor Chernov, leader of the Socialist-Revolutionists and bitter enemy of the Social-Democrats, visited Capri in 1911, and obtained Gorky's consent to write for the proposed new organ, *Zavety* (*Legacies*), and other Socialist-Revolutionary publications. Gorky's connexion with *Zavety* was of short duration, however. In a letter to the Ukrainian writer, Mikhail Kotzyubinsky, he had a *postscriptum*: "*Zavety* have chagrined me greatly, and I no longer dance with them. My past relations with them will have to be a *pas seul*." The probable reason for this rupture was the appearance in *Zavety* of Ropshin-Savinkov's novel, *To chevo nie bylo* (*What Never Happened*), which was regarded in many quarters as a calumny of the revolutionary movement.

The Department of the Police received information, or rather misinformation, about Gorky leaving the Social-Democratic Party and joining the Socialist-Revolutionists. This was in 1911, apparently in connexion with Chernov's visit at Capri. During the following year the Department was advised of attempts made at Moscow to organize Narodnik groups and publish a Narodnik review, *Zavety*, following the example of the St. Petersburg *narodniks* who centred around Korolenko's *Russkoye Bogatstvo*. The report cited rumours to the effect that "part of the money for the publication of *Zavety* has been given by Maxim Gorky, who is alleged to have broken with the Social-Democrats and joined the Socialist-Revolutionists. The latter have made previous attempts at winning over Gorky,

and his present attachment to the *narodniks* is regarded by them as a step in the desired direction. They await with great interest what Maxim Gorky will have to say in the pages of the new *narodnik* magazine. In view of the inert activity of the present-day *Russkoye Bogatstvo,* they expect that *Zavety* will play for the *narodnik* movement the rôle of a reviving factor. . . .''

The Central Spider continued to weave its web. The Department of Police was receiving information about Gorky's correspondents in Russia, intercepting the letters on either side. Thus its agents in the province of Simbirsk advised, in 1911, that the Simbirsk Social-Democratic daily, *Zhizn (Life),* had appealed to Gorky for support, complaining of lack of funds. From his Capri retreat Gorky reprimanded the editors of the paper for writing shoddy and illiterate articles, and suggested that before presuming to teach others they ought to go to school themselves. Gorky's occasional articles on political themes were carefully noted by the police and their gist boiled down to a paragraph. An example follows:

In Number 6 of *Budushcheye (l'Avenir),* published by Vladimir Burtsev in Paris, there appeared an extremely tendentious and indecent article by Maxim Gorky, under the title: " A Letter to a Monarchist." In this letter Gorky, after stating that monarchism seems to him a blunder in general, and a particularly pernicious one for Russia, brands the members of the Imperial Russian House as " a family of foreigners, descendants of Karl Ulrich, prince of Holstein, who ruled Russia under the name of Peter III ! " He has the impudence to add that our safely prospering dynasty " has been mercilessly draining our country, and three times within the last hundred years it has brought it to the verge of a national catastrophe." Further on in his article Gorky allows himself the outrageous impertinence of passing insolent remarks about the sacred person of our emperor, and in conclusion he points out that " the coming revolution will amaze even you, half-beasts, with its cruelty, most of which will have to be traced to the unhealthy zoological elements which you have aroused in man: during the last five years, you have done all you could to make men lose their conception of the value of life,

their own and that of others; you have done everything to awaken the beast in man."

After reading this note, Gorky wrote the following comment:

The article in question is my *Letter to a Monarchist,* which I wrote in response to a letter from V. I. Breyev, who was then the president of the Nizhni Novgorod chapter of the Union of True Russian Men. In his letter Breyev offered to "make peace" between me and Nicholas II.

BACK IN RUSSIA (1914–1917)

GORKY'S return to Russia, early in 1914 (by amnesty), was enthusiastically greeted by the radical elements. A letter from " Moscow Students " told him, in part: " You have now come back to us, just on the eve of our awakening from a long and tortured sleep. . . . Our hope is growing firmer in the approach of spring, which we shall meet together with you." Numerous greetings from workmen reached him. One of them, signed by a " Group of Workmen," said: " We believe that your presence in our motherland and your spiritual work will increase our strength, and will enable us, proletarians, to throw off the hateful yoke of reigning darkness." Gorky avoided public celebrations, and a few days after his arrival he retired to Finland, where he settled at a summer villa near the village of Mustamyaki.

Just as in 1906 Gorky had left Russia secretly, so he recrossed the border eight years later, without the formalities of passport and visa. The police was caught napping again. Only three days after his arrival, when he was already in Finland, did the Department of Police learn this, and it frantically demanded an explanation from the frontier gendarmerie, as to how Gorky, still under indictment, had managed to slip through their hands. The Finland gendarmerie was given orders to keep a strict watch over " the Nizhni Novgorod guildsman, Alexey Peshkov, alias Maxim Gorky." The watch must have been far from perfect, for shortly after his arrival the Department reprimanded the police for having failed to note that Gorky had left Mustamyaki, had been to St. Petersburg and Moscow, and came back unobserved. Yet exaggerated

rumours of his persecution spread abroad, and in March, 1914, *La Bataille Syndicaliste* commented:

There is hardly anything more abominable than the prejudiced hatred of the Autocracy for Maxim Gorky, who does honour to Russian letters, and represents civilization, whereas the rulers of Russia personify the most infamous barbarism in Europe. Maxim Gorky, a sick man, whose days are probably numbered, has recently returned to Russia, in the hope of a peaceful existence free from persecution. He had been given assurances that by virtue of the amnesty he was cleared of all former accusations. These were lying words, a snare of the Russian bureaucracy. From the outset the police subjected him to a humiliating surveillance. Again Gorky is compelled to leave this savage land, through which he once tramped with his friend Chaliapin. His novel, *Mother*, is still persecuted. . . .

As a matter of fact, though the several indictments against Gorky were never officially annulled, he was not molested by the Authorities. One of the standing indictments arose in connexion with *Mother*. Upon its publication, 1907–1908, the Prefect of St. Petersburg posted a curious announcement: " By order of the St. Petersburg District Court: WANTED — the Nizhni Novgorod guildsman of the dyers' guild, Alexey Maximovich Peshkov (Maxim Gorky), indicted under articles 1 and 4 of statutes 129, 73, and 132 of the Criminal Code."

The name of Gorky continued to serve as a scarecrow in reactionary circles. In February, 1914, the Berlin police, ever working in accord with their Russian confrères, deported Lunacharsky, following a lecture that he delivered about Gorky. At home, his isolation and reticence failed to please the throngs of reporters and curiosity seekers, who dogged his steps and spied on his privacy at the Finnish villa. Young Suvorin's *Vecherneye Vremya* (*Evening Time*) printed sensational insinuations, alleging that Gorky's ill health did not prevent him from taking part in gay orgies, both in Italy and in Germany, and further asserting that uninvited visitors at his villa were threatened by armed guards. The Department of Police added to its voluminous Gorky file a letter from the " widow of an Actual State Secretary " of Irkutsk, in which she hurled ac-

cusations of disloyalty against Gorky, linking his name with that of the " Grandmother of the Revolution," Katerina Breshkovskaya.

In April of that year the local report to the Department stated that continuous " observation of Alexey Peshkov since January has brought no results that might indicate any criminal activity on the part of said Peshkov." A relaxation of the surveillance seemed to be in order. On June 20th, the chief of the Finland gendarmerie informed the Department that Gorky had rented Lange's villa at the Kerevalo village for a whole year, and queried: " In view of this circumstance, and considering the large expense involved in police surveillance, ought we to continue it? " In reply, he was instructed to verify periodically Gorky's presence at the villa, and to have the nearest station-master report to him of Gorky's journeys. Accordingly, the chief sent in regularly bi-monthly reports on the whereabouts of the writer. He stayed in Finland practically all the year. Only once did he leave that country for a trip, on November 14th, to Kiev, where Maria Andreyeva played at the Solovtsov Theatre. The chief of the Kiev gendarmerie had this to communicate: " According to reports from our agents, Gorky's quarters were visited by representatives of the local tailors' union, who are Social-Democrats by conviction. When they asked him how he regarded the current war, he answered that he could not say anything, because he was ' tangled up ' on this question himself."

Gorky was, of course, opposed to the war, on principle. Yet the police, all its zeal notwithstanding, was unable to indict Gorky for any definite act of disloyalty. There was not a particle of truth in the reports of some German papers (notably *Hamburger Fremdenblatt*, February 6, 1916) about Gorky's arrest as a result of his public speeches advocating immediate peace with Germany. To be sure, he was as outspokenly internationalistic as it was possible under conditions of wartime censorship, and in that vein he conducted the review *Letopis* (*Annals*), the first issue of which appeared in December, 1915. Victims of war hysteria thought even the Draconian censorship of autocratic Russia inexcusably mild, and they made the

Letopis the butt of their ultra-patriotic attacks. The Department of Police could not, nor did it wish to, ignore the clamour for Gorky's blood. It kept on file letters and clippings, the following anonymous communication being quite characteristic:

Sir: Are you aware of the criminal activity of a group of people centering around the defeatist review *Letopis* and the Society for the Study of Jewish Life? These people, headed by Maxim Gorky and hiding behind the would-be legal activity of that society, are collecting money in large amounts, which are spent on far from charitable aims. As a matter of fact, they have been showering on the Russian public proclamations and all sorts of appeals on the Jewish and other questions. Their aim is to discredit all the actions of our Government, and to arouse distrust and hatred for it among the intelligentsia and workmen, in whose midst these leaflets are intensively circulated. Under the guise of conferences with self-taught contributors, Maxim Gorky has been arranging meetings at the offices of the defeatist *Letopis*, or in the rooms of his publishing house *Parus* (*Sail*), or at the residence of Tikhonov, or Sukhanov (pseudonym), or Bazarov (ditto), or Lodyzhnikov, publisher of revolutionary brochures abroad. which are even today circulating in Berlin. . . . As a matter of fact, instead of self-taught contributors these meetings are attended by delegates of various revolutionary labour organizations, prevailingly Bolshevik. These very persons frequently appear at workmen's clubs and other circles, under different nicknames, of course, where they call on the workers to strike and to join the defeatists. *Via* Finland, where he rents a yearly villa, Gorky carries on relations with Russian defeatist emigrants in Switzerland and Norway.

Do you not think it might be worth while to verify these matters of which all St. Petersburg has been talking for a long time?

The writer of this letter must have been an experienced St. Petersburg journalist, intimately acquainted with the *Letopis* circle; much of his information was plausible enough to engage the attention of the Authorities. The Department of Police investigated the charges of the anonymous informant. The St. Petersburg Secret Service gave detailed reports about

all the editors and contributors of *Letopis;* they discovered no " criminal activity " connected with the " Society for the Study of Jewish Life." " On the other hand," so ran the report, " we have information from our agents that Peshkov (Gorky) is, indeed, in favour of pro-Jewish agitation in Russia ; that he is a rabid supporter of all kind of collections for party purposes, and endeavours to carry out the same at every opportunity." This " information " was hardly worth a straw to the Department. As to defeatist propaganda and Bolshevik meetings, alas, " they had no proofs for these offences! " The suspects were, apparently, too dexterous to leave " proofs " for the Invisible Thread, on the strength of which they might be arrested and brought to account. General Globachev, Chief of the St. Petersburg Secret Service, wrote an additional report to the Department of Police in connexion with that anonymous letter. He tried to minimize the importance of Gorky's group. Though *Letopis* (he argued) was of Bolshevik and therefore defeatist tendencies, its editors and contributors kept apart from party organizations, " being more cultivated and materially much better off than the workmen who filled the rank and file of the Social-Democratic Party." The review had no printing shop of its own, hence it could not possibly print any anti-governmental proclamations and appeals. Even if Gorky did carry on relations with political emigrants, " they could not be of great importance, because Gorky has become ' bourgeois,' as they say in party circles, his glamour as a Social-Democrat has grown dim, and he has altogether discontinued all active work."

Lenin's sister, A. Yelizarova, has recently published portions of the secret correspondence between the Russian and foreign bureaus of the Bolshevik Central Committee. In one of her letters to her brother, signed " James," and written in invisible ink, Yelizarova reported on an interview she had with Gorky in the name of the Central Committee. It appears that he " produced on her an excellent impression," that despite his vacillations and incurable conciliatory policy he was in sympathy with Bolshevik internationalism. His *Letopis* and *Parus* (the publishing house) pursued two aims: " 1. Internationalism,

and 2. The abolition of all the remnants of Asianism in our life." Gorky promised to help them publish some of their literature, as articles and in book form. " We are now waiting to see whom they will invite from our group as contributors. There is no doubt that only conditions of censorship are in the way. What is your opinion? Shall we offer them your paper *On Opportunism*? To my mind, we should." The " conditions of censorship " apparently prevailed to the end, for in her letter dated April 7, 1916, " James " informs Lenin that an article by Zinoviev submitted by her to *Letopis* could not be printed because of the censor. When she told the editor that Zinoviev gave him the right to make whatever changes were necessary, he "promised to reconsider." By that time the caution of Gorky as editor, and his collaboration with " dubious " radicals must have dampened Yelizarova's enthusiasm for him. She explains his vagaries by the fact that he " can be easily bent one way or another, and he has a forgiving soul."

Yelizarova reported, incidentally, Gorky's occasional meetings with workmen. At one of these Gorky offered a resolution in favour of the seizure of the Government by revolutionary means. The resolution was adopted. The anonymous informer was not altogether wrong after all!

Military disasters, internal disorders, Rasputinism, were dragging Imperial Russia down to the bottom of Sheol. But the old order was still wriggling, and desperately fighting against the inevitable end. One of its last convulsions may be seen in a letter addressed to the " Society of 1914," in a patriotic daily:

Maxim Gorky has invaded the entire Volga region with his publications. Not only with his writings, but also with his publications. Because Maxim the Great is not only the king of hooligans, but a commercial publisher to boot. An army officer who has been travelling on the Volga reports that the Volga region is groaning and moaning because of this flood of Maxim's "bitterness." Everybody cries out: " Rid us of Gorky! Rid us of defeatist literature! "

It is worth noting that the defeatist literature is directed

with especial zeal into plants working for the country's defence. All the publications and stenograms [of the Duma — A.K.] hammer into the heads of the munition workers the following " axiom ":

The war is wanted only by the bourgeois governments of France, England, Russia, and of their enemies, Germany and Austria.

The proletarians of *all* countries have no need of any war.

Next they deal with the question of peace in such a way as to make it impossible to repeat even approximately those " ideas " in the press.

Aside from stenograms of the speeches of the defeatist Duma wing and the writings of Gorky, they zealously circulate through the Volga towns and even villages (in rural reading-rooms) the defeatist journal, *Letopis*, published by the same Maxim the Great.

The letter goes on to wonder why this " infamous work of the defeatists goes unpunished in these trying days," though it is no less than " state treason." He suggests that " the Kaiser must rejoice hugely " at this activity, and asserts that Gorky's plays are at the present moment very popular in Berlin, as are his articles, reprinted in Austria and Germany with " flattering introductions by Hauptmann and Ostwald."

The letter appeared on December 10, 1916, and its effect on the Authorities can be seen from the fact that three days later the director of the Department of Police requested the chief of the Press Bureau to investigate the matter and report whether there is truth in the accusations of that letter. His findings were to be incorporated in a memorial to the minister of the interior. The chief of the Press Bureau had the censor Trofimovich prepare a statement concerning the nature of the *Letopis*. He defined the review as one of " an extremely oppositional tendency, with a Social-Democratic hue "; its attitude toward the war should be classified as defeatist; the editors highly praised Western, especially German, culture, and wrote sympathetically of agitation in favour of French, English, and Italian workmen; the journal condemned all patriotic Russian literature, and zealously championed the interests of the Jews.

Furthermore, the Department of Police sent inquiries to the governors of nine Volga provinces regarding the influence of *Letopis* and Gorky. Nearly all of them replied reassuringly. The governors of Kazan, Astrakhan, and Simbirsk sent in the names of all the *Letopis* subscribers in their provinces, but they minimized the importance of Gorky's publications. The same opinion was expressed by the governors of Samara, Nizhni Novgorod, Saratov, Tver, and Kostroma.

Meanwhile Rasputin was murdered, and the Romanov structure began to topple with bewildering speed. The Department of Police had its hands full with more compelling issues than that of Gorky and his review. He was no longer troubled. For thirty years Gorky had felt the meshes of the Invisible Thread; in 1917 it snapped, with the fall of the Exalted Spider.

IN THE REVOLUTIONARY TURMOIL:
II. GORKY AND LENIN

BETWEEN REVOLUTIONS

GORKY has told me definitely that he never belonged to any political party. In the revolutionary movement he was merely a " sympathizer," a very active one, to be sure, with time and pen and money and personal freedom (perpetual police surveillance and sporadic prison cells), but broad enough to support simultaneously Bolsheviks, Mensheviks, Socialist-Revolutionists, and even Liberals. Yet already at the outset, as soon as he parted company with the romantic *Narodniks,* Gorky's sympathies were preferably directed toward the revolutionary current headed by Lenin. To refresh the reader's memory, I may be permitted to state again that early in the century he became connected with the *Iskra* group, at that time Lenin's mouthpiece, and gave it lavish support, personally and through opulent friends. He became closely acquainted with Lenin's " Minister of Finance," Leonid Krasin, whom he brought in contact with the Moscow millionaire, Savva Morozov, " angel " of the Moscow Art Theatre, of revolutionary terrorists, and similar causes which are not ordinarily within the province of rich manufacturers. In November, 1905, Gorky organized the daily, *Novaya Zhizn,* with Maria Andreyeva as official publisher and N. Minsky, as formal editor. Actually, beginning with its sixth issue, the short-lived paper was edited by Lenin.

Gorky's intimate friendship with Lenin began in 1907, at the London conference of the Russian Social-Democratic Party. He listened to the debates of the representative factions in their final attempt at party union. The fight centred between Plekhanov, spokesman for the Mensheviks, and Lenin, leader

of the Bolsheviks, with Trotsky occupying the unenviable
middle. Whichever faction won, the nominal victory was less
important than the fact of the Party having now split definitively and irreparably. Gorky found himself heartily in accord
with Lenin's platform of a proletarian revolution, free from
opportunistic negotiations with bourgeois Liberals. He felt
that the differences between the two factions were not merely
theoretical, and with his sense of reality he followed the simple
dynamics of Lenin rather than the doctrinaire casuistry of the
brilliant Plekhanov.

Thereafter the two men kept up a lively correspondence,
which lasted, with one interval, until the return of Gorky to
Russia, on December 31, 1913. Lenin admired Gorky's talent,
and was happy to make use of it for the Cause, provided the
latter did not harm the former. When A. Lunacharsky, then
with Gorky in Capri, suggested to have Gorky take charge of
the literary department in the Bolshevik organ, *Proletary,*
Lenin wrote to him:

Your plan . . . is excellent and gladdens me exceedingly. It
has been precisely my dream to establish a permanent literary-
critical department in the *Proletary,* and hand it over to
A. M—ch [Alexey Maximovich; Gorky]. But I was afraid,
dreadfully afraid to suggest this directly, because I do not
know the nature of A. M—ch's work at present, nor his working capacity. Should he be engaged in a big and serious work,
it would be silly and criminal to interfere and disturb him,
if such trifles as journalism may disrupt that work! On this
point I feel very strongly. You are right there on the spot . . . .
and can see better. *If you think that we shall not harm the
work of A. M — ch* by harnessing him to regular party work
(the latter will certainly gain enormously!), then try to arrange the matter.

In the same vein he wrote to Gorky, in reply to his offer
of writing small pieces for the *Proletary,* admonishing him
not to tear himself away from his " big work." From the very
first, Lenin's letters express a warm solicitude for Gorky's
health and literary activity. He willingly accepts the invita-

tion of Gorky and Maria Andreyeva to pay them a visit at Capri, and promises to do so as soon as the affairs of the *Proletary* will permit him and Krupskaya (his wife) to leave Geneva. How unlimited is his confidence in his Capri friends, can be seen from his letter to both of them, in which he entrusts Maria Andreyeva with the organization of the delicate and dangerous task of smuggling quantities of the *Proletary* into Russia. Indeed, Gorky's second wife (or mistress, in the eyes of pious New York hotel-keepers and newspapermen), a woman of versatile gifts and a polyglot education, played an active and extremely useful part in the Bolshevik organization.

While admiring Gorky's talent as a writer of fiction, Lenin has serious misgivings concerning the solidity of his friend's political notions. In this field the Bolshevik leader suffers no nonsense, and he takes his correspondent to task in letter after letter for his theoretical and practical vagaries. Gorky's non-partisanship permitted him a revolutionary catholicity, and he advocated the co-operation of differing persons and groups. At times in a mild banter, at others curtly, Lenin resented such suggestions. Trotsky as a contributor to the *Proletary?* Well, the editorial board had sent him a collective invitation to write for the journal, and apparently this impersonal form peeved Trotsky, for a similarly impersonal note reached the editors to the effect that " at the request of Comrade Trotsky " they were advised of his refusal to contribute to the *Proletary*. Lenin branded this as a pose, adding that Trotsky had always been a *poseur*. Thereafter he prefixed the very name of Trotsky with a sobriquet which the editors of Lenin's letters thought wise to delete. When Gorky wrote sympathetically about a book of essays by Lenin's former comrades whom he now suspected of " idealism," he received a decisive reply: " I should rather let myself be quartered than consent to take part in an organ that preaches such things." Yet Gorky persisted, year in and year out, in seeking a reunion of the Social-Democratic factions, and as late as in 1911 — that is, eight years after the initial split — he urged an all-party conference. Lenin had to adopt a resolute tone: " Our unification with Mensheviks of

Martov's ilk is *absolutely* hopeless, as I have already told you when you were here [in Paris]. Should we undertake the arrangement of a conference for the sake of such a hopeless project, it would result in sheer disgrace (personally, I should refuse even a private conference with Martov)." This in spite of Lenin's erstwhile friendship with Martov, and in spite of the esteem in which he held Martov's intelligence to the end of his life (" What a pity that Martov is not with us ! " he once said to Gorky, about 1920. " What a wonderful comrade he is, what a clean man ! " And hearing of Martov's remark that there were only two Bolsheviks in Russia — Lenin and Kollontay, he laughed heartily and sighed). Once in power, Lenin was willing to employ all sorts of compromise, and was far more tolerant of opposition than his puny successors are today, but when organizing the revolution he was adamant in eschewing heresies and however slight defections. " Take my word," he wrote to Gorky : " what we need at present is differentiation, not unification ! "

As a matter of fact, Gorky's contributions never appeared in the *Proletary*. The one article he sent in betrayed a heretical predilection toward idealism, and Lenin returned it with the request either to change it and purge it of heresy, or publish it elsewhere. A polemic ensued, which not only disrupted for a time the relations between the two men, but which, in its ramifications, produced a serious rift within the Bolshevik faction. In Gorky's article Lenin detected a note of sympathy for the views of the Empiriomonist group, which subsequently seceded into a Bolshevik sub-faction known as *Vperyodovtsy*, for their periodical *Vperyod !* (*Forward !*). In returning the article, Lenin wrote a lengthy explanation of his stand in the matter, emphasizing his toleration for all philosophical views, but refusing to open the pages of the *Proletary* for philosophic discussion, especially if it touched on debatable points. He urged Gorky to help him keep the philosophic divergencies from splitting the faction, by ventilating them in other publications than the *Proletary*, which must preserve a united front. The fight, however, soon grew in bitterness, and the *Proletary* was forced to launch a campaign against the heretics, the

initial shot being fired in L
Different Roads."

The main leader of t
Bogdanov, associate edito
versatile scholar, who c
edge of sciences and hun
a victim of fearless la
organism). He was join
rov, P. Yushkevich, a
faction, who published
port of the revision of
suggested by Ernst M
ism, George Plekhan
articles, in which mar
sarcasm of an experienced ......

disagreeing with Plekhanov on many basic q__
upheld him on this point vigorously, even though such men as
Bogdanov and Lunacharsky were his close collaborators and
adherents. After a careful perusal of the " thrice accursed
Machists " he became convinced that they were on a dangerous
and absolutely erroneous road. While reading their latest collective work, *Studies in the Philosophy of Marxism*, he (so he
wrote to Gorky) " had fits of indignation. No, that is not
Marxism! These empiriocritics, empiriomonists, and empirio-
symbolists are getting into a bog. To assure the reader that
' faith ' in the reality of the external world is ' mystic ' (Bazarov), to confuse in the most atrocious manner materialism and
Kantianism (Bazarov and Bogdanov), to preach a species of
agnosticism (empiriocriticism) and of idealism (empiriomon-
ism), to instruct our workmen in ' religious atheism ' and the
' adoration ' of higher human potentialities (Lunacharsky), to
declare Engels' dialectic teaching as mystic (Berman), to
quaff from the stinking source of some French ' positivists ' —
agnostics or metaphysicians, the devil take them, with their
' symbolic theory of knowledge ' (Yushkevich)! No, that is
too much."

The battle was on. In the realm of ideas Lenin allowed no
mercy or compromise. Gorky pleaded for peace and concilia-

f Bolshevik unity. Lenin replied that he
respected Gorky's feeling, but that he re-
profoundly erroneous": "You must under-
f course you will understand, that once a party
become convinced of the utter wrongness and harm-
of a certain doctrine, he is obliged to come out against
should not have raised a storm, had I not become abso-
ly persuaded (and every day, as I acquaint myself with
the primary sources of the wisdom of Bazarov, Bogdanov, &
Co., I am more and more persuaded) that their writings from
branch to root, to Mach and Avenarius, are absurd, pernicious,
philistine, wholly priestish, from beginning to end. Plekhanov
is *entirely* right in the substance of his opposition against them,
only he does not know how, or does not want to, or is too
lazy to say it *concretely,* pithily, simply, without unnecessarily
scaring off the readers by philosophic niceties. Well, I am
going to say it *in my way,* at all costs. Now, what sort of
' reconciliation ' can there be, my dearest A. M.? Don't you
see, it is ridiculous even to mention it. The battle is *absolutely*
inevitable."

Meanwhile Bogdanov had gone to Capri, and Gorky kept
on asking Lenin to come too, and talk matters over. But
Lenin refused: " It would be useless and harmful for me to
come: I *cannot,* and am not going to argue with men who
have gone off to preach the fusion of scientific socialism with
religion. . . . This cannot be discussed, and it is foolish to
work up one's nerves to no purpose. . . ." In a postscript:
" Especial greetings to Maria Feodorovna [Andreyeva]: she is
not, I hope, for god, eh?" He was hoping, indeed, that as a
practical helper in the party, Andreyeva was free from literary
and idealistic deviations. But now came a telegram, signed by
Gorky *and* Andreyeva, with a final plea for him to come and
thus prevent a rupture. Lenin wired his refusal, and in the
letter which followed it he excused himself for not being in a
position to accept their invitation (he did go to Capri, after
all), and reiterated his demand that the philosophic discussions
must not be confused with the political work of the Bolshevik
faction. He therefore urged Lunacharsky and other " literati "

to continue their support of the *Proletary:* " All of us are responsible before the Russians." He also charged Bogdanov to obtain money for the organization : " Our comrades in Russia are howling from lack of funds! "

Thus Lenin tried to separate the skin from the bones. That he realized the delicacy of such an operation is evident from an earlier letter to Gorky, in which he admitted that " such a separation was difficult, painful, when performed on live persons," and he asked for Gorky's help, as a specialist in psychology. Soon the differences transcended mere philosophic quibbles, and caused a rift in the Bolshevik faction, which was never fully healed.

The whole dispute need arrest our attention only insofar as it is germane to our subject-matter, that is, Maxim Gorky. Now Gorky is primarily an observant artist; he loses his force and originality as soon as he ventures into provinces outside of fiction. Yet as a citizen and revolutionary he has been tempted again and again to voice his views on philosophic and political questions, both directly, in the form of editorials and interviews, and indirectly, through the mouths of his fiction characters. As a publicist he seldom satisfied any of his critics. Literary men objected to the intrusion of didactic tracts into his narrative, and revolutionary publicists found his ideology jejune and dilettantish. His novel, *Mother,* is a case in point; and so are his *American Sketches.* Gorky himself admits the weakness of his digressions, but he just cannot help reacting to contemporary events and currents of thought. In this way he became involved in the religious controversy.

The abortive revolution of 1905 produced a mood of the mystic sort that usually follows defeat. The Russian intelligentsia, having valiantly fought for a constitutional form of government in behalf of the common people, was disenchanted both in the consitution and in the people, when the former proved a farce and the latter a rough element devoid of kid gloves. They began to desert the revolutionary ranks in large numbers, some of them joining the victorious reactionaries, others turning their backs on idealism and altruism and proclaiming the principle of self-gratification (Artsybashev's *Sanin*

enjoyed a tremendous vogue), while a considerable element, in quantity and quality, deflected into transcendentalism. Merezhkovsky, Filosofov, Hippius, Bulgakov, Berdyayev, and other prominent artists and thinkers formed an influential group, generally known as *bogoiskateli* — god-seekers. The leading idea that might be gathered from their obscure and often divergent though always colourful phraseology, was the quest of a synthesis between man and God, heaven and earth, the spirit and the flesh. So widespread did that mystic mood become that its echoes reverberated even through the ranks of professional terrorists (Ropshin-Savinkov, in his *Pale Horse* and *What Never Happened*) and orthodox Marxians of Lenin's own faction. We have seen how Lenin treated these heretics.

Small wonder that Gorky, whose intimacy with crass and cruel reality never quite destroyed his congenital romanticism and nostalgia after his grandmother's Fairyland and genial God, did not stand up against the current. He could not stomach the Merezhkovsky crowd, with its personal God and unctious theology. What was more, his religious mood was not generated by disappointment in the revolution and the masses; on the contrary, it emanated from a strengthened faith in collective humanity. Rejecting *bogoiskatelstvo*, the quest of a god beyond man and reality, he championed *bogostroitelstvo,* the " building " or creation of god *by* man, using the word " god " to mean the synthetic perfection of man's potentialities. In 1907, the *Mercure de France* sent out a questionnaire on religion to a number of internationally known men. In his answer, Gorky definitely states his enmity for the existing religions, of " Moses, Christ, and Mahomet," which engendered antagonism in mankind, and whose same and sole idea is " the subordination of man to forces supposed to lie outside of himself." The downfall of these religions he regards as ineluctable and highly desirable. At the same time he sees the formation of a new type of man, that of a " perfect being " boasting " a harmonious development of all his faculties, without any mutual contradictions " (cf. his unfinished *Muzhik*). This anticipation (four years previously Gorky expressed it in his poetic essay, *Man*) prompts him to define religious feeling as

" a happy and proud awareness of a harmonious link that joins man to the universe. This feeling is born of an aspiration for synthesis, inherent in every individual; it is nourished by experience . . . . and is gradually transformed into 'pathos' through the joyous sensation of inner freedom, which has awakened in man."

This somewhat misty definition of religion is made clearer in his novel, *The Confession*, a medium where Gorky feels more at home. Matvey, the hero of the story, seeks God. From early childhood to maturity he yearns for God, and follows a variety of tortuous paths in his quest, living in monasteries and hermitages, communing with sectarians of all descriptions, trying to find inspiration in the labour movement. The book draws to an end in a minor key; Matvey is disheartened; his quest is futile. Then he witnesses a significant scene. A mob of worshippers await the procession bringing a miracle-working icon of the Virgin. The enthusiastic crowd infect with their faith a young girl who has been unable to use her legs. With tears and joyous exclamations they urge her to rise and walk, in the name of the all-merciful Mother. As the icon comes closer and the general ecstasy waxes supreme, the girl makes an effort, rises, and actually makes a few feeble steps. At this manifestation of the efficacy of collective will Matvey realizes that the God he has been seeking all his life abides in the " all-powerful, immortal people." He prays: " Thou art my God and the creator of all gods, which thou weavest out of the beauties of thy spirit in the travail and rebellion of thy seeking. There shall be no other gods but thee, for thou art the one God, creator of miracles. Thus I believe and confess! "

The Confession is one of Gorky's finest achievements. Written in a heightened, biblical tone, abounding in colourful descriptions and poetic images, the novel is at the same time free from Gorky's early extravagances. The characters are drawn full length and forcefully against an authentic Russian background, and the prose has the rich and racy quality of old *byliny*. But the majority of Russia's critics judged the book not by these qualities so much as by what it purported to teach. Here was a novel voicing the *bogostroitelstvo* tendencies of the

Bogdanov-Bazarov-Lunacharsky group of empiriomonists, Machists, and other doubters of philosophic materialism. Lunacharsky discussed *The Confession* in a long article, giving it a Marxian interpretation, and assuming the air of a knowing guide. Afraid that Gorky's idealization of the people might be taken for a variant of Social-Revolutionary *narodnichestvo*, Lunacharsky emphasized Gorky's preference for the proletarian people. " The collective might," he wrote, " the beautiful ecstasy of collective life, the miracle-working power of the collective — that is what the author believes in, that is what he calls on us to believe in. But has he not said himself that the people are at present disunited and subdued? Has he not told us that one must look for collectivism only among the newly born people, in factories and foundries? Yes, only there, only in the agglomeration of a class-minded collective, in the slow building up of an all-proletarian organization, is one to find the real work of transforming men into mankind, if only the preliminary work. . . . So Gorky presents his miracle as a symbol of the future, as a pale specimen — pale in comparison with the future, but brilliant in comparison with the surrounding present."

The *bogoiskateli* were eager to find in Gorky a congenial note. D. Filosofov who shortly before had published a paper, *The End of Gorky,* reviewed the novel sympathetically, underlining its motive of " social religiosity," as the proper solution of the problem of the individual. The final scene and the revelation of the new and only God-people did not please Filosofov; here he felt that the artist had given place to the thinker, the disciple of Lunacharsky, hence his " fall." But the critic was hopeful. " No matter," he wrote, " how much Gorky will try to persuade us that he is an orthodox Marxian, that he professes the religion of Lunacharsky . . . . we shall no longer believe him. His new works show too clearly that he himself, the writer, the artist-Gorky, is far deeper, more serious and important than those acquired theories which he so zealously preaches, thereby doing harm to himself and his work, and consequently to all of us, his readers. One would like to trust that Gorky will, at length, come out of the swaddling

clothes of Lunacharsky's religion, and together with all of the Russian intelligentsia will tread the true path." Amen . . .

To the materialistic Marxians Gorky's novel was another symptom of the noxious disintegration in the ranks of the faithful. The veteran Plekhanov regarded the issue grave enough to warrant a series of articles under the general title, *About the So-Called Religious Quests in Russia,* in which he subjected these to a devastating criticism, using his dialectic scalpel with equal intransigeance on Tolstoy and Gorky, on Lunacharsky and the " evangelists — decadents " — Merezhkovsky, Minsky, and their variants. The dreaded polemist treated Gorky rather mildly, relatively speaking. After paying tribute to Gorky's " remarkable and brilliant " talent, and to certain " wonderful " pages in *The Confession,* in which one hears " Goethe motives " of the unity of man with nature, he takes him to task for meddling in theories. Even Gogol, Dostoyevsky, and Tolstoy, " these giants in the field of creative art, display infantile weakness whenever they approach abstract questions." The same happens with Gorky, whose *Mother* and other " revolutionary " productions Plekhanov has time and again ridiculed as diluted socialism (he made one exception for Gorky's play, *Enemies*). Plekhanov recalls Krylov's fable about the pike that attempted to ply the cat's trade and in consequence had its tail nibbled off by the mice. He is especially annoyed by Gorky's indebtedness to Lunacharsky, whom Plekhanov subjects to a merciless thrashing. Gorky, he says, " preaches what Lunacharsky does. But he knows less (by this I do not mean to say that Lunacharsky knows much) ; he is more naïve (by which I do not mean to suggest that Lunacharsky is devoid of naïveté) ; he is less versed in the contemporary theory of socialism (which does not in the least imply that Lunacharsky is well versed in it). For this reason his effort at clothing socialism in the robe of religiosity proves even a greater failure." Comparing Gorky and Lunacharsky to Mont Blanc and a haystack respectively, he laments the fact that the former should have fallen under the influence of the latter. Lunacharsky preaches a religion minus God, and Gorky follows him in raising humanity to the rank of a divinity, thus

replacing one fetish by another. " They start out by declaring God a fiction, and end by proclaiming man a god. But since humanity is not a fiction, why call it a god? Why should it be regarded flattering for humanity to be identified with one of its own fictions? " And Plekhanov clinches the argument by quoting such an ultimate authority as Engels, namely:

There is no need for us to have recourse to the abstraction of God, in order to grasp the grandeur of man; we have no need in the roundabout way of first placing on man the stamp of God before we may feel respect for man.

On this question Lenin, as we have seen, fully agreed with his enemy, Plekhanov. Upon the publication of *The Confession* he wrote to Gorky " a letter of chagrin," as he later told him in person, but did not send it, in view of the Machist schism which had meanwhile taken place. Unfortunately, that letter has not been discovered among Lenin's papers, and we can only judge of its contents from his other utterances on the subject. Succinctly he expressed his attitude in the resolution passed by the conference of the Bolshevik Centre (Paris, June, 1909): " Whereas at the present moment, in the atmosphere of a slump in the social movement, the growth of religious moods among counter-revolutionary bourgeois intelligentsia has lent an important public meaning to questions of this sort [" *bogostroitelstvo* tendencies "]; and whereas in connexion with this growth of religious moods individual Social-Democrats have been attempting to involve Social-Democracy in the preaching of faith and *bogostroitelstvo,* and even to ascribe to scientific socialism the character of a religious creed, — the enlarged group of the *Proletary* declares that they regard this current, propagated with particular ardour in the articles of Comrade Lunacharsky, as a current which breaks with the foundations of Marxism, and by the substance of its sermon . . . . brings harm to the work of the revolutionary Social-Democracy for the enlightenment of the working masses, and furthermore that the Bolshevik faction has nothing in common with such a distortion of scientific socialism." The resolution proceeded to name specifically Lunacharsky's article

on *The Confession,* classifying it as "a form of war against proletarian, Marxian socialism, waged by petty-bourgeois tendencies."

The Bogdanov-Lunacharsky group, forced out of the *Proletary,* that is, the Bolshevik Centre, began to publish their own organ, *Vperyod!* Aside from the philosophical dissenters, the so-called Machists, the *Vperyodovtsy* included Bolsheviks of the *otzovist* political hue, that is, those who advocated the *recall* of the Bolshevik members from the Imperial Duma, and its boycott. The *Proletary* group, while recognizing the futility of the pseudo-parliamentary Duma, yet insisted on utilizing it as a platform, from which they might address the masses and educate them. Lenin fought vigorously the leftism of the *Otzovists,* and ridiculed it out of existence, just as about a decade later he laughed to death the " infantile disease of leftism " represented by Bukharin and other extremists.

The *Vperyodovtsy* enjoyed Gorky's support. Among other things, he helped them organize at his villa in Capri a school for Russian workmen, a fantastic undertaking even for the Russian revolutionary movement, replete with romance and adventure. A Bolshevik workman from the Urals, Mikhail Vilonov, had on his record numerous prison sentences and almost as many escapes from prison. After one of his flights he was caught, and so thoroughly beaten up by the police that he contracted tuberculosis. The Party helped him flee abroad, and get to Capri. So delightful was the climate, and so stimulating the society of Gorky and his friends, that Vilonov resolved that other workmen must get a taste of that paradise. Though still convalescent, he returned to Russia, risking his limb and life, and obtained the sanction of the Party to send groups of intelligent factory workmen to Capri, where they were to go through an intensive schooling and return home as graduate propagandists. The first group, of some twenty men, arrived at Capri in the summer of 1909, after considerable vicissitudes. The Authorities got wind of the project, and issued orders for the arrest of Vilonov and his party. With the rather limited resources at their disposal they had to dodge the police, and buy their way across the frontier clandestinely.

Their strategy was often rather naïve. Thus, at the border town they were to call at the home of a socialist midwife, the password being: " My wife has given birth to triplets." Imagine the astonishment of the maid who had to open the door to a score of men, each one of whom declared on his admission that he was a father of three! Safely abroad, these innocents made several stops in various capitals. In Vienna Comrade Trotsky, one of the proposed lecturers at the Capri " university," met the group and guided them through the local museums.

The school consisted of lectures and practical revolutionary work. Among the lecturers were Bogdanov, on political economy; Pokrovsky, on history; Lunacharsky, history of the labour movement and revolutions; Alexinsky, on Syndicalism and finance; Gorky, history of Russian literature, and so forth. Of other men invited to come and lecture for the school, Plekhanov, characteristically enough for his superior airs, failed even to reply; Trotsky promised to come, but was unable to; Kautsky wrote back that he was too busy, and that he worked better with his pen than with his mouth; Lenin entered into a long correspondence with the students, of which more later. It was a lively school, the pupils refusing to swallow the wisdom of the lecturers whole, but engaging in heated arguments and discussions. The future propagandist was to be not only intimately acquainted with the technique of revolutionary organization, but was also to be in readiness to meet opponents from other parties and factions. With this in view the school often arranged mock debates, the faculty and students impersonating various political parties. Gorky was given the rôle of an extreme reactionary, one of the Black Hundreds. The most popular course of lectures proved to be the one on the history of art, read by Lunacharsky, who later took the students on a tour through Rome. They also enjoyed Gorky's lectures, especially those on Gogol and Pushkin. Nor should one omit mentioning the thrill received by these proletarians from contact with men of all arts and professions, who constantly flocked to Gorky's villa and readily displayed their talents.

Gorky's enthusiasm over his guests was boundless. In his letters to the Ukrainian writer, Kotsyubinsky, he wrote rhapsodically about the superb lads whose companionship he cherished beyond words. Forced to live away from Russia, he drew keen pleasure from this contact with the brave youth of his homeland, the pledge of a better future. Alas, essentially non-political, Gorky was forcibly involved in party wrangle and squabble, which poisoned the joyous atmosphere of the school, and eventually destroyed it. Lenin was responsible for this turn of affairs: he was always ingenious, and nearly always successful, in his methods of attack against his enemies, and as such he regarded the Capri school. The invitation to come and lecture for the school he curtly rejected, stating that he could not travel together with the *Otzovist* lecturers, who would endeavour to swerve their audience from the right road. The students, rough and ready workmen, were puzzled by the previously unsuspected differences among the Bolshevik leaders, and they resented Lenin's refusal. Seven of them, who were from Moscow, had a conference, and sent Lenin a formal summons, in the name of the Moscow Committee, to appear at Capri, threatening, in case of his persistent refusal, to complain of his breach of discipline before the Central Committee. Lenin must have chuckled at this specimen of Bolshevik tactics on the part of the fledglings, for he sent them a lengthy letter in which he spoke in plain terms of the errors of Bogdanov's group, and of their dangers for the Party. He told them that they were fine lads, but as yet " not experienced in political struggle," and insinuated that he would be happy to teach them " if they should care to come over to Paris." The correspondence continued for some time, and the siren call had its effect: the students decided to go to Paris, on the completion of their five months' course at Capri.

Lenin was not content, however, with this victory; he feared that the infection of the Bogdanov heresy might set in the innocent minds too deep for any subsequent effect of his antidote. The heresy had to be dealt with pontifically; the case called for anathematization. Accordingly he had a resolution passed by the conference of the Bolshevik Centre referred to

above which stated that the founders of the Capri school, A. Bogdanov in particular, organized it in opposition to the *Proletary*, that these founders represented not the faction as a whole but the currents of *otzovism* and *bogostroitelstvo* only, and that the Bolshevik faction therefore " could not bear the responsibility for that school." In other words, the school was outlawed, as far as official Bolshevism was concerned. This step, coupled with Lenin's further letters to the students, resulted in a split among the latter, and five of them abruptly left Capri for Paris. With them went the author of the plan, Mikhail Vilonov. The *Proletary* published an extra leaflet under the title: *A Shameful Failure,* which was a scathing denunciation of the Capri school, and a sensational account of the split. The Bogdanov group of students, on the other hand, were embittered by the cavalier tactics of Lenin's Centre, and loyally remained at Capri till the end of the course, after which they too joined the Paris school, where beside Lenin, Zinoviev, and Kamenev, they were addressed also by such leading Mensheviks as Martov and Dan. Some of the Bogdanovists persisted in their heresies even after Paris, for indeed, Bogdanov appealed to the young heads as a more militant revolutionary than Lenin, whose policy of participation in the Duma and postponement of the uprising struck them as opportunism and compromise.

Gorky suffered poignantly from these dissensions. He saw only the aim of enlightening the workmen and equipping them with cultural baggage to take back to their destitute home environment. The intra-factional nuances of opinion did not seem to him to matter seriously in the general scheme. Even the intransigeant Lenin could appreciate Gorky's state of mind, especially after he had talked things over with Vilonov, who had come to Paris with the secessionists. The following letter of Lenin to Gorky (which is for some reason not included in the State publication of Lenin's letters) reveals along with his well-known adamantine faith in his cause, a warmth of understanding with which the Bolshevik leader is seldom credited:

My dear Alexey Maximovich! I had been fully convinced that you and Comrade Mikhail [Vilonov] were the staunchest members of the new faction, with whom it would have been absurd for me to attempt friendly communication. Today for the first time I saw Comrade Mikhail, and had a hearty chat with him both on business matters and about you, whereupon I realized how cruelly I had erred. . . . I had regarded the school *only* as the centre of the new faction. It appears that I was wrong — not in the sense that it was not the centre of the new faction (the school was and still is such a centre), but in the sense that that was not all, not the whole truth. Subjectively, certain individuals have made such a centre out of the school; objectively, the school served as such, but aside and above that, it has scooped out some genuine advanced workmen out of the thick of Russia's toilers. It has transpired that beside the conflict between the old faction and the new one, there has evolved at Capri a conflict between a handful of Social-Democratic intelligentsia and honest-to-goodness Russian workmen who will *by all means* bring the Social-Democracy out on the right road, no matter what happens, and they will do so in despite of all our *émigré* wrangles and squabbles, our " affairs," and so on and so forth.

. . . From the words of Mikhail I see, my dear Alexey Maximovich, how depressed you must feel. You have chanced to get a glimpse of the Labour movement and Social-Democracy from such an angle, in such manifestations and forms, which more than once in the history of Russia and western Europe have reduced intellectual sceptics to despair concerning the Labour movement and Social-Democracy. I am certain that this will not happen to you, and after my talk with Mikhail I should like to grasp your hand firmly. With your gift of an artist you have so tremendously benefited the Labour movement in Russia — and not only in Russia, and you will so much benefit it in the future, that it is inadmissible for you to fall under the oppressive moods caused by episodes of our " campaign abroad." There are certain conditions under which the Labour movement brings about unavoidably such a " campaign abroad," and splits, and quarrels, and fights of groups and circles. That is due not to the inner weakness of the Labour movement or to the inner errors of the Social-Democracy, but

is due to the extreme variability and multifariousness of the elements, out of which the working class is obliged to forge its own party. Such a party they will manage to forge, in all events; they will forge a splendid Social-Democracy in Russia, they will forge it sooner than it may appear sometimes from the point of view of the thrice accursed *émigré* position, they will forge it more certainly than it would seem to those who judge by some external occurrences and single episodes.

. . . . I finally grasp your hand and the hand of Maria Feodorovna, for now I am enabled to hope that you and I shall yet meet not as enemies.

Meanwhile the fight between *Proletary* and *Vperyod!* went on with all the vehemence that an unhealthy *émigré* atmosphere can produce. The non-Bolshevik and non-Socialist press made a sensation of this internal split, and featured with especial glee the rumour that Gorky had been expelled from the Party. Lenin had the Berlin *Vorwärts* deny this rumour, but other periodicals refused to print his refutation. He then published in the *Proletary* a note on *The Fairy-Tale of the Bourgeois Press Concerning the Expulsion of Gorky,* in which he attributed the slanderous campaign to the desire of the bourgeois parties to fan the intra-factional strife, and to see Gorky desert the ranks (the fact that Gorky never was an actual member of any party was not mentioned either by Lenin or his opponents). The note ended thus: " The effort of the bourgeois newspapers is futile. Comrade Gorky, through his great works, has linked himself with the Labour movement of Russia and the whole world too firmly to respond to their hullabaloo with anything but contempt."

Toward 1910 Lenin had the satisfaction to see the " Leftists " dwindle into a shadow. Both the Machists and the *Otzovists* were losing ground, and their literary efforts showed signs of despair. Their latest declaration of faith was full of contradictions and veiled admissions of errors. Lenin gave it a murderous estimate, which he concluded with the following reference to Gorky's place in that group:

However, one cannot say that the contents of their platform is entirely negative. Behind some of its words may be found

also a certain positive content. This positive content may be expressed in one word: Gorky. Indeed, there is no use denying the fact . . . . that Gorky belongs to the adherents of that group. And Gorky is undoubtedly the biggest representative of proletarian art, for which he has done much and may do even more. Any faction of the Social-Democratic Party may justly be proud of Gorky's adherence, but to use this as a basis for the inclusion of " proletarian art " in the *platform* means to hand this platform a testimony of poverty, means to reduce that group to a literary circle which convicts itself of authoritarianism.

Lenin refers to the passages in the declaration which insinuate that the fight against Machism and *otzovism* was waged in the name of individual authorities (i. e., Lenin and Plekhanov). He points out that the use of Gorky's authority in the interests of the *Vperyod!* group is unwarranted. In proletarian art Gorky is " without doubt an authority " and " an enormous plus, despite his sympathies for Machism and *otzovism*." But the projection of his name in a political platform is " a minus, because this platform endeavours to perpetuate and utilize the weak side of a great authority, the very thing that forms a negative quantity in the sum total of his beneficial work for the proletariat."

In the summer of the same year Lenin paid a visit to Capri. The school had been killed — an attempt at its revival at Bologna (with Trotsky's participation) also failed. Lenin was apparently spared the embarrassment of meeting at Gorky's villa the men who might have reminded him of his murderous work. Lenin needed relaxation, and he obtained it in some degree at Capri, where aside from business conversations with his hosts he also enjoyed a bit of play. Gorky recalls in this connexion:

He [Lenin] had a certain magnetism which attracted the hearts and sympathies of men of toil. He spoke no Italian, but the fishermen of Capri, who had seen Chaliapin and many other prominent Russians, from the first sensed in Lenin, by some wonderful intuition, a man apart from the rest. His laughter was enchanting, the " genial " laughter of a man who,

while discerning the clumsiness of human stupidity and the
acrobatic tricks of our intellect, knew how to enjoy the childlike naïveté of those " simple of heart."

The old fisherman, Giovanni Spadaro, said of him: " Only
an honest man can laugh as he does."

Rocking in a row-boat on the sky-blue transparent water,
Lenin yearned to fish " off the finger," that is, with a line but
without a rod. The fishermen explained to him that he must
pull in as soon as his finger began to feel the tremor of the
line:

" *Cosi: drin-drin. Capisce?* "

At once he pulled out a fish, and shouted with the ecstasy of
a child, with the fire of a sportsman:

" *Aha! Drin-drin.*"

The fishermen laughed uproariously and joyfully, also like
children, and they nicknamed our fisherman: " Signor Drin-
Drin."

Long after he had left they kept on inquiring: " How is
Signor Drin-Drin? The tsar won't catch him, will he? "

Friendly relations between the two men were restored. Many
points were cleared up in face to face talks, and Gorky expressed his regret at Lenin's former reticence — in not sending
him the letter about *The Confession,* and particularly in refusing to lecture for the school. Lenin agreed to be more direct
in the future, and indeed, in his subsequent letters he did not
spare Gorky's sensitiveness, whenever the issue demanded
plain words. It is evident from their correspondence that
Gorky recanted, in substance, his Bogdanov-Lunacharsky heresies, but still he gave Lenin many opportunities for severe
though friendly censure, mainly because of his inability to be
rigidly rectilineal in his revolutionary allegiances.

Thus, at Capri Gorky spoke to Lenin about his " isolation "
in the Russian periodical press, and expressed his wish for a
review of his own, where he might feel at home. Lenin sympathized with the idea of a congenial magazine. Under existing
conditions no openly socialistic organ could be had in Russia,
and the leading revolutionary thinkers had to seek the hospitality of liberal or radical journals. The four influential
monthly reviews, which Lenin characterizes in the letter

quoted below, were: *Vestnik Evropy,* an old publication, of moderately liberal views; *Russkaya Mysl,* edited by Peter Struve, modern in form (Bryusov was its literary editor), and championing under this form a variety of religious and imperialistic notions; *Russkoye Bogatstvo,* edited by Korolenko, of *narodnik* tendencies grown inanely moderate; and *Sovremenny Mir,* Marxian in purpose, prevailingly Menshevik in program, but catholic enough to publish papers by liberals along with articles by Plekhanov and stories by Gorky. After Lenin's departure from Capri, Gorky was won over by Alexander Amfiteatrov to become a regular contributor to a new review, *Sovremennik (Contemporary).*

Amfiteatrov, a giant with a flowing beard, was a picturesque figure in old Russia. He had prepared for an operatic career, and having switched over to journalism, he brought along the temperament of a matinée idol. Clever and brilliant, urbane and ingenious, he used his racy style in a captivating manner, and was sought after by leading publishers. Politically unstable, he had no compunction about working for Alexey Suvorin's reactionary daily, the notorious *Novoye Vremya,* from which he lightly went over to the radical *Rossiya.* A biting satire on Nicholas II and his Romanov kin, under the transparent title *The Obmanov Gentry* (*obman* means fraud), which appeared in *Rossiya,* caused the confiscation of that issue, the suspension of the paper, and the arrest and exile of the author, Amfiteatrov. Influential friends helped him obtain permission to go abroad, where he published a nondescript radical journal, *Krasnoye Znamya (Red Flag).*

Lenin's reaction to Gorky's alliance with Amfiteatrov is quite illuminating of Lenin's unrelenting exactitude in shades of political opinion, and, again, of his mentorial treatment of his politically wayward correspondent. I quote some passages from his letter of November 22, 1910:

Today I read an advertisement . . . about the *Sovremennik,* to be published " with the closest and *exclusive* (that's the word used! Illiterate but the more pretentious and significant for that) co-operation of Amfiteatrov," and with the promise of your regular contributions.

What is the meaning of all this? My word! " A large
monthly " review, with departments of " politics, science, history, public affairs " — why this is altogether different from
the *Miscellanies* that aimed at the concentration of the best
forces of our *belles-lettres* [he, apparently, refers to the
Znaniye Miscellanies, of which Gorky had been the actual
editor]. Why, such a review either must have a quite definitive,
serious, sustained outlook, or it will inevitably disgrace itself
and disgrace its contributors. . . . A review without an outlook is an uncouth absurdity, scandalous and pernicious. And
what kind of an outlook can there be " with the exclusive co-
operation " of Amfiteatrov? . . . . In my opinion, a politico-
economic big monthly with the exclusive co-operation of
Amfiteatrov is a thing many times worse than a separate
faction of Machists-*Otzovists.* The trouble with that faction
was and is the fact that its ideology departed and departs from
Marxism, from Social-Democracy, without actually breaking
with Marxism, but only bungling and groping.

An Amfiteatrov review (what a good thing his *Krasnoye
Znamya* did, in dying so timely! [It stopped with the fifth
issue]) is a political step, a political undertaking lacking the
slightest awareness of the fact that general " leftism " is not
enough for politics, that after 1905 it is wrong, impossible, unthinkable to talk seriously of politics without a clarified attitude toward Marxism and Social-Democracy.

It looks rotten. I am in a sad state of mind.

Lenin's misgivings about *Sevremennik* were justified; it did
have a motley array of contributors, and its lack of a clear-cut
political line disgusted Lenin. When Gorky tried to mollify his
anger, pleading in the name of political realism for the need of
a broader activity among the ranks of democracy, Lenin
snapped back: " You seem to tease me: ' realism, democracy,
activity '! Do you think these are good words? They are
abominable words, and are being utilized by all bourgeois
tricksters the world over, by the Kadets and Socialist-Revolutionists at home, by Briand and Millerand here [in France],
by Lloyd George in England, and so forth. Both the words are
abominable, inflated, and the contents [of *Sovremennik*]
promise to be Socialist-Revolutionary-Kadet. Bad, bad."

In the same way Gorky's repeated efforts at arranging a conference of all Social-Democratic factions, with a view to reunion, met with Lenin's admonition not to bother about unification when there was a greater need in further differentiation. Alliance with the Mensheviks of Martov's hue he regarded as " *absolutely* hopeless," and said so emphatically in his letters and when they met in person. As to Plekhanov, Lenin, indeed, rejoiced at the possibility of co-operating with him on many points, especially after the former had left the Mensheviks; during 1910–1913 Plekhanov contributed to various Bolshevik publications, notably to the Moscow *Mysl* (*Thought*), and to the St. Petersburg *Zvezda* (*Star*) and *Pravda* (*Truth*). Yet Lenin was reluctant to go beyond this journalistic *rapprochement*. Nor did he completely trust the Bolshevik members of the Duma, for apparently they failed to follow in full the instructions of the Centre, i.e., of Lenin. The idea of uniting with Martov, Plekhanov, and the Duma faction repelled him, and he wrote to Gorky in mock-horror: " I am frightened, as god lives, I am frightened! "

Lenin's frank strictures of Gorky's political vagueness must have proved fruitful. At any rate, the mentor had the satisfaction of praising now and then his pupil's sanity. As we shall yet see, however, the differences between the two men, intellectual and temperamental, re-emerged time and again, assuming on occasion, especially after 1917, a serious form.

Aside from political discussion, the Lenin-Gorky correspondence contains some personal touches of inestimable value, if only on one side, since Gorky's letters will probably not be published till after his death. The intimacy of their friendship is attested by the frequency and ease with which they exchange small services, requests for favours, chidings and confidential news. Lenin, for example, had constant difficulties with the legal publication of his papers and those of his faction; what appeared abroad was too limited in size and accessibility for the Russian readers. We read of his joy and pride in the two Bolshevik " legal " periodicals they succeeded in launching, in 1910, at Moscow (*Mysl*) and St. Petersburg (*Zvezda*). But it was more difficult to keep these alive than launch them, what

with financial troubles and the tsar's censors, who systematically confiscated separate issues, imposed fines and limitations,
and finally suspended both. He frequently wrote to Gorky
about these matters, urging him to help with his literary contributions, and thanking him again and again for doing so.

There is a curious detail in this connexion. In 1907 Lenin
wrote a book, *The Agrarian Programme of the Social Democracy during the First Russian Revolution, 1905–1907.* His
efforts at finding a publisher proved futile, and the book appeared in print only after November, 1917. In a letter to
Gorky, written in January, 1911, Lenin said toward the end:
" Look here, can you not place my book on the agrarian question with *Znaniye?* Talk it over with Pyatnitsky. I can't find
a publisher, do what I may. I feel like crying: ' Help ! ' " Now,
as we may recall, Gorky had become a shareholder in the publishing house of *Znaniye* back in 1900, and had gradually gained
control over the business. *Znaniye* did remarkably well. When
Gorky left Russia, he handed the affairs over to K. P. Pyatnitsky, in whom he had implicit faith, and to whom he dedicated his most successful literary and dramatic venture, *At the
Bottom.* It was natural therefore for Lenin to request Gorky's
intercession with his own manager. In fact, he made another
request in his very next letter, a frantic appeal to save *Mysl,*
just killed by the Moscow censor. He asked whether Pyatnitsky might not help in the purely technical side of publishing
Mysl in St. Petersburg, without incurring any risk, financial or
legal: the journal was to be paid for by the Party, and its contents were to be carefully censored before going into print. In
the same letter he suggested that Pyatnitsky publish two books,
one by Kautsky, the other being Peary's account of his expedition to the North Pole, in the translation of Nakhamkes, better known as Steklov.

Before this second letter reached Gorky, Lenin was informed
by Maria Andreyeva that Gorky was " out of *Znaniye.*" " Does
that mean a complete break with Pyatnitsky ? " queried Lenin,
not without peevishness, in view of his pending requests. I
have not been able to find out the details of this rupture:
Gorky was reluctant to speak of the matter. He always feels

ashamed, when someone he has trusted disappoints him. As a matter of fact, he is a poor judge of people, and his abundant experience in being deceived and misused by would-be friends and protégés might have rendered him immune against credulity, were he not an incurable believer in Man. All he told me was that he had sunk practically all his possessions in *Znaniye*, and retrieved nothing. Pyatnitsky, apparently, used his trust for his own benefit, and forced Gorky out of the business. How much Lenin took this misventure to heart, can be seen from the vehement passage in one of his subsequent letters to Gorky:

As to Pyatnitsky, I am for suing him. There is no use standing on ceremony. It would be unpardonable to indulge in sentimentalities. Socialists are not at all opposed to state courts. We are *for* making use of legal forms. Marx and Bebel appealed to court *even* against their social opponents. One must know *how* to do it, but do it one must. *Pyatnitsky must be condemned in court,* without hesitation or scruple. Should you hear any reproach for that, spit into the mug of those who dare reproach you. Only hypocrites will condemn you. It would be *unpardonable* to yield to Pyatnitsky, to let him off because you are afraid of lawsuits. . . .

Of course, Gorky did not sue Pyatnitsky.

In April, 1912 the Bolsheviks began to publish a daily paper in St. Petersburg, under the title of *Pravda* (*Truth*). This was a daring venture, and the wonder is that this daily managed to drag out its existence till July, 1913, when it was definitely suspended by the Authorities, to be resurrected only in 1917. Its circulation grew steadily, so that the contributors began to be paid — an unusual procedure for revolutionary publications! Lenin wrote to Gorky that he had received an inquiry from the office of *Pravda* as to whether Gorky would not be offended if they offered him twenty-five copecks per line for his regular contributions. Lenin explained that *Pravda* ordinarily paid two copecks per line, and urged Gorky not to be " offended " and to accept the offer in a " comradely way."

A cautious conspirator, Lenin had so much faith in Gorky's discretion that he did not hesitate to communicate to him most

confidential bits of information. In the summer of 1912 Lenin moved from Paris to the ancient capital of Poland, Cracow, whither he was followed by Zinoviev and Kamenev. He explained to Gorky the reasons for this peregrination, merely using the phrase " between us " parenthetically. The Central Committee of the Party decided to organize secretly its headquarters at Cracow, chiefly because it was closer to the Russian border, and therefore made it easier to establish communications and to edit the daily *Pravda*. Later Lenin mentioned another advantage of Cracow, namely the hatred of the Poles for official Russia, which prompted them to be lenient toward its enemies, the Russian revolutionists. Indeed, Lenin enjoyed there a greater freedom than elsewhere on the Continent, until the outbreak of the war, when he was arrested and finally deported into Switzerland. Incidentally, Lenin proved to be a poor prophet, making the following remark in a letter dated January, 1913: " War between Austria and Russia would be a useful thing for the revolution (throughout eastern Europe), but it is hardly probable that Francis Joseph and Nicholasha will accord us this pleasure." On the other hand, he predicted correctly that in case of war the P.P.S. (Polish Socialist Party) would fight on the side of Austria and against Russia; that was precisely what Joseph Pilsudski and his Legions did in 1914.

Lenin kept Gorky regularly informed of his personal and Party affairs. Thus: " Things are brewing hot in the Baltic fleet! A special delegate came to me in Paris (between us), who was sent by an assembly of sailors. . . . There is no organization, I feel like weeping!! If you have any connexions with naval officers, we must exert every effort to arrange something. The sailors are in a fighting mood, but they may perish in vain again." This was written in the fall of 1912, and the " again " probably referred to the sporadic outbreaks in the army and navy in 1905–1906.

His sojourn in the Dual Empire drew Lenin's attention to the question of nationalities, and in this connexion he informed Gorky of " a wonderful Georgian who was gathering Austrian and other material for a long article " on that question. The

" wonderful Georgian " was Joseph Stalin, who had just escaped from his place of exile in Narym, and came to Cracow. The convenience of the place was well utilized by the Bolsheviki. In June, 1913, Lenin wrote to Gorky (" arch-confidentially ") of a pending conference of the group of Duma deputies and possibly some workmen, at Poronin, near Cracow: " Please, drop me a line whether you can come here (for a series of lectures or conversations or studies, whichever you may like) or not. It would be fine! In seven kilometres from here, by rail, there is Zakopane — a very good resort. . . . If your health permits, come over for a while, won't you? After London [the Conference of 1907] and the Capri school it might do you good to see some more workmen." Gorky was unable to go to Cracow.

We have seen how vehement Lenin waxed against Pyatnitsky. Even more so was his solicitude about Gorky's health; his tone was that of a frantic mother over her sick child. Thus: " I am reading your P. S.: ' My hands are shivering from cold,' and I feel outraged. What execrable houses your Capri has! Why, it is monstrous! Even we, here [in Paris], have steam heat, it is quite warm, while your hands are freezing. You must rebel, raise a riot! " His letters ended frequently with severe exhortations about taking care of his health, " resting well," and seeing a good physician. Here is a specimen passage: " What do you mean, my dear sir, by behaving so abominably? Overworked, tired, nervous! That's rank disorderliness. At least at Capri, especially in the winter when you have probably fewer invaders, you ought to lead a regular mode of living. Is there no one to look after you, and is that why you are going to pieces? As god lives, that's bad! Take yourself in hand and get under a strict régime, please do! It is quite inadmissible to be sick at this day and age. Have you, by chance, begun to work nights? When I visited at Capri you were saying that it was only I who introduced disorder, and that before my arrival you went to bed early. There! Get rested and establish a proper régime, without fail."

In February, 1913, on the occasion of the 300th anniversary of the Romanov dynasty, an amnesty was granted for political

offences if these had been committed only in print. Gorky began to plan his return to Russia, notwithstanding his poor health. Lenin appreciated his nostalgia, and urged him to follow his inclination, counselling him, however, to ascertain first whether he might not be persecuted for the Capri school. As to his possible scruples about accepting the tsar's pardon, Lenin advised " realism ": " I hope you are not holding the view that one ought not ' accept amnesty.' This is a wrong view: at the present moment a revolutionist can do much more from the interior of Russia. . . . I take it that you will call on us when you go home: we are on your way! For a revolutionary writer the opportunity to ramble through Russia (the new Russia) is an opportunity for a hundredfold stronger blow at the Romanovs & Co. later on. . . ."

Gorky decided to return to Russia for the winter. Meanwhile his old tuberculosis renewed its attack on his lungs with such severity that the attending physicians gave him " just three weeks," as he told me years later. Lenin became uneasy. " I am dreadfully alarmed," he wrote to Gorky. " Are you doing the right thing in staying on at Capri without proper treatment? The Germans have splendid sanatoriums, for example, at. . . . And you intend to go to Russia, straight from Capri, for the winter???? I am terribly afraid that this may harm your health and undermine your working capacity. . . . Please, do take a trip to a first-rate physician in Switzerland (I can get names and addresses) or Germany, and get about two months of *serious* treatment in a *good* sanatorium. I declare, to squander for no purpose state property, that is, to be sick and undermine one's working strength, is something altogether inadmissible." After discussing other matters, the letter concludes: " I earnestly beseech you *to undertake a serious treatment.* As god lives, it is *quite possible* to be cured, but to neglect the case is downright godless and criminal."

A young Russian physician, I. I. Manukhin, formerly a member of the Party, happened to call on Gorky at this stage, and suggested his newly discovered method of treating tuberculosis by means of intense X-rays. Gorky submitted (" I had nothing to lose," he said to me), and the treatment proved so

successful that in December he was on his way to Russia. But Lenin had serious misgivings. " The news," he wrote him, " of a ' Bolshevik,' even if only an ex-Bolshevik, treating you by a *new* method, is very, very disquieting to me. God save us from comrade-physicians in general, and from Bolshevik physicians in particular! Upon my word, in ninety-one cases out of a hundred comrade-physicians are ' asses,' as one *good* physician once told me. . . . To try on oneself the discoveries of a Bolshevik — that's terrible!! . . . Look here, if you go back in the winter, be sure in any event to see some first-class physicians in Switzerland and in Vienna — it will be unpardonable if you don't do that. How is your health now? "

These solicitous notes were intermingled with similarly paternal (or maternal?) rebukes for his correspondent's ideational vagaries, at times coming almost in the same breath. Thus, after reading a paper by Lunacharsky, *Between Fear and Hope,* sent to him by Gorky, Lenin wrote banteringly: " And ' your ' Lunacharsky is a fine one!! Oh, what a fine one! In Maeterlinck he finds ' scientific mysticism.' . . . Or perhaps Lunacharsky and Bogdanov are no longer yours? Joking aside. Be well. Scribble a couple of words. *Rest* well." Apparently Gorky was tireless in his efforts to revive factional unity. In December, 1912, Lenin wrote to him:

Your joy at the return of the *Vperyodovtsy* to the fold I am ready to share with all my heart, provided . . . provided you are right in assuming that " Machism, *bogostroitelstvo,* and other tricks are gone for good." . . . Thus far it is more a pious desire than a fact. Do you recall our " last *rendez-vous* " at Capri, in 1908, with Bogdanov, Bazarov, and Lunacharsky? Do you remember my suggestion that we should have to part company for two or three years, and Maria Feodorovna, who presided, savagely protested and called me to order? Well, it has now lasted four and a half, almost five, years. And that is not a long time for such a deep disintegration as had taken place in the period of 1908–1911. I do not know whether Bogdanov, Bazarov, Volsky (one half an anarchist), Lunacharsky, Alexinsky are capable of *learning a lesson* from the depressing experience of 1908–1911. Have they understood

that *Marxism* is something more serious and profound than it had seemed to them? That one must not make sport of it, as Alexinsky had done time and again, or ill-treat it as a dead thing, the way the rest of them did? *If* they have understood, a thousand salutations to them, and all the personal animus (unavoidably introduced by the bitterness of the fight) shall go to the dustbin in a trice. But if they have not understood, if they have not learned a lesson, well, then do not blame me: " friendship is friendship, but duty is duty [a Russian proverb]." For their attempts at vilifying Marxism, or to embroil the policies of our workers' party, we shall fight, and fight without sparing ourselves.

As a matter of fact, of these men Lunacharsky alone eventually rejoined the Lenin faction whole-heartedly; Bogdanov and Bazarov remained wavering to the end, and Alexinsky went over to the most reactionary enemies of Soviet Russia.

There were occasions, however, when Lenin's reprimands had not a shade of jesting about them. Gorky's " maladroit articles " in non-Bolshevik periodicals brought about repeated scoldings. The following case is characteristic. In the fall of 1913 Gorky protested in a Moscow daily against the presentation by the Moscow Art Theatre of Dostoyevsky's *Demons* (*Possessed*), branding the idea as " dubious ethically and certainly noxious socially." A heated polemic followed in the press, compelling Gorky to come out with a fresh article, under the title *More about Karamazovism,* in which he spoke of " the frailty of the Russian character," " the pitiful instability of the Russian mind and its predilection for all sorts of infection," for " self-contempt which takes the place of self-criticism," for " senseless anarchism and variegated convulsions." The article might have pleased Lenin hugely, as a sign of Gorky's recovery from the Lunacharsky " fog," were it not for a short passage which " infuriated " Lenin, as he admitted later. It ran like this:

As to *bogoiskatelstvo,* it is best to let it go for a while — it is a useless occupation: why seek what isn't? Not having sown, you cannot reap. You have no God, you have not yet created one. One does not seek gods, one creates them. . . .

This relapse of Gorky into a shade of *bogostroitelstvo* after an intensive course of treatments administered to him by Lenin, exasperated the "physician" acutely. He wrote the recidivist a long letter bristling with exclamation marks and underscored phrases. After quoting the fatal passage, he exclaimed:

It follows that you are against *bogoiskatelstvo* only "for a while!!" It follows that you are against *bogoiskatelstvo only* in order to replace it by *bogostroitelstvo!!* Now isn't it terrible that such a thing should *follow* from your words? *Bogoiskatelstvo* differs from *bogostroitelstvo* or *bogosozidatelstvo* (god-creating) . . . not a whit more than a yellow devil differs from a blue devil. To talk about *bogoiskatelstvo* not for the sake of condemning *all kinds* of devils and gods, all sorts of mental necrophilism (any godkin is necrophilia, be it the cleanest, most ideal, not "sought" but "buildable" godkin — it does not matter), but merely in order to express a preference for a blue devil as against a yellow one, is a hundred times worse than not to talk at all.

In the freest countries, in countries like America and Switzerland, where your appeal to "democracy, to the people, to the public spirit, to science" is *quite* out of place, the people and workmen are being stupefied with especial zeal precisely by the idea of a cleanly, spiritual, "buildable" godkin. Precisely because any religious idea, any idea about any kind of a godkin, even the slightest flirtation with a godkin, is the vilest turpitude, accepted with particular tolerance (and often even with goodwill) by the *democratic* bourgeoisie, precisely for that reason it is the most dangerous abomination, the nastiest "infection." A million of sins, obscenities, violences and *physical* infections are much easier discovered by the crowd and are therefore far less dangerous than the *subtle,* spiritual idea of a godkin arrayed in the smartest "ideational" finery. A Catholic priest deflowering little girls (I have just read of one in a German paper) is *far less* dangerous for the "democracy" than a priest without a cassock, a priest without a crude religion, a democratic priest full of ideas, who preaches the creation and building of a godkin. Because it is *easy* to expose, condemn, and chase out the former priest, while it *is not* so simple to chase out the latter, it is a thousand times

more difficult to expose him, and not one " frail and pitifully unstable " burgher will be willing to " condemn " him.

And you, knowing as you do the " frailty and pitiful instability " of the (Russian: why Russian? Is the Italian better?) *philistine* mind, you tempt this mind with the sweetest poison, most aptly covered up by lollipops and all sorts of coloured bits of paper!

Upon my word, this is terrible.

. . . Isn't *bogostroitelstvo* the *worst* kind of " self-contempt "? Any man engaged in *god*-building, or even allowing such building, *contemns himself* in the worst manner, through engaging not in " deeds " but *precisely* in self-contemplation, self-admiration, and at that such a man " contemplates " the filthiest, dullest, most slavish traits of his self, divinized by *bogostroitelstvo*.

. . . Reading into your article, and *probing* how such a *slip* could have cropped forth, I am at a loss. What is it? The residue of *The Confession,* of which you *yourself* disapproved? Its echo? Or something else — for example, a clumsy attempt at *lowering* yourself from the height of a proletarian viewpoint down to an *all-democratic* point of view? Perhaps in order to talk to " democracy in general " you wished (pardon my expression) to lisp a bit, as one lisps with children? Maybe for the sake of " popular exposition " for the *burghers* you felt like admitting for a moment *their* prejudices?

But don't you see that this is a *wrong* method in every sense and every respect?

. . . Why do you do that?

It hurts devilishly.

P.P.S. Do take serious *treatments,* really, in order that you might travel in the winter without *catching colds* (it is dangerous in the winter).

For the first time in years this letter was signed not " Your Lenin," but " Your V. Ulyanov." It was a furious letter, its madly racing handwriting, twice and three times underlined words and phrases, and numerous exclamation and interrogation points, making one visualize the big-headed, stocky little man spitting fire from his mobile mouth and dancing eyes, now and then puncturing a phrase with that memorable gesture

of his — striking the left fist with the right one. The very next day, in another letter, Lenin said: . . . " Don't be angry that I became infuriated [yesterday]. Maybe I *mis*understood you? Maybe you used the words ' for a while ' *jokingly?* Maybe you did not mean seriously what you wrote about *bogostroitelstvo??* For god's sake, take good treatments. Your Lenin."

Alas, these desperate " maybe's " were like straws for a drowning man. Gorky, apparently, was chafing under the ferule of his censor. True enough, he wrote back that he was " greatly vexed," that he " could not understand how the phrase ' for a while ' had slipped in," but along with this " apology " he attempted a lengthy defence of *bogostroitelstvo*. Lenin retorted with a long letter, of which the first four pages have not been made public; the remainder, however, is sufficiently eloquent. The tone is no longer furious, the emphatic outbursts fewer, but the clear-cut dryness is murderous. He points out Gorky's confusion of ideas, reminding him of a conversation they had at Capri, when Lenin reproached him for having broken (" or seemingly broken ") with the *Vperyodovtsy*, without having grasped their basic ideas. In his present " defence " he notes a similar confusion. He quotes Gorky's letter, and proceeds with his comment:

" God is a complex of ideas worked out by a tribe, or a nation, or humanity, which awaken and organize social feelings, aiming to link the individual with society, and to bridle zoological individualism."

This theory is obviously allied with the theory or theories of Bogdanov and Lunacharsky. And it is obviously incorrect, and obviously reactionary. Like the Christian Socialists (the worst variety and distortion of " socialism "), you are employing a method which (despite your best intentions) repeats the hocus-pocus of priestery: out of the idea of god is removed its *historic* and *actual* substance (filth, prejudices, the sanction of darkness and wretchedness, on the one side, and of feudal bondage and the monarchy, on the other), and in place of this reality is inserted a goody-goody philistine phrase

(god — " ideas which awaken and organize social feelings ").
. . . . By virtue of the correlation [of social forces and classes]
it *follows* (in despite of your will, and regardless of your
cognition) that you have coloured and sugared the idea of
Clericals, of Purishkevich [one of the blackest reactionaries
in Russia], Nicholas II, and the Struve gentry, because *in
reality* the idea of god helps *them* to keep the people in
bondage. By having prettified the idea of god, you have prettified the chains by which they bind the dark workmen and
muzhiks. . . .

It is not true that god is a complex of ideas that awaken
and organize social feelings. That is the Bogdanov brand of
idealism, which befogs the material origin of ideas. God is
(historically and actually) first of all a complex of ideas that
rise from the oppression of man both by external nature and
by class tyranny, ideas which *perpetuate* this oppression and
lull to sleep the class struggle. . . . At present, both in Europe
and in Russia *any,* however refined and well-intentioned, defence or justification of the idea of god, is a justification of
reaction.

Your whole definition of god is through and through reactionary and bourgeois. . . .

Why is it reactionary? Because it colours the priestly-feudal
idea of " bridling " zoology. In reality " zoological individualism " was bridled not by the idea of god, but by the primitive
herd and the primitive commune. The idea of god has *always*
lulled to sleep and dulled " social feelings," substituting dead
things for live, *always* being an idea of slavery (the worst,
most hopeless slavery). Never has the idea of god " linked the
individual with society," but it has always fettered the oppressed *classes* with faith in the *divinity* of their oppressors. . . .

You say : " *Bogostroitelstvo* is a process of further growth and
accumulation of social principles in the individual and society."
That's downright horrible! If Russia were free, the whole
bourgeoisie would raise you on their shields for such words,
for this sociology and theology of a purely bourgeois type and
character.

Well, enough for the present, my letter is too long as it is.
Once more I firmly grasp your hand and wish you good health.

Your V. I.

Neither Lenin, nor Ulyanov, but V. I[Ilyich?]. That is the last letter of Lenin to Gorky in the published collection of Lenin's letters. Presumably it disrupted their relations for nearly five years, when they met in Russia under changed conditions. Gorky proved a poor disciple. In fact, even among the Bolsheviks there was hardly one man who was able to follow Lenin to the dot at all times. And Gorky was not a party member, and an artist to boot!

Incidentally, when Gorky published a collection of his *Articles, 1905–1916,* he deleted from the article on " Karamazovism " the fatal passage that had " infuriated " Lenin.

WAR AND REVOLUTION

DURING the World War Gorky edited a monthly review, *Letopis* (*Annals*). The chauvinistic press and various patriotic societies, as we have seen, branded the publication as pro-German, defeatist, and traitorous, and called upon the Government repeatedly to deal with it as with an enemy of the nation. The official censorship, however, found no concrete basis for persecuting *Letopis,* and when the Authorities did resolve to suspend its publication, late in 1916, the murder of Rasputin and other cataclysmic events engaged their attention elsewhere. The truth is that *Letopis* pleased neither the champions of the war nor the defeatists; it was hated by the bourgeoisie and despised by Lenin. Free from the latter's tutelage, Gorky succumbed to his weakness for " unification rather than differentiation," and surrounded himself with men of whose kind Lenin had said that he would rather let himself be quartered than stay in their company. Incidentally, among the contributors of *Letopis* were Bazarov and Lunacharsky. On the whole, the magazine stood on an international Socialist platform and, within the limits of war censorship, opposed the war on general principles. In conversation Gorky denies having ever entertained defeatist views, and no one who knows his warm, unreasoning love for Russia may doubt his denial. His own papers in the review rarely touched on politics; the issue which absorbed his interest more and more intensely was the cultural backwardness of the people, and the urgency of a war against this " inner enemy." Apparently, Gorky's burning faith in the revolution as a panacea against *all* national evils had cooled off. The

overthrow of the monarchy, in March, 1917, and the subsequent demoralization of the army and civil population under the Kerensky régime, roused in Gorky a mixed reaction. His natural joy at the fall of an obsolete and corrupt order was not unmixed with apprehension for the ability of the people to maintain order and humaneness under such apocalyptic circumstances as war and revolution interlaced. He even forgot his anti-war attitude for a moment, and in an open letter printed in all newspapers he spoke of the mission of the revolution to carry on the war to a successful conclusion, as long as it was of a defensive nature. Lenin commented on this eruption of Gorky's inconsistency:

One experiences a bitter feeling while reading this letter, so utterly permeated with the prejudices of the average citizen. The writer of these lines, on his visits to Capri, had occasion to reproach Gorky for his political errors, and warn him against repeating them. Gorky parried these reprimands with his inimitably charming smile and candid statement: " I know that I am a poor Marxian. Besides, we artists are all of us somewhat irresponsible persons." . . . Against such a declaration it is not easy to argue. . . .

The letter may have been a *lapsus* in the early days of the revolution, when banners and slogans and phrases went to one's head. He wrote in a more " responsible " vein in his *Thoughts out of Season,* which appeared in his daily paper, *Novaya Zhizn,* resurrected from its death, twelve years previously. *Letopis* soon gave up its ghost, both because of the disruption of printing facilities, and because a monthly review could not keep up with the quickened tempo of Russian life. The April issue of *Letopis* carried an article by Gorky, which struck the keynote for his subsequent *Thoughts out of Season.* The very opening of the article is typical of his attitude:

The Russian people have been wedded to Liberty. Let us trust that out of this union new strong men will be born in our land which is exhausted both physically and spiritually. Let us firmly believe that in the Russian man will flare up in

a bright flame the forces of his reason and will, forces that have been extinguished and crushed by the age-long yoke of a police régime.

This faith in the " reason and will " of the people was none too " firm " in Gorky's heart, to judge by what followed in that article and in the *Thoughts*. More emphatic sounded his references to such legacies of the old order as the extant " filth, rust, and all kinds of poison," as the " many-headed hydra of ignorance, barbarism, stupidity, vileness, and Hamism," as millions and millions of " politically illiterate and socially un-educated masses." The political victory in itself was a trifle in comparison with the enormous tasks ahead of the victors. In fact, the political victory was nothing to boast of:

We have overthrown the old order, but we have succeeded in doing so not because we are powerful, but because that order, aside from corrupting us, was itself corrupted through and through, and collapsed under the first co-ordinated jolt. The very fact that it had taken us so long to decide on that jolt in face of the ruination of the country and violation of the people, that very long-suffering of ours testifies to our weakness.

Gorky reiterated his faith in Man — " the most valuable creative force " potentially. Man must be armed with reason, with knowledge, with culture. Such was Gorky's " platform," his refrain, and the evolving events served as illustrations for his misgivings, and provoked his repeated admonitions and exhortations. The overthrow of the monarchy might mean, he warned, that the revolution " had merely driven the skin dis-ease inside the body." He commented on growing manifesta-tions of national anarchy, of cruelty and folly, of vulgar licence and disrespect for higher values, and proceeded to harp on the greatest need, the only thing that could save the country from destruction — culture. " Citizens, culture is in danger! " This slogan he suggested in place of the glib and hackneyed cry: " Citizens, the fatherland is in danger! " Not content with his sermons, Gorky organized a " Free Association for the De-velopment and Spread of Positive Sciences," and a society of

"Culture and Liberty," vigorously recruiting men of culture to assist him in this work. Both organizations lasted only a short time in the turbulent conditions of the moment, but Gorky kept up the fight to the end of his stay in Russia, and beyond.

That note of Gorky sounded like a still, small voice in the storm that overwhelmed the country. Even in *Novaya Zhizn* the editor's words were muted, and they drowned in the brasses of political discussions. His co-editors and contributors were practically the same as on the *Letopis*, who found it much more difficult to profess no definite line of political action now than under Tsarism, when vagueness was often the safest means to get by the censor. *Novaya Zhizn* rapidly became the most widely read paper in Russia, yet it did not align itself with any of the parties or factions which emerged into the open after March. Its prevailing tone resembled most closely a variant of Bolshevism, but decidedly not the Lenin variant. Though it opposed the imperialistic notions of Milyukov and the rest of the bourgeoisie; though it systematically attacked Kerensky for his vacillating policy and vain efforts at riding simultaneously such spirited steeds as those of labour and capital, of war and revolution; though it had nothing good to say of the Socialist-Revolutionists, Mensheviks, the Plekhanov group, and other spokesmen of the "revolutionary democracy" who tried to support the impossible duarchy of the Provisional Government and the Petrograd Soviet, a duarchy that actually spelled anarchy — the paper fought as vigorously Lenin's program of the immediate seizure of all power by the Soviets and the launching of a proletarian state. As a result, *Novaya Zhizn*, despite its immense circulation, pleased no one and was abused generally. While the majority of the press branded it Bolshevik, pro-Lenin, hence pro-German, the Leninist journals upbraided the paper the more virulently because of its seeming kinship, in accordance with Lenin's old dictum, Differentiation rather than unification.

Gorky was uncomfortable as editor of the daily. On the one hand, he disliked heartily interfactional strife, and never ceased his efforts at reunion. A curious meeting took place one

evening in the editorial rooms of *Novaya Zhizn,* at which three Bolshevik " generals-to-be " were present — Ryazanov, Lunacharsky, and the newly converted Trotsky. In his *Notes on the Revolution,* N. Sukhanov, one of Gorky's co-editors, reports that they discussed the possibility of editing the paper with the co-operation of the three visitors. It transpired, however, that the editors leaned more toward Martov, who had recently organized a tiny group of " Internationalists," than toward Trotsky. The latter then curtly remarked that, indeed, the position of *Novaya Zhizn* came much closer to Martov than to " revolutionary socialism," and that consequently nothing remained for him to do but organize a daily paper together with Lenin. A few years later Trotsky explained, in this connexion, that he and Lenin had agreed, before that meeting, to " capture " Gorky's paper, and failing this, to establish jointly their own organ.[1]

On the other hand, politics irked Gorky; he could not digest such large doses of it as he was now compelled to take, in the capacity of an editor of a big and influential daily. His single note of " culture " was merely tolerated, out of respect for his revolutionary past. When his text of a manifesto " To the World Nations " was presented to the Executive Committee of the Petrograd Soviet, it was rejected as " inopportune." " It contained not a gramme of politics," complains N. Sukhanov, whose text was finally accepted and published. Gorky's only appearance before the Soviet was met with thunderous applause, but his message dealt with a purely cultural matter: in the name of the Petrograd artists he suggested a change in the place of burial for the victims of the March revolution. His request was declined. He did succeed in having the Soviet's Executive Committee circulate his text of an appeal to the people for the preservation of monuments.[2]

---

[1] This episode is discussed in *A Letter from Trotsky,* Appendix, II.

[2] The text of the Appeal is characteristic of Gorky's anxiety in those days:

" Citizens, the old masters are gone, leaving behind them an enormous inheritance. It now belongs to the whole nation.

" Citizens, guard this inheritance, guard the palaces, they will become

The political program of his newspaper, however vague in its positive tenets, was on its negative side definite enough to make it unpalatable for all other groups, parties, and papers. Its Bolshevik leanings were particularly obnoxious to the bourgeois intelligentsia, who did not scruple about accusing the *Novaya Zhizn* group, and Gorky at its head, of all imaginable crimes, including, of course, that of being a paid agent of Germany. Gorky pleaded for tolerance, mildly suggesting that though alliterate, criticism and calumny were not the same thing. It is doubtful whether he was capable of a philosophical indifference to attacks, an attitude which was indispensable for the head of a paper that roasted everybody but supported no one wholly. In his voluminous *Notes on the Revolution*, Nicholas Sukhanov, member of the Executive Committee of the Petrograd Soviet and co-editor of *Novaya Zhizn*, speaks of the difficult position of Gorky who, while being held answerable for the policy of his paper, was actually in doubt as to the correctness of this policy. Let me quote a graphic passage from Sukhanov:

From morning till night Gorky spent his time among the bourgeois intelligentsia — scientists, artists, writers. As ever, *all* social groups pounced on Gorky, fighting for him and endeavouring to appropriate him. The nature of his activity at the time threw him for the most part with those of the intelligentsia that had been scared out of their wits and reacted to Gorky accordingly. *Novaya Zhizn* and its policies affected decisively his relations with the people he met in his " Free Association for the Development and Spread of Positive Sciences " and in the literary and artistic circles and societies, to which he devoted his activity. He was regarded in those

---

palaces of your national art, guard the pictures, statues, buildings — these are the embodiment of your spiritual power and of that of your ancestors.

" Art consists of those fine things which gifted men have created even under the oppression of despotism, and which testify to the power and beauty of the human mind.

" Citizens, do not touch a single stone, guard your monuments, buildings, old objects, documents — all these are your history, your pride. Remember that this is the soil from which your new national art will grow forth.

" The Executive Committee of the Soviet of Workers' Deputies."

places with wonderment, as a victim of his shady colleagues on the newspaper. They argued with him incessantly and perseverantly.

Manufacturers also called on him, and demonstrated to him as clearly as $2 \times 2 = 4$ that the workmen were criminal idlers, who were destroying the national industry, and culture along with it. They pointed out that Gorky, by championing a Bolshevik line of action in a big influential paper, was personally aiding the criminal cause. They cited facts, often true facts. These produced on Gorky a strong impression. Regarding the destruction of industry by the workmen, Gorky was approached incidentally by such an authority as the subsequent Bolshevik, Krasin. In the following years Krasin proved one of the pillars of the Soviet economic policy, but at that time he spoke quite in tune with the Konovalovs, Lvovs, and the yellow bourgeois press. To Gorky he sounded very convincing. After such seances Gorky demanded that *Novaya Zhizn* throw light on " the other side of the problem."

Dubious as to the stand of his paper on internal questions, Gorky was particularly embarrassed by its foreign policy, its accentuated internationalism and savage attacks on Allied diplomacy. In substance, the views of *Novaya Zhizn* did not differ from those of *Letopis,* except that with the removal of the tsar's censorship they were voiced in plain words and not in the traditionally veiled, Æsopian language of pre-revolutionary Russia. *Novaya Zhizn* spared neither Sir George Buchanan and His Majesty's ministers, nor Monsieur Paléologue and his Poincaré-Millerandesque France. Kerensky's vacillating government was forced to take measures against the inconsiderate journal. Gorky winced under the howling campaign of all respectable Russia against the " traitorous " tone of his paper. He demanded of his co-editors a clear statement of their foreign policy. Why, he asked, this vicious exposé of Allied imperialism? Surely they did not advocate a separate peace, as they were accused by the bourgeois press? That phrase, " a separate peace," was then the most terror-inspiring heresy, and even Lenin pleaded not guilty of such a hellish notion.

Alas, no " clear statement " could come from the muddle-headed, hypercritical, arch-radical, but hopelessly indefinite and undecided editors of *Novaya Zhizn*. All the seven volumes of Sukhanov's *Notes* fail to make clear his stand or that of his group. Sukhanov, in reproaching Gorky for his lack of a definite policy, overlooks the beam in his own eye. He does, however, pay tribute to Gorky's chivalry. Gorky, he admits, was the sole owner and master of the paper, and had the power to dictate its policy, or, if he cared for his personal peace and comfort, to give up entirely this burdensome and messy undertaking. Yet, though suffering abuse and inner doubts and qualms, Gorky remained at his post to the very end, and according to Sukhanov, " not once did he interfere " with the editorial policy of the paper. He did one thing to calm his conscience: in June, 1917, he requested that henceforth the names of his three colleagues appear jointly with his own as those of the responsible editors.

The policy, or rather lack of a clear policy on the part of *Novaya Zhizn* was characteristic of the transition period between the political revolution of March, and the social revolution of November, 1917. The intervening months revealed the unlimited capacity of the intelligentsia for theoretical disputes and inconsequential eloquence, and their utter failure to grasp the actuality. They were well-read in history and political thought, and knew precisely the *à priori* course that Russia was to follow. From the reactionary Purishkevich to the conservative Guchkov and the liberal Milyukov, from the Socialist-Revolutionist Chernov to papa Plekhanov of the Social-Democrats and all the Menshevik shades from Dan to Martov — the political leaders were unanimous in regarding the March events as a repetition of 1848 in western Europe, that is to say, as a victory of constitutionalism and middle-class democracy. The Lvov-Milyukov-Guchkov cabinet was, accordingly, accepted as logical and proper, and the presence in their midst of the " socialist " Kerensky was merely tolerated as a complimentary gesture in the direction of the revolutionary masses. The socialist parties not only did not aspire to places in the cabinet, but they firmly resented any

notion of their participating in a government which by all rules and precedents could not be anything but bourgeois. Russia was freed from autocracy and the remnants of feudalism, and its next stage was categorically indicated by the experience of other countries: feudalism must be succeeded by capitalism, under a respectable parliamentary régime, with the predominance of the middle class taken for granted.

The only dissonance in this touching concord of views was caused by Lenin and his handful of adherents. From the very beginning of the outbreak he gauged the situation differently. Notwithstanding all theories and precedents, the Russian revolution did not augur to him a transition to the rule of the middle class. Russia has been a land of extremes, in every respect; anything middle seems foreign there. Its middle class was numerically insignificant, and its moral influence was *nil*. The stolid masses had been kept in subjection and ignorance for generations, and had not been prepared for gradual, evolutionary processes. When in the midst of a stupendous war the autocratic order proved corrupt to its core and criminally inefficient, it collapsed suddenly and utterly. The March revolution was a military *coup d'état,* if there ever was one, except that it was promulgated not from the top but from the bottom. The enormous mass of privates, more than eighty per cent of them peasants, and with a considerable sprinkling of city workers and intellectuals, simply refused to carry out the orders of their officers, broke their allegiance to the tsar, and backed the cause of the people, traditionally represented by a few scores of starving housewives in the capital. The political leaders appeared on the stage the morning after, and endeavoured to formulate neatly what had taken place. The Lvov-Milyukov-Guchkov cabinet proved the acceptable formula — for the intelligentsia. The untutored soldiery and peasantry and factory hands sent their representatives, not to the lofty Provisional Government but to the humble Soviet of Workers, Soldiers, and Peasants. On the one hand, then, there was the Lvov-Milyukov-Guchkov government, the spokesman of a relatively non-existing middle class, and on the other, the

Soviet, the voice of some ninety-five per cent of the nation. The Provisional Government wished to rule, but it had no backing, except for that of political leaders who had no one to lead. The Soviet was backed by practically the whole people, but it was chary of ruling. Its leaders, fine and eloquent gentlemen like Dan, Lieber, Gotz, Martov, Chernov, Chkheidze, and others, engaged in tirelessly assuring this all-powerful body that it must not attempt to rule the country, because that would be against all historic precedent. This paradox continued for months, the Provisional Government reduced to a grim joke, the Soviet bursting with cumulative power but reluctant to use it. The Government gradually passed into the hands of Kerensky, an artful juggler, a second-rate lawyer presuming to play the part of a Napoleon, who danced between the war and the revolution, capital and labour, landowners and peasants, the war-weary delegates from the front and the emissaries of the Allies (shades of Elihu Root, Albert Thomas, Arthur Henderson!) who urged an offensive at any price. Reluctantly the Soviet delegated some of its members into the coalition ministries of Kerensky, where they held themselves as tentative hostages of the " revolutionary democracy," and acted shamefacedly and apologetically.

Even before he crossed the border into Russia, in April, 1917, Lenin formulated his slogan: " All power to the Soviets! " From the day of his arrival at Petrograd he launched into a fierce campaign for the popularization of that slogan. He was opposed not only by all respectable leaders and organs who branded him as a madman and a German agent, but even by the nearly-Bolshevik group of *Novaya Zhizn,* and by some of his closest associates, who saw in his platform a dangerous bit of demagogy. At the All-Russian Congress of Soviets, in June, Lenin made a speech, in which he referred to the claim of Tseretelli, Menshevik member of Kerensky's cabinet, that " there was not one political party in Russia, which would consent to assume the full authority of government." Said Lenin: " My answer is: There is such a party! No party may decline this burden, and our party does not decline it. At any moment it is ready to take over the complete authority of

government (*applause and laughter*). You may laugh as much as you like." Lenin became the butt of caricaturists and columnists. To plead openly for power — that was impudent and un-Russian. Boris Godunov, back in the sixteenth century, after astutely paving the way for his election as tsar, had the politeness to refuse the offer three times before he finally yielded to the tearful entreaties of the head of the church and representative Muscovites. This attitude toward public office is not only due to a certain provincial desire to be coaxed, but may be also explained by the traditional anarchism of the Russian people, which resents government and any coercion as sin. Legend has it that when the ancient Russians, tired of disorder and strife, decided to have a government, they sent messengers across the sea to the Norsemen, and invited them to come and rule over them; they appeared less scrupulous about causing foreigners to sin. Lenin, with but a handful of followers, declaring his readiness to assume power at any moment, seemed excruciatingly funny, and impertinent to boot.

Bazarov, in a leading editorial in *Novaya Zhizn*, warned against Lenin's " communistic hysteria," and Ryazanov, today a pillar of Bolshevism,[3] wrote there that " Leninism is a product not of faith in the revolution, but of lack of faith in it." V. Kerzhentsev, later a prominent Soviet diplomat, branded Lenin's platform as a reversion to Bakunin's " riotism." In July, on the morrow of the first unsuccessful attempt of the Bolsheviks at an uprising, Sukhanov wrote in the characteristically vacillating manner of Gorky's paper: " In contradistinction to the Bolsheviks, we do not include the struggle for power in our program. We say that in doing so they are committing a mistake, but there is no doubt that a refusal of authority at this moment would be a similar mistake." Small wonder that the Bolshevik *Pravda* sneered at " the hesitations of the petty bourgeois chatterers from *Novaya Zhizn*." When Ryazanov appealed to the Leninists and Trotskyists " to compromise," and Gorky's paper renewed its efforts to unite all

---

[3] In 1931 Ryazanov lost favour with Stalin, and consequently was stripped of his power.

factions, *Pravda* dismissed these sentiments as " a soap bubble."

The July " rehearsal " of the Bolshevik forces proved a fiasco. Kerensky's government made use of this false step, by declaring the Bolsheviks traitors and issuing orders for the arrest of their leaders. The bourgeois press excelled itself in showering abuse and accusations against them and their " sympathizers " — " Gorky's circus riders and cannibals, who are more harmful than the Bolsheviks, because the latter reveal their intentions openly, whereas the *Novaya Zhizn* chaps hide under the mask of culture " (Milyukov's *Rech*). Lenin, Kamenev, and Zinoviev went into hiding, and in a joint letter they requested Gorky's paper for " hospitality," in view of the suspension of their own publications. To be sure, hospitality was given, but more broadly than suited Lenin's taste. On the one hand, the paper printed Trotsky's open letter to the Provisional Government, in which he declared his complete harmony with the views of Lenin, Kamenev, and Zinoviev, and therefore demanded that he be arrested and punished on par with them (his wish was granted, and his next letter was mailed from jail). On the other hand, *Novaya Zhizn* published a series of articles by Martov, who started out with the statement that the July attempt spelled " the defeat of the working class." During the August elections to the Soviet, *Novaya Zhizn* appealed to the voters to reject the Bolshevik candidates, and to vote for the Internationalists, that nondescript *mélange* of semi-Mensheviks and semi-Bolsheviks, which for a while included such strange bedfellows as Martov, Sukhanov, Ryazanov, and even Lunacharsky. The Bolshevik sheet, *Proletary,* lost all patience with the catholicity of Gorky's daily and accused it, unjustly of course, of " perpetually vacillating between revolution and counter-revolution, between war and peace, between labour and capital, between landowners and peasants."

Not being a politician, Gorky, as we have noted, lacked the brazen indifference to abuse and calumny so indispensable for a public man. He was annoyed by these attacks from every side, but he was apparently more hurt by the insinuations from

the respectable Right than by the sneers from Lenin's camp: in any event, of the former he took frequent cognizance, and cried out in protest. To the accusation by Milyukov's *Rech* of suspicious elasticity in his political convictions, Gorky replied with touching candidness:

For seventeen years I have considered myself a Social-Democrat, and have served as much as I could the great purposes of that party. At the same time I did not deny my services to other parties, unwilling to spurn any vital cause. I have never sympathized with people who become fossilized and petrified under the pressure of the faith they confess. . . .

I shall say more: in every group and party I regard myself as a heretic. In my political views there are, most likely, a number of contradictions, which I cannot and do not want to reconcile. I feel that for the sake of my inner harmony, for the sake of my mental peace and comfort, I should have to kill utterly that part of my soul which loves most passionately and achingly the live, sinful, and — by your leave — wretchedly pitiful Russian man.

He thus chose to parry the numerous reproaches for his inconsistencies with an admission of guilt. In regard to the Germans, for instance, he never broke the bounds of decency, unlike such of his former friends as Leonid Andreyev and Alexander Kuprin, who now preached with foam at their mouths undying hatred for the Huns. In *Novaya Zhizn*, Gorky had the temerity to speak with sympathy of the sporadic fraternization between Russian and German soldiers, in which he saw the awakening of " a feeling of disgust at the senseless slaughter." This sentiment aroused a savage howl in the press and in the circles of the intelligentsia. Ivanov-Razumnik, a literary critic of the sociological school and a Left Socialist-Revolutionist of the " Scythian " shade, reminded Gorky that he was not alway immune from anti-German feelings, citing the fact that early in the war Gorky had lent his signature to a protest against the German scholars who championed the cause of their fatherland. In his reply Gorky began with the lame assertion that he did not " remember " such a protest, and that he must have signed it without reading the text. For

one who knows what a prodigious memory Gorky has, such a statement sounds preposterous.[4] But after the opening quaking sentences Gorky rallied, and boldly admitted that he " was ready to sign any protest, provided it condemned the participation of men of science in a fratricidal and senseless war."

The very name of Maxim Gorky served as a magnet for foes and friends, for proposals and protests, for the whole gamut of public emotions evinced at such a critical period as war combined with revolution. In the diaries of contemporary men and women one finds the name of Gorky inflected in every imaginable way and in every conceivable connexion. He was used, incidentally, as a receptacle for all sorts of notions. For example, the Bulgarian minister to Germany, D. Rizov, wrote to Gorky a long letter, requesting him to act as mediator for the arrangement of an armistice between the fighting nations. That was early in June. What the prevailing attitude toward the war at that time was, and how Gorky had to reckon with that attitude, can be seen from the fact that in reprinting Rizov's sane and courteous letter in *Novaya Zhizn,* Gorky prefaced it with a few lines, in which he labelled the letter as " infamous and silly," concluding: " It goes without saying that I do not intend to answer Rizov." This preface did not save Gorky from a shower of mud and chuckling insinuations that there must have been good reasons for Rizov to address Gorky and not a lesser friend of Germany. The notorious Sherlock Holmes of the revolution, Vladimir Burtsev, who succeeded in exposing the *agent-provocateur* Azev, but whose detective mania prompted him to many groundless accusations, now included Gorky in his list of suspects. He finally blurted out definitely that Gorky was a German agent, a betrayer of

---

[4] In fact we find among Lenin's notes that he was chagrined by Gorky's signing " a nasty scrap of paper by Russian liberals " against the misconduct of certain Germans, whereas he should have protested against the brutality of *all* imperialists. A. Elizarova, in her confidential letter to Lenin, written from Petrograd in December, 1915, reported that Gorky had asked her to assure her brother that " he never was a chauvinist, that his name appeared on the anti-German declaration without his knowledge, but that it was inexpedient for him to protest against it, for personal reasons. The other signatories would have been offended if he disavowed his signature."

his motherland. Gorky demanded an explanation. " Motherland," he wrote, " means one's people. I have been serving my
people for a quarter of a century, and it is not for you, miserable man, to judge and accuse me." The congress of United
Trade Unions, held at that time in Petrograd, voted a protest
against Burtsev's slander of Gorky, " the pride of Russian
literature, and the unrelenting champion of the toiling masses."
Also the Press Bureau of Paris requested through the Russian
embassy that Burtsev furnish proofs for his grave accusation
of Gorky. But the time was not propitious for smoothing out
personal matters: November was approaching.

Toward the end of the summer the Provisional Government —
that is, Kerensky's would-be dictatorship — was becoming more
and more isolated, enjoying neither respect nor fear. The
failure of the offensive, which could have been foreseen by any
observer of the morale at the Russian front, dealt a blow to
the prestige of Kerensky at home and abroad. His desperate
effort to galvanize into martial action the demoralized and
freedom-drunk soldiery brought no results, except that they
gained him the sobriquet of Persuader-in-Chief, which suited
him better than that of Commander-in-Chief — one of the
many titles he assumed in those interregnum days. The Bolshevik fiasco in July prompted Kerensky to persecute vigorously the Left elements and to seek the support of the
conservative and well-to-do classes. His contact with the
masses and the rank-and-file army receded into the mist of
meaningless phrases. No practical legislation was enacted, and
the crying need for land and labour reforms was dodged by
referring all questions to the Constituent Assembly, whose
convocation was postponed time and again. The much sought
after conservatives raised their heads, made ever growing demands on the bewildered " dictator," and finally gave vent to
their sentiments in the uprising of General Kornilov, whose
purpose was to put an end to the Soviets and establish a military dictatorship of the orthodox variety. Kerensky's part in
this affair has not been quite cleared up as yet, and his own
verbose memoirs fail to dissipate the suspicion that he had
personally supported Kornilov's plan for a dictatorship of

three, of which Kerensky was to be one. In any event, he raised an alarm at the eleventh hour, and called upon the "revolutionary democracy" to save the revolution from the attack of Kornilov and those with him. Kornilov's insurrection proved a tempest in a glass of water, and his march against red Petrograd petered out into nothing, for the simple reason that none of the Russian soldiers were willing to follow him, and the Savage Division, composed of Caucasian mountaineers, obeyed their general only until they found out his intentions. But the Kornilov affair undoubtedly played into the hands of the Bolsheviks, whose constant warning against co-operation with the non-proletarian parties now seemed to have been amply justified.

From his hiding place in a Finnish hamlet Lenin directed the campaign with resolution and confidence, the very qualities which his opponents sorely lacked. After the Kornilov affair the slogan "All Power to the Soviets!" found many ready ears, and the subsequent elections to the Soviets gave the Bolsheviks a decisive majority in both capitals. The Petrograd Soviet elected as president Leon Trotsky, who had by now definitely aligned himself with Lenin, once his enemy. Henceforth the Soviet assumed a new tone, an authoritativeness, a clear-cut aspiration after power, and an undisguised contempt for the ephemeral "government" of Kerensky. The latter thundered against the Petrograd Soviet, accused the Bolsheviks of treason, of plotting against the existing government, of preparing an insurrection. The Bolsheviks denied nothing, acted non-committally, and went on organizing the capture of military and civil authority.

What was the stand of *Novaya Zhizn* in those critical days? They could no longer jest at the hallucinations of the isolated madmen, since the growing popularity and power of the Leninists compelled earnest consideration. Trotsky's Soviet no longer debated as to whether it was right or wrong for it to take over the government, but proceeded to prepare for this transaction, and was already issuing orders to the army and civilians, orders which were obeyed, unlike those of Kerensky. *Novaya Zhizn* had to admit the pending transition of authority

into the hands of the " democracy," but it still refused to treat
the Bolsheviks as a serious quantity *in themselves*. Bazarov
asked: " Will the Bolsheviks be in a position to transform
themselves from a party of extreme opposition into a governing
party, even if we grant the condition that the entire democracy
will join their platform? " It did not occur to him for a moment
that the Bolsheviks might assume the responsibility alone, but
he answered in the negative the question of their effectiveness,
even if they should be supported by all other socialist parties
— the " democracy." It was already middle October, about a
fortnight before the victory of Lenin, yet Bazarov could not
resist poking fun at Lenin's faith in the masses, expressed in
his slogan " All Power to the Soviets! " classifying this faith
as " sentimental goody-goodiness," and " revolutionary Mani-
lovism." Gogol must have turned in his grave at this comparison of his syrupy jellyfish with the most dynamic Russian of
modern times. Bazarov concluded his leader with the following
prophecy: " The moment of the political victory of the Bolsheviks will be the beginning of the end of Bolshevism, and
at the same time the beginning of the end of the revolution."
Had he meant to say that once in power the Bolsheviks would
be forced to modify their doctrine, and to put an end to the
revolution by inaugurating a constructive era, he might have
been right, for such has been the fate of most revolutionary
parties when they attained their immediate goal. But, of
course, Bazarov had in mind something more devastating; he
meant to sound as the Cassandra of the Russian revolution.

At the end of October the editorial policy of *Novaya Zhizn*
was formulated as favouring " the transfer of all power into
the hands of the democracy, and at the same time warning the
Left portion of the democracy against isolated action." The
paper's theoretician, Bazarov, continued to speak derisively
of the Bolshevik resolutions for the " immediate " seizure of
power by the Soviets, with promises for an " immediate " arrangement of an armistice, an " immediate " settlement of the
land question, and similar boastful illusions. The frantic
refrain of the editorials was: " Democracy must consolidate

all its forces," and this refrain grew more and more nervous as the Bolshevik insurrection loomed inevitable and near.

There was so much open talk about the insurrection that one hardly felt like taking it seriously. Kerensky's government was prepared to meet the pending "demonstration" with proper measures, and was not in the least alarmed. *Rech* predicted that if the Bolsheviks risked coming out into the streets, they would be crushed without difficulty, and spoke hopefully of the Provisional Government which " shall this time show enough determination to give, at last, a proper moral and physical setback to unbridled anarchism; a storm is pending, but perhaps it will clear the atmosphere." The hope that the Bolshevik adventure would provoke another Kornilov reaction was shared by other bourgeois organs, but most of them were less patient than *Rech,* and advocated immediate drastic steps against the Bolsheviks (Andreyev's *Russkaya Volya*), while Suvorin's sheet wrote unmincingly that " one does not give battle to German agents: one arrests them." The implication was that there was only a handful of these scoundrels, whose arrest would put an end to the affair. The Menshevik *Rabochaya Gazeta* (*Labour Gazette*) wrote of the Bolshevik leaders: " Is it possible that these men do not realize that never before have the Petrograd proletariat and garrison been so isolated from all other social elements? Is it possible that they do not understand that even the workmen and soldiers will not follow them *en masse,* and that their slogans are apt to lure into the streets only a few handfuls of hot-headed workmen and soldiers, who will be smashed ineluctably? " Other socialist papers wrote in the same vein. *Novaya Zhizn* warned that the proposed " insurrection, with its most probable result of civil war, would alleviate and solve nothing; there is only one party whose purposes it would serve, namely, the party of Kornilov." The Internationalists issued an appeal signed by Martov, Sukhanov, and others, " To the Workmen and Soldiers," in which they were urged to refuse taking part in the " demonstration " prepared by the Bolsheviks. The Socialist-Revolutionary mayor of Petrograd, Shreider, shortly after-

wards a member of Lenin's cabinet, published a similar appeal. Gorky wrote in *Novaya Zhizn* for October 31 an editorial: "One Must Not Be Silent" (a paraphrase of Tolstoy's "I Cannot Be Silent," written ten years previously against the wholesale executions of political offenders), in which he wrote in a style curiously reminiscent of Leonid Andreyev's:

Ever more persistent rumours are spreading to the effect that on November 2 a "Bolshevik rising" will take place; in other words, that the hideous scenes of July 16–18 may be repeated. That means that once more there will appear motor-lorries overfilled with men with rifles and revolvers in their trembling hands, and these rifles will shoot at shop windows, at people, at random. They will shoot only because the men armed with them will try to kill their fear. All dark instincts of the crowd irritated by disorder, by the falsehood and filth of politics, will flare up and ooze forth poisonous malice, hatred, vengeance. People will be killing one another, in their inability to destroy their own bestial stupidity.

The unorganized crowd will creep out into the streets, hardly understanding what it wants, while under its cover adventurers, thieves, professional assassins will set out to "create the history of the Russian revolution."

In brief, there will be repeated that bloody, senseless slaughter, which we have already witnessed, and which has undermined through our whole land the moral importance of the revolution, and has shaken its cultural meaning.

It is very probable that this time the events will assume a more bloody and riotous character, and will deal the revolution a heavier blow.

Who wants all that, and for what purpose? The Central Committee of the Bolsheviks is, apparently, taking no part in the planned adventure, for up to now it has not confirmed the rumours about the pending uprising, though it has not denied them either.

It may be pertinent to ask: Is it possible that there are adventurers who, seeing the slump of revolutionary energy among the class-conscious part of the proletariat, intend to rouse this energy by means of copious bloodletting?

Or are these adventurers desirous of hastening the stroke of the counter-revolution, and, with this in view, are endeavour-

ing to disorganize the forces that have been organized with such difficulty?

The Central Committee of the Bolsheviks is under obligation to refute the rumours about the rising on November 2. It must do this, if indeed it is a strong and freely functioning political organ capable of directing the masses, and not a will-less toy in the moods of a bestialized mob, if it is not a tool in the hands of shameless adventurers or demented fanatics.

As a matter of fact, the Bolshevik leaders refused to commit themselves definitely on this question. Who ever heard of conspirators discussing their plans in public? Trotsky preferred action to words. In those days he was most indefatigable in his work of organizing the Petrograd army and workmen. According to his enemy, Sukhanov, Trotsky seemed ubiquitous, rushing from the revolutionary headquarters to one factory after another, to barracks after barracks: " Every Petrograd workman and soldier knew him and heard him. His influence, both among the masses and in headquarters, was overwhelming. He was the central figure of those days and the main hero of that singular page of history." At Trotsky's initiative, the Soviet organized a Military-Revolutionary Committee, which proceeded energetically to arm the sympathizing workmen and to prepare the soldiers and sailors for the moment when Kerensky's government would fall into their hands like an over-ripe apple. On the other hand, neither Trotsky nor other Bolshevik leaders were willing to admit their intentions, when pressed to do so by representatives of the " revolutionary democracy." They dodged the question. A characteristically ambiguous statement was made at the Central Executive Committee of the Soviet by Ryazanov, who had meanwhile joined Lenin's group (Lenin complimented Ryazanov highly on this statement). Replying to the socialist supporters of the Provisional Government, who spoke of the need to defend the revolution from the right and the left, he said:

As long as this defence remains in the hands of the coalition [of the socialists and the parties of the Right], it will be in as helpless a condition as it is now. With this in view,

we have organized the Military-Revolutionary Committee, against which the Mensheviks voted. . . . You lack the determination to tell the Government, Get out! Well, then, don't talk of being in earnest about desiring to defend the revolution. If you wish to be taken seriously, you must hand over to the Soviets the defence and the whole authority. . . . We have been asked here as to when we intend to start our insurrection, but Dan [leading Menshevik] knows that we are Marxian and therefore do not prepare an insurrection. The insurrection is being prepared by the policy which you have been supporting these seven months. The insurrection is being prepared by those who generate despair and indifferentism among the masses. If this policy will continue to be what it is now, and if as a result there will be an insurrection, then we shall be in the first ranks of the insurrectionists. . . .

Ryazanov is a learned and orthodox Marxian — in 1930, on the occasion of his sixtieth birthday, Soviet Russia celebrated him as *the* historian of Marxism. It is natural therefore that he tried to justify the pending insurrection by the logic of " objective conditions." He disclaimed all initiative on the part of the Bolsheviks. The united opposition to the " Bolshevik adventure " had its effect not only on Ryazanov's tone: it frightened some of Lenin's closest associates. During those very November days Kamenev published in *Novaya Zhizn* (the Bolshevik *Novy Put'* (*New Road*) refused to print it) a public letter, in which he spoke for himself, for Zinoviev, and a number of " expert comrades." They were " decidedly against the Party taking the initiative for any armed uprising in the near future." Such a step they regarded " inadmissible and fatal for the proletariat and the revolution . . . an act of despair." In later years both Trotsky and Stalin were fond of citing this " courage " of Kamenev and Zinoviev. At the time their conduct showed that not only were the Bolsheviks isolated from other parties, but that within the Central Committee itself there were grave differences of opinion. Lenin became alarmed at this rift in his own ranks, and from his hiding place he sent out a projectile, one of his *Letters to My Comrades*. Unlike Trotsky, Ryazanov, and other diplomatic leaders, Lenin dotted all i's. " To reject the insurrection," he wrote,

" is to reject the transfer of power to the Soviets, is to place all hopes and expectations in the kindly bourgeoisie, which has ' promised' the convocation of the Constituent Assembly. Either you join the liberals and openly disavow the slogan, All Power to the Soviets, or — insurrection. There is no middle course. Either you fold your useless arms on your empty breasts and wait, swearing your ' faith' in the Constituent Assembly, for Rodzianko & Co. to betray Petrograd and strangle the revolution, or — insurrection." As to the argument that the Bolsheviks were isolated, that declarations against the insurrection had been issued by the Mensheviks, and the Internationalists, and the Left Socialist-Revolutionists, and the *Novaya Zhizn* group, and the Central Executive Committee of the Soviet, Lenin wrote: " Up to now we have dealt blows to those who hesitate, and have thereby won the sympathy of the people and the majority of the Soviets; now we are to profit by our conquest of the Soviets and desert for the camp of the hesitators. What a fine career for Bolshevism! . . ." In the end he dismissed all arguments with a cavalier shrug of his shoulders: " One blockhead can ask ten times more questions than ten clever minds can answer. . . . We have never denied the difficulties of assuming authority, but we are not going to let the difficulties of a revolution frighten us."

The issue of *Novaya Zhizn* for November 4 carried a greeting to Maxim Gorky from his co-workers on the paper. The occasion was the twenty-fifth anniversary of his literary activity. No one else seemed to have noticed this event at the time. Sukhanov tells us that four days previously he arrived at the session of the Petrograd Soviet, and intended to make a motion for a message of congratulation to Gorky. His behaviour in this connexion is again typical of his vacillating group and newspaper. He found it awkward to make that motion, because of his connexion with *Novaya Zhizn,* of whose members Lenin said that they were " contemptible little fools," and of whom the Bolshevik *Novy Put'* wrote that " the revolution neither buries nor pities its corpses." Sukhanov feared that if the motion emanated from him it would be howled down by his enemies. Would not Trotsky, the president of the Soviet, be

willing to make the proposition? After all, Gorky was not only an editor but the foremost proletarian writer, of whose art Lenin himself thought most highly. But Sukhanov hesitated to ask Trotsky directly. He came up to the speakers' platform, and sought out Ryazanov, until recently a regular contributor to *Novaya Zhizn*. Ryazanov mumbled something in confusion, declined to make the motion himself, but promised to approach Trotsky on the subject, as soon as the latter finished his speech. Sukhanov waited in vain for several hours. It is doubtful whether Trotsky would have entertained that motion. In the first place he was then in the midst of carrying out the final arrangements for the " insurrection," and would have hardly felt like distracting the attention of his audience with irrelevant matters. In the second place, on that very day *Novaya Zhizn* printed Gorky's " One Must Not Be Silent," whose caustic tone and anti-insurrection sentiment made a eulogy of Gorky by a Bolshevik leader a bit unpropitious.[5] Lastly, Trotsky, whose prodigious versatility includes a *penchant* for literary criticism, has always treated Gorky's writings with reserve, and even his revolutionary proclivities provoked Trotsky's derisive appellation of " the psalm-singer of the revolution."

In this connection I may quote a letter written to me recently by Trotsky:

. . . . Gorky's *Novaya Zhizn* presented in 1917, to put it mildly, a downright misunderstanding. One of his chief collaborators was Sukhanov, whom you seem to know through his book. The other contributors were of the same type. They were an extremely honest lot, who sincerely wished to carry on " revolutionary " and " Left " politics, but of their own brand, that is, that which emanated from their literary schemes

[5] From a letter of Trotsky's to me:

" You are of course quite right in surmising that under no circumstances would I have consented to speak about Gorky's anniversary from the platform of the Petrograd Soviet in the fall of 1917. This time Sukhanov did the right thing in giving up one of his fanciful whims — to inveigle me, on the eve of the October [O.S.] uprising, into a celebration of Gorky who stood on the opposite side of the barricade."

and not what grew out of the objective conditions of society and its revolutionary crisis. In order to put into practice the revolutionary-" cultural," " rationally "-socialistic, and similar policies of Gorky, Sukhanov, and their brethren, it would have been necessary as a preliminary step to prepare in retorts and cucurbits the kind of a proletariat, and in fact of all other social classes, that would fit such policies. Since that had not been done, *Novaya Zhizn* remained a smart, or rather smartish, uselessness. . . .

By his whole makeup Gorky is not a revolutionist and not a politician. He is a culturist. To be sure, the cultural criterion is the broadest and commonest criterion of historical development, but it must be applied broadly. Taine figured out how many window-panes the French revolution had broken, and on the basis of these figures he condemned it utterly. That was a narrow-culturist, and in the last account a reactionary, approach. Having lowered temporarily the cultural level of the country, the Great Revolution of the eighteenth century prepared the gigantic cultural leap of the nineteenth century. Hence, from the cultural point of view, and not from that of a narrow-culturist criterion, the French revolution is completely vindicated. Of course, Gorky is broader, bolder, and mentally more magnanimous than Taine. But he stumbled more than once in his narrow-culturist approach to public events, the October revolution being one of them.

. . . . I recall having on a certain occasion dubbed him " culture's psalmodist," meaning to say thereby that in the capacity of an exceedingly Left socialistic psalmist he chanted in tune with the priests of liberalism who attacked the October revolution for the decline of culture [Trotsky refers to the Greek-Orthodox liturgy, in which the psalm-singer assists the officiating priest]. It goes without saying that this definition (" culture's psalmodist ") does not in the least exhaust Gorky, and it was used in a period of keen struggle against him. But in any event the definition underlines one very substantial trait of Gorky's mental image. It was that trait which separated us, despite my great fondness for Gorky and, I take it, Gorky's far from hostile feelings toward me.

The " insurrection " was finally staged, with the swiftness and ease of a comic opera. On November 4, the Petrograd regi-

ments voted to obey only the orders of the Military-Revolutionary Committee, Trotsky's child. On November 6, Kerensky declared his intention to sue in court those responsible for " the attempt to rouse the mob against the existing order." At the same time the Provisional Government summoned troops from outside the capital for its defence; actually only pupils of the military schools and the Woman Battalion appeared at the Winter Palace to express their loyalty to Kerensky. On the same day the Military-Revolutionary Committee issued orders to the soldiers, whose terse, unmistakably Trotskyist, style differed characteristically from the highfalutin' Napoleonic style of Kerensky's orders. Thus: " No hesitation or doubt. Firmness, steadiness, perserverance, determination. Long live the revolution." November 7 (October 25, O.S.) was the decisive day. At 2 A.M., the Military-Revolutionary Committee began to occupy public institutions and plants. At 4 A.M., Kerensky appealed to the cossack regiments " in the name of the motherland's liberty, honour, and glory to give aid to the revolutionary democracy and Provisional Government, and to save perishing Russia." The cossacks refused. At 10 A.M., the Committee declared: " The Provisional Government has been overthrown." Kerensky left for Gatchina, to make a last and futile attempt at mustering some cossack regiments to come to his help. At 2:35 P.M., Trotsky announced at the session of the Petrograd Soviet that " the Provisional Government no longer existed," and he aroused a wild enthusiasm when he disclosed the presence of Lenin and other erstwhile fugitive leaders. Lenin's speech was short: " Comrades, the workers' and peasants' revolution, whose need has been advocated all the time by the Bolsheviks, has been accomplished. A new phase is beginning in the history of Russia, and this third revolution shall in its final account lead to the victory of socialism. In Russia we must at once engage in the building up of a proletarian socialistic state. Long live the world socialistic revolution! "

Had anyone predicted at that time that the Bolshevik rule would last more than a few months at best, he would have been laughed at. Not even Lenin and Trotsky were confident that their *coup* would outlast the record of the Paris Commune.

Yes, said Trotsky, in effect, we shall have to go, but when we do, we shall bang the door so that the noise will reverberate for generations. It was difficult at that time to foresee that the Bolshevik rulers would prove plastic enough to endure longer than any contemporary political party in the world and in face of terrific odds, chiefly by virtue of their readiness for change and modification at the behest of the omnipotent dictator — life. More plausible seemed the supposition that the Bolshevik victory was an accident, an untoward episode due to the laxity of the Provisional Government, a temporary usurpation of power by a power-greedy band of nobodies who would shortly be swept out by organized common sense. Accordingly, no one took the Bolshevik " government " seriously, and no self-respecting party or individual thought of lending it support or co-operation any more than they would a snow man.

Novaya Zhizn, from the moment of the insurrection, took a tone of sharp opposition to the Bolsheviks. It referred to their government always in quotation marks, and prefaced the name of Lenin with the mocking " Citizen," instead of " Comrade." The editorials bore such lugubrious titles as " On the Verge of a Precipice," " The Breath of Death," " Demagogy of Impotence," " Madness " — the last one applied to the appointment as commander-in-chief of Sub-lieutenant Abram Krylenko (the present Commissar of Justice). At the same time the paper persistently harped on the need of " a united revolutionary front," and as late as November 11, it carried an appeal to this effect, addressed to " Workers, Soldiers, Peasants." For a time, indeed, the Bolsheviks themselves sought the co-operation of other socialist parties, and negotiated with their representatives. The unwillingness of Lenin to yield to these any important concessions as the price of co-operation and support, brought a temporary breach among his close associates: the ever vacillating Kamenev and Zinoviev, joined by Rykov, Milyutin, and Nogin, resigned from the Central Committee of the party. The last three resigned also as People's Commissars. Two other Commissars resigned. Their stand was supported by a number of prominent Bolsheviks, among them

Ryazanov and Larin. In the end Lenin admitted a few Left Socialist-Revolutionists as Commissars, and this strange union lasted till the Brest-Litovsk Treaty, after which the Bolsheviks were abandoned even by these dubious allies.

As for Gorky, his pen had never before been so venomous as in his attack against the triumphant Bolsheviks. He was outraged by the fact that as soon as they came to power they adopted against their opponents the same repressive measures from which they had so recently suffered themselves. His position was more awkward than ever. The ruling party had nothing but contempt for him and his associates, the " onefourth Bolsheviks," as Lenin called the *Novaya Zhizn* crowd. The non-Bolshevik intelligentsia, who had stigmatized Gorky as worse than a Bolshevik, because hiding " under the mask of culture," now held him responsible for the "national calamity." His former friends and protégés turned their backs on him, as on one stricken with the plague. Leonid Andreyev, who in his first autobiographical note avowed his indebtedness to Gorky, his " only faithful friend " who awakened in him " a real interest in literature and a realization of the importance and grave responsibility of a writer's mission "; whose acquaintance he regarded as " the greatest stroke of good fortune that could befall a writer," and so on, and so forth, was now repelled by the very name of Gorky. . . . In his diaries during and after the war Andreyev wrote in such an unreservedly negative vein concerning Gorky that Madame Andreyev has felt bound to refuse me the right to publish those passages.

Since he was held " responsible " for the advent of the Bolsheviks, he was constantly pestered with requests for intercession with his " friends." The recently unearthed diary of Zinaida Hippius for 1914–1918 has many bitter passages about Gorky. The wife of Merezhkovsky and spiritual sister of Filosofov, Madame Hippius voiced the views of the intellectual *élite* of Petrograd. They have always regarded Gorky as a *parvenu,* and his efforts in behalf of culture, redoubled after March, 1917, roused their contempt and apprehensions. In connexion with the activity of the " aesthete trio," as she called the committee of Gorky, Chaliapin, and Alexander

Benois, Zinaida Hippius wrote in her diary: " Yes, he [Gorky] is a sweet, gentle Hottentot, who has been presented with a silk hat and beads." When I spoke to Madame Hippius not long ago, before the discovery of her diary, she said apropos of Gorky: " We have always regarded him as a negro in a silk hat." Apparently this simile has been employed in that milieu consistently. In November, 1917, she jotted down some notes on a visit of Gorky to their friend X, during which he was asked to intercede for Konovalov and other ministers of Kerensky's cabinet, who were then in prison. One cannot vouch for the accuracy of the description (the lady was nervous and virulent), but it typifies the attitude of the intelligentsia to Gorky:

Gorky called on X. He produces a *terrible* impression. He seems all dark, black. . . . He talks as if he were barking. Poor Madame Konovalov felt quite depressed in his presence (she is a dear Frenchwoman, and her only offence in the eyes of Gorky is, perhaps, the fact that her husband is a " bourgeois and Kadet "). Altogether there was a stony atmosphere. He absolutely refuses to intercede for the ministers.

" I am . . . organically . . . unable . . . to talk to these . . . scoundrels. To Lenin and Trotsky."

He had just been talking of Lunacharsky (a contributor to *Novaya Zhizn;* as to Lenin — he was once quite a " comrade " of Gorky), so I suggested that he approach Lunacharsky on the subject. No use. He kept on returning to an article which he had already written . . . for *Novaya Zhizn,* for tomorrow's issue. To hell with articles! K. went to see Madame Konovalov home, and the heaviness became even denser. Dima [Filosofov] was on the point of leaving. . . . Then I pounced on Gorky. None of your articles, I said, in *Novaya Zhizn,* will place you apart from the Bolsheviks, the " scoundrels," as you call them; you must get away from that company. Aside from the " shadow " which falls on you because of your nearness to the Bolsheviks, what of your own self? I asked. What does your *own conscience* say?

He got up, barked something huskily:

" If I should . . . get away . . . to whom shall I go? "

Dmitri [Merezhkovsky] quickly retorted:

" If there is nothing to eat, should one eat human flesh? "

The article to which Hippius refers is probably the one in *Novaya Zhizn* for November 20. It deserves to be reproduced entire, for it sheds light both on Gorky's point of view and on the political moment:

The socialist ministers, freed by Lenin and Trotsky from the Peter and Paul Fortress, have gone to their homes, leaving their colleagues Bernatsky, Konovalov, Tereshchenko, and others, in the hands of people who have not the slightest conception of personal freedom, of the rights of man.

Lenin, Trotsky, and those with them, have already been poisoned by the corruptive virus of power, which is evident from their disgraceful treatment of the freedom of speech and person, and of all those rights for whose triumph democracy has struggled.

The blind fanatics and unconscionable adventurers are rushing headlong, supposedly on the road toward the " social revolution," but in reality on the road to anarchy, to the destruction of the proletariat and the revolution.

Along this road Lenin and his henchmen deem it right to commit every crime, such as the slaughter near Petrograd, the bombardment of Moscow, the abolition of the freedom of speech, senseless arrests — all the abominations once perpetrated by Plehve and Stolypin.

To be sure, Stolypin and Plehve acted against the democracy, against all that was live and decent in Russia, whereas Lenin is, for the time being, followed by a considerable portion of the workmen. But I am confident that the workmen's sense, their understanding of their historical tasks, will soon open their eyes to all the illusoriness of Lenin's promises, to all the depth of his madness, and to his Nechayev-Bakunin brand of anarchism.

The workmen cannot fail to understand that it is on their skins, on their blood, that Lenin is performing a certain experiment, that he is trying to raise the revolutionary mood of the proletariat to the extreme point and to see what may come out of that.

Of course, he does not believe in the possibility of a proletarian victory in Russia under present conditions, but perhaps he hopes for a miracle.

The workmen must know that there are no miracles in

real life, that they are to expect hunger, the complete disorganization of industry, the ruin of transportation, prolonged bloody anarchy, and in its wake — a not less bloody and gloomy reaction.

That is where the proletariat is being led by its present leader. It behooves us to realize that Lenin is not an omnipotent magician, but a cold-blooded trickster, who spares neither the honour nor the lives of the proletariat.

The workmen must not permit adventurers and madmen to heap on the heads of the proletariat shameful, senseless, and bloody crimes, for which not Lenin will pay, but the proletariat alone.

I ask:

Does the Russian democracy remember for the triumph of what ideas it has struggled against the despotism of the monarchy?

Does it regard itself capable of continuing this struggle even now?

Does it remember that when the Romanov police hurled its leaders into jails and hard-labour camps, it branded this fighting method as vile?

Wherein does the attitude of Lenin toward the freedom of speech differ from the similar attitude of Stolypin, Plehve, and other semi-humans?

Does not Lenin's government seize and cast into prison its opponents in the same way as the Romanov government had done?

Why are Bernatsky, Konovalov, and other members of the coalition government kept in the Fortress — are they in any way more criminal than their colleagues the Socialists, whom Lenin has set free?

The only honest answer to these questions must be an immediate demand for the release of the ministers and other innocent prisoners, and also for the full restoration of the freedom of speech.

Next, the sensible elements of the democracy must draw their further conclusions — they must decide whether the road of conspirators and Nechayevan anarchists is their road.

That was strong enough to please even a Zinaida Hippius; certainly no other publication still extant at that time had the

temerity to chastise the Bolshevik leaders in such outspoken terms. In his subsequent articles Gorky reiterated his comparison of these leaders with Nechayev, the quaintly unscrupulous revolutionist, sponsored for a while by Bakunin, who served as a prototype for Dostoyevsky's young Verkhovensky, in his *Demons* (or *Possessed*). Lenin, according to him, was introducing socialism " by Nechayev's method — ' full steam ahead across the bog.' " Both Lenin and Trotsky and their followers on the road to " destruction in the quagmires of reality " apparently agreed with Nechayev that " ' a Russian is most easily infatuated by the right to dishonour,' hence they were cold-bloodedly dishonouring the revolution, and dishonouring the working class by forcing it to perpetrate bloody massacres, by egging it on to outrages and arrests of innocent men. . . ." Gorky wrote with bitter contempt for those hesitators who, while abusing their leaders behind their backs and now deserting them, now rejoining them, ended up by " humbly serving the will of the dogmatists "; he probably had in mind Kamenev, Zinoviev, Lunacharsky, Ryazanov, and other " wobblies." He spoke of the Leninists as men who imagined themselves " Napoleons of socialism," and for whose destructive work " the Russian people will pay in oceans of blood." His characterization of Lenin is particularly worth noting, in view of their former, and subsequent friendship:

Lenin himself is, of course, a man of exceptional force. For twenty-five years he has stood in the front ranks of the fighters for the victory of socialism, he is one of the biggest and brightest figures in international Social-Democracy. A man of parts, he possesses all the qualities of a " leader," not excluding the indispensable quality of amoralism and of a purely aristocratic merciless attitude toward the lives of the common masses.

Lenin as a " leader " and Russian aristocrat (certain mental traits of this defunct class are not alien to him), deems himself in the right to perform over the Russian people a cruel experiment, doomed to failure in advance.

Exhausted and ruined by war, the people have already paid for that experiment with thousands of lives, and will now be made to pay with tens of thousands more. . . .

This inevitable tragedy does not embarrass Lenin, slave of his dogma, nor his sycophants — his slaves. Life, in all its complexity, is unknown to Lenin. He does not know the mass of the people, he has not lived with them; only from books has he learned how one can raise this mass on its haunches, and how one can most easily infuriate its instincts. The working class is for Lenin what ore is to the metallist. Is it possible, under the existing conditions, to cast a socialistic state out of this ore? Apparently, it is not possible; yet — why not try? What does Lenin risk, if the experiment should fail?

He is working as a chemist does in his laboratory, with the difference that the chemist employs dead matter with results valuable for life, whereas Lenin works over living material and leads the revolution to perdition. The thinking workmen who are following Lenin should realize that over the Russian working class is being performed a merciless experiment, which will destroy the best forces of the workmen, and will arrest for a long time the moral development of the Russian revolution.

Some of the things in this article may have been said in the heat of polemic, but essentially Gorky has not changed his estimate of Lenin, except that at one time he extolled the very traits which at another time he condemned. Lenin, it seems, took no notice of Gorky's attacks, but the minor Olympians began to feel restive under the stings of Gorky's lash. His vehement protests against the mistreatment of non-Bolsheviks and non-proletarians by the new rulers, gained him the label of a traitor to the cause of the people, one who " after serving democracy for twenty years " had finally " taken off his mask." To this Gorky replied that he " had never been blinded by the excellent qualities of the Russian people, had never genuflected before democracy, and had never regarded it as something so sacred as to preclude altogether criticism and condemnation." He reminded them that back in 1911, he wrote that it was just as wrong for a proletarian to boast of his class as for a noble to brag of his, and went on:

Now that a certain portion of the working masses, provoked by the demented masters of their will, are manifesting the spirit and methods of a caste, employing violence and terror, the very violence against which their best leaders and com-

rades had fought so valiantly and so long, now, it is plain, I cannot march in the ranks of this portion of the working class.

I think that to gag with one's fist the mouth of *Rech* and other bourgeois newspapers only because they are inimical to democracy, is disgraceful for democracy. Does the democracy feel that it is not right in its actions, and fears the criticism of its enemies? Are the Kadets so powerful in their ideas that one can defeat them only by means of physical violence? Deprivation of the freedom of the press is physical violence, and is unworthy of democracy.

To keep in jail the venerable revolutionist Burtsev, the man who has dealt the monarchy many a good blow, to keep him in jail only because he is carried away by his rôle of sewer-cleaner for our political parties, is disgraceful for democracy. . . .

To threaten with terrorism and massacres those who are unwilling to take part in Mr. Trotsky's mad dance over the ruins of Russia, is disgraceful and criminal.

Thus Gorky continued to play his customary rôle of challenging the powers that be in behalf of the oppressed. Under the tsar he raised his voice for the revolutionary and oppositional elements in general; under Kerensky he pleaded for tolerance toward both the survivors of the extreme Right and the hunted representatives of the extreme Left, notably the Bolshevik leaders; now, after November, it became his ungrateful task to exhort the erstwhile persecuted minority against mistreating their opponents, the very men who consistently slung mud at Gorky, and continued to do so in despite of his efforts in their behalf. That spiomaniac Burtsev, for example, who had accused Gorky of being a German agent and who has not ceased slandering him to this very day, became the object of Gorky's special anxiety. In the issue of *Novaya Zhizn* for November 27, Gorky had a conspicuously boxed paragraph to the effect that on the previous day there had elapsed thirty-five years since the first arrest of Burtsev by the tsar's police, and now this fighter for freedom, this " historical figure " was held prisoner by revolutionary Russia!

The Bolshevik *Pravda* took Gorky to task for " speaking the language of the workmen's enemies," for over-emphasizing the negative features of the new order, features which " are

inevitably connected with the breaking down of thousand-year-old form of government," and caustically queried: " When at the future bright festival of nations former involuntary enemies will merge in one brotherly impulse, will that peace banquet welcome Gorky, who has so hurriedly deserted the ranks of genuine revolutionary democracy? " Gorky replied rather sceptically to the last query: " It goes without saying that neither the author of that article nor I shall live to see the ' bright festival ' — it is too remote, and many decades of stubborn, workaday, cultural labour will be required for the creation of such a festival. As to a festival, at which the despotism of half-literate masses will celebrate its easy victory, while the human individual will remain oppressed as before, as ever — at such a ' festival ' I have nothing to do, and it is no festival to me."

A decade later life answered *Pravda's* question in its own way. Gorky returned to the land of the Soviets, a venerable sexagenarian, and received the enthusiastic homage of official Russia and the triumphant proletariat. The jubilarian was time and again moved to tears by the tokens of universal affection and admiration, and in his brief acknowledgements of speeches and greetings he had nothing but superlatives for the achievements of the Union of Soviets. He has been reclaimed by Bolshevik Russia, while the " bright festival of nations " still remains a remote dream. And Gorky? Has he changed his mind about the " despotism of half-literate masses "? Has he found the " human individual " less " oppressed " in Stalin's tsardom? Or has he learned to ignore politics, as a field alien to him, and is concentrating his interest on culture alone?

At any rate, as long as *Novaya Zhizn* was allowed to exist, its editors never relaxed their severe censure of Lenin's régime. " No matter in whose hands the government be," declared Gorky, " I maintain the human right to regard it critically." He admitted his misgivings about the Russian common people, " slaves of yesterday," being in a position to rule without displaying " unbridled despotism " in lording it over their fellow-men. These misgivings were, of course, interpreted by the Bol-

shevik press as a sign of Gorky's "betrayal" of the working class, of his having "sold himself to the Kadets." Gorky calmly reiterated what he had been saying and writing for many years, namely his faith in the industrial proletariat, as "an aristocracy amidst a democracy," whose rôle was to offset the backwardness of an overwhelmingly stagnant peasant country by serving as the vanguard of progress and culture, and helping the conquest of nature and its subjugation to man, Gorky's glorified Man. Because of this high estimate of the workmen he deplored their exploitation by the "Anarcho-Communists and fantasts," the Commissars for whom the Russian people served as "material for an experiment." This became Gorky's favourite theme, with such variations as this one: Russia is for the Commissars "the horse inoculated by bacteriologists with typhus, with a view to having the horse work out in its blood a serum against typhus. . . . It does not occur to them that the exhausted, half-starved wretch of a horse may give up its ghost." Again and again he would end his philippics with a warning to the workmen that they were misused by their leaders as "material for an inhuman experiment," and urged them to bethink seriously their attitude toward the government of the People's Commissars.

The year 1918 arrived, the Bolsheviks were not ousted, and their leaders continued to perpetrate deeds which outraged their opponents, and often shocked and vexed even their friends and sympathizers. Most conspicuous among these deeds were the dismissal of the Constituent Assembly and the signing of the Brest-Litovsk Treaty.

The Constituent Assembly had been one of the sacred shibboleths in the revolutionary movement of Russia, and one of the campaign slogans of the Bolsheviks was the immediate convocation of this body, for the determination of the will of the people in regard to the form of government and all important national problems. Indeed, shortly upon their coming into power they announced elections, and set the date for opening the Assembly, in January. The elections gave the majority to the Socialist-Revolutionists. When this became evident, Lenin resolved that "the sabbath was made

for man, and not man for the sabbath " — he knew how to quote his bible. Russia had already started out as a Soviet state, and no assembly could be allowed to impose its will on the recent victors in the fight for the Soviets. But what about the majority, the will of the people? Lenin was determined to set up a dictatorship of the advanced minority over the ignorant majority. Accordingly, he did not hesitate to disperse the Constituent Assembly shortly after it met and elected as president Chernov, leader of the Socialist-Revolutionist Centre. *Novaya Zhizn* had hoped that Lenin would not dare to raise his hand against the sacred symbol of the revolution, and his audacity aroused a storm of indignation in its editorials. When an attempted street manifestation in honour of the Assembly was suppressed by force of arms, Gorky wrote an article, in which he compared this January " massacre " with the Red Sunday of January, 1905. Nothing could have been more murderous than this analogy between the tsar's cossacks and the Bolshevik red soldiers and sailors.

The Brest-Litovsk Treaty with the Central Powers was branded by Lenin himself as " lewd." It was not only that by this treaty Russia lost enormous stretches of territory, rich in soil and minerals and well equipped with transportation facilities, and obliged itself besides to pay a large indemnity. The treaty had a universal significance, in that it enabled the Central Powers to withdraw their armies from the east and hurl them against the western front, and in that their occupation of the Ukraine promised vast supplies of food and raw material for their desperately indigent armies and civilians. Now that the passions have subsided, one may ask coolly whether Lenin could have acted differently. Tired of negotiating with the Soviet delegates, whose main purpose was to address over the heads of the diplomatists and generals the masses of Germany and Austria, the Central Powers presented Russia with an ultimatum, and invaded the country after the refusal of Trotsky's delegation to sign the treaty. The German troops, for whose sympathy with the non-resisting Soviets Trotsky had hoped in vain, marched inland, and swiftly moved toward the capital. The Russian army had been demoralized, long

before the Bolsheviks assumed authority; in fact, one may
say that its demoralization was the primal cause of the Bolshevik victory. From the revelations of Colonel Raymond
Robbins it is evident that Lenin and Trotsky made desperate
efforts, without success, to secure the military help of the
Allies for the repulsion of the advancing Germans. Lenin had
to choose between the romantic phrases of the hot-headed comrades who favoured war to the last breath against Germany,
and submission to the iron fist of the " lewd " treaty. He dismissed the former sentiment as " revolutionary cant," and
signed what turned out to be " a scrap of paper," in order to
obtain, as he said, " a breathing spell."

Novaya Zhizn commented on this event in an editorial under the heading " A Disgraceful Finale," in which it said, among
other things: " We are facing a band of adventurers who, for
the sake of their personal interests, for the sake of prolong-
ing, if only for a few weeks, the agony of their perishing autocracy, are ready for anything. They are ready for the most
shameful betrayal of the interests of the country and the revolution, the interests of socialism, the interests of the unfortunate Russian proletariat, in whose name they are committing
their infamies on the vacant throne of the Romanovs, preparing
for their truster a horrible Golgotha." The next day, a signed
article by Sukhanov stated that " the surrender of the Council
of Commissars is a disgraceful suicide of the Russian revolution and a betrayal of the cause of the international proletariat." This resulted in the suspension of *Novaya Zhizn* for
eight days, curiously enough by the order of a Left Socialist-
Revolutionist, that is a member of the party which shortly broke
with the Bolsheviks because of the Brest-Litovsk Treaty. At
first the editors were requested to publish a statement of their
disagreement with Sukhanov's view, but when they refused to
do so, a permit to resume the publication of the paper was
issued all the same by the Authorities. Soviet censorship was
still comparatively lax. Under the Stalin régime, with all opposition even within the party ruthlessly crushed, such laxity
would be unthinkable. While Lenin was alive, he suffered opposition " within the family," extending this term far enough

to include even *Novaya Zhizn*. One may recall that simultaneously with Bazarov and Sukhanov, such Bolsheviks as Radek and Bukharin viciously attacked Lenin's policy in Party press and conferences. Incidentally, Bukharin, who later fell into disfavour with Stalin because of his leanings to the Right, was at that time the spokesman for the Left wing, and accused Lenin of deviating from Communism in the direction of State Capitalism. It was in the spring of 1918, anticipating the introduction of NEP by three years, that Lenin mildly retorted to Bukharin: " But State Capitalism is an enormous step forward, and should we succeed in promulgating it, it would mean a gigantic victory! "

But though tolerated, *Novaya Zhizn* was regarded with suspicion and hostility. There can hardly be any doubt that the name of Gorky condoned many sins, and that only his revolutionary past and his popularity with the masses saved the paper from the fate of other non-Bolshevik publications. Yet Gorky's own utterances were so outspokenly bitter against the new masters of the land, that he generated a growing antagonism among the Bolsheviks. The satrap of Petrograd, Zinoviev, possessing none of the bigness of Lenin whom he followed when the risk of doing so was lowest, made use of his position to degrade Gorky in the eyes of the masses. He accused him of supplying grist to the mill of the bourgeoisie through his attacks against the Bolsheviks, and challenged him to a public debate. Gorky wrote in reply: " I am unable to meet Mr. Zinoviev's request. I am no orator, I dislike public appearances, and am not sufficiently adroit to vie in eloquence with professional demagogues. . . . Mr. Zinoviev asserts that in condemning acts of cruelty, coarseness, and the like, committed by the people, I am ' tickling the heels of the bourgeoisie.' This is a coarse and stupid trick, but nothing else could be expected from Zinovievs. It is too bad, however, that he failed to mention before the workmen that when condemning some of their actions I constantly tell them that the workmen are being corrupted by such demagogues as Zinoviev. . . ." The fight between Zinoviev and Gorky was quite unequal, considering the fact that the all-powerful administrator addressed

immense crowds, of which only a very small portion could read
what Gorky had to say in his reputedly treacherous paper. As
a result, Gorky received a number of crude letters from groups
of workers and sailors, in which he was warned to " lay off "
criticizing the Authorities, otherwise they would " close up "
his journal. Such demands provoked even more truculent criticism from the pen of Gorky. It came to pass that on several
occasions the type-setters refused to print certain articles in
Novaya Zhizn, as inimical to the Government, and the paper
did not come out, or was printed in a very limited number, or
appeared in a considerably reduced size. The position of Gorky,
a son of the masses who was now treated by the masses as an
enemy, was becoming grotesque. He stubbornly kept up the
struggle and declared that " the men working on *Novaya Zhizn*
had fought the autocracy of scoundrels and crooks not for the
sake of seeing it replaced by an autocracy of savages." The
central organ of the Bolshevik party, *Pravda,* did not scruple
about insinuating suspicions concerning the financial sources
of *Novaya Zhizn.* Conceptions of decency in polemics were
reduced to a rather low level, if Gorky was constrained to make
a detailed statement as to paper's resources. After naming
E. Grubbe as the man who had loaned him 275,000 rubles at
the outset, and adding that he had put into the paper also part
of the honorarium for his collected works published by *Niva*
(Field), he went on to inform the *Pravda* crowd: " During
the years 1901–1917, hundreds of thousands of rubles passed
through my hands for the cause of the Social-Democratic Party.
My own share amounted to tens of thousands of rubles, but
the greater part came from the pockets of the ' bourgeoisie.'
Iskra [the central organ of the party] was published with the
money of Savva Morozov, who naturally gave the money not
as a loan, but as a donation. Your calumnious and filthy sallies
against *Novaya Zhizn* disgrace not my paper, but yourselves."

The inevitable finally happened. Soviet Russia was facing
a hostile world from the outside and numerous attempts at
exploding the new order from the inside. Abandoned and opposed by every party and faction, the Bolsheviks faced complete isolation, at home and abroad, and they decided to meet

the issue squarely. The issue amounted to war against all and everything. Outnumbered by their adversaries, the Bolsheviks nevertheless accepted the challenge. The country was set on a war basis, with the screws of the dictatorship tightened to the last degree. The vestiges of democratic privileges were wiped out, and chief among these was freedom of opinion, a privilege which, by the way, has not been restored as yet by the Bolsheviks, since they still regard themselves in a state of war with the rest of humanity. Under those circumstances, coupled with shortage of paper and electric power and the frequent sabotage of the type-setters, *Novaya Zhizn* finally gave up its ghost.

One cannot but surmise that Gorky felt relieved when the protracted agony of his journal was thus terminated. For almost one year and a half he had lent his name and responsibility to an undertaking, which on the whole was more irksome than pleasurable to him. A sense of chivalry, as we have noted, kept him at the helm, and indeed, but for him the good ship of *Novaya Zhizn* would have been sunk much sooner, for neither Kerensky nor Lenin would have suffered its mordant pugnacity. His anxieties connected with the paper interfered both with his literary work and with his cultural activities in general. With the suspension of the paper, Gorky's remaining years in Russia were given entirely to the non-political task of rescuing, preserving, and fostering whatever cultural values Russia possessed.

RESCUING CULTURAL VALUES

GORKY faced a gigantic task, and a delicate one at that, even though it was non-political. Regarding lack of culture as the source of all Russia's evils, he now set to work on what seemed a virginal field. The upper layer of society, the intelligentsia, those who formed the resplendent veneer of Russia, receded into the background after November, 1917, perforce or through voluntary boycott and sabotage. The great masses of the people, now for the first time commanding the concern of the ruling class, were prevailingly backward, illiterate, indolent, and unfamiliar with the most elementary features of western civilization. Gorky headed a number of organizations of multifarious cultural purposes, not the least of these being adult education; the thirst for knowledge among adults become so prodigious after the revolution that it taxed all the available cultivated men and women in trying to supply the demand.

The untutored masses, on coming into power, naturally reacted with hatred to whatever reminded them of the former ruling classes. Untiringly Gorky pleaded for the preservation and care of extant monuments and art treasures, reiterating in plain words the ABC argument that though these things had belonged to their oppressors, they were now the property of the people. Especially arduous became his task under the Bolsheviks, when the confiscation and nationalization of private collections and valuables demanded organized supervision, not so much against peculation as against vandalism, both wilful and unintentional. Bakunin believed that " *Die Lust der Zerstörung ist eine schaffende Lust* "; he was an aristocrat, and

saw the common people through the mist of idealization. Gorky knew his people intimately, and while he observed their charming, poetic, kindly traits, he was also aware of the beast lurking behind their childlike naïveté. It was no surprise for him to learn of precious libraries and archives destroyed by the masses, as paper for their cigarettes and for worse uses. The need of guarding the national treasures was brought home to him again and again by such personal observations as this:

In 1919, a conference of " poor villagers " was held in Petrograd. Several thousand peasants from the northern provinces of Russia arrived, and hundreds of them were quartered at the Winter Palace of the Romanovs. After the conference was over and these men had gone, it transpired that they had polluted not only all the bathtubs of the palace, but also an enormous quantity of most precious vases — Sèvres, Saxon, and Oriental — employing them as bed-chambers. That was done not from necessity — the palace lavatories proved to be in good order and the plumbing functioned properly. No, this hooliganism was the expression of a desire to spoil, to sully beautiful things. During the two revolutions and the war I have observed hundreds of times this dark, vindictive yearning of people to break, mutilate, mock, and vilify the beautiful.

More difficult than any of these phases of Gorky's activity was that of caring for the human material among the cultural values of Russia. No longer engaged in political faultfinding, Gorky was welcomed by the Bolsheviks as a worker along intellectual and artistic lines. His co-operation, however limited, was a matter of boastful pride to them. But he met grave obstacles when he championed not monuments or books or paintings or cathedrals, but living scientists, poets, and playwrights, if these did not happen to be Bolsheviks. The intelligentsia, in the early years of the Bolshevik régime, were a stench in the nostrils of the masses, both because for a long time a considerable portion of the intellectuals practised sabotage against the new order, and also because they filled the ranks of the interventionists. The finger of blame was pointed at them for the national calamities and vicissitudes — for the reduction of the former empire to a small inland state sur-

rounded by glowering enemies, for Clemenceau's "sanitary
cordon," the blockade that aimed at starving the Soviets into
submission, for the armies that invaded Russian territory at
every frontier and thus shattered Lenin's hope for a " breathing spell," for the shot fired at Lenin by a Socialist-Revolutionist, for the shortage of food and all commodities. It was
therefore extremely awkward to intercede in behalf of these
men, suspected, and often justly, of hostility toward the régime.

The plight of the intellectuals during the years before the
introduction of the NEP was indescribably more dreadful
than that of other citizens in the Soviet republic. To be sure,
all classes suffered from wars of intervention, civil wars and
their concomitant atrocities and devastation, from the disorganization of transport, the practical standstill of industry,
the undercultivation of the soil, and the resultant hunger in
the cities. In what modern terms can be estimated such a privation as the necessity of undergoing surgical operations, on the
part of wounded soldiers, women and children, without any
anaesthetics, owing to the will of civilized Christendom that no
quinine or other medicaments shall enter the land of the im-
pious Bolsheviks? Yet it is even more difficult to plumb the
sufferings of the men of liberal professions, which were not only
material and physical but also mental and spiritual. The
composer Glazunov, pale, emaciated, and ragged, begged
H. G. Wells, on the latter's flying visit to Russia, for help from
the West; he did not ask for food or clothes, though he needed
both direly, but he implored for paper, on which he might
write down his compositions. One could understand that. But
how about the grievance of the great physiologist, Ivan Pavlov?
Not that he had to perform his laboratory experiments in a
room without heat or electricity, dressed in furs — coat, cap,
and gloves. Nor even that he had to tend to his own little patch
of potatoes and guard it carefully from greedy colleagues who
might be tempted to fill their sunken stomachs with Pavlov's
delicacy and thus deprive him of his only sustenance. His only
complaint was that his precious time had to be wasted on
janitor duties. One must recall that in those days of absolute
equality every citizen had to work, and no work but manual

was acceptable in the eyes of those " who had been nothing and had become everything " (the words of the Russian " International "). As late as in August, 1920, one could read an announcement on the walls of the Academy of Sciences to the effect that every employé whether scientist or doorman, was to take turns in watching for six hours at a stretch the firewood stacked on the pavement in front of the Academy. Let one try to imagine the bitterness of Zinaida Hippius as she recorded in her diary (the *Black Book*) of having taken her turn of standing guard in the street for three hours. It was the time when the Bolsheviks expected a raid on Petrograd from the Whites. And Hippius awaited the coming of the Whites as of saviours!

Here is a characteristic entry by Zinaida Hippius:

Dima [Filosofov] was, after all, conscripted into forced (" social ") labour. Tomorrow at 6 A.M. — to haul beams.

It wasn't beams at all. Unhappy Dima did not get back home today till 4 P.M., soaking-wet literally to his knees. He is so emaciated, weak, terrible, that one can hardly take heart to look at him. Although he occupies quite a prominent position at the Public Library, he spends more time in watching wood-laden barges on the Canal than in work with books. Watching wood is part of his service.

This morning he was driven far outside of the city, along the Irina Road, with a company of other conscripts, to dig trenches. Horrible weather, thawing, slush, wet snow.

While I was pulling off Dima's boots and rubbing his legs with a brush, he narrated how they were gathered up, how they were driven. . . .

At the appointed place they gave him a pickax. Shocking, unnecessary, and fruitless. Everyone knew that it was compulsory needlessness (I recall Dostoyevsky's *Dead House*, his observation that the most depressing thing about convict labour was the awareness that one's labour was of no use. Here it is even worse: the *repulsiveness* of this needless work).

No one had dug anything, and no one in fact saw to it that they should dig, that any trenches should be made. Frankest mockery.

After many hours of standing in the water of thawing snow,

the " convicts " were allowed to receive, with lengthy cere-
monies, one pound of bread apiece from the stout, well-fed
taskmaster. . . . Dima has brought home this black bread,
bristling with straw.

Assyrian slavery. But no, neither Assyrian slavery, nor Siberian hard labour, but something quite unexampled. Half-
naked men, reeling from hunger, are driven together for heavy,
needless toil, driven in snow, rain, cold, darkness. . . . Have
such things happened before?

The intellectuals thus, in addition to the general suffering,
had to bear the cross of moral and mental humiliation, and of
being treated with, sometimes well-founded, suspicion, as enemies of the new order. No wonder that the number of " brain
workers " who perished during those trying years exceeded by
five or six times the number of victims from the average citizenry, endowed with a tougher hide, with a greater power of
resistance. In 1919 alone, the Academy of sciences recorded the
death of nearly fifty members; there must have been many
more of whose whereabouts the Academy had no information.
Allowing for natural causes of death from old age, there was
still a staggering number of known deaths among Academicians
" from lack of nourishment " and " physical over-exertion "
(*Report* of the Academy). Every branch of mental activity
suffered great and premature losses. How little the new rulers
understood the value of intellectual workers, can be seen from
the obvious truths which Gorky found himself constrained to
emphasize at that time for the benefit of the " lowbrows." In
a paper under the title *What Is Science?* he stressed such
points as these:

The basic wealth of a country consists of the amount of
brains, the number of intellectual forces nurtured and accumulated by the nation. . . . It is extremely important that the
people possess a sufficient quantity of scientific workers, and
that the lives of these men be not wasted without sense. . . .
If we compel a skilful metal engraver to clean cesspools, if a
goldsmith is made to forge anchors, and a chemist is driven to
dig trenches, we are guilty not only of stupidity but also of a
crime. . . . One must realize that the labour of a scholar is

the possession of all humanity, and that science is the realm of the highest disinterestedness. Scientific workers must be valued as the nation's most productive and precious energy, and it is therefore necessary to create such conditions, under which the growth of this energy might be facilitated in every way. The premature invalidation or death of a scholar is an enormous loss for the country, and this should be particularly clear to a government of workmen. . . . Herein is published the list of scholars who died within the last few months; you will note how great is the loss of scientific energy in our land. If this process of the dying out of scholars will continue at such speed, our country may be completely deprived of its brains. . . . In these difficult days the life of a scientist is terrible in its physical conditions and is morally tormenting, since it is painful for one who feels capable of raising a mountain to be deprived of the possibility to lift even a handful of sand. When such a disgraceful obstacle as the lack of light for work, as cold and hunger, stands in the way of a great scientific invention which might enrich the country and give happiness to its masses of people, then it is criminal. For in that very fact one feels the want of understanding the deep significance and indubitable usefulness of creative scientific endeavour.

Today Soviet scientists assert that never before has scientific research been so lavishly supported and encouraged by the State as it is now. It was obviously different in the early years of the present order. The more astonishing and admirable appears the fact that in face of all those odds Russian intellectuals, in their majority, did not lose their creative urge. In face of utter isolation (attempts at re-establishing relations with Western intellectuals proved futile), of excruciating privations, of painfully humiliating lack of sympathy and confidence on the part of the ruling class, the Russian brain workers persevered in producing results in laboratory and field, in exploration and invention, in musical and literary composition. What nerve it required, to cite one illustration, to write down treatises or novels on scraps of wrapping paper, or on the reverse of old manuscripts, with no chance of publication, in view of the shortage of printing material and facilities! Picture those literary soirées in Petrograd and Moscow, where

the foremost writers, finding no way to see their work in print and yet unable to remain silent, read from fantastic bits of paper their prose and verse to immense audiences hungry not for bread alone.

Perhaps the following poem by Anna Radlova may give an idea of the contemporary mood among those who, unlike Zinaida Hippius, did not merely stew in their own gall:

AUTUMN 1919

Surely there are lemon groves somewhere,
Winters plentiful of nascent grain,
Violet skies unbearably hot,
Genial thousand-year relics of saints in lacy cathedrals.
And men strut there, golden empty bells in their breasts.
Lord, Thou art most just of all judges,
Why, then, hast ordained our life so dark and mean,
With no easy roads but the road to Thy beyond?
Why have we no flowers, nor wine, nor bread,
The skies over us a rearing black lid?
Answers God: " More intoxicating than wine,
Hotter than fire, more secretive than earth, deeper than water,
More consoling than sleep,
Sweeter than all earthly fruits —
There has been given unto you Love,
Warm and salty as blood."

(tr. by A. K.)

Gorky's efforts to alleviate the lot of the intelligentsia were not confined to the writing of exhortations. He succeeded in obtaining the Government's sanction and support of the Commission for the Improvement of the Conditions of Scholars, which managed to issue special food rations for mental workers, and to organize a Scholars' Home with dormitories and lecture halls, also sanatoria and summer resorts. A few shops were opened for the specific purpose of supplying these men with shoes, linen, and clothes. Under similar conditions a Writers' Home was established, and a Home of the Arts. The Authorities, however, were more wary concerning the members of these Homes than those of the Scholars' Home, and accord-

ingly more restrictive about their privileges. For the members of his own profession Gorky was able to do more. He was authorized to publish at the expense of the state a series of *World Literature,* which were to include masterpieces of all times and lands for distribution among the people. It was a grandiose undertaking, and as its head, Gorky rejoiced at the opportunity of helping his fellow-writers, by compensating them for translations from foreign languages and the work of editing these.

Korney Chukovsky, a brilliant critic and educator, translator of Kipling, Walt Whitman, and others, recalls some interesting bits from his contact with Gorky in those days:

We writers met Gorky quite often at the time, for it somehow came to pass that Gorky had become the unofficial president of all Petrograd authors. He was the head of *World Literature,* Home of the Arts, Section of Historical Paintings, Union of Workers of the Verbal Arts, and so on, and so on, and so on. He not only presided at all our " Commissions," but had taken upon his shoulders all our troubles and needs, so that if one of us had a baby born, Gorky obtained a nipple, if one fell sick with typhus, he interceded for getting for him a place in the hospital, and if one wished to go to the country for a while, he wrote letters to various institutions for permits to use the Sestroretsk resort.

I think that if one should collect all the letters written by Gorky to various institutions in behalf of Russian writers, there would accrue a goodly five or six volumes: in those days Gorky wrote no novels or stories — only these endless letters.

. . . Once a poetess called on him. After she left, he remarked: " The devil alone can understand them! They have no firewood, no light, no bread, yet they go on as though everything was as usual." It appeared that a few days ago the poetess had given birth to a child. Gorky got busy, and she received a permit: " Milkwoman so and so is hereby authorized to deliver milk to the wife of Maxim Gorky, so and so " — the name of the poetess was given.

. . . On another occasion I told him that a considerable food-ration was coming to him for a lecture he gave at the Murmansk Railroad Club. He asked me whether the ration

might not be transferred to a certain woman translator, who was in great need. " How shall we designate her relation to you? " " Put her down as my sister."

Gorky had an enormous family of adopted wives, sisters, and sons. Zinovy Sverdlov was not an exceptional case. S. Marshak recalls that as an ailing boy he was enabled to attend the Yalta gymnasia, in Crimea, through the efforts of Gorky. " There goes Maxim Gorky's son," people pointed at him, and he adds that the number of such " sons " was considerable.

Chukovsky goes on to say:

We must definitely admit that if we survived those bread-less, typhoidal years, we owe it in a large measure to our " kin-ship " with Maxim Gorky, to whom all of us, great and small, became in those days a kindred family. I often chanced to see Gorky intercede for authors who had viciously baited him before the revolution.

Chukovsky fails to add that many of these proceeded even more viciously to sling mud at Gorky as soon as they crossed the border of Soviet Russia.

Such measures as Gorky managed to undertake for the needy intelligentsia brought some help, to be sure, but in a hardly perceptible degree. The general want was mounting with the passing of months and the tightening of the blockade. Gorky issued an appeal to the intellectuals of the world, and although the war fumes of hatred and callousness had not been dispersed as yet, his voice did not remain unanswered. Not inconsiderable funds were gathered in the United States by the society of " Friends of Gorky," and even in starving Germany Gerhardt Hauptmann organized some help for Russia's intellectuals. Gorky caused a breach in the international blockade of his country.

How he took to heart the suffering of Russia's scholars! In the summer of 1925, an American novelist once accompanied me to afternoon tea at Gorky's villa, in Sorrento. In his study Gorky showed me a letter from R. L. Dana, concerning the " Friends of Gorky " relief fund. This brought to his memory

the dreadful Petrograd days, and he gave a few graphic details of those experiences with such emotional force that the eyes of my American companion filled with tears, though he understood not a word of Gorky's Russian. Here are some of his phrases as I jotted them down at the time:

In 1920 we hungered terribly. More than one hundred scholars died from lack of nourishment. You can hardly realize what it means to starve for fats and sweets. With the first American relief money — one thousand dollars! — we sent an expedition to Central Asia for sweets. A case of pressed peaches arrived. It was opened. There they stood — old men, scientists, international celebrities, their trembling hands instinctively stretched out for the delicacy, their eyes burning with greed. . . . Yes, the organism felt the need of sugar. I recall Professor Hvolson lecturing on Einstein, clinging with his hands to the pulpit, and swaying to and fro, as if he were on the deck of a steamer on a stormy sea. In those days it was an effort to rise, or to stand up straight. Yes, it was pretty hard. There, I can see Sergy Oldenburg, Permanent Secretary of the Academy of Sciences, flaunting his felt boots — a luxury. And there, in the Scholars' Home, I see Professor Shimkevich, Rector of the Petrograd University; he is huddled up in a corner with a bowl of some gruel or other, he devours his food avidly, his eyes travelling about the room like those of a baby afraid lest someone take away its goody.

Did the intelligentsia appreciate Gorky's efforts? Not all of them. I have heard Petrograd professors and writers speak with profound gratitude of what Gorky had done for them and many others. But most of the *émigrés* spit venom at the very mention of Gorky's name. Prominent writers whom I approached on the question refused to discuss it, and hastened to change the subject. During Russia's trials those writers were either abroad, or taking a more or less active part in the White movement, in the armies of Denikin, or Yudenich, or Wrangel. Their prevailing attitude toward Gorky found expression in the pamphlet of Yevgeny Chirikov, *The Smerdyakov of the Russian Revolution,* in which he compares Gorky to that nauseating lackey in Dostoyevsky's *Brothers Karamazov.* Chirikov, like

Kuprin, Bunin, Shmelev and other present day Bolsheviko-phobes, once belonged to the group of the *Znaniye* publishing house, of which Gorky had been the actual head. In this pamphlet Chirikov endeavoured to rob Gorky even of his past glory, recalling such sins of his as coarseness, conceit, ingratitude for the intelligentsia, who helped him rise from the " bottom " to the heights of Russian literature, and alleging that as head of the *Znaniye* he virtually robbed his fellow-writers of their profits. His main point of accusation, however, was Gorky's subservience to Lenin, and his unprincipled and unscrupulous change of policy from that of a prosecutor of Bolshevism to that of its champion. Chirikov ascribed to Gorky most base and selfish motives, in explanation of his stand, and concluded his pamphlet with pathetic vehemence:

. . . the rôle of Gorky, an infamous, humiliating, and criminal rôle, the rôle at one and the same time of a Cain, Judas, and Pilate toward his own people. Once you are with assassins, you are an assassin yourself; once you are with traitors, you too are a traitor! You have helped to betray, you have helped to kill, and then you took the part of the judge of your motherland, Pilate-like washing your hands. . . .

For us you remain, when all is said, the Cain, Judas, Pilate of the Russian people, the Smerdyakov of the Russian revolution, who has sold his conscience!

The fact that in the latter part of 1918 Gorky abandoned his warfare against the Bolsheviks, and plunged head and soul into co-operation with them in the field of enlightenment, was sufficient in the eyes of the intransigeant intelligentsia to brand him with the mark of the devil. To them anyone who stooped to work with the Bolsheviks was a traitor. Valery Bryusov, who after November dedicated his brilliant poetic gift and his extraordinary erudition to educational work, had " sold himself." The seventy-five-year-old A. F. Koni, member of the Imperial Senate, volunteered to read lectures for the Red Army; consequently he " sold himself for groats " (Hippius). The same simple explanation was applied to the reported " surrender " of Alexander Blok, Andrey Bely, Alexey Tolstoy, and

other prominent men. Yet no one was vilified so eagerly and so abundantly as Maxim Gorky. A collection of the fantastic gossip about his offences against decency at that time would make a sensational " best seller." Nicholas Roerich, the celebrated painter, told me some of the hair-raising things that were circulating about Gorky at that time, and he assured me that though obviously mythical they were asserted by people for whose integrity under normal circumstances Roerich would not hesitate to vouch. One must visualize the nerve-racking atmosphere of Petrograd during those years to understand the virulence and credulity of such exemplars of intellectual aristocracism as Merezhkovsky and Hippius, for example. They readily picked up and repeated every bit of gossip and slander that reached their ears in the dilapidated, feverish city, where starving people wandered like shadows over broken pavements, tearing down fences and deserted houses — for fuel, or surreptitiously selling heirlooms in the market-place, and always sniffing the air for rumours of approaching deliverers, Yudenichs' troops or British torpedo-boats. In that poisonous environment, a shifting of values imperceptibly took place, one additional eighth of a pound of *Ersatz* black bread superseding all other interests in the most fastidious minds, and mutual relations reverting to the stage when *homo homini lupus erat.*

The diary of Zinaida Hippius is instructive precisely because it reflects the morbid state of mind of the intelligentsia at that time. It is hardly conceivable that this keen, clever, urbane, and discriminating author would normally entertain such notions as she jotted down furtively and hurriedly in dreary Petrograd, fearful of detection by prowling Bolsheviks, yet unable to keep her malice and hatred unuttered. Gorky appears there melodramatically villainous. We are told, for example, of his relations with a certain I. I., the initials obviously suggesting Dr. I. I. Manukhin, whose X-ray treatment saved Gorky from death, back in 1913. I. I. lives in the same building with the Merezhkovsky family, and shares their conditions of hunger and cold and darkness and subjection to Bolshevik searching raids at all unearthly hours. His brother

is arrested, and I. I. calls on Gorky, to plead for his intercession. He happens to come during dinner-time. Hippius has I. I.
say to her: " They did not invite me to join, and anyway, I
should not have consented for anything in the world to take
a piece of Gorky's food into my mouth. But I admit, I was
hungry, and felt quite disagreeable: there were cutlets, and
fresh cucumbers, and huckleberry pudding. . . ." I. I., like the
Merezhkovskys, has not seen for months any other food than
stale gruel and watery soup. Hippius goes on: " Poor I. I., who
once *literally saved Gorky from death!* For that he is now allowed to watch Gorky dine. Only this, because to his request
concerning his brother Gorky said: ' I am sick and tired of
you. Well, let them shoot your brother.' "

This sounds incredible, in view of Gorky's proverbial hospitality. His house has always been open, and his table ever at
the disposal of casual visitors, whether it was in Nizhni Novgorod, or Petrograd, or Sorrento, in days of opulence or in
time of famine. Of Dr. Manukhin he speaks to this day with
admiration and affection. Zinaida Hippius has been uncon-
sciously, let us believe, affected by the gossip in intelligentsia
circles about Gorky's " high life " amid the ruins of Petrograd.
Baroness Marie Budberg, who has since become Gorky's
secretary, gave me enough details for the visualization of that
" high life." His apartment was so cold that they were all
huddled in one room which they managed somehow to heat
from time to time. Semi-starvation was the rule, except for occasional gifts of food that were brought from the country by
personal friends. Gorky was constantly besieged by petitioners
of the most bewildering variety, from a professor requesting
a requisition note for a pair of spectacles, to the poetess
Grushko who wanted a ration of milk for her baby. Valentina
Hodasevich, who painted one of Gorky's best portraits, recounted to me some of the requests that came to him, personally
and by mail, in which tragedy mingled with comedy. For not
only did relatives plead for invariably innocent prisoners of the
Cheka, and mothers for milk or medicine for their babies,
and professors for spectacles or boots, but, according to Hodasevich, there were urgent demands for an adequate treatise

on the Immaculate Conception, and for advice as to the efficacy of certain medical prescriptions, and — from remote Siberia — as to the reliability of such and such an astronomer. Korney Chukovsky tells us that two days after his fiftieth birthday Gorky received a letter from a prisoner: " Dear writer, will there be no amnesty on the occasion of your saint's day? I am in jail for the murder of my wife on the fifth day after our wedding, because . . . . (here followed very intimate details). So can't you have an amnesty arranged for me? " In 1920, a total stranger wired Gorky that at the station of Kilyayevo he had been robbed of two pairs of trousers and sixteen thousand rubles: what was Gorky going to do about it? Among the pleaders for his intercession there came a lady who, Gorky recalls, had on her body about four pounds of silver and two pounds of gold, and was asking help for her two husbands who had been jailed " by mistake." Gorky promised to inquire about the two unfortunates, whereupon the lady demanded to know how much he was going to charge her for his intercession. " Aren't we humourists? " queried Gorky, when he concluded the story.

Apropos of the comical side of that period, Gorky described to me one scene in his inimitable way, which, alas, cannot be reproduced from my bare jottings, minus his mimicry, impersonation, and apt vocabulary.

There were always [he said, in effect] twenty-five to thirty people at our table, in Petrograd. One evening a squad of Red soldiers broke in, searching for bombs. The soldiers were hungry. So were we all, had been so for some time. But it so happened that at eight o'clock on that evening a chap brought us a wonderful gift: potatoes, beets, three lake whitefish, and a goodly slab of bacon. At midnight, Olga Fomishna (our German cook) brought the whole business in a gigantic pan, and put it on the table. We had been wrangling with the soldiers over the silly matter of looking for bombs at my residence, but at the sight of the pan they became speechless. Their eyes fairly popped out, and their mouths drooled. " Sit down, boys! " They did, even their leader. A little vaudeville!

All the time there was a mingling of tragedy with vaudeville.

The number of people for whom Gorky interceded with local and central authorities was not recorded. It is known, however, that both official Petrograd and Moscow lost all patience with Gorky and spoke mockingly of his unrevolutionary softness. The time was not propitious for humanitarian sentiments. Gorky was aware of this, yet he proceeded to show his " softness " untiringly, at the cost of his popularity with the ruling party, and to the detriment of his health. Baroness Budberg told me of a case, when Gorky, in pleading with Lenin for some destitute scholars, lost his calm, began to shout at Lenin, and then swooned: " he nearly died from heart failure." When I asked Gorky about that scene, he growled into his moustachios: " Yes, it did come to shouting and banging on the table. Our faces were flushed." On another occasion Gorky tried to save four arrested Grand Dukes from execution by the Petrograd Cheka. He repeatedly communicated with Lenin by long-distance telephone, and finally got his consent to release the prisoners on Gorky's pledge. To avoid red tape procrastination, Gorky went to Moscow, obtained Lenin's signed order, and immediately returned to Petrograd. Just before reaching the last station, he learned that during the night the Grand Dukes had been shot by the order of Zinoviev. Gorky told me that when Lenin was informed of this precipitous execution, " he had a veritable fit, rolled on the floor and howled."

It was unpleasant enough to bargain and haggle with the small and big dictators, but when such an ordeal proved fruitless, the pain was acute. For months and months Gorky implored the Authorities to issue a permit for Alexander Blok to go abroad for treatment in a sanitarium. Blok, perhaps the greatest Russian poet since Pushkin, was suffering from acute scurvy and an ailing heart, but according to Gorky, his main trouble was that " he had lost his will to live." A change of environment and a proper régime might have saved him. At last the permit arrived. It was too late. Alexander Blok had died on the previous night.

The physical and mental exertion weighed heavily on Gorky. His heart troubled him, his old enemy, tuberculosis of the lungs, raised its head, and the wretched and insufficient food

resulted in scurvy; he almost lost his teeth. The " little vaudeville " demanded a high fee. I have put down a bit of reminiscence, as Gorky boomed it in a muffled basso, his eyes musing
deep in their sockets:

Morning. Scurvy, your teeth are loose, you hate to get up.
You come down into the dining-room, and find two or three
dozen complainers, cold and hungry people. You go outdoors,
hardly able to drag your feet. You call at the Scholars' Home,
or at the Commission of Experts on Art Treasures. Things are
stolen; sailors destroy works of art. Sick at heart you leave
the place, perch on a curb, and remain there for half an hour,
forty minutes. . . . Only to stay away from the damnable
mess.

" High life," indeed.

Gorky's activity in connexion with the *World Literature*
publications did not find favour in the eyes of the irreconcilables. Some of Zinaida Hippius' most venomous lines deal
with this " charity, the copper penny donated by Gorky to
Merezhkovsky." It seems, from her diary, that she and her
husband did only proof-reading for the organization; perhaps
they refused closer co-operation. In any event, Hippius complains that " one could not have a spree with that copper. It
would be more profitable to sell one's old pants." The lady has
always had a weakness for affecting masculinity; her portrait
by Bakst shows her in satin breeches. She signs her critical
writings " Anton Krayny," and writes of herself in the mas-
culine gender. Merezhkovsky, the mystic, the prophet, the
clairvoyant that he likes to affect, in his notebook for 1919–
1920, does not fall below his wife in recounting such " facts "
as the sale of the flesh of executed prisoners in the streets of
Petrograd by their executors. He solemnly states that " Lenin
is an autocrat, and Gorky, his high priest." Gorky's *World
Literature* undertaking he labels " a charity home for Russian
writers dying from hunger," and the compensation he regards
" sufficient for a slow death from starvation." I am tempted
to quote one more gem from his notebook: " In Moscow they
have invented a new mode of capital punishment: they put the

man into a sack filled with lice, and the lice devour him. Into such a sack has Gorky put the soul of Russia."

One must grant the probability of Gorky's lack of tact in his dealings with the stricken intelligentsia. His inherent brusqueness might have been a bit accentuated when circumstances raised him to the rôle of protector of those who had been accustomed to treat him as a plebeian upstart. Only recently it has transpired that Alexander Blok, hypersensitive that he was, felt ill at ease while working with and for Gorky on *World Literature*. Granted also that Gorky's personal ills and disappointments might have been reflected in his gruff manner when associating with his fellow-writers. With these reservations, one cannot help subscribing to the opinion of the historian of Russian literature, Prince D. S. Svyatopolk-Mirsky, son of the Minister who had Gorky arrested in 1905, when he writes that Gorky's

activity in those dreadful years was extraordinarily useful and salutary. He played the part he pretended to of defender of culture and civilization as well as he could have done. The debt of Russian culture to him is very great. Everything that was done between 1918 and 1921 to save the writers and other higher intellectuals from starvation was due to Gorky. . . . His great place in modern Russian letters is entirely due to his personal part in the salvaging of Russian civilization when it was in danger of going down.

What about the accusation of Gorky as being Lenin's " high priest " and Smerdyakov? How can one explain, or justify, his sharp turn from a bitter enemy of the experimenters over the organism of the Russian people into an upholder of their régime? The simplest way to answer the second question would be to refer to Gorky's own admission of heresy and contradictions in his party allegiances. We have noted his inconsistencies, and his impatience at being held to account for them, even by Lenin. A free-lance in politics, he did not feel bound by doctrine or discipline to adhere to certain views when he was prone to discard them. But was not his anti-Lenin campaign vehemently passionate? Was not this vehemence a proof of his

deep conviction in this matter, which for that reason one might have expected to show a greater endurance? Not necessarily. The depth of one's conviction may be measured by the serene calm of its exposition, while hysteric screams and abusing terms for the opponent may betray a momentary mood, a passion uncooled by clear knowledge.

Gorky is accused by his enemies of having deserted his stand for reasons of personal expediency, of having bowed before the Bolsheviks, when their power was in ascendance. Even Trotsky writes to me: " Gorky became reconciled to the October revolution only after it had weathered the civil war, and showed its first cultural results." The facts in the case point to a reverse implication. Throughout the summer of 1917, when the Bolsheviks were numerically insignificant and were universally mocked and abused and ostracized, Gorky and his journal, though in disagreement with Lenin's platform, had the temerity to treat the Bolsheviks humanely and tolerantly, thereby incurring the enmity of all parties and of the whole press. From November, 1917 to about September, 1918, when the Bolsheviks appeared to be celebrating an easy and uncontested victory, Gorky challenged their undisputed authority and attacked it, more pugnaciously perhaps then wisely. When he did switch over to their side, the Bolsheviks were in a most precarious position. Lenin was lying wounded by a Socialist-Revolutionist, the culprit, Dora Kaplan, representing the militant opposition of the only party which, or at least a branch of which, had hitherto co-operated with the Soviet Government. The capital had been moved to Moscow, from fear that Petrograd could be easily captured by the Germans or the Finns or any other organized force. And Moscow was becoming more and more like a tiny island threatened by encroaching waves of hostility. It was no longer the capital of the largest contiguous empire in the world, stretching from the Baltic to the Pacific, and from the Arctic to the Black Sea and the border of China, but merely the centre of a small inland state, as it had been some four centuries earlier. On every side the Soviets faced armed enemies, whose strangling vice had the stamps of both the Allies and the Central Powers. Soon the victorious Allies

were to monopolize the waging of a holy war against Russia, and to pour men and tanks and aeroplanes and money and uniforms and moral propaganda into the campaign. The Soviets had to fight, unorganized and unequipped, on sixteen fronts, not counting inner enemies and the Czecho-Slovaks who tried to blow up the state from within (to be rewarded at the diplomatic table of the Allies with independence for their country). In the face of inner disruption and starvation, and the armed hostility of the West, the fate of Soviet Russia seemed doomed beyond the slightest peradventure. Gorky was not blind to all this when he threw his lot with the Bolshevik régime.

The last phrase does not mean that Gorky joined the Bolshevik Party, or that he recanted his views concerning its tactics. Chirikov voiced the indignation of the irreconcilables in his attack on Gorky's appeal, *Follow Us!*, which he addressed to the intelligentsia in 1919. That within a few months after the suspension of *Novaya Zhizn*, its editor should be paraded along with Lenin, Radek, Zinoviev, as " the most prominent representative of the Soviet order "! Worse yet: this very editor of an anti-Bolshevik paper now called upon the intellectuals of Russia and the world to " follow us," that is Lenin and Gorky! To be sure, in their growing isolation the Bolsheviks could not help rejoicing at Gorky's offer of co-operation. " We have gained one of the greatest victories: we have won over Maxim Gorky! " they wrote, and at every opportunity they flaunted the " conversion " of Gorky. That was rather pathetic.

Gorky's *Follow Us!* did not indicate that he no longer saw the recklessness of the Bolshevik experiment and its cruel methods. It did show that he had come to prefer the " madness of the brave " to the safety and sanity of the Western world. The armistice imposed by the Allies on Germany, whose conditions were " ten times harder than those of the Brest-Litovsk Peace," sobered Gorky from his illusions about Western democracies. The following excerpts are expressive of his new attitude:

. . . From day to day the cynicism of the inhuman policy of the imperialists becomes clearer, and threatens more and

more openly the peoples of Europe with new wars and new bloodshed.

President Wilson, who yesterday was the eloquent champion of the freedom of peoples and the rights of democracy, is equipping a powerful army for the " Restoration of Order " in Revolutionary Russia, where the people have already realized their lawful right to take the power into their own hands, and are striving according to their capacity to lay the foundation for a new political order. I will not deny that this constructive work has been preceded by an often unnecessary destruction. But I, more than anyone else, am justified and in a position to explain, that the cultural metamorphosis which is going on under particularly difficult circumstances, and which calls for heroic exertions of strength, is now gradually taking a form and a compass which have been up to the present unknown in human history. This is not an exaggeration. But a short time ago an opponent of the Soviet government and still in many respects not in agreement with its methods of work, I can yet say that in the future the historian, when judging the work which the Russian workers have accomplished in one year, will be able to feel nothing but admiration for the immensity of the present cultural activity. . . .

. . . . now that the damnable war has disclosed the complete shabbiness, inhumanity, and cynicism of the old system, now its death sentence has been pronounced. We Russians, a people without traditions and on that account bolder, more rebellious and less bound by the prejudices of the past, have been the first to tread the path that leads to the destruction of the outworn conditions of capitalist society, and we are convinced that we have a claim on the help and sympathy of the proletariat of the entire world, and also of those who, even before the war, criticized sharply the present conditions of society.

If this criticism was honest, then all honourable men in Europe and America must recognize our right to shape our destiny in the manner we think necessary. If any of the intellectual workers take a true interest in the solving of the great social problem, they must protest against those who strive for the re-establishment of the old régime, who wish to destroy the Russian revolution by the shedding of Russian blood, to subject Russia to their rule in order later to exploit

it as they have exploited Turkey and China, and as they are now preparing to exploit Germany. . . .

Existing under the menace of conquest by the robbers, they [the New Russia] proclaim to the workers and honourable men of the world: Follow us to a new life, for the creation of which we are working without sparing ourselves or anything or anyone else. For this we are toiling, erring, and suffering with an eager hope for success, leaving our acts to the just decision of history. Follow us in our struggle against the old order, in our work for a new form of life, for the freedom and beauty of life.

Discounting the hyperbolic tone of this obviously propagandic appeal, we may discern Gorky's anxiety for the fate of the New Russia. The preparations for a grandiose intervention in Soviet Russia, under the banner of a crusade of civilization against savagery, naturally disquieted every Russian who had not been blinded by personal chagrin into hatred of his people and country. With all its shortcomings, errors, and excesses, the Bolshevik order was preferable to interference from outside, with the prospective restoration of the old régime. The names of the generals and admirals who headed the crusade were a sufficient pledge for its reactionary aims, and the initial actions of these leaders gave the local population a pungent whiff of the punitive atrocities that were in store for it in the case of a successful restoration. Furthermore, when the Bolsheviks had lived long enough to celebrate their first anniversary in power, it became clear to Gorky that they could not be treated as ephemeral caliphs-for-one-hour. Once in the saddle, the Bolshevik leaders became conscious of their responsible destiny, that of the only political group which had the audacity and will to take over the dreadful heritage of the tsar and that arch-demoralizer of the army and nation, the lawyer Kerensky. Gorky could not help observing that along with their sweepingly destructive measures the Bolsheviks were displaying the quite un-Russian faculty of bridling anarchy, restoring order and discipline, and cementing the centrifugal members of the loose national organism.

Above all, Gorky was won over by the attitude of the new

government toward cultural activities. The Autocracy had thwarted educational efforts, especially among the common people, because it regarded, with good reason, enlightenment as its doom. The Bolshevik dictatorship, politically as despotic and repressive as tsarism, has adopted from the outset a diametrically contrasting educational policy. The fight against illiteracy was set forth as one of the primary national issues. Literary, scientific, and artistic undertakings have been receiving the support of the State in a proportion which not only far exceeds that of the pre-revolutionary budget of Russia, but is superior to that of any contemporary national budget, in the most opulent states. Is there any wonder that Gorky, who never tired of emphasizing the crying need of Russia for cultural development, eagerly welcomed the opportunity for such work so generously afforded by the Soviet government?

Gorky's personal relations with Lenin were resumed, in consequence of Gorky's change of policy, from boycott to co-operation. From the time of Gorky's return to Russia, at the end of 1913, to the attempt against the life of Lenin, late in 1918, the two men neither met nor exchanged letters. Before the revolution of 1917, as we have seen, Gorky rebelled against Lenin's guidance along strictly factional lines; these were too narrowly exacting even for the closest followers of Lenin. Their differences during and after the revolution have been sufficiently dwelt upon in these pages. They were not differences that could be brushed aside at a stroke, unless indeed Gorky could have been transformed into a Smerdyakov or a " high priest " of Lenin. In his obituary note on Lenin, written in the calm atmosphere of his Sorrento retreat, Gorky sums up his divergences from the Bolsheviks, clearly and succinctly:

During 1917–1921 my relations with Lenin were far from what I should have liked them to be, but they could not be otherwise.

Lenin was a politician. He was in full possession of that artificially but precisely mastered rectilinearity of vision, which is indispensable for the helmsman of such an enormous, heavy ship as is the leaden peasant-Russia.

I have an organic disgust for politics, and I am a rather

doubtful Marxist, because I have little faith in the wisdom of masses in general and of the peasant mass, in particular.

When Lenin, on his return to Russia, in 1917, published his " theses," it appeared to me that in these theses he was sacrificing to the Russian peasantry the whole, numerically insignificant but in quality heroical, army of politically educated workmen and sincerely revolutionary intelligentsia. The only active force in Russia was to be thrown like a handful of salt into the insipid morass of the village, where it would dissolve without a trace, without altering aught in the spirit, living mode, or history of the Russian people.

The scientific, technical — the qualified and specialized — intelligentsia, is, in my opinion, revolutionary in its essence, and together with the socialistic intelligentsia from among the workmen, they are, for me, the most precious force that Russia has accumulated. There was no other force capable of ruling and organizing rustic Russia of 1917. But these forces, negligible in quantity and dismembered by contradictions, could accomplish their task only on condition that a firm inner unity existed. A gigantic problem faced them: to master the anarchy of the village, to cultivate the muzhik's will, teach him how to work rationally, transform his economy, and thereby move the country swiftly forward. All this could be achieved only by means of subjecting the instincts of the village to the organizing reason of the city.

I considered as the foremost task of the revolution the creation of conditions which would foster the growth of the country's cultural forces. [Gorky enumerates his efforts in this direction, from the Capri school to the Free Association for the Growth and Spread of Positive Sciences, adding that the last one was " destroyed by the October revolution, and its funds were confiscated."]

For the sake of greater clearness, I will say that the basic obstacle in the way of Russia becoming Europeanized and cultured is the overwhelming preponderance of the illiterate village over the city, the zoologic individualism of the peasantry and the almost complete absence among them of social emotions. The dictatorship of politically educated workmen in close union with the intelligentsia was to my mind the only possible way out of the difficult situation, which was further

complicated by the war, in that the war increased the anarchism of the village.

I disagree with the Communists in their low estimation of the part played by the intelligentsia in the Russian revolution. The revolution was prepared precisely by the intelligentsia, which included also all the " Bolsheviks " who had educated hundreds of workmen in the spirit of social heroism and high intellectuality. The Russian intelligentsia — both of scientists and workmen — was, is, and will remain for a long time yet, the only draught-horse harnessed to the ponderous cart of Russian history. In spite of all the jolts and shocks it has experienced, the mind of the masses still remains a force which demands direction from the outside.

To this day Gorky harbours resentment against the Bolsheviks' tactics toward those who do not belong to the inner orthodoxy of the Party; he has never been reconciled to their suppression of free speech, to their at times idiotic censorship of the printed word. In consequence, the Bolsheviks have treated him, until quite recently, as a valuable friend, but at the same time as a heretic, at best only as a " fellow-traveller," to use the phrase coined by Trotsky for mere sympathizers of the Soviet order. It is pertinent, in this connexion, to quote further from Gorky's *Lenin*:

Before 1918, before the vile attempt at murdering him, I had not met Lenin in Russia, and had not even seen him from a distance. I called on him, when he was still unable to use his arm freely, and could hardly move his perforated neck. In answer to my words of indignation, he spoke unwillingly, as of something of which he was tired and bored:

" It's a scuffle. What are you going to do about it? Everybody acts in the only way he knows how."

Our meeting was very friendly, but of course the all-seeing little eyes of Ilyich [Lenin's patronymic, by which he was popularly called] looked at me, the sheep " gone astray," with evident regret. A very familiar look for me — for some thirty years I have been looked at in that way. I expect with certainty that I shall be accompanied into my grave with the same look. . . .

A few minutes later Lenin was saying heatedly:

" He who is not with us is against us. Individuals who are independent of history are a fantasy. Even if we grant that such people existed at one time, they are not to be found now; they cannot be. No one wants them. Everyone, to the last man, is sucked into the whirlpool of actuality, more entangled than it has ever been before.

" You say that I am simplifying life too much? That this simplification threatens to destroy culture, eh? "

The ironic, characteristic " hm . . . hm."

His sharp eyes become even sharper, and he proceeds in a lowered voice:

" Well, do you think that millions of muzhiks armed with rifles are no threat to culture, no? Do you imagine that the Constituent Assembly could have managed their anarchism? You, who are making so much noise, and justly, about the anarchism of the village, you should understand our work better than anybody else. The Russian common people have to be shown something very simple, something that is accessible to their brains. Soviets and Communism, that's simple.

" The union of workmen and the intelligentsia, what? That is not bad, not at all. Tell the intelligentsia to come to us. According to you, they sincerely serve the interests of justice, don't they? Then why do they keep away? Come over to us: it is we who have undertaken the colossal task of raising the people to their feet, of telling the world the whole truth about life; it is we who point out to nations the direct road to a humane life, the road out of slavery, penury, humiliation."

He laughed, and said without malice:

" That's why the intelligentsia gave it to me in the neck."

And when the temperature of our conversation approached the normal, he said with vexation and sorrow:

" Am I disputing the fact that we need the intelligentsia? But you see, don't you, in what a hostile frame of mind they are, how poorly they understand the demands of the moment? They fail to see that without us they are helpless, they cannot reach the masses. It will be their fault if we shall smash too many pots."

No one could appreciate more than Lenin the dire need of men of skill and brains in his gigantic task, and no one knew

more than Gorky how destitute the Russian people were of such men, and how true was Lenin's remark about the helplessness of the intelligentsia " without them." For generations the noblest sons and daughters of Russia endeavoured to get close to the people and rouse them from apathy and humility. They were not understood. The Bolsheviks were the first to talk the people's language, and though often hated and cursed by the peasants, they have not been resented as outsiders, as " fooling gentry." By co-operating with the Bolsheviks the intelligentsia has the only chance for getting in direct touch with the people and put into practice their professed love for this mysterious *narod*.

In spite of his justified mistrust for the over-squeamish intelligentsia, Lenin felt overjoyed at meeting and utilizing men of brains. Gorky tells us of Lenin's patriotic pride in the flexible dexterity of the Russian mind, after he would talk to inventors or generals of artillery or members of the Academy. He was proud of such a Russian product as Trotsky, of whom he said, " banging the table with his fist ": " Could they show me another man capable of organizing within one year an almost exemplary army, and in addition, to win the respect of military specialists? We have such a man. We — have everything! We shall have wonders! " Though on another occasion he said to Gorky: . . . " We are a gifted people, for the most part, but of a lazy mind. A clever Russian is nearly always either a Jew, or one with the admixture of Jewish blood." He might have had in mind, among others, Martov, the son of a Hebrew editor, his lifelong opponent, of whom, as already noted, he said to Gorky: " What a pity that Martov is not with us, what a pity! He is such a marvellous comrade, such a clean man! "

Of his intercessions for victims of the Cheka, Gorky has this to say:

I troubled Lenin very often with all sorts of requests, and at times I felt that my pleas for people aroused in him a certain pity for me, almost a contempt. He would ask me:

" Does it not occur to you that you are busying yourself with nonsense, with trifles? "

But I was doing what seemed to me necessary, and the cross, angry glances of the man who knew the number of the proletariat's enemies, did not repulse me. He would shake his head in commiseration, and say:

" You are compromising yourself in the eyes of the workmen and comrades."

I pointed out that the comrades, the workmen, being in a state of vehemence and touchiness, often treated liberty and the lives of valuable individuals too lightly and " simply." That, in my opinion, not only compromised the fine and difficult cause of the revolution by superfluous and at times absurd cruelty, but was objectively harmful for this cause, as it repelled not a small number of big forces from aiding it.

" Hm-hm," growled Lenin sceptically, reflecting on the numerous facts of the intelligentsia's treason to the cause of the workmen.

" Between us," he said, " don't you think that most often they betray us from cowardice, from fear of embarrassment in case their beloved theory should suffer in its collision with practice? We are not afraid of that. Theories and hypotheses are for us not anything ' sacred,' but a working instrument."

And yet I do not recall an instant when Ilyich refused a request of mine. If it happened, indeed, that my pleas were not complied with, it was not because of his fault, but because of those damnable " mechanical shortcomings," of which the clumsy machine of Russia's statehood has always suffered abundantly. One may also allow for someone's malicious unwillingness to alleviate the fate of human beings, or save their lives. Vengeance and malice may often act also by inertia. And then, there are, of course, small, psychically unhealthy people with a morbid thirst for the enjoyment of suffering on the part of their fellow-men.

One easily surmises that Gorky referred to the typical case of Zinoviev and the four Grand Dukes.

What appealed to Gorky in Lenin from the beginning to the end, through all the stages of their friendship and frictions, was his iron will, so rarely encountered among the well-intentioned but impractical intelligentsia. Whenever such a man arose in Russia, he was suspected of being un-Russian or an

ally of the devil. Recall the example of Peter the Great. Another un-Russian trait attracted Gorky in Lenin: his hatred for suffering. Russian life and literature seem to have sanctified pain and sadness; one thinks of Russia's melancholy steppes, sorrowful folk-songs, of Dostoyevsky's sadists and masochists. Gorky tells us of Lenin's profound and aggressive " hatred, revulsion, and contempt for unhappiness, grief, and human sufferings," of his " flaming conviction that unhappiness is not an immutable basis of existence, but an abomination which people must and can sweep out of life." " For me personally," writes Gorky,

Lenin is not only the marvellously perfect incarnation of a will directed toward a goal which no one before him has dared to face practically. For me he is one of the " just " men, one of the monstrous, fairy-like, and unexpected men in Russian history, men of will and talent, such as Peter the Great, Mikhail Lomonosov, Lev Tolstoy, and others of that calibre. I think that such men are possible only in Russia, whose life and history always remind me of Sodom and Gomorrah.

Gorky's skill as a portraitist has enabled him to give us a most graphic description of Lenin's exterior, which he was in a position to observe at close range, after he had moved to Moscow, in 1920:

Robust and thick-set, with the cranium of Socrates and the all-seeing eyes of a past-master in ingenious shrewdness, he often assumed an odd and somewhat comical pose: he threw his head back, and bending it toward one shoulder, he thrust his fingers somewhere under his armpits, behind his vest. There was something marvellously dear and funny in that pose, something of a triumphant rooster, and at such a moment he all radiated joy, a great child of this damned world, a fine man who found it necessary to bring himself as a sacrifice to enmity and hatred, for the sake of attaining the goal of love and beauty.
His movements were light and agile, and a spare but strong gesture harmonized perfectly with his speech, also spare of words and surcharged with ideas. On his Mongolian face burned and played the keen eyes of an indefatigable hunter after falsehood and sorrow in life, they burned, contracting, wink-

ing, smiling ironically, flashing with anger. The flash of those eyes made his speech even more torrid and terribly clear. At times it seemed that it was the indomitable energy of his mind which spurted from his eyes as sparks, and the words, saturated with it, seemed to scintillate in the air. His speech always produced the physical sensation of irrefutable truth, and although this truth was often unacceptable for me, I still could not help feeling its power.

All his life Gorky has fought smugness and philistinism, the desire of the average man to keep things as they are, his fear of novelty, of the unusual and daring. He has ardently supported the revolutionary movement, in the hope that it would stir the slough of contentment and provoke the passion for creative change and excelling feats. Lenin impersonated for him the spirit of that revolution. He wrote:

The fundamental hue and cry of the majority is:
" Do not interfere with our living as we have been accustomed to live."
Vladimir Lenin has succeeded, like no one before him, in preventing people most ingeniously from living their customary lives.

Gorky resolved to co-operate with the Bolsheviks at the lowest ebb of their career. He had the satisfaction of seeing Soviet Russia emerge, at the end of 1920, victorious on all fronts. The triumph of the amateurish Red Army over professional troops was due to a superior morale based on a question of life or death. More important than the military issue of the conflict, was the resultant reintegration of what had been the Russian empire as a largely voluntary union of Soviet republics. Except for the Baltic states, Poland and Bessarabia, the former territory remained intact. Russia forced the world to recognize its might and its right to independence.

At the same time, the liberation from intervention and invasion was attained at the price of a terrific strain of the nation. Six years of warfare — foreign and civilian — left the country exhausted and undernourished, its agriculture, industry, and transportation disrupted, its population greatly dimin-

ished in numbers, with a lower birth-rate, and an alarming proportion of physically and mentally deficient babies born in these calamitous years. Even in normal times the Communist experiment — briefly, the nationalization of all production and distribution — would require not only an idealistic and intelligent majority, but also material self-sufficiency, in the absence of world co-operation. Boundlessly rich in natural resources, yet fabulously backward in technique and average culture, Russia could not cope with the situation, when international endeavour bled her white. The presence of invaders on home soil, the menace of restoring the old order, stimulated the masses for a superhuman feat of driving out the enemies and pooling the available pittance of food and ammunition. With the passing of this danger the country relapsed into prostration. The cities produced practically nothing in exchange for grain, and the peasantry adopted the traditional Russian method of passive resistance: they cultivated just enough ground to meet their personal needs. The cities faced hunger. On the horizon began to loom the periodic catastrophe of medieval Russia — famine, from time to time a visiting scourge of the land, but now, coupled with other vicissitudes, and above all with large stretches of undercultivated ground, a fatal blow.

What saved Russia from ruin and bankruptcy, was Lenin's sagacity in sharply turning about, and against the protests of the Left Communists introducing State Capitalism in the form of the NEP. It was this New Economic Policy that brought the unparalleled recuperation of the country, in spite of the fact that Russia, unlike the rest of the Continent, received no outside help, but on the contrary met with united interference. Yet one must also remember that the immediate alleviation of the famine victims was due in a large measure to the efforts of such disinterested friends of humanity as the late Fridtjof Nansen and the Quakers, and to the gigantic undertaking of the American Relief Administration. Maxim Gorky sent out a stirring appeal, and Herbert Hoover responded without much delay, and after preliminary negotiations were over, the ARA began to feed starving children and adults. Were it not for these tokens of humanity still being capable of altruism,

with the blood of the world war still undried, the famine would have reaped far more than the five million lives it did snuff out.

Gorky's variegated, non-political activity was balm to the heart of Lenin. He was always fond of Gorky, even during their bitterest fights. When in 1918 Lenin was asked for a final decision regarding the fate of *Novaya Zhizn*, he said to his intimate co-workers:

> Of course, we must suspend *Novaya Zhizn*. Under present conditions, when we are to raise the whole country for the defence of the revolution, any intelligentsia-pessimism is extremely harmful. Yet Gorky is one of us. He is too closely knit with the labour class and the labour movement, and he comes from the " lowly " himself. He will come back to us, beyond doubt. Such things happened to him before, as in 1908, during the *Otzovists*. He has been afflicted by such political zigzags.

Time and again Lenin, in conversation with those near to him, emphasized the up-hill road which Gorky had to cover in his craving for knowledge, suggesting that this experience must make him congenial to the new, peasant-worker intelligentsia, who are also forced to acquire culture at the cost of great hardships. He regarded Gorky as a splendid asset in the building of New Russia, and urged the Party to have Gorky frequently appear in large public gatherings, and to make phonograph records of his speeches. Gorky received from him a list of suggested themes for such records, among them on anti-Semitism, on the intelligentsia, science, and the revolution, on technical experts, and the like. Gorky, always shy of oratory, promised to write down these speeches, but never did.

Gorky's trips to Moscow from Petrograd always gladdened Lenin, both because he liked him personally and because through him he felt the pulse of Russia's intellectuals. These trips helped greatly in the establishment of various cultural undertakings and institutions. On one of his arrivals Gorky was asked to take part in an intimate celebration of Lenin's fiftieth birthday by his close co-workers. Somehow Lenin was lured to this assembly, and when he learned of its purpose, he

became quite angry, and threatened to have their names registered and propose before the Central Committee to penalize them for useless and vain waste of time. We are told that on that occasion Gorky's informal verbal portrait of Lenin moved the assembly profoundly, and the two men merged in a prolonged embrace.

Anxious for Gorky's health, Lenin often invited him to Moscow for a rest. Here are two such invitations, recently made public:

5/VII/1919

Dear Alexey Maximovich:

Upon my word, you've been staying too long in Pieter, it seems to me. It isn't good to stay in one place. One gets tired and bored. Give your consent to a ride down here, eh? We'll arrange for that.

Your Lenin.

18/VII/1919

Dear Alexey Maximovich:

Come down for a rest. I often get away for two days to the country, where I can arrange to have you stay both for a short and a long time.

Come down, upon my word!

Wire *when*. We shall get a compartment for you, to make the ride more comfortable. As god lives, it will do you good to change the air for a space. I am awaiting your answer!

Your Lenin.

One cannot help wondering at Gorky's power of endurance. Repeatedly condemned to death by expert physicians, he defied their science, and went on living under most unhealthful conditions. The physical privations and the mental chagrin of those unforgettable years finally began to affect Gorky's amazing organism. Lenin, himself groaning under the strain, raged against Gorky's negligence and for more than a year urged him to go abroad and see specialists. On August 9, 1921, ill from overwork and lack of food, Lenin wrote to Gorky in the tone of his letters to him eight years previously, addressed from Cracow to Capri:

so tired that I cannot do a thing to save my life.
ou spit blood, yet you don't go!! Upon my word,
h unfair and extravagant. In Europe, in a good sana-
you will be treated properly, and will be able to ac-
sh thrice as much work. Upon my word. Whereas with
re you get neither treatment nor any work done, nothing
fuss and vanity, futile vanity. Go away from here, get
ell. Don't be stubborn, I beg of you!

> Your Lenin.

Truly Lenin was a thrifty master, trying to avoid the dissipation of national assets, and finding time in the midst of his bewildering tasks for paying attention to individuals. Gorky tells us that Lenin had written many such letters to a variety of comrades. Gorky was reluctant to desert Russia at such a moment. At last, he was literally " taken " abroad, and brought to a German sanatorium, with the prospect of speedy death more likely than that of recovery.

Gorky once said to me:

Alexey Peshkov has been unreservedly at the disposal of Maxim Gorky. On numerous occasions Peshkov yielded to Gorky, and made sacrifices. But there abides a third self in me, and that is the Russian, who cannot help reacting to environmental conditions. This one, of course, caused the other two much trouble and suffering.

RECENT YEARS

RECENT YEARS

$\mathbf{T}$HE extraordinary organism of Gorky once more emerged victorious from the shadows. A snapshot taken of him in the streets of Berlin, shortly on his arrival there late in 1921, shows a gaunt cadaver, with a face reduced to nose and cheek-bones, the sepulchral caverns feebly lit by eyes that spoke from their depths of the agony of weariness. Yet even then his will to live and create belied the played-out exterior. Excerpts from a letter of his were printed in the *Annals of the Writers' Home* in Petrograd (January 15, 1922), in which he keenly commented on what he saw in Germany, on the country's magnificent efforts at economic and cultural recovery. Of his own health he wrote half jestingly:

The highly esteemed Professor Kraus, having thoroughly examined my ancient organism, has found it in a far from decent condition: the sack of the heart has for some reason grown to the pleura, and of the lungs there remains only one third, not more, of which I could convince myself from the X-ray photograph. But the worst is my nervousness and all manner of over-fatigue. The state of the lungs does not permit for the time being any treatment of the heart, so that in place of Nauheim I am going to the Black Forest for two or three months. I cannot say that all this pleases me, for I am eager to work. Very eager. The atmosphere here is so stimulating to work, the Germans are working so zealously, valiantly, and sensibly, that, you know, one's respect involuntarily grows for them, despite their being " bourgeois."

When Barrett H. Clark came to interview the " dying " man at his little Black Forest villa near Freiburg, he winced under

the grip of the handshake, given him by the " invalid " who had just come in from working in his landlady's garden. By this time Gorky has become accustomed to his miraculous recuperations from " fatal " attacks. He has been prepared for death so many times that, as I gather from conversations with him, he faces the inevitable end with a yawn of indifference. On the other hand, his uncanny power of recovery has prompted his enemies to accuse him of shamming. The tsar's police doubted his illness, when friends interceded for the betterment of his prison conditions, or for permitting him to go to Crimea. In recent years the *émigrés* have jeered at Gorky's absence from Russia under the pretext of ill health.

As soon as he was in a position to get along without the supervision of his " highly esteemed " German physicians, Gorky made his way to the land of his warmest affection, Italy. He finally settled — if this congenital nomad can ever settle — at Capo di Sorrento, far away from tourist-ridden Sorrento. He shares the Il Sorito villa with its owner, Duke Serracapriola, whose grandfather, while in diplomatic service in Russia, married a Princess Vyazemsky. The democratic duke, with his rusticated bare-legged daughters, mingles freely with the always large and nondescript household of Signor Massimo Gorky. The genial climate, the bountiful soil (" Plant an umbrella, and it will blossom into fruit," boasts Gorky), the Bay with its Vesuvius and jewelled islands, the simple proud natives whose chants betray the oriental drop in their blood, the old Roman and Saracen ruins, the Pagan-Christian *mélange* of local pageants and festivities, are balm to the tired body and mind of the Russian wanderer. For the first time in many years he is enabled to extricate himself from the Russian maelstrom, and to enjoy creative labour and relaxing play.

The Mussolini régime has made itself felt only slightly. Once Gorky's villa was searched. So was his secretary, Baroness Budberg, as she was leaving Italy, and the letters and manuscripts she had with her were taken by the police. P. Kerzhentsev, then Soviet ambassador at Rome, assures us that the White *émigrés* were responsible for those indignities. Gorky wrote a letter of protest to Mussolini, and was on the point of

leaving Italy. Mussolini gave explanations to Kerzhentsev, and promised that such a "misunderstanding" would not occur again. This was the only unpleasantness to happen to Gorky in Italy, and he has eagerly dismissed it from his mind.

The congeniality of the place has brought out Gorky's amazing capacity for work. His literary output at Capo di Sorrento includes thousands of pages of fiction (short stories and novels), reminiscences, critical essays, introductions to various works, journalistic articles, aside from his editorial activity and prodigious correspondence. He is usually editing some periodical review or some series of publications — translations from Western literatures or from those of the numerous nationalities of the Soviet Union. He receives hundreds of letters and manuscripts from known and unknown people, and he regards the reading and answering of these with the utmost earnestness.

To be sure, some of the letters contain trifles or curious grotesques. One chap attends Ostrovsky's play, *The Forest*, is moved deeply, and in four days he writes a play, which beside being rank plagiarism on Ostrovsky is hopelessly illiterate. Another gentleman recommends himself as a professional thief, whose name "has been renowned for a long time among detectives of three countries." An urgent request arrives from an unknown person to hand over the inclosed letter immediately to the author of *Cathedral Folk*, Nikolay Leskov. Gorky shows the letter to his visitor, and exclaims in comical despair: "And how can I hand the thing to Leskov, and *immediately* at that?" (Leskov has been dead for more than thirty years.)

But most of his correspondents emanate from the very thick of Soviet life, from among village and factory journalists and aspiring authors, in whose awkward attempts Gorky discerns the face of New Russia. Mindful of his own vicissitudes as an author, he takes meticulous care about reading manuscripts by beginners and discussing their good and bad sides with their perpetrators. Both as correspondent and as editor he has always been unsparing of his time and labour in hunting down the slightest lapse and suggesting corrections and changes. When the editor of a popular magazine begged Gorky to be more

lenient with manuscripts coming from peasants or artisans, he was severely reprimanded: " It is a shame and a crime to breed mediocrity among the people! One must not divert a workman from his regular trade for the sake of cheap success. It is wrong to develop conceit among these people — it debases them." Indeed, Gorky's great friendliness for writers from the lower classes has made him the more exacting for that. Among the papers of the late Neverov, author of *The City of Bread*, was found a letter from Gorky, in which the young writer was severely criticized for some early story. The scathing letter had a characteristic conclusion:

No, you must try to write something else, you can do better. No leisure? Uncongenial environment? I understand that, and am not hurrying you. But I hope, no — I am sure that you will write well. Meanwhile, here are my good wishes. Perhaps you need some money? Or books? Let me know.

Chekhov's advice to eliminate adjectives and " qualifications " were not wasted on Gorky, for we find him counselling young writers in a similar vein. Thus he tells A. Demidov: " You should not write: ' I saw a beautiful yellow flower.' Say simply: ' I saw a yellow flower.' But you must so arrange the composition that out of the sum total of words and hints the reader shall of his own accord feel that your flower is beautiful." He feels the need of instructing the young writers in such obvious truths and to guard them, on the one hand, against the strait jacket of Party bigotry, and on the other, against literary fads and extremist innovations. To the poet, A. Severny, a student of the school for Worker-and-Peasant Correspondents, he writes:

You must study the technique of writing. Without technique you can't even plane off a cobbler's last. Read well into our old masters — Pushkin, Lermontov, and the like. Don't be afraid of them: they will not change your ideology, and will surely help your technique. Do not get infatuated with word-tricksters. Truth and simplicity are kindred sisters, and beauty is their third sister. Work longer over your compositions, over your self, unsparingly.

To another young author he writes somewhat sententiously:

Young Russian literature has a tremendous task: to depict
the old life in the fulness of its abomination, to help in the
creation of a new life and a new psychology, to call men to
valiant, heroic work in every field, and to self-transformation.
I am not preaching " tendencies." The world is material for
the artist, who is a man always dissatisfied with reality and
with himself. Note this: with himself too.

In a recently published collection of autobiographies by
Soviet writers, there is hardly one case of an author who fails
to acknowledge his indebtedness to Gorky. This in spite of the
fact that Gorky can be harsh and mordant in his relations.
He once let me read a letter which he had just written to a
Moscow professor (A. Fatov), calling him to task for certain
unfair methods in his literary biographies. It was devastating,
and I could not but feel pity for the victim of Gorky's indignation. In the domain of Russian letters Gorky feels and acts
as a shareholder, whose heavy investments make him deeply
concerned about the good as well as the bad sides of the
enterprise.

It should be noted that Gorky's literary interests are not
confined to his native land. There is hardly a contemporary
writer, with the exception perhaps of Willa Cather, who is so
intimately familiar with his fellow-craftsmen as Gorky. With
what loving pride he dwells on the excellencies of Knut Hamsun and Romain Rolland, on an apt scene in an Ambrose
Bierce story, on a specifically remembered chapter of Dreiser's
Sister Carrie, on a brilliant passage in Ben Hecht, on the groping men of Sherwood Anderson, on some subtle merit of Zona
Gale. He is perfectly at home in Western prose and poetry,
even though he has to depend on translations, and the emergence of a Panait Istrati is to him as much a source of joy as
that of a Russian roofer, Kazin, bursting into refreshingly
vigorous lyrics. V. Desnitsky recollects a " comically puzzled
expression " on Gorky's face during his conversation with
Rainer Maria Rilke, who visited him at Capri. They were discussing contemporaries. Through Maria Andreyeva the host

showered his visitor with questions as to his familiarity with a number of German and French writers. Rilke's answers were to the effect that he had met this man once or twice, that he was not acquainted with the other, that the third had sent him his book, that the fourth was a charming fellow and they were quite friends, and so on. Gorky, irritated by his inability to approach his interlocutor directly, urged Andreyeva to get out of his distinguished visitor whether he had read the writings of his magnificent friends. Rilke's answers brought Gorky " into a state of bewilderment and even melancholy ": No, he had not read this one — that is not in his special field; the other one had not sent him his book; the third. . . . To Gorky it is unpardonable for an author not to read his fellow-citizens of the republic of letters.

All of these are time-devouring tasks, and if you add to them Gorky's close familiarity with the last word in science, philosophy, sociology, psychology, as well as with the last speech by Marcel Cachin or Senator Borah, you cannot help marvelling as to how he manages to do all these things, and do them to the best of his ability: from his early childhood he believed in performing his task as best as he could, whether it was baking bread or hauling cargo or editing a magazine or composing a story.

Yet — he also knows how to play. About two in the afternoon his work is usually over. At that time I always found him in his large, cool study, ready to talk leisurely and with gusto on any subject of interest. If not in his study, he could be discovered at the end of the garden, perched on the edge of a bluff and watching some fisherman's boat or some nimble rock-hewer suspended over a declivity and working away with his pick on a sheer wall. You sit down by the long, slightly stooping, easily doubled up torso, and listen to his apt remarks on human toil, which as a rule rouse in him memories of his own rich experience as a workman. Then he is at his best. A bell summons us to tea, the invariable afternoon pastime at the large table in the dining-room, with sometimes a score and seldom fewer than a dozen people in attendance. There are usually visitors — writers, artists, diplomatists, from Naples

or Rome, from Russia or the United States. An early evening meal follows, after which there is music, or reading (by the host or some visitor), or an outdoor party in the garden with lanterns and games, or a stroll to the Point. Occasionally, Gorky suggests a trip to Sorrento, to an open-air theatre. When left alone at last, the " invalid " stays up for a long time on the balcony, inhaling the odours of the night and listening to its multiple still voices.

In a sense, Capo di Sorrento has come to serve as a Yasnaya Polyana. Like Tolstoy in his time, Gorky draws to his abode questing Russians and foreigners, particularly writers. It is the ambition of every young Soviet author to make a pilgrimage to the " foremost proletarian writer " and unburden himself before him. Of course, no comparison between Tolstoy and Gorky is attempted here. Aside from their personal dissimilarity, there is a glaring difference in the messages these men have to offer to their callers. Where Tolstoy preached passive anarchism and the rejection of civilization and culture, both in the form of technical progress and of modern art, Gorky advocates dynamic collectivism and cultural advance, in technology and in the arts. One cannot gainsay, however, the resemblance between the two men as unofficial spokesmen for their people in the eyes of the outside world, with due allowance for the greater respect and reverence enjoyed by Tolstoy.

As spokesman for Russia, Gorky has courted no end of difficulties. His readiness to speak his mind on the spur of the moment, his aptness for heresies and inconsistencies, in brief, his lack of the elementary prerequisites for a politician, should have served as excellent reasons for Gorky to limit his utterances to literary subjects only. But though he admits it to be a weakness, and though he has suffered for it considerably, he cannot resist the temptation to make public his views on life in its various manifestations. He told me how often he had wished he had not said the things he did say on political questions. Thus in 1922, during the celebrated trial of the Socialist-Revolutionists in Moscow, he was prevailed upon by certain leaders of that party to come out with a public statement against the Bolshevik intolerance and the threatened execu-

tion of the defendants. The trial showed beyond peradventure that the Socialist-Revolutionists were responsible for a number of terroristic acts against Soviet officials, including Lenin, and against public institutions and utilities. The Bolsheviks could ill afford such activities within the country, while they encountered a hostile world without; those activities had to be stopped short. The expected death sentences were changed, however, to imprisonment of the arrested leaders as hostages, their fate to depend on the subsequent behaviour of their Party. This verdict had been decided upon in advance in the official spheres, as Trotsky implies in his *My Life*. Gorky's precipitous accusations placed him in an awkward position with the Bolsheviks, who saw in his statement another symptom of his recidivous vacillation.

But it is not only as an *advocatus diaboli* that Gorky has represented Soviet Russia. We have seen how effectively he appealed to the world to come to the help of the starving intellectuals. While official Washington was not on speaking terms with Moscow, Secretary Hoover found it possible to negotiate through Gorky about feeding the famine victims. In 1927, a declaration signed by " Russian Authors " was circulated abroad, which complained of the wretched state of literature and literary workers in the Soviet Union. All literary societies and unions existing in the Union immediately refuted these allegations, branding the declaration as a calumny. Nevertheless the *émigré* press raised a great ado in this connexion. Bunin and Balmont transmitted the declaration to Romain Rolland, and requested him to issue a protest against the persecution of literature in Soviet Russia. Rolland wrote to Gorky for information; his note and Gorky's letter were published in *L'Europe* for March, 1928. They bear reproducing here, if we recall that as late as 1930, the *Saturday Review of Literature* printed, without comment, a " Russian Letter " by a *ci-devant*, which spoke of the suppression of free fiction in Soviet Russia, and of the utter degradation and corruption of the current fiction passed by the censor. The encouraging features noted in Gorky's letter have undoubtedly advanced upward since that time.

Rolland's letter in *L'Europe:*

Wishing to verify certain facts relating to my polemic with Konstantin Balmont and Ivan Bunin, I addressed myself to Maxim Gorky. Here is a striking picture, sketched by him in a few lines, which portrays the conditions of present-day Russian literature.

Romain Rolland.

Gorky's answer:

My dear friend,

I have read the " Letter of Russian Authors Living in Russia." I am inclined to doubt that authors could have written it. Authors could not have written that " the classics are forbidden in Russia," when the Gosizdat [State Publishing House] has just published — and excellently too — the works of Dostoyevsky (including his " counter-revolutionary " *Demons*), Gogol, and Pushkin, and is preparing for publication the works of Turgenev and the complete writings of Lev Tolstoy in ninety volumes (one of the editors is Tolstoy's close friend, Chertkov). At this moment they are printing selected works of Bunin, Kuprin, Shmelev, nor are they forgetting older writers, like Mamin-Sibiryak, Garin-Mikhaylovsky, and others.

From library reports, in which Tolstoy, Dostoyevsky, and Gogol stand first, the Authors might also know that the classics are not forbidden.

Every year young Russian writers visit me abroad. It is hard to associate " penury " with distant travels abroad. It seems to me that I have the honour to enjoy the confidence of the young. But to my question, in intimate conversations, as to who, what group, could have written that letter, I received in answer only a sceptical shrug of the shoulders.

They are writing to you that there is no longer any literature in Russia. What an odd assertion! I am amazed at the abundance of young authors. At the present moment there are hundreds of writers in Russia; their number is rapidly increasing, which I can explain only by the giftedness of my people as a whole. The Russian people are at last beginning to realize their " I," their value, and their right to a free expression of their creative powers in all the fields of life.

This year has brought forth several notable writers, who give great promises. Namely, Fadeyev, author of the novel *Razgrom* [*Débacle;* in an English version — *Nineteen*]; Leonid Borisov, Nina Smirnova, the poet N. Tikhonov, who has written an excellent book.

There are such talented writers as Leonid Leonov, Babel, Vsevolod Ivanov — who is now editing the monthly *Krasnaya Nov* [*Red Virgin Soil*], although he is not a Communist. They have all won prominence, as have also Konstantin Fedin, Vladimir Lidin, Boris Pilnyak, Sergey Semenov, a workman endowed with an original talent, who is under the influence of Knut Hamsun. Zoshchenko is dissipating himself in short sketches, which does not in the least diminish his talent; there is no doubt that he will gradually pass from humour to satire. Side by side with him stands Katayev, author of *The Embezzlers,* a story written in Gogol's manner. I note the rapid growth of Alexander Yakovlev, Kaverin.

It is difficult for me to enumerate to you all those who deserve not only mention, but praise.

Among the non-revolutionary writers I may mention Sergeyev-Tsensky, Mikhail Prishvin, Konstantin Trenev, Nikandrov, Veresayev, Ivan Volnov, Olga Forsh, Alexey Chapygin (who has recently published a magnificent novel, *Stepan Razin*), the poet Sergey Klychkov — all of them working very, very successfully. Alexey Tolstoy is writing with zeal, as ever a splendid narrator. Ivan Novikov has just published a volume of tales.

In my opinion, two exceptional masters stand today at the head of Russian literature: Sergeyev-Tsensky and Mikhail Prishvin. The latter has recently sent you his last book, *V Pogonye za schastyem* [*In Pursuit of Happiness*].

It is quite possible, it is even certain, that I have forgotten to mention to you a number of gifted writers. I have not had the time to read them all. I am afraid to weary you by an enumeration of the writers who contribute to the review *Sibirskiye Ogni* [*Siberian Lights*], among whom there are very capable men.

Nor have I spoken about the poets, in whose midst there are many prominent ones, like Pasternak, Tikhonov, Aseyev, Zharov, Kazin, Selvinsky, Oreshin, and others.

Whole new literatures are being created by the peoples of

the Caucasus, the Circassians and Ossets, also by the Tatars of Kazan.

Yes, there is a fine literature living and growing in present-day Russia. Admiring it, I am grieved by the fact that Europe pays so little attention to this great movement, to these creative forces, that it so diligently and with so much enmity searches for evil things in Russia, overlooking the good things.

Undoubtedly (and this I admit), the quantity of good things existing there is insufficient, considering that it is a country of one hundred and fifty million people. But one must not forget that it is only ten years since the Russian people conquered with one stroke the cultural heights and conceived a thirst for culture. Russia already has villages of one hundred and forty inhabitants who subscribe to thirty-two periodicals. Newspapers, magazines, popular brochures on scientific questions, are appearing in thousands of copies. I am convinced that hundreds of prose and verse writers, who are now just beginning their literary career, will in five or ten years become brilliant stylists.

M. Gorky.

January 29, 1928.

This is, obviously, a private letter; as a public statement it is slipshod and incomplete, though in substance correct. Incidentally, in reference to the library reports, Gorky either errs or misrepresents through modesty. Reports from State, municipal, workers', peasants', and soldiers' libraries showed, by 1928, that Gorky had gradually superseded all other authors in demand. His popularity has perceptibly grown since, owing to the celebration of his sixtieth birthday and his subsequent visit to Russia.

A great deal of controversy was aroused by another public statement of Gorky, on the occasion of the tenth anniversary of the Soviet order. From a distant perspective he tried to appraise in cautious terms the changes that had taken place in Russia. The growing solidity of the Soviet power gave him hope in its " founding a basis for the construction of a new world ":

As such a basis I regard the release of the enslaved will to live, that is, the will to act, for life is action. . . .

It seems to me that in the Soviet Union people are beginning to work, conscious of the significance of labour for the State, conscious of the fact that labour alone is the direct and the shortest road to liberty and culture. The Russian workman is earning for himself not a wretched, niggardly subsistence, as used to be the case: he is earning for himself a state. He is aware of gradually becoming master of the whole country and leader of the peasantry on the road to freedom. . . . The Russian workman, remembering the legacy of his leader, Vladimir Lenin, is successfully learning to rule the State — this is a fact whose importance cannot be exaggerated. . . .

He then proceeds to make clear that he does not overlook the dark sides of the new order, but that knowing as he does the average Russian workman, having studied him for more than half a century, he wonders not so much at his negative traits as at the fact that he is not much worse:

I know the builder of contemporary Russian life from the days of his youth. He began as an " abused errand-boy," a stepson of the horrible Russian life, then he passed through the revolutionary underground into prison, exile, convict-labour, then he made a great revolution, one which has, indeed, " shaken the old world," and will continue shaking it until its downfall. After that he carried on for three years a victorious civil war, at the end of which he undertook the most difficult task of restoring the economic ruins of Russia, a task for which he had not been tutored, just as he had not been taught how to beat the highly learned generals on the numerous fronts. . . . He has had no time for cultivating in himself the qualities claimed by our refined intelligentsia, who so easily leaped over into the camp of his enemies, thereby proving that their " qualities " — as, for example, socialism or humanism — were purely verbal.

Curiously enough, in this *Greeting* to the triumphant Bolshevik state, Gorky managed to reiterate his old pet notions, for which he had been chastised many a time by orthodox party leaders. Into this *Greeting*, solemnly published in the official *Izvestia* and the semi-official *Pravda*, he smuggled his twenty-five-year-old *Chelovyek* (*Man*), and even — now that

both Plekhanov and Lenin were dead — his much-spanked *bogostroitelstvo*:

Years ago, in the period of gloomy reaction, 1907–1910, I called man a " god-builder," putting into this word the meaning that man, in himself and out in the world, creates and embodies the faculty to create, miracles, justice, beauty, and all other faculties with which Idealists endow the power alleged to exist outside of man. He knows that outside of his reason and will there are no miraculous forces, except for the forces of nature, which he must master in order to make them serve his reason and will, and thus ease his labour and life. He is confident that " only man is, everything else is his point of view and his handiwork."

Such a man the world has not seen heretofore, and it is this man who has undertaken the great task of educating the toiling masses " after his image and likeness "; this task he is performing with extraordinary success. . . .

After denouncing the former " lovers of the people " who now spit and fume at their fetish, Gorky ends up rhapsodically:

My joy and my pride is the new Russian man, builder of the new state.

To this small yet great man, who is to be found in all the remote nooks of the land, in factories and villages lost in the steppes and the frozen marshes of Siberia, in the mountains of the Caucasus and the tundras of the north; to this often very lonely man working amidst people who as yet understand him with difficulty; to the shaper of his state, who modestly does his seemingly unimportant work which is of vast historical significance; to him I send my heart-felt greeting.

Comrade! Know and trust that you are the most needful man on earth. By doing your small work you have begun to create a really new world.

Learn and teach.

I firmly grip your hand, comrade!

The *émigré* press naturally met Gorky's *Greeting* with a storm of indignation and abuse. The *Manchester Guardian* published, along with an abridged version of Gorky's statement, also an abridged answer by F. Dan, editor of the Menshevik

bi-monthly, *Socialistichesky Vestnik* (*Socialist Messenger*), published in Berlin. The Mensheviks have been the most reserved among the Russian anti-Bolsheviks abroad, and Dan's protest against Gorky was also distinguished by comparative politeness. He began by allowing for the " privilege of an artist in politics," be it G. B. Shaw's glorification of Mussolini, or M. Gorky's panegyrics to the Bolshevik dictatorship. But he went on to say that Gorky was " abusing his privilege " by praising the very men whom ten years previously he condemned as " shameless adventurers and demented fanatics." He referred, of course, to Gorky's articles in *Novaya Zhizn*, in particular to the one under the title *One Must Not Be Silent*. More virulent than Dan was Kerensky's Paris periodical, *Dni* (*Days*), which published a series of condemnatory letters against Gorky, alleged to have come anonymously from Russia.

Gorky felt obliged to reply, in the *Izvestiya*, to his denouncers, in a letter addressed *To the Anonyms and the Pseudonyms*. Dan's objection to his change of front he met with the direct admission that in 1917 he " was wrong," in fearing that the dictatorship of the proletariat would " pulverize and annihilate " the advanced Bolshevik workmen, whom he considered as " the only truly revolutionary force." The subsequent ten years dissipated his fears by demonstrating the creative activity of the Russian workmen, " an activity that has been in all sorts of ways interfered with by ' cultured Europe,' diligently egged on by the Russian *émigrés*." He admired the achievements of the Soviet workers, but he denied any desire to " flatter " them; in all his life he never tried to " please " any group or individual. The changes promulgated by the Soviet government he regarded as more significant than the reforms of Peter the Great:

It is not Peter the Great who is acting now in the Soviet Union, but the Great Ivan, the workman and peasant beneath one cap, and the work concerns not " reforms," but a radical transformation of all the foundations of our old life. I know that Russia had and has much that is bad; I have reasons to believe that I know that better than the authors of the an-

onymous letters. But never and nowhere has the good been so good as it is at present in Russia.

Needless to say, Gorky's " explanations " served only to enhance his isolation among the *émigrés*. By the reverse token, his acclaim in Soviet Russia grew more and more united. This became apparent in 1928, during the celebration of his sixtieth birthday (on March 28). Ten years before, Gorky's fiftieth birthday passed unnoticed. Russia was struggling for its existence and suffering indescribable hardships. Gorky was then still raging against the " adventurers " in his *Novaya Zhizn*. Korney Chukovsky tells us that in March, 1919, a handful of Gorky's co-workers on *World Literature,* together with some of the type-setters and help, " celebrated " Gorky's jubilee. " Champagne glasses were filled with tea (without sugar), and each guest received a luxurious cookie, the size of a five-copeck piece." Among those present was the poet, Alexander Blok, who recorded in Chukovsky's notebook : " This jubilee day of Alexey Maximovich is radiant and fully saturated; not an empty day, but a musical day." In the terminology of the author of *Twelve,* who died from lack of will to struggle against life's tedium, those words were significant. But one of the guests proved a traditional jubilee orator, and with a champagne glass in his outstretched hand he began to deliver himself of grandiloquent banalities concerning Gorky's evangelical love for the humiliated and offended, and the tender halo with which he surrounded his heroes. Gorky fidgeted for a while, and finally interrupted the orator rather curtly, and made him stop. He then turned to a seven-year-old boy who was in the room, treated him to his cookie, and softly admonished him : " Don't ever celebrate jubilees. When you will be fifty, tell the world that you are forty-nine, or fifty-one. . . . And the refreshments you shall then eat by yourself." Another writer present, Yevgeny Zamyatin, was reminded by the occasion of Finland, where women serve as public bath-attendants. He noted down: " Once while in Finland I went to a bath-house. Behold, a woman came up to me, an uddered-like Finn. She began to wash me, rub here and pour there. I felt embarrassed,

and did not know what to do with myself. But the attendant did not wince: she was a habitual. The jubilarian must have felt as I did. As to those who do the pouring, they don't mind: they're habituals! "

In March, 1928, Gorky's sixtieth birthday was celebrated as a national event; as regards official sanction and solemnity it certainly eclipsed the one hundredth birth of Tolstoy, commemorated in September of the same year. The absence of the jubilarian did not diminish the enthusiasm of the speeches and articles in his honour; if anything it spared him embarrassment. It was easier for him to blush in his Capo di Sorrento retreat, while reading the messages and the special issues of *Izvestiya, Pravda,* and various illustrated weeklies. With all his sincere dislike of public celebrations, Gorky could not help feeling happy at this recognition accorded him after thirty-five years of literary work. It must have gratified him, too, to be greeted not only as a writer but also as a man and a fighter. Along with the homage of André Gide, Jacob Wassermann, Stanislavsky, and other men of letters and the stage, he was honoured by the State, by public organizations, by groups and individuals of no relation to the muses. The multiplicity of his appeal became apparent on that occasion. Rykov in the name of the Soviet Union, Bukharin in the name of the Party, vied with the Lenin Institute, the Academy of Arts, the Academy of Sciences, the All-Russian Labour and Professional Unions, and a legion of other institutes and societies who claimed the kinship of Gorky. It goes without saying that numerous groups of workmen expressed their joy and pride at the triumph of one of " their own "; in fact, nearly all the greetings emphasized the merit of Gorky as a " proletarian writer."

I am inclined to believe that Gorky, with his inordinate reverence for science and scientists, was moved most deeply by the messages he received on that occasion from Russia's scientific institutions. In his acknowledgement of the message sent by A. P. Karpinsky, President of the Academy of Sciences, Gorky spoke of his " profound admiration and esteem for Russia's science and scientists," which he had felt even in his youth, when " as a semi-savage " he " first learned about the won-

derful achievements of positive sciences and the indefatigable efforts of scientists, which lend strength to man's mind and will." He concluded:

It is not for me to speak of the strenuous work of Russian scientists during the last ten years, which has been so stupendously fruitful; but as a Russian, I reverently and gratefully bow my head before you and all who work in the domain of science.

The universally esteemed Sergey Oldenburg, then Permanent Secretary of the Academy of Sciences, had two articles on Gorky published on his birthday, one in the *Izvestiya,* and one in the *Pravda.* In *Gorky and Science,* he reviewed Gorky's literary work, and concluded that had he not become an artist he would have been a scientist, because he possesses " the main prerequisite for scientific work," namely, " his whole being has incessantly demanded a conscious attitude toward life's phenomena and the surrounding world." In his other paper, *Maxim Gorky and Scientists,* Professor Oldenburg wrote of the warm affection and gratitude with which Russian men of science remembered Gorky's work in their behalf during the hungry years of 1918, 1919, and 1920. It was Gorky's influence with Lenin that made it possible then to obtain extra rations for them, despite the prevailing " suspicion " of intellectuals among the ruling class. In normal times it is difficult to realize what that extra ration meant in the period when " the value of one pound of black bread could hardly be estimated, since it often became equivalent to the value of life itself." Oldenburg added that though himself sick and underfed, Gorky was tireless in providing for the scientists, aside from the extra ration, also books, apparatus, and even commissions for trips abroad. " Alas," he admits parenthetically, " one cannot conceal the fact that not a small number of our scientists made use of their commissions for the desertion of their motherland." An illuminating detail for the understanding of Gorky's ungrateful task as pleader for the " traitorous intelligentsia."

A digression may be in order here in connexion with Gorky's title of a " proletarian writer." The Bolshevik revolution pro-

duced its Savonarolas who have championed the wiping out of whatever was not one hundred per cent communist, Marxian, proletarian. A group of Bolsheviks harped continually on the need of creating and supporting a " proletarian culture," a " proletarian literature," a " proletarian theatre," and so on, infinitely. Both Lenin and Trotsky ridiculed this phraseology, particularly Lenin, who in his wonted curt manner urged to put a stop to this " chatter," and to endeavour to catch up with bourgeois culture before dreaming of superseding it with a proletarian culture. Yet the word " proletarian " continued to have a magnetic attraction in a country of " proletarian dictatorship." There arose a literary school, known as *Napostovtsy*, from the name of its publication, *Na postu* (*At the Post*), whose loud intolerance atoned for its aridity and poverty of talent. Standing " at the post " as defenders of proletarian ideology, these men assert that in a proletarian state there is no room for non-proletarian literature, for writers who are mere " fellow-travellers " of the new order and not its wholehearted supporters. As I have said, they were more loud than gifted or logical, but as elsewhere a cry in the name of loyalty finds a hearing with the rank and file.

Gorky did not escape scrutiny at the hands of these zealots. In a number of articles and in literary text-books he was subjected to an inquisition and found wanting as a proletarian writer. Among the evidence against him was advanced the fact that as a child he was brought up in a petty-bourgeois family, and that most of the years before he became a writer he spent as a tramp and a Jack-of-all-trades, rather than as a legitimate factory worker. As to his writings, it was pointed out that he failed in drawing proletarian characters, rendering them sweetish and unreal. He was reproached for devoting his post-revolutionary fiction to problems and scenes of the past, rather than portraying the glorious present. Of course, he was taken to account for his heresies, defections, and disloyalties. He was declared a fellow-traveller, and one who lived abroad, in the bourgeois West, to boot.

In October, 1927, a solemn session was held by the Section of Literature and Art of the Communistic Academy in Moscow,

to commemorate the thirty-fifth anniversary of Gorky's literary activity. After the acceptance of a formal congratulatory message to Gorky, the meeting was opened to addresses and discussion, which proved so lively that it was necessary to prolong it on a subsequent evening. The minutes were published in the *Vestnik* (*Messenger*) of the Communistic Academy, and they reveal, along with earnest and vital critical analysis, a goodly amount of academic piffle, of the Marxian brand. The comparatively lenient tone of the discussion may be explained by the absence of the representative of the *Napostovtsy*, who was unable to appear because of illness.

The Russian masses, meanwhile, showed a growing interest in Gorky's books, as witnessed by library reports. Some of the " class-conscious " groups wondered at the attacks on Gorky's proletarianism, especially in view of Lenin's reiterated statement to the effect that he regarded Gorky as the foremost proletarian writer. One such group in a small Volga town decided to take the bull by the horns; they wrote a letter to Gorky, asking him whether he was a proletarian writer or not. Gorky's reply is characteristic of his conscientious treatment of correspondents, and is at the same time an interesting profession of faith. It follows in part:

Dear Comrades!
Personally I am not interested in the disputes of the critics as to whether I am a " proletarian or non-proletarian writer." In the mass of congratulations I am getting from the workmen of every corner of the Union they call me in one accord " our own," " proletarian," and " comrade." The voice of the workmen is, of course, more imposing to me than the critics' voices. I am very proud of the fact that the workmen regard me as one of their own, as their " comrade ": this is a great honour for me, and is my genuine pride.

As to the term " proletarian," it does not, to my mind, quite correspond to the actual state of the toiling masses in the Soviet Union. By " proletarian," as you know, we mean a class of men who live by their personal earnings and who have no other means of existence. Can this label apply to the workmen and peasants of the Soviet Union, to the mass of toilers who have taken into their hands the political power in our land,

and who are gradually taking possession of the whole economy, of all the treasures of our country?

You ask: " By what tokens may one define a true proletarian writer?" I think that these tokens are not many. Among them are: the writer's active hatred for everything that oppresses man from the outside and from within, everything that prevents the free development and growth of man's faculties; his merciless hatred for idlers, parasites, toadies, vulgarians, and in general for scoundrels of all sorts and forms. The writer's respect for man as the source of creative energy, the creator of all things, of all wonders on earth; for man as a fighter against the elemental forces of nature, and the creator of a new, " second " nature by means of his toil, his science and technique, in order to free himself from the useless waste of his physical strength, a waste inevitably senseless and cynical under conditions of a class-state. The writer's poetization of collective labour which aims to create new forms of life, forms which absolutely exclude the mastery of man over man and the absurd exploitation of his strength. The writer's appraisal of woman as not only the source of physiological enjoyment, but as a faithful comrade and help in the difficult business of life. His attitude toward children as to persons before whom we are all responsible for everything we do. The writer's effort to heighten in every way the readers' dynamic relation to life, to inspire them with sureness of their power, of their ability to conquer in themselves and outside of themselves everything that prevents men from grasping and becoming aware of the great meaning of life, the tremendous importance and joy of labour.

This is, in brief, my view of the kind of a writer that is needed by the labouring world. . . .

Despite his reputed, and avowed, inconsistencies, Gorky manages to adhere in substance to the views he has been voicing throughout the four decades of his literary expression. His fluctuations and contradictions, however sensational and striking they appeared at the time, had to do with detail, with method, with strategy and tactics, rather than with the goal. To be sure, there is a much greater responsibility about choosing and practising the means than about cleaving to a lofty

but often abstract end. Gorky's errors abundantly prove his weakness as a man of action, a politician.

Again and again we can see in the case of Gorky how deep the gulf is growing between the moribund Old Russia, unenviably dragging out its days in exile, and the nascent New Russia. While the Soviet Union celebrated the sexagenarian author, stressing the dubious (since it is accidental) merit of his common birth and his common occupations, the *émigrés* used the occasion for heaping abuse upon the " plebeian " upstart. Konstantin Balmont, once an exile from tsaristic Russia, for his revolutionary poems, at the same time as Gorky was, the composer (with Grechaninov) of the revolutionary hymn in 1917, now stooped to sling mud at Gorky, repeatedly insulting him with the apellation " commoner." Another ex-radical and democrat, Alexander Yablonovsky, wrote on Gorky's birthday in the Paris Monarchist daily, *Vozrozhdeniye (Renascence)* : " Of Gorky one may say directly, without beating about the bush and timid ambiguity: he is a dishonourable man and undoubtedly an accomplice of the Sovietist criminals." He goes on to speak in the name of the exiles: " Russian writers have nothing to do with this jubilee, because it is precisely our literature and writers that Gorky has betrayed like Judas Iscariot."

I have already spoken of the *émigrés'* unreserved hostility toward Gorky, of their reluctance to discuss him with me, as if it were a painful and nauseating subject. Still their behaviour on this occasion, the celebration of a big writer, whatever his views and personal conduct, puzzled me. I wrote for an explanation to Mikhail Osorgin, a distinguished author of fiction (*Quiet Street*) and essays, one of the few anti-Bolshevik *émigrés* who do not lose their head and decency when discussing Soviet affairs. M. Osorgin contributes to the liberal and radical press abroad and, incidentally, he edited a special Gorky edition of Kerensky's *Dni,* which was comparatively tolerant and readable. As he seems to me one of the finest representatives of the tragically uprooted Russian intelligentsia, I shall translate a few passages from his valuable estimate of the " Gorky

affair," which he was good enough to write to me in answer to my inquiry:

The attitude toward Gorky in pre-revolutionary Russia was not an even one. He was considered a gifted and prominent writer, but was not respected as a thinker, which he tried to be. Neither by education nor by his cultural upbringing did Gorky ever belong to the inner, exclusive caste of the " intelligentsia "; one always felt in him an " autodidact " who had fallen under the Marxians' influence. . . . Gorky was liked, but not respected. In the eyes of our " creators of public opinion " he was a talented writer, culturally of the level of an average " class-conscious workman," well-read, of a colossal memory, utterly incapable of digesting the mass of fragmentary information he swallowed and of working out an independent *Weltanschauung*, above all incapable of refraining from puerile philosophizing and over-loading his art with " ideas."

One must add that Gorky was always greatly hurt by his " entourage "; he was always surrounded by numerous people of the hanger-on variety, who exploited his name and his purse. . . . The multitudinous gossip and rumours spread about him to this day have more often than not emanated from this entourage. Few individuals suffered so much from " friends " as did Gorky, who is either too credulous or too careless in the choice of his intimates.

You are quite right in stating that during the first years of the revolution Gorky helped the starving intelligentsia. He was very close to the ruling circles, and particularly friendly with Lenin; he never failed to utilize this relationship for the sake of writers, scientists, artists. One may say unhesitatingly that Gorky has saved hundreds of intellectual workers from hunger, humiliation, even death. . . . I know personally of Gorky's efforts in behalf of people threatened with dire punishment (even execution), of his appeals to Lenin and other men of authority. No doubt, he was prompted by humane feelings, and he was not afraid to annoy officials and institutions with his petitions about people whom he at times did not know personally and only trusted their champions. His pleas on some occasions suffered severe defeat, perhaps because his powerful friends regarded his political acumen critically. The

Petrograd writers know that were it not for the intercession of Maxim Gorky their lot during the revolutionary years would have been much more lamentable. . . .

Why do the *émigrés* treat Gorky " cannibalistically," to use your expression?

There are many general causes. First of all, of course, for his friendship with the representatives of the Soviet government, for his acceptance, even adoration, of the revolution. He is being blamed for the fact that, with his connexions and the (moral) authority which he enjoys in the USSR, he has never [?] come out in the press openly and sharply against Sovietist despotism, imprisonment, executions, suppression of the printed word. In the numerous interviews he has given for foreign newspapers he has willingly (and with good reason) emphasized the positive features of the revolution, the awakening of thought in the broad layers of the population, the thirst for knowledge, the greater accessibility of education for the formerly oppressed classes, the amazing vitality of Russia, its perspectives. Yet he never mentions the dark sides of Russian life, in particular the irresponsible conduct of the band of rulers who have hurled Russia into the horrors of Terrorism, and who have made violence the only method of government. It is generally known that Gorky himself is an enemy of violence and Terror, that he is aware of the depressing conditions of the Russian working class, that he is personally unable to live or work in Russia. This has been interpreted as pusillanimity unpardonable in a writer and citizen. In his justification one must say that such interviews he was obliged to give for the purpose of counteracting the constant declarations of the *émigrés* regarding the destruction of Russia, the demoralization of its people — those plaintive groans which lower our national dignity in the eyes of foreigners.

Gorky has been baited and slandered for a long time; but such has been the lot of nearly all those who have " accepted the revolution." To Gorky's credit be it said that for many years he has ignored the calumnious sallies. It is regrettable that lately (before his trip home) he ventured, without defending himself, to hurl unjust, unfounded, and wholesale accusations against the *émigrés,* and the *émigré* writers in particular. This lowered him in the eyes of those who had regarded him

with respect and sympathy. The worst thing is that he made these statements in Soviet newspapers, that is, in a land where no one can retort him, and where no one is going to verify the truth of his sweeping condemnations.

One particularly harsh treatment of Gorky by the *émigrés* had a rather accidental pretext. One of the Russian newspapers printed a private letter of Gorky to his friends, in which he expressed his regret at the death of Dzerzhinsky, the main instigator of Terror, the former head of the Cheka, with whom Gorky was once tied by friendship. The letter was *a customary condolence written upon the receipt of a death announcement.* The name of Dzerzhinsky is hateful not only to the *émigrés,* but to all Russia. Whatever the personal traits of this strange and terrible man, with his name are associated memories of thousands of men tortured and shot. The memory of these men is too fresh to permit even the most dispassionate persons to recall Dzerzhinsky with anything but a curse, and of course Gorky cannot help understanding this. The publication of his *private* letter was extremely disagreeable to Gorky himself, judging at least from his letter in the *Izvestiya* in which he complained against such a treatment of his private correspondence. As to the *émigrés,* they met Gorky's letter with bitter and vehement condemnation; in this case they were certainly right. . . .

M. Osorgin's statement, quoted here in part, speaks for itself, and in view of his urbane generosity it would not be fair to take issue with him, even if I were impelled to do so. One or two points may be made clearer, perhaps. The case of Dzerzhinsky is not so simple as it appears on the surface. Those who knew him intimately, like Lenin or Gorky, were aware of his almost effeminate tenderness toward living creatures. In taking upon himself the headship of a department whose office it was to extirpate mercilessly everyone and everything suspected of putting sticks in the spokes of the revolutionary wheel, Dzerzhinsky showed a loyalty to the cause, which rose above personal sentiments and instincts. When Lenin and his associates resolved on Terror as a means to combat the internal enemies, they may have been wrong, unethical, but they did so not from blood-thirstiness. The revo-

lution must be saved, even if it be through violence. Someone had to do the dirty work, and Felix Dzerzhinsky undertook to do it, despite his hypersensitiveness. If we pay tribute to heroes who give themselves unsparingly for an ideal, we must not slight those who pour out on the altar what may be more precious to them than their very life, namely — for the lack of a better word — their soul.

Gorky's chagrin at the publication of his private letters was expressed in a truculent note, in which incidentally he spoke his mind about the unceremonious manners of certain Soviet high functionaries. It read in part:

Of late my private letters to writers have been made public in the press. I recall that in former days writers waited more or less patiently for the death of their correspondent, and only after his funeral they published his letters. I should ask my fellow-writers also to wait a while, and not place me in a comic and awkward position while I am alive. . . . It is possible that they are led into error by A. Lunacharsky and N. Piksanov, who have erroneously included me among the authors already dead. Only by such an error can I explain the fact that having decided to publish *Selected Works* by M. Gorky, Lunacharsky and Piksanov fail to ask the author whether he approves of such a publication, and which of his works he might " select " himself. . . .

Regretting the fact that Gorky finally broke his silence and began to attack his attackers, M. Osorgin has probably in mind, above all, Gorky's introduction to D. A. Gorbov's book, *On the Literature of the White Émigrés*. In this paper Gorky, indeed, seems to give vent to his pent-up and long-controlled wrath against the vilifiers of Soviet Russia. That his darts may incidentally have also a personal tinge, can be only conjectured from the fact that among the Whites whom he mentions by name are Merezhkovsky, Hippius, Filosofov, and other unsqueamish slanderers of Gorky. This may and may not be so; the important thing is that the burden of Gorky's philippic against the *émigrés* can hardly be controverted. To be sure, there are Osorgins among the prominent *émigrés,* but these could be numbered on the fingers of one hand.

Gorky speaks, in that Introduction, of the brutalities of the interventionist armies and of the analogous motives in the utterances of the exiled intelligentsia. He wonders at the sudden display of so much hatred and malice on the part of the intelligentsia who have always protested their lofty idealism, their altruism, and above all their love for the people. Such an astonishing number of Russian writers who had glorified extravagantly the people, Dostoyevsky's " god-bearing " people, Tolstoy's Christ-like people, lost their " love " for this *narod* overnight, and began to speak of Russia as a " bitch," and of its people as adorned with the snout of a pig. Refined poets now sang of holy hatred, of sacred vengeance, of " hanging the villains in silence." Gorky, being of the people, never felt the need of declaring his " love for the people." He tells us that in 1917 he had grave misgivings at the sight of the rustic people raising their angry faces over the Russian land. Those faces frightened the intelligentsia, the people's " nightingale," and the nightingale " fluttered off into the bushes." The Bolsheviks proved the only force unafraid to cope with the anarchic people set loose. Gorky admits that at the time he feared that the holy people would sweep away the Bolsheviks along with the intellingentsia and organized workmen, and he credits the " inhuman energy of Lenin and his associates " with having prevented this from happening. He arraigns the intelligentsia who were guilty of sabotage, who abandoned their land, and have engaged in egging on foreign interventionists and in nursing their peevish grievances. Their soil-lessness, verbosity, and wingless malice he compares with the constructive work going on in the New Russia, and concludes:

The *émigrés* often reproach the Bolsheviks for " distorting Marx," for not living " according to Marx." That is, of course, not quite the case, but — why not go further? They are even more sinful, they do not intend to live even " according to Darwin," boldly endeavouring to destroy the struggle for existence among men, in order to transfer the forces absorbed by this senseless struggle to the struggle of man with nature, for the subjugation of its elemental energies to the rational interests of humanity.

Meanwhile the intelligentsia across the border are pining away in ennui and idleness, rapidly exhausting the remnants of their strength, and essentially regretting only one thing: those " heart-felt evenings," when sitting around the samovar they oozed eloquence on such themes as the tyranny of Autocracy, love for the people, and the inadequate arrangement of the universe as a whole.

It is quite possible that if Prometheus, having stolen some new fire illuminating the mysteries of life, appeared to them and interfered with their tea-drinking, they would curse Prometheus too.

Gorky's *Greeting* for the tenth anniversary of the Bolshevik revolution, the national celebration of his sixtieth birthday, and his controversy with the *émigrés,* combined to make clear his stand with regard to the Soviet Union. Though not uncritical, though not orthodox-communistic, it was a decidedly sympathetic stand. Since the sympathy appeared mutual, the inevitable conclusion had to be drawn as to Gorky's co-operation in the building of a new life at home. What form was this co-operation to take? If Gorky's value lies in his literary production, then the best he might do for his country would be to devote his remaining years to creative work. But to the young Soviet state Gorky is not merely a big writer. He is a symbolic figure, a demonstration of the potential rise of the masses to the heights of cultural achievement, a bridge from the past to the future across a feverish, groping present. When children admire a toy they are not content with beholding it; they crave to hold and touch it. The Russian masses cry: " We want Gorky! " They want his tangible presence. And so do the intellectuals, and the political leaders. Most of the articles and messages regarding Gorky, before and during his celebration, had the refrain: Gorky must come back. President Karpinsky of the Academy of Sciences, its Permanent Secretary, Oldenburg, Commissar of Education Lunacharsky, President of the People's Commissars, Rykov, editor of the *Pravda,* Bukharin, and other spokesmen of the Soviet Union voiced the same request: Gorky must come home, and see with his own eyes what has been done during his absence. In an article,

What We Want of Gorky, Nikolay Bukharin pointed out the need of such a writer as Gorky to portray contemporary life. Among Gorky's qualifications he underlined his being " an advocate of culture and labour. He has always valued and esteemed labour above everything else in the world. Perhaps no one feels so keenly the pathos of constructive, creative labour, as Gorky does; no one is aware of the enormous revolutionary, transforming meaning of labour as is this proletarian writer." Bukharin describes the present moment: " The fever of construction is at its highest. Our Soviet ant-hill is stirring as never before. Men are moving ponderous rocks, do foolish things, make mistakes, correct them, err again and rectify again, learn and study, remake everything around them, and remake themselves — yet we have not had as yet a broad canvas of this great epoch! " He goes on deploring the state of literature, the absence of all-embracing observers, of adequate evaluators of the complex moment, and concludes: " With all his qualifications, Gorky is in a position to fill the enormous gap. He is awaited as a kindred artist by our Union, our working class, and our Party, with which Gorky has been connected for many, many years. That is why we expect his arrival: he must come to us for work, for a great, fine, glorious labour! "

Gorky could not ignore the siren call. He had been postponing his return year after year, for reasons of health and literary work. During his celebration, A. Halatov published in the *Pravda* a passage from Gorky's letter to him:

Early next May I am going to Russia, and shall travel all summer through the places where I used to live. That is decided. I am going home, in order to see what has been done there during the five years [seven?] of my sojourn in Europe. I feel like writing a book about the New Russia. For this I have already accumulated a deal of most interesting material. I need to visit and observe — unseen — factories, clubs, villages, beer-halls, construction places, Komsomols [Young Communists], college students, classrooms, colonies for socially dangerous children, worker-correspondents and village-correspondents, women-delegates, the new Mussulman women,

and so forth, and so on. This is a most serious undertaking. When I think of it, my hair stands on end from excitement.

These lines were reprinted everywhere in Russia, with enthusiastic comments, though a good deal of doubt still prevailed as to whether Gorky's promise would go beyond good intentions. The *émigré* press made sneering remarks. The *Vozrozhdeniye* carried an article full of insinuations about Gorky's " enviable health," which had time and again served him as a pretext for staying away from the USSR. It presented the repeated deferments of his return to Russia as a farcical race on the same spot, entitled " I am coming — I am not coming," and mentioned with glee Mayakovsky's verses, in which with his wonted crudeness the poet taunted Gorky as a deserter, and proffered him comfortable living quarters in Moscow. The Riga daily, *Sevodnya (Today)*, reported that Katherina Pavlovna, Gorky's first wife, made a special trip to Sorrento, with the object of advising her former husband, in the name of the Politbureau (the inner sanctum of the Soviet government), that his further staying away from home was " regarded as desertion, treason and disloyalty to the world proletariat."

Gorky did go to Russia, in the spring of 1928. Had he, indeed, cared for his health and proper working conditions, he would not have kept his promise. Russia's climate and the prospective festivities augured ill for a sixty-year-old consumptive engaged in writing a novel of *Forty Years (Klim Samgin)*. But, as I have already quoted him, Alexey Peshkov usually yields to Maxim Gorky, and these twain are at the command of the Russian citizen in him. The risk he ran in succumbing to the eagerly proffered embrace of Russia, was well realized by his leading compatriots. In a message of welcome published in the *Pravda*, there was a warning to his admirers:

A wave of ardent welcome is rising from every side toward Gorky. A well-deserved personal triumph awaits him. In the dense throng that will encompass him everyone will wish to push forward, to have a closer look at Gorky, to shake hands with him, to say a few words to him. He has already been

elected as honorary member by numerous societies and circles. An eager desire will be shown for his presence at many meetings. An understandable and legitimate desire. But we wish to warn Gorky's admirers: he presents a cultured value in himself, and one should treat him as a cultural value. We must spare Gorky's health and strength.

The ordeal faced by Gorky on his arrival would have taxed the endurance of a younger and stronger man. He was wanted everywhere and all the time, and he did not have the heart to refuse. What sustained him at the endless receptions, mass meetings, banquets, visits to factories, institutions, army barracks, special performances, and solemn sessions of Government bodies, was the infectious enthusiasm of his compatriots and his own affection for those very Russians whom he had observed and castigated for nearly four decades. Nor may one discount the effect of the joy which he was human enough to experience at this hearty acclamation by a country where not long ago he had known prison and persecution. Now as he travelled east and south and north he came upon Gorky Streets, Gorky Squares, Gorky Schools, Gorky Colonies for Homeless Children, not to forget the Gorky Cars, as fourth-class railroad cars are generally known in Russia. It was balm to the weary heart of the old wanderer to see tokens of devotion in places revisited, to be awarded membership cards by the bakers' union and the builders' union and endless other unions, to be presented with gifts, manufactured by the proletarian aristocracy of the land, to be given a rifle and elected honorary member by the Red Army. . .

Whatever Gorky did manage to see of the new order in the midst of the festive turmoil stirred him deeply. He kept on repeating: " Amazing! Astonishing! " To the sophisticated Muscovites he felt obliged to apologize for his unrelieved ecstasy. " You," he said at a meeting of the State Publishing House, " do not realize, living in your own country, what an enormous work has been done here. This enormous work I see on each street, even in the Moscow pedestrian whose gait is so different from what it was ten years ago. . . . Yes, I am an optimist. Yes, that is my biological peculiarity." The things

he saw showed that the revolution had struck deep roots in the very mind of the people, that the average man had been jolted out of apathy and stagnation, and that Gorky's pet aversion, smug Philistia, had been dethroned. He who had known the darkness, the savagery, the lack of human dignity among the bulk of the people, could not react reservedly to such signs of cultural growth as factory clubs and theatres, as village reading huts with radios, as the latinization of oriental alphabets, or the removal of veils by the women of Turkmenistan and Uzbekistan, or the efforts at redeeming prostitutes and criminals by means of teaching them some trade in wholesome surroundings. On visiting one such place, his eyes met a placard on the gate: " A flaming greeting to Maxim Gorky from former Chelkashes and Malvas who have come to the road of an honest life through the Labour Commune." At the end of his visit, moved to the point of tears, Gorky inscribed in the visitors' book: " As one who was once a socially dangerous person, I testify: what is being done here is altogether amazing and profoundly significant. M. Gorky."

On his trip down the Volga, to see the Volga-Don canal still in construction, Gorky was greeted by throngs at every stopping place, and requested to make a speech. His words were of necessity few and often trite, the refrain being: " Study, be patient, work! Above all — work! " He was often moved deeply by the tokens of affection, and his eyes readily filled with tears. The correspondent of a Menshevik paper abroad wrote sarcastically that the rumour of Gorky's copious tears spread across the Lower Volga as he was sailing down from Nizhni Novgorod, provoking the remark: " Gorky is coming! Look out, the Volga may overflow! " At Saratov, where the steamer arrived at four in the morning, Gorky was met by a crowd of stevedores, who wanted to have a chat with a one time colleague. They complained of their hardships, low wages and difficult toil. According to the reporter of the Saratov *Povolzhskaya Pravda* (*Volga Truth*), Gorky said to them:

" My dear friends, do you realize that stevedores in foreign lands live under much worse conditions? And remember that

here we shall have before very long golden rivers flowing. I divide men into three categories: pessimists, sceptics, and optimists. As pessimists I regard those who maintain that $2 \times 2 = 3$, as sceptics those for whom $2 \times 2 = 4$, and as optimists those to whom $2 \times 2 = 5$. My friends, I belong to the optimists, and I call on you to follow my example."

We do not know how the stevedores took Gorky's amazing arithmetic. His " general impression " of the New Russia he summed up in a short speech before the Conference of Workers' Universities:

. . . " Everything seems to have been rejuvenated from within. Gone are the Russian softness, the melancholy of the spirit, that specifically Russian gravitation toward sadness which used to be celebrated as our beauty. Yet what beauty was there in that? Rather was that our misfortune. We were squeezed hard, and naturally we squeaked. But now everybody talks here in a fine baritone. On this I congratulate you from the depth of my heart! "

In the fall Gorky's health began to ebb. At the advice of physicians he left Russia once more for Italy. The following spring he returned to Moscow, and again resumed his Capo di Sorrento residence in the winter. This arrangement promises to work well indefinitely. In any event it permits Gorky to put out some creative fiction, though goodness knows when he may be able to make use of his " accumulated material " for his book on the New Russia. He is still writing his *Klim Samgin,* the third volume of which, recently published, brings the story to the middle of 1906; and he intends to conclude the novel with the death of Lenin! One may doubt whether Gorky will cope successfully with his " material," even if time and health should allow him to undertake such a work. He has never done well in portraying contemporary events.

The unrelieved enthusiasm of the first visit has given room to calm and critical activity. When in and out of Russia Gorky takes a close interest in a number of cultural undertakings in the Union. Among these should be mentioned the periodicals

Za Rubezhom (*Abroad*), a review of foreign literature, and *Nashi Dostizheniya* (*Our Achievements*), of which he is the editor. It occurred to him, on his first visit, that both the Soviet Union and the outside world should be regularly informed of Russia's accomplishments along material and spiritual lines. His periodical is to counterbalance the enormous amount of " self-criticism " fostered in the Soviet press and utilized one-sidedly by the enemies abroad. The eulogistic tone of the early issues of *Nashi Dostizheniya* has been lately varied by notes of criticism in regard to certain " achievements," which is, of course, a gratifying improvement.

It is gratifying because nothing seems so unsuitable to Gorky as the rôle of a professional Yes-man. " I have come into this world — to disagree " has been his fighting motto from his naïve teens to his youthful sixties. He cannot, he must not, accept any order of things as perfect and exempt from criticism. With all allowances for the extraordinary circumstances under which the Soviet Union has been forging ahead, and with all due consideration for its gigantic plan of building a new life in face of universal opposition, one cannot ignore its palpable shortcomings. Who but Gorky, with his immense moral authority, can raise his voice against bigotry and intolerance, which are among the conspicuous vices of the Stalin régime? Gorky's enemies complain that he has failed to do so. The truth is that, under the circumstances, he has been doing much in that direction, increasingly so. To be sure, his critical assaults have been confined to cultural problems. The province of politics is too tight a compartment for any but a Simon-pure Stalinist to breathe in, and Gorky's political utterances in recent months have been lamentably of the " made to order " variety. Furthermore, even in his own, literary, field, Gorky's voice does not always bear weight with the one hundred per cent loyalists. Thus, when Boris Pilnyak was attacked savagely for having inadvertently allowed a story of his to be printed abroad, after it had been forbidden by the Soviet censor, Gorky came to his defence. He pointed out that Russian culture is still too poor to dissipate extravagantly its assets. Pilnyak

may not be a communist, he is only a " fellow-traveller," but he is a talented writer, and should be treated sparingly. Gorky's intercession did not prevent the dismissal of Pilnyak from the post of President of the Soviet Writers' Union. But his voice of protest did sound forth, and will sound in the future, one may hope. That is the important thing: a dissenting voice under a dictatorship.

MAXIM GORKY AND HIS RUSSIA
(Conclusion)

MAXIM GORKY AND HIS RUSSIA

GORKY must be taken, for better or for worse, as a didactic writer. He is always imbued with a social idea, which he is anxious to convey to his readers, and his literary output may be approached with regard to the proportion and intensity of the message preached in each individual work. It hardly need be suggested that the quality of his work is in inverse proportion to the degree and obviousness of its didacticism. Yet one should remember that it was this latter trait that enhanced his value in the eyes of the masses and their fighting vanguard, and lent him the public significance which cannot be discounted by any purely aesthetic considerations.

" I have come into this world — to disagree." This line of an early poem of his might have been his life slogan. His hatred for things-as-they-are came to the surface quite early, while he lived under " settled " conditions with his relatives. An early hatred endures longer, and this perhaps may explain the comparative violence of Gorky's aversion for smugness, for sedate and respectable, convention-bound and God-fearing Philistia, in whose midst he suffocated in his childhood and boyhood. He refused to " agree " to the squalor and ignorance of that milieu, to such accepted traditions as wife-beating, vodka-swilling, fighting, swearing, and gossiping, and his disagreement often took a pugnacious form, at the expense of his much thrashed and pommelled skin. His flight from Nizhni Novgorod and the ensuing vagabondage answered not only a longing for the gipsy trail, but primarily an urge to escape from the settled smugness of his relatives, employers, and even the dogmatic intelligentsia.

It was natural for the first attempts of his pen to voice an unbridled yearning for freedom. *Makar Chudra* and *Old Woman Izergil,* along with Gorky's realistic observations, contain legends, in which extreme individualism is glorified with naïve exaggeration. The same motive, resentment of smugness, may explain the general tone of idealization in his subsequent stories, portraying the tramps. Though he did not endow his tramps with positive traits, though he did not omit to picture the drudgery and humiliating privations that go with vagabondage, he managed to lend that life a comparative attractiveness over middle-class indifferent security. His *Chelkash* shows the superiority of a thief and smuggler over a peasant whose aspirations are confined to a piece of land and a healthy wife. In *Konovalov, Heartache, The Orlovs, A Shady Tramp, Malva,* even in the unrelieved drabness of *Ex-Men* and *At the Bottom* (*Lower Depths*) and his other writings of that period, the author stresses, by implication or directly, the advantage of being free from the thraldom of things and conventions. Gorky is particularly successful in making this mode of existence alluring, when he rescues his characters from the prison of walls and roofs, and places them in the great outdoors, on the shores of the " laughing " sea or in the boundless steppe (unless it be cold and raining: *Once in Autumn*). Indirectly these tales served as a protest against existing conditions, and proved infectious. Here is a characteristic testimony by Count Alexey Tolstoy, from the reminiscences of his own youth in Samara:

There is no doubt: Gorky prepared the revolutionary temperament in the intelligentsia (and partly in the proletariat) on the eve of the revolution of 1905. The romantic sensation of freedom, of wild abandon, crept into every cranny. As soon as summer vacations began, our youth would go off " barefooting " to the places bespoken by Gorky. Those who were unable to go away arranged for domestic hoboing. Directly from their offices they would rush in boats across the Volga, where they built bonfires, drank vodka, sang songs about Stenka Razin, and philosophized, sprawled trouserless on the green slope.

The inadequacy of the tramps as spokesmen of his sentiments was felt by Gorky. In *Ex-Men,* and especially in *At the Bottom,* hoboland is stripped of its tinselled romance. These men and women, having escaped from a prison, are too hollow to replace it with aught of their own, and consequently are doomed to wriggle in hopeless nothingness. Gorky had made sufficient use of his fellow-tramps as an implied critique of middle-class existence, and proceeded to a direct attack of his enemy. His first two novels, *Foma Gordeyev* and *Three of Them,* and his first play *Smug Citizens,* are a many-sided arraignment of human pettiness, avarice, craven incuriousness and its concomitants — mulish obscurantism and immobility. These traits are shown not only in the ideal of the average man for the possession of a haberdashery store and a nice wife and nice children (*Three of Them*); not only in the greed and spiritless arrogance of wealthy merchants (*Foma Gordeyev*), and in the tedious vegetation of the lower middle-class *Smug Citizens,* the old Bessemenovs, but even in the would-be intelligentsia, in the young Peter Bessemenov. Individual freedom, unreservedly glorified in Gorky's early stories, is ridiculed in the person of Peter, who hides his small selfishness under high-sounding phrases. In all of these characters we are asked to feel the common denominator of stagnation, tenacity in upholding things-as-they-are, hence opposition to progress, to all efforts at liberating man's latent possibilities.

Gorky was keenly discontented with the rôle of an adverse critic. Like Gogol, he reproached himself for depicting only undesirable characters. Having risen from the lower depths, he felt his mission to be not only in their portrayal and condemnation, but also in guidance toward a positive goal. The Russian reader expected such guidance from the writer. But there can hardly be two opinions as to the fact that though glibly certain in his journalistic sermons and creeds, Gorky has failed so far in creating a convincing positive character in his fiction. Foma Gordeyev, the hero of the novel by that name, voices the author's sentiments in his attack on the soulless merchants, but he fails to define his aims. We know what he does not want, but we do not, nor does he or the author know

what he does want. By comparison, the negative character, Mayakin, gains immeasurably as a clear-minded, rectilineal protagonist of Big Business. The first hint at a positive character may be seen in Nil, the workman in *Smug Citizens*, the only " strong " individual in the play, who speaks of the joy and power he experiences while hammering the red-hot metal. But Nil is needlessly rude and callous, and proletarian critics have justly resented his choice as a representative workman. It was logical that by that time (1901) Gorky should have centred his sympathies and hopes on the Russian workman, the vanguard of the revolution. For by that time Gorky had known prison and persecution as a political suspect, and had become an active and lavish supporter of the revolutionary movement. All Russia was reciting his allegories, which sometimes passed the censor, but whose hidden meaning never missed the eager reader, trained to read between the lines. " Madness of the Brave," for example, became the slogan of the radical youth. The phrase was picked out of Gorky's *Song of the Falcon*, in which the smug Eel, securely crawling in the dank crevice, is contrasted by the adventurous Falcon, who perishes in battle, and whose bruised and bleeding body is embraced by the waves of the sea, and lauded in song. In 1901, in the midst of student disturbances throughout Russia, Gorky published his *Song of the Stormy Petrel,* whose appearance in the Marxian *Zhizn* caused the suspension of that review. The concluding verse of that *Song:* " There shall be a storm! Let the storm break mightily! " became another revolutionary slogan of the day. Two years later appeared Gorky's essay, *Man,* the grandiloquent statement of his *Weltanschauung,* which he has followed, reiterated, and elaborated ever since. It was a hymn to Man, his potential power, limitless in its creativeness, with the aid of his two servants, Thought and Labour. To be sure, a similar hymn to *Chelovyek* (Man) had been previously proclaimed by Satin, one of the denizens *At the Bottom ;* but that note sounded accidental in the play, and Satin was drunk, besides.

Gorky's first attempt at portraying positive characters and a positive ideal was the novel, *Mother,* published after the revo-

lution of 1905, and acclaimed since by the workers of all countries. Gorky himself has come to agree with most of his critics,
namely, that the novel suffers from weakness of characterization and too obvious didacticism. He undertook there to show
the first steps of the factory workers toward class-consciousness
and revolutionary action. His leading characters appeared too
saccharine even to such a Marxian critic as Plekhanov. In the
novel, *Summer,* Gorky attempted to show the awakening new
village, by drawing a group of old and new peasants, organized
by a disguised Social-Democrat. The novel ends in a note of
hilarious optimism concerning the nascent Russia. The publication of Gorky's play, *Enemies* (its presentation was, of
course, forbidden by the Authorities), produced a strong impression. Aside from giving a clear-cut differentiation of the
interests of the employers and employés, the "enemies," he
succeeded in presenting the workmen as the coming force.
Far from being sweetishly idealized as in *Mother,* these men
are simple, even homely, unostentatiously self-sacrificing, and
calmly certain of victory. To this list of "positive" works
should be added *From the Life of a Superfluous Man (The
Spy),* in which the revolutionary movement is only indirectly
hinted, and *The Confession,* which ends in an apotheosis
to collective humanity, whose organized will breaks all obstacles, and creates "miracles." In practically all of these
productions one sees the growth of Gorky's talent, his gradual
liberation from bookish gaudiness, and his improving power
of description, which at times, as in *Summer* and *The Confession,* reaches sheer magnificence. At the same time they all
suffer (to a lesser degree, *Enemies*) from "tendentiousness,"
the author's thesis in each case pinned on extraneously, without
organically merging with the story.

We have reached the middle of Gorky's road. He was now
about forty, with nearly two decades of literary work behind
him, and living at Capri, where the remoteness of the Russian
turmoil and the comparative solitude furnished him with a
sorely needed perspective. He looked with dissatisfaction at his
recent productions, and could not help realizing that he was
losing ground with his critics. The Marxians found fault with

his unorthodoxy and " unreal " characters. The non-Socialists were proclaiming " The End of Gorky " (Dmitry Filosofov). The latter carried more weight with Gorky because of their higher literary acumen, and because they represented the intelligentsia, for whom he has always felt a nostalgia not unmixed with revulsion. In his non-fiction writings he has praised the rôle of the intelligentsia in the enlightenment and awakening of the people, and to this day he differentiates between those who deserted Russia and joined the unhealthy emigration, and the intellectual workers who have stayed at their posts and shared the vicissitudes of the people. But Gorky the artist has never been able to portray the intelligentsia sympathetically; as a rule they appear verbose, conceited, hypocritical in their " immodestly " protested love for the people, and incapable of action. Yezhov, in *Foma Gordeyev*, exclaims:

" I should gather the remnants of my outraged soul and together with the blood of my heart I should spit into the mugs of our intelligentsia, the devil take them! I should say to them: ' You vermin! You regard yourselves the sap of my country! The fact of your existence is repaid with the blood and tears of generations and generations of Russian people! You nits! How costly you are to your country! What have you done for her? ' "

Practically the same sentiment prevails through Gorky's writings, to *Klim Samgin*, the unfinished novel, which thus far presents a devastating picture of the vain and futile Russian intelligentsia. In his two plays produced shortly before his first departure from Russia, *Summerfolk* and *Children of the Sun*, his treatment of the intelligentsia as aliens amidst their people aroused considerable indignation against the author, and contributed to the popularity of the cry: " The End of Gorky! "

At Capri begins the greatness of Gorky. His initial success had come so swiftly, and was followed by such a feverish activity, literary and political, that he had had no breathing spell for leisure and self-evaluation. In peaceful Capri the exile began to find that which he sorely lacked at home: perspective.

Like Gogol, Turgenev, Henry James, he was able to get a fuller vision of the native belfry from the vantage of distance. In Russia Gorky had stood so close to things that he was in danger of overlooking the forest because of the trees. Capri enabled him to discern more clearly the complexity of his country, of its people and problems. More important, the remoteness of the audience and its plaudits gave back to Gorky his inherent sense of self-criticism and self-analysis. Tendencies, problems, messages, editorial comments were suppressed and pushed to the background, though not altogether obliterated. Not so much to guide and teach as to describe and narrate, became Gorky's more modest goal in the seclusion of Capri. It is there that he wrote his most robust and vivid pages, re-creating unforgettably the Russia he knew and carried in his amazingly retentive memory. It is there that he began his autobiographic writings, masterly in style and portraiture, because builded on his two basic assets — memory and experience. Capri proved congenial for intro- and retrospection. The result was his as yet unexcelled masterpiece, *Childhood*. This unassuming record of his early life was epically free from sermons and problems, despite the occasional asides as to " why " he was describing the " leaden abominations " of Russian reality. Gorky found himself — a rare case for a writer in the second half of his life and career. It became clear that his strength lay in autobiography, not in the Proustian sense of introvert self-analysis, but as an extrovert record of observation and experience. This holds true of his earlier writings, whenever they were not weakened by what Tolstoy resented as " inventions," but this is especially evident in his work since *Childhood*. His subsequent autobiographic books, such as *In the World* and *My Universities,* his *Notes* and *Reminiscences,* his novels *Okurov Town* and *Matvey Kozhemyakin,* most of his *Stories* of later years, and his *Recollections* of dead contemporaries, most notably of Tolstoy, Andreyev, and Bugrov, have placed Gorky as a memoirist of unequalled power. In a sense he anticipated the memoirist tendency in present-day literature the world over, and the biographical style of Strachey-Maurois-Ludwig and their epigoni.

As suggested, the nature of Gorky's observations is extrovert. In consequence, his personal record, however interesting,
dwindles in relative importance before the huge panorama of
Russia, of which it becomes a tiny particle. The great value
of Gorky's later literary work lies precisely in his empirical
portrayal of the Russia he knows best, that is, of the lower and
middle classes. No longer anxious to use his characters as
spokesmen, positive or negative, Gorky now goes about his
work with the joy of a skilful painter who delights in his
subject-matter for its own sake, with no ax to grind. He re-
sumes, for example, his tramp memories, but how much more
alive his hobos are now that they do not proclaim Nietzschean
aphorisms or sing hymns to Man! " I do not condemn: I testify," is the motto of Matvey Kozhemyakin's memoirs, in the
book of the same title, and this motto might be used for most
of Gorky's fiction beginning with *Childhood*. His " testimony "
is most apt, curiously enough perhaps, not with regard to Russian tramps, or peasants, or workmen, or intellectuals, but concerning Russia's merchants, and even more so, concerning
common " townspeople," for lack of a better equivalent of the
Russian word *meshchanye,* applied to the class midway between peasants and merchants, a word that means burghers
and also, figuratively, smug Philistines.

Gorky's merchants, or business men, are a picturesque group.
In *Foma Gordeyev, Okurov Town, Matvey Kozhemyakin,*
various reminiscences, and his last two novels, *The Artamonov
Business (Decadence),* and *Klim Samgin* the author draws
on his abundant observations in Nizhni Novgorod, Kazan,
Samara, Moscow. He has known well the merchant class,
until recently hardly touched by the Europeanizing reforms
of Peter the Great, adhering to ancient customs and traditions, and spurning the " German " dress and haircut. He
knew intimately some typical Volga and Moscow millionaires, prototypes of his Taras Gordeyev and Ilya Artamonov,
men of a " broad nature," capable of bestiality and magnanimity, of gipsy abandon and callous greed, of smashing
expensive mirrors in restaurants, harnessing ballerinas to
their carriages, and of giving millions for cultural needs.

Strange individuals, "queer," as they would be branded in the United States, men like the multi-millionaire Bugrov, known as the Grand Prince of Nizhni Novgorod, who indulged in all kinds of vice, and at the same time gave money for the revolution, at Gorky's request, and built a home for Gorky's erstwhile comrades, the Barefooted Brigade. Or Savva Morozov, of Moscow, a cultured capitalist, who backed the Moscow Art Theatre and worked there as electrician, and spent huge sums to aid the revolution, whose aim, he well knew, was the destruction of Morozov's class. Or the ship-owner Meshkov, who permitted one of his Volga steamers to be used as a floating conference of the Socialist-Revolutionists, with Mikhaylovsky and Katherina Breshkovskaya on board. Or Savva Mamontov, who fathered Chaliapin, and built an opera house for him, when the Imperial Opera hesitated about accepting the hobo-bass. Or Tredyakov, Shchukin, and other Moscow merchants, patrons of modern art, not only domestic but foreign; they housed the finest collections of Cézanne, Gaugin, Matisse, Picasso, before these commanded attention in the West. Gorky portrays them with curiosity, understanding, and enough sympathy to make us see beneath their queerness. They all suffer from a similar malady, the tedium of life.

The same tedium lords it over the life of those one rung below the merchants, the " townspeople " — small shopkeepers, clerks, artisans, and nondescripts. *Okurov Town* may be regarded as Gorky's best novel. Its sequel, *Matvey Kozhemyakin*, is just as significant, only it suffers from uninevitable length. Okurov is a composite town of Arzamas and scores of other Russian Zenith Cities, with its equivalents of American Babbitts. But Okurov is not wedded to the civilization of bathtubs and Rotary Clubs; it is backward, Asiatic. Its denizens are obliged to be more inventive in their efforts to escape from boredom and themselves than in the rush and speed of American life. The Okurovans' chief diversion is sadism. They beat their wives and children, they indulge in public fist-fights, they prove exceedingly ingenious as tormentors of human beings and animals. Their sense of humour is expressed

in such innocent jokes as throwing dust into the eyes of blind beggars (to test whether their blindness is genuine), as hurling a dog into a lime pit, as oiling the wooden sidewalks to make pedestrians slip, and the like. The jokes of the adults do not differ much from those of the children, who vie with their elders in cruelties inflicted on birds and dogs and inoffensive people. The grown-ups look on with a chuckle as the children throw rotten eggs through open windows, or bait and stone a demented ex-official, or tie an old bucket to the tail of a dog and chase it through the streets. Mutual suspicion reigns supreme, and hatred, and envy. Emotions and sentiments are twisted into depravity and callousness. Bigotry, chauvinism, and intolerance take the place of civic virtues. Parochial stagnation breeds complacency and contempt for the rest of the world. The spokesman of these people, one-eyed Tiunov, states with pride that they are the true representatives of Russia, that Russia consists in the main of such towns as Okurov. Someone asks him, What about Moscow? Tiunov replies:

"Well, what about Moscow? Let us say, for instance, that your feet are shod in torn remnants of boots, your shirt has not been washed for a whole year, your trousers scarcely cover your shame, your belly — like your pockets — has naught but rubbish and crumbs, whereas your hat may be a fine one, say — a beaver hat! That's your Moscow!"

Gorky's *Okurov Town* is one of the gloomiest pictures of Russia since Gogol's *Dead Souls*. " Okurovism," " Okurov-dom " have become generic words for provincial Russia, as much as " Main Street " is for provincial America. While the novels (*Matvey Kozhemyakin,* though written as a sequel, is really introductory to *Okurov Town*) are composed with epic calm, quite *sine ira,* their author has used the conclusions as a passionate " text " in his non-fiction sermons. By contrast with his subsequently acquired culture and familiarity with the Western world, the remembrance of Okurovdom irked him extremely. In a number of essays Gorky expressed his hatred for the Okurov elements of Russian life, as Asiatic traits. Russia's

backwardness, mysticism, passivity, Tolstoyanism, he came to regard as oriental features which must be combated and substituted by European, Western ways. This has been the burden of his publicistic writings for the last twenty years. In conversation he is even more emphatic about his preference for " Europe " as against " Asia," the *Two Souls*, as he defined his division of humanity in an essay written in 1915. He is extravagant in his praises of American technologic progress, dismissing all strictures about the inferiority of spiritual values in American life as superficial and temporary. In the advancement of machinery and material comfort he sees a pledge for man's eventual conquest of the forces of nature, and their subjugation to man's interests. By the same token, he exalts the city over the village. His fierce opposition to the Bolsheviks in the first year of their rule was based on his fear that rural, savage Russia would overwhelm the thin crust of city workers and intellectuals, and drown the country in anarchy and chaos. In a booklet, *On the Russian Peasantry*, published in 1922, he outraged most of his contemporaries brought up on an idealized conception of the Russian villagers. He recounted there fact after fact from the recent revolutionary experience, that showed the stupidity, puerility, ignorance, and above all the cruelty, of the Russian peasant. The Russian village appears to him more hopelessly Asiatic than Okurov Town. He dreads Asia.

In 1925, during the close co-operation between the Chinese Nationalists and Moscow, Gorky spoke in an alarmed tone of this alliance. To my question whether he did not see in the union of Russia and China a possible guaranty of world peace, he mumbled: " Possibly, possibly. . . . But don't you see that the success of that union would spell the triumph of the village over the city, of Asia over Europe! " During the same year he had an opportunity to give counsel to the Mongolian Soviet Republic, and he did not mince words about accentuating the superiority of Europe over Asia.

. . . It seems to me [he wrote for the Mongolian official organ] that the most useful thing would be to introduce to

your people the principle of action. Europe may thank its active way of looking at life for everything good that it possesses and that may be recommended to other races.

" Desire is the source of suffering," was taught by Buddha. In the field of science, of art, and of technique Europe has accomplished far more than the other continents, and it has done so just because Europe has never been afraid of suffering, and has always desired something better than what it already had.

Europe has known how to awaken among its masses the impulse toward justice and liberty, and for that alone we must forgive its many sins and crimes.

Gorky's refrain of " Culture! More Culture! " has wearied the ears of his compatriots, but he continues to harp on the subject of Russia's abominations that are Asia, and her need of culture, which is Europe. Nowhere is the discrepancy between Gorky the artist and Gorky the publicist so apparent as in this issue. Notwithstanding his protestations and efforts, he is never so weak, banal, and bookish as when he speaks and writes on Europe and Europeans. His *Italian Tales*, in which he glorifies the Western mind as he sees it in his beloved Italians, sound like a translation from a second-rate foreigner. His sketches on Anatole France or Romain Rolland have the forced air of a school-theme written to order. Obversely, he is exuberantly alert and forceful when he speaks or writes of his Asiatic Russia. Let a visiting accordionist strike up a Volga song, and his great eyes of a sad dog, set over the most Asiatic cheek-bones this side of the Urals, grow moist with nostalgia. Not his vapid intellectuals, nor his Westernized, Socialist workmen reveal his power, but precisely his savage, backward, abominable Asiatic Russians, whom theoretically he condemns and flagellates. His *Childhood* is not only written in a robust style smelling of earth and woods; it is one of the sunniest books in literature, despite its scenes of gory violence and degrading squalor. On the publication of *Okurov Town*, reactionary critics greeted the conversion of Gorky to conservative patriotism, so colourful did the dreadful Town appear to these innocent readers. Both Tolstoy and

Chekhov praised highly Gorky's *Goltva Fair,* perhaps the only non-problem sketch of the early Gorky, in which he showed his power in describing autochthonous, Asiatic Russia. As the years go by, and Gorky's rich impressions settle down in his prodigious memory, he lovingly puts down portrait after portrait of " queer " Russians he had met in Okurovdom. With his reason he hates them, but with his heart he loves them dearly, and he ends a series of such portraits with a revealing reverie:

I felt like naming this collection " A Book About Russians As They Had Been." But . . . I am not quite certain of my own sentiment: do I wish these people to become different? Absolutely alien to nationalism, patriotism, and other ailments of one's spiritual vision, I yet see the Russian people as exceptionally, fantastically gifted, original. Even fools in Russia are foolish in an original way, in a peculiar manner, and as to loafers — these are positively geniuses. I am sure that by their fancifulness, by the unexpectedness of their twists, by the significant form, so to speak, of their thoughts and feelings, the Russian people are the most grateful material for an artist.

This is a most significant confession. Gorky has painted joyfully and with consummate skill the Russia he knows, independently of what he wrote as a ratiocinating publicist. That Russia is rapidly disappearing under the onslaught of the violent Europeanizers — the Bolsheviks. The ardent hope of Soviet Russia that Gorky's return will enable him to write a " great novel " of the new life, is ill founded, whatever good intentions Gorky himself may entertain on this score. He neither knows this New Russia, nor does he sympathize with it except with his reason. His *Klim Samgin* is planned to end with 1923, and the parts of the novel that have already appeared do not augur the fulfilment of the expectation of his Soviet admirers. Gorky belongs with " Asiatic " Russia, and he still has enough to give us of that colourful though hateful past. His literary work stamps the conclusion of a period in Russian history, a period rich in contradictions and conflicts. Alexander Blok, author of *The Twelve,* a prophetic symphony

of the revolution, has poignantly defined the place of Gorky in the hearts of his contemporaries:

If there is something great, boundless, vast, painfully gripping and promising, which we have been wont to associate with the name of Russia, then it is Gorky whom we must regard as having expressed all that in a stupendous degree.

APPENDICES

APPENDIX I

MAXIM GORKY IN THE UNITED STATES

AS it is now established by documents, the idea of sending Gorky to America to secure goodwill and financial support for the revolutionary movement in Russia belonged to Leonid Krasin, the ingenious " minister of finance " of the Bolshevik faction, and later Soviet ambassador in Paris and London. Krasin had the Party send its representative, N. Burenin, along with Gorky and Maria Andreyeva, to act as organizer and treasurer. Although the trip proved a financial and moral failure, Bolshevik records speak of moneys received from America, through Comrade Burenin.

Gorky's mission augured success. American public opinion had been overwhelmingly opposed to the Russian Autocracy, both in its war with Japan and in its struggle against the people. Gorky's name had figured prominently and sympathetically in press dispatches ever since the Red Sunday. Incidentally, the Hearst papers published, on January 24, 1905, a long cablegram from St. Petersburg, under the signature of Maxim Gorky, dated one day after the fateful Sunday.[1] During

[1] The dispatch began with the words: " The Russian revolution has commenced. The bloody dawn of the day of freedom will be followed by more slaughter, but in the end the people will triumph." Elsewhere it read: " Yesterday's awful proceedings have accomplished what years of propaganda did not accomplish: the confidence in the tsar — the strongest article of faith of the common people in Russia — has been destroyed. . . . In one volley the soldiers of the tsar have destroyed the power of his name. On Saturday morning the tsar was the object of his people's worship. With the roar of the guns he became the known enemy of those who would have gladly laid down their lives for him."

Gorky's imprisonment at the Peter and Paul Fortress, leading American editors (Richard Watson Gilder of the *Century*, Charles Scribner of *Scribner's*, W. C. Allen of *Harper's*) declared their readiness to join the movement in behalf of Gorky, launched by Dr. Theodore Barth of the Berlin *Nation*. Gorky's sojourn in this country promised to be a series of banquets and public meetings, with the participation of many literary and political notables. An invitation to the White House from President Roosevelt was rumoured to be pending.

Official Russia, desperately negotiating at the time for a foreign loan, did not relish the popularity of Gorky who was received and fêted as the spokesman of its enemy, the Russian people. The Washington embassy got busy exerting effort after effort to expose Gorky's influence by discrediting him personally. Their attempt to have the immigration officers bar Gorky's entrance into the country, as an anarchist, had to be given up. In answer to the customary question of the Authorities as to whether he was an anarchist and an enemy of law and order, Gorky declared: "No, I am a Socialist. I am for law and order, and therefore I am fighting the tsarist government, which is nothing but organized anarchy." The embassy then tried to play on the malleability of the American press, by "inspiring" it in the desired direction. Thus they managed to suggest here and there the contention that it was "inadmissible" to collect American dollars for arms against a "friendly" government. Mark Twain, as yet a vigorous champion of the Russian revolution, parried that argument by reminding his compatriots of the help they received from France during their revolutionary struggle. In 1906, the word "revolution" was still acceptable in the average American household, even among the D.A.R. This explains the ineffectiveness of the next "inspiration" which came in the form of a message from St. Petersburg, warning Gorky's admirers that he was not a liberal or reformer, but a dangerous and desperate "social revolutionist." The Russian embassy then decided to play its trump card, designed to strike at the most vulnerable spot of the average American — his scrupulosity in regard to sex morality. All they had to do was to intimate that the

woman who had been received as Gorky's wife was not legally married to him, and their purpose was momentarily gained.

The student of opinion will be highly instructed by a perusal of the American press, which recorded within a few days the meteoric swiftness of Gorky's rise and fall in the public estimate. His arrival on April 10 was greeted with unanimous enthusiasm. Front page headlines spoke of admiring crowds at the pier, their number varying from " more than one thousand " (in the *Sun*) to generous " thousands " (in the *New York American*). The disposition toward the Russian visitor and his " young charming wife " was on the whole sunny, from the reporter's story to the cartoon and editorial. Even the *New York World,* which was subsequently accused of having deliberately plotted Gorky's downfall, treated him at first in a friendly manner. The *World* reported at length on the dinner arranged at Club A the day after Gorky's arrival. The toastmaster, Robert Hunter, appealed for funds to help the Russian revolutionists, announcing among the members of the committee to raise money William Dean Howells, Samuel Clemens, Robert Collier, Finley Peter Dunne, and Jane Addams. Others present at the dinner, according to the *World,* were Arthur Brisbane, Ernest Poole, Walter Weyl, Leroy N. Scott, David Graham Phillips, " and other well-known thinkers." Gaylord Wilshire, a mild Socialist and editor of *Wilshire's Magazine,* acted as host at a party for Gorky, to which were invited H. G. Wells, Edwin Markham, Professors Charles Beard and Franklin Giddings, Christian Brinton, and John Spargo. The *World* reporter referred to " Madame Gorky, the charming wife of the noted Russian," who acted as interpreter for her husband. The sly reporter, on learning of Gorky's admiration for Schopenhauer and Nietzsche, tried to trap him : " It was suggested that Nietzsche was an atheist. M. Gorky merely shrugged his shoulders and said nothing either as to his own belief or that of Nietzsche." That was too bad.

On April 12, the *World* carried a cartoon: " Let There Be Light! " The Statue of Liberty was graciously bending down to Gorky and igniting his torch which bore a tag: " For My

People." Friday, the 13th, the *World's* tone was still friendly.
A cartoon, " A Yankee in Czar Nicholas' Court," showed
Mark Twain pushing the tottering throne of the Romanovs,
with the startled Nicky falling into space and dropping his
sceptre. In the same issue an editorial commented on the
fact that some of the gentlemen who attended the Gorky dinner had not long before sat at a banquet in honour of Sergey
Witte. " He [Gorky] is the voice of the underworld of Russia,
a world repulsive, vicious, and depraved, and a world human
in its strivings and resentment against the enthroned wrongs
of centuries."

The bomb exploded on the next day. The *World* reproduced
on its front page two photographs, one of Gorky and his
" family," the other of Gorky and the " so-called Mme Gorky
who is not Mme Gorky at all but a Russian actress, Andreyeva,
with whom he has been living since his separation from his
wife a few years ago." The text explained that Gorky and his
wife had separated without any bitterness, but had not been
legally divorced because of the exceeding difficulties in obtaining a divorce through the Greek Orthodox church. The
inspiring touch of the Russian embassy could be felt in the
passage relative to Gorky's living in Finland with Andreyeva:

Gorky's political admirers in Russia paid little attention to
the matter, but the common people who knew the story used
to say:
" Here is your ideal that you always boast of, and see — he
leaves his wife for an actress! "

The Sunday papers, of course, reprinted the *World* story,
with a variety of embellishments. The immediate result of the
revelation was the eviction of the Gorky group from the Hotel
Belleclaire. With just pride the *World* reported: " Gorky's
eviction was a foregone conclusion as soon as the guests of the
Belleclaire opened their *Worlds* this morning." When Mr. Wilshire pleaded with the proprietor, the latter cut him short:
" This is not Europe. I am running a family hotel, and I can't
have these people in my house any longer." The immoral
foreigners moved to the Lafayette-Brevoort, where, according

to the *World,* " the situation had been previously explained."
In the evening, however, the proprietor ejected his suspicious
guests, but in view of the lateness of the hour he was kind
enough to secure rooms for them at the Hotel Rhinelander.
The manager of the Lafayette-Brevoort voiced the notorious
piety of New York hotel-keepers, when he explained to the
reporters that he " could not possibly tolerate the presence of
any persons whose characters were questioned in the slightest
manner " (*New York Times*). During the same night the
Gorkys were put out on the street by the proprietor of
the Rhinelander, who claimed that his pious colleague from the
Lafayette-Brevoort had foisted the foreigners on him without
revealing their identity. There they stood, a bewildered group,
on the sidewalk of a foreign city, in the dead of the night.
The *Herald* reported that Gorky was " laughingly saying that
if necessary he would sleep in the streets, as he had done
before." They were ultimately given shelter by Mr. and Mrs.
John Martin.

Needless to say, the scandal bore the fruit anticipated by
the Russian embassy. Gorky's prestige sank at once to the
lowest depths, and society turned its back upon him and his
mission. Even such a brave soul as Alice Stone Blackwell
found it necessary to cancel a meeting in honour of Gorky
that was to be held at Faneuil Hall in Boston. The *Times*
quoted Miss Blackwell as saying: " I do not want to judge
Mr. Gorky, but apparently his views on morality and ours
somewhat differ, and consequently. . . ." John Dewey, who
enjoyed Gorky's company in the Adirondacks, at the Martins' place, tells me an illuminating bit: " A group of women
had asked my wife if she would give the use of our apartment to Mme. Andreyeva to speak on the condition of women
in Russia; a sensational newspaper reported that this was a
reception to her, and the Barnard girls were the guests. As
this was after the Gorkys had been expelled from the hotel,
there was considerable newspaper furore for a few days."

That the American press would make full use of the sensation could have been expected, of course. The *World* was the
first to print the story of Gorky's irregular relations with

Andreyeva, which had been an open secret, as the *Herald* and *Evening Post* testified. We shall presently see what motives Mr. Upton Sinclair ascribes to the *World* in initiating the scandal. Mrs. Gaylor Wilshire tells me that when she reproached one of the *World* people for having " broken faith " in regard to the Gorky matter, he retorted: " It was ' news,' wasn't it ? " Which cannot be gainsaid. Incidentally, the Hearst papers tried to put the soft pedal on the story, not, of course, from noble considerations but because they had contracted for Gorky's contributions. The *New York American* even attempted to counter the damaging sensation by one intended to rehabilitate their contributor. On April 15, it carried a story studded with such fantasies as these:

> Maxim Gorky *is* married to the charming young actress . . . . and he has been divorced from the woman to whom he has formerly been married. . . . The strangely dramatic feature of the situation. . . . Gorky cannot disclose the details of the marriage and divorce. . . . without placing in deadly danger the lives of scores, and perhaps thousands of his fellow-countrymen. . . . It is here made known for the first time that there exists in Russia today a provisional republican government. . . . with a set of laws. . . . Thousands of men and women live in accordance with those laws. Gorky received his divorce under those laws.

This canard was too obvious even for the Hearst papers, and they did not press the point. Curiously enough, *Wilshire's Magazine* (May, 1906), which certainly knew better, did not hesitate to quote the *American* version approvingly.

It is only fair to state that editorially the metropolitan papers treated the affair with relative moderation. The *Times* self-righteously advised Gorky that " society had promptly avenged itself upon him for a social offence," and ponderously deducted that Gorky was " in fact undergoing the punishment of precisely that government of public opinion which he had come to this country for the purpose of helping to establish in his own." Other respectable organs chided not so much Gorky as his erstwhile sympathizers in this country.

Thus the *Sun* caustically commented on the incident, under the heading, " Propriety and Amateur Revolutionists ":

> Our amateur revolutionists who only yesterday were so keen for the overthrow of the Russian political system and so enthusiastic in their laudation of Maxim Gorky. . . . seem to have cooled considerably in their devotion to him since the announcement was made that his female companion on his visit to this country is not his legally wedded wife. . . .
>
> At the sudden cooling of enthusiasm for him Gorky is probably amazed. His sole purpose is to overthrow certain existing conditions, the downfall of which must inevitably involve serious social disturbances. He means to wipe out many conventions. Now, to find his success threatened by the mere non-observance of one convention, cannot but have a disturbing effect on his mind. To learn that his new found disciples are eager to follow his program of blood and violence, but balk at his domestic arrangements, is enough to set the head of any revolutionary in a whirl. Not a few now dead and canonized patriots of every race would grin if they might see the strict line the Russian's American supporters are drawing between his political beliefs and his personal and domestic practices.
>
> Must revolution, to have the support of American amateurs, hereafter clothe itself in immaculate and conventional respectability and observe rigidly the tenets of morality and conduct set up in the land to which it appeals for aid and sympathy?

Even the *World*, so proud of its scoop on the front page, spoke editorially not so much against Gorky as against his fickle admirers:

> Maxim Gorky has reason to be bewildered at his reception in America. . . . So long as Gorky was known merely as a political revolutionist he was welcomed with effusion. So soon as he was shown to be living in unconventional private relations — not so soon as it was known but so soon as it was printed — he was hounded from hotel to hotel, deserted by those who had most enthusiastically befriended him, and fairly driven to take refuge in concealment.
>
> Americans are right in reverencing the marriage institution. The family is the basis of the Republic and the unit of society.

But it is too firmly entrenched, too strongly guarded, to be successfully assailed by one revolutionary agitator or endangered by free speech and fair play.

Those who welcomed Gorky knowing his opinions and who spurn him now are at the least guilty of inconsistency. Considering the tolerance that domestic irregularities so often find, may there not also be in this change of front something of hypocrisy? [2]

Less dignified " organs of public opinion " were unreserved in their salacious innuendoes. It was the San Francisco earthquake that of a sudden shifted the greed for sensation elsewhere, and the Gorky topic vanished from the pages of the daily press. In the non-daily periodicals it reverberated for some time to come. Mr. Wallace Irwin referred to it in a lighter vein as late as June, 1906 (*The Literary Horrors Club,* in the *Bookman*) :

> There came a Russian accent next,
>   Belike a popping cork.
> I think 'twas Maxim Gorky who
>   Was showing how to Gork.

Dr. Franklin H. Giddings voiced the pro-Gorky sentiment of the American public in a forceful article on *The Social Lynching of Gorky and Andreyeva,* which appeared in *The Independent*.

The mighty American people [so ran the opening paragraph], called and set apart by Destiny to be the biggest thing on earth, has made another record. It has had two spasms in one short week. In the State of Missouri it has physically lynched three negroes, accused of rape, but actually innocent. In the city of New York it has morally and socially lynched two distinguished visitors, Maxim Gorky and Madame Andreyeva, for unconventional marital relations.

[2] An American author of prominence, intimately connected with the Gorky episode, writes to me: " Gordon Bennett, who was having an affair at the time with a lady of the old Russian régime, cabled from abroad to the *Herald* to play up the story of ' Gorky's mistress.' " My correspondent does not wish to be quoted by name.

Dr. Giddings took the stand that the relations between Gorky and Andreyeva were essentially moral and marital, and in support of his view he cited Dante and Petrarch, Milton, Shelley, Goethe, Wagner (*Tristan and Isolde!*), John Stuart Mill, Herbert Spencer, and finally George Eliot, whose relations with Lewes were a case in point:

In all decency and consistency, therefore, the ladies and gentlemen who have taken part in the social boycotting of the Gorkys should instantly with a long pair of tongs pick up any stray copies of *Adam Bede* or *Romola* that may be lying about their houses, and cast them into the fire, preferably with a pinch of brimstone.

He went on to take issue with the American press for "queering" Gorky, paying special tribute, transparently veiled, to the *Sun* for raising an alarmed cry that "the purity of our inns was threatened," and to the *Times,* which admonished Gorky to bow before the force of "public opinion" whose power is *nil* in his own country. He reminded the press that

Maxim Gorky came to this country not for the purpose of putting himself on exhibition, as many a literary character has done at one time or another, not for the purpose of lining his pockets with American gold, but for the purpose of obtaining sympathy and financial assistance for a people struggling against terrific odds, as the American people once struggled, for political and individual liberty.

The Independent, by the way, reacted to the episode in two editorials, one before the appearance of Dr. Giddings' article, and one simultaneously with it. In the former, Gorky was roasted for coming to these pious shores "with his mistress, a Russian actress, instead of his wife." The editorial poked fun at the "conventional and respectable ladies" who were shocked by Gorky's conduct, yet who previously "used to press their money upon the Russian committees with the stipulation that it be used for dynamite. They were anxious to aid and abet murder, but they could not countenance

matrimonial irregularities." It did not conceal its chuckle over the failure of Gorky to collect funds for the revolutionary movement, for with the establishment of the Duma it saw a chance for "peaceful and orderly evolution," and believed that such "work could be better carried on by such a liberal as Miliyukov rather than a revolutionist like Gorky."

One week later, commenting on Dr. Giddings' article in the same issue, *The Independent* assumed a tone of superior moral tolerance.

It is not true [the editorial ruled] that it is nobody's business whether Mr. Gorky and the lady with him are really husband and wife. To be sure, the presumption was, and is, that they are; but marriage is so sacred an institution, and looseness is so detestable, and so properly condemned by society, that we have the right to know whether those who seek our hospitality are living in virtual marriage or are masquerading.

The writer then pleads for tolerance toward Gorky, on the basis of the difficulty of obtaining a divorce in Russia. "We may well be grateful that we live in a land of reasonable laws, which provide safe sanctions for marriage, as they do for property," consequently, "in a country like ours, with decent codes, the common law marriage of Mr. and Mrs. Gorky would be indefensible." "But Russia is not America. We cannot utterly condemn Mr. and Mrs. Gorky for doing what is done many a time in this country, simply because they could not do there what they could have done here. The socially strict Queen Victoria could receive the Shah of Persia, who had a harem of wives, and the very religious Emperor of Germany visits the Sultan of Turkey."

This effort at being righteous and magnanimous at the same time was pitiful enough. The facts in the case were quite clear. Gorky and Andreyeva had been living like man and wife for over three years, without trying to conceal their intimacy from their friends and the public. Katherina Pavlovna, Gorky's legal wife, has remained his devoted friend to this day, and as Gorky has told me, excellent relations exist between Katherina Pavlovna, Maria Andreyeva, and Baroness Budberg, his present

secretary. Such conditions have been rather common among the Russian intelligentsia, both because of their broadmindedness, and because, indeed, divorce in Russia was a troublesome and nasty affair. The Greek Orthodox church sanctioned divorce only when adultery was claimed and proved by one of the parties. Rather than go through public scandal, many couples preferred to separate and marry without the benefit of the clergy, and society regarded them as quite *comme il faut*. The American reaction to their matrimonial relations was both unexpected (though not wholly, as we shall see presently) and painful to Gorky and Andreyeva.

How the whole episode looked to an intelligent outsider, may be seen from H. G. Wells' account, as it appeared at the time in *Harper's Weekly* (reprinted in his *The Future in America*). The account is thorough enough and yet personal enough to deserve reproduction:

. . . I assisted at the coming of Maxim Gorky, and witnessed many intimate details of what Professor Giddings, that courageous publicist, has called his " lynching."

Here . . . is a case I fail altogether to understand. The surface values of that affair have a touch of the preposterous. I set them down in infinite perplexity.

My first week in New York was in the period of Gorky's advent. Expectation was at a high pitch, and one might have foretold a stupendous, a history-making campaign. The American nation seemed concentrated upon one great and ennobling idea, the freedom of Russia, and upon Gorky as the embodiment of that idea. A protest was to be made against cruelty and violence and massacre. That great figure of Liberty with the torch was to make it flare visibly half way round the world, reproving tyranny.

Gorky arrived, and the *éclat* was immense. We dined him, we were photographed in his company by flashlight. I very gladly shared that honour, for Gorky is not only a great master of the art I practice, but a splendid personality. He is one of those people to whom the camera does no justice, whose work as I know it in an English translation, forceful as it is, fails very largely to convey his peculiar quality. His is a big, quiet figure; there is a curious power of appeal in his face, a large

simplicity in his voice and gesture. He was dressed, when I met him, in peasant clothing, in a belted blue shirt, trousers of some shiny black material, and boots, and save for a few common greetings, he has no other language than Russian. So it was necessary that he should bring with him some one he could trust to interpret him to the world. And having, too, much of the practical helplessness of his type of genius, he could not come without his right hand, that brave and honourable lady, Madame Andreyeva, who has been now for years, in everything but the severest legal sense, his wife. Russia has no Dakota, and although his legal wife has long since found a companion, the Orthodox Church in Russia has no divorce facilities for men in the revolutionary camp. So Madame Andreyeva stands to him as George Eliot stood to George Lewes, and I suppose the two of them had almost forgotten the technical illegality of their tie, until it burst upon them and the American public in a monstrous storm of exposure.

It was like a summer thunderstorm. At one moment Gorky was in an immense sunshine, a plenipotentiary from oppression to liberty, at the next he was being almost literally pelted through the streets.

I do not know what motive actuated a certain section of the American press to initiate this pelting of Maxim Gorky. A passion for moral purity may have prompted it, but certainly no passion for purity ever before begot so brazen and abundant a torrent of lies. . . . The irregularity of Madame Andreyeva's position was a mere point of departure. The journalists went on to invent a deserted wife and children; they declared Madame Andreyeva was an " actress," and loaded her with all the unpleasant implications of that unfortunate word; they spoke of her generally as " the woman Andreyeva"; they called upon the Commissioner of Immigration to deport her as a " female of bad character," quite influential people wrote to him to that effect; they published the name of the hotel that sheltered her, and organized a boycott. Whoever dared to countenance the victims was denounced. Professor Dewar [Dewey?] of Columbia had given them a reception; " Dewar must go," said the headlines. Mark Twain, who had assisted in the great welcome, was invited to recant and contribute unfriendly comments. The Gorkys were pursued with insult from hotel to hotel. Hotel after hotel turned them out. They found

themselves at last after midnight in the streets of New York city with every door closed against them. Infected persons could not have been treated more abominably in a town smitten with a panic of plague.

This change happened in the course of twenty-four hours. On one day Gorky was at the zenith, on the next he had been swept from the world. To me it was astounding — it was terrifying. I wanted to talk to Gorky about it, to find out the hidden springs of this amazing change. I spent a Sunday evening looking for him with an ever deepening respect for the power of the American press. I had a quaint conversation with the clerk of the hotel in Fifth Avenue from which he had first been driven. Europeans can scarcely hope to imagine the moral attitudes at which American hotels are conducted. . . . I went thence to seek Mr. Abraham Cahan in East Side, and thence to other people I knew, but in vain. Gorky was obliterated.

I thought this affair was a whirlwind of foolish misunderstanding, such as may happen in any capital, and that presently his entirely tolerable relationship would be explained. But for all the rest of my time in New York this insensate campaign went on. There was no attempt of any importance to stem the tide, and to this day large sections of the American public must be under the impression that this great writer is a depraved man of pleasure accompanied by a favorite cocotte. The writers of paragraphs racked their brains to invent new and smart ways of insulting Madame Andreyeva. The chaste entertainers of the music-halls of the Tenderloin district introduced allusions. And amidst this riot of personalities Russia was forgotten. The massacres, the chaos of cruelty and blundering, the tyranny, the women outraged, the children tortured and slain; all that was forgotten. In Boston, in Chicago, it was the same. At the bare suggestion of Gorky's coming, the same outbreak occurred, the same display of imbecile, gross lying, the same absolute disregard of the tragic cause he had come to plead.

One gleam of comedy in this remarkable outbreak I recall. Some one in ineffectual protest had asked what Americans would have said if Benjamin Franklin had encountered such ignominies on his similar mission of appeal to Paris before the War of Independence. " Benjamin Franklin," retorted one bright young Chicago journalist, " was a man of very different

moral character from Gorky " — and proceeded to explain how Chicago was prepared to defend the purity of her homes against the invader. Benjamin Franklin, it is true, *was* a person of very different morals from Gorky — but I don't think that bright young man in Chicago had a very sound idea of where the difference lay. . . .

I spent my last evening on American soil in the hospitable home in Staten Island that sheltered Gorky and Madame Andreyeva. After dinner we sat together in the deepening twilight upon a broad veranda that looks out upon one of the most beautiful views in the world, upon serene large spaces of land and sea, upon slopes of pleasant window-lit, tree-set wooden houses, upon the glittering clusters of lights and the black and luminous shipping that comes and goes about the Narrows and the Upper Bay. Half masked by a hill contour to the left was the light of the torch of Liberty. . . . Gorky's big form fell into shadow, Madame Andreyeva sat at his feet, translating methodically, sentence by sentence, into clear French, whatever he said, translating our speeches into Russian. He told us stories — of the soul of the Russian, of Russian religious sects, of kindnesses and cruelties, of his great despair.

Ever and again, in the pauses, my eyes would go to where New York, far away, glittered like a brighter and more numerous Pleiades.

I gauged something of the real magnitude of this one man's disappointment, the immense expectation of his arrival, the impossible dream of his mission. He had come, the Russian peasant in person, out of a terrific confusion of bloodshed, squalor, injustice — to tell America, the land of light and achieved freedom, of all these evil things. She would receive him, help him, understand truly what he meant with his " Rossia." I could imagine how he had felt as he came in the big steamer to her, up that large converging display of space and teeming energy. There she glowed tonight across the water, a queen among cities, as if indeed she was the light of the world. Nothing, I think, can ever rob that splendid harbor approach of its invincible quality of promise. . . . And to him she had shown herself no more than the luminous hive of multitudes of base and busy, greedy and childish little men. . . .

On the whole correct, Mr. Wells' account fails to mention the rôle played in the affair by the Russian embassy, a fact that has been established beyond doubt. For a circumstantial light on this episode, I wish to quote from a letter written to me by Mr. Ivan Narodny:

A few months after my arrival in the United States, in 1906, I received a letter from my friend, Nicholas E. Burenin, from Helsingfors, saying that he was coming with Maxim Gorky to America as his secretary and manager. " I wish," he wrote, " that you would help us with your publicity and press connections as much as you can. We shall be the guests of Mr. Gaylord Wilshire. . . ."

I had come to this country to do publicity work for the Russian revolution, and was stopping at the Club A, at 3 Fifth Avenue, which was a radical journalistic and literary association, with such members as Mark Twain, Jack London, Upton Sinclair, Ernest Poole, Leroy Scott, Robert Hunter, and many others. I had already launched a successful press campaign in New York for the revolutionary cause . . . when Mr. Zinovy Peshkov, Maxim Gorky's adopted son, called on me one day, explained that he was employed in the office of Mr. Wilshire, and asked me whether I would help them out in the planned tour of Gorky to raise funds for the cause of the Bolshevik Party. I assured him that I should be only too happy to do everything I could for his father, and showed him Burenin's letter.

I told the members of Club A of Gorky's coming, and they said that they would be glad to launch Gorky's campaign from the Club. . . . It was decided to give at the Club a gala dinner for Gorky on the morrow of his arrival, to which were invited Mark Twain, Robert Collier, Arthur Brisbane, William Dean Howells, and others.

. . . . Gorky's coming to America had the widest publicity that any Russian revolutionist or author ever received, and the Russian embassy at Washington was greatly annoyed about it.

A Russian banker, V. Zaharov, who was at that time in this country and kept in close touch with the tsar's embassy in Washington, called me up by long-distance telephone on the day preceding Gorky's landing, and advised me that Baron Rosen, the Ambassador, and Colonel Nikolayev, of the diplo-

matic Intelligence, were planning a vicious campaign against the delegate of the revolution.

" You know," telephoned my friend, " that Gorky is coming with Mme Andreyeva as his wife, whereas Gorky has a wife and a child in Russia. He is not divorced from his first wife, and in American terms his present wife is nothing but his mistress. The embassy is going to use this point in the press as soon as Gorky and Andreyeva land. Nikolayev has a photograph of Gorky's first wife and child and a number of data to raise a terrific scandal in the newspapers. You know how easily such things are done, so you had better warn Gorky, and have him take proper steps to frustrate Nikolayev's plot."

I gave out this information to Ernest Poole and other members of Club A, and later I told it to George Kennan. They all advised me to meet Gorky before he lands, explain to him the situation, and invite him to stay at Club A, while Mme Andreyeva would be the guest of Mr. Wilshire at the Hotel Belleclaire, where quarters were arranged for them. . . . I managed to get on board ship with the newspaper men. . . . and told Burenin of Zaharov's information and of our Club's suggestion. Burenin discussed the matter with Gorky, and told me that Alexey Maximovich [Gorky] was not going to change his plans because of the embassy's plot.

Maxim Gorky landed as a hero, and went to the suite arranged for him by Wilshire at the Hotel Belleclaire. No questions were raised about Mme Andreyeva and his relations to her.

The next day the dinner at Club A took place. There were only men, about fifteen in all, as I recall. Mark Twain sat between me and Gorky, I acting as interpreter between the two authors. Mark Twain was humorous and brilliant, as usual, while Gorky was telling the venerable American author how popular his books were in Russia.

Robert Hunter and I composed the manifesto that was signed by Gorky, Chaykovsky, and myself, and given that evening to the press. The dinner was an elated affair and lasted late after midnight. I suggested to Comrade Burenin once more that he urge Gorky to stay apart from Mme Andreyeva, especially since Bradford Merrill, then chief of the *New York World,* had telephoned to me that he was going to use the story about Gorky's undivorced wife and her picture, both supplied by

Colonel Nikolayev. Apparently Gorky paid no attention to these warnings.

Sure enough, next day the *World* brought out the first sensational news about Gorky's family affairs, and this was followed by a regular series of similar stories, all furnished by the embassy. On the morrow of the release of the stories, Burenin came to me, pale and excited, told me that Gorky and Andreyeva had been put out of their hotel, that they were unable to get rooms in any other hotel, and asked for my help. I discussed the matter with members of Club A, and they invited Gorky to come and stay in a room next to mine, while Miss Bensley arranged for a suite of rooms at the home of Mr. John Martin, on Staten Island.

That night Gorky came to our Club, and Mme Andreyeva went to Staten Island. For three days the reporters were unable to reach either of them, as we kept their whereabouts secret.

Thus his hailed American tour collapsed. We discussed with Gorky and Burenin all sort of plans to remedy the situation, but there was nothing to be done. Gorky was, so it seemed to me, disappointed by the silence of Mark Twain and other American authors in the matter. I hinted that much to Mark Twain, and he said:

" Gracious! What could I do after Gorky failed to listen to your warnings, and did not come to the Club? You know the spirit of our press. My protest would have been published as a letter on the back page, and would have done no good."

Gorky and Andreyeva never doubted for a moment that official Russia was behind the whole intrigue. Incidentally, Marie Feyodorovna Andreyeva tells me, in a rather reticent letter, of her angle in the case. I quote it in part:

After the Moscow uprising of 1905, both Alexey Maximovich and I were forced to migrate abroad for political reasons.

A. M. journeyed to the United States for public activity, and I accompanied him as a private person, with absolutely no intention to take part in his public life, his receptions and appearances.

Unfortunately at that time not only A. M., but even I did not know the English language. For this reason we, quite unexpectedly, found ourselves " invited " by a certain Mr. Wil-

shire, as his alleged " guests." This Mr. Wilshire engaged for us a suite in Hotel Belleclaire. . . . By the way, A. M. paid for his rooms, and I paid for mine.

A. M. went out, received callers, attended meetings, dinners, and so forth, while I, as an absolutely private person, did not appear with him anywhere, being of the opinion that this would be awkward for myself and unnecessary for the purposes of A. M.

Quite unexpectedly Mr. Wilshire appointed a " reception " in my suite. Unfamiliar with American customs, we were bewildered and astonished, when for two or three hours utter strangers kept on coming in a line, shaking hands with us, and saying something or other. As I have said, I knew no English then, and my French, German, and Italian were of no help. I asked A. M.'s secretary: " What is the matter? Why are these people passing in line? " He knew nothing about it either, and the reception arranged by Mr. Wilshire was a surprise for him. As it appeared later, among the visitors were many known and even celebrated men.

That was the only time when, against my will and without warning, I was made to appear officially at a reception.

Written twenty-odd years after the event, this letter still suggests the apologetic note of one who unwittingly caused the collapse of a grand plan and considerable damage to the reputation and coffers of a revolutionary movement. Maria Andreyeva tasted her fill of American publicity engineered by the Yellow Press. The mud-slinging campaign to which she was subjected was too harrowing for her to be atoned by the few tokens of sympathy some discriminating New Yorkers showed her and her husband. One of these tokens was the enthusiastic ovation given Gorky and Andreyeva at the Grand Central Palace by the Russian colony. Another sign that not all America went Pecksniffian was shown by the hospitality offered the two victims by Mr. and Mrs. John Martin, first at their home on Staten Island, and later at their place in the Adirondacks, where Gorky spent some six peaceful and productive months. I deem it germane to quote from a letter of Prestonia Mann (Mrs. John) Martin, which she was kind enough to send me in answer to my inquiry to her recollection of the case:

We knew nothing about the merits of the Gorky case at the time we received them in our home, except that a distinguished foreigner was being treated with outrageous rudeness in our country, and we wished to make some amends. The seeming irregularity in Gorky's marriage relation was to us sufficiently explained away by the knowledge [rather misinformation. — A. K.] that under the tsarist régime revolutionists were denied all the sacraments and " blessings " of the Orthodox Church. . . .

I may say that although we gave ourselves no further concern about the matter, on our part, the social odium cast by our conventional fellow-citizens upon us, persists in some quarters to this day. Our friends, pretty generally, stood by us, and in some quarters we were absurdly lauded as moral heroes.

Most of our friends believed that the whole trouble was started by a newspaper woman employed by the *World,* in revenge for Gorky's somewhat injudicious promise to write only for the Hearst papers. The *World* deliberately determined to spoil his mission to America, and as far as financial help for the Russian revolution was concerned, they pretty well succeeded. . . .

Personally I derived great pleasure from the contact with two lofty natures, and we were glad to do what we could to mitigate their embarrassments and troubles while they were in our country.

Mrs. Martin's surmise as to the rôle of the *World* in the Gorky affair has been shared by a number of contemporaries. Among others, Mr. Morris Hillquit, Gorky's lawyer at the time, writes to me:

Ostensibly the persecution was instigated by some of our daily papers. The fact that Gorky had rather unwisely tied himself up with the *New York American* to the exclusion of all other newspapers, seemed to me at the time to afford an explanation of the latters' attitude.

Granted the plausibility of this suggestion, and the part played in the matter by the Russian embassy, one might still wonder at the vehemence of Gorky's persecution by the press and the public, were it not for an additional highly probable

regarding Gorky, would be amusing, were not their purblind inconsistency so contemptible.

Who can gainsay the correct estimate of the Russian " theorists and *intellectuels* " and of the American " nincompoops," in the light of recent history? In any event, the name of the " nincompoops " who turned about face in regard to Gorky as a result of his " indiscretions " was legion. Typical of this crowd was Ambrose Bierce, once an admirer of Gorky — he wired him his congratulations upon his release from the Peter and Paul Fortress a year previously. Now, in the summer of 1906, Bierce wrote from Washington, D. C., to George Sterling, in San Francisco:

. . . You are wrong about Gorky — he has none of the " artist " in him. He is not only a peasant, but an anarchist and an advocate of assassination — by others; like most of his tribe, he does not care to take the risk himself. His " career " in this country has been that of a yellow dog. Hearst's newspapers and . . . are the only friends that remain to him of all those that acclaimed him when he landed. And all the sturdy lying of the former cannot rehabilitate him. It isn't merely the woman matter. You'd understand if you were on this side of the country. I was myself a dupe in the matter. . . .

If allowances must be made for the provincialism and inflated conceit, personal and national, of second-rate scribblers, what of the coryphaei of American letters, William Dean Howells and Mark Twain?

Mr. Abraham Cahan, mentioned in H. G. Wells' article, who had much to do with Gorky's reception in New York, recalls a few enlightening details in a letter to me:

William Dean Howells, of whom I saw a great deal in those days, invited me to the house one day and asked me to act as interpreter at a great Gorky dinner that had been organized with Howells as the prospective toastmaster. A few days later I received a letter from him informing me that the whole thing was off. That was two days after the *New York World* exploded with a story that the lady with whom Gorky was travel-

ling was not his wife. . . . Well, Howells and Mark Twain, who was his partner in the undertaking and also his great fellow-admirer of Gorky, were in a blue funk and dropped Gorky like a hot potato; the projected banquet did not take place.

One day (that was some time before the *World* printed the story) on my way from the hotel where Gorky was stopping I met Howells and Mark Twain who were just going there. As we exchanged greetings Howells stopped long enough to ask me what sort of an impression Gorky made on me. I said something nice about him. I could see from Howells' accents that he was looking forward to a very interesting meeting, and also that he and Mark Twain seemed to be overjoyed at the opportunity to show the famous Russian writer the hospitality of the literary world of America and their appreciation of Gorky's art and Russian literature in general. This, also, was the spirit in which Howells spoke to me about Gorky upon the occasion when he asked me to interpret their speeches to Gorky and Gorky's to them.

In a letter to J. H. Howells, William Dean Howells wrote characteristically of the affair:

Dear Joe:

Mark Twain and I have been having a lively time about the Russian novelist and revolutionist, Maxim Gorky; we were going to give him a great literary dinner, but he has been put out of three hotels with the lady who was not his wife, and Mark Twain has been literally swamped in reporters wanting to know " how about it." I mention it, thinking you may see something about it in the papers; it seems to have blown over, together with the revolutionist committee which Gorky has hopelessly damaged. He is wrong, but I feel sorry for him; he has suffered enough in his own country, except for the false relations which cannot be tolerated here. He is a simple soul and a great writer, but he cannot do impossible things.

More pathetic was the plight of Mark Twain, since his enthusiasm for Gorky and his mission had been much more outspoken than that of the reserved Howells. Twain's biographer, Albert Bigelow Paine, records the humourist's warm

interest in Gorky and the success of his tour. He cites Twain's letter to the veteran revolutionist, Chaykovsky, which was read at a mass meeting in the Grand Central Palace:

My sympathies are with the Russian revolution, of course. It goes without saying. I hope it will succeed and now that I have talked with you I take heart to believe it will. Government by falsified promises, by lies, by treachery, and by the butcher-knife, for the aggrandizement of a single family of drones and its idle and vicious kin, has been borne quite long enough in Russia, I should think. And it is to be hoped that the roused nation, now rising in its strength, will presently put an end to it and set up a republic in its place. Some of us, even the white-headed, may live to see the blessed day when tsars and grand dukes will be as scarce there as I trust they are in heaven.

Mark Twain staggered under the blow of the *World* story. Mr. Paine quotes him as saying to Dan Beard: " Gorky has made an awful mistake, Dan. He might as well have come over here in his shirt-tail." In a recently published letter which he wrote at the time to Charlotte Teller, Twain said:

Gorky is a puzzle and a vexation to me. He came here in a distinctly diplomatic capacity — a function which demands (and necessitates) delicacy, tact, deference to people's prejudices. He came on a great mission, a majestic mission. The succor of an abused and suffering nation. As to his diplomacy, it does not resemble Talleyrand's, Gortchakov's, Metternich's; it is new, it is original; it has not its like in history. He hits the public in the face with his hat and then holds it out for contributions. It is not ludicrous, it is pitiful.

As to his patriotism, his lofty talk of lifting up and healing his bleeding nation — it can't stand the strain of a trifling temporary inconvenience. He has made a grave blunder and persistently refuses to rectify it.

From the point of view of expedient common sense Mark Twain's argument is irrefutable. The American author knew his public, when he remarked, according to Mr. Paine: " The American public opinion is a delicate fabric. It shrivels like

the webs of the morning at the slightest touch." His biographer cites a memorandum made by Mark Twain on that occasion:

Laws can be evaded and punishment escaped, but an openly transgressed custom brings sure punishment. The penalty may be unfair, unrighteous, illogical, and a cruelty; no matter, it will be inflicted just the same. Certainly, then, there can be but one wise thing for a visiting stranger to do — find out what the country's customs are and refrain from offending against them.

The efforts which have been made in Gorky's justification are entitled to all respect because of the magnanimity of the motive back of them, but I think that the ink was wasted. Custom is custom: it is built of brass, boiler-iron, granite; facts, reasonings, arguments have no more effect upon it than the idle winds have upon Gibraltar.

In his *Ordeal of Mark Twain,* Van Wyck Brooks quotes the last sentence of this " memorandum " with a comment which for noble pathos stands apart in American critical literature:

What would Emerson or Thoreau have said, fifty years before, of such an argument, such an assertion of the futility of the individual reason in the face of " brass, boiler-iron, granite " and mob emotion? It is perhaps the most pitifully abject confession ever written by a famous writer.

I have been interested in the reaction of other liberal-minded Americans to the Gorky affair. Perhaps the three following opinions are sufficiently representative. Mr. Ernest Poole, who stood very close to Gorky during his visit, has written me a lengthy account of the case, decidedly sympathetic to Gorky, yet he has this to say: " It was a tactless blunder, of course, to bring with him Madame Andreyeva." Mr. Arthur Brisbane informed me that Maxim Gorky and his wife stopped for several days at his house in Hempstead, Long Island, and that he " enjoyed talking with him." When I pressed Mr. Brisbane for his attitude toward the affair, he wrote back:

. . . If I had approved of the treatment that Gorky received on his arrival here, I should not have invited Gorky to my house.

I think he acted foolishly, or rather ignorantly. Some of those who criticized and boycotted him acted stupidly, others brutally.

However, I do not judge of other men in public print, and have nothing to contribute on the subject. . . . It is long past, and of no consequence.

Quite naturally I wished to know H. L. Mencken's stand in this matter. To my initial inquiry he answered:

I didn't begin doing books regularly until 1908. Thus, I had no active part in the controversy over Gorky. Later on, I often referred to it but never in a formal article. It seems to me that Clemens was eternally disgraced by his action in the matter. I have said so more than once, but only in scattered paragraphs.

Upon the perusal of my material for this paper, Mr. Mencken was good enough to write me again:

. . . . Gorky, after all, provoked his own troubles. It seems to me that he carried himself with the greatest stupidity. When he horned into the local politics of the country, especially at a time of public excitement, he laid himself open to all sorts of reprisals. Certainly he must have been well aware, when he came to America, that unofficial marriages were not countenanced here.

In answer to my inquiry as to his recollection of the case, Mr. Upton Sinclair has referred me to a chapter in his *Brass Check*, where he treats the matter with his customary passion and aptness for neat deductions. His testimony, as that of an eye-witness and contemporary, warrants quoting at length:

. . . A group of American Socialists went out on the revenue-cutter " Hudson " to meet Gorky's steamer in the harbor; among them I remember Gaylord Wilshire, Abraham Cahan, Leroy Scott. There were also reporters from all the newspapers, and on the way down the bay a reporter of the *World* came

to Wilshire and asked if he had heard a report to the effect that the lady who was coming as Gorky's wife, Madame Andreyeva, was not legally his wife. Wilshire answered by explaining to the reporter the situation existing in Russia [follows thin stuff about revolutionists refusing to enrich the church through marriage and divorce revenues and " having their own marriage code," with which Gorky had complied. — A. K.]. . . . The reporters of other papers had gathered about, listening to this explanation, and they all agreed that the American public had no concern with the marriage customs of Russia, and that this story had nothing to do with Gorky's present mission.

Gorky went to the Hotel Belleclaire, as Wilshire's guest. From the moment of his arrival he was the object of several different intrigues. In the first place there was the embassy of the tsar, who was hanging and shooting Gorky's partisans in Russia, and naturally spared no labor or treasure to destroy him in America. A spy of the embassy afterwards confessed that it was he who took the story about Gorky's unorthodox marriage to the New York newspapers, and who later on succeeded in persuading the *World* to make use of it.

Then there were representatives of various newspaper syndicates and magazines and publishing-houses, which wanted Gorky's writings, and were besieging his friends. And then there were two different groups of radicals, competing for his favor — the " Friends of Russian Freedom," settlement-workers and folks of that sort, many of whom have since become Socialists, but who in those days were carefully bourgeois and painfully respectable, confining their revolutionary aims strictly to Russia; and the American Socialists, who knew that Gorky was an internationalist like themselves, and wished to use his prestige for the benefit of the American movement, as well as for the Russian movement.

It happened that at this time Moyer and Haywood were being tried for their lives, and this case was the test upon which the right and left wings were divided. Gaylord Wilshire, who was then publishing a Socialist magazine in New York, drafted a telegram of sympathy to Moyer and Haywood, and submitted it to Madame Andreyeva, proposing that Gorky should sign it. Which, of course, threw the " Friends of Russian Freedom " into a panic. If Gorky supported Moyer and Hay-

wood, he would get no money from the liberal millionaires of New York, the Schiffs and the Strausses and the Guggenheims and the rest, who might be persuaded to subsidize the Russian revolution, but who had no interest in industrial freedom for America! The matter was explained to Gorky, and he gave his decision: he was an international Socialist, and he would protest against the railroading of two radical labor leaders to the gallows. He signed the telegram, and it was sent, and next morning, of course, the New York newspapers were horrified, and the Russian embassy got busy, and President Roosevelt cancelled a reception for Gorky at the White House!

But the worse mistake that Gorky made was in his contracts for his writings. He fell into the . . . trap . . . he signed a contract with the *New York Journal* and thereby incurred the furious enmity of the *New York World!* So then the editors of the *World* remembered that story which they had got from the Russian embassy; or may be the embassy reminded them of it again. By this story they could destroy entirely the news-value of Gorky's writings; they could render worthless the contract with their hated rival! That incidentally they would help to hold one or two hundred million people in slavery and torment for an indefinite number of years — that weighed with the staff of the *World* not a feather-weight.

Next morning the *World* came out with a scare-story on the front page, to the effect that Maxim Gorky had insulted the American people by coming to visit them and introducing his mistress as his wife. And instantly, of course, the news-channels were opened wide — the Russian embassy saw to that. (Do you recollect the fact that the general manager of the Associated Press went to Russia and received a decoration from the tsar?)

From Maine to California, American provincialism quivered with indignation and horror. That night Gorky and his " mistress " were invited to leave the Hotel Belleclaire. They went to another hotel, and were refused admittance there. They went to an apartment-house and were refused admittance there. They spent a good part of the small hours of the morning wandering about the streets of New York, until friends picked them up and whisked them away to a place which has never been revealed. And next morning this shameful and humiliating story was flaunted on the front page of the newspapers — especially, of course, the *New York World*.

A perfect flood of abuse was poured over the head of poor, bewildered Gorky; the clergy began to preach sermons about him, and our great, wise, virtuous statesmen, who were maintaining a " House of Mirth " in Albany, and high-class houses of prostitution in every State capital and in the National capital, joined in denunciations of this display of " foreign licentiousness." So Gorky's mission fell absolutely flat. . . . Even now the story is raked up, to serve the slave-drivers of the world. Gorky is defending his revolution against allied world-capitalism; the United States Senate is officially collecting scandal concerning the Bolsheviki; and Senator Knute Nelson, aged servant of privilege from Minnesota, puts these words on the Associated Press wires: " That horrible creature Maxim Gorky — he is about as immoral as a man can be."

In a subsequent letter Mr. Sinclair was kind enough to elucidate the matter, or at least a certain angle of it, quite succinctly:

Gorky was the victim of a quarrel going on between the out-and-out Socialists and the Liberals who called themselves the " Friends of Russian Freedom." The Socialists, of course, wanted to exploit Gorky in the Moyer-Haywood fight. It was up to Gorky to choose whether he wanted to go with the Reds or with the Settlement Workers. He chose the former and was treated accordingly. So far as the marital part is concerned, I think he was guiltless, because he had no idea he was doing anything wrong.

It is patent that Gorky was, indeed, a " victim." Even at the time, the *World* learned that the ill-fated telegram to Moyer and Haywood was composed by Gaylord Wilshire and signed by him in Gorky's name. Mr. Wilshire read the text of his telegram to Zinovy Peshkov, who approved of it as " expressing Gorky's sentiments." This circumstance clears Gorky of at least one *gaucherie*.

As far as the American conscience was concerned the Gorky case had its educative value. It caused considerable searching of the heart among the critically minded citizens. At the same time the affair revealed Gorky's utter unfitness for the rôle of politician and diplomatist. Not even his warmest admirer can deny that on that occasion he displayed grievous tactless-

ness. It was not his concern to test the spiritual courage of a country that has its own Emersons and Thoreaus and Menckens and Van Wyck Brookses. His mission was delicate enough and important enough to warrant concessions to foreign standards and customs. There is hardly any doubt that Lenin would have disapproved of Gorky's dubious bravado both in flaunting his irregular matrimony and in meddling with the domestic troubles of a strange land by way of inconsequential gestures. In his letters to Gorky, Lenin persistently endeavoured to cure his correspondent of his naïve romanticism. Lenin the *Realpolitiker,* who did not hesitate to make use of the services of Ludendorff and Hindenburg for his cause, who chastised Trotsky and Bukharin for their " revolutionary cant," would certainly have been in favour of sacrificing a few gestures for the sake of obtaining the dollars of the Schiffs and Guggenheims.

How did Gorky react to his treatment? His double pain, caused by the defeat of his mission and by the humiliation of Andreyeva, could not but affect his judgement. His early statements to the reporters, in which he tried to shield the honour of Andreyeva, sounded a plea for toleration in the name of the American principles of liberty and broadmindedness. The futility of his appeal crushed him. He faced the inexorable Moloch of custom and public opinion, with the pandering press on the one hand and the tacit submissiveness of men of the calibre of Howells and Twain. It meant to him the poverty of spiritual courage commensurate with the country's material wealth. Accordingly, he had no use for the efforts of the American Socialists at improving the material well-being of the workmen. " Already," he said to Mr. John Martin, " your workmen have a plethora of material goods; their souls are stuffed with fatness; they, like the rest of America, have no souls." He was impatient with the campaign for public ownership of utilities and similar meliorative issues: " I do not care," he said, " to see the men better off — but better." And when asked as to what kind of activity he regarded necessary for social advancement, he replied: " Circulate cheap editions of the classics, the great histories, novels,

poems, dramas; provide picture exhibitions for the wage earners and lectures on natural science." Mr. Martin, who took Gorky around a good deal, tells us that his guest " was more depressed by the mental squalor of the well-to-do classes in America than by the physical squalor of the poor inhabitants of lower New York," and that " he was impressed much more by the scantiness of the supply of books in rural libraries as he saw them, than by the grandeur of the library buildings in the cities."

As the months went by, the Gorky sensation began to wear off, in favour of fresher scandal. The press seemed to have forgotten the Russian author, who was now quietly working on his novel, *Mother,* in the Adirondacks. But before long Gorky aggravated his first offence by another: he forfeited the dignity of martyrdom by breaking his silence. His *American Sketches* could be nothing but sketchy at best, based as they were on brief and superficial observations. With the author's chagrin still raw, they hardly vouched objectivity. The publication, in *Appleton's Magazine* (August, 1906), of *The City of Mammon,* was obviously in bad taste. Gorky's enthusiastic remarks, upon his arrival, about New York, its buildings and crowds, were still fresh in the memory, and now they were reversed completely in his ponderous philippic. Now the buildings were " stern, cheerless and morose," " prisons," with no flowers in their windows:

From afar the city looks like a huge jaw with black, uneven teeth. It belches forth clouds of smoke to the sky, and sniffs like a glutton suffering from over-corpulency. When you enter it you feel that you have fallen into a stomach of brick and iron which has swallowed up millions of people, and churns, grinds, and digests them.

. . . . Along the sidewalks people walk hurriedly, in every direction. . . . Their faces are motionlessly calm — apparently none of them is aware of the misfortune of being a slave of life, of being fodder to the city-monster. In sad conceit they regard themselves as masters of their fates, in their eyes gleams at times the sense of independence, but evidently they do not realize that theirs is only the independence of the ax in the

hands of the woodsman, of the hammer in the hands of the blacksmith, of the brick in the hands of the unseen mason who, with a sly grin, builds for all one enormous but crowded jail. There are many energetic faces among them, but in each face you notice before everything else its teeth. No inner freedom, freedom of the spirit, shines in their eyes. This energy without freedom resembles the cold gleam of a knife that has not yet had time to be dulled. Theirs is the freedom of blind tools in the hands of the Yellow Devil — Gold.

It is the first time that I have seen such a monstrous city, and never before have people seemed to me so insignificant, so enslaved. Yet at the same time I have nowhere seen them so tragicomically self-satisfied as in this greedy and dirty stomach of the glutton that has fallen into idiocy from greed and with a savage roar is devouring men's brains and nerves.

Small wonder that this fresh indiscretion served as grist for the mills of the patriots from the *Bookman*, and the Bierces. In a letter to George Sterling, Ambrose Bierce wrote:

. . . . Did you see Gorky's estimate of us in *Appleton's*? Having been a few weeks in the land, whose language he knows not a word of, he knows (by intuition of genius and a wee bit help from Gaylord Wilshire and his gang) all about us, and tells it in generalities of vituperation as applicable to one country as to another. He is a dandy bomb-thrower, but he handles the stink-pot only indifferently well. . . .

Twenty years later Gorky spoke of his *City of the Yellow Devil* (the title of *The City of Mammon* in the original) with regret. " I was a Russian rustic then," he admitted. In the interval Gorky has become a champion of Western civilization, particularly of the marvels of technology in the modern city. To him, as to all Sovietist Russians, New York is today the epitome of industrialization, of that ideal state which, in the parlance of Lenin's aspiring followers, is synonymous with Americanization. At his Sorrento teas he often takes issue with detractors of present-day America, and it is curious to watch him persuade visiting Americans not to lament the mechanization of their life, but to regard all their devices for comfort as pledges of the ultimate liberation of man from

the tyranny of toil and nature. He even tries to suggest a pseudo-scientific approval of chewing gum, though he admits that upon his arrival in New York the sight of milling jaws disconcerted him.

He has retained no bitterness in connexion with his visit to this country. As we were discussing the Tennessee " monkey trial " that was taking place at that time, Gorky justified the Bryanists and his moral censors in 1906 as men acting from a " biological urge " to defend their Puritanic traditions against the onslaught of alien races and alien ideas. He recalls with pleasure many incidents from his sojourn in the United States, such as the " good time " he had with John Dewey or his visit to the Baldwin Locomotive Plant. His eyes gleam softly as he speaks of the delightful hours at the Martins' place in the Adirondacks. In the evening they would climb trees, and from his perch Gorky would teach them Russian phrases. One of these was: *Lyubitye drug druga — love one another.*

Incidentally he still speaks with admiration of Ambrose Bierce's Civil War stories, and enjoys relating their contents to his listeners. He tells of having converted Tolstoy, who disapproved of Bierce, to one of the latter's stories dealing with a Northern officer going mad while in ambush.

APPENDIX II

A LETTER FROM TROTSKY

I WAS curious to have Trotsky's version of his visit, together with Lunacharsky and Ryazanov, to the editors of *Novaya Zhizn*. In answer to my inquiry Trotsky was considerate enough to write at some length. Coming as it does from the pen of a contemporary history maker, the letter strikes me as valuable enough to be reproduced almost fully. Trotsky's estimate of Sukhanov is characteristic of the official Bolshevik attitude toward their semi-friends from Gorky's newspaper. Incidentally, Sukhanov was arrested in the fall of 1930 for alleged counter-revolutionary activities, and in the following winter he, with Bazarov, Groman, and other " specialists," was a defendant in the sensational " Menshevik " trial.

You are interested to know [writes Trotsky] how correctly Sukhanov reports our conference, in May, 1917, at the editorial offices of *Novaya Zhizn,* of which Gorky was the formal chief. In order to make my further points clear, I must say a few words about the general nature of Sukhanov's *Notes on the Revolution*. With all its drawbacks (verbosity, impressionism, political shortsightedness), which at times make the reading of this work intolerable, one cannot deny the author's conscientiousness, a feature that makes the *Notes* a valuable source for the historian. Jurists know, however, that the conscientiousness of a witness does not by any means assure the reliability of his testimony. One must, in addition, consider the level of the witness' intelligence, the keenness of his sight, hear-

ing, memory, the state of his mind at the moment in question, and so forth. Sukhanov is an impressionist of the intelligentsia variety, and like most of these he is incapable of understanding the political psychology of people of a different makeup. Despite the fact that in 1917 he personally belonged to the left wing of the Conciliators, hence stood very closely to the Bolsheviks, he was and is by his Hamletian makeup the very antipode of a Bolshevik. He is always antagonized by inwardly complete people who firmly know what they want and whither they are going. As a result, in his *Notes* Sukhanov quite conscientiously piles up error upon error, whenever he attempts to understand the motives of the Bolsheviks' actions, or to lay bare their hidden promptings. At times he gives the impression of deliberately entangling simple and clear issues. As a matter of fact he is constitutionally incapable, at all events in politics, of discovering the shortest distance between two points.

Sukhanov exerts himself quite a bit to present my line as opposed to that of Lenin. Exceedingly sensitive to peripheral moods and rumours of the intelligentsia circles. . . . Sukhanov naturally lived in hopes that there would arise differences between Lenin and Trotsky, the more so since such a contingency might, if only in part, ease the unenviable position of the *Novaya Zhizn* between the Social-Patriots and the Bolsheviks. In his *Notes* Sukhanov still lives in the atmosphere of those unfulfilled hopes, expressing them in the form of reminiscent conjectures in retrospect. He endeavours to interpret personal peculiarities and those of temperament and style as a particular course of political action.

In connexion with the still-born Bolshevik manifestation of June 10, and especially in connexion with the armed demonstrations of the July days, Sukhanov tries to show, at great length, that whereas Lenin at that time strove for the direct seizure of the Government by means of conspiracy and insurrection, Trotsky, contrariwise, aspired for gaining the actual power of the Soviets represented by the then dominant parties of the Socialist-Revolutionists and the Mensheviks. All that has not the shadow of a foundation.

At the first congress of the Soviets, on June 4, Tseretelli in passing remarked: " At the present moment there is not a single party in Russia, which might be willing to take over the Government." From his seat Lenin shouted: " There is such a

party ! " Lenin disliked interrupting speakers or being interrupted when he spoke. Only serious considerations could have urged him on that occasion to break his wonted restraint. According to Tseretelli's logic, in a moment of great national difficulties one should above all try to foist the government on someone else. This, indeed, constituted the wisdom of the Conciliators who after the March revolution foisted the Government upon the Liberals. Tseretelli painted the unattractive fear of responsibility in the colours of political disinterestedness and extraordinary perspicacity. Such cowardly priggishness is intolerable for a revolutionist who believes in the mission of his party. A revolutionary party which spurns authority under difficult conditions deserves nothing but contempt. . . .

At the same congress, speaking after Minister of Agriculture Peshekhonov [a moderate Socialist. — A. K.], I said: " I do not belong to Peshekhonov's party, but if I were told that the Cabinet will consist of twelve Peshekhonovs, I should regard this as an enormous step forward." [1]

I doubt whether at the time of those events my words about a Cabinet of Peshekhonovs could have been construed as the antithesis of Lenin's readiness to take over the Government. Sukhanov concocts this alleged hypothesis — retrospectively. The planned Bolshevik manifestation of June 10 in favour of the Soviets, Sukhanov interprets as a preparation for the seizure of the Government, and he writes: " Two or three days before the ' manifestation ' Lenin declared publicly his readiness to assume authority. At the same time Trotsky stated his desire to see twelve Peshekhonovs in the Government seats. Quite a difference. Still I take it that Trotsky was in on the affair of June 10. . . . Even then Lenin was hardly inclined to launch the decisive battle without the help of the dubious ' Interregionary.' [2] For Trotsky was his equal, a monumental partner

[1] In his brochure, *Why I Did Not Emigrate* (Berlin, 1923), Peshekhonov states that Trotsky's phrase made him and his wife immune against Bolshevik outrages, when they lived in Red Odessa during the 1919 days of Terror. — A. K.

[2] Sukhanov calls me a " dubious Interregionary " (i.e., member of the Inter-Regionary Organization), implying apparently that in reality I was a Bolshevik. That in any event is correct. In the Inter-Regionary Organization I stayed on for the sole purpose of merging it with the Bolshevik party, which indeed took place in August.

in a monumental game; in his own party Lenin had no one to match him for a long, long time."

The whole passage is full of contradictions. According to Sukhanov, Lenin actually planned the very thing of which Tseretelli accused him: " the immediate seizure of the Government by a proletarian minority." The proof of such a Blanquism Sukhanov, extraordinarily enough, sees in the words of Lenin as to the readiness of the Bolsheviks to assume authority in spite of all difficulties. If Lenin had actually intended to seize the government by means of a conspiracy on June 10, he would have scarcely warned of this his enemies at the plenary session of the congress, on June 4. Need one recall that from the first day of his arrival at Petrograd Lenin admonished his party to regard the overthrow of the Provisional Government as a task that must be preceded by the Bolsheviks gaining a majority in the Soviets? In April Lenin resolutely opposed those Bolsheviks who advocated the slogan " Down with the Provisional Government! " as the issue of the moment. Lenin's remark on June 4 had only one meaning: we, the Bolsheviks, are ready to take over the Government even today, provided the workmen and soldiers give us their confidence; herein we differ from the Conciliators who, though enjoying the trust of the workmen and soldiers, lack the temerity to assume authority.

Sukhanov contraposes Trotsky against Lenin, as a realist versus a Blanquist. " While rejecting Lenin, one might yet quite approve of Trotsky's formulation of the question." At the same time Sukhanov asserts that " Trotsky was in on the affair of June 10," that is, on a conspiracy for the seizure of the Government. Sukhanov thus discovers two non-existing lines of thought and action, and does not deny himself the pleasure of converging the two lines into one, so as to be able to accuse me of being an adventurer. An odd and somewhat platonic revenge on the part of the Left intelligentsia for their frustrated hopes in a split between Lenin and Trotsky.

The central slogan on the Bolshevik banners prepared for the cancelled manifestation of June 10, and used later on June 18, was " Down with the Ten Capitalist Ministers! " As an aesthete Sukhanov admires the simple expressiveness of the slogan, but as a politician he fails to grasp its meaning. Beside the ten " Capitalist Ministers " the Government included also

six Conciliators. These were not attacked by the Bolshevik banners. On the contrary, the banners implied that the Capitalist Ministers should be replaced by Socialists, representatives of the Soviet majority. It was this idea of the Bolshevik banners that I voiced before the congress of Soviets, namely: break your coalition with the Liberals, remove the bourgeois ministers, and substitute for them your Peshekhonovs. While urging the Soviet majority to take over the power, the Bolsheviks, of course, did not in the least bind their hands as regards the Peshekhonovs; on the contrary, they did not conceal their intention of relentlessly fighting them within the Soviet democracy to the end of conquering the Soviet majority and the Government. All this is quite elementary. Only the previously indicated traits of Sukhanov, not so much as an individual but as a type, may explain how this participant and observer of the events could make such a jumble of so serious yet so simple an issue.

In the light of the episode just analysed you may find it easier to understand Sukhanov's false interpretation of my conference with the editors of *Novaya Zhizn,* concerning which you inquire. The moral of my collision with the group of Maxim Gorky is expressed by Sukhanov in the concluding sentence which he ascribes to me: " Now I see that nothing remains for me to do but to organize a daily paper together with Lenin." It follows that only my failure to come to terms with Gorky and Sukhanov — that is, with men whom I never regarded either as politicians or as revolutionists — forced me to find my way to Lenin. The fallacy of this idea is too obviously patent.

How characteristic for Sukhanov, let me note in passing, is the phrase: " to organize a daily paper together with Lenin," as if the tasks of the revolutionary moment were summed up in a newspaper. It must be clear to anyone with a minimum of imagination that I was incapable of such a way of thinking and formulating the issues.

In order to explain my visit to Gorky's group I must remind you that I reached Petrograd early in May, more than two months after the uprising, a whole month after Lenin's arrival. Much had already taken shape and form during that time. I felt the need of a direct empirical, so to speak, orientation not only in the basic forces of the revolution, the workmen and soldiers, but also in all the groupings and political shades of

the " cultivated " public. My visit to the *Novaya Zhizn* was a bit of political reconnoitring on my part, for the purpose of ascertaining the positive and negative forces of this " Left " group, the chances for the secession of some elements or others, and so forth. A brief talk with them convinced me of the utter hopelessness of this circle of literary wiseacres, for whom the revolution was confined to a leading editorial. Since, furthermore, they accused the Bolsheviks of " self-isolation," blaming for this Lenin and his April Theses, I most probably did tell them that their words gave me additional proof of Lenin's perfectly correct stand in isolating the party from them, or rather in isolating them from the party. Sukhanov's version is apparently based on this conclusion of mine, which I had to emphasize with especial force in order to affect properly the other participants, Ryazanov and Lunacharsky, at the time opposed to an alliance with Lenin.

INDEX

of persons, periodicals, and Gorky's writings mentioned in the text

Date Due